EDUCATIONAL PSYCHOLOGY

EDUCATIONAL PSYCHOLOGY FIFTH EDITION

HERBERT J. KLAUSMEIER
University of Wisconsin—Madison

1817

HARPER & ROW, PUBLISHERS, New York
Cambridge, Philadelphia, San Francisco,
London, Mexico City, São Paulo, Singapore, Sydney

Sponsoring Editor: George A. Middendorf
Project Editor: Jo-Ann Goldfarb
Text Design: Michel Craig
Cover Design & Cover Illustration: Jack Ribik
Text Art: Vantage Art, Inc.
Photo Research: Mira Schachne
Production: William Lane
Compositor: Ruttle, Shaw & Wetherill, Inc.
Printer and Binder: R. R. Donnelley & Sons Company

PHOTO CREDITS

The majority of photos in this book were provided by the following people: Jean S. Dyer, co-ordinator of public information/relations, Madison Metropolitan School District, Madison, Wisconsin; Robert S. Essock, audiovisual specialist, Samuel Gompers Middle School, Madison, Wisconsin; and Thomas J. Grade, audiovisual specialist, James Madison Memorial High School, Madison, Wisconsin. Following are the exceptions: Page 4: UPI; p. 123 (left): Courtesy, Clark, Phipps, Clark & Harris, Inc.; p. 123 (middle): Archives of the History of American Psychology; p. 123 (right): American Psychological Association; p. 180: Strickler, Monkmeyer; p. 357 (top): Forsyth, Monkmeyer; p. 464 (left, right), p. 465 (left): Archives of the History of American Psychology; p. 465 (right): Courtesy, Stanford University; p. 531: Courtesy, W. W. Norton & Co., Inc.; p. 532: UPI.

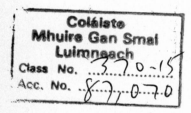
Educational Psychology, Fifth Edition
Copyright © 1985 by Herbert J. Klausmeier

This book was previously published as *Learning and Human Abilities: Educational Psychology*.

Library of Congress Cataloging in Publication Data
Klausmeier, Herbert J. (Herbert John), 1915–
  Educational psychology.

  Rev. ed. of: Learning and human abilities. 4th ed. 1975.
  Bibliography: p.
  Includes indexes.
  1. Educational psychology. I. Klausmeier, Herbert J. (Herbert John), 1915–   . Learning and human abilities.   II. Title.
LB1051.K67 1985   370.15   84-12809
ISBN 0-06-043696-4

86 87 9 8 7 6 5 4 3

CONTENTS

PREFACE

This is the fifth edition of the very widely used book previously titled *Learning and Human Abilities: Educational Psychology*. This totally new fifth edition is written specifically for the introductory course in educational psychology. In keeping with this focus, it is given a new title, *Educational Psychology*. Its purpose is to aid prospective teachers and practicing educators—teachers, counselors, administrators, and others—in learning and applying concepts that contribute to excellence in education.

NATURE OF THE CONTENTS

The material is up to date, as may be inferred by scanning the Suggestions for Further Reading at the end of a few chapters and a page or two of the References listed toward the end of the book. The content is comprehensive, directly applicable to educational practice, and meaningfully organized into four parts of 16 chapters.

Part One consists of Chapter 1, which presents an introduction to the study of educational psychology. In this chapter, I preview the content and research methods of educational psychology, describe what I have done to make the content readily learnable, and indicate how the student may use the book.

Part Two surveys five highly important foundation areas of educational practice: aims and objectives of education (Chapter 2), theories of child and adolescent development (Chapter 3), theories and conditions of learning (Chapter 4), individual and group differences, including provisions for exceptional children (Chapter 5), and instructional theory, instructional technology, and classroom leadership (Chapter 6). These chapters provide an overview of the powerful theories and models that underlie the principles of learning and teaching described in Part Three.

Part Three begins with motivation for learning (Chapter 7). The principles of classroom motivation given in this chapter are applicable to the learning and teaching of verbal information (Chapter 8), concepts and principles (Chapter 9), problem solving and creativity (Chapter 10), motor and vocal skills (Chapter 11), attitudes and values (Chapter 12), and personality integration and self-discipline (Chapter 13). Chapter 14 presents principles of retention and transfer that are relevant for the learning outcomes discussed in prior chapters. In Chapters 7 through 14, I first integrate key information from child development, learning theory, and individual differences and then follow this with a set of principles that teachers apply in fostering their students' learning. Strategies that aid the university student in becoming a more effective learner as well as a more successful teacher are given throughout the chapters. Reviewers of this edition and users of the prior editions regard the principles for fostering student learning and the learning strategies as especially noteworthy contributions to the improvement of learning and teaching.

Our interest in Part Four is with measurement (Chapter 15) and evaluation (Chapter 16). The focus is on measurement devices and evaluation procedures directed toward promoting student learning, achieving excellence in teaching, and continually improving the school's educative processes. Chapter 16, as earlier chapters, assumes that the teachers of a school cannot greatly improve their school's educative processes without effective leadership by the principal and greater support from the district office, the school board, parents, and society at large than they presently receive. For this reason, I give more attention than other authors to evaluating the school's total educative processes.

UNIQUE, CREATIVE FEATURES

The truly unique and creative features of this text that distinguish it from all others are the organizational pattern of the chapter material that enhances initial learning and retention and the related design elements built into the book that make the pattern readily perceivable. Complementing these features are other learning aids that heighten motivation as well as enhance learning. Although some persons may regard the organizational pattern and design elements as obvious, many university students have not had the opportunity to learn to use text-embedded learning aids with high effectiveness. Therefore, we take time here to identify the most salient aids of this book and to indicate a few ways of using them to ensure that students will receive maximum benefit from their study. (This book is carefully designed to be self-contained; there is no workbook or study guide.)

Except for introductory Chapter 1, the concepts of each chapter are organized into taxonomies, also referred to as *conceptual structures*. There is one *primary taxonomy* at the beginning of each chapter, and there are two or more *secondary taxonomies* within each chapter. Here is the primary taxonomy of Chapter 2:

AIMS AND OBJECTIVES OF EDUCATION

NATIONAL AIMS OF EDUCATION

DOMAINS OF EDUCATIONAL OBJECTIVES

OBJECTIVES FOR CURRICULUM PLANNING AND TEACHING

MINIMUM COMPETENCY OBJECTIVES

Notice that it consists of one generic concept, *aims and objectives of education,* and four superordinate concepts, one for each main part of Chapter 2: *national aims of education, domains of educational objectives, objectives for curriculum planning and teaching,* and *minimum competency objectives.* Each of these superordinate concepts is repeated later as a first-order heading at the beginning of each main part of the chapter.

Here is the first *secondary taxonomy* of Chapter 2:

NATIONAL AIMS OF EDUCATION

Aims of Elementary Education

Aims of Secondary Education

Objectives of the National Assessment of Educational Progress

Observe that a secondary taxonomy consists of a superordinate concept and its several subordinate concepts, in this case, *national aims of education* (superordinate), *aims of elementary education, aims of secondary education,* and *objectives of the National Assessment of Educational Progress* (subordinate). These subordinate concepts are then repeated later as second-order headings. Both the superordinate and the subordinate concepts are red. However, the subordinate concepts at the next lower levels appear in black and only as third-order or fourth-order headings in the text, not in the page margin. The use of color and the kind and size of lettering in first-, second-, and third-order headings for the first main part of Chapter 2, and the page number where the heading appears, is as follows:

NATIONAL AIMS OF EDUCATION (p. 26)

Aims of Elementary Education (p. 26)

Aims of Secondary Education (p. 27)

Cardinal Principles of Secondary Education (p. 28)

High School Competencies as Aims (p. 30)

Objectives of the National Assessment of Educational Progress (p. 31)

It is imperative that students readily recognize and use these different levels of concepts and the headings that name the concepts.

How do we use this organizational pattern and the design to maximize initial learning and subsequent retention? Examining the primary taxonomy at the beginning of the chapter and then the secondary taxonomies in the chapter enables us to preview the content of any chapter very quickly and thoroughly. The preview tells us that concepts rather than other outcomes are to be learned, and it indicates the particular concepts to be learned. By returning to the chapter-opening taxonomy after the preview and rehearsing the taxonomy for a few seconds before starting to study, we are able to begin constructing and internalizing our own *conceptual network* of the chapter content, referred to also as a *schema*. We relate our own experiences and knowledge to this schema before starting to study and, when studying, relate the new chapter material to the schema. Later, when wanting to recall and use the chapter material, we first retrieve the primary conceptual structure of the chapter (the generic and superordinate concepts) from long-term memory and then the secondary structures that now include our own related experiences and the new chapter material that we have learned.

We should note in passing that the generic concepts named by the chapter titles (for example, *Aims and Objectives of Education, Motivation*) are very general and inclusive as are the superordinate concepts (for example, *Aims of Elementary Education, Recent Cognitive Theories of Motivation*). So also are the generic and superordinate concepts of major taxonomies (for example, *living things, plants, animals*). The subordinate concepts in the taxonomies of this text, like those of other taxonomies, are less general and less inclusive. Nevertheless, principles of learning and teaching, as well as factual information, are presented as examples or elaborations of some of the subordinate concepts.

OTHER AIDS TO LEARNING

A cartoon at the beginning of each chapter introduces the chapter theme in a light, humorous vein. The importance of teachers in influencing people's selection of a life career is reflected in vignettes "What's Right With The Schools?". These vignettes help us appreciate our own roles as teachers and encourage us to feel good about being in education and studying educational psychology. A picture or a collection of pictures appears in most chapters and makes a major chapter theme more salient and vivid. Figures within the chapter enable us to grasp big ideas quickly and to recall them later.

Questions placed at the end of each main section of a chapter call for application, elaboration, integration, and other high-level intellectual skills rather than for recall of the text information. Responding to the questions provides for review and strengthens our conceptual network, thereby preventing forgetting.

Portions of the chapter, such as a set of principles for fostering student learning or a list of learning aids, are highlighted by use of large lettering, red color, and screening. This highlighting alerts us to the fact that here is a considerable amount of important, condensed information. Another design aid is that each superordinate concept appears as a running head at the top of each right-hand page of the chapter, starting with a page where the concept is first mentioned. This helps us locate information for previewing and reviewing.

A concise summary at the end of each chapter gives the gist of the chapter. Immediately preceding the summary there is a question that lists all of the secondary taxonomies of the chapter. This question encourages the students to synthesize and to apply what they have learned.

The Suggestions for Further Reading at the end of each chapter are of four kinds: ideas for improving educational practices, reports of original research, summaries of research, and explanations of theory. They range in comprehensibility from easy to difficult, depending upon the reader's psychological and educational background. Accordingly, it is advisable to read a title and annotation carefully before making a selection and to preview the selection before making a final decision about its substance or difficulty.

Before turning to other considerations, we should consider a few of the less perceptible design elements that greatly contribute to readability and comprehension. First, the graphs and tables, with very few exceptions, appear on the same page where they are discussed. Second, there are no supplementary pieces of printed information inserted here and there throughout a chapter. Both of these elements facilitate readability and comprehension in that we are not called on to shift our attention from what we have just read, study the material, and then locate the place where we stopped reading and try to recall what we had read. Also, I did not place words and phrases drawn from the paragraphs in the page margins. Attending to unconnected and unrelated words and phrases in the margin may help us recall the specific words, but it also impedes constructing a meaningful schema that incorporates the major chapter concepts.

As we shall see later in Chapters 1, 4, 8, and 14, many different researchers have found that using conceptual structures and other text-embedded aids increases initial learning and later retention by a very great amount. The employment of learning strategies and study skills adds another large increment. Moreover, being able to use learning strategies and strategies for studying enables teachers to demonstrate them to their own students, a very significant contribution to successful teaching. In this book, the following strategies are explained in the chapters where they are best related to the other chapter content: metacognitive and cognitive strategies in general, strategies for comprehending prose, divergent and creative problem-solving strategies, strategies for learning motor skills, metamemory strategies in general, retrieval strategies, and study skills that promote initial acquisition and retention.

ACKNOWLEDGMENTS

Many substantive ideas of this book, as well as the internal chapter organization and design, draw heavily on research conducted by myself and my research teams at the Wisconsin Center for Education Research. I should like to recognize the continuous research support since 1956 from federal agencies and the University of Wisconsin, and from philanthropic foundations for intermittent time periods. This support has enabled me to conduct both experimental and longitudinal research on central concerns of educational psychology and also on the improvement of elementary and secondary education. The improvement research, along with my teaching experience at the elementary, secondary, and university levels, has reaffirmed my conviction regarding the importance of effective teaching and of educators, parents, and the public in general working together to improve education. These two ideas are reflected throughout this book. I regard learning to improve education and becoming a more effective learner as the primary objective of taking the introductory course in educational psychology.

I am appreciative of the ideas that many persons contributed to this text. I have given the usual acknowledgment for information from published sources. My thanks go to my former graduate advisees and to other members of my research teams. Persons whose names follow were involved with me as team members in planning and conducting the research, and most of them published their first monograph, article, or book either individually or as a coauthor with me: Ronald Ady, Patricia Allen, Michael Bernard, Kay Bull, Joe Byers, John Check, Donna Rae Clasen, J. Kent Davis, Zackaria Ethnathios, John Feldhusen, Katherine Feldman, August Flammer, William Franzen, Chris Flizak, Dorothy Frayer, Wayne Fredrick, John Gaa, Elizabeth Ghatala, William Goodwin, Gerald Gleason, Barbara Gruendemann, Terence Janicki, Jan Jeter, Selena Katz, Barbara Kennedy, Thomas Klausmeier, Peter Lamal, Irvin Lehmann, Elmer Lemke, Carol Lindeman, Leo Loughlin, Daniel Lynch, Richard Marliave, Frank May, Julia McGivern, Nancy McMurray, Dean Meinke, Gerald Miller, Gregory Mize, John Mulhern, Barbara Nelson, Gordon K. Nelson, Ralph Pippert, Daniel Probst, Mary Quilling, Winston Rampaul, Richard Ripple, Laila Russell, Joan Schilling, Joseph Scott, Thomas Sipple, Terrence Snowden, Juanita Sorenson, James Swanson, Glenn Tagatz, Joan Wakefield, James Wardrop, William Wiersma, Suzanne Wiviott, and Dan Woolpert.

Recognition is also due the instructors and my own students who used prior editions and offered comments regarding this one. Three scholars selected by the publisher provided many helpful suggestions regarding the breadth and accuracy of the information that is presented. I am indebted to teachers who read the manuscript and offered their ideas for making it readable and relevant.

Thomas W. Klausmeier, a dedicated and enthusiastic teacher, merits my deepest appreciation for a critical analysis of the earlier editions of this book, an exhaustive review of this edition, and preparation of the material on discipline in this edition.

Special recognition is due my secretary, Arlene Knudsen, for the dedication with which she undertook the typing of the manuscript and aiding me in compiling the references, securing the permissions, and proofing.

The publisher's staff is commended for the care given to designing and editing this book.

AN INVITATION

The publisher, and I as well, recognize that most instructors are eagerly seeking creative approaches in textbooks that directly facilitate learning by their students, and particularly in textbooks in educational psychology. We recognize, too, that there may be some questioning as to whether a book can truly make the large leap forward in facilitating the learning of educational psychology that is outlined in this preface. Based on my many experiments with public school and university students, I am confident that this book marks the beginning of a new era in text learnability and that instructors will not be in any way disappointed with it. Their students will readily use the conceptual structures, facilitative design elements, and other learning aids with great success and satisfaction. In this regard, I invite any comments from students and instructors that they may be kind enough to send to me or the publisher.

HERBERT J. KLAUSMEIER

EDUCATIONAL PSYCHOLOGY

PART ONE

THE NATURE OF EDUCATIONAL PSYCHOLOGY

1 INTRODUCTION TO THE STUDY OF EDUCATIONAL PSYCHOLOGY

CHAPTER 1

INTRODUCTION TO THE STUDY OF EDUCATIONAL PSYCHOLOGY

This book is about learning and development in educational settings. It starts with the aims of education and continues through to the measurement and evaluation of the results of education. It is concerned with human learning and development in all their richness and variety, the processes by which the helpless newborn baby progresses into a thinking, doing, feeling adult. Learning and development culminate in persons who can use machines to do much of their physical work, who can organize ideas that influence not only their individual lives but also the lives of others, who can create and perform in the fine arts, who can deftly remove a malignant tumor to restore health, and who, perhaps most important of all, have compassion and respect for their fellow human beings.

This book presents a very positive picture of what teachers and education can do for children and youth. This confidence derives from a vast accumulation of research which shows that the school environment can be managed to facilitate learning and development. Teachers are getting uninterested students to want to learn. Situations are being organized to nurture the cognitive development of students, to make their learning of psychomotor skills more effective, to build favorable attitudes, and to develop buoyant personalities. Consider a few of the enduring contributions that the American system of education makes to its citizenry.

WHAT'S RIGHT WITH THE SCHOOLS
A Tribute to Jim Harris, Who Believed in Me

ERMA BOMBECK

Erma Bombeck is an enormously popular and witty exploiter of everyday themes. Her self-deprecating humor appeals particularly to women caught on the merry-go-round of middle-class American life. Bombeck's "At Wit's End" column, syndicated by Field Enterprises, is used by nearly 1,000 newspapers in the U.S. and Canada, and she is author of six highly successful books, typified in the title, *If Life Is a Bowl of Cherries, Then What Am I Doing in the Pits?*

Not only have teachers influenced my life, but I have since married one and given birth to another.

My father died when I was 9 and my mother went to work. That left me with a grandmother who played euchre every afternoon, a tearoom that was hot in the summer and cold in the winter, and a boy's bike I was too short to ride.

Teachers were my entire life. They looked at me. They talked to me. They spent time with me. They ate with me. They played ball with me. But mostly they spent their time convincing me I was better than I thought I was.

The September before my graduation from a vocational school, my journalism teacher, Jim Harris, pulled me aside and made his last impassioned plea: I must go to college. I must not become a school secretary for the Dayton Board of Education. My parents opposed his viewpoint because it was a waste of time for a girl to go to college.

Jim Harris and his wife offered to loan me money for college. It was then that I knew he meant what he said. Against my parents' will, I worked my way through college.

When my first book was published in 1967, the earth did not move. Not for anyone except me. I was sitting in the book section of a department store, directing people to the restroom mostly, when I looked up and there stood my high school journalism teacher, Jim Harris, with a look I will never forget.

We didn't say anything. I just handed him the book and said, "You're on page 186." The tribute was to the four men in my life who always told me I could do what I knew I couldn't. Jim Harris was the first one to have the kindness to "laugh when I sat down at the typewriter."

He opened the door for me to 900 newspapers, a contract with ABC, and six books.

You don't get that many laughs as a school secretary for the Dayton Board of Education.

SOURCE: *Phi Delta Kappan,* 1980, *62*(4). Back cover page.

Hyman, Wright, and Reed (1975) conducted a pioneer study of the achievements and other characteristics of about 80,000 persons ranging in age from 25 to 72. These persons were taught in many different American schools and colleges during several historical periods. They had reached varying levels of educational attainment in differing educational environments. The results were clear that being educated in American schools "increases knowledge, deepens receptivity to further knowledge, and stimulates active seeking for new information long after the first formal schooling" (Hyman et al., 1975, p. 1). These positive effects were directly related to the number of years spent in school. More recently, Walberg and Fredrick (1982) reviewed all the available research and found positive correlations of .40 to .50 between achievement and years of schooling and days of instruction. Similarly, Welch, Anderson, and Harris (1982) found that the number of semesters of mathematics studied influenced the mathematics achievement of 17-year-olds more than all factors combined related to their home and community background.

Hyman and Wright (1979) also analyzed their data to determine the enduring effects of education on values and character. They concluded that education produces many and lasting good effects. The good effects include valuing due process of law; freedom of information even when it is controversial; humanitarian alleviation of pain, suffering, and deprivation; and morality and good conduct over surface manners. As the amount of education increases, a higher proportion of the population holds these values. Rest, Davison, and Robbins (1978) reported that persons with more education are more concerned about their own ethical behavior and about the rights and feelings of others.

These studies relate amount of education to achievement and personality variables. Other studies are directed toward identifying the conditions in the school which make education more effective. Reviews of research by Edmonds (1982) and Purkey and Smith (1982) indicate that seven conditions characterize effective schools: well-defined school goals, high expectations for student achievement on the part of the school staff, a system for monitoring student progress, a sense of order, good discipline, control by the staff over instructional decisions, and strong instructional leadership by the principal, teachers, or some other persons in the school. Most of these conditions were found in diverse settings, including effective American elementary schools (Madaus, Airasian, & Kellagan, 1980) and effective inner-city schools of London (Rutter, Maughan, Mortimore, Ouston, & Smith, 1979).

That many American schools are effective in providing excellent educational opportunity for many students is undeniable (Hodgkinson, 1982). However, there is still an urgent need for improvement, especially for raising student achievement in the academic subjects (National Commission on Excellence in Education, 1983).

Educational psychology offers much for improving school effectiveness, because it is the science that studies student learning and development in educational settings. Student behaviors and the process of education set the boundaries of the content and method of educational psychology. Research and theorizing in educational psychology have moved from the experimental laboratory to the schools. The learning of reading, mathematics, and other subject matter is of high research interest. Moreover, educational psychologists are developing models of instruction that teachers use to guide their daily practices. Educational psychology, then, has a central role in generating knowledge in the foundations of educational practice, principles of learning and teaching, and principles of measurement and evaluation, as is discussed in the three main parts of this book.

As knowledge about students and effective instruction has greatly increased in recent years, the course in educational psychology required of teachers has become a practical course. Principles and applications relevant to guiding student learning and development are given major attention. Practitioners acquire information that enables them to analyze their teaching-learning situations more intelligently, to make wiser decisions when working with students, and to start developing their own ways to improve educational practices.

CONTRIBUTIONS OF EDUCATIONAL PSYCHOLOGY TO THE IMPROVEMENT OF EDUCATION

The three primary contributions of educational psychology to the improvement of educational practice may be summarized as follows: Knowledge in the foundations of educational practice contributes to a better understanding of the principles of learning and teaching. Applying the principles of learning and teaching makes classroom instruction effective and thereby enhances student learning. Applying the principles of measurement and evaluation enables teachers to assess and to monitor student progress effectively. The ensuing discussion of each primary contribution provides an organizing framework for the three parts of the book.

Knowledge in
Foundations of Educational Practice

Educational psychology provides basic knowledge in five foundations of educational practice: aims and objectives of education, theories of child and adolescent development, theories and conditions of learning, individual and group differences, and instructional theory, technology, and leadership. Educational history, philosophy, and sociology also contribute to each foundation area. Nevertheless, educational psychology makes unique and highly significant contributions.

Aims and Objectives of Education

Broad aims of education are formulated to influence education nationwide. These aims provide the context for a school district to formulate program objectives, such as the objectives of the reading program for grades 1–6 or those of the science program for grades 9–12. Course objectives are derived from program objectives, and the objectives of the units of each course are directly related to the course objectives. One goal of educational psychology is to clarify the nature of program, course, and unit objectives and to explain how objectives are used in planning and guiding daily instruction. This kind of knowledge aids teachers in preparing the course and unit objectives that they use to guide student learning.

Theories of Child and Adolescent Development

How children respond to instruction and what they are capable of learning change as they develop. We are getting a better understanding of developmental processes through the study of questions such as these: Are there identifiable stages of intellectual development that are common to all children and adolescents? How reliably can a child's development be predicted and how well can it be guided? How does the interaction of heredity, environment, and an individual's own self-direction influence the individual student's development? Knowing the course of development during the school years provides guidelines for understanding and working with students of a particular school level, such as primary or high school.

Theories and Conditions of Learning

Learning theorists are interested in the acquisition and retention of information, skills, values, and other broad classes of human behavior. They study human learning in order to understand the changes in an individual's knowledge, skill, and other behavior resulting from experience, study, or practice. Some theorists, including educational psychologists, are trying to gain a more complete understanding of conditions internal and external to the learner that influence learning and retention. Two internal conditions of the learner are motivation and prior experience, while two external conditions are the amount of time the student spends in active learning and the quality of instruction the student receives. Understanding learning processes and the conditions of learning enables teachers to guide student learning effectively.

Individual and Group Differences

At the same time that a better understanding of child and adolescent development and of learning is being gained, psychological and educational differences among individuals and among groups are being investigated. Much of our knowledge of these differences comes from studies using intelligence tests. Presently, however, intelligence testing is being supplemented with other procedures. For example, the mental processes and the strategies of learning that contribute to wide differences among students in reading and other achievement areas are being identified. Reliable means are also being developed for identifying differences among students in learning styles, creativity, the performing arts, and leadership. These latter are very important in the school curriculum but are not highly correlated with intelligence as measured by current tests.

Progress continues to be made in identifying differences between and among groups and within groups. For example, the differences between groups such as males and females and blacks and whites are being continually reexamined. A much better understanding of exceptional children and their educational needs is emerging. The interaction of biological and environmental factors in determining differences continues to be examined. As we shall see in Chapter 5, knowledge of the range of differences among individuals and between groups continues to grow. However, there is still some uncertainty about how to provide for the differences.

Instructional Theory, Technology, and Leadership

In recent years, educational psychologists have exercised strong leadership in formulating instructional theory. Instructional theory now ranks in importance with learning theory and developmental theory for guiding the instructional practices of teachers. In addition, research is being conducted on many questions related to instructional technology and leadership: How can instructional media, such as films, recordings, and books be adapted more effectively to each student's rate and style of learning? How can the desirable effects of TV viewing be enhanced and the undesirable effects be eliminated or ameliorated? How can computer-assisted learning techniques be used to increase students' achievement of the basic skills? What kind of instructional leadership and classroom management skills are required for effective teaching and how can they be developed? This research provides many possibilities for improving teaching methods.

Each of the five foundation areas encompasses far more scientific information than could be presented in Chapters 2–6 of this book. Accordingly, the information in these chapters has been selected for its direct relevance to education and to understanding principles of learning and teaching.

Principles of Learning and Teaching

Educational psychology provides principles of learning and teaching related to students' motivation for learning; their attainment of learning outcomes, such as concepts, motor skills, and attitudes; their retention of what is initially learned; and their transfer of it to other situations. The big ideas related to each of these areas follow as an advance organizer for the principles and illustrative applications that are given in Chapters 7–14.

Motivation for Learning

Motivation is a general term for goal-seeking or need-satisfying behavior. The strength of motivation is judged by how well a student attends to learning activities and persists in completing them. Principles of classroom motivation are directed initially toward securing students' attention and encouraging them to set learning goals. As these and other motivational principles are put into practice, students exercise more self-management of their learning activities, thus decreasing their need for teacher management and control.

Outcomes of Learning

Three major kinds of learning outcomes in subject fields such as mathematics, science, social studies, and English are verbal information, concepts and principles, and problem-solving skills, including creativity. Relatively little motor or vocal skill is involved in acquiring these outcomes. Accordingly, they are considered to be in the *cognitive domain.*

Motor skill is a second kind of learning outcome and is associated with curricular areas such as industrial arts, physical education, typing, instrumental music, and shorthand. The learning of a motor skill requires practice guided by an internalized motor program. Thus, this important class of learning outcome is considered to be in the *psychomotor domain.* There are, of course, both cognitive and psychomotor learning outcomes in subject fields such as music and typing.

A third type of learning outcome is in the *affective domain.* Students acquire attitudes and values at home, in school, and in their neighborhoods. These learning outcomes, more than those in the cognitive and psychomotor domains, involve feelings, such as liking, disliking, acceptance, and rejection. Personality integration is also learned and involves both feelings of self-esteem and positive regard for the welfare of others. Self-discipline accompanies healthy personality integration.

Principles of learning and teaching differ somewhat for each of these three classes of learning outcomes. Moreover, the applications of any given principle differ for each level of schooling. Accordingly, teachers must find applications of the principles to the subject matter field and level of schooling in which they are interested. In addition, we should recognize that the three domains of learning outcomes are not mutually exclusive. Typically, some feeling accompanies the learning of a motor skill as well as the learning of principles. Similarly, information as well as feeling is involved in learning an attitude.

Retention and Transfer

When children first correctly spell a word or solve a problem, we say that they have learned that particular outcome. When children correctly repeat the performance some time later, we say they have retained what they learned earlier. *Transfer of learning* takes place when that which is learned in one situation is used in a different situation in school or out of school.

Learning with meaning, intending to remember, and organizing material are key processes that promote long-term retention. Student self-regulation of activities to facilitate retention and transfer is a primary teaching goal. Conditions that affect retention and transfer are examined in Chapter 14.

Principles of Measurement and Evaluation

Educational measurement involves collecting information about students' characteristics and achievements. The results of *measurement* are expressed in numbers, such as the percentage correct on a test or the rating of a term paper. *Evaluation* is more inclusive than measurement because it may be based on qualitative information resulting from observation (Bill's interest has changed from science to math) as well as on quantitative information resulting from measurement (Mary scored 90% on the test). Moreover, evaluation requires making value judgments about students' characteristics or achievements (Mary's rate of progress is appropriate in terms of her learning handicap; Bill is not achieving as well as expected). Notice that making a value judgment requires relating the quantitative and qualitative information to a criterion, such as appropriateness or effectiveness.

Evaluation of student progress is necessarily related to specific learning outcomes, such as understanding a principle or developing a vocal skill. These specific outcomes are usually stated as the objectives of a course or of an instructional unit, in terms of a student's goals of the course or unit, or of a combination of the two. Evaluating student achievement of learning outcomes is an essential part of evaluating the effectiveness of educational programs.

RESEARCH METHODS OF EDUCATIONAL PSYCHOLOGY

Educational psychologists seek knowledge about human beings rather than about lower animals. They gain new knowledge of learning, development, and educational practices through studies conducted in the schools. Five methods of research frequently used in educational psychology, as well as examples of studies in which the methods are used, follow in outline form:

I. Descriptive Method
   A. Objective: To describe a situation, event, or area of interest accurately.
   B. Examples
      1. Observations are made of the proportion of instructional time that students actually spend on learning tasks.
      2. Questionnaires are administered and are followed with face-to-face interviews to identify the learning strategies that students use to comprehend what they read.
      3. An opinion survey is conducted to identify public perception about the importance of education to success.
      4. Tests are administered to a national sample of students of ages 9, 13, and 17 at five-year intervals to ascertain whether the level of achievement increases or decreases.
II. Practical Method
   A. Objective: To solve problems of learning and teaching, counseling, and other processes, by using procedures such as

(a) developing and testing new instructional materials or methods and (b) identifying and testing new or refined applications of models and principles of learning, development, instruction, or evaluation.

   B. Examples

     1. A mathematics program with record keeping and testing done by microcomputer is developed, put into practice, and evaluated.

     2. A program whereby both Spanish- and English-speaking children receive part of their instruction in Spanish and part in English is worked out and evaluated.

     3. An arrangement whereby each high school teacher serves as an advisor to 15 to 20 students is planned, put into practice, and tested.

III. Developmental Method

   A. Objective: To relate human growth or change to increasing age.

   B. Examples

     1. A longitudinal study is conducted to determine the changes that occur in children's ability to classify objects. In the study, the same measurements of the same children when enrolled in kindergarten, grade 1, grade 2, and grade 3 are taken at one-year intervals.

     2. A cross-sectional study is conducted to identify the changes that occur in students' comprehension of scientific concepts. In the study, the same tests are administered during the same week to a different group of students enrolled respectively in grades 10, 11, and 12.

IV. Correlational Method

   A. Objective: To identify the extent to which two or more characteristics of the same individuals are related. The relationship, or *correlation,* may be positive, such as between height and weight, or negative, such as between driving speed and safety.

   B. Examples

     1. The reading achievement of students is correlated with their achievement in other subject fields.

     2. The test scores of students at the beginning of a course are correlated with their scores at the end of the course to determine the relationship between what students already know and how they achieve.

V. Experimental and Quasi-experimental Methods

   A. Objective: To identify cause-and-effect relationships by conducting experiments in which one or more experimental groups receive one or more treatments that one or more control groups do not receive.

   B. Examples

     1. An experiment is conducted with students of grades 1, 2, and 3 to determine the effectiveness of teaching reading in a new, clearly described way (to experimental groups) in comparison with the current, clearly described way (to control groups).

     2. An experiment is carried out to determine whether requiring students of high, average, and low ability to achieve a mastery criterion of 90% correct on their tests in order to progress from one unit to the next has the same effect on the attitudes of all three groups as permitting the students to move ahead when the teacher judges their learning of the unit adequate.

     3. An experiment is conducted to determine the extent to which the speed of learning concepts can be accelerated through use of a clearly specified instructional procedure.

Many studies employing these five methods are reported in this book. A few studies based on other methods are also reported.

FEATURES OF THIS TEXT THAT AID LEARNING

Educational psychology provides practical information about learning and teaching in the form of principles. This being the case, the principles of learning from text material should be applied in educational psychology textbooks. Features of this text that will facilitate your learning are as follows: the meaningful conceptual structure of the content, the learning aids appearing in each chapter, research findings included in the text, and the sets of principles given in Chapters 7–14.

A great deal of research has been conducted on learning aids of the type included in this text, aids that are made highly effective by the meaningful conceptual structure of the content of this text. For example, Anderson, Pichert, and Shirey (1983) demonstrated that having a content schema, or internalized conceptual structure of the content, such as is given in the chapters of this book, markedly facilitated comprehension and recall. Loman and Mayer (1983) found that headings and similar signals of content increased the recall of conceptual information and improved problem solving. Brooks, Dansereau, Spurlin, and Holley (1983) also found headings to have a highly beneficial effect on both initial learning and recall of scientific information by college students. However, college students who were instructed regarding how to use the headings performed better than those who were not. The headings represented concepts, as is the case in this book. Inasmuch as you probably have not had prior experience with text material being organized into conceptual structures and, therefore, have not been able to use learning aids as employed in this text, the suggestions for using the conceptual structures and aids that follow should be very helpful.

Meaningful Conceptual Organization

The main learning outcomes from your study of educational psychology are concepts and principles and their applications to you as learner and teacher. Before turning to how the content is organized into conceptual structures and how principles of teaching and learning are presented, we will consider what a concept is and how concepts and principles are related.

A *concept* is a person's organized information about an entity or a class of entities: objects (*tree, ball*), events (*birthday, Rose Bowl Parade*), ideas (*equal rights, fair play*), or processes (*thinking, reading*). Having a concept enables a person to discriminate the particular entity or class of entities from other entities and classes of entities (*tree* from *shrub*) and also to relate it or them to other entities and classes of entities (*tree* to *shrub*). Accordingly, concepts are the mental tools with which we think.

Notice that a concept consists of a person's information about something and that each concept has a name. The name of the concept may be a single word or a phrase. To the extent that persons who speak the same language have the same organized information about a word that stands for a given concept, including the meaning of the word, they can use the word to communicate with one another. Thus, if the words in this paragraph have the same meaning for the reader as for the author, the author is communicating with the reader.

We may now relate concepts to principles, another major outcome of the study of educational psychology. *Principles* contain two or more concepts and express a relationship among the concepts, for example, "*i* comes before *e* except after *c*"; "water solidifies at 32°F"; "a reinforcement strengthens the response made immediately before the reinforcement." Accordingly, the concepts incorporated in a principle must be understood in order to understand the principle. Finally, both concepts and principles are used in solving problems. Thus, solving problems of learning and teaching requires the understanding and application of concepts and principles. Principles of learning and teaching are made clear in Part Three of this book.

Let us now turn to the conceptual structure of the content. The titles of each part of this book, of each chapter beginning with Chapter 2, and of each main part of a chapter name a concept. These concepts have been carefully organized into hierarchical conceptual structures: a structure for the entire content of the book, a structure for each of the three contributions of educational psychology to the improvement of educational practice (Parts Two, Three, and Four), a structure for each chapter (2–16), and a structure for each main part of each chapter.

With very few exceptions, each conceptual structure contains the names of one higher-order, or *superordinate,* concept and the names of two or more lower-order, or *subordinate,* concepts. The subordinate concepts are usually *coordinate* to each other. This same pattern of superordinate, subordinate, and coordinate concepts is found in taxonomies, such as those of the plant and animal kingdom. Indeed, understanding these superordinate, subordinate, and coordinate relationships among concepts makes it possible to acquire and relate a great amount of important knowledge that would be exceedingly difficult to acquire by learning each concept separately.

We can clarify the meaning and use of the conceptual structures by turning to the conceptual structure of Part Two of the book.

You may wish to examine page 23 which gives the structure. There you will see that the title, "Foundations of Educational Practice" indicates, or names, the superordinate concept of Part Two and that the subordinate concepts are indicated by the five chapter titles: Aims and Objectives of Education; Theories of Child and Adolescent Development; Theories and Conditions of Learning; Individual and Group Differences; and Instructional Theory, Technology, and Leadership. Each of these titles is the name of a foundation of educational practice.

How does your study of this conceptual structure for just a few seconds facilitate your subsequent study and learning? First, it enables you to grasp quickly the five foundations of educational practice to which educational psychology contributes. Second, it alerts you that your learning task in Chapters 2–6 is to increase your understanding of these five concepts. In this regard, you may have already decided that you understand some of the concepts better than others. Third, it sets boundaries to your learning task, thereby preventing unnecessary searching and guessing as to what the foundations of educational practice are. Fourth, and perhaps most important, it enables you to begin to construct your own *internal conceptual network*, or *schema*, of these foundations of educational practice. This book provides *conceptual structures*, or taxonomies, consisting of names of related concepts, but your *conceptual network* is your own internalized meaning and organization of one or more structures. Your conceptual network enables you to relate the more specific information of each chapter to it.

The content of each chapter after this first one is organized into conceptual structures corresponding to a taxonomy that has concepts hierarchically arranged into four successively higher levels. The chapter title names the highest-level, or generic, concept, while the main headings name the second-highest-level concepts, usually two to six per chapter. For each second-level concept, there are usually two to six third-level concepts; there are fourth-level concepts for some but not all third-level concepts. The third- and fourth-level concepts are also named by the headings that appear in the chapter so that you can easily identify them. You may wish to refer to the beginning of Chapter 4 (p. 89), to see how the conceptual structure at the beginning of each chapter is presented. You will notice that the superordinate concept is *theories and conditions of learning* and that the second-level concepts are the five different theories and conditions of learning: *conditioning, observational learning, meaningful verbal learning, learning as information processing,* and *purposeful learning.* Now turn to page 90 and see the next level of the taxonomy and how it is indicated. *Conditioning* is the higher second-level concept and its two subordinate (third-level) concepts are *classical conditioning* and *operant conditioning.* Each of the other four second-level concepts of the chapter and its subordinate concepts are indicated in this same manner at the place where the second-order concept is introduced.

Research on learning text information presented in Chapter 8 of this book explains how having a conceptual network, or schema, enables the reader to organize new information effectively. In addition, forming a conceptual network of the content of a chapter, such as that of Chapter 4, before starting to read the chapter, and then later forming a network of each main part before beginning to read enables you to relate the new information to what you already know. Organizing new material meaningfully and relating the new information to what you already know are the two most effective strategies for learning that have been identified up to the present time.

Moreover, upon completing your study of Chapter 4 and hearing or seeing the words *theories and conditions of learning,* you will be able to recall the five subordinate concepts, or theories, and much of the specific information related to each theory. Accordingly, you will learn educational psychology by forming a network of big ideas or concepts first, then of closely related subordinate concepts, and finally of specific information. At no time will you be presented with a large amount of unrelated, piecemeal information that is impossible for you to organize and relate.

Two other points are in order regarding this organization of the content. The conceptual structures located at the beginning of and within each chapter enable the reader to set realistic learning goals in terms of how much of the chapter to study in one session. They also may be used for surveying the content of a chapter and raising questions or using other learning strategies that you may have acquired before starting to read.

There are a few exceptions in this book to the superordinate-subordinate conceptual structures. The exceptions occur in a chapter or in part of a chapter where knowledge about something is either too incomplete or too unrelated to be organized as a conceptual structure. In these instances, the content is organized according to topics. Although the organization consists of a series of topics rather than a taxonomy, the name of each topic also represents a concept to which you can attach meaning as you may have already observed from your study of this chapter.

Learning Aids

The primary aid to learning the content of each chapter is the listing of one superordinate and several subordinate concepts of the chapter in color at the beginning of the chapter and the listing of one superordinate and several subordinate concepts of each main part of the chapter in color at the beginning of each main part. With only one or two exceptions, fewer than seven subordinate concepts have been included in any one list. Most contain two to five. This was done because the majority of people cannot hold more than seven items, or chunks, of information in their short-term memory. If they attend to something else before the items are stored in memory, they cannot recall all of them later. As a further aid in organizing and relating ideas, the third-level concepts appear in red and the fourth-level concepts in black, but they are not brought together in lists.

Other aids to learning the content of this book are figures, tables, special highlighted text, cartoons, and photographs. The figures, tables, and highlighted text condense or elaborate information in the text and, in order not to interrupt your train of thought, immediately follow the text to which they relate. The opening chapter cartoon introduces the chapter theme in a light, humorous vein, while the photographs reinforce big ideas of the chapter.

The question section at the end of each main part of each chapter also aids your initial learning and retention. One type of question invites you to identify relationships among items of information given in the text, to analyze the information, and/or to evaluate it. A second type calls for you to integrate the text ideas with what you already know by relating them to your own experiences as a learner or to your own perceptions of how to guide the learning activities of students. Answering questions of this kind markedly facilitates initial learning and retention. As a matter of fact, Ellis, Konoske, Wulfeck, and Montague (1982) found postquestions to have a greater facilitative effect than instructions to the students about how and what to learn. The postquestions combined with the instructions had a greater positive effect than either one alone.

LEARNING AIDS IN THIS TEXT

1. Lists placed at the beginning of and within each chapter to indicate the superordinate and subordinate concepts of the chapter.
2. Figures.
3. Tables.
4. Special highlighted text.
5. Questions requiring analysis, evaluation, and application at the end of each main part of a chapter.
6. Cartoons and photographs that dramatize a main chapter theme.

The conceptual structure and the questions will help you use your time effectively for studying each chapter. How many parts of each chapter to study at one sitting varies with the amount of time you have for study, your ability to study with concentration, and what you already know about the content.

You can get a quick estimate of the type, amount, and difficulty of the content of a chapter by examining the opening chapter list of concepts and the in-chapter lists. After getting this estimate and taking into account other conditions that affect your study, you may wish to complete only one or two parts of a chapter in one study session. When you return to the chapter, examine the list at the beginning of the chapter and at the beginning of each part that you studied. Recall your responses to the questions. Then examine the list for the next part of the chapter that you will be studying and begin your reading. This strategy will work better for more students than trying to complete an entire chapter in one study session.

Findings from Recent Research

We gain knowledge in many ways. One of the most important ways is research. Results from research conducted in school settings are a very important part of educational psychology.

As you might surmise, there are hundreds of research articles and many books related to nearly every chapter of this book. Unfortunately, only part of the research could be included because of space constraints. Accordingly, representative research studies are reported. In addition to the research reported in the chapters, original research studies of exceptional significance are listed for some chapters in the "Suggestions for Further Reading" at the end of the chapter.

Scholars during recent years have reviewed all of the original research—hundreds of studies in some instances—on most of the big ideas of this book. Some of these reviews are also listed at the end of some chapters. They are very helpful in gaining an overview of recent advances in theory and practice. We pause briefly to note that books and articles describing effective instructional practices are also included in the "Suggestions for Further Reading."

Principles for Fostering Classroom Learning

Cookbooks provide detailed step-by-step directions for preparing each of many items. Cookbooks are effective because the ingredients and measuring devices are identical or nearly so for all cookbook users. Students and teachers are not identical. Not even one teacher and one student interact identically in all situations on a given day in school. Accordingly, this text presents a relatively small number of principles for fostering student learning rather than many detailed prescriptions. The principle indicates a general action. The teacher analyzes the specific situation and identifies the specific actions to be taken based on the principle.

As an aid to the reader, a set of these principles is given in the last parts of Chapters 7–14, except that strategies for comprehending verbal information rather than a set of principles are given in Chapter 8. These principles are drawn from the research and theory presented in the chapter and from the foundation areas presented in Chapters 2–6. They are intended as general guidelines for teaching. Some applications of the principle are given to guide the reader in finding similar applications.

The number of principles has been deliberately held to seven or less to facilitate your being able to study and rehearse the list for a few seconds before starting your reading. The principles for fostering classroom motivation given in Chapter 7 follow:

**PRINCIPLES FOR
FOSTERING CLASSROOM MOTIVATION**

1. Establish a learning-oriented environment.
2. Utilize students' needs and intrinsic motives.
3. Make the subject matter interesting.
4. Help each student set and attain goals.
5. Aid students to assume increasing responsibility for their learning activities.
6. Provide informative feedback and, as necessary, external control.

USES OF THIS TEXT

This book has been written to meet the interests and educational needs of all students who enroll in courses where the book is used as the basic text. It may be used in several ways.

First, this book is intended to help you extend your knowledge about child and adolescent development, theories of learning, individual differences, instructional theory and instructional leadership, principles of learning and teaching, measurement, and evaluation. Education is a very large and exceedingly important enterprise. All students enrolled in educational psychology can profitably extend their knowledge about these important aspects of education.

Second, this book is designed to help you understand your own interests, capabilities, and learning strategies. You may acquire new learning strategies and be able to apply them in this course and in other courses. Moreover, you may wish to demonstrate your strategies to younger students so that they, too, can become more effective learners. Understanding your characteristics as a learner, the learning process, motivation, strategies of learning, and principles of learning and teaching will stand you in good stead as a citizen, a parent, and an educator.

Third, this book is a source of practical ideas on how to teach. Principles and suggestions are given in Chapters 7–14 on how to guide student learning. Chapters 15 and 16 give suggestions for developing your skills in measurement and evaluation. Using this book as a source of practical ideas on how to teach requires you to make applications of the concepts and principles. Writing the answers to the *application* questions at the end of each main part of each chapter will help you generate ideas for use in your formal or informal teaching. Keeping these written responses in a notebook will prove especially helpful for future reference in the event that you cannot apply your ideas immediately.

Finally, this book is a reference work to which you can return when you need specific information to help you solve a personal learning or teaching problem. As you read and study a chapter or a topic, you may not have the opportunity to make the applications immediately. However, you may subsequently encounter a challenge in learning the material of another course or in solving a problem encountered when teaching. This text, the references, and the "Suggestions for Further Reading" provide up-to-date information that you can use in independent study or research on a topic of immediate interest.

SUMMARY

Education continues to contribute significantly to the intellectual, moral, and social development of children and adolescents. Despite widely publicized criticisms of education, the overwhelming majority of the public regards education as extremely important to achieving success in life. Educational psychology has much to offer to the continuing improvement of education.

Much of the theory and practice of education is based on five foundations of educational practice: the formulation of educational objectives that serve as guides to learning and teaching, child and adolescent development, principles and conditions of learning, individual and group differences, and instructional theory and instructional leadership. In turn, knowledge from these foundation areas contributes to the identification of sound principles of learning and teaching.

The study of educational psychology provides much practical information in the form of principles of learning and teaching. One important area is motivation for learning. Other principles guide instructional practices related to the outcomes of learning. One domain of learning outcomes is *cognitive* and includes verbal information, concepts and principles, and problem solving and creativity. Another is *psychomotor* and includes motor and vocal skills. The third domain is *affective* and includes attitudes and values, and personality integration. Self-discipline and positive regard for the individuality and welfare of others are important elements of personality integration. Principles for fostering retention and transfer are applicable to all of these outcomes of learning. Securing high student motivation, achieving the outcomes of learning in the three domains, and fostering long-term retention and transfer as widely accepted goals of teachers. The study of educational psychology contributes to the achievement of these goals.

Another major emphasis in educational psychology is measuring student progress in achieving learning outcomes and evaluating the effectiveness of educational programs. Skill in measurement and evaluation greatly facilitates student learning and thereby successful teaching.

Practical and theoretical knowledge is gained through research. The research methods of educational psychology—experimental, correlational, developmental, descriptive, and practical—are similar to those of the other social sciences. These methods are used selectively to extend knowledge in the foundation areas, to generate more reliable principles of learning and teaching, and to solve problems of education.

A unique feature of this text is the incorporation of principles of learning and teaching to facilitate your initial learning, long-term retention, and use of the material. The principles are embodied in ways that extensive research has shown to facilitate the learning of text material. First, the entire content of the book is carefully organized into conceptual structures rather than loosely related topics. Second, these conceptual structures are listed at the beginning of each chapter and each main part of each chapter, including in the page margins, to enable you to secure a quick overview of the content of a chapter and an estimate of your familiarity with it. Third, two kinds of questions at the end of each main part of each chapter encourage you either to analyze and evaluate what you have read or to relate ideas to your own experiences as a learner or to your own perceptions of how to guide the learning activities of students. Responding to these questions will foster long-term retention and use of the ideas. Fourth, research results have been selected and included in the text. From thousands of original research studies and research summaries, the most representative and significant for improving educational practice have been included. Fifth, a short set of principles of learning and teaching is presented in each of Chapters 7–14.

An appendix on statistics at the end of the book provides a brief introduction to statistical terms and methods.

SUGGESTIONS FOR FURTHER READING

Clifford, M. M. Educational Psychology. In Corsini, R. J. (Ed.), *Encyclopedia of Psychology*, Vol. 1, New York: Wiley, 1984, pp. 413–416.

Gives an overview of the original and present status of the main concepts of educational psychology. This four-volume encyclopedia provides most recent information on every main concept included in this text as well as on many other concepts of high interest to educators.

Cuban, L. *How teachers taught: Constancy and change in American classrooms: 1890–1980*. New York: Longman, 1984.

Examines stability and change in teaching practices and describes what teachers can and cannot do.

Eisner, E. (Ed.). Teaching as art and craft. *Educational Leadership*, January, 1983.

This special issue of *Educational Leadership* has several interesting articles on teaching as an art.

Flanagan, J. C. The contribution of educational institutions to the quality of life of Americans. *International Review of Applied Psychology*, 1983, *32*, 275–288.

A follow-up of 1000 grade 9 students when 30 years of age. Reports the quality-of-life values held by this group, the percentage satisfied or very satisfied with their present status regarding each value, and the many contributions of education to the attainment of the values.

Gallup, G. H. The 15th annual Gallup Poll of the public's attitude toward education. *Phi Delta Kappan*, 1983, *65*(1), 33–47.

Reports the attitudes of Americans toward many aspects of public education in 1983, and also in earlier years. For example, in 1978, 36% of the individuals polled regarded college education as very important; in 1983, 58% did. The percentage of persons who would vote to raise taxes for public schools was 36 in 1972, 30 in 1981, and 39 in 1983.

Good, T. L., Biddle, B. J., & Brophy, J. E. *Teachers make a difference*. Lanham, Md.: University Press of America, 1982.

This book documents the fact that teachers and schools can and do make a big difference in the educational progress of students.

Hodgkinson, H. L. What's STILL right with education. *Phi Delta Kappan*, 1982, *64*(4), 231–235.

Hodgkinson indicates that our educational system is one of our strongest American institutions. It is designed for every student, and yet its very best students are as good as those of any nation in the world.

Isaac, S., & Michael, W. B. *Handbook in research and evaluation* (2nd ed.). San Diego, Calif.: Edits Publishers, 1981.

Chapter 1 describes different kinds of evaluation studies and indicates how evaluation studies are conducted. Chapter 3 describes research methods and indicates how research is planned and conducted.

Lyson, T. A., & Falk, W. W. Recruitment to school teaching: The relationship between high school plans and early adult attainments. *American Educational Research Journal*, 1984, *21*, 181–193.

A fascinating follow-up of the high school class of 1972 identifying the relationship between plans for entering teaching and becoming teachers.

Rubin, L. Artistry in teaching. *Educational Leadership*, 1983, *40*(4), 44–49.

Rubin explains the difference between exciting and dreary classes and shows what teachers can do to make their classes exciting for the learners and themselves. (This issue of this journal has other excellent articles on teaching.)

PART TWO

FOUNDATIONS OF EDUCATIONAL PRACTICE

SALLY FORTH CARTOON COPYRIGHT BY FIELD ENTERPRISES, INC.

CHAPTER 2

AIMS AND OBJECTIVES OF EDUCATION

- NATIONAL AIMS OF EDUCATION
- DOMAINS OF EDUCATIONAL OBJECTIVES
- OBJECTIVES FOR CURRICULUM PLANNING AND TEACHING
- MINIMUM COMPETENCY OBJECTIVES

The national aims of education take into account a number of key questions of interest to citizens generally. Should education through the twelfth grade prepare some students for college attendance? for further education in a technical school or community college? for employment immediately after high school graduation? Should some students be permitted or even encouraged to leave school before high school graduation? What should be the role of the school in educating for personality development, health, family life, and citizenship? Should education ensure that every student has equal opportunity to achieve the aims of education?

Less comprehensive objectives to guide educational practice in local schools have been formulated in each of three domains: *cognitive, psychomotor,* and *affective.* A widely used taxonomy of objectives is available in each of the three domains.

The objectives for curriculum planning and teaching include objectives in the three domains and also reflect the broad aims of education. They raise questions of high concern to teachers. Who should determine the objectives that students should achieve in each program area of the school, for example, the objectives of mathematics, kindergarten through grade 6, or of high school English? Should teachers be responsible for selecting or writing the objectives of their own courses? To what extent should students take responsibility for identifying their own learning objectives? Each teacher is called upon to make decisions about educational objectives and in many instances to formulate and write them.

Minimum competency objectives and related minimum competency testing are common in many states. However, there are still many unresolved issues about the effects of minimum competency objectives and related testing.

The purpose of this chapter is to aid teachers and others in making wise decisions about educational objectives. The decisions that are made influence what students learn and the role of the teacher in the educative process.

Aims of Elementary Education

Aims of Secondary Education

Objectives of the National Assessment of Educational Progress

NATIONAL AIMS OF EDUCATION

What should the schools teach? Are there certain aims of education that contribute more than others to individual development and to strengthening democratic life and government? National groups formulate aims of education that they believe will contribute to individual development and citizenship. The aims are stated in general terms so that school-board members, parents, and others will readily understand them. Widely accepted aims of elementary and secondary education follow to illustrate how aims are stated and what they include. As you read, check them mentally to see if you would support them as indicators of the purposes of elementary and secondary schools.

Aims of Elementary Education

Aims of elementary education were formulated by the Mid-Century Committee on Outcomes in Elementary Education (Kearney, 1953). These aims are very widely accepted. Figure 2.1 shows the aims organized in a three-dimensional framework.

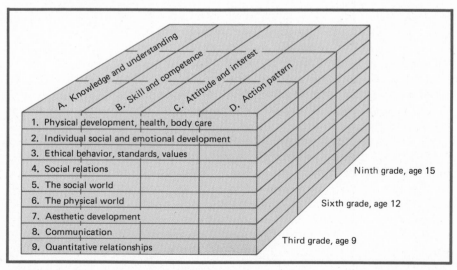

Figure 2.1 Aims of elementary education.
Source: Kearney, 1953, p. 38.

The first dimension is a growth scale. It is called the growth dimension because students are expected to attain objectives related to the aims at successively higher levels with each year of school. For convenience, the growth dimension is related to grades in school. Grades 7–9 are included to indicate the desired continuity between elementary and postelementary education.

The second dimension is represented by broad program areas of the elementary school. The nine areas are physical development, health, body care; individual social and emotional development; ethical behavior, standards, values; social relations; the social world; the physical world; aesthetic development; communication; and quantitative relationships. Students are to make continuous progress in all of these program areas throughout elementary school.

The third dimension consists of four classes of learning outcomes: knowledge and understanding, skill and competence, attitude and interest, and action pattern. These four areas of learning outcomes are generally accepted as including everything of importance that students should learn. The framework indicates that students should achieve these outcomes at successively higher levels in all nine program areas as they progress through elementary school.

Determining conditions, though not indicated in Figure 2.1, include the biological inheritance of the individual student and the social-psychological climate of the school. Both of these can change over a period of time. For example, students mature physically about two years earlier than they did fifty years ago. Similarly, the social-psychological climate of the elementary school changes. It changed for some students when small rural schools were consolidated into larger ones and when city schools carried out court-ordered desegregation by busing children from their neighborhood schools.

When subject-matter specialists and other persons first encounter the nine program areas, they may be perplexed because the program areas do not seem to fit neatly into separate subject fields. It is true that the communication area can readily be associated with reading, spelling, and English; quantitative relationships are usually part of mathematics; the physical world is included in science and geography, and so on. However, aims of education generally do not specify how the curriculum should be organized. Each elementary school that accepts the aims assumes the responsibility for organizing its curriculum to achieve them. The same is true for secondary schools.

Aims of Secondary Education

One statement of educational aims that had great influence on secondary education in the present century is the Cardinal Principles of Secondary Education (1918) and subsequent revisions of it. A recent set of aims stated in the form of competencies that all college-bound students should attain will probably have a marked effect for the remainder of this century (College Board, 1983). Both of these sets of high school aims merit further consideration.

Cardinal Principles of Secondary Education

The Cardinal Principles of Secondary Education (1918) departed from the earlier idea that the primary aim of secondary education was preparation for college or university. This departure occurred because the commission that formulated the principles believed that secondary education should be helpful to all students, not only to those intending to pursue higher education. In formulating the principles, the commission tried to take into account the needs of society, the characteristics of the students to be educated, and the available knowledge about educational theory and practice. The Cardinal Principles of Secondary Education reflect the democratic ideal that the individual and society find fulfillment in each other. The seven cardinal aims to be achieved in the education of every high school boy and girl are:

1. Health
2. Command of fundamental processes
3. Worthy home membership
4. Vocation
5. Civic education
6. Worthy use of leisure
7. Ethical character

The cardinal principles were modified slightly by various national groups from 1927 to 1970. A thorough updating was carried out in the 1970s as a project of the National Education Association (Shane, 1977). This project was planned in connection with the 200th anniversary celebration of the Declaration of Independence. A panel of adults and high school juniors and seniors were interviewed to get their ideas regarding what the aims of secondary education should be for the remainder of this century.

Shane (1977) found wide acceptance of the original seven cardinal principles by the adults and high school students. However, new emphases were added to take into account the changes in society that have occurred during the past half century and other changes that are expected to occur till the year 2000. The new emphases for two of the cardinal principles—health and command of the fundamental processes—follow. You may wish to add your own ideas to these two and to the other five.

Health (in addition to physical health)

Mental and emotional health.

Interpersonal and intercultural attitudes regarding matters of health.

An understanding of dietary needs and problems that goes beyond earlier simple nutrition education to include such matters as dangers in food additives and health concerns associated with family living, sexuality, and divorce.

Drug education.

Command of fundamental processes
(in addition to reading, writing, mathematics)

Humanistic processes, including human relations, group-process skills, and intercultural and multiethnic relationships.

Nonacademic skills, including knowledge of sources of information, the role of computers, and interdisciplinary understandings.

Problem-solving skills, including gathering, analyzing, synthesizing, and evaluating information.

The preceding additions reflect two very important trends in American secondary education. First, the school should provide ever-increasing, essential services to youth that the family, church, and other organizations have ceased to provide. Second, the school should provide a model for educating the present generation of adolescents in desired social changes, for example, equal educational opportunities for women, students with learning handicaps, and students from minority groups.

The responses of the students interviewed by Shane (1977) to what they thought might be done to improve secondary education reflect the previous trends. Shane's summary of their main ideas follows:

> Although their thoughts were phrased in many different ways, three points came through clearly. First, in a world that youth find frustrating, distressing, and sometimes frightening, the need for *coping* skills and techniques was expressed. Made uneasy by the widespread malaise and troubles of the present—the profound global turmoil of which the media constantly reminded them—the students clearly recognized the importance of good guidance and better preparation in their schooling so that they could live good and useful lives in a world of inter- and intra-dependence.
>
> A second quality that youth sought in its schools is more difficult to capture in words. The young people wanted schools that *cared* about them. The [interview] tapes sometimes poignantly revealed loneliness. The image of the "good" teacher was not merely one who was bright, good-looking, or well informed. It was a person who radiated warmth and genuine interest in students. Parents who substituted things rather than giving of their time and of themselves, parents who didn't seem to care, and absentee parents also troubled many boys and girls. Some spoke of having no one other than their peer group for companionship and of no place other than the streets for a "home."
>
> Finally, the young sought help in *communicating*. They were not speaking here of better language instruction or of forensic skills, but of the opportunity to have someone to talk with, someone to whom they could listen, someone to whom and with whom they could communicate and share their feelings, hopes, and concerns.
>
> Reduced to their basic meanings, the comments made by youth indicate that they hope for schools characterized by a climate of love and of understanding that will build the inner security that the troubled present and an uncertain future require. *Coping, caring, communicating: the three words suggest a premise charged with emotion. The schools youth seek are schools that provide coping skills for facing a world that is often harsh and sometimes frightening; schools that are warmly humane because*

teachers care; and schools that give an opportunity to communicate inner feelings without fear of ridicule or reprisal. This is easy to say, but truly difficult to realize in practice. (Shane, 1977, pp. 68–69)

High School Competencies as Aims

In 1980 the College Board started a study designed to identify the competencies that entering college students should have developed in order to be successful in college. Many different school and college educators served on various committees to identify the competencies, also referred to as what students need to know and should be able to do. The conclusions of the committees were subsequently reported in a 46-page booklet (College Board, 1983). Attaining the competencies should be the aim of high school education for college-bound students, according to the College Board.

The committees identified competencies in six *basic academic areas:* reading, writing, speaking and listening, mathematics, reasoning, and studying. Other competencies were formulated related to computers and observing. However, these are not considered as basic academic competencies. Students are to acquire the basic academic competencies, and also other competencies, through study of the *basic academic subjects:* English, the arts, mathematics, science, social studies, and foreign language. In general, study in the fine arts and foreign language does not contribute as directly to the basic academic competencies as the other four subjects.

Having attained the basic academic competencies is regarded as essential for achieving success in any field of study at the college level. However, the attainment of basic competency is not specific to the study of any particular subject in high school. This will become more apparent by examining one competency in each of the six basic areas (College Board, 1983, pp. 7–10):

> **Reading.** The ability to identify and comprehend the main and subordinate ideas in a written work and to summarize the ideas in one's own words.

> **Writing.** The ability to conceive ideas about a topic for the purpose of writing.

> **Speaking and Listening.** The ability to engage critically and constructively in the exchange of ideas, particularly during class discussions and conferences with instructors.

> **Mathematics.** The ability to perform, with reasonable accuracy, the computations of addition, subtraction, multiplication, and division using natural numbers, fractions, decimals, and integers.

> **Reasoning.** The ability to identify and formulate problems, as well as the ability to propose and evaluate ways to solve them.

Studying. The ability to set study goals and priorities consistent with stated course objectives and one's own progress, to establish surroundings and habits conducive to learning independently or with others, and to follow a schedule that accounts for both short- and long-term projects.

One feature that sets off the preceding recommendations of the College Board is that no suggestions are made as to the number of credits or courses that a student should take to be graduated from high school. Instead, the school is to decide the level of competence it desires of the students. A second feature is that the competencies are stated in a manner that high school students and their parents, as well as educators, can understand. Accordingly, the booklet listing and explaining the competencies can be used at home as well as at school. An important goal of the project is that all high school students, including the educationally disadvantaged, should be fully aware of what they need to know and be able to do to be successful in college. Moreover, the students should then develop the competencies during their high school years so as not to be disadvantaged educationally upon entering a four-year college, or later, upon attempting to enter graduate school.

Objectives of the National
Assessment of Educational Progress

The aims of elementary education and secondary education were formulated to influence national opinion on the purposes of American education. More detailed objectives were developed to assess student achievement throughout the United States and to determine whether it increases, decreases, or remains constant across extended periods of time. The National Assessment of Educational Progress called upon a national panel of educators and citizens in the development of the objectives.

The National Assessment of Educational Progress assesses student achievement at approximately five-year intervals in each of ten program areas: art, career and occupational development, citizenship, literature, mathematics, music, reading, science, social studies, and writing. Work groups, including citizens, teachers, and subject-matter scholars, prepare the educational objectives for each program. Tests are constructed to measure the achievement of the objectives by students of ages 9, 13, and 17. Neither the objectives nor the related achievement tests are expected to change much; test results obtained in the future will be compared with the results of the earlier assessments that started in the late 1960s.

Examples of objectives for citizenship and science follow (National Assessment of Educational Progress, 1972a, p. 13; 1972b, p. 19). The objectives in these and other program areas are typically organized into sets that include one comprehensive objective for all levels of schooling and related objectives for ages 9, 13, and 17. As you examine the objectives, give careful consideration to how student achievement of each age-level objective contributes to the achievement of the comprehensive objective.

Comprehensive Citizenship Objective
Is ethical and dependable in work, school, and social situations.

Related objectives for age levels
Students are ethical and dependable in work, school, and social situations:

Age 9: They are considerate and prompt in keeping appointments. They keep promises and can be trusted with work and school responsibilities appropriate to their age. They correct their own errors and do not blame others for their mistakes. They try to see that credit is given where due, and that everyone gets a fair share of participation and reward. They admit the limits of their own knowledge and experience and accept corrections and decisions of authorities. They try to choose other students for special roles and tasks on the basis of the student's interest and ability rather than solely on the basis of friendship or popularity.

Age 13 (in addition to Age 9): At school or work, they follow agreed upon procedures and schedules and persevere until a job is completed. They are willing to work extra hours on occasion and to undertake additional responsibilities. They start new tasks without having to be told, check work for mistakes, and use initiative to find better ways of achieving work goals.

Age 17 (in addition to Ages 9 and 13): They assume integrity and good intentions of other citizens and public officials unless there is clear contrary evidence.

Comprehensive Science Objective
Understand that measurement is an important feature of science.

Related science objectives for age levels
Age 9: Understands that quantitative measurements of natural phenomena can be made.

Age 13: Describes how quantitative measurements provide clearer and more precise representations of natural phenomena than do qualitative descriptions.

Age 17: Explains or demonstrates that quantitative measurements, when feasible, provide the basis for description, hypothesis testing, and prediction; explains that mathematics and statistics provide valuable tools for deriving information from quantitative data; explains that all data are not equally precise.

The objectives of the National Assessment for Educational Progress may have considerable impact on the course of American education. For example, if achievement goes down in basic skills, such as reading and writing, during a five-year period schools may give more time and emphasis to these areas and less to art, music, or other program areas.

2.1 Examine the nine program areas of elementary education given in Figure 2.1. Do you think all nine areas should receive equal attention today in grades 4–8 in terms of the amount of instructional time given to them each year? Indicate which should receive more or less time than others and give the reasons for your answer.

2.2 Review the seven Cardinal Principles of Secondary Education. Which of the seven aims were given the least instructional time when you were in high school? Why do you think these areas received less instructional time than others?

2.3 The changes from 1918 in the emphases regarding health as an aim of secondary education were indicated. How well do you think present secondary schools can respond to these new emphases? Explain.

2.4 High school students indicated that schools can be improved if they teach more coping skills and if they become more caring and personalized. Why do you think high schools have difficulty in dealing with coping, caring, and communicating?

2.5 In recent years, there has been greater public demand than during the 1970s for schools to produce high educational achievement. Why do you think this has occurred?

DOMAINS OF EDUCATIONAL OBJECTIVES

Cognitive Domain
Psychomotor Domain
Affective Domain

The aims of elementary and secondary education provide general directions for education. On the other hand, the objectives of the National Assessment of Educational Progress are sufficiently specific to enable experts in test construction to develop related achievement tests and questionnaires. However, they only sample from the many possible objectives of only 10 program areas. Local-school curriculum developers and teachers need objectives that are more specific than the aims of elementary and secondary education and more complete than the objectives of the National Assessment to indicate what students should learn. Systematic guidelines for formulating objectives to meet this need have been organized according to three domains: *cognitive* (Bloom, 1956), *psychomotor* (Kibler, Barker, & Miles, 1970), and *affective* (Krathwohl, Bloom, & Masia, 1964).

Objectives in the *cognitive domain* deal with gaining and recalling information and with the intellectual skills of comprehending, applying, analyzing, synthesizing, and evaluating information. Many objectives in

English, mathematics, science, and social studies are in the cognitive domain. Objectives in the *psychomotor domain* imply the learning of skilled movements. Dancing, swimming, and typing are psychomotor activities. Objectives in the *affective domain* include feelings, such as are involved in the learning of attitudes, interests, and values. In general, all teachers desire their students to achieve objectives in the affective domain.

The three domains are not mutually exclusive. There is some affect, or feeling, associated with learning both cognitive and psychomotor outcomes. Similarly, learning and performing psychomotor skills involve some cognitive activity. Despite the overlapping, you will find it useful to identify how objectives of your subject-matter specialty may be related to the three domains.

Cognitive Domain

What thought processes, or intellectual skills, should students continually develop to higher levels? What subject-matter content should students learn? How is an educational objective formulated to specify both process and content? The most widely used approach to answering these questions is based on a taxonomy of six educational objectives in the cognitive domain (Bloom, 1956).

According to this taxonomy, the learning of information in any subject field proceeds from simple to increasingly complex operations: *acquiring and recalling, comprehending, applying, analyzing, synthesizing,* and *evaluating.* In the taxonomy, acquiring and recalling information are called *knowledge;* the other five operations are called *intellectual skills.* Educational objectives, stated in terms of desired changes in student behavior, are formulated to correspond to the six categories of knowledge and intellectual skills.

The idea that each of the intellectual skills is increasingly complex is now being questioned. For example, acquiring and comprehending some kinds of information, such as a scientific or mathematical theory, is regarded as more complex than synthesizing or evaluating other information, such as a news story or a TV soap opera (Furst, 1981). Therefore, introducing objectives that require synthesis or evaluation of certain kinds of information should not be delayed until objectives involving application and analysis of other kinds of information have been achieved.

In the next paragraphs, each of the six kinds of objectives is first defined. Then, illustrative objectives are given. Proceed slowly through each of the areas of the taxonomy and think of at least one more example for each objective. This will help you to capture the value of using this taxonomy in formulating educational objectives.

Knowledge Objectives (Memory)

Knowledge objectives call for the student to learn information and then either to recall or to recognize it at a later time. Recall may be of specific facts, methods, or principles.

The Bloom taxonomy of educational objectives in the cognitive domain calls for students to recall knowledge and to learn to comprehend, apply, analyze, synthesize, and evaluate information. Should all teachers be experts in these intellectual skills? When and how should they teach the skills to their students?

Examples. The student will be able to (a) recognize the correct spelling of *believe,* (b) recall the procedure for identifying the correct spelling of a word in a dictionary, (c) recall the rule "*i* before *e* except after *c*."

Comprehension Objectives

Comprehension objectives indicate that students will be able to understand and use information. However, relating the comprehended information to other information is not required to attain a comprehension objective.

Examples. The student will be able to (a) read musical scores, (b) give a literal translation of a sentence from Spanish to English, (c) give examples of air pollution.

Application Objectives

Application objectives indicate that the student should learn to use abstractions, such as ideas, rules, or methods, in particular situations.

Examples. The student will be able to (a) use the concept of *tree* to identify particular plants as trees, (b) apply the rule "*i* before *e* except after *c*" in spelling the new word *receipt,* (c) prepare a weekly menu based on principles of diet and nutrition.

Analysis Objectives

Analysis objectives specify that the student will learn to break down a communication, or other whole, into its constituent parts.

> **Examples.** The student will be able to (a) distinguish a conclusion in a research study from the specific findings that support it, (b) recognize the causes of air pollution, (c) identify the likenesses and differences between short stories and novels.

Synthesis Objectives

Synthesis objectives call for the student to learn to put together elements or parts to form a whole. The whole may be a communication, a plan, or a set of abstract relations.

> **Examples.** The student will be able to (a) write an essay, story, or poem, (b) formulate hypotheses for an experiment, (c) design an experiment for testing hypotheses.

Evaluation Objectives

Evaluation objectives indicate that the student will learn to make value judgments about something in terms of specified criteria. The criteria may be given to the student or formulated by the student.

> **Examples.** The student will be able to (a) evaluate a paragraph in terms of its coherence, (b) judge the pros and cons of capital punishment, and (c) compare two theories of learning in terms of their usability in guiding instruction.

As indicated earlier in this chapter, this taxonomy is used extensively in formulating objectives when planning instruction for a unit, semester, or a year, but it can also be used to generate questions and activities when teaching. As you have probably experienced personally, in some classes, questions and activities call almost solely for recall and comprehension. In other classes, questions calling for higher intellectual skills are emphasized. Redfield and Rosseau (1981) analyzed 14 studies dealing with teachers' use of lower- and higher-level questions and found that higher-level questioning produced considerably higher student achievement.

Sanders (1965) worked with teachers for several semesters to improve their use of questions and problem-solving activities. As a result, students developed their higher-level intellectual skills more fully. The following questions and activities, related to the social studies concept *gerrymandering* illustrate the teachers' efforts (Sanders, 1965, pp. 3–5):

Comprehension. What is meant by *gerrymandering?*

Application. The mayor recently appointed a committee to study the fairness of the boundaries of the election districts in our community. Gather information about the present districts and the population in each. Determine whether the present city election districts are adequate. (The student is expected to apply principles of democracy studied in class to this new problem.)

Analysis. Analyze the reasoning in this quotation: "Human beings lack the ability to be fair when their own interests are involved. Party X controls the legislature, and now it has taken upon itself the responsibility of redrawing the boundaries of the legislative election districts. We know in advance that our party will suffer."

Synthesis. If current election districts in our community are inadequate, suggest how they might be redrawn. (This activity must follow the preceding application question.)

Evaluation. Would you favor having your political party engage in gerrymandering if it had the opportunity?

Psychomotor Domain

Kibler, Barker, and Miles (1970) classified movements and skills of the psychomotor domain. One purpose of their classification was to provide a framework for identifying educational objectives. Another was to define the major classes of motor and vocal skills. This classification was not intended to be hierarchical like the taxonomy in the cognitive domain. Nevertheless, it is based on theory and research in child development that indicates the following four-phase sequence of development during infancy and early childhood: gross bodily movements → finely coordinated movements → nonverbal communication → speech. In the following pages, each of these four classes of motor and vocal behaviors is defined, the subclasses of each class are indicated, and illustrative objectives are presented.

Gross Bodily Movements

This category involves movements of entire limbs in isolation or in conjunction with other parts of the body. The movements are carried out by a person alone, by a person in conjunction with another object, or between two or more persons. Some coordination of movements with the eye or ear is necessary. However, the primary emphasis is on strength, speed, or precision involving gross movements.

Movements Involving the Upper Limbs: Skills such as throwing, catching, and pulling oneself up.

> To be able to throw a baseball 50 feet.
> To be able to do 5 chin-ups.

Movements Involving the Lower Limbs: Skills such as running, jumping, marching, and kicking.

To be able to run the 100-yard dash in 20 seconds.

To be able to march in step with a drum beat.

Movements Involving Two or More Bodily Units: Skills such as swimming, diving, gymnastics, and dancing.

To be able to swim 50 yards.

To be able to execute the basic ballet positions.

Finely Coordinated Movements

This class requires coordinated movements of the extremities, usually in conjunction with the eye or ear. The movements are usually performed in combination with some external object. The degree of learning necessary to perform coordinated skills differentiates them from the gross bodily movements of the first classification.

Hand-Finger Movements. Skills characterized by the sense of touch rather than by the sense of sight.

To be able to translate a paragraph in Braille accurately.

To be able to differentiate between a nickel and a penny solely by touch.

Hand-Eye Coordination. Skills such as playing a musical instrument, typing, writing, sewing, painting, sculpting, and weaving.

To be able to print the letters of the alphabet.

To be able to type 60 words per minute.

Hand-Ear Coordination. Skills found primarily in applied music (not reading music), broadcast media, and other performing arts.

To be able to tap the rhythm of a song.

To be able to find the same note on the piano that is played on the violin.

Hand-Eye-Foot Coordination. Skills requiring coordinated movements by hands, feet, and fingers in conjunction with the eye, such as physical education activities and the operation of technical equipment and machinery.

To be able to kick a football 40 yards.

To be able to operate a sheet-metal lathe safely.

Other Combinations of Hand-Foot-Eye-Ear Movements. Skills such as piano tuning (eye-ear-hand), playing the organ, harp, and trap drums (eye-ear-hand-foot), and driving a car (eye-ear-hand-foot).

To be able to drive a car.

To be able to read and play a piece of piano music.

Nonverbal Communication

Nonverbal communication behaviors include facial expressions, gestures, bodily movements, or a combination of the three.

Facial Expressions. Activities that focus primarily on the mouth and eyes as communicators of moods or messages.
  To be able to exhibit a range of facial expressions.
  To be able to portray the emotion *love* by facial expressions.

Gestures. Movements that involve the use of hands and arms to communicate specific messages, as in public speaking, theater, and dance.
  To be able to communicate messages in hand-sign language.
  To be able to communicate by the use of gestures.

Bodily Movements. Skills involving the movement of the trunk and other limbs in communicating a message, as in pantomime.
  To be able to portray, without words, a tennis player serving an ace.
  To be able to pantomime an enthusiastic teacher getting students' attention as they arrive at class.

Speech

This category involves actual speech production, in oral language communication, public speaking, and speech correction.

Sound Production. The ability to produce *meaningful* sounds.
  To be able to produce consonant sounds.
  To be able to repeat sounds that are heard.

Sound-Word Formulation. The ability to coordinate sounds into meaningful words and messages.
  To be able to say *lose* and *loose* so that their meaning may be distinguished by a listener.
  To be able to repeat a commercial without mispronouncing any words.

Sound Projection. The ability to project sounds at a level adequate for reception and decoding by a listener.
  To be able to read aloud so that a class of 25 can hear.
  To be able to make a speech that a group of 100 in an auditorium can hear.

Sound-Gesture Coordination. The ability to coordinate facial expression, movement, and gestures with verbal messages.
  To be able to shorten a verbal explanation of evolution by adding gestures and bodily movements.

To be able to transmit the instructions for conducting an experiment more meaningfully by adding gestures.

Affective Domain

The importance of education in the affective domain should not be
minimized as sometimes occurs when there is a strong demand for higher
academic standards. In general, persons who want high academic standards
also want good affective education. They want a good learning environment in the school, positive attitudes toward self and others, and good discipline. Combs (1982) explains why we cannot divorce affective education
from the total educative process.

Messick (1979) includes not only affects, or feelings, in the affective
domain but also interests, attitudes, beliefs, motives, and values. Only the
affects, such as joy and anger, are primarily feelings. The other outcomes
have a strong cognitive basis in addition to feelings. For example, an attitude involves not only positive versus negative feelings about something
but also information about it. Interests reflect positive feelings for activities undertaken for their own sake, but together with the feelings are knowledge about the activity and usually capability for performing it. Values
reflect concepts and principles as well as feelings.

We should recognize that students initially learn and also modify their
interests, attitudes, and other outcomes in the affective domain throughout the school years. They are not mastered during a short period of time
and maintained thereafter, as are some outcomes in the cognitive domain.
Indeed, we want the individual to learn favorable attitudes toward mathematics in kindergarten and to strengthen these favorable attitudes throughout the school years. Therefore, objectives in the affective domain should
be considered as continuing objectives to be attained initially and then
strengthened.

A widely accepted taxonomy is available to aid teachers and others
formulate objectives in the affective domain (Krathwohl, Bloom, & Masia,
1964). This taxonomy takes into account cognitive processes as well as
feelings but focuses on outcomes not typically included as objectives in
the cognitive domain. Its focus is on attitudes and values and does not
specifically include interests and motives as proposed by Messick. The
taxonomy involves the internalization of cognitions and related affects.
Internalization progresses from receiving information through responding,
valuing, organization, and characterization (see Figure 2.2).

Educational objectives for each level of the taxonomy may be formulated. A definition of each level of internalization and two sets of examples of objectives follow. One set of examples deals with aesthetics,
and the other with interpersonal relationships.

Receiving

The learner becomes aware of the existence of something in the environment and shows a willingness to attend to it. After some experiences
with it, the learner consciously attends to it rather than to other things.

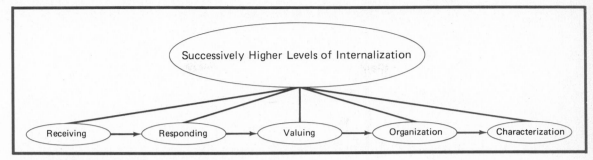

Figure 2.2 Internalization in the affective domain.

> **Examples.** (a) The student will attend to color, material, artistic con-
> trol, and other factors that serve to differentiate works of modern
> abstract art. (b) The student will attend to the differences among
> persons of varied ethnic and racial backgrounds.

Responding

Here the learner moves from selectively attending to responding. The
responding is passive at first but changes to willingness and then to satisfaction from responding. For example, initial obedience to an adult's suggestion to read changes to choosing to read in one's free time.

> **Examples.** (a) The student will choose to visit art exhibits and galleries
> in free time. (b) The student will work and play with peers of varied
> cultural backgrounds.

Valuing

At this level of internalization, the learner acquires values. Each value
relates to many situations and events. Initially there is merely acceptance
of a value. Eventually there is commitment to the value which serves as a
guide to one's behavior in many situations.

> **Examples.** (a) The student will express positive attitudes about aes-
> thetics in the school and community. (b) The student will encourage
> others to accept individual students of all ethnic backgrounds.

Organization

Here the learner conceptualizes a set of values and organizes them
into an internally consistent system.

> **Examples.** (a) The student will conceptualize and describe the place of
> personal expression and aesthetic appreciation in his or her per-
> sonal growth. (b) The student will formulate judgments about the
> ways that equality of educational opportunity can be successfully
> achieved in the United States.

Characterization

The learner has developed a generalized system of values. This value system consistently guides and thus characterizes the individual's behavior. Decisions regarding right and wrong, important and unimportant, and other values are made readily without experiencing internal conflict and debate.

> **Examples.** (a) The student will develop values and ideals that guide his or her aesthetic aspects of life. (b) The student will develop democratic values and ideals that guide his or her relationships and interactions with others.

Most class time is given to achieving objectives in the cognitive and psychomotor domains. However, it is appropriate to formulate objectives in the affective domain as well when preparing course and unit objectives. The objectives may be stated in either of two ways. One way is to indicate the feeling directly, for example, the student enjoys reading; the student likes to ski. The other way indicates what the student does that implies the feeling, for example, the student reads voluntarily; the student goes skiing at every opportunity.

A partial list of objectives prepared by a primary school teacher, a middle school teacher, and a high school teacher when enrolled in the author's course follow to show how the teachers related affective objectives to other objectives:

Primary school unit:
metamorphosis of the monarch butterfly
Cognitive Objectives
> Given a set of butterflies, the student will correctly identify the monarch butterfly.
> Given 4 picture cards, the student will sequence in the proper order the development of the monarch butterfly from egg to adult butterfly.
> The student will be able to tell what is happening as the life cycle progresses from egg to adult butterfly.

Affective Objectives
> The student will demonstrate interest in learning about butterflies and other insects.
> The student will observe butterflies and other insects out-of-doors.

Middle school unit: use of the hand calculator
Cognitive and Psychomotor Objectives
> The student will be able to name the parts of the calculator.
> The student will be able to use a calculator to perform the basic operations of addition, subtraction, multiplication, and division.
> The student will increase speed of computation.
> The student will use the calculator in math and science courses for faster and easier computation.

The student will be able to use math outside of school to solve everyday problems.

Affective Objectives

The student will feel better because of the developed ability to solve multidigit problems quickly.

The student will volunteer favorable comments about math and math classes.

Senior high school unit: batik

Cognitive and Psychomotor Objectives

The student will be able to recognize works of batik.

The student will be able to define the terminology related to batik.

The student will produce an original batik.

Affective Objectives

The student will express opinions that indicate the importance of batik in the art of another culture.

The student will demonstrate enthusiasm when producing batik.

The student will develop standards for comparing the artistic merits of two or more batiks.

2.6 Formulate an objective related to your major field of interest for each of the following:

    a. Knowledge
    b. Comprehension
    c. Application
    d. Analysis
    e. Synthesis
    f. Evaluation

2.7 List four or five subject fields that emphasize objectives in the psychomotor domain and four or five that do not.

2.8 For the concept *educational objective*, formulate an appropriate question or activity for each intellectual skill of the Bloom taxonomy.

2.9 Why is it important for teachers to include objectives in the affective domain together with their cognitive or psychomotor objectives?

OBJECTIVES FOR
CURRICULUM PLANNING AND TEACHING

Objectives at Six Levels of Specificity

Objectives Based on Subject-Matter Taxonomies

Course Objectives

Unit Objectives

Behavioral and Performance Objectives

What kinds of objectives help teachers plan a course? To what extent should teachers formulate their own course and unit objectives? Should course and unit objectives be placed in the hands of students to guide their learning activities? The answers to these and similar questions regarding objectives properly vary from one subject field to another and according to the age of the students and the preference of the teacher. They will help you to make wise decisions about educational objectives and to formulate program, course, and unit objectives. We begin by identifying the relationship among objectives stated at different levels of specificity. As you read, notice that as objectives are stated with greater specificity they indicate more precisely what is to be learned.

Objectives at Six Levels of Specificity

As we saw earlier in this chapter, broad educational aims, or objectives, are formulated to indicate the common purposes of education throughout the nation. Generally, school district officials include such aims in their statements of educational philosophy. Every teacher of a district should be aware of these district aims.

At the next lower level of generality, program objectives are developed for each main curricular area and for other programmatic areas, such as health or career education. Every local school of the district should have program objectives, for example, in health and reading, that apply to all school levels, primary through high school. They are essential for achieving continuity in student learning from one grade to the next and also from one school level to the next. Therefore, teachers should be aware of the program objectives for the areas they teach.

Most courses are set up for either a semester or a year. Each course is typically organized into units. Course objectives indicate the main subject-matter knowledge and skills to be learned and are therefore more general than unit objectives.

A unit may be as short as one week or as long as nine weeks. A unit has two or more objectives that are used to focus students' learning activities over short periods of time. Each unit objective must be related to its more comprehensive course objective so that students, upon achieving the unit objectives, organize and integrate the unit outcomes into a more complete whole. When unit objectives are not related to the course objective, students achieve only the unit objectives. For example, many elementary students who master unit objectives in reading, but do not work toward achieving program and course objectives, do not learn to read. They acquire the many unrelated facts and verbal skills specified by the unit objectives, but then quickly forget them.

Unit objectives are stated in quite general terms in many subject fields. However, highly specific behavioral and performance objectives are used in some subject fields that involve the learning of clearly defined skills or a large amount of factual information. In general, behavioral and performance objectives cannot be formulated readily for outcomes in the affective domain. Similarly, they are not well suited for certain outcomes in the cognitive domain, such as understanding concepts and principles and producing creative ideas.

The relationship among objectives at six different levels of specificity may be seen by examining one science objective at each level (Doherty & Peters, 1978, p. 4):

SIX LEVELS OF OBJECTIVES

1. Aim of Science Education: The student knows and is able to apply basic scientific and technological processes.
2. Program Objective of Science Education: The student is able to use the conventional language, instruments, and operations of science.
3. Course Objective of General Science: The student is able to classify organisms according to their conventional taxonomic categories based on first-hand observations, illustrations, and descriptions.
4. Unit Objective: The student is able to correctly classify cuttings of the following trees as needleleaf: hemlocks, pines, spruces, firs, larches, cypresses, redwoods, and cedars.
5. Behavioral Objective: Given cuttings of ten trees, seven of which are needleleaf, the student is able to correctly identify which of the trees are needleleaves.
6. Performance Objective: Given cuttings of ten trees, seven of which are needleleaf, the student is able to correctly identify at least six of the seven as belonging to the class of needleleaves.

Notice that the behavioral objective is more detailed than the unit objective. The behavioral objective indicates not only the desired student behavior but also the method of measurement. In addition, the performance objective explicitly states the desired level, or criterion, of student proficiency (six of seven).

Let us identify who generally formulates objectives at these six levels. Committees of curriculum coordinators and representative teachers of a school district typically formulate both the aims and the program objectives for the schools of the district. The course objectives are formulated by individual teachers or by school committees with representation from the school district office. Unit objectives are more often formulated by individual teachers or school committees than by school district groups.

Objectives Based on Subject-Matter Taxonomies

An educational objective at any level indicates student behavior and also the content of what is to be learned. Hence, specifying the content of a field precedes writing program, course, and unit objectives. A taxonomy provides one excellent means for specifying the subject matter of a field (Doherty & Peters, 1978). It classifies the content of the particular field of study into categories with which teachers are most familiar. We can get a better idea of the nature of program objectives and course objectives and how they are related by examining part of a subject-matter taxonomy and then some program and course objectives related to the taxonomy.

Four major concepts of a health education taxonomy are mental health, physical health, community health, and safe living. The first five of eight subclasses of concepts in the major category, mental health, follow to illustrate how a taxonomy is organized and what is included in it (Doherty & Peters, 1978, p. 45). A taxonomy of this kind permits objectives to be developed on any topic of the taxonomy that may be desired.

1. 1.1 Definition of mental health
    1.2 Relationship to physical health
    1.3 Relationship to community health
    1.4 Determinants of mental health
         1.41 Physiological determinants—physical and hereditary
         1.42 Environmental determinants—physical and societal
         1.43 Psychological determinants
               1.431 Concept of self and others
               1.432 Psychological needs and motivation
               1.433 Sources and expression of emotions
               1.434 Outlook on life and values
    1.5 Behavior influenced by mental health
         1.51 Communicating
         1.52 Decison making
         1.53 Risk taking—positive or negative
         1.54 Behaving responsibly or irresponsibly
         1.55 Adjusting (adapting)
         1.56 Problem solving

Comprehensive taxonomies of this kind are useful to the staff of any local school that has not recently identified and organized the subject matter of the content field. Interested persons can compare it with their own ideas of the content of the field and how it should be organized, and course unit objectives may be keyed to the taxonomy of each subject field.

The program objective (Doherty & Peters, 1978, p. 44) and two related course objectives (Doherty & Hathaway, 1974a, p. 74) for mental health follow:

Program objective
The student has the knowledge and skills needed to ensure the physical and mental health of himself and others.

Related course objectives
The student knows that discussing problems and concerns with family members can bring about understanding and aid in problem solving.
The student knows that effective communication among family members about sexuality can lead to personal understanding and understanding of the feelings of others.

Course Objectives

We see that the preceding course objectives are stated in general terms that teachers can use in planning their instructional strategies and materials and their evaluation tools and procedures. They are written at a fairly general level, and there are usually several objectives for each course. Each course objective includes the desired student behavior or activity and the content to be learned:

Music (Doherty & Hathaway, 1974b, p. 126)

The student is able to accept guidance and direction in solving problems of psychomotor performance.

The student is able to analyze his or her performance problems and to take appropriate practice measures to resolve them.

Social science (Peters & Doherty, 1976, p. 386)

The student knows ways that consumer lending or credit policies influence demand and supply in markets for other goods (commodities, services).

The student is able to use appropriate concepts and models for analysis of interdependencies of supplies-demands-prices in financial and commodity markets.

Physical education (Doherty & Hathaway, 1974c, p. 386)

The student knows the appropriate form for shots used in table tennis, including forehand, backhand, chop, and smash.

The student is able to execute the skills in table tennis using the appropriate form.

Second language (Doherty & Hathaway, 1973, p. 19)

The student values the use of second language skills in leisure time activities.

The student values the role a second language plays in meeting society's needs for communication among countries and cultures.

Unit Objectives

Because unit objectives are more specific than course objectives, the typical procedure is to have several unit objectives for each course objective. The examples that follow indicate differences in the way that unit objectives are stated and used in two high schools (Klausmeier, Lipham, & Daresh, 1983).

In both schools, courses are organized into units that count one-tenth of a credit toward high school graduation. The large majority of the students take a full semester to complete five units and thereby earn one-half credit toward meeting graduation requirements. The use of the unit objectives varies considerably between the two schools.

In High School A, the student must decide whether to work for an A, B, or C at the beginning of each unit. Credit is not awarded for less than a C. There are unit objectives for each letter grade. (Students who achieve their objectives in less than three weeks may work on an advanced unit that is not one of the ten units included in the year course.) Two objectives for each letter grade of a unit of a biology course follow:

Grade C
Identify the parts of an amoeba, euglena, and paramecium.
List seven diseases caused by fungi.

Grade B
Describe the economic importance of protozoans.
Describe the characteristics of the four classes of fungi.

Grade A
Describe sexual reproduction in protozoans.
Describe the life cycle of an alga that exhibits alternation of generations.

The preceding objectives, as well as all the other objectives of the unit, are included in a unit learning guide that is distributed to the students on the first day of the unit. Each student decides which letter-grade objectives to work toward and then discusses this decision with the teacher. The teacher accepts the decision or discusses it further with the student.

At High School B, very different from High School A, the objectives of each unit are the same for every student, and the student must demonstrate mastery of all the objectives to receive credit for passing the unit. However, students may take unequal amounts of time to complete each unit and thereby complete unequal numbers of units during a semester. The objectives of a unit in English follow:

Course objective
The learner will develop the skills needed for writing unified and well-developed paragraphs.

Unit objectives
The learner will:
Analyze the way in which a sentence is developed from a core pattern.
Write three sentences using at least three levels of development and label each level (*developmental level* refers to the increasingly complex structure of sentences).
Analyze the levels of development used in four sample paragraphs provided by the teacher.
Select three suitable topics for paragraph writing.
Write topic sentences for each of the topics which he or she selected and have them approved by the teacher.

Write three paragraphs which contain at least three levels of development and label those levels.

Behavioral and Performance Objectives

The use of highly specific behavioral and performance objectives to guide instruction follows directly from a behavioristic stimulus-response psychology of learning. According to this psychology, whether a student has learned can be inferred only from observing a change in the student's observable behavior, not from inferring a change in the amount of information the student has acquired or a change in how the student organizes the information. Another aspect of behavioristic psychology is that learning cumulates by very small, discrete steps. In accordance with this psychology of learning, objectives are formulated that call for students to learn highly specific information and skills. Moreover, the students are to display what they have learned, that is, their responses to the objectives in directly observable performances.

Some teachers who teach facts and skills, such as in typing, auto mechanics, reading, spelling, and arithmetic computation, consistently use behavioral or performance objectives. These objectives are either formulated by the teacher or they are included in the printed instructional material that the teacher uses. These objectives are distributed to the students to guide their individual study. On the other hand, performance objectives are no longer widely accepted for guiding student learning in the affective domain or for teaching creativity, problem solving, and other high-level outcomes in the cognitive domain. This part of the chapter is designed, first, to enable the reader to gain a more thorough understanding of behavioral and performance objectives and, second, to aid the person who is interested to gain skill in formulating them.

You will recall that a performance objective has three main components: (1) it indicates the observable behavior, or response, that the learner is to display, (2) it provides the condition, or conditions, under which the learner's response is to be made, (3) it states explicitly the criterion for determining whether the learner has achieved an acceptable level or quality of response. Thus, a performance objective implies both the learning activity and the measurement technique. A behavioral objective does not include the explicitly stated criterion.

Observable Learner Behavior

A performance objective specifies the behavior that the learner is to display upon attaining the objective. Furthermore, the behavior is stated in such unambiguous terms that a teacher, an older student, or even a parent will agree on the exact behavior being sought. To state the objective exactly, a verb that indicates directly observable behavior or readily inferable behavior is used. Verbs that indicate behaviors for some of the categories of objectives in the cognitive and affective domains follow in Table 2.1.

TABLE 2.1 VERBS THAT INDICATE BEHAVIORS FOR PERFORMANCE OBJECTIVES

PERFORMANCE OBJECTIVES	VERBS
COGNITIVE DOMAIN	
Knowledge	define, distinguish, identify, name, recall, recite, recognize, write.
Application	adapt, adopt, apply, employ, implement, interrelate, select, utilize.
Evaluation	appraise, assess, contrast, decide, evaluate, judge, test, validate.
AFFECTIVE DOMAIN	
Satisfaction in response	acclaim, applaud, approve, commend.
Commitment	demonstrate, endorse, sanction, uphold, debate, deny, protest, reject.
Organization of a value system	delimit, integrate, interrelate, organize, plan.

Conditions for Display of Behavior

A performance objective gives the condition under which the behavior is to be displayed. The condition might be that the learner can use materials or other aids in learning and displaying the desired behavior, or it might be that no aid can be used. Examples of display conditions follow:

> Given the textbook . . .
> Given a day with winds less than five miles per hour and a dry track . . .
> Without the aid of class notes or the text . . .
> Without reference to materials on mouth-to-mouth resuscitation . . .

Assessment Criteria

A performance objective explicitly states the standard, or criterion, for assessing whether the learner has attained the desired behavior. Thus, it provides the means whereby the teacher determines whether or not the learner's response is satisfactory. It also gives the learner a specific standard for personal achievement. The criteria may take many forms:

> Given an official 440-yard track that is dry and a day with winds less than five miles per hour, the student will run the 440-yard distance *in less time than in the immediate prior trial.*
> With a language notebook available as a reference, the student will write a paragraph *that includes a topic sentence, development by contrast, and a conclusion.*

With the use of the car's maintenance manual, the student will replace and adjust the fan belt *so that the car operates according to factory specifications*.

It should be clear that behavioral and performance objectives are neither good nor bad. Rather, they are useful or not useful in aiding particular teachers and students to attain particular learning outcomes. Part of their utility depends upon whether the objective calls for a highly specific performance, such as spelling *receive,* or whether it calls for a comprehensive performance, such as spelling all words correctly that conform to the rule "*i* before *e* except after *c.*" The proponents of behavioral and performance objectives in their early writings objected to the latter kind of performance because it did not clearly specify the exact learning tasks to either the teacher or the learner.

How can the interested and concerned teacher decide whether to use many specified behavioral or performance objectives for each unit of instruction, less specific unit objectives, or only course objectives? Educators do not agree on the answer to this question. The early claim of Gagné (1967), Glaser (1967), Mager (1968), and Popham (1969) was that performance objectives markedly enhance both immediate and cumulative learning by indicating to the teacher and the student precisely what is to be learned, the sequence in which the successive items are to be learned, and the means for determining whether or not the learning has occurred. On the other hand, Arnstine (1964), Atkin (1968), and Eisner (1967) stated that behavioral objectives restrict students to learning specific information and skills and actually prevent them from achieving many of the more important outcomes of instruction, such as creativity, curiosity, and initiative for independent learning.

Each of these claims applies better to certain learning outcomes than to others. The first argument relates better to outcomes such as learning to type or to spell, and the second to outcomes such as understanding a principle at successively higher levels or finding a solution to a social problem. But more important, most of the early pro and con claims were logical and hypothetical. Definitive studies had not been conducted in a variety of school subject matters at all school levels to secure empirical information. Melton's conclusion warrants careful attention:

> The development of two distinct schools of thought, respectively supporting and opposing the use of behavioral objectives, has encouraged useful debate, but it has also encouraged an oversimplification of issues by often failing to distinguish clearly between substantiated and unsubstantiated claims. Much effort has been wasted in attempting to find a simple, universal answer as to whether behavioral objectives should or should not be used, and an alternative approach is required. It is suggested that this should be one that treats behavioral objectives simply as one of several tools available to educators, with research directed toward determining not only their advantages and limitations, but also the conditions under which they can be used most

effectively. It would then be the responsibility of individual educators to determine whether or not the objectives are likely to be useful in their own particular situation. (Melton, 1978, p. 299)

2.10 How are program, course, and unit objectives related?

2.11 Explain what a subject-matter taxonomy is and how it is used in formulating objectives.

2.12 Write a course objective and two related unit objectives for the school level and subject field of your interest.

2.13 Examine the unit objectives of the biology course at High School A and the unit objectives in writing at High School B. Do you regard one set of objectives as more motivational for students than the other? Explain. Does one set include more high-level intellectual skills than the other? Identify the higher-level skills in two or three of the objectives.

2.14 Objectives may be stated in several ways. Indicate how they should be stated for a course in your teaching field. Indicate why your preferred way is better than the other ways.

MINIMUM COMPETENCY OBJECTIVES

Most states have laws that indicate that a student must demonstrate a stated level of proficiency on an approved test, or tests, in order to graduate from high school. The level of proficiency is moderate, and the number of different areas tested, such as mathematics, reading, writing, and spelling, is not large. The tests used for this purpose are called *minimum competency tests*.

Minimum competency testing started in some states in 1975. At about the same time, the decline in educational achievement at all levels of schooling, but particularly at the high school level, was widely publicized. State legislators apparently believed that minimum competency testing would result in higher student achievement. Moreover, parents and the public at large, including employers, saw a need for higher standards. They believed that many high school graduates were not being prepared well enough to hold down a job, to start specialized technical training, or to enter college.

After competency testing went into effect, some parents of students who did not pass the test for high school graduation took their case to the courts. The courts concluded that the schools must teach students the knowledge and skills included in the competency tests to make competency testing enforceable. The development of curricula guided by clearly stated minimum competency objectives was called for. Many statements of minimum competency objectives for elementary school through high school have been formulated. The objectives are stated in the form of performance objectives.

In closing, we should note that minimum competency testing has become widespread. However, its final effects on the quality of education, including the level of student achievement, are not yet established. Measurement experts, teachers, administrators, and parents are still divided about it. The many pro and con arguments cannot be enumerated here. However, prospective teachers should be aware that, in some schools, instruction in academic subjects is largely guided by minimum competency objectives and related minimum competency testing. Chapter 15 of this book discusses minimum competency testing further.

2.15 Minimum competency objectives indicate what every student should achieve to advance from one unit, grade, or school level to another and to graduate from high school. In which curricular or program areas of the elementary school do you think minimum competency objectives and a related minimum achievement level should be established? Middle school or junior high school? High school? Which students, if any, should not be required to meet the established minimum level achievement?

2.16 Do you think individual teachers could enforce minimum achievement standards if there were no school district regulations or state laws requiring students to achieve a clearly stated minimum level? Explain.

2.17 Review and Application. Recall the most important information about each of the following concepts and identify at least one possible use of the information by you as a learner, a teacher, or both:

National Aims of Education
    Aims of Elementary Education
    Aims of Secondary Education
    Objectives of the National Assessment of Educational Progress
Domains of Educational Objectives
    Cognitive Domain
    Psychomotor Domain
    Affective Domain
Objectives for Curriculum Planning and Teaching
    Objectives at Six Levels of Specificity
    Objectives Based on Subject-Matter Taxonomies
    Course Objectives
    Unit Objectives
    Behavioral and Performance Objectives
Minimum Competency Objectives

SUMMARY

Aims of elementary and secondary education are formulated by various groups for the purpose of reaching nationwide consensus on the main purposes of education. Individual schools and school districts include some or all of these aims in their statements of educational philosophy. The aims are usually not sufficiently specific to indicate whether program areas such as driver education, swimming, Russian language, and drug education will or will not be included in the school's curriculum.

The program objectives of a school include three domains: *cognitive, psychomotor,* and *affective.* The six classes of educational objectives in the *cognitive domain* involve gaining and recalling information and the intellectual skills of comprehending, applying, analyzing, synthesizing, and evaluating information. Objectives in the *affective domain* involve feelings and also cognitions. Objectives in the *psychomotor domain* refer to outcomes involving gross bodily movements, finely coordinated movements, nonverbal communication, and speech.

The objectives that are formulated for use in curricular planning and in teaching are related to one another and range in specificity. Program objectives are least specific, course objectives based on one or more program objectives are more specific, and unit objectives based on each course objective are most specific. Each objective at any of these levels indicates both the desired student behavior and the content to be learned; however, it may or may not specify the criterion for determining an acceptable level of performance. Taxonomies of objectives that have been prepared in the cognitive, psychomotor, and affective domains are very helpful in identifying desired student behaviors, while subject-matter taxonomies contribute to identifying the content that the students should learn.

Early recommendations regarding the formulation of behavioral and performance objectives called for many precisely stated objectives, each objective indicating a highly specific learning outcome. A performance objective, whether highly specific or more general, indicates the learner's observable behavior, the conditions for the display of the behavior when learned, and the criterion for determining whether or not the learner has achieved the objective. Many arguments have been made both for and against the presentation of both behavioral and performance objectives to students as guides to their learning activities. Educators are encouraged to get a full understanding of all forms of objectives and to try out the forms that appear to be most applicable to their particular teaching situation.

Minimum competency testing has become widespread. In order to fail or retain a student who does not pass the test, a school must demonstrate that the student has had the opportunity to learn what is covered by the test. Minimum competency objectives are prepared to guide this aspect of the school's curriculum.

SUGGESTIONS FOR FURTHER READING

Bloom, B. S., Hastings, J. T., & Madaus, G. F. *Handbook on formative and summative evaluation of student learning.* New York: McGraw-Hill, 1971.

Section three of part 1 of this book has four chapters that state objectives and provide related evaluation techniques matched to the knowledge, comprehension, application, analysis, synthesis, and evaluation objectives in the cognitive domain and to the first four levels of internationalization in the affective domain. Part 2 has objectives pertaining to levels of schooling and subject fields.

Cogan, J. J. Should the U. S. mimic Japanese education? Let's look before we leap. *Phi Delta Kappan,* 1984, *65,* 463–468.

Presents the Japanese national goals of education, the strengths and weaknesses of its national system, and elements of the system that should and should not be imitated by the United States. This issue of this journal has other articles on national aims of education: "Soviet education and the development of Communist ethics," "Educational policy in China and India," and "U. S. schooling through Chinese eyes."

College Board. *Academic preparation for college: What students need to know and be able to do.* New York: The College Board, 1983.

An excellent statement of the basic academic competencies (objectives of schooling) in reading, writing, speaking and listening, mathematics, reasoning, and studying that college-bound students should attain. Computer competencies and observing competencies are also indicated. This complete list of competencies is a good self-evaluation checklist for the student already in college.

Harrow, A. J. *A taxonomy of the psychomotor domain.* New York: McKay, 1972.

A taxonomy for classifying objectives in the psychomotor domain and illustrative objectives are presented.

Heddens, J. W. Elementary education. In H. E. Mitzel, J. H. Best, & W. Rabinowitz (Eds.), *Encyclopedia of educational research* (5th ed., Vol. 2). New York: The Free Press, 1982.

A good overview of the program of elementary education. Other levels of schooling described in this encyclopedia include "Junior High and Middle School Education" by C. F. Toepfer, Jr., and "Secondary Education" by S. M. Holton.

Kibler, R. J., Barker, L. L., & Miles, D. T. *Behavioral objectives and instruction.* Boston: Allyn & Bacon, 1970.

Taxonomies for classifying objectives in the cognitive, psychomotor, and affective domains are presented with illustrative objectives.

CHAPTER 3

THEORIES OF CHILD AND ADOLESCENT DEVELOPMENT

PIAGETIAN THEORY
OF COGNITIVE
DEVELOPMENT

BRUNER'S VIEW
OF COGNITIVE
DEVELOPMENT

DEVELOPMENT
OF METACOGNITION

DEVELOPMENTAL
TASKS AND
EDUCATION

We may think of *maturation* as growth that results in progressive changes in a person's physical and neural structures. Normal growth of the structures requires a stimulating environment and informal activity rather than an impoverished environment and no activity. *Learning,* on the other hand, is the process that results in relatively permanent changes in knowledge skill, or other behavior based on practice. Guided practice increases the rate of learning, whereas it does not appreciably increase the rate of maturation.

Developmental theorists are interested in describing and explaining the relationship between earlier and later behavior, mainly in terms of growth processes. Many treat learning as either dependent on, or incidental to, growth processes. However, other developmental psychologists take a broader view and consider development to be a product of maturation and learning and accordingly give considerable attention to learning. As we shall see in Chapter 4, learning theorists typically take growth processes as a given and try to formulate theories and principles that apply equally well to individuals of all developmental levels. However, the educational psychologist, as well as the teacher, must relate both maturation and learning to instruction.

In this chapter, we shall examine Piaget's theory of cognitive development and some of its enduring principles. Then we shall turn to a longitudinal study of cognitive development, kindergarten through grade 9, and alternatives to Piaget's description and explanation of development. The next two parts of the chapter outline the main ideas of Bruner and Flavell. Bruner gives more emphasis than Piaget to continuity of development and to cultural factors that influence development, including language and education. Flavell goes beyond Piaget's conceptions of development with his ideas about metacognition, or knowing about knowing. The last part of the chapter presents Havighurst's stimulating ideas about developmental tasks and the role of the school in aiding boys and girls of about ages 6–18 to achieve the developmental tasks of middle childhood and adolescence. Havighurst, more than other theorists, relates development to education.

Before turning to Piagetian theory, recognize that the purpose of this chapter is to present only comprehensive theories of development. Specific areas of development, such as conceptual, motor, moral, and attitudinal development, are discussed later in Chapters 9–12. Similarly, the relation of classroom discipline to the development of an integrated personality is discussed in Chapter 13.

Development Progresses Through Four Qualitatively Different Stages

An Alternative to Piaget's Four-Stage Description of Development

An Alternative to Piaget's Explanation of Development

PIAGETIAN THEORY OF COGNITIVE DEVELOPMENT

Piagetian theory (Piaget, 1970; Flavell, 1977) is a complex and comprehensive theory of human cognitive development. It indicates that human cognitive development from birth to maturity progresses through four clearly delineated stages. Certain cognitive structures are specified as underlying and making possible the child's progression from one stage to the next. Each stage has its own unique observable characteristics. The changes that occur in the unobservable structures and in the accompanying observable behaviors from one stage to the next are qualitative.

Development Progresses Through
Four Qualitatively Different Stages

Piaget (1970) indicates that individuals continuously interact with their environments. Each interaction always has two adaptive aspects: assimilation and accommodation. Related to cognitive development, *assimilation* implies incorporating experiences into a person's existing cognitive structure. *Accommodation* implies changing the cognitive structure to fit new experiences. In the process of assimilating and accommodating, the cognitive system itself changes and cognitive development occurs.

Cognitive development proceeds in an orderly fashion through four successive stages. All individuals progress through the four stages in the same fixed order, or invariant sequence. The main descriptive features of each stage follow. However, they are not broken into substages as Piaget has done.

Sensorimotor Stage: Birth to Age 2

In this stage, the individual interacts with the environment through the sense organs and by means of motor actions. At first, the infant has no awareness of the body, sensory relationships, or environmental objects. At the end of the stage, the child is able to grasp objects, move by walking, and imitate sounds and actions. Sensory experiences—sight, sound, touch, and taste—become coordinated during this period, and speech begins. By the end of the period, young children's motor actions are more coordinated. For example, they can pick up toys by performing several simultaneous actions: bending their knees, retaining their balance, reaching, and grasping. If they have not correctly estimated the task, they can vary their actions.

Another accomplishment of the sensorimotor period is the development of *object permanence*. When a 4- or 5-month-old baby playing with a toy such as a ball rolls it out of sight (say, behind a pillow), the baby does not search for it even if it is easily within reach or within crawling distance. It is as if the object has ceased to exist once it leaves the baby's field of vision. The infant's schema, or internal representation, of objects at this age does not include the realization that they are permanent. Toward the end of the sensorimotor period, however, a child regards objects as having permanence and accordingly seeks toys and other objects that have disappeared from view.

The main qualitative features of cognitive development during the sensorimotor stage may be summarized as follows:

**QUALITATIVE FEATURES
OF SENSORIMOTOR THOUGHT**

Thinking occurs primarily through motor and sensory actions.
Coordination of sensory activities improves.
Coordination of motor activities improves.
Objects and people, including self, are differentiated from one another and are recognized as permanent.
Talking and symbolic thinking begin.

Preoperational Stage: Age 2 to Age 7

A major characteristic of the child in the preoperational period is the rapid development of language. Children learn the names for many items in the immediate environment from age 2 to about age 7. They speak in sentences and have a large vocabulary by the end of the period.

Another characteristic of the preoperational child is *egocentrism*. Children believe that reality is as they see it. They are not aware that other points of view exist. We sometimes speak of an egocentric adult, but there is a difference. The egocentric adult can take another person's point of view, but the preoperational child cannot.

Preoperational children center on one feature or attribute of something and cannot change their perceptions to focus on another one. They group objects in only one way, rather than in multiple ways. In a classical experiment, Piaget presented a 5-year-old child with a box containing 27 wooden beads, 20 white and 7 brown. When asked if there were more white or more brown beads, the child correctly responded "white." However, when asked if there were more white or more wooden beads, the child did not understand the question. Once the beads are thought of by the child as brown or white, they cannot be thought of in other terms, such as wooden or not wooden. The child *centers* on the dimension of color and is unable to *decenter* to consider the composition of the beads.

The preoperational child also does not understand the effect of *reversing* operations. For example, if water is poured from a tall, thin container into a short, broad container and then back again, the child does not understand that the second inverse operation essentially negates the effects of the first one.

Another characteristic of the preoperational child is the failure to *conserve* numerousness, quantity, length, weight, and other properties of things. Thus, the preoperational child does not understand that ten marbles are the same number whether the marbles are arranged in a circle or in a straight line. Similarly, the child does not perceive that a piece of clay has the same weight when rolled into a ball as when patted into pancake form. The child does not perceive that a cup of water has the same quantity in a tall, thin glass as in a short, squat glass.

The main qualitative characteristics of the preoperational period may be recapitulated as follows:

QUALITATIVE FEATURES OF PREOPERATIONAL THOUGHT

Language and symbolic thought increase very markedly.
Egocentric speech and thought predominate.
Centration and irreversibility, rather than decentration and reversibility, characterize perception and thought.
Failure to conserve is found throughout the period.
Some objects are grouped and classified on one basis but cannot be reclassified on another basis.

Concrete Operations Stage: Age 7 to Age 11

There are four qualitative changes from the preoperational period to the period of concrete operations. They involve inferring rather than acting on the surface characteristics of things, decentration rather than centration, reversibility rather than irreversibility, and greatly increased use of number and numerical relationships. These four sets of operations are the interiorized *concrete* operations of the period.

Inferring relations among things, rather than simply perceiving the surface characteristics of things, may be illustrated with the conservation of liquid quantity. To the concrete operational child, a tall, narrow glass appears to contain more water than a short, broad one. However, the child infers that the quantity is still the same, since only the water contained in the short glass is poured into the tall one.

Decentering may be illustrated with the same situation. The concrete operational child observes the height of the glass as one source of information for inferring, but also observes the width, or diameter. Instead of centering only on the height, the child decenters, taking both width and height into consideration.

The concrete operational child understands and can carry out reverse mental operations. Thus, the child recognizes that carrying out an inverse, or reverse, action returns the situation to its original state. For example, if 6 is subtracted from 14 to get 8, then adding 6 to 8 has the effect of negating the first operation.

Another important concrete operation involves the child's ability to operate on things quantitatively. Thus, the child counts the actual number of items of a group rather than merely estimates them as being more or less. Things are put in order—first, second, and so on.

Being able to carry out the preceding operations is accompanied by remarkable progress in classifying. Things are classified by two or more properties. Also, reclassification is done. In reclassification, a red circle is first classified as a circle and later as a red object. Superordinate and coordinate relationships among concepts are understood. By the end of the concrete operations stage, concepts become the tools of thought and are used in understanding principles and in solving problems.

During this period, the child's egocentrism wanes. Children increasingly are able to take another's viewpoint, and speech becomes increasingly socialized and less egocentric. Understanding and taking another child's viewpoint are common in peer groups of the concrete operations period.

The main qualitative features of the concrete operations stage may be summarized as follows:

QUALITATIVE FEATURES OF CONCRETE OPERATIONAL THOUGHT

Inferring replaces acting only on the surface characteristics of things.
Decentering and reversible operations are performed.
Symbolic thinking, including use of numbers, progresses rapidly.
Quantitative reasoning with numbers increases.
Concepts are formed; two or more classes of things are combined into a superordinate class; superordinate classes are broken down into two or more subordinate classes.
Social behavior replaces egocentrism.

Formal Operations Stage: Age 12 to Adult

In the stage of formal operations, boys and girls are able to think logically about things existing only in their minds. They reach logical conclusions about an object, process, or event without having had direct experience with it. Abstract number concepts, as well as other kinds of abstract concepts, are used as tools of thought.

Individuals in the formal operations stage are capable of carrying out the formal operations employed in conducting experiments. They can formulate abstract hypotheses, make predictions, define terms operationally, test hypotheses, and draw conclusions.

A frequently cited demonstration will clarify thought processes at this level. The student is given four bottles containing colorless liquids. The experimenter produces a smaller bottle containing x, another colorless liquid, and adds some of x to a liquid in a sixth bottle, causing the latter to turn yellow. The child is asked to produce the same color, using four bottles of liquids and the liquid x. Children at the concrete operational stage typically try only the simple combinations, that is, bottle 1 with x, 2 with x, 3 with x, and 4 with x, thinking that they have done everything possible. If advised to try several bottles at once, the child does so randomly and may or may not hit on the proper combination. If, by luck, the child produces yellow, the child usually becomes confused when trying to retrace and repeat the steps. Adolescents at the formal operations stage, however, approach the problem differently. After trying the simple combinations, they attempt complex combinations in an orderly, systematic way: x with bottles 1 and 2, x with 1 and 3, x with 1 and 4, and so on. After finding one solution to the problem, they may also continue to look for other solutions.

The qualitative features of the formal operations stage may be summarized as follows:

QUALITATIVE FEATURES OF FORMAL OPERATIONAL THOUGHT

Abstract thinking occurs in the absence of things and events.
A complete range of possibilities or hypotheses can be considered.
Abstract ideas are analyzed, synthesized, and evaluated.
Concepts that are completely removed from concrete contexts are formed; concepts of proportion, energy, noun, and the atom, for example, are learned.

Identifying the preceding qualitative changes that characterize cognitive development from infancy through adolescence is a significant contribution of Piagetian theory. Persons generally agree that qualitative changes occur. The idea that each item of development, such as classifying things or understanding number, progresses in an orderly manner is another important contribution with which there is little disagreement. However, the basic premise that nearly all of the preceding developmental items of each stage emerge at about the same time at the beginning of each stage, progress at about the same rate during each stage, and reach full functional maturity at the same time toward the end of each stage has not been confirmed by our recent longitudinal study. A considerable amount of information from this longitudinal study and an alternative description of cognitive development follow. The purpose here is not to minimize Piaget's contributions. Rather, it is to provide an accurate, research-based description of cognitive development that will enable educators to gain a better understanding of a child's cognitive development and to guide it wisely.

An Alternative to Piaget's
Four-Stage Description of Development

In a large-scale longitudinal study we investigated Piaget's two most basic ideas of cognitive development during the concrete operations stage (Klausmeier & Sipple, 1982). One purpose of the study was to test the accuracy of his description of development during the concrete operations stage. The second purpose was to test the validity of his construct of cognitive structures that purportedly explains development during the concrete operations stage.

Three groups of children—100 each—participated in the study for four years. One group was enrolled successively in kindergarten–grade 3; another group was enrolled successively in grade 3–grade 6; and a third group was enrolled successively in grade 6–grade 9.

In the first year of the study, the children of the first two groups were administered 12 concrete operations tasks and 16 tests of the cognitive structures that, according to Piaget, underlie the concrete operations stage. The students who remained through the next years were tested annually with the same tests administered in the first year. The third group of grade 6–grade 9 was administered the cognitive structures tests only, since most of the Piagetian tasks were found to be very easy for grade 6 students.

The 12 concrete operations tasks were individually administered to each child of the first two groups in the same week of the school year at 12-month intervals. These tasks were adapted by Hooper, Brainerd, and Sipple (1975) from tasks reported in earlier experiments. The categories of tasks and the name of each task of the category follow:

> Three tasks that measure the ability to classify objects: dichotomous sorting, some-all relationships, class inclusion.
> Three tasks that measure the ability to arrange objects in a logical order: seriation, transitivity of length, transitivity of weight.
> Four tasks that measure the ability to conserve properties of things: identity conservation of length, equivalence conservation of length, identity conservation of weight, equivalence conservation of weight.
> Two tasks to measure the ability to relate objects and their number: cardinality of number, conservation of number.

Another classification task, combinatorial reasoning, that purportedly emerges with the onset of the formal operations period, was also administered annually.

The participating children were also administered tests constructed by Brainerd (1972) to measure their performances on the eight groupement structures of the concrete operations stage. Four of the groupement structures deal with the logical composition of classes and their inverse, for example, the addition of primary classes and the subtraction of primary classes; and four with the composition and the reciprocity of relations, for example, the addition of difference relations and the reciprocity of difference relations.

It is not necessary to know the details of what each Piagetian task and each groupement test measure in order to understand the results of this longitudinal study. Rather, it should be recognized that the 13 Piagetian tasks measure 12 observable performances that Piagetian theory indicates are descriptive of the concrete operations stage and one of the formal operations stage. The 16 groupement tests measure 8 cognitive structures (two tests for each structure) which develop and, according to Piagetian theory, make possible the observable performances of the concrete operations stage. (A description of each task and each test is given in Klausmeier and Associates, 1979).

The grade at which each developmental item measured by the 13 Piagetian tasks and by the 16 groupement tests reached full functional maturity is given in Table 3.1. Full functional maturity of a developmental item was defined on a Piagetian task or a groupement test as a mean score on the test of 85% correct or higher. Piagetian stage theory indicates that the large majority of the 12 developmental items of the concrete operations stage as measured by the respective 12 Piagetian tasks reach full functional maturity in the same grade, about grade 5, or age 11–12. Notice, however, that the mean percentage correct was 85 or higher for 2 concrete operations tasks in kindergarten, for 9 of them in grade 2–grade 5, and for another one in grade 6. Hence, kindergarten children were already functioning fully at the concrete operations stage on 2 of the concrete operations tasks. However, this same level of functioning on some of the other concrete operations tasks was not reached by the children until grades 5 and 6.

Turning to the groupement structures, we see that the mean percentage correct was 85 or higher for 2 groupements in kindergarten, for 10 others in grade 1–grade 6, and for 4 others in grade 9 (not all 4 groupements were as high as 85 in grade 9). According to Piagetian theory, all the groupements of the concrete operations stage reach full functional maturity at about the same time. Clearly, this wide range, extending from kindergarten through grade 9, does not support the theory, since some of the structures were already as fully functional in kindergarten children as others were in grade 9 adolescents. Thus, kindergarten children, based on the functioning of some structures, were already as far into the concrete operations stage as grade 9 students were, based on other structures.

The preceding mean scores indicate the average performances of the longitudinal groups of students when they were enrolled in successively higher grades. Correlation methods are based on each individual student's scores and indicate the relationships among the scores. Correlations using the measures administered each year to the participating children of kindergarten–grade 6 were computed. Factor analyses were performed on the

TABLE 3.1 FIRST GRADE AT WHICH PERCENTAGE CORRECT ON MEASURES OF CONCRETE OPERATIONS TASKS AND GROUPEMENTS WAS 85 OR HIGHER

CONCRETE OPERATIONS TASKS			GROUPEMENTS		
MEASURE	GRADE	MEAN PERCENTAGE CORRECT	MEASURE	GRADE	MEAN PERCENTAGE CORRECT
Some-all	KG	95	Reciprocity of difference relations	KG	85
Transivitity of weight	KG	89	Reciprocity of equiva-lence relations	KG	86
Conservation of number	2	97	Subtraction of primary classes	1	94
Identity conservation of length	2	85	Subtraction of secondary classes	1	96
Equivalence conserva-tion of length	3	91	Addition of difference relations	1	87
Identity conservation of weight	3	91	Addition of equivalence relations	1	85
Dichotomous sorting	3	90	Bi-univocal reciprocity of relations	1	87
Class inclusion	3	87	Bi-univocal multiplication of relations	2	85
Transivity of length	3	92	Co-univocal reciprocity of relations	2	90
Cardinality	5	85	Co-univocal division of classes	3	89
Equivalence conserva-tion of weight	5	89	Co-univocal multiplica-tion of relations	5	95
Combinatorial reasoning	5	86	Co-univocal multiplica-tion of classes	6	85
Seriation	6	86	Addition of primary classes	9	78
			Addition of secondary classes	9	76
			Bi-univocal multiplica-tion of classes	9	63
			Bi-univocal division of classes	9	85

correlations for three different sets of measures: the Piagetian tasks, the groupement tests, and the combined Piagetian tasks and groupement tests. (The many correlations for each year and from one year to the next are not indicated here but are reported in Sipple, Allen, and Klausmeier [1979]. Similarly, the many factor loadings are reported in Sipple and Klausmeier [1981]). We may now turn to the main findings and see whether they confirm or disconfirm the descriptive and the explanatory aspects of Piagetian stage theory.

Piagetian theory specifies that children's performances of the Piagetian tasks develop in an integrated, synchronous pattern from kindergarten through grade 6. If they actually develop in this pattern, high correlations among the 12 Piagetian tasks should be found, and one and the same factor should be identified through factor analysis for five or more consecutive grades, corresponding roughly to ages 7–11.

Instead of these predictions, many low correlations were found among the Piagetian tasks, as well as some that were moderately high. Five different factors were identified rather than one factor as predicted. One was a classification factor and involved the three Piagetian classification tasks. Two others were conservation factors: conservation of length and conservation of weight. A fourth factor was number and included cardinality and conservation of number. The final one was relations.

This factor organization indicates that there is a parallel and synchronous development of five substantively related sets of concrete operations tasks rather than an integrated and synchronous development of all 12 separate tasks. It indicates that any given child's developmental progression with respect to any one of the 12 concrete operations tasks is quite different from the same child's progression with respect to all other tasks except those of the related set.

From these results, we see that useful information is not gained by identifying a child's status as being in the stage of concrete operations unless the child's status with respect to each related set of concrete operations tasks is also identified. Perhaps more important, a very serious error will be made if a teacher or parent assumes that a child should be able to perform all the concrete operations tasks equally well. Assuredly, the practitioner should be aware that these 12 fundamental and clearly defined tasks of the concrete operations stage do not develop in an integrated, synchronous pattern as might be inferred from the description of the concrete operations stage in Piagetian theory.

The analyses of the groupement data also showed that the eight groupements do not develop in an integrated, synchronous pattern; rather, they develop as eight separate items. The most important finding from the analysis of the combined concrete operations tasks and the groupement tests was that the performances of the concrete operations stage and the groupement structures developed in an uncorrelated fashion, rather than in a highly correlated manner as is implied by Piagetian theory. Accordingly, we infer that the cognitive structure proposed by Piaget is not valid for explaining the course of cognitive development during the concrete operations stage. Other scholars including Brainerd (1978), Flavell (1977), Feldman and Toulmin (1976), and Smedslund (1977) express a similar reservation. However, the reservations of these scholars are not yet appearing in the books and articles read by teachers.

The longitudinal study supports the following alternative views regarding development. Each related set of the concrete operations tasks (for example, number, classification, and conservation of length) and each related set of cognitive structures (for example, the addition and the subtraction of primary classes) have their own developmental pattern. There is parallel and integrated development of small sets of related developmental items of the concrete operations stage rather than integrated and synchronous development of all the items. Moreover, some items achieve full functional maturity starting as early as kindergarten, and others do not achieve it even in grade 9. Thus, the four stages and the related qualitative changes given earlier in the chapter are useful for describing intellectual development only if they are applied to substantively related areas of development.

In Chapter 9 of this book, we will see that some concepts are learned much earlier than other concepts. For example, children fully understand the concept *tree* much earlier than the concept *noun*. Thus, the understanding of concepts progresses in the same manner as achieving the related sets of Piagetian tasks and the groupements (as demonstrated by the longitudinal study). Accordingly, teachers should not expect a child of any given age to be at the same level of development in all curricular areas such as reading, spelling, science, social studies, and mathematics. Even within a subject field such as mathematics, they should not expect the same child to be equally proficient, for example, in classifying objects, in understanding number relations, and in understanding spatial relations. Variability in development within each child is much greater than the Piagetian stage description of cognitive development implies; and the differences among children of the same age in their levels of development are much greater than the description of the four Piagetian stages of development takes into account.

An Alternative to Piaget's Explanation of Development

In the preceding section, we observed an empirically validated alternative to the Piagetian four-stage description of cognitive development. The Piagetian explanatory concept of cognitive structures underlying the observable behavior was not supported empirically either. We may now examine a revision of the theory that replaces the cognitive structure concept with information-processing concepts (Case, 1981).

As a starting point, Case (1981) accepts certain principles of Piagetian theory. The first is that qualitative differences occur in thinking. The second is that children progress from one stage of thinking to the next in an invariant sequence: each new set of operations builds upon the prior ones (a logical necessity not empirically validated). A third principle is that a child is not ready to perform a particular task until the underlying capabilities for performing the task emerge. Case then proceeds to redefine the essential features of each of the four stages and to replace the Piagetian construct of cognitive structures with concepts drawn from cognitive information-processing theory.

Case (1981) proposes that the structure of each stage can be thought of as a set of executive strategies. An *executive strategy* (to be discussed in Chapter 4) consists of the operations necessary for performing the tasks of a stage and the means for monitoring them. According to this view, the child develops a strategy for performing a particular task, such as classifying objects on the basis of their color. In order for a child to classify at a qualitatively higher level, a new strategy must be available that incorporates elements of the prior strategy but also contains new elements. For example, to classify on the basis of color and shape rather than color only, the child must have a strategy using color but must also develop a new strategy taking shape into account. The Piagetian progression from centering to decentering is accounted for in terms of this kind of change in learning strategies rather than in terms of the changes in the cognitive structures from the preoperational stage to the concrete-operations stage.

Case (1981) proposes that progression from one stage to another not only requires more advanced strategies but also an increased short-term memory capacity to store information and an increased capability to use the strategies to process information. The capacity of short-term memory increases with age. Moreover, the more advanced learning strategies enable more information to be processed in short-term memory in less time. Thus, progression from the preoperational to the concrete operations stage is based on increased memory capacity, more advanced learning strategies and executive control, and an accompanying ability to process an increasing amount of information in less time. (A discussion of information-processing theory is given in Chapter 4.)

A few concerns are in order regarding the views of Case. First, Case's revision maintains the idea that Piaget's four stages accurately describe intellectual development. However, as demonstrated by the longitudinal study earlier in this chapter, the descriptive aspect of the four stages applies accurately only to correlated sets of developmental items. Second, Case's revision has a very strong maturational flavor, implying a strong hereditary basis for the progression from one stage to another. In this regard, Case (1981) states that change from one stage to the next "is dependent primarily on maturation; that is, it is relatively independent of any specific experiences" (Case, 1981, p. 158). The present author disagrees with this point of view and, like Bruner, Flavell, and Havighurst, to be considered next, ascribes much importance to learning and other environmental conditions in determining both the rate of intellectual development and the fields of human activity in which individuals express their intellectual abilities.

3.1 Describe and give an example of each of the five qualitative features of sensorimotor thinking.

3.2 Describe and give an example of each of the following qualitative features of preoperational thought: egocentrism, centration rather than decentration, irreversibility rather than reversibility, failure to conserve, and inability to reclassify.

3.3 Trace the qualitative changes in classifying that occur from the sensorimotor stage through the concrete operations stage.

3.4 How are the thought operations of the formal operations stage different from those of the concrete operations stage?

3.5 Piaget's description of the concrete operations stage implies that the majority of the observable behaviors of the concrete operations stage as represented by various Piagetian tasks emerge at about the same time, progress at about the same rate, and reach full functional maturity at about the same time. Using Table 3.1, draw two or three generalizations indicating how intellectual development actually progresses.

3.6 The groupements are the internal structures hypothesized by Piaget as underlying, or making possible, the observable behaviors of the concrete operations stage. Accordingly, all the groupements should achieve full functional maturity at about the same time as the Piagetian task performances. Using Table 3.1, summarize the information regarding this Piagetian hypothesis.

3.7 If cognitive development progresses during the concrete operations period in a highly integrated manner, all the tasks of the concrete operations stage should develop in a highly integrated pattern. Using the longitudinal findings based on factor analysis, summarize how the Piagetian tasks of the concrete operations actually develop.

3.8 If the groupements actually make possible the performance of various concrete operations tasks, the groupements and the Piagetian tasks should develop in a highly integrated pattern. Summarize the findings of the longitudinal study based on the factor analysis regarding this proposition.

3.9 Identify consequences undesirable to a 7-year-old child in the first grade if a teacher infers that the child is equally capable of classifying, using quantitative relationships, and conserving. Identify the even more seriously adverse effects of inferring that all children of age 7 are equally ready to learn the same subject-matter knowledge and skills.

3.10 How can educators use the idea of qualitative changes in thinking processes, rather than the idea of stages of development, with highly desirable consequences?

3.11 Compare Case's ideas about information processing as a basis for explaining the qualitative changes that occur in thinking processes with Piaget's ideas about cognitive structures as a basis for explaining them.

BRUNER'S VIEW OF COGNITIVE DEVELOPMENT

Development Progresses in an Integrative Manner

Development Is Continuous

Development Is Strongly Influenced by Culture

Bruner's theory of cognitive development focuses on the means by which human beings interact with the environment and internally represent their experiences. Continuity of development and cultural determinants of development, including language and schooling, are also of central importance (Bruner, Olver, & Greenfield, 1966).

Development Progresses
in an Integrative Manner

Bruner explains three ways of knowing something. One way, the *enactive*, involves doing something and then representing the motor experience internally. A second way, the *ikonic*, involves sensing things visually, aurally, and by the other senses, and then storing the resulting images internally. A third mode of knowing, the *symbolic*, involves knowing something by interacting with the environment through language and then representing the meaning of it internally. The three modes of interacting with the environment emerge quite early in life in the order given: enactive, ikonic, and symbolic. Upon successive emergence, they become integrated and continue to be used throughout life, rather than disappearing. Excerpts from Bruner's explanations of the three modes follow:

> We can talk of three ways in which somebody "knows" something: through doing it, through a picture or image of it, and through some such symbolic means as language. A first approach to understanding the distinction between the three can be achieved by viewing each as if it were external— though our eventual object is to view representations as internal. With respect to a particular knot, we learn the act of tying it and, when we "know" the knot, we know it by the habitual pattern of action we have mastered. The habit by which the knot is represented is serially organized, governed by some sort of schema that holds its successive segments together, and is in some sense related to other acts that either facilitate it or interfere with it. There is a fair amount of sensorimotor feedback involved in carrying out the act in question, yet what is crucial is that such a representation is executed in the medium of action.
>
> Representation in imagery is just that: the picture of the knot in question, its final phase or some intermediate phase, or, indeed, even a motion picture of the knot being formed. It is obvious, yet worth saying, that to have a picture before one (or in one's head) is not necessarily to be able to execute the act it represents . . . A picture is a selective analogue of what it stands for, and only in a trivial sense is it a "copy" of its referent . . .
>
> The representation of a knot in symbolic terms is not so readily stated, for it involves at the outset a choice of the code in which the knot is to be described. For symbolic representation, whether in natural or mathematical "language," requires the translation of what is to be represented into discrete terms that may then be formed into "utterances" or "strings" or "sentences," or whatever the medium uses to combine the discrete elements by rule. Note, too, that whatever symbolic code one uses, it is also necessary to specify whether one is describing a process of tying a knot or the knot itself (at some stage of being tied). There is, moreover, a choice in the linguistic description of a knot whether to be highly concrete or to describe this knot as one of a general class of knots. However one settles these choices, what remains is that a symbolic representation has built-in features that are specialized and distinctive. (Bruner, Olver, & Greenfield, 1966, pp. 6, 7. Reprinted by permission)

Development Is Continuous

Bruner's ideas are similar to Piaget's in that both propose that cognitive development occurs in phases that are qualitatively different from one

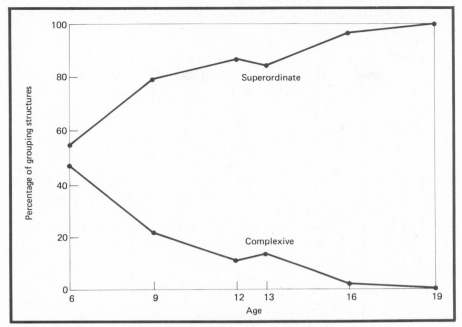

Figure 3.1 Percentages of students using two types of grouping structures.
Source: Bruner, Olver, & Greenfield, 1966, p. 77.

another. However, Bruner provides for much greater continuity and relatedness from one phase to the next.

The idea of continuity of development is reflected in Figure 3.1. In an
experiment, individuals of ages 6, 9, 12, 13, 16, and 19 were given the same
tasks. Initially, the subject was asked how two things represented by the
words *banana* and *peach* were alike and different. Additional items — *potato,
meat, milk, water, air, germs* — were added consecutively, and the same
question was asked until all eight items were presented. Providing an answer to these successive questions involved classifying the items, or forming concepts. A final contrast item, *stones*, was presented, and the subject
was asked only how it differed from the preceding items.

The responses of the subjects in terms of how they judged the things
to be alike were put into two categories, superordinate and complexive. In
superordinate classifying, a superordinate concept that included all the
items given was formed by identifying one or more common attributes of
the given items. For example, *banana, peach, potato* and *meat* were classified as edible things because they all can be eaten. *Complexive grouping*
was at a more primitive level; a superordinate concept was not formed of all
the items and a nondefining attribute of the items was used for classifying.
For example, *banana* and *peach* were classified as alike because they are

both yellow; *banana, peach,* and *potato* because they are both round, and *potato* and *meat* because they are both heavy.

Note in Figure 3.1 that while superordinate and complexive groupings are used by about 52% and 48% of the subjects at age 6, the comparable percentages are about 80 and 20 at age 13. These results do not support a stage description of development, inasmuch as for all ages, 6–19, there is a gradual increment in the superordinate groupings and a gradual decrement in complexive groupings. A stage theory would indicate sharper changes at some point in the two types of groupings from ages 6 to 19.

Development Is Strongly Influenced by Culture

In addition to assigning more importance to continuity, Bruner also emphasizes the importance of language in cognitive development much more than Piaget does. As implied by the idea of symbolic interaction, Bruner regards language as a primary factor in child and adolescent cognitive development. For example, children at any age who do not have the names of the superordinate concepts use complexive groupings and perform much less well than those who do have the names.

Finally, Bruner considers schooling to be more important than Piaget does. Although Piaget recognizes social transmission and informal learning experiences as contributing to cognitive growth, Bruner indicates that cultural groups, through their schools, provide the tools for cognitive growth. Accordingly, children of different cultural groups differ in their average rate of development and also differ qualitatively, as indicated in their different patterns of thinking about the physical and social environment. Bruner makes clear his disagreement with Piagetian theory:

> Our point of departure is, then, a human organism with capacities for representing the world in three modes, each of which is constrained by the inherent nature of the human capacities supporting it. Man is seen to grow by the process of internalizing the ways of acting, imaging, and symbolizing that "exist" in his culture, ways that amplify his powers. He then develops these powers in a fashion that reflects the uses to which he puts his own life. The development of those powers, it seems to me, will depend massively on three embedded predicaments. The first has to do with the supply of "amplifiers" that a culture has in stock—images, skills, conceptions, and the rest. The second consideration is the nature of the life led by an individual, the demands placed on him. The third (and most specialized) consideration is the extent to which the individual is incited to explore the sources of the concordance or discordance among his three modes of knowing—actions, image, and symbol. (Bruner, Olver, & Greenfield, 1966, pp. 320–321. Reprinted by permission)

3.12 Give an illustration of each of Bruner's three modes of knowing something: enactive, ikonic, and symbolic.

3.13 Give an example of an adult learning something, such as weaving or demonstrating a tennis serve, through an integration of all three ways of knowing.

3.14 Compare Bruner's ideas regarding continuity of development and the integration of the three modes of knowing with Piaget's four discrete stages of intellectual development.

3.15 Compare Bruner's ideas regarding the role of language, learning, and cultural factors in intellectual development with those of Case and Piaget regarding the role of maturation and biological factors.

DEVELOPMENT OF METACOGNITION

Cognition and Metacognition

Self-Regulation of Cognitive Activity

Metacognition refers to one's own knowledge about knowing. *Cognitive monitoring* refers to regulating one's own use of knowledge and cognitive strategies in achieving learning goals (Flavell, 1979).

Cognition and Metacognition

It may be well to illustrate the difference between cognition and metacognition and between cognitive strategies and metacognitive strategies. *Cognition* involves becoming aware of something and understanding it, for example, the American form of representative government. *Metacognition* refers to being aware of what one knows about the American form of government and also of one's own capabilities for learning about it. *Cognitive strategies,* such as organizing material and relating it to what one already knows, are used to gain information about the American form of government. A *metacognitive strategy* is used to decide which strategies to use to get further information or even whether to get it.

Self-Regulation of Cognitive Activity

Flavell (1979) indicates that regulating one's own cognitive activities occurs through the interaction of four types of phenomena: metacognitive knowledge, metacognitive experiences, tasks to be performed, and strategies. Figure 3.2 depicts the interactions.

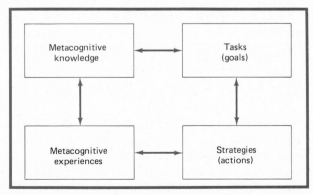

Figure 3.2 Factors involved in self-regulation of learning activities.

A person's *metacognitive knowledge* includes what one knows and believes about the variables that affect both the course and the outcomes of goal-directed, cognitive activities (Flavell, 1979). Three categories of knowledge variables are person, task, and strategy. The metacognitive knowledge for carrying out a particular sequence of learning activities is depicted in Figure 3.3.

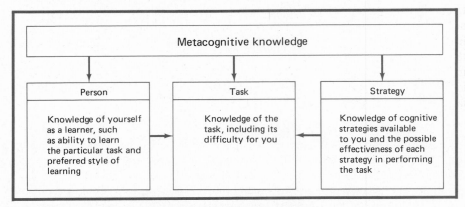

Figure 3.3 Metacognitive knowledge and task performance.

The interaction of the three kinds of metacognitive knowledge may be illustrated. You believe that you do not have an appropriate strategy for solving a physics problem. Therefore, you believe that you cannot complete the task without assistance. You decide to go to your classmate or the professor to see if one of them can aid you in identifying an appropriate problem-solving strategy. This is your metastrategy for identifying a helpful cognitive strategy.

A *metacognitive experience* is a conscious experience and is essential for the self-regulation of cognitive activities, from the time one attends to a situation until a goal is either achieved or discarded. Flavell (1979) presumes that metacognitive experiencing is likely to occur in three kinds of situations. One is any situation that stimulates careful, conscious thinking, such as writing a term paper or essay exam. Another is a novel situation where each step must be considered carefully beforehand and evaluated along the way. A final situation is one in which decisions are accompanied with some risk to the individual.

Flavell (1979) assigns other functions to metacognitive experiencing that are related to motivation and to learning. In regard to motivation, consciously thinking about something can activate the goal-setting process and subsequently direct goal-setting activities. Thus, if you believe that you are not well prepared to take a test, you set a goal of preparing for the test, make plans to study for it, and then carry out the plans. In regard to learning, new knowledge that you acquire modifies your metacognitive knowledge base.

Through metacognitive experiencing, you may add, delete, or revise some of your ideas as you think, or experience, mentally. For example, you may now mentally review Piaget's theory, Bruner's theory, and metacognition and decide, as Flavell did, that neither of the first two theories accounts well for metacognition as an aspect of intellectual development.

Preschool and elementary school children are limited in their knowledge about cognitive strategies, for example, strategies for learning to read, to acquire concepts, to solve problems, and to set goals. Adolescents and adults are more knowledgeable. However, even the most eminent scholars in the field, including Flavell, have only limited knowledge at present about the learning and development of cognitive and metacognitive strategies from infancy through adolescence. The reason for this nearly universal ignorance is that this very critical area of child and adolescent development has been ignored in both developmental and learning psychology until very recently.

3.16 Explain the difference between metacognition and cognitive monitoring, or the self-regulation of cognitive activities.

3.17 Indicate the strategies that you employ in studying text material and explain the metastrategy that controls your use of the particular strategies.

3.18 Assume that you will take a 20-item, multiple-choice test on the material of this chapter three days from now. Think about how the following factors influence your self-regulation of your learning activities: (a) your knowledge about learning and about yourself as a learner (metacognitive knowledge), (b) your conscious thinking about the task and setting a goal related to how well you will learn and achieve on the test (metacognitive experience), (c) your knowledge of the nature of the task (estimating the difficulty of the task for you), and (d) your knowledge of methods for learning the material and preparing for the test (cognitive strategies). Outline your learning and test-preparation activities, and indicate how you will use (a)–(d) in self-regulating the activities.

3.19 Give possible reasons why some high school and college students prefer to be told how to proceed rather than to engage in self-regulation of their learning activities.

3.20 At what school level do you think students should be taught ideas about metacognition and cognitive monitoring? Explain.

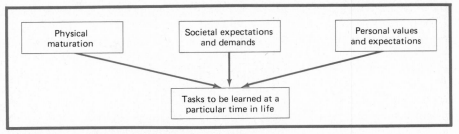

Figure 3.4 Determinants of developmental tasks.

DEVELOPMENTAL TASKS AND EDUCATION

Havighurst (1953, 1972) identified three major factors contributing to the individual's development: physical maturation, expectations of the social groups of which one is a member, and one's personal values and aspirations. These correspond to the biological, cultural, and psychological determinants of development. These inner and outer forces (see Figure 3.4) produce a series of developmental tasks of life that must be mastered at an appropriate time if the individual is to be a happy and successful human being at a particular time and also later.

According to Havighurst (1972):

> The tasks the individual must learn — *the developmental tasks* of life — are those things that constitute healthy and satisfactory growth in our society. They are the things a person must learn if he is to be judged and to judge himself to be a reasonably happy and successful person. *A developmental task is a task which arises at or about a certain period in the life of the individual, successful achievement of which leads to his happiness and to success with later tasks, while failure leads to unhappiness in the individual, disapproval by the society, and difficulty with later tasks.* (p. 2)

Two very important points follow from this definition. First, failure in a task at one age will cause partial or complete failure in the achievement of a related task at a later age. Thus, not learning to read independently during childhood will cause reading and perhaps other problems during adolescence. Second, there are teachable moments for each developmental task. For every person, there is a proper time to learn to read, to prepare for a career, and to become economically independent.

The idea of developmental tasks is especially powerful and useful to educators because it takes into account the external conditions that stimulate growth, maturation that partially determines the rate and upper limits of growth, and the self as the regulator of personal development. Furthermore, growth in various areas of development, such as the physical, intellectual, emotional, social, and moral, is treated in an integrative fashion at successive periods in a person's life.

The relation of developmental tasks to education is direct and clear.

Successful achievement of a developmental task leads to happiness and to success with later tasks while failure leads to unhappiness, disapproval from others, and difficulty with later tasks. With which tasks can the school most directly aid the child in experiencing success?

First, many societal expectations about desirable directions of growth are transmitted to a child through the school. Parents also transmit their expectations about the role of the school to a child. These societal expectations are powerful determinants of some of the developmental tasks. Growing children internalize these expectations as a crucial element of their self-concepts. Second, since developmental tasks are successfully achieved through learning, they serve as a focus for directing educational processes. Furthermore, they can be used in diagnosing difficulties of children who are late in achieving mastery of particular tasks.

The developmental tasks are arranged according to six periods of life that have been recognized and widely accepted for centuries: infancy and early childhood, middle childhood, adolescence, early adulthood, middle age, and later maturity. The chronological age at which individuals of the same social class or other group first experience a certain developmental task varies considerably because of the maturational and other characteristics of the individual interacting with the expectations of the particular group. Thus, there are wide differences in the age at which persons of the same social class achieve given tasks, such as preparing for marriage and achieving personal independence. The differences are even wider among persons of different social classes.

In this part of the text, developmental tasks of infancy and early childhood and those of early adulthood are only listed because of space limitations. More information, however, about the tasks of middle childhood and adolescence is provided.

Tasks of Infancy and
Early Childhood: Birth to Age 6

The tasks that must be learned during infancy and early childhood follow (Havighurst, 1972, pp. 9–17):

1. Learning to walk.
2. Learning to take solid foods.
3. Learning to talk.
4. Learning to control the elimination of body wastes.
5. Learning sex differences and sexual modesty.
6. Forming concepts and learning language to describe social and physical reality.
7. Getting ready to read.
8. Learning to distinguish right and wrong and beginning to develop a conscience.

Tasks of Middle Childhood: Age 6 to Age 12

Middle childhood is characterized by three great outward pushes, or thrusts. One thrust is from the home into the peer group. Another is into the world of games and work requiring neuromuscular skills. The third thrust is mental into the world of adult concepts, logic, symbolism, and communication. The developmental tasks that must be learned during middle childhood accompany these thrusts:

1. Learning physical skills necessary for ordinary games.
2. Building wholesome attitudes toward oneself as a growing organism.
3. Learning to get along with age-mates.
4. Learning an appropriate masculine or feminine social role.
5. Developing fundamental skills in reading, writing, and calculating.
6. Developing concepts necessary for everyday living.
7. Developing conscience, morality, and a scale of values.
8. Achieving personal independence.
9. Developing attitudes toward social groups and institutions.

The first developmental task, quoted directly from Havighurst (1972, pp. 19, 20), indicates how he analyzes each task.

1. Learning physical skills necessary for ordinary games.
Nature of the task. To learn the physical skills that are necessary for the games and physical activities highly valued in childhood—such skills as throwing and catching, kicking, tumbling, swimming, and handling simple tools.
Biological basis. This is a period of general growth of muscle and bone, with possibly some neural maturation to make muscular coordina-

tion easier. In general, large muscle coordination precedes that of the small muscles, and therefore the refinements of neuromuscular skill come at the end rather than at the beginning of this period.

Psychological basis. The peer group rewards a child for success and punishes him by indifference or disdain for failure in this task.

Cultural basis. Boys are expected to learn these skills to a higher degree than girls. A girl can do rather poorly on them and still hold status in the peer group, while a boy who does poorly is called a "sissy" and loses status. Boys of all social classes are expected to acquire physical skills.

Educational implications. The peer culture teaches these skills so successfully to most boys and girls that the school can be content with trying to help the ones who have special difficulty with the task. This special help may take the form of arranging play groups of the more awkward youngsters, so that they can learn at their own rates without being punished by faster-moving age-mates.

2. Building wholesome attitudes toward oneself as a growing organism. This task requires developing habits of care of the body and of cleanliness and safety. These habits are accompanied by a wholesome attitude that includes a sense of physical normality and adequacy, the ability to enjoy using the body, and a wholesome attitude toward sex.

Havighurst sees a number of educational implications in this task. Health habits should be taught routinely during the elementary school years. Glamorous figures in athletics and the movies might be used as examples. Sex education should be agreed upon by the school and parents, with the school doing what the parents feel they cannot do well. The facts of human reproduction should be taught before puberty.

3. Learning to get along with age-mates. This task has two demands. One is to learn the give-and-take of social life among peers. Another is to learn to make friends and to get along with enemies. From these demands, the child's social personality emerges and continues without major change throughout life.

4. Learning an appropriate masculine or feminine social role. This task requires learning to act the role that is expected and being rewarded for being a boy or girl. The role changes somewhat from early to late middle-childhood because of maturational processes and related societal expectations.

The anatomical differences between boys and girls are small during middle childhood. Girls are as well built for physical activities as boys. Many girls are as tall and as strong as boys. However, starting at about age 9 or 10, the body chemistry of boys and girls becomes differentiated, since girls mature about two years earlier than boys.

American culture still expects some differences in the physical activities and motor skills of boys and girls during the elementary school years. However, we are moving rapidly toward greater equality between the sexes.

The differences between the sex roles of boys and girls are fewer than they have been in the past.

Havighurst believes that having more male teachers in the elementary schools will have a good influence on boys. It will give them a closer relationship with male models at a time when they are learning how men and women behave.

5. Developing fundamental skills in reading, writing, and calculating. Handwriting, spelling, and reading do not improve for most students after age 12 (Havighurst, 1972). This being the case, it is critical that every child learn these basic skills during the elementary school years. Not to learn these skills causes many problems in postelementary schooling. Learning to calculate — add, subtract, multiply, and divide — is also critical during the elementary school years.

6. Developing concepts necessary for everyday living. This task requires learning the basic concepts necessary to think effectively about ordinary occupational, civic, scientific, and social matters. The learning of concepts with which to think and to understand is equal in importance to the learning of basic skills.

At about age 10–12, many children can learn abstract concepts and principles when provided good instruction. In learning concepts and principles, they need to see and to do, not merely to listen and to read. The child who can read and who has a good store of basic concepts in mathematics, science, and social studies can handle middle school subject matter with relative ease.

7. Developing conscience, morality, and a scale of values. Three critical areas of learning are required here: inner moral control, respect for moral rules, and a budding value system. Achieving this task during middle childhood has a profound effect on the happiness and success of the individual throughout the life span. The school influences the child's morality in several ways. One is through its teachings about morality. Another is through teachers' punishments and rewards. The teachers' examples are also important. Finally, the child's experience in the peer group is influential.

8. Achieving personal independence. In mastering this task, children take increasing responsibility for their personal safety, for planning their use of time, and for choosing their friends. A difficult task of teachers and parents is to find a proper balance between encouraging children to assume personal initiative and responsibility and giving them too much freedom too soon. Havighurst (1972) offers the following advice:

> If the elementary school aims to promote the personal independence of its pupils, it will teach them how to study and learn independently; it will give them opportunity to plan a part of the school program and to discuss and criticize the results of their planning; all under a kind of supervision that supports children when they make mistakes, and sets limits for their growing independence to protect them from going too far. (p. 33)

9. Developing attitudes toward social groups and institutions. This task involves developing attitudes that contribute to the maintenance and refinement of our democratic form of government and life. The school aids this development by inculcating the basic democratic social attitudes considered desirable for all Americans. Included here are religious and racial tolerance, respect for freedom of speech and other civil rights, democratic political practices, and international cooperation.

Tasks of Adolescence: Age 12 to Age 18

Boys and girls reach their full physical maturity during the adolescent period, but growth of the self is a very different matter. It is dependent in part upon biological maturation, but it is also influenced by societal expectations and opportunities. As a result of the uncertainty of present societal expectations and opportunities, many middle school and high school students are experiencing difficulty with one or more of the developmental tasks of adolescence. These biological and social tasks follow:

1. Achieving new and more mature relations with age-mates of both sexes.
2. Achieving a masculine or feminine social role.
3. Accepting one's physique and using the body effectively.
4. Achieving emotional independence from parents and other adults.
5. Preparing for marriage and family life.
6. Preparing for a career.
7. Acquiring a set of values and an ethical system.
8. Desiring and achieving socially responsible behavior.

1. Achieving new and more mature relations with age-mates of both sexes. There are three main subtasks here. One is that boys and girls learn to look upon girls as women and boys as men and thus to become adults among adults. A second subtask is to learn to work with others for a common purpose, disregarding personal feelings. The final subtask is to learn to lead without dominating. Havighurst (1972) indicates that success in accomplishing these tasks means a reasonably good social adjustment throughout life, whereas failure results in an unhappy adult life. There are, however, delays in achieving the task fully. The delays are not apt to have serious permanent consequences, though they may mean a relatively unhappy adolescent period.

2. Achieving a masculine or feminine social role. This task involves accepting and learning a socially approved adult masculine or feminine social role. Both feminine and masculine roles have changed greatly since 1950. For example, women who work outside the home are increasing in numbers and in positions of high status and influence. Women also have become more free in their sexual behavior. Accordingly, adolescent girls have many more choices. They can choose to go into business or a profession, to be married with or without becoming a mother, or to do many things not widely done earlier.

The masculine sex role is also less restrictive. Doing housework and caring for young children are more common. Careers in nursing, primary school teaching, and other fields once dominated by women are opening to men.

3. Accepting one's physique and using the body effectively. The subtasks here are to accept one's body and to use and protect it effectively and with personal satisfaction. Two important considerations are the wide differences in the age at which individuals mature and the kinds of psychological problems that accompany the differential rate of physical development.

Girls reach puberty about two years earlier than boys, and nearly all girls have reached their mature height at age 16. Boys continue to grow until 18, and some even later. This average difference between girls and boys presents fewer difficulties than the large differences within each sex. Both very early and very late developers of both sexes have problems accepting their physique. The early developer's concerns are alleviated much earlier in life than those of the late developer. Both boys and girls who regard themselves as different in any characteristic associated with sexual attractiveness — acne, flabbiness, height, hair growth, facial features, sexual organs — experience difficulty in body acceptance.

4. Achieving emotional independence from parents and other adults. The three facets of this task are to achieve increasing independence from parents, to maintain affection for parents without remaining dependent on them, and to develop respect for older adults without depending on them. This task is a source of confusion and worry in some homes. The adolescent wants to be independent yet also cherishes support and guidance. The parents want the child to achieve economic and personal independence but yet also do not want to be ignored by the child or to be replaced in influence by peers or other adults. In this kind of confusion, there is often rebellion by the adolescent and rejection by the parents.

Havighurst (1972) points out some implications of the generation conflict for education that are often overlooked. Generation conflict, a common theme in literature, can be studied in English classes. Social change as it affects successive generations can fit readily into social studies classes. Teachers can play a useful role in the process of psychological weaning by understanding the reasons for attachments that some students form for them and by helping these students to the next stage of development. Finally, teachers, counselors, and administrators can help parents understand the problem of generation conflict and attack it constructively. They can, for example, hold individual conferences with parents and form parent-teacher study groups.

5. Preparing for marriage and family life. The two basic subtasks here are developing a positive attitude toward family life and children and getting the knowledge necessary for home management and child rearing. How this task is achieved depends upon the concept of marriage and family life held by the individual and the social group. Marriage and family are taking on an increasingly greater variety of forms. The number of one-parent homes,

homes in which both parents work, and children born to unmarried mothers will probably continue to increase.

6. Preparing for a career. It is possible that the United States, as well as Western countries generally, is providing fewer opportunities for each successive generation to prepare for fruitful careers. At present, three disturbing conditions are becoming prevalent. First, there is a decrease in the ethical value assigned to work and to preparing for an occupation. Second, economic independence is very nearly impossible for the vast majority of young people below the age of 20. Third, the number of career opportunities available is decreasing relatively as the number of candidates, including women entering careers, continues to increase. These conditions will probably limit the opportunity for the upward mobility of many children of the poor and of minority groups. New and more equitable solutions to the current situation are clearly needed.

7. Acquiring a set of values and an ethical system. Identifying and acquiring a stable system of values and ethics are very difficult for modern adolescents. The traditional ideology of earlier generations is not credible to a large number of the present generation nor to many teachers. To earlier generations of Americans, the physical world and humankind were consistent with their dominant values. They perceived the wealth and natural resources of the country as beneficial to all people. The present generation perceives many contradictions between this earlier value system and the present reality of ready access to the better things of life for some but poverty and lack of opportunity for others. The discrepancy between the ideal and current practice is very great, and traditional values are rejected.

A possible solution for the schools involves two steps (Havighurst, 1972). The first is to help students acquire instrumental, aesthetic, and ethical values—rather than accept traditional values—that will maintain the positive qualities of a highly productive economy and bring more beauty and love into the lives of people. The second step is to help students learn how to apply these values in their personal and civic lives.

8. Desiring and achieving socially responsible behavior. Two goals associated with this task are to participate as a responsible adult in the life of the community, region, and nation and to take into account the values of society in one's personal behavior. Achieving socially responsible behavior requires both making some sacrifices and experiencing desired consequences for the sacrifices. Thus, the adolescent must learn to give up some things for the greater good and then also be rewarded with social approval and the privileges of adulthood.

Altruism is commonly observed in adolescents. They want action and are ready to assume social obligations. They are likely to be impatient with the slowness of effecting desired improvements. When this pattern occurs, they are attracted either to group activism or to uncommitted privatism and individualism. Possible approaches for dealing with this pervasive situation include cooperative group learning activities in school and cooperative study of American and other forms of government.

Tasks of Early Adulthood: Age 18 to Age 30

The eight tasks of early adulthood are:

1. Selecting a mate.
2. Learning to live with a marriage partner.
3. Starting a family.
4. Rearing children.
5. Managing a home.
6. Getting started in an occupation.
7. Taking on civic responsibility.
8. Finding a congenial social group.

Most young adults experience the first full-time job, the first furnishing of an apartment or house, the first extended time away from home, marriage, parenthood, and similar memorable events during this period. Young adults are usually eager to learn how to manage these events successfully and are able to learn quickly. Havighurst believes much more attention and help should be given to them in this period.

3.21 The developmental tasks of each period of life (a) are based on the external demands placed on the individual, the biological maturation of the individual, and the self as the regulator of personal development and (b) take into account the various areas of growth—physical, intellectual, social, emotional, and moral—in an integrative manner. React to the statement that developmental tasks provide educators useful knowledge about child and adolescent development.

3.22 Why are certain developmental tasks widely experienced during a given developmental period, for example, developing fundamental skills in reading during middle childhood, ages 6–12, even though they may not be equally well mastered by all children during the middle childhood years?

3.23 Kelly, at age 12, is completing grade 6 and has mastered the nine developmental tasks of middle childhood reasonably well. Give a short characterization of Kelly's behaviors related to each of the nine tasks.

3.24 Bill, before entering junior high school, has mastered all the developmental tasks of middle childhood reasonably well except two: (a) developing fundamental skills in reading, writing, and calculating, and (b) developing conscience, morality, and a scale of values. Predict how well Bill will get along in grade 7 of the junior high school.

3.25 Return to the eight developmental tasks of adolescence: (a) Select those that you think most adolescents today have mastered reasonably well upon high school graduation. (b) Select those with which most adolescents are still experiencing concern or difficulty upon high school graduation.

3.26 Prepare for middle school students a short explanation as to why there is typically a generation conflict between students and their parents. Recommend books that they can read that illustrate the conflict and how it is resolved.

3.27 Return to the developmental tasks of early adulthood: (a) Are all of them equally important to you? (b) Which of the tasks do high school graduates who do not go to college experience earlier than most college students?

3.28 Which of the tasks does your college course work help you to achieve?

3.29 Review and Application. Recall the most important information about each of the following concepts and identify at least one possible use of the information by you as a learner, as a teacher, or both:

> Piagetian Theory of Cognitive Development
>> Development Progresses Through Four Qualitatively Different Stages
>> An Alternative to Piaget's Four-Stage Description of Development
>> An Alternative to Piaget's Explanation of Development
> Bruner's View of Cognitive Development
>> Development Progresses in an Integrative Manner
>> Development Is Continuous
>> Development Is Strongly Influenced by Culture
> Development of Metacognition
>> Cognition and Metacognition
>> Self-Regulation of Cognitive Activity
> Developmental Tasks and Education
>> Tasks of Infancy and Early Childhood: Birth to Age 6
>> Tasks of Middle Childhood: Age 6 to Age 12
>> Tasks of Adolescence: Age 12 to Age 18
>> Tasks of Early Adulthood: Age 18 to Age 30

SUMMARY

Piaget described human development as occurring in four clearly delineated stages: sensorimotor, preoperational, concrete operations, and formal operations. He also indicated the cognitive structures that make possible the child's progression from one stage to the next. That qualitative changes occur in development, that development progresses in an orderly manner, and that the child constructs knowledge rather than receives it passively represent some of the many enduring ideas of Piagetian theory. However, Piaget's stage description of development, based heavily on his observing his three children in the 1920s and 1930s, and his logical ideas about cognitive structures are giving way as large-scale, cross-sectional and longitudinal studies of children's development are being conducted. Variability within the same child in various areas of development and differences among children of the same age in any area of development are far greater than Piagetian stage theory takes into account.

Bruner describes and explains development in terms of internal and external operations: enactive, ikonic, and symbolic. Bruner sees more continuity in development than Piaget and also gives more weight to environmental conditions as determinants of development. Bruner indicates that cultural groups, through their language and their schools, provide the tools for cognitive growth and that differences in these tools account for some of the qualitative differences in the thought processes of children of different cultural groups.

Flavell, the early American interpreter of Piaget, has shifted considerable attention from Piagetian theory to metacognition, that is, knowing about knowing. Metacognitive development is concerned with children's acquiring knowledge about their own learning characteristics, the learning tasks they encounter, their strategies for learning the tasks, and the control or regulation of their learning goals and activities.

Havighurst, similar to Bruner, indicates that the interactions of three major factors contribute to the individual's development: physical maturation, expectations of the social groups of which one is a member, and one's own personal values and aspirations. Using these ideas, Havighurst specifies developmental tasks for broad age groups, including infancy and early childhood, middle childhood, adolescence, and early adulthood. The developmental tasks take into account all areas of development: intellectual, emotional, moral, physical, and social. Achieving the developmental tasks of each age level leads to present and future happiness and success, while failure to do so has the opposite effect. Havighurst proposes that education provides the principal means for boys and girls to achieve many of the developmental tasks. Accordingly, the developmental tasks of each period provide a very useful framework for relating major ideas about human development to education.

SUGGESTIONS FOR FURTHER READING

Bruner, J. S. *Beyond the information given.* New York: Norton, 1973.

Chapters 18 and 19 of this book are reprints of Bruner's key papers dealing with the course of cognitive growth. The enactive, iconic, and symbolic modes of representation are explained.

DiVesta, F. J. Cognitive development. In H. E. Mitzel, J. H. Best, & W. Rabinowitz (Eds.), *Encyclopedia of educational research* (5th ed., Vol. 1). New York: The Free Press, 1982.

Piaget's stages of development are summarized, and more recent interests including metacognition are explored. Levels of development described in this encyclopedia include "Infant Development" by P. M. Schwartz, "Early Childhood Development" by C. A. Cartwright and D. L. Peters, "Middle Years Development" by P. Minuchin, "Preadolescent Development" by W. Bolden, "Adolescent Development" by D. Rogers, "Adult Development" by D. Thompson, and "Aging" by J. H. Britton and J. O. Britton.

Farley, F. H., & Gordon, N. J. (Eds.), *Psychology and education: The state of the union.* Berkeley, Calif.: McCutchan, 1981.

The titles and authors of chapters on development are chap. 5, "Social Cognition" by N. J. Gordon; chap. 6, "Intellectual Development:

A Systematic Reinterpretation" by R. Case; and chap. 8. "Psychological Models of Educational Growth" by L. P. Nucci and H. J. Walberg.

Flavell, J. F. Cognitive monitoring. In W. P. Dickson (Ed.), *Children's oral communication skills*. New York: Academic Press, 1981, pp. 35–60.

Presents a model for the self-regulation of one's own communication and cognition and gives educational implications.

Gordon, E. W. (Ed.). *Review of research in education* (Vol. 11). Washington, D.C.: American Educational Research Association, 1984.

A. M. Clark reviews research and theory in chap. 4, "Early experience and cognitive development," and S. F. Hamilton in chap. 6, "The secondary school in the ecology of adolescent development."

Grady, M. P. *Teaching and brain research*. New York: Longman, 1984.

Discusses the implications of changes in brain structures and functions for classroom instruction, kindergarten through grade 12.

Havighurst, R. J. *Developmental tasks and education* (3rd ed.). New York: Longman, 1972.

Chapter 1 presents an introduction to life, learning, and development, while chap. 4 explains the characteristics of developmental tasks. Other chapters describe the tasks of infancy and early childhood (chap. 2), middle childhood (chap. 3), adolescence (chap. 5), early adulthood (chap. 6), middle age (chap. 7), and later maturity (chap. 8).

Miller, P. H. *Theories of developmental psychology*. New York: W. H. Freeman, 1983.

Compares, contrasts, and analyzes the strengths and weaknesses of Piagetian, information processing, social learning, and other theories of development.

Siegel, L. S., & Brainerd, C. J. *Alternatives to Piaget: Critical essays on the theory*. New York: Academic Press, 1978.

Various scholars analyze elements of Piagetian theory and present current research that does not support the theory. The authors steer a middle course between recognizing weaknesses of the theory and totally rejecting it.

CHAPTER 4

THEORIES AND CONDITIONS OF LEARNING

CONDITIONING

OBSERVATIONAL LEARNING

MEANINGFUL VERBAL LEARNING

LEARNING AS INFORMATION PROCESSING

PURPOSEFUL LEARNING

Learning may be regarded as a relatively permanent change in knowledge, skill, or other behavior that results from practice and is not simply attributable to maturation. The primary task of the school is to aid students learn effectively. Accordingly, knowledge of learning is one of the most important foundations of effective teaching.

At the outset, we should recognize that there is not one theory of learning; there are many theories. Two association theories, discussed first in this chapter, are conditioning and observational learning. The early experiments on which these theories are based involved simple forms of learning, such as elementary motor and verbal skills and approach and avoidance behaviors.

A second kind of learning theory is cognitive. The cognitive theory presented in this chapter addresses how we learn factual information and concepts and principles. It is based on experiments conducted with human beings of school age.

In the last decade, information-processing theory has become prominent. It is based on experiments with human beings and on experiments that simulate human learning with the computer. The experiments are directed toward gaining a better understanding of the acquisition, processing, and retention of information of all kinds. Information-processing theory is neither an association nor a cognitive theory, as these terms are conventionally used in psychology. However, some psychologists explain information-processing theory from an association frame of reference and others from a cognitive view. The explanation in this chapter is cognitive rather than association. This approach is taken because most school learning involves cognitive processes other than association.

In the last part of the chapter, conditions that may be managed by the teacher to make learning effective are discussed in terms of implementing a sequence of purposeful learning. Teaching procedures to make learning purposeful for students are not based on any one theory. Rather, purposeful learning draws primarily on observational learning, cognitive learning, and information-processing theory. The sequence of purposeful learning provides a framework for the more specific principles of learning and teaching given in Chapters 7–14.

Throughout the chapter, only the most basic ideas of each theory are presented. However, the relevant ideas from the theory are incorporated in the sequence of purposeful learning in this chapter, and again later in the principles of learning and teaching in Chapters 7–14.

Classical Conditioning

Operant Conditioning

CONDITIONING

A young child strokes a furry pet, apparently without fear. Later, an adult strikes a bell sharply immediately behind the child. The child cries in fright, an unconditioned response to the harsh sound. Now, each time the pet is presented, the adult strikes the bell sharply. After this pattern is repeated a number of times, the pet is presented by itself and the child cries. The child, by another person's manipulation of the two stimulus events—the presentation of the pet and of the harsh sound of the bell—has acquired a conditioned response of crying to a previously unfeared stimulus. Other furry pets of similar color are now presented. The child responds with crying to these also. The conditioned response of crying has now generalized to other stimuli of the same class.

A toddler avoids a hot stove after touching it (*avoidance learning*) and seeks milk as food after having drunk milk when hungry (*approach learning*). Here, the child has learned to suppress or to continue responses on the basis of the consequences of these responses. These examples are typical applications of principles of conditioning to human learning.

Classical Conditioning

Figure 4.1 schematizes first-order and higher-order classical conditioning. As noted in *first-order conditioning,* a neutral *stimulus,* in this case, the sound of a metronome, is presented almost simultaneously with the *unconditioned stimulus* (US), food. The sight of food leads to the *unconditioned response* (UR) of salivation in a hungry organism. By presenting both stimuli repeatedly and withdrawing the food gradually, the sound of the metronome alone eventually elicits the response of salivation. The metronome sound is now the *conditioned stimulus* (CS) and salivation is the *conditioned response* (CR).

We should notice that the organism has already made the response to food. Accordingly, a new response was not learned. Rather, the learning

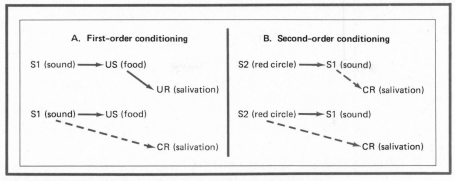

Figure 4.1 Schematic arrangement of classical conditioning.

process consisted of associating the already available response with a new stimulus. Therefore, control of the organism's behavior occurred through the manipulation of environmental stimuli, namely, food and the sound of the metronome. Moreover, the organism had to be experiencing a need for food in order for the conditioning to occur.

In *higher-order conditioning,* the sound of the metronome produces the *conditioned response* (CR) of salivation and now serves the same function as did the previous *unconditioned stimulus* (US), food. A new neutral *stimulus,* a red circle, is now presented immediately preceding the sound of the metronome. Through repeated presentations of the red circle and the sound of the metronome, the sight of the red circle elicits the response of salivation in the absence of the metronome sound.

The stimuli do not produce the response directly in either first-order or higher-order conditioning. Rather, the stimuli lead to internal cues or movements which subsequently lead to the response of salivation. We shall not treat the internal events in more detail because the results are the same, independent of what happens internally.

Teachers typically do not employ classical conditioning techniques in the classroom. However, psychologists use the theory to explain how emotional reactions to various stimuli may be learned. For example, children learn emotional reactions, such as fear, toward previously neutral stimuli, such as dentists or nurses, after experiencing pain caused by the dentists or nurses. Similarly, adults may develop a positive feeling toward an acquaintance (initially a neutral stimulus) who agrees with them and a negative feeling toward one who disagrees.

Classical conditioning has other applications. For example, some psychologists and special education teachers use classical conditioning techniques as a means of counterconditioning emotional reactions. The counterconditioning takes two forms: changing a negative response (e.g., fear of mice) to positive or neutral; and changing a positive response (e.g., enjoyment of junk foods) to negative. Typically, other techniques such as modeling, reasoning, and reinforcement are employed in counterconditioning along with the manipulation of the stimuli and the responses.

Operant Conditioning

Operant conditioning, as formulated by Skinner (1938, 1953), dominated the psychology of learning and related educational practices for many decades. Today, cognitive psychology and information processing are more prominent. Nevertheless, principles of operant conditioning are still used with remarkable success in training animals and in some school situations.

Principles of Operant Conditioning

In classical conditioning, a previously neutral stimulus, through repeated presentations with an unconditioned stimulus, becomes a conditioned stimulus and elicits a conditioned response: the conditioned stimulus comes to elicit the response. By contrast, in *operant conditioning,* the response must be made before a *positive reinforcer,* such as food, is given, or before a *negative reinforcer,* such as isolation from a peer group, is removed. Thus, in operant conditioning, when a response is followed by either a positive reinforcer or the removal of a negative reinforcer, the response that is made immediately prior to the reinforcer is strengthened. For example, a hungry child says "please" and is then given food. Each time this sequence is repeated, the probability increases that the hungry child will say "please" to get food. Food serves as a positive reinforcer of the "please" response, or *operant.* As an illustration of negative reinforcement, a teacher isolates a child from playing with other children until the child copies a page from a book. When the page is copied, the teacher terminates the isolation. Termination of the isolation increases the probability that child will copy from a book when asked to do so again.

A further comment is in order regarding operant behavior, positive reinforcers, and negative reinforcers. An *operant behavior* is any behavior carried out by an organism to obtain a reinforcer, for example, a hungry child says "please" to get food. A *positive reinforcer* is any event — for example, giving a child food — following a behavior that increases the probability that the behavior, or class of behaviors, will be performed again under similar conditions. Receiving positive reinforcers typically produces a favorable feeling, or *affect,* that accounts for the strengthening effect on the operant behavior. Accordingly, positive reinforcements are often referred to as *rewards.* A *negative reinforcer* is any event involving the termination or removal of an aversive stimulus, for example, the teacher's terminating the child's isolation, following a behavior that strengthens the behavior. We should be aware that the aversive stimulus is terminated or removed and that the behavior that preceded the termination is strengthened, for example, the child's copying the page from the book.

It is appropriate to recognize that both a positive reinforcer and a negative reinforcer may provide informative feedback to a human being. The human being recognizes that the behavior reinforced is, for example, appropriate, correct, or approved. Accordingly, cognitive theorists, such as Wittrock and Lumsdaine (1977), propose that the positive effects of reinforcement on human beings are more readily explained by information-processing theory than by operant conditioning theory.

Earlier we saw that the removal of an aversive stimulus strengthens the response that leads to its removal. This removal is different, however, from punishing, or administering an aversive stimulus, following undesired behavior. Punishing a student after engaging in undesired behavior is intended to terminate or to weaken the undesired behavior. However, the effects of punishment cannot be predicted reliably. A number of different effects are possible. First, when an adult punishes a child for an act, the child may not commit the act again depending upon the intensity of the punishment and other variables. However, this weakening effect of punishment is not nearly so predictable as is the strengthening effect of positive reinforcers. Second, punishment may have a suppressing effect on the act only in the presence of the punisher. The child may repeat the act in the absence of the punisher, particularly if the child has not developed another action to replace the punished one. Third, the punished child may *model* (imitate) the behavior of the punisher and accordingly use the same form of punishment on others. Fourth, the punisher may become an aversive stimulus for the child by becoming associated with the punishment. The child then avoids the punisher and escapes from the situation, if possible.

In the discussion of classical conditioning, we saw how higher-order conditioning occurs. It also occurs in operant conditioning. For example, presenting food to a hungry child who says "please" increases the probability of the child's continuing to say "please." In the next step, a neutral stimulus, for example, the words "good boy" are presented with the presentation of the food. After a number of times, the words alone have the same effect as the presentation of the food in maintaining the strength of the "please" response. The words "good boy" are now the *conditioned reinforcer* for the response "please." Another important point can now be made. A *secondary reinforcer* may generalize to reinforce responses other than the one with which it was initially associated. Accordingly, "good boy" reinforces responses other than saying "please," for instance, sharing a toy or hanging clothes up neatly.

Social reinforcers are used in the schools on many occasions. Positive social reinforcers include complimentary words; physical or verbal responses of endearment; and approval in the form of applause, group laughter, or attention. Social reinforcers are not injurious to the student and have been found to increase intrinsic motivation for tasks such as learning to read and to write.

The main generalizations about operant conditioning may now be summarized. A positive reinforcer closely following an operant behavior increases the probability that the behavior will occur again. When a negative reinforcer is removed immediately after the behavior that led to the removal, the probability that the behavior will occur again also increases. Higher-order conditioning occurs in operant conditioning. When a neutral stimulus is paired with a positive reinforcing stimulus, the neutral stimulus acquires reinforcing power.

Shaping Behavior

According to operant conditioning, the final behavior that is desired is shaped through a series of successive approximations. To achieve this, each act that gets closer to the final behavior is reinforced. In an early classical experiment, human beings were given score points as reinforcers of behaviors that terminated in successive scratching of the ear (Verplanck, 1956). At first, the experimenter reinforced any movement of the subject; this reinforcement strengthened the movement response. The next step was to reinforce any movement of the arms; then the movement of the hand toward the head; and, finally, scratching the ear. This use of operant conditioning principles to shape behavior through successive approximations of the desired final behavior has been replicated in hundreds of later experiments.

Although Skinnerian theory is not as useful as other theories for explaining how we learn initially, we shall see in Chapter 5 that special education teachers use conditioning principles, along with cognitive approaches, in teaching children with learning problems and with behavioral handicaps (Gardner, 1977). In Chapter 6, we shall see that Emmer and Evertson (1980) apply the principles in their prescriptions to teachers for gaining and maintaining classroom control. Finally, many schools in which discipline is poor are attempting to control student conduct by publicizing rules of conduct, providing reinforcement to students for obeying the rules, and punishing students for violations, including through suspension. In general, this strategy is being employed only after many other approaches have failed.

The extent to which conditioning theory contributes to the understanding of learning continues to be a source of some disagreement. Bower and Hilgard (1981) provide an extensive analysis of the merits and the limitations of the theory. Wingfield (1979) makes two very good points about the relationship between reinforcement and learning. Reinforcement may be a powerful way to encourage performance and to control behavior, but it cannot either produce initial learning or explain the learning process.

4.1 Describe how you would teach a child to respond to the word "good" as a social reinforcer, using techniques based on classical conditioning. Based on operant conditioning.

4.2 Give one or two examples of each of the four effects of punishment that you have observed: extinction of the punished behavior, modeling of the punisher's behavior, suppression of the punished behavior in the presence of the punisher, and negative attitudes toward the punisher.

4.3 Identify an appropriate situation for a teacher to employ principles of operant conditioning.

Social learning theory explains how chunks of behavior are learned initially. What do students learn by observing their teachers, including parents?

OBSERVATIONAL LEARNING

Models Observed and Imitated

Effects of Observational Learning

Processes and Conditions of Observational Learning

John, for the first time, observes his father hug his mother when his father and mother come home in the evening. His mother and father appear happier. The next time John comes into the house, he, too, hugs his mother. Mary, for the first time, observes other adolescents' reactions to a popular singer on TV. Mary buys a record and reacts in the same way when she and her friends listen to it. Jim hears a phrase in a foreign language for the first time and tries to say it exactly as his teacher did. These incidents illustrate the pervasive effects of observational learning. Bandura (1977) provides a lucid explanation of observational learning as part of his comprehensive social learning theory.

Models Observed and Imitated

The models that students observe and imitate may be persons, pictures, or verbal descriptions. The actions and words of the models may or may not be deliberately designed to be imitated. Television uses many means to influence people's attitudes and behaviors. In fact, observational learning that accompanies television viewing has great impact on the social behavior of many students.

In schools and in many homes, attention is given to providing exemplary models. Such models demonstrate *prosocial behaviors,* that is, behaviors that adults responsible for the education of children desire children to learn. This socializing aspect of observational learning is far more critical than is generally assumed. Indeed, many antisocial and self-damaging behaviors, as well as prosocial behaviors, are acquired through imitating models.

Effects of Observational Learning

The primary effect of observational learning is the acquisition of behavior that the individual has not learned before. Another effect is either to inhibit or disinhibit behavior that has been learned earlier.

Modeling Effect

An observer attends to a model. Later, in the absence of the model, the observer produces behaviors for the first time that match the behaviors of the model. For instance, some preschoolers were shown a film of a model performing various aggressive acts, such as hitting and pushing, that the children had not previously exhibited. Without direct, external reinforcement of any kind, the young children later performed aggressive behaviors of the kind they had observed in the model (Bandura, Ross, & Ross, 1963). For this modeling effect to occur, the model must demonstrate behavior that is new to the observer, but it must be behavior of appropriate difficulty for the observer to perform.

Disinhibitory and Inhibitory Effects

Observing a model may serve either to disinhibit or inhibit responses that the observer already has made before. For example, aggressive behavior in children is generally disapproved by adults and, to some extent, inhibited by the child. Observation of a model displaying aggressive behavior, however, weakens the inhibition. The result is that the child then expresses the earlier learned aggressive behaviors that the model portrayed. Furthermore, other aggressive behaviors that had been inhibited may be released and expressed. Other forms of behavior have also been shown to be disinhibited in individuals who have observed models displaying the behavior (Bandura, 1977).

The inhibiting of behavior already learned may also occur as a result of observing, for example, when the model is subjected to painful consequences following a certain behavior. The observer may then inhibit behavior perceived to be associated with the painful results.

Processes and Conditions of Observational Learning

Teachers use modeling techniques to facilitate student learning. The techniques are most productive when they accord with recently gained knowledge about the processes involved in learning through observation. The four kinds of processes identified by Bandura (1977) and the relationships among them are shown in Figure 4.2.

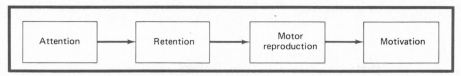

Figure 4.2 Four processes in observational learning.
Source: Bandura, 1977, p. 23.

Attention

The model must be attended to for observational learning to occur. Consider an effective demonstration of handwriting. For observational learning to occur, the students must attend to and perceive the forms of the letters and words and also the movements of the hand.

Which models are likely to be attended to and imitated? The persons with whom the observer associates become models more than others. Thus, younger students tend to smoke marijuana if they associate with other persons who use it. Models who are attractive to the observer and whose behaviors produce desired consequences are attended to more than others. Thus, the dress, speech, and actions of TV heroes and heroines are attended to and imitated by many adolescents, but those of teachers and parents often are not. In real life, neither the appearance of parents and teachers nor the consequences of their activities attract the adolescent.

Characteristics of the observers are related to attending. Two very important ones are the observer's capability to learn the modeled information or skill and the observer's feelings and attitudes toward the model. We attend to instructions for painting a house or repairing furniture if we think we are capable of performing the skills. Similarly, we are more likely to attend to persons and ideas if there is an accompanying positive feeling than if there is a negative feeling.

Retention

Attending to something, according to Bandura (1977), must be followed by retention for observational learning to occur. Retention is necessary because whatever is acquired when attending is necessarily used after the model is no longer present. What is attended to is represented internally and stored either in the form of visual images or symbolically. Thus, the teacher's handwritten words and movements are represented as visual images, while the accompanying verbal instructions are encoded as word meanings. These representations are subsequently retrieved and guide the learner's performances of the modeled behavior.

The developmental level of the learner is especially important in the retention phase of observational learning. In the early years of life, a child's imitative responses follow immediately after observing a model's actions, since the child has limited capability for retention. As learning and development continue, children are able to remember and recall what they have observed earlier for increasingly longer time periods.

Motor Reproduction

The third process in observational learning involves transforming the internal representation of the observed behavior into appropriate actions. You will recall from the earlier handwriting example that the handwritten words, the movements of the hand, and the verbal instructions are represented internally. This internal representation provides the cognitive basis for motor reproduction. The observer retrieves this representation from memory and mentally selects and organizes the information that will guide the movements.

The learner's capability to perform the whole skill and its component parts is a very important determinant of how effectively motor reproduction proceeds. Preschool children can learn to hit, scratch, and bite other children, but they cannot write their names comprehensibly. They cannot carry out the component movements. Elementary school children can throw a baseball reasonably well, but they have more difficulty hitting it. The essential coordination and strength are missing. Nongolfers of any age have difficulties modeling the pro's drive off the tee since they cannot reproduce the pro's movements.

Bandura (1977) indicates that complex verbal and motor skills are not learned solely through observational learning. The observer acquires an internal program through observational learning that guides the observer's subsequent practice. Increased proficiency in the skill comes with practice that is guided by the internal program. Moreover, guidance of the practice by a teacher typically facilitates skill development.

Motivation

According to Bandura (1982), the observer's motivation for matching and reproducing the observed behavior is the expectancy that it will be effective in gaining benefits, avoiding problems, or achieving other consequences desired by the observer. Hence, an observer is likely to reproduce the model's behavior if the observer believes that reproducing it will have desired consequences, especially increasing the observer's effectiveness.

It is appropriate here to indicate Bandura's sharp departure from Skinner's ideas about operant conditioning. First, observational learning accounts for the initial learning of responses; whereas operant conditioning explains the strengthening of responses that have already been learned. Second, observational learning indicates that the expectancy of desired results is the motivation for performing the behavior; whereas operant conditioning specifies that reinforcement automatically strengthens responses without any mediation by the organism. Thus, thinking, or mediation, is an integral aspect of observational learning.

Bandura (1977) does not deny that the behavior of lower animals, very young children, and other persons under certain circumstances can be shaped and controlled by the use of conditioning techniques. However, he indicates that the important task of learning theory is to describe and explain learning as it occurs in everyday life, including in the schools. If a teacher's planned demonstration or incidental modeling does not produce the desired effects on students, learning theory should be able to help diagnose the causes. Bandura indicates that the failure of students to match the teacher's behavior may occur for any of five reasons: First, the students do not attend to the relevant activities of the model. Second, they do not encode or represent their observations adequately. Third, they fail either to store or to retrieve what was observed. Fourth, they are incapable of performing what was observed. Finally, they do not have sufficient incentives for matching the model's behavior.

4.4 Give an example of each of the following effects of observational learning: modeling, inhibitory, disinhibitory.

4.5 Michael is learning to speak Spanish by listening to a recording and saying what he hears. Relate Michael's learning to the attention, retention, motor reproduction, and motivation processes involved in observational learning.

4.6 Janet is getting piano lessons that include live demonstrations of piano playing, but her piano playing is not improving. Using observational learning theory, indicate what Janet's teacher should look for in diagnosing Janet's lack of progress.

MEANINGFUL VERBAL LEARNING

Meaningful Reception Learning

Advance Organizers for Meaningful Learning

Meaningful Discovery Learning

Ausubel (1963) was one of the first modern cognitive psychologists to focus specifically on the meaningful learning of verbal information presented in texts and in other kinds of instructional material used in the schools. Mayer (1979) regards the meaningful learning approach as especially promising for eliminating rote memorization by students, including those in college. Before proceeding further, we should recognize that Ausubel's theory is also referred to as subsumption theory. The idea of subsumption will be discussed later.

According to Ausubel's theory, verbal information becomes available to the learner by either *reception* or *discovery*. The new information is learned either *meaningfully* or *by rote*. Therefore, four basic kinds of learning are indicated: *meaningful reception, rote reception, meaningful discovery*, and *rote discovery*. Information that is acquired meaningfully is assimilated into the existing cognitive structure and is remembered well. Information acquired by rote is not assimilated and is quickly forgotten. (*Cognitive structure* is the total content and organization of a person's ideas. Applied to a subject field, it is the content and organization of the person's ideas in the particular subject field.)

In *reception learning,* the content of what is to be learned is received by reading or listening. For example, in the preceding paragraph, four types of learning are stated. Only reception learning is required to recognize that there are four types of learning. Conversely, in *discovery learning*, the learner gets information independently; it is not provided to the learner.

Reception and *discovery* are the processes by which information becomes available to the learner. *Meaningfully* and *by rote* refer to how the learner acts on the information. If the learner attempts to memorize the new information verbatim, the process is *rote*. For example, memorizing the information presented thus far about the four types of learning is rote. On the other hand, relating it to what you already know and thereby assimilating it into your existing cognitive structure are *meaningful processes*. Ausubel formulated meaningful learning theory as a reaction against unnecessary and ineffective rote learning. Accordingly, no further attention is given to rote processes here.

Meaningful Reception Learning

As persons acquire knowledge in several subject-matter fields, they develop cognitive structures related to each field. New information is then assimilated into the cognitive structure by subsumption and other processes. These processes are used by Ausubel to explain meaningful learning.

New information is related to higher-order concepts and principles already in the cognitive structure by either derivative or correlative subsumption. In *derivative subsumption*, the meaning of the new idea is derivable from the higher-order concepts. For example, a child already knows the principle "Cats climb trees." Now, new information is heard: "The neighbor's cat is climbing the tree." This new information is subsumed by the higher-order principle. Stated differently, the meaning of the new information is *derived* by relating it to the principle, is subsumed by the principle, and is thereby assimilated into the cognitive structure.

Correlative subsumption occurs when new information extends or modifies the higher-order concept already learned. For example, a child has a concept of *triangle* as a closed, plane, simple figure with three sides. The child now reads that an equilateral triangle is a closed, plane, simple figure with three sides of equal length. By correlating this new information with the higher-order concept already known, the child's concept of *triangle* is extended so that it includes equilateral triangle as a kind of triangle. Stated in terms of meaning, the new concept, *equilateral triangle*, is readily understood, subsumed by triangle, and assimilated into the cognitive structure regarding triangles.

We see that by derivative and correlative subsumption, new information is related to and subsumed by a more inclusive idea. Ausubel calls this *subordinate learning*. How is a higher-order concept learned initially? It is learned by proceeding inductively from particular instances that have been learned to a new and more general concept. For example, a child perceives that each *red, blue,* and *green* is a color and arrives at the superordinate concept *color*. This kind of learning is called *superordinate learning*.

A new principle may also be learned when there is no related subordinate or superordinate concept in the existing cognitive structure, but there is information to which the principle can be related. This is called *com-binatorial learning* by Ausubel. As an example, a student may learn how atoms function by observing a physical model that depicts their functioning. Similarly, the principles underlying mathematical equations may be understood by observing how weight and distance are related in making a seesaw work. For combinatorial reasoning to occur, learners must have some general knowledge first to understand the model and then the new principle. According to Ausubel, students learn many new generalizations and principles in science, social studies, and other fields in this manner.

Advance Organizers for Meaningful Learning

We have seen that the learning of new material is facilitated when the learner has an appropriate cognitive structure to which to relate the new material. It follows that providing learners higher-order concepts and principles in advance of the new material will facilitate learning the new material.

An *advance organizer* (Ausubel, 1963) is a small amount of verbal or visual information that is presented to the learner in advance of the new material. One kind of advance organizer provides information to activate a cognitive structure that the students already have. This facilitates combinatorial and superordinate learning. Another kind of organizer provides a new concept, principle, or other cognitive structure that the learner is to assimilate. New information is then related to this organization by derivative or correlative subsumption.

In research using advance organizers, the advance material does not contain any of the new material to be learned. In instructional practice, however, it is wise to include some of the new information whenever it helps the student grasp the relationship between the advance organizer and the new material.

A description of an advance organizer that proved very effective in aiding students learn transformational grammar follows:

> In order to describe something, we usually look at the whole thing and then look at the parts. Knowing the parts and how they fit together helps us in our description. If we are dealing with a number of things, we frequently put them into groups in order to make our description clearer and more organized. During the next two weeks, you will be using this approach in learning to describe English sentences.
>
> One of the first things you will learn is that all sentences can be described in terms of certain basic sentence patterns. There are nine basic sentence patterns in the English language. These nine patterns might be compared to the primary colors that an artist uses. All hues can be obtained from mixtures of red, blue, and yellow, which are the three primary colors. Similarly, every sentence you read can be described as taking the form of one of the nine basic sentence patterns, or as a combination or rearrangement of the nine basic sentence patterns. . . .
>
> In all nine basic sentences, the subject group is always a noun phrase. In other sentences, which are rearrangements or combinations of basic sentences, the subject group may or may not be a noun phrase; in basic sentences it is always a noun phrase.

As you learn about noun phrases, you will discover that the last word in all noun phrases is a noun. What is a noun? Rather than depending on the traditional definition of noun as the "name of a person, place, or thing," you will learn to use the noun test-sentence. If a word fits in the noun test-sentence, it can be used as a noun. In a later lesson you will be given other ways which will help you identify nouns. (Blount, Klausmeier, Johnson, Fredrick, & Ramsay, 1967, p. 38)

Lawton and Wanska (1979) extended the idea of advance organizer to include not only substantive information but also process information. Children of grade 1, grade 3, and grade 5 participated in their study. Four groups were formed randomly for each grade. One group received a content organizer that included only higher-order concepts. A second group received only a process organizer that gave rules for classifying. A third group received both of the preceding organizers. A control group received material unrelated to the learning task. The learning activity consisted of hearing and seeing information about dwellings, tools, and other items of three different primitive groups of people. One part of the learning task was to learn to classify the items. Understanding relationships between superordinate and subordinate concepts was the other part. The children were tested at the time of the experiment and again five months later. On both the initial test and the retention test, the rank order of performance from highest to lowest was the combined organizer, the process organizer, the content organizer, and control. The mean, or average, initial acquisition and retention scores of the students receiving the combined organizer were from about 50% to 300% higher than the means of the control groups and from 25% to 100% higher than those of the other two groups.

Bernard (1975) used two different kinds of substantive information in advance organizers with grade 12 students. One kind of content was higher-order concepts. The other was an explanation of a taxonomy, including the relationships among the concepts of a taxonomy. The students who received the combined higher-order concepts and the taxonomy ideas scored 68% on a test of understanding the concepts included in the new material, while the control group scored 52% correct. Mayer (1983) found that an advance organizer and studying a passage either on radar or on Ohm's Law one time resulted in recall of principles and in problem-solving performance equal to study of the passage three times without the advance organizer. In a comprehensive review of 135 studies of advance organizers conducted in grades 3–8, grades 9–12, and college, Luiten, Ames, and Ackerson (1980) reported facilitative effects at all levels, the highest being at the college level and the lowest at grades 9–12.

Time constraints prevent teachers from preparing written advance organizers for the many different units and separate lessons they teach. Thus, the main opportunity to capitalize on the use of advance organizers is in oral presentations to the students. Perhaps the most important aspect of developing an advance organizer is to provide a concise conceptual framework in words, pictures, or both that the students easily understand

and to which the new information can be related. Although advance organizers used in research contain none of the new information, teachers should include new information as necessary to make sure that the students understand and can use the organizers effectively.

Meaningful Discovery Learning

In *meaningful discovery learning,* the learner gains information independently rather than receiving it in final form as in meaningful reception learning. The information gained independently is related to the learner's existing cognitive structure.

Ausubel (Ausubel, Novak, & Hanesian, 1978) regards discovery learning as particularly appropriate for older students in learning how new knowledge is discovered in various disciplines. It is also used in the preschool and early elementary school years when children are forming many basic concepts with little or no adult guidance. Similarly, older learners use it in the early stages of acquiring the concepts of a discipline new to them. However, Ausubel does not consider discovery learning either feasible or economical for learning large bodies of subject matter by students who are capable of learning concepts and principles by meaningful reception processes.

Ausubel views discovery learning, including guided discovery learning, in a more restricted manner than most psychologists and educators. Considerable importance is given to discovery learning in Chapter 10 on problem solving and creativity.

4.7 Indicate one or two outcomes that you have learned by meaningful reception learning, meaningful discovery learning, and rote reception learning.

4.8 Give an example of subordinate learning, superordinate learning, and combinatorial learning.

4.9 Describe how an advance organizer that includes only substantive information facilitates the learning of new information.

4.10 Using Ausubel's ideas about meaningful reception learning, explain how the sets of concepts presented at the beginning of each chapter and of each part of a chapter of this book should aid you in learning the new information of the chapter.

LEARNING AS INFORMATION PROCESSING

Computer and Human Information Processing

Phases of Human Information Processing

Mental Operations in Information Processing

Executive Control of Information Processing

For decades, learning was defined solely as a change in observable behavior resulting from practice. At present, cognitive psychologists agree that learning results in a change in observable behavior. However, they also regard learning as a change in the individual's knowledge—both the amount of knowledge and how it is organized. The mental processes that students employ in learning mathematics, science, and other fields of knowledge are of particular interest to cognitive psychology. A better understanding of these mental processes is being gained by relating learning to information processing. The interpretation of information processing presented here focuses on the internal cognitive operations and includes the control of the operations by the individual. For this reason, it is called *cognitive information processing*.

Computer and Human Information Processing

Some psychologists turn to the computer to simulate human learning processes. They are achieving considerable success in simulating less complex thinking processes and in formulating models of human information processing (Bower & Hilgard, 1981). Our interest here is the integration of cognitive psychology and computer information processing.

Computers input, process, and output information very rapidly without making errors. The main features of computer information processing are portrayed in Figure 4.3.

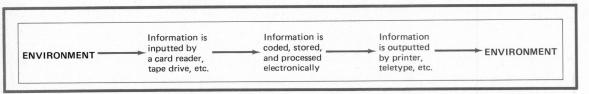

Figure 4.3 Major phases of computer information processing.

These input-process-output operations provide an analogy of human learning processes. We may examine the analogy further. First, the computer takes in information from the environment from a card reader or other device. Human beings take in information through their sense organs. The information is coded, stored, retrieved from storage, and processed electronically by the computer. Second, the computer processing of the information is controlled and monitored by a program that has also been put into the computer. Human beings encode, store, and process information; however, this sequence is controlled and monitored by programs that they learn. Finally, after the information is processed by the computer, it is outputted to the environment through a device such as a line printer in the form of a computer printout. After human beings process information, they may generate and make vocal responses, such as speaking, or muscular movements, such as typing. In some instances, human beings do not respond overtly; instead, they store the processed information in long-term memory.

We observe that the programs for controlling and monitoring the information processing are inputted to the computer, but they are learned by the human being. The cognitive psychologist is interested in the nature of these human programs—how they are learned and how they function in the processing, storage, and retrieval of information. The "pure" information-processing psychologists generally limit their explanations of human learning to what they have simulated by computer. Cognitive psychologists use the analogy of computer information processing, but they do not limit their explanations to the processes simulated by a computer.

Cognitive theorists are now making detailed analyses of what occurs internally as a person learns. One area of high interest is the *phases*, or steps, of the information-processing sequence. These phases are referred to by some authors as either mechanisms or structures. A second area is the mental operations involved in each phase. A third concern is the internal control and monitoring of the mental operations.

Phases of Human Information Processing

Shiffrin and Atkinson (1969) and Atkinson and Shiffrin (1971) outlined models of long-term and short-term memory on which most current information-processing models are based. Extensions, refinements, and elaborations of these original models and of later models are found in various books and chapters on learning, including Anderson (1980), Bower and Hilgard (1981), and Wickelgren, (1981). The model in Figure 4.4 attempts to summarize the most important ideas from these and other sources that are cited.

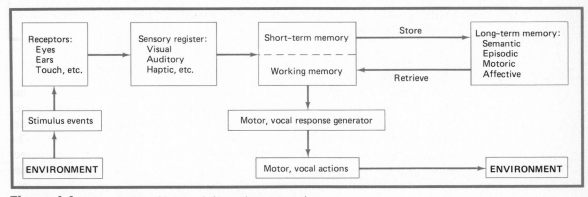

Figure 4.4 Major phases of human information processing.

The phases—sensory register, short-term memory, and long-term memory—are not to be regarded as separate and clearly identified locations or structures of the brain. Rather, consider them to be phases of the temporal processing sequence. Similarly, do not regard the information flow as an actually observed transfer of neural information from one phase to another. Instead, consider the flow to represent the acquisition, processing, storing, retrieval, and action sequence.

Sensory Register

We receive stimulation from our environment that activates our receptors and is transformed into neural information. This information persists in a structure, or structures, called the *sensory register*. It persists in the sensory register for a very short period of time, a few hundredths of a second (Sperling, 1960). All of the information that is sensed is registered. However, only part of it is attended to, transformed, and entered into short-term memory.

Short-Term Memory

It is helpful to think of *short-term memory* in two ways. First, it is that phase of information processing during which information from the sensory register is stored. Second, the actual processing of the information takes place in *working memory*. We shall clarify these points.

Information received in short-term store is held for a limited time, up to as much as 30 seconds (Shiffrin & Atkinson, 1969). It may be held longer if it is rehearsed or operated on in some other way. Another way to think of the duration of short-term memory is in terms of the amount of information that can be stored. On the average, persons can receive and retain only seven items of information, plus or minus two (Miller, 1956). An item of information may be a single picture or word, or it may be a chunk of information, such as the meaning of a sentence.

In addition to the storage aspect of short-term memory, there is also a *working memory*. All conscious processing of information occurs in working memory. The various operations performed on information in working memory are indicated in the next part of this chapter.

Long-Term Memory

Some of the information received in short-term memory is not processed and is lost. Some of it is processed and is transferred to long-term memory. Shiffrin and Atkinson (1969) regard *long-term memory* as permanent. According to this interpretation, failure to recall something learned earlier is attributed to failure to retrieve it (to find it in long-term memory and bring it to a conscious level). However, Loftus and Loftus (1980) do not agree that everything stored in long-term memory is permanent, never lost. Their experiments indicate that some information is lost as it is replaced with other information, and some is lost as organization and reorganization occur.

Tulving (1972) established a clear distinction for two kinds of long-term memory: episodic and semantic. We store events that we have personally experienced at particular times in *episodic memory,* for example, our first day of school or seeing the running of the Kentucky Derby. We store in *semantic memory* everything associated with language, for example, our meanings of words, our rules of grammar, and our organized knowledge about word meanings.

Two other kinds of memory have been identified and described: motoric (Singer, 1978) and affective (Zajonc, 1980). As we prepare to write something, we retrieve a program for writing from *motoric memory* that guides our writing movements. When we see someone we know, we retrieve some kind of feeling toward the person from *affective memory.*

Vocal and Motor Response Generator

Some of the information that is processed in short-term memory is transferred to long-term memory, where it remains. For example, we solve a problem mentally and store the problem and its solution. At other times, we respond overtly by writing out a solution, by speaking, or by making other movements. A *response generator* transforms input from working memory into impulses that guide the effectors in producing overt responses.

Mental Operations in Information Processing

Some cognitive psychologists, for example, Ausubel, Novak, and Hanesian (1978), Bandura (1977), Klausmeier and Associates (1979), Miller and Johnson-Laird (1976), and Tolman (1949) have studied learning processes mainly to ascertain how knowledge, skills, and attitudes are initially acquired. Others, including Atkinson and Shiffrin (1971), Loftus and Loftus (1980), Shiffrin and Atkinson (1969), and Tulving (1972) have been more interested in the storage and retrieval of information. In this chapter, our concern is mainly initial acquisition. In Chapter 14, long-term storage and retrieval are discussed in detail. However, some attention is necessarily given here to long-term memory, because much initial learning involves retrieval of earlier learned information from long-term memory.

One set of internal mental processes closely associated with the different phases of information processing is shown in Figure 4.5.

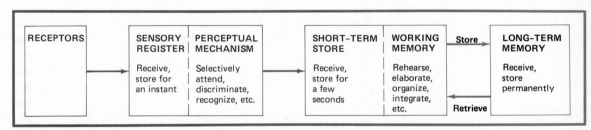

Figure 4.5 Phases and mental processes of human information processing.

Attending to the environment is essential for acquiring information by means of the receptors. Only certain aspects of the environment are attended to. Furthermore, not all the information that is received in the sensory register is subsequently encoded, or transformed neurally, and stored in short-term memory. Persons selectively perceive only a portion of what is received in the sensory register. What they perceive is related to their prior experiences, including their feelings regarding the particular stimulus. In this regard, children at age 12 are selective and can concentrate exclusively on task-relevant information, whereas children at age 9 are relatively nonselective (Hale & Alderman, 1978).

The processes carried out in the short-term memory phase are stated in different ways. Persons interested in the learning of meaningful prose material frequently use the terms *rehearse, organize, elaborate,* and *integrate.* Thus, we *rehearse* the last items we have read. We *organize* by connecting two or more items of the new material before relating them to what is already known. We *elaborate* by relating new information to what we already know. Siegler (1983) indicated that what one already knows influences what and how one learns. Peterson, Swing, Braverman, and Buss (1982) found elaboration to facilitate achievement markedly. We *integrate* by combining items into a more complete knowledge structure. Integration of information in working memory is essential for encoding prose material into long-term memory (Masson & Miller, 1983). From a strict information-processing point of view, these are the only processes necessary for explaining initial learning. Furthermore, this processing during the working memory phase is also considered as the *encoding,* or coding, process. *Encoded information,* that is, whatever is learned initially, is stored in long-term memory.

Guilford (1967) uses different terminology to indicate the mental operations involved in learning and remembering. He proposes five mental operations: *cognizing, remembering, convergent thinking, divergent thinking,* and *evaluating.* Guilford's ideas are widely used today in educational programs for gifted and creative students.

We may relate Guilford's operations to the information-processing operations mentioned earlier. *Cognizing,* which includes recognizing and understanding, subsumes attending and selective perception, since one necessarily attends before recognizing something. *Remembering* in Guilford's system includes only storage and retrieval, not other information-processing operations. *Divergent thinking* is the operation by which novel ideas are generated. *Convergent thinking* leads to the production of correct answers or solutions. *Evaluating* involves reaching decisions concerning correctness and adequacy. Divergent thinking, convergent thinking and evaluation are the information-processing operations that substitute for rehearsing, elaborating, organizing, and integrating.

Executive Control of Information Processing

How do we consciously control our internal mental processes? The concept used in cognitive information processing to explain this aspect of learning is *executive control.*

You will recall from the earlier discussion that a program is prepared and inputted into a computer, which then controls the processing of the information that is inputted. The program contains the control instructions that guide the computer's electronic processing of information. Recognize also that the electrical energy that activates the computer is supplied from an external source. The executive control of the human being necessarily includes the activating process as well as the control processes. Accordingly, there are two aspects of the internal, or executive, control of our own learning. One is the control of motivation, and the other is the control of the information flow and the related mental operations.

Executive control (see Figure 4.6) completes the model of cognitive information processing, parts of which were introduced earlier.

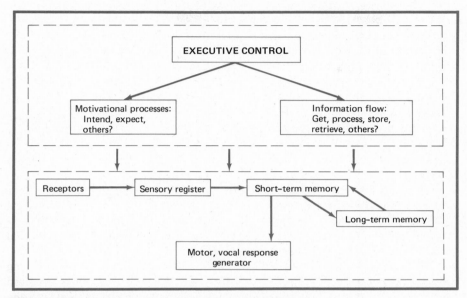

Figure 4.6 Executive control of information processing.

Intend is the term employed by Miller and Johnson-Laird (1976) to indicate the process for consciously controlling the direction of one's thinking. These authors imply further that intentions arise in connection with carrying out a plan to reach a goal, such as getting to class at 11:00 A.M., or gaining an understanding of cognitive information processing. The relationship between *intend, perceive,* and *remember* in their theory is depicted in Figure 4.7.

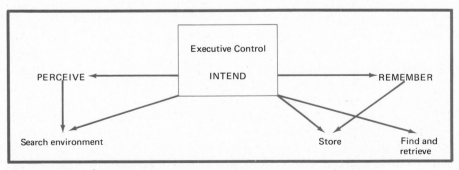

Figure 4.7 Intend, perceive, and remember in information processing.

Imagine that you intend to write a letter to a friend. This intention activates the processes that control the input, flow, storage, and retrieval of information. One control instruction related to perceiving is to search the environment for relevant information, perhaps writing materials, a correct address, and a prior letter from your friend. A control instruction related to remembering is to find relevant information in long-term memory concerning what to write. You generate instructions for finding and retrieving relevant information from long-term memory and other instructions for storing what you write throughout the letter-writing sequence. When you complete the letter, one control instruction is to store the fact that you have written the letter, and another is to store some of its contents.

Atkinson and Shiffrin (1971) did not propose an overall control mechanism, such as executive control, in their formulation of short-term memory. Rather, they indicated that all of the processes carried out in working memory "can be called into play at the subject's discretion, with enormous consequences for performance" (p. 82).

You may find it interesting at this point to recall the main phases of the information-processing sequence, starting with attending and continuing through generating overt actions. Knowledge regarding the phases can be very helpful to educators in two ways. First, we can now arrange instruction in accordance with the control and the flow of information. Second, we have a better basis for determining when a student may be having difficulty and also the nature of the difficulty. In prior decades, we often recognized that a student was having a problem of attention, motivation, initial learning, or retention. Now we can take into account whether it is a problem of sensory reception, short-term memory capacity, rehearsal, organization, executive control, or a similar specific process. Siegler (1980) regards better understanding of initial learning processes as a very significant contribution of information-processing theory to the improvement of children's learning.

4.11 Describe how human information processing is both similar to and different from computer information processing.

4.12 Trace the flow of information from the time Amy is told to write *dog* until she completes writing the word.

4.13 Indicate one or more processes that are involved in each phase of information processing—sensory register, short-term memory, long-term memory, response generator—as Amy carries out the internal and overt activities.

4.14 Explain how executive control of Amy's internal and overt activities functions.

Purposeful Learning by an Individual

Purposeful Learning in a Classroom Setting

PURPOSEFUL LEARNING

Purposeful learning is goal-directed. A *goal* is an end or condition toward which motivated activity is directed. We are continually setting goals and learn while attaining our goals. As we shall see, some purposeful learning is accomplished without instruction. However, instruction can make purposeful learning more effective.

Purposeful Learning by an Individual

Figure 4.8 shows a sequence of purposeful learning by an individual.

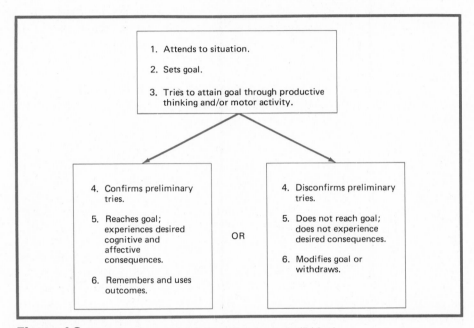

Figure 4.8 Sequence in purposeful learning by an individual.

This sequence indicates how individuals acquire many of their concepts and their motor and verbal skills. We shall consider two situations which exemplify this sequence.

Let us assume that a young child, Bill, already rides a tricycle well. After receiving a bicycle, he is highly motivated to learn to ride it and sets as his goal (not using the word *goal*, of course) to ride it as well as his friend can ride his bicycle. He has now experienced the first two phases outlined in Figure 4.8: attending to the situation and setting a goal.

Bill now attends even more closely to the situation, the bicycle, himself, and his desire and ability to ride it. He makes preliminary trials almost immediately. Some delayed imitation may be involved, that is, imitating the actions of his friend (his *model*) whom he has previously observed riding a bicycle. These early trials, much like a person's early tries at automobile driving, are usually characterized by lack of speed and coordination. Bill at first may not get on the bicycle properly and may not put his foot pedal in proper position to start off. After several trials, he will probably master the skills of starting, making a complete revolution first with one pedal and then continuing to make the revolution with the other pedal. The next big task is to maintain body balance. Falls frequently occur at this point. Depending upon his size and other characteristics, Bill may learn quickly, or he may try for weeks to get this part of the skill accomplished. After mastering body balance. Bill continues his trials. He drops inappropriate responses and confirms and improves the ones which he interprets as useful.

As soon as Bill achieves his goal of being able to ride the bike as well as his friend, he has experienced the desired consequence of his efforts. He may experience other consequences, such as feeling successful or securing the admiration and approval of his parents or friends. The feelings that accompany goal attainment are the affective component in the learning sequence. This component first entered when Bill originally wanted to learn and continued throughout the entire learning sequence. It results in Bill's learning to like or dislike bicycle riding.

Suppose that, with his best effort, Bill is not able to ride the bicycle. He may engage in any one of a variety of behaviors depending upon whether he places the blame for not reaching his goal on himself or on an external cause. He may try to find a different method. He may quit. He may substitute a different goal. For example, he may return to his tricycle and attempt new ways of riding it.

A young child learning to ride a bicycle, even for a short distance, makes many trials. In contrast, consider an example of purposeful verbal learning which may be accomplished in a few trials. Suppose that Mary is reading about a basketball game. She encounters the following sentence and finds an unfamiliar word, *crucial:* "Sue scored her only point at a crucial moment in the game." Examine how the sequence of purposeful learning in Figure 4.8 applies.

Mary attends to the unknown word and sets as her initial goal getting its pronunciation. Her first try to pronounce the word starts almost simultaneously. In trying to get the pronunciation, Mary may look at the individual letters in the word and try to sound them out. Or, she may try to divide the word into syllables and pronounce the syllables. She may read the sentence again to try to get the meaning of the word as an aid to recognizing it. If Mary already has learned the typical strategies for identifying new words, she will probably attempt all three: using phonetic analysis, using structural analysis, and using the context. After several trials, she will pronounce the word either correctly or incorrectly.

Uninstructed, Mary confirms the pronunciation that makes the most sense to her. It is possible that from the context the word might be *critical* rather than *crucial.* Regardless of whether Mary pronounces the word as *critical* or *crucial*, she has reached her goal and experiences the desired consequence.

Crucial is a difficult word. It is possible that Mary may realize that she cannot get its pronunciation. In this case, she does not reach the goal and may quit without further effort. The consequence of not being able to recognize this one word may not be so high that she experiences any negative affect.

Purposeful Learning in a Classroom Setting

How may a teacher proceed in making learning purposeful for all the students in a classroom setting? An instructional strategy for implementing the purposeful learning sequence is presented in Figure 4.9.

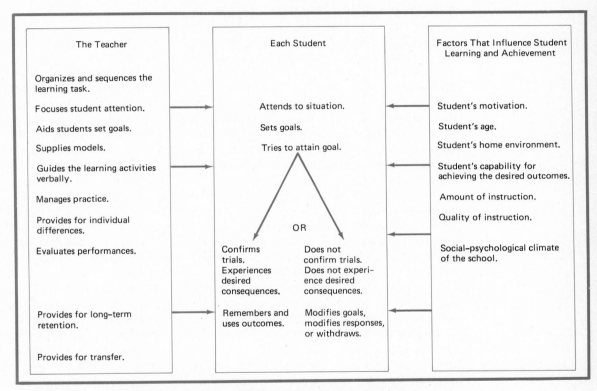

Figure 4.9 Sequence of purposeful learning and a related instructional strategy.

The figure indicates (a) the earlier sequence in purposeful learning by an individual student; (b) a ten-step teaching strategy that correlates with the sequence of purposeful learning; and (c) seven conditions of the student and the learning environment that influence how well the student learns.

The purpose here is to provide an overview of the instructional strategy. The seven factors that influence student learning and achievement are described further in Chapters 5, 6, and 7. Applications of the ten steps to specific learning outcomes are given in Chapters 8–13. Discussion of the ten steps follows:

1. Organize and sequence the learning tasks. Completing a learning task involves acquiring certain knowledge, skills, attitudes, or some combination of them. In completing learning tasks, students typically use materials, such as textbooks and films; and they carry out activities, such as reading, listening, discussing, doing paper-and-pencil exercises, or performing motor or vocal activities. Organizing learning tasks, materials, and activities that are interesting and meaningful to the learner is one important element of a teaching strategy. Another is arranging the tasks in a sequence that results in continuity and cumulative learning from one task to the next. Some organizing and ordering of the tasks in an appropriate sequence must be done before teaching begins, so that student attention can be gained and focused effectively.

2. Focus student attention on the learning tasks and means of attaining them. Students must know what the learning tasks are and the possible means of attaining them in order to start the sequence of purposeful learning. Therefore, the teacher uses visuals, print material, class discussion, and other techniques to focus student attention on the tasks. The extent to which the students share in determining the tasks and the activities for attaining them varies with the age and experience of the students, the nature of the tasks—for example, required or elective—and other conditions of each particular teaching-learning situation. Effective motivational and classroom management techniques are essential for focusing student attention on the learning tasks.

3. Aid students to set goals. Wanting to attain a goal serves as a motive for purposeful learning. A plan is needed to achieve a goal. A plan includes the activities and a related time schedule for completing them. In setting goals with the students, the teacher helps them verbalize their goals and develop tentative plans for achieving them. Having a goal in mind and intending to complete the activities to achieve it provide the motivation for persisting in the learning activities until the goal is attained.

Goal setting and related planning necessarily vary according to the type of learning outcome and the age of the student. For example, a third-grade child sets a goal of learning to spell 20 new words by the end of the week. A college freshman sets a goal of completing the requirements for teacher certification in five years. The activities to achieve these two goals and the time schedule for completing them differ in explicitness and in other ways.

4. Supply models. Observing a model performance facilitates the learning of new knowledge and skills (Bandura, 1977). The modeled presentations may take the form of live demonstrations, verbal descriptions, films, or pictures. Thus, the child who has not written the word *teacher* may profit from seeing the word in written form and also from watching the teacher or another child write it. By observing a performance of a verbal, oral, or motor skill, students avoid many incorrect preliminary trials.

5. Guide students' learning activities verbally. Guiding the initial trials of students is essential to their achieving any desired learning outcome and avoiding habitual verbal, vocal, and motor skills errors. Guidance may be given by supplying models. Here, we are concerned with verbal guidance. Early verbal guidance directs the learners' attention to more adequate skills or knowledge, aids the learners in understanding the nature of a successful performance, provides encouragement to continue, and relieves possible anxiety that may arise if the learners are uncertain about their ability to perform the task. Throughout the purposeful learning sequence, teachers try to manage classroom learning activities, student knowledge of progress, and other instructional conditions to make instruction effective.

6. Manage practice effectively. Practice is essential for improving verbal and motor skills. Effective practice usually requires both productive thinking and motor activity by the learner. Teachers make practice effective by providing models, managing the length and spacing of practice sessions, and arranging for offering feedback and correction.

7. Provide for individual differences. Providing for individual differences is a key teacher activity, since students of the same age or grade vary greatly in their interests and readiness to learn the same subject matter. There are three major ways to provide for individual differences. One is to make it possible for students to set and achieve goals of different difficulty levels. Thus, one student's goal is to read five paragraphs and another's is to read a whole book. A second method is to use different materials and activities whereby students achieve the same goal. For example, one student learns about Nigeria through independent study and reading; another replaces the reading with seeing films and listening to tapes. A third method is to vary the amount of time that students spend to achieve a common goal. To illustrate, one student achieves the common goal in two weeks and moves ahead to something else, while another takes four weeks and also does homework.

8. Evaluate student performance and provide feedback. Evaluating the progress of students and aiding them to overcome errors facilitate goal attainment by eliminating inadequate or incorrect responses and by providing encouragement to continue. Providing means for students to measure their own progress and encouraging them to take initiative for improvement work successfully with many students. Lack of progress and simultaneous failure in reaching goals are principal contributors to students' losing their zest for learning and their interest in subject matter and schooling. Helping students overcome the undesirable effects of failure after trying hard is one of the most important challenges facing teachers today.

9. Provide for retention. Systematic review of verbal material and spaced practice of skills are essential for ensuring retention. One way to aid retention is to arrange rehearsal immediately after initial learning, followed with review some time later. Another is to arrange for the students to use their recently acquired information and skill in performing activities different from the initial learning activities; for example, children learn a spelling list and then use the words in their written work.

10. Provide for transfer. Helping students apply knowledge and skills in new situations facilitates both long-term retention and use. Actual situations in which new knowledge and skills are put to use are more effective than verbal descriptions of applications. Nevertheless, verbal descriptions and simulations are much more helpful than assuming automatic transfer. As you are aware, knowledge about learning or teaching does not automatically yield effective instructional practices.

4.15 Is purposeful learning by a student equally possible in situations where the teacher employs (a) a cognitive information-processing approach, (b) meaningful reception learning, (c) observational learning, (d) conditioning? Explain.

4.16 The sequence in purposeful learning includes attending, setting a goal, trying to attain the goal, confirming preliminary trials, reaching the goal, and remembering and using what is learned. Indicate how these six steps should be implemented by a college freshman who misspells many words in written assignments.

4.17 Assume that you are to teach a group of 25 students to spell the same list of 100 words during a 4-week period. The students differ in spelling ability, and no student can spell any of the words correctly. Indicate one or two things that you would do to implement each of the following 10 steps of the teaching strategy:

a. Organize and sequence the learning tasks.
b. Focus student attention on the learning tasks and means of attaining them.
c. Aid students to set goals.
d. Supply models.
e. Guide students' learning activities verbally.
f. Manage practice effectively.
g. Provide for individual differences.
h. Evaluate student performance and provide feedback.
i. Provide for retention.
j. Provide for transfer.

4.18 Review and Application. Recall the most important information about each of the following concepts and identify at least one possible use of the information by you as a learner, a teacher, or both:

Conditioning
   Classical Conditioning
   Operant Conditioning
Observational Learning
   Models Observed and Imitated
   Effects of Observational Learning
   Processes and Conditions of Observational Learning

SUMMARY

Conditioning theory includes principles of classical and operant conditioning. These principles were initially formulated in animal laboratories and were then extended to human behavior. The repeated use of concrete rewards and aversive stimuli that may cause physical or psychological pain is being discontinued. On the other hand, social reinforcement of desired behavior is widely accepted and practiced with good results. In addition, behavior modification based on operant conditioning principles is used in educational programs of students with learning and behavioral handicaps, particularly to increase deficit behavior.

Bandura demonstrated that many actions and attitudes are initially learned by observing models. The processes of observational learning include attending to the model, remembering what was observed, and reproducing what was observed, based on the expectancy that the behavior will be effective in achieving desired consequences. Hence, the motivation for observational learning is cognitive, that is, expecting a desired consequence. Teachers aid students acquire attitudes, prosocial behaviors, and skills through demonstrating behaviors that they desire their students to observe and learn.

Ausubel identified four types of learning: meaningful reception, meaningful discovery, rote reception, and rote discovery. Students who can read reasonably well and who have already learned the basic concepts of a subject field acquire a great deal of new information through meaningful reception learning. In meaningful reception learning, potentially meaningful material is presented to the students, and they learn it by relating the new material to what they already know.

Cognitive information-processing theory is directed toward understanding the mental processes involved in acquiring, processing, and retrieving information. In addition, the internal control of one's own mental processes is of high interest. Cognitive information-processing theory provides many useful ideas for arranging instruction and for diagnosing a student's learning difficulties.

Human beings, during their life span, acquire many different kinds of learning outcomes, including elementary motor and verbal skills in infancy and highly complex forms of problem solving and creativity during the school years. Each learning theory presented in this chapter contributes to our understanding of how different kinds of learning outcomes are attained. Most of our knowledge and skills are acquired through a sequence of purposeful, goal-directed activities. In purposeful learning, a person attends to a situation and sets a goal to achieve a desired outcome. The individual tries to achieve the goal through productive thinking, motor activity, or both. As the person tries to achieve the goal, efforts that lead toward the goal are confirmed and others are disconfirmed. Reaching the goal produces satisfaction. Moreover, the outcomes that are learned throughout the sequence are likely to be remembered and used. Not reaching the goal is followed by goal modification, goal substitution, or withdrawal. An instructional strategy based on this purposeful learning sequence calls for organizing and sequencing the learning tasks, focusing student attention, aiding students to set goals, providing material resources and guidance to students, arranging for feedback throughout the learning sequence, and fostering retention and transfer.

SUGGESTIONS FOR FURTHER READING

Bandura, A. *Social learning theory*. Englewood Cliffs, N.J.: Prentice-Hall, 1977.

Bandura presents his updated theory of observational learning in this book.

Bower, G. H., & Hilgard, E. R. *Theories of learning* (5th ed.). Englewood Cliffs, N.J.: Prentice-Hall, 1981.

Each major learning theory is first discussed in a scholarly manner from a sympathetic perspective. A critical discussion and evaluation of the theory follow.

Grady, M. P. *Teaching and brain research*. New York: Longman, 1984.

Discusses the implications of changes in brain structures and functions for classroom instruction, kindergarten through grade 12.

Horton, D. L., & Mills, C. B. Human learning and memory. In M. R. Rozenzweig & L. W. Porter (Eds.), *Annual review of psychology* (Vol. 35), 1984, 361–394.

A scholarly review of encoding processes, retrieval processes, and kinds of long-term memory storage.

Mayer, R. E. *The promise of cognitive psychology*. San Francisco: Freeman, 1981.

Chapter 2 gives a succinct and easy-to-understand description of the information-processing system.

Murray, F. B., & Mosberg, L. Cognition and memory. In H. E. Mitzel, J. H. Best, and W. Rabinowitz (Eds.), *Encyclopedia of educational research* (5th ed., Vol. 1). New York: The Free Press, 1982.

A brief introduction to cognitive learning theory, information processing, and memory. Other topics on learning in this encyclopedia include "Learning" by R. E. Mayer, "Perception" by S. H. Bartley and C. Daniel, and "Readiness" by N. J. Gordon.

Sahakian, W. S. *Introduction to the psychology of learning* (2nd ed.). Itasca, Ill.: F. E. Peacock, 1984.

Presents a short chapter summary of each main learning theory, including classical conditioning, operant behaviorism, and information processing.

Schunk, D. H. Self-efficacy perspective on achievement behavior. *Educational Psychologist*, 1984, *19*, 48–58.

A scholarly discussion and update of Bandura's ideas about the relationship of self-efficacy to motivation and achievement.

Skinner, B. F. *The technology of teaching*. New York: Appleton-Century-Crofts, 1968.

Skinner presents his views of teaching, based on the implementation of principles of operant conditioning.

Wittrock, M. C. Learning and memory. In F. H. Farley & N. J. Gordon (Eds.), *Psychology and education: The state of the union*. Berkeley, Calif.: McCutchan, 1981.

In Chapter 9 of this book of readings, Wittrock presents principles of cognitive learning and points out their implications for education.

CHAPTER 5

INDIVIDUAL AND GROUP DIFFERENCES

RANGE OF HUMAN DIFFERENCES

DIFFERENCES AMONG INDIVIDUALS

DIFFERENCES AMONG GROUPS

DETERMINANTS OF INDIVIDUAL AND GROUP DIFFERENCES

EXCEPTIONAL CHILDREN

Each child of a given age is more alike than different from children of the same age in terms of the needs of the human species. But there are also large differences among children of the same age in educational and psychological characteristics that result from differences in their maturational and learning processes. The task of the school is to provide for the common needs of students while taking into account the unique characteristics of each individual. No easy solution to the task has yet been found; however, knowledge of the range and kind of differences is becoming more complete.

In this chapter, the range in the capabilities of normally developing human beings is examined first. This subject is followed by a description of the differences among individuals in intellectual abilities, styles of learning, and educational achievements. (Differences in motivation and in learning strategies that affect educational achievement are presented respectively in Chapters 7 and 8.) Many studies have been carried out recently regarding the differences between the average performances and abilities of groups of persons, such as males and females and members of various socioeconomic, racial, and ethnic groups. After these group differences are examined, the genetic and environmental determinants of individual and group differences are discussed.

The last part of the chapter is devoted to learning handicaps and giftedness. These two areas of differences are not discussed elsewhere in the book; accordingly, educational provisions are indicated. Federal and state programs in these two areas, along with other federal and state programs to eliminate sex, ethnic, and racial discrimination, have greatly increased the teacher's responsibilities.

RANGE OF HUMAN DIFFERENCES

How much do individuals differ from one another? This question is not easy to answer. One method for answering it is to identify the very high and very low performances of individuals of about the same age. The difference between these highest and lowest measures yields the *range of difference*. A *range ratio* is derived by dividing the highest measure by the lowest.

Wechsler (1952) derived range ratios for many human characteristics. He included the second highest and the second lowest of 1000 cases in his computations, rather than the very highest and very lowest, in order to eliminate the abnormally high and low individuals. Some ratios of high interest to educators follow in Table 5.1.

TABLE 5.1 RANGE RATIOS FOR SELECTED HUMAN CAPABILITIES

CAPABILITY	RANGE RATIO
High jump	2.01:1
Tapping	2.20:1
Simple reaction time	2.24:1
Learning simple tasks	2.42:1
Memory span	2.50:1
Card sorting	2.50:1
Latent reflex time	2.50:1
Intelligence quotient	2.86:1
Swiftness of blow	2.93:1
Learning difficult tasks	3.87:1

SOURCE: Wechsler, 1952.

Gettinger and White (1980), studying capabilities closer to educational practice, identified the range of differences in the amount of time required by grade 5 students to reach the same level of achievement in a social studies unit that extended eight days. The range ratio was 5:1 when the students used the instructional units of their own school. In other words, the fastest learner took one-fifth as much time as the slowest learner. The ratio was 9:1 when social studies units from a different school were used.

In another study, Gettinger and White (1979) identified the number of trials that elementary school students made to reach the same predetermined achievement criterion. Units of instruction from six academic areas were

Kenneth Bancroft Clark (1914–   ), president of the American Psychological Association in 1971. Clark's research is focused on the self and related problems of ego and racial identification. He is a leading researcher and author in the advancement of human dignity and human rights.

Anne Anastasi (1908–   ), president of the American Psychological Association in 1972. Anastasi's main interest is individual differences, including the measurement of differences. Her textbooks on individual differences and psychological testing have been very well received.

Leona Elizabeth Tyler (1906–   ), president of the American Psychological Association in 1973. Tyler's interests include individual differences and counseling. Her textbooks in these fields have received wide acclaim.

Distinguished contributors to understanding individual differences.

used in this study. The range ratio in the number of trials varied for the different units from 6:1 to 9:1. It should be noted that the ratios obtained for the number of trials and the amount of time are directly related to the criterion of achievement that is established. The higher the criterion that is established, the larger is the ratio. Moreover, the number of trials and the amount of time required to reach the criterion reflect differences among students not only in ability to learn but also in motivation, interest, and other characteristics. Modifying some of these characteristics will also affect the ratio.

Figure 5.1 shows the range in five areas of development of 40 boys and of 40 girls at an average age of 125 months. The range in their ages was from 119 to 132 months. These boys and girls were selected from a much larger school population, so that both the boys and girls would be of the same age and have a mean IQ of 100 (see lowest line in Figure 5.1). Three points may be made about the range of performances and the means of the boys and

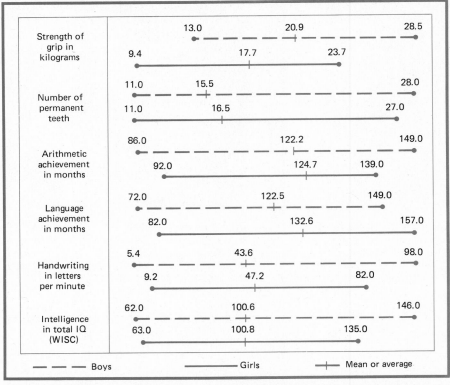

Figure 5.1 Range and mean scores for strength of grip, number of permanent teeth, arithmetic achievement, language achievement, and handwriting speed of 40 boys and 40 girls at an average chronological age of 125 months.

girls shown in Figure 5.1. First, the range in the five areas of development is about the same for the boys and the girls, a little lower for the girls. Second, the range between the lowest and highest child is very large, for example, from 9.4 to 28.5 (19.1) kilograms in strength of grip, from 72 to 157 (85) months of age in language achievement, and from 5.4 to 98.0 (92.6) letters per minute in handwriting speed. Third, in comparison with the range for each sex, the differences between the means of the boys and the girls are quite small: 3.2 in strength of grip favoring the boys, 1.0 in number of permanent teeth favoring the girls, 2.5 months in arithmetic achievement favoring the girls, 10.1 months in language achievement favoring the girls, and 3.6 letters per minute in handwriting favoring the girls.

A different way to identify the range in differences is to examine when students of different ages achieve the same level of performance. Klausmeier and Allen (1978) studied cognitive learning in normally developing children and youth of grades 1–12. Three percent of the grade 3 students and 52% of the grade 6 students had achieved a mature understanding of the concept *equilateral triangle;* however, 21% of the grade 12 students had not. Stated differently, about one-fifth of the grade 12 students had not learned this concept as well as about one-half of the grade 6 students and one-thirtieth of the grade 3 students.

5.1 A range ratio in IQ of 2.86 represents a high IQ of about 149 and a low of about 52. Indicate how you think two children of age 8 with these IQ scores will perform in reading or arithmetic computation.

5.2 The range in the amount of time required by grade 5 students to learn the same material is at least 5:1. What are some implications of this for teaching?

5.3 Compare the differences between the means of boys and girls in arithmetic, language arts, and handwriting given in Figure 5.1 with the range of the differences between the highest and lowest student of the same sex. What are some implications of these differences for instruction?

DIFFERENCES AMONG INDIVIDUALS

Intellectual Abilities
Styles of Learning
Educational Achievements

Differences among students that are frequently taken into account in the educative process are intellectual abilities, learning styles and cognitive styles, educational achievement, motivation, learning strategies, attitudes, and personality integration. The first three areas will be examined in this chapter. Motivation is discussed in Chapter 7, learning strategies in Chapter 8, attitudes in Chapter 12, and personality integration in Chapter 13.

Intellectual Abilities

Views about the nature of intellectual abilities continue to change. For many decades, the idea of a general intellectual ability was very popular. Then, the idea of a few primary mental abilities was added. Next, a structure of 120 specific abilities was proposed. At present, a major attempt is being made to identify the basic mental processes and learning strategies that underlie intellectual performances. As we shall see, most research on differences among individuals and between groups has used tests of general intellectual ability.

General Intellectual Ability

The testing of intelligence began on a widespread basis in 1916 in the United States when Terman (1916) adapted the earlier version of an intelligence test by Binet and Simon. Terman thought of intelligence as the ability to carry on abstract thinking. Thorndike (1926) defined intelligence as the ability to make good responses from the point of view of truth or fact. Taking a broader perspective, Wechsler (1958) developed an intelligence test to measure the aggregate or global capacity of the individual to act purposefully, to think rationally, and to deal effectively with the environment. The Wechsler Scale included performance tests as well as typical verbal and mathematical tests. Perhaps more than any others, Burt, Jones, Miller, and Moodie (1934) conceived of intelligence as inborn, while Hunt (1961) viewed it as almost totally determined by environmental conditions.

Terman's Stanford Binet Scale was widely accepted when first introduced in America in 1916. Terman regarded intelligence as determined almost solely by heredity. Accordingly, he believed that the rate of intellectual development was fixed by heredity and therefore did not change from birth onward. One outcome of educators' accepting this point of view was the tracking system in education that became widespread in the 1920s and continues in some schools today. Students starting junior high school were put in one or another educational track, based on their scores on an intelligence test. Educators assumed that students should remain in the particular track for the remainder of their school years, since their ability to learn could not be changed.

When the Stanford Binet was revised in 1937, a very wide range among individuals in IQ from below 35 to above 170 was reported (see Figure 5.2).

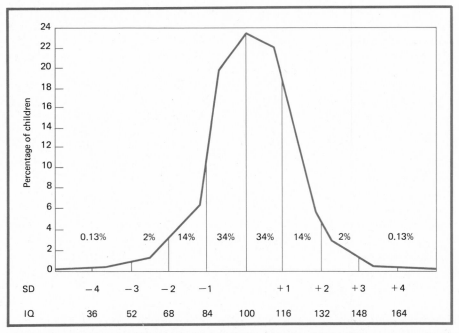

Figure 5.2 Normal distribution of Stanford-Binet IQs for 2904 children of ages 2–18. Source: Terman & Merrill, 1937, p. 37.

The distribution shown in Figure 5.2 is based on a normal curve in which 68% of all cases fall within +1 and −1 standard deviation units from the mean, 14% between +1 and +2 standard deviation units, 14% between −1 and −2 standard deviation units, and 2% above and 2% below two standard deviation units from the mean. Not only IQ but all abilities and achievements of an unselected population of human beings of the same age are assumed to be normally distributed. The majority of the 1937 Stanford Binet standardization group had IQs between 84 and 116, with slightly more than 68% of the total group in this IQ range. Approximately 14% had IQs between 116 and 132, 14% between 68 and 84, 2% above 132, and 2% below 68. The average IQ score actually obtained in the standardization process and shown in Figure 5.2 is slightly above 100.

At present, educators regard a measure of general intelligence as useful in predicting how a student will achieve in academic subject fields. However, an increasing number of scholars, including Ebel (1979) and Guilford (1979), are skeptical about the use of general intellectual ability tests with normally developing students. Their skepticism stems from the possible misuses of IQ test scores, particularly with disadvantaged students. Nevertheless, as Wechsler (1975) has pointed out, the misuse is not inevitable and can be avoided. Indeed, Messé, Crano, Messé, and Rice (1979) found that the correlations between a measure of general intellectual ability and primary school teachers' ratings of children's achievement in reading and mathematics were slightly higher for students of low socioeconomic status than for those of high socioeconomic status. Thus, the IQ score can be used to understand and help any student, rather than to categorize and label the student.

Before proceeding to primary mental abilities, we should recognize that the concept of general intellectual ability has been expanded to include both hereditary and environmental factors. Cattell (1971) proposed two kinds of general intelligence, fluid and crystallized. *Fluid intelligence* is genetically determined and sets the upper limit of the individual's ability. How well the inherited ability is used and what forms it takes depend on cultural factors, including learning. *Crystallized intelligence* is based on environmental factors, and its observable expression is based on learning. Accordingly, fluid ability is necessary, but it is not sufficient for the development of crystallized intelligence. Moreover, fluid intelligence peaks at about age 25, but crystallized intelligence continues to rise as long as persons continue to learn. Figure 5.3 gives examples of both kinds of abilities. Information and vocabulary are two kinds of crystallized abilities, while digit span and arithmetic reasoning are fluid abilities. In both males and females, information and vocabulary are still increasing at age 36. On the other hand, digit span starts decreasing in both males and females at about 25, while arithmetic reasoning ability levels off in males at about age 26 and starts decreasing in females at about age 26.

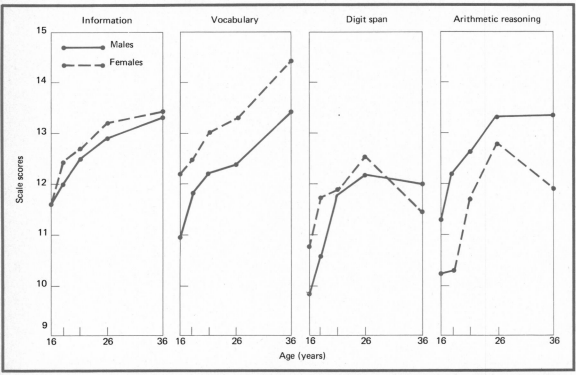

Figure 5.3 Means by age and sex for Wechsler scales in two selected crystallized abilities (information and vocabulary) and in fluid abilities (digit span and arithmetic reasoning).
Source: Bayley, 1970, pp. 1184–1185.

Primary Mental Abilities

Thurstone (1938) identified seven primary mental abilities and devised tests to measure them (Thurstone & Thurstone, 1963). The seven primary mental abilities are shown in Table 5.2.

Thurstone's identification of primary mental abilities refutes the idea underlying general intellectual ability that persons are equally able in all academic areas. Instead, most individuals vary markedly in verbal, numerical, spatial, and other abilities. Thus, the powerful and practically important concept of intraindividual, or within-individual, variability in abilities is fully established. We expect some but not most students to achieve at the same level in all subject fields. For example, it is possible for a student to be in the top one-fourth of the students of the same grade in one ability, such as spatial or mathematical, and to be in the bottom one-fourth of the same students in another ability, such as word fluency or perceptual speed.

The primary abilities emerge and reach full functional maturity at different rates (see Figure 5.4). For example, perceptual speed approaches

TABLE 5.2 PRIMARY MENTAL ABILITIES

ABILITY	DESCRIPTION
Verbal comprehension	The ability to understand the meaning of words; vocabulary tests represent this factor.
Word fluency	The ability to think of words rapidly, as in solving anagrams or thinking of words that rhyme.
Number	The ability to work with numbers and perform computations.
Spatial	The ability to visualize space-form relationships, as in recognizing the same figure presented in different orientations.
Memory	The ability to recall verbal stimuli, such as word pairs or sentences.
Perceptual speed	The ability to grasp visual details quickly and to see similarities and differences between pictured objects.
Reasoning	The ability to find a general rule on the basis of presented instances, as in determining how a number series is constructed after being presented with only a portion of that series.

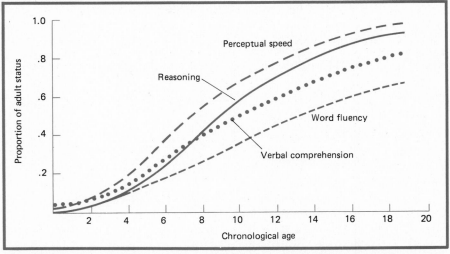

Figure 5.4 Growth of four primary mental abilities. The scale of 1.0 represents mature adult functioning.
Source: Thurstone, 1955.

full functional maturity corresponding to that of adult status by age 20, whereas word fluency and verbal comprehension only reach a level, respectively, of about 60% and 80% of adult status by 20. Our verbal growth continues long after we have peaked in perceptual speed.

Specific Abilities

Guilford does not accept the concept of a unitary general intellectual ability or of a few primary mental abilities. His model (1967) is the foremost illustration of the systematic identification of specific intellectual abilities. Developed initially in the early 1950s, the model has become increasingly significant in recent years as national attention is directed to educating gifted students.

Guilford (1967) defines an *ability* as a union of an operation, a content, and a product. In Guilford's structure of intellect, depicted in Figure 5.5, there are five operations, four types of content, and six products; therefore, $5 \times 4 \times 6 = 120$ possible cognitive abilities. Most of the 120 abilities have been identified (Guilford & Hoepfner, 1966; Hoepfner, Guilford, & Bradley, 1968; Hoffman, Guilford, Hoepfner, & Doherty, 1968). The range and

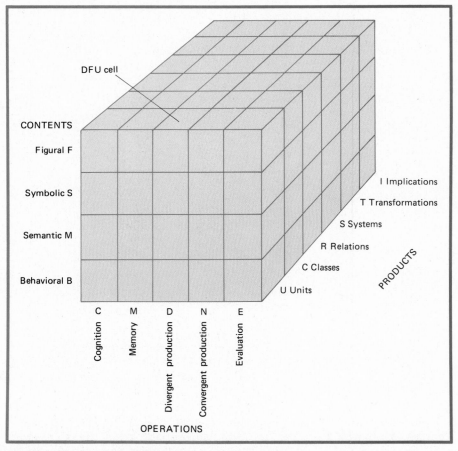

Figure 5.5 Model of the structure of intellect.
Source: Adapted from Guilford & Hoepfner, 1966, p. 3.

distribution of each of these abilities are assumed to be that of the normal curve shown earlier in Figure 5.2. Furthermore, the within-individual variation in these specific abilities is very large.

A brief overview of Guilford's operations, contents, and products follows (Guilford & Hoepfner, 1966, p. 4):

OPERATIONS, CONTENTS, AND PRODUCTS OF GUILFORD'S STRUCTURE OF INTELLECT

MENTAL OPERATIONS
Processes that the organism performs on *information*—information being defined as anything the organism discriminates.

Cognition. Immediate discovery, awareness, rediscovery, or recognition of information; also, comprehension or understanding of it.

Memory. Retention and retrieval of information.

Divergent Production. Generation of information from given information, where the emphasis is upon the variety and quantity of output produced. This operation is most clearly involved in creativity.

Convergent Production. Generation of information from given information, where the emphasis is upon achieving correct or conventionally accepted outcomes.

Evaluation. Reaching decisions or making judgments concerning criterion satisfaction (correctness, suitability, adequacy, desirability, etc.).

CONTENTS THAT ARE PROCESSED MENTALLY
Figural. Concrete information as perceived and recalled in the form of visual images and aural, olfactory, kinesthetic, and other sensory representations.

Symbolic. Information in the form of denotative signs, such as letters, numbers, and musical notations, that have no significance in and of themselves but to which meanings can be attached.

Semantic. Information in the form of meanings which commonly are represented by words.

Behavioral. Information, mostly nonverbal, in human interactions where the attitudes, needs, desires, moods, intentions, perceptions, thoughts, of other people and of ourselves are involved.

PRODUCTS THAT RESULT FROM PROCESSING
Units. Smallest but complete items of information having a "thing" character.

Classes. Items considered to be equivalent by virtue of their common properties; the meanings of words that name classes of things are concepts.

Relations. Connections between items and classes of items; principles and rules indicate relationships among concepts.

Systems. Organized or structured aggregates of units, classes, or relations; models and theories include specific information, concepts, and principles.

Transformations. Redefinition, shifts, or modification of existing information.

Implications. Extrapolations of information in the form of expectancies, predictions, known or suspected antecedents, concomitants, or consequences.

Guilford proposes three types of intelligence, each associated with different contents. *Concrete intelligence* involves figural content. Mechanics, operators of machines, architects, and artists tend to be high on concrete intelligence. *Abstract intelligence* requires the processing of symbolic and semantic content. Learning to recognize words, to spell, to operate with numbers, and to understand verbal and mathematical concepts involves abstract intelligence. In present-day group intelligence tests, most of the test items measure verbal and mathematical content. *Social intelligence* pertains to behavioral content, that is, awareness and feelings regarding the behavior of others and oneself. Teachers, social workers, and political leaders require higher social intelligence than many other professional groups.

There is some doubt today that each of the 120 proposed abilities is in fact a separate ability (Harris & Harris, 1973). Despite this doubt, the structure of intellect makes two very significant contributions to our thinking about intelligence. First, the fact that many specific abilities have been reliably identified poses a direct challenge to the notion that all human beings can be placed from high to low on a single intellectual ability and should be treated accordingly in educational and vocational settings. Second, the ideas regarding behavioral content and divergent production were not included in prior concepts of intelligence. The behavioral area is now regarded as an important area of intellectual functioning, and much educational effort in the field of creativity is guided by Guilford's work on divergent production.

Figure 5.6 shows the 18 divergent production abilities for three of the

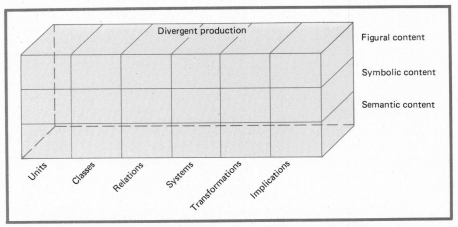

Figure 5.6 Divergent production factors in the structure of intellect.
Source: Guilford, 1967, p. 139. Copyright 1967 by McGraw-Hill Book Company. Used with permission of McGraw-Hill Book Company.

contents and all six products. Chapter 10 indicates how educational programs designed to foster creativity attempt to develop these creative abilities. Examples of the kinds of tests used to measure divergent production abilities are given in Chapter 15.

Other Abilities

A major effort is underway to identify the basic mental processes that underlie learning in the cognitive domain. Carroll (1981) and Sternberg (1979) are representative of this endeavor. Their efforts are guided by the recent advances in cognitive psychology and information processing. Sternberg and Detterman (1982) report a number of studies in which learning processes and learning strategies that underlie intelligence have been improved. However, commercially produced tests are not available for measuring these processes and strategies.

Styles of Learning

An *ability* is the capability to perform tasks. A *style* refers to the learner's preferred mode and desired conditions of learning, such as preferring to acquire information visually rather than aurally and requiring quiet when studying rather than tolerating sound, such as background music or other persons talking. *Cognitive styles* refer to how one perceives, or cognizes, situations.

Learning Styles

Dunn and Dunn (1978), and teachers working with them, identified students' learning styles, or needs and preferences when learning. They also identified ways to adapt the physical environment of the classroom and instructional approaches to students' learning styles. Price worked with the Dunns in developing an inventory to measure learning styles (Dunn, Dunn, & Price, 1983). The inventory is described in Chapter 15 of this book. An explanation of the styles is given here to indicate the differences among students in learning styles.

There are four major areas of learning styles. The four areas involve the student's needs and preferences associated with the environment for learning, the student's motivation, the sociological aspects of the learning environment, and the student's physical needs while learning and studying. The four areas and the styles in each area are shown in Figure 5.7.

A checklist of learning styles based on Dunn and Dunn (1978) follows. As you read it, mentally check the ones that correspond to the way you prefer to study when you use a textbook or other printed material. Comparing your preferences and needs with those of a friend will indicate differences in profiles.

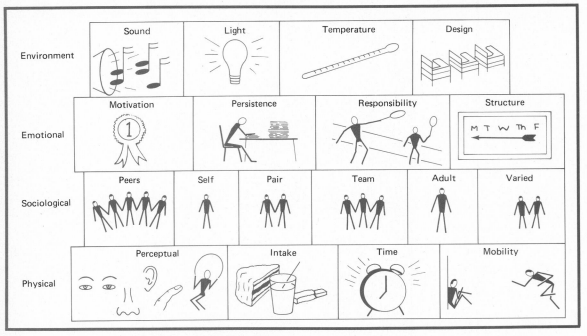

Figure 5.7 Learning styles.
Source: Dunn & Dunn, 1978, p. 4.

CHECKLIST OF LEARNING STYLES

ENVIRONMENTAL CONDITIONS
1. Needs quiet.
   Tolerates sound.
2. Requires bright light.
   Requires low light.
3. Needs cool environment.
   Needs warm environment.
4. Requires formal design of furniture, such as a desk and chair.
   Requires informal design of furniture that permits lounging.

EMOTIONAL-MOTIVATIONAL STATES OF THE INDIVIDUAL
5. Self-motivated.
   Unmotivated.
6. Persistent.
   Not persistent.
7. Responsible.
   Not very responsible.
8. Needs structured learning conditions, including specific assignments and rules.
   Needs little structure.

SOCIOLOGICAL PREFERENCE OF THE INDIVIDUAL
9. Prefers learning alone.
   Prefers learning with one peer.
   Prefers learning with two peers.
   Prefers learning with several peers.
   Prefers learning with adults.
   Prefers learning through several ways.

PHYSICAL CHARACTERISTICS AND NEEDS OF THE INDIVIDUAL
10. Has auditory preference.
    Has visual preference.
    Has tactile preference.
    Has kinesthetic preference.
11. Requires food intake, such as nibbling food or sipping soft drink.
    Does not require food intake.
12. Functions best in morning.
    Functions best in late morning.
    Functions best in afternoon.
    Functions best in evening.
13. Needs mobility, that is, to move about.
    Does not need mobility.

Checking your own styles probably resulted in preferences related to each of the four areas. Thus, each student has a profile of learning styles, not one style. Dunn and Dunn (1978) describe physical arrangements and intellectual approaches that take into account each individual student's profile. They also offer suggestions for small groups of students whose profiles are similar. They base their suggestions on research that shows student achievement and attitudes to be better when teachers take into account students' learning styles (Dunn, 1983).

Cognitive Styles

A *cognitive style* is a preferred way of reacting to environmental stimuli and may be regarded as a subclass of learning styles. Messick and Associates (1976) identified learning styles based on their review of the literature. Styles not identified by Dunn and Dunn include two cognitive styles: reflective versus impulsive responding to environmental situations and field-dependence versus field-independence.

Persons with an *impulsive style* react quickly to situations (Kagan, 1966). They give answers quickly without thinking through the situation first and tend to make errors by responding quickly. Persons with a *reflective style* react in opposite patterns.

Field-independent and field-dependent styles were identified by Witkin (1949), and research is continuing on them (Witkin, Moore, Goodenough, & Cox, 1977). The basic difference between the field-independent and field-dependent style is in perceiving and ordering the stimulus world. The *field-independent* person interprets and restructures environmental situations. The *field-dependent* person tends not to restructure situations but to accept them as experienced. The effects of these basic differences are reflected in many ways that are of interest to education (Witkin et al., 1977).

Field-dependent persons are attentive to social cues, accept other people readily, and like to be with people. Field-independent persons are less attentive to social cues and prefer to work with ideas and abstract principles. Field-dependent persons get along well with others, while field-independent persons have fewer warm, interpersonal relations.

Persons with field-dependent styles tend to be interested in social studies, while the field-independent are more interested in mathematics and science. Field-dependent students learn abstract concepts in all subject fields less well than do the field-independent. The field-dependent require more externally defined goals and extrinsic rewards, whereas the field-independent tend to set their own goals, find desired consequences of achieving their goals, and do not require external reinforcements.

Field dependence and field independence are reflected in career interests. Academically oriented, field-independent persons tend to be attracted to careers in mathematics and science, including teaching in these fields. Practically oriented field independence is reflected in vocations such as carpentry, farming, mechanics, and forest service. The interests of field-dependent persons lie in careers such as social work, counseling, elementary school teaching, and social studies teaching. Table 5.3 shows that even within career areas, interests and choices vary according to these styles.

TABLE 5.3 CAREER INTERESTS AND COGNITIVE STYLES

FIELD DEPENDENCE	FIELD INDEPENDENCE
Clinical psychology	Experimental psychology
Psychiatric nursing	Surgical nursing
Psychiatric practice favoring interpersonal relations with patients	Psychiatric practice favoring impersonal forms of therapy
Business personnel director Business education teacher	Business production manager
Social studies teacher	Natural science teacher
Elementary school teacher	Industrial arts teacher
Art students with informal art style	Art students with formal art style

SOURCE: Witkin, Moore, Goodenough, & Cox, 1977, p. 44.

Witkin et al. (1977) conclude that cognitive styles are very important determinants of academic learning and also of social behavior. When fully developed, cognitive styles tend to be stable over long periods of time. They are *bipolar*, in that persons are not high in both sets of opposite behaviors, for example, field independence and field dependence. Despite this fact, there is *continuity* of cognitive style, meaning that most persons are not pure types in all situations. On tests of cognitive style, more persons are in the middle range than toward either *pole,* or end of the test-score distribution. Finally, styles are not value-laden. Being high or low in either field independence or field dependence is not to be evaluated as good or bad, better or worse on criteria such as happiness and success in a life career.

Educational Achievements

The two most widely used indices of differences in educational achievement are grade point average and educational achievement test scores. Educational achievement tests provide more usable information regarding the range of differences in achievement in elementary and secondary schools, inasmuch as grades are not given in all schools at all school levels. Moreover, factors such as attendance and effort enter into the grades assigned by some teachers but not by others.

Table 5.4 shows the range in reading achievement at the beginning of grades 2, 3, and 4, as measured by the Metropolitan Achievement Tests.

TABLE 5.4 RAW SCORES* AND PERCENTILE RANKS IN READING FOR BEGINNING OF GRADES 2, 3, AND 4 (METROPOLITAN ACHIEVEMENT TESTS, PRIMARY 2, 1978 EDITION)

PERCENTILE RANK	GRADE 2	GRADE 3	GRADE 4
99	52	55	55
90	49	52	53
75	39	49	51
50	23	41	47
25	11	28	35
10	6	17	24
1	1	10	12

* The number of items correct out of 60.
SOURCE: Prescott, Balow, Hogan, & Farr, 1978.

A score of 10 correct of 60 items at the beginning of grade 3 is equivalent to a percentile rank of 1. A score of 55 is equivalent to a percentile rank of 99. In other words, 1% of the students who participated in the standardization of this test had scores of 10 or lower, while 99% had scores lower than 55.

Another way to examine Table 5.4 is in terms of the percentage of correct items. To illustrate, 1% of the beginning grade 3 children got approximately 91% correct, 55 of 60, and 1% got about 17% correct, 10 of 60. The range in the percentage correct by the middle half of the students, that is, those between the 25th and 75th percentile, is also large. In grade 2, it is from 18% to 65%; in grade 3, 47% to 82%; and in grade 4, 58% to 85%.

The test publisher recommends that a beginning grade 4 student who scores 12 or lower should have instruction pitched at a preprimer level, while another student who scores 55 or higher should have reading instruction at the level of average grade 5 students.

Table 5.5 gives the range in language achievement at the beginning of grades 9, 10, 11, and 12, as measured by the Iowa Tests of Educational Development. The range in the number of items correct for the 1st and 99th percentile ranks is very large. For example, at the beginning of grade 10, it is between 15 and 74, and at the beginning of grade 12, it is between 18 and 83.

TABLE 5.5 RAW SCORES* AND PERCENTILE RANKS IN LANGUAGE ACHIEVEMENT FOR BEGINNING OF GRADES 9, 10, 11, AND 12 (IOWA TESTS OF EDUCATIONAL DEVELOPMENT, 1974 EDITION)

PERCENTILE RANK	GRADE 9	GRADE 10	GRADE 11	GRADE 12
99	70	74	80	83
90	58	63	68	72
75	45	52	58	63
50	33	38	45	50
25	24	28	32	36
10	19	21	24	27
1	14	15	17	18

* The number of items correct out of 94.
SOURCE: Science Research Associates, 1974.

These wide ranges reflect not only differences in ability to learn but in other variables as well, such as motivation and learning styles. Both the lowest achiever and the highest achiever have a unique combination of these and other characteristics that contributes to their particular achievement levels. It is because of these wide ranges in achievement that many persons propose departing from one-teacher, age-graded, classroom-group instruction to the forms of education described in Chapter 6 that are more adaptive to individual differences.

5.4 Outline how general intellectual ability is distributed in an unselected, heterogeneous population of students.

5.5 Differentiate between fluid and crystallized intelligence.

5.6 Compare the use of a general intellectual ability test and the primary mental abilities tests for identifying strengths and weaknesses of the individual student.

5.7 Compare the use of tests of Guilford's structure of intellect with the primary mental abilities tests for gaining information about social intelligence and creativity.

5.8 How is intellectual ability different from a learning style?

5.9 Return to the learning style checklist. Select each style that you think a teacher (a) should try to change, for example, unmotivated, and (b) should try to accommodate, for example, self-motivated.

5.10 Prepare a brief description of a young adult of age 22 whose cognitive style is field-dependent.

5.11 React to the following statements regarding cognitive styles: (a) they are important determinants of academic learning and social behavior; (b) they are bipolar; (c) they are not value-laden.

5.12 Table 5.4 gives the range in raw scores and corresponding percentile ranks on a standardized achievement test in elementary reading for grades 2–4, while Table 5.5 gives the raw scores and corresponding percentile ranks in language achievement for grades 9–12. Using either table, draw one conclusion regarding the range of differences in each grade and another conclusion regarding the amount of increase in achievement from grade to grade.

5.13 What can a school do to decrease the range in educational achievement among students while still aiding the high achievers to achieve as high and as much as possible? Explain.

DIFFERENCES AMONG GROUPS

Sex Differences

Social Class Differences

Racial and
Ethnic Differences

In the previous part of this chapter, we saw the wide range in educational achievement among individuals of the same grade. The range between the highest achiever and the lowest achiever of any given grade is much greater than the difference between the average achievement of two groups of students, such as males and females or blacks and whites enrolled in a particular grade. Therefore, focusing on the small differences in the averages of groups, such as males and females, tends to conceal the differences within each of the groups. These points need to be kept in mind as group differences are examined.

Sex Differences

Psychological Differences

Maccoby (1966) reviewed approximately 1600 studies that provided some information about psychological differences between males and females. Subsequently, Maccoby and Jacklin (1974) arrived at three kinds of conclusions regarding sexual differences: widely confirmed differences, questionable differences, and unfounded differences. Block (1976) examined the same studies and other information. She confirmed some of the conclusions of Maccoby and Jacklin and drew others. Here, we shall indicate the differences confirmed by Maccoby and Jacklin that Block agreed with and the differences unconfirmed by Maccoby and Jacklin that she judged to be confirmed (Block, 1976, p. 307):

Differences confirmed by Maccoby and Jacklin and by Block
Girls are higher than boys in verbal abilities, such as reading, vocabulary comprehension, and spelling.

Boys are higher than girls in (a) spatial abilities, (b) quantitative abilities, and (c) aggressiveness.

Other differences confirmed by Block
Girls (a) are higher than boys in tactile sensitivity, (b) express more fear, (c) are more anxious, (d) have lower task confidence, (e) seek more help and assurance, (f) maintain closer proximity to friends, and (g) are more compliant with adults at younger ages.

Boys (a) are higher than girls in solving problems, (b) are more dominant, (c) have a stronger self-concept, (d) are more active, and (e) are more impulsive.

Before proceeding further, recall that the preceding conclusions are based on the *average* of test scores or other performances of different groups of boys and girls used in the various studies. The conclusions give no indication of the amount of the difference between the boys and girls or of the percentage of one sex that was higher than the average of the other sex. Finally we should recognize that the majority of studies were completed before 1970 and that our perceptions of male and female roles have changed since then.

Differences in Aptitudes and Career Interests
Your associates may demonstrate achievements and interests in line with the high school students who intended to go to college and participated in the 1980 College Admission Testing Program of the College Board (Educational Testing Service, 1980b). About 1 million high school students took the Scholastic Aptitude Test (SAT) in 1980; 51.8% of them were females. In Table 5.6 we may examine the average scores of the boys and the girls of 1980 and also those of other years to observe both sex differences and the downward trends in the average scores of both sexes at five-year intervals.

TABLE 5.6 MEAN SCHOLASTIC APTITUDE TEST SCORES OF HIGH SCHOOL BOYS AND GIRLS

YEAR	VERBAL APTITUDE			MATHEMATICAL APTITUDE		
	MALE	FEMALE	DIFFERENCE	MALE	FEMALE	DIFFERENCE
1970	459	461	+2F	509	465	−44F
1975	437	431	−6F	495	449	−46F
1980	428	420	−8F	491	445	−46F

SOURCE: Educational Testing Service, 1980b, p. 5. Copyright © 1980 by College Entrance Examination Board. All rights reserved.

The differences were obtained by subtracting the males' score from the females' score. Notice that the mean verbal aptitude of the girls was slightly lower than the mean of the boys in 1975 and 1980, whereas the mathematical aptitude of the boys was considerably higher for all three years.

A smaller group of the high school girls and boys took a Test of Standard Written English (TSWE). The girls' mean was higher than that of the boys in 1980, but the difference between the girls and boys narrowed from 1975 to 1980, as shown in Figure 5.8.

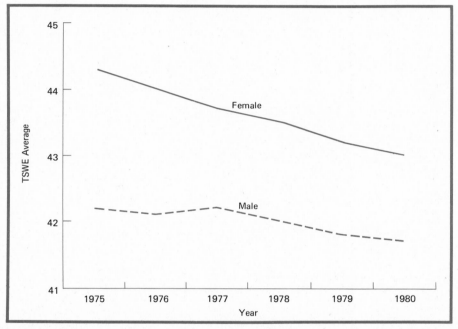

Figure 5.8 Means of boys and girls on Test of Standard Written English.
Source: Educational Testing Service, 1980b, p. 5. Copyright © 1980 by College Entrance Examination Board. All rights reserved.

The differences in the academic achievement of the boys and girls of 1980 as reflected in the letter grades that were awarded to them are shown in Figure 5.9. Notice that the mean grades of the girls in English and foreign languages are considerably higher than those of boys, whereas the grades of the boys are barely higher than those of girls in mathematics and physical science. Thus, these letter-grade differences do not agree with the aptitude test results in the verbal and mathematical areas, but they do accord with Block's conclusions regarding sex differences and also with Witkin's conclusions about field-independent and field-dependent cognitive styles.

The first choices of the high school boys and girls of 1980 concerning their intended areas of study in colleges also reflect some sex differences

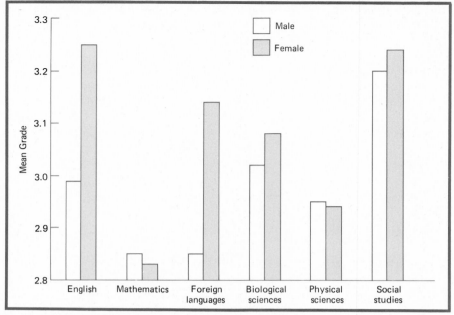

Figure 5.9 Mean grades of boys and girls for six academic subjects.
Source: Educational Testing Service, 1980b, p. 6. Copyright © 1980 by College Entrance
Examination Board. All rights reserved.

that might or might not be predicted on the basis of the earlier conclusions
about psychological sex differences. The top five choices of boys and girls
and the percentage of each sex making the choices are given in Table 5.7.

TABLE 5.7 TOP FIVE INTENDED AREAS OF STUDY

	% MALES	% FEMALES	% TOTAL
Business and commerce	18.5	18.8	18.6
Health and medical	9.2	19.5	14.7
Engineering	20.4	2.9	11.1
Social Sciences	7.7	7.8	7.8
Education	2.8	9.0	6.1

SOURCE: Educational Testing Service, 1980b, p. 9. Copyright © 1980 by College Entrance Examination Board. All rights reserved.

That boys made a first choice of engineering in a ratio of about 7:1 over girls
might have been expected. However, that a higher percentage of the girls
than the boys chose business and commerce would probably not be. The
interest of girls in business and commerce tripled from 1973 to 1980
(Educational Testing Service, 1980b, p. 9).

Table 5.7 listed the top five choices. Table 5.8 lists the intended areas
of study sought primarily by one sex (above 60%) and suggests that some
long-standing sex differences in career choices are persisting.

**TABLE 5.8 INTENDED AREAS OF
STUDY PRIMARILY SOUGHT BY ONE SEX**

PREDOMINANTLY MALE		PREDOMINANTLY FEMALE	
Military science	87%	Home economics	93%
Engineering	84%	Library science	92%
Geography	74%	Foreign languages	85%
Architecture/		Psychology	81%
Environmental design	73%	Education	79%
Physical sciences	71%	Art	75%
Forestry/		Theater arts	74%
Conservation	68%	English literature	72%
Agriculture	61%	Health and medical	71%
		Ethnic studies	65%

Differences in Reading and Mathematics

The information presented thus far shows that the findings regarding sex differences are identical neither in their direction favoring males or females nor in the size of the average differences. Some persons are now trying to ascertain the environmental conditions that contribute to sex differences. These environmental conditions may vary from one situation to another in which the studies are conducted. One main area of interest is the difference between males and females in reading and in mathematics.

Bank, Biddle, and Good (1980) reviewed many studies of reading achievement conducted in the United States and in other countries. They reported that girls do not achieve higher than boys in reading in Germany and Japan. Using all the studies, they concluded that the earlier physical maturation of girls and the large proportion of female elementary school teachers in the United States were not determinants of the higher achievement in reading by American girls. Two possible, but not likely, determinants of higher reading achievement by girls were teacher discrimination against boys and the perceptions of boys and girls that reading is a feminine activity. Two other determinants were accepted as more likely than these. One was that teachers respond to the behavior of boys and girls differently because boys and girls behave differently. Boys and girls bring different interests and behaviors to the class. For example, because boys come to school less interested in reading than girls, teachers respond differently to boys and girls on the basis of their interests (the teachers respond; they do not discriminate). The second hypothesis is that teachers' learning styles serve the purpose of girls' reading achievements more than that of boys' reading achievements. Bank et al. (1980) conclude that any one of these last four teaching-learning conditions might contribute to girls' higher reading achievement in a particular classroom setting. However, there is no convincing evidence that the national pattern in reading that favors American girls is determined by any one of them singly, or even all four in combination.

Many careers involve the completion of advanced course work requiring higher mathematical achievement, spatial ability, or both. Girls' consistently lower performances in these areas is a deterrent to their entering and succeeding in these careers.

Fennema and Sherman (1978) did not find significant sex differences in mathematics achievement in grade 8. However, significant differences were found when the same boys and girls were in grade 11 (Sherman, 1980). The difference in visual spatial ability between the girls and the boys, favoring the boys, was significant in grade 8 and also in grade 11. Sherman (1980) concluded that the marked differences between boys and girls in mathematics achievement that developed from grade 8 to grade 11 were partially determined by the sex-related difference in spatial ability but also by sociocultural influences that assign mathematics to the male domain. One indicator of the sociocultural influence was that the girls had a much sharper decline in favorable attitudes toward mathematics than the boys from grade 8 to grade 11. This finding of a sex-related, sociocultural factor as a determinant of girls' lower math achievement and interest in math confirmed earlier results found by Sherman and Fennema (1977).

Later investigations of math achievement and spatial abilities tend to confirm the preceding conclusions. For example, Pallas and Alexander (1983) concluded that the difference in the mean SAT math scores favoring males was very likely due to the fact that they take more math courses in high school. Wattanawaha and Clements (1982) reported that the mean spatial ability performances of junior high school boys were consistently higher than those of girls.

We may conclude that the differences in the average achievements, aptitudes, and behaviors of boys and girls are quite small in comparison with the very large range of differences between the members of the same sex. Moreover, the differences are not the same for boys and girls of all ages or in all locales, and some appear to be changing from one decade to the next. In this regard, Paulsen and Johnson (1983) found girls in grade 11 to have more favorable attitudes toward math than boys, and equally favorable attitudes in grades 4 and 8. Clearly, reliable predictions based only on gender cannot be made about any individual student's intelligence, educational achievements, or career interests.

Social Class Differences

Social class is indicated by the status given to groups of persons in a society by other persons of the same society. Warner, Havighurst, and Loeb (1944) found that persons of a large community could be classified into the following six social class groups: upper-upper, upper, upper-middle, middle, upper-lower, and lower-lower. *Socioeconomic status* of the family, as measured by income, occupation of parents, and amount of education of parents, was found to be an important determinant of social class. These criteria and others are generally used in determining an individual's social class today.

Differences directly related to education have been found in the conceptualizing skills and the geometry achievements of children of higher-socioeconomic status (Wiviott, 1970) and of lower-socioeconomic status (Nelson & Klausmeier, 1974) enrolled in grades 5, 8, and 11. The students of higher-socioeconomic status used more sophisticated conceptualizing skills at all three grade levels. First, they classified the examples of concepts presented to them by identifying the attributes of the examples accurately. Second, they identified the subordinate and superordinate relationships among the examples of the concepts and used them in their classifications. Table 5.9 shows that the average geometry scores of the students of higher-socioeconomic status were consistently higher for all three grades.

TABLE 5.9 AVERAGE SCORES IN GEOMETRY RELATED TO SOCIOECONOMIC STATUS

	LOWER-SOCIOECONOMIC STATUS	HIGHER-SOCIOECONOMIC STATUS
Grade 5	21.4	33.3
Grade 8	28.8	37.9
Grade 11	28.4	47.2

SOURCE: Nelson & Klausmeier, 1974.

We observe that the average score of the students of higher-socioeconomic status of grade 5 is higher than that of the lower-socioeconomic groups of any grade. Moreover, the mean of the grade 11 students of lower-socioeconomic status is lower than that of the grade 8 students. The results of these two studies suggest that more students of lower-socioeconomic status than of higher-socioeconomic status do not learn mature conceptualizing skills. The lack of conceptualizing skills greatly retards their educational achievement in school subjects that require understanding concepts.

Much federal legislation starting in the 1960s was directed toward eliminating teacher discrimination against children of lower-socioeconomic levels, and it has proven beneficial in many instances. For example, Haller and Davis (1980) found that the socioeconomic level of the children and the teachers played only a minor role in assigning children of grades 4, 5, and 6 of four separate school districts to groups for reading instruction. Rehberg and Rosenthal (1978) reported similar findings at the high school level.

Although the schools are rapidly eliminating social class discrimination in learning opportunity, children and youth of the lower social classes remain lower than the middle class in IQ and educational achievement, but higher in aggression, delinquency, and mental health problems (Minton & Schneider, 1980). We should recognize that these are average differences, and that the differences within each social class are much larger than the average between any two social classes. Moreover, conditions in our society remain unfavorable for many children and youth of the lower social classes.

Home conditions, as well as socioeconomic status, contribute to educational achievement. The range in achievement among students from families of the same socioeconomic status, for example, middle class, is much larger than the difference between the average achievement of children of lower- and middle-socioeconomic status. Factors in the home and family found to retard cognitive development both during the elementary school years and the secondary school years are less favorable parental attitudes toward school and education, lower parental expectations for their children, and a less favorable intellectual climate of the home (Mize & Klausmeier, 1977; Klausmeier & Allen, 1978).

Racial and Ethnic Differences

The racial and ethnic origin of many American children cannot be clearly delineated because of the cross-marriages that have occurred for many generations between persons of different national groups and racial groups. Therefore, the terms are used here either synonymously or in accordance with how particular researchers classify their subjects.

Lesser, Fifer, and Clark (1965) administered tests to 320 children of ages 6–8 from four ethnic groups of New York City. The children were classified as Chinese, Jewish, black, and Puerto Rican. The children were also classified as lower class and middle class. There were equal numbers of boys and girls. The tests measured verbal, reasoning, number, and spatial (space) abilities. The results are shown in Figure 5.10.

Children of the lower social class of all four ethnic groups had lower mean test scores than those of the middle class. The difference in mean test scores between the lower and middle social classes was somewhat larger for blacks than for the other ethnic groups. Consistent differences in the mean test scores were not found among the ethnic groups. However, the patterns of the means of the four tests within each group were different. The verbal score of the Jewish group was the highest of their four scores and the spatial the lowest, whereas the spatial score of the Chinese was the highest of their four scores and the verbal the lowest. The verbal score of the blacks was the highest of their four scores, but the differences among their four scores were not as large as those among the Jewish and Chinese groups. The patterns of the Puerto Rican group were also distinct from the other groups but most like that of the Chinese.

Backman (1972) examined the patterns of aptitudes and achievements of grade 12 boys and girls of various ethnic backgrounds who attended high schools that were representative of all the high schools in the United States. There were 1236 Jewish whites, 1051 non–Jewish whites, 488 blacks, and 150 Orientals in this study. Social class was based on father's occupation and education, mother's education, family income, value of the family home, availability of a room and desk, number of books in the home, and access to specific appliances, such as TV and telephone.

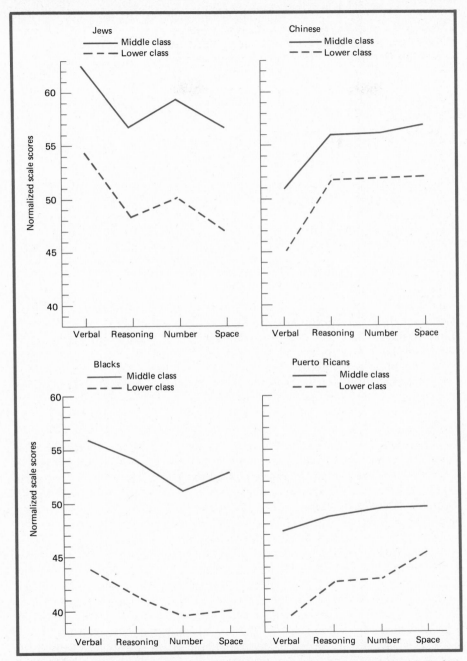

Figure 5.10 Mean test performances of middle- and lower-class children from four different racial and ethnic groups.
Source: G. S. Lesser, G. Fifer, & D. H. Clark, 1965.

TABLE 5.10 MEAN MENTAL ABILITY SCORES OF FOUR RACIAL AND ETHNIC GROUPS, TWO SOCIAL CLASSES, AND MALES AND FEMALES

GROUP	MENTAL ABILITIES					
	VKN	ENG	MAT	VIS	PSA	MEM
ETHNICITY						
Jewish white	57.1	50.8	58.6	46.0	51.0	47.8
Non–Jewish white	51.9	51.1	52.1	51.8	49.5	50.9
Black	46.0	47.5	47.3	45.1	50.9	50.4
Oriental	49.0	52.5	59.1	49.4	50.3	51.6
SOCIOECONOMIC STATUS						
Upper-middle	53.0	50.6	56.2	48.9	50.5	50.0
Lower-middle	49.0	50.3	52.4	47.2	50.3	50.3
SEX						
Male	53.7	40.9	63.9	54.5	49.1	44.3
Female	48.3	60.0	44.6	41.7	51.7	56.0

SOURCE: Backman, 1972, p. 6.

Table 5.10 gives the means for each of the four ethnic groups, for the upper-middle and lower-middle social classes into which all the students were classified, and for males and females. Three tests measured achievement and three measured aptitude as follows: VKN—the general information that the student had acquired, ENG—achievement in grammar and language, MAT—high school mathematics achievement, VIS—spatial aptitude, PSA—perceptual speed, and MEM—short-term recall of verbal symbols.

In this study, the girls were found to be considerably higher than the boys in English achievement and memory ability, but considerably lower in mathematics achievement and spatial ability. The differences favoring the upper-middle class over the lower-middle class were relatively small. Blacks were lowest of the four racial-ethnic groups, except in perceptual speed and memory.

Hennessy and Merrifield (1976, 1978) provide information regarding the aptitudes of 2985 college-bound urban high school seniors. The students were classified as black, Hispanic, Caucasian-Jewish, and Caucasian-gentile. Three basic aptitudes for college academic success were identified: verbal, reasoning, and technology. *Verbal aptitude* included achievement in areas such as reading and English usage. *Reasoning aptitude* was similar to that measured by Thurstone's primary mental ability called *inductive reasoning* and was regarded as least influenced by learning and environmental conditions. The *technology aptitude* involved both algebra achievement and spatial ability.

No significant differences in the verbal area were found between the two Caucasian groups or between the black and Hispanic groups. However, large differences favoring the Caucasian groups were found between the black group and the Caucasian groups and between the Hispanic group and the Caucasian groups. The Caucasian groups were also significantly higher in reasoning than the black group and the Hispanic group. The differences in technology aptitude among the ethnic groups were smaller than in verbal aptitude and reasoning. However, significant differences were found.

There are large inconsistencies between Backman's findings and those of Hennessy and Merrifield regarding racial and ethnic differences. These inconsistencies may result because Backman's study included all seniors, while the study by Hennessy and Merrifield included only those who intended to go to college. There are inconsistencies between these two studies and the study by Lesser et al. (1965), which was conducted with children of ages 6–8. Discrepancies regarding group differences are commonly found from one study to the next, and the precise source of the discrepancy cannot be identified. However, the age of the participating students, the location in which the study is conducted, the year in which the study is done, the tests used, and the methods of analyzing the data are among the many factors that may lead to inconsistent findings. In this regard and contrary to widespread opinion, Fulkerson, Furr, and Brown (1983) found expectancy for success to be lower for blacks than for whites in grade 3 but to be as high in grade 9. The blacks' expectancy for success rose from grade 3 to grade 6 to grade 9, while that of the whites remained constant. The difference in math achievement between the two groups was not significant in any grade.

The effects of desegregation on differences in educational achievements appear to be situational rather than generalizable to all situations, as is indicated in a review of the available studies (Bradley & Bradley, 1977). With some notable exceptions, desegregation achieved by busing, by permitting students to enroll voluntarily in any school of the district, and by creating central schools that enroll all the children of a grade or two of the district has resulted in higher achievement. On the other hand, and again with some exceptions, closing inner-city schools has not. Considering all the studies of the effects of desegregation, one person might generalize that desegregation has resulted in higher achievement, while another person might not. Needed are detailed analyses of conditions in specific classrooms, schools, and school districts that do and do not yield higher achievement by children of clearly defined characteristics.

5.14 Maccoby and Jacklin and Block found that in the majority of studies, the means for boys were higher in spatial abilities, quantitative abilities, and aggressiveness. Explain why it would be possible for the means in these areas to be higher for girls than for boys in some classes of 25–30.

5.15 The mean verbal aptitude of over 500,000 high school girls who took the Scholastic Aptitude Test (SAT) in 1980 was lower than that of the boys.

Do you think the mean verbal aptitude of all high school girls in 1980 was also lower than that of all high school boys? Give your reasoning.

5.16 The mean letter grade of the girls who took the SAT in 1980 was higher than the mean letter grade of boys in English, foreign languages, biological sciences, and social studies. The mean letter grade of the boys was higher in mathematics and physical sciences. Compare these grades with the SAT test scores. Do you think factors other than achievement may have been used in assigning grades in any or all of the six subjects? Explain.

5.17 The differences among the 1980 high school males and females in career choices, for example, military science and home economics respectively, are much larger than the differences in achievement and ability. What do you think contributes the differences in career choices?

5.18 Which of the intended areas of studies of high school males and females of 1980 do you think will remain predominantly male or female in the foreseeable future? Give your rationale.

5.19 Compare your own observations to the conclusions of Bank et al. regarding environmental conditions that do and do not contribute to higher reading achievement by girls in the United States.

5.20 Fennema and Sherman attribute the higher achievement of high school boys in mathematics to their higher spatial ability and to sociocultural influences. Do you think sociocultural influences would tend to depress the girls' achievements or to heighten the boys' achievements? Explain.

5.21 The mean educational achievement and the mean mental ability of the successively higher social classes—lower, middle, upper—are consistently higher. What conditions associated with social class membership contribute to this phenomenon?

5.22 The differences found among racial groups and ethnic groups vary somewhat from one study to another. Indicate the main factors that are not the same in the studies that might lead to the different results.

Hereditary Influence

Environmental Influence

DETERMINANTS OF
INDIVIDUAL AND GROUP DIFFERENCES

Most research on the genetic and environmental determinants of psychological differences among individuals and between groups involves the use of tests of general intelligence or of primary mental abilities. Many scholars do not attempt to assign a certain portion of an identified difference to either heredity or environment. However, a few do, and it is the controversial conclusions that are disseminated widely in the mass media.

Hereditary Influence

Heredity determines the mental abilities of individuals to an unspecifiable extent. This judgment is based on correlations between the IQ scores of samples of persons with differing degrees of genetic relationship. Figure 5.11 summarizes 52 studies of genetic relationships:

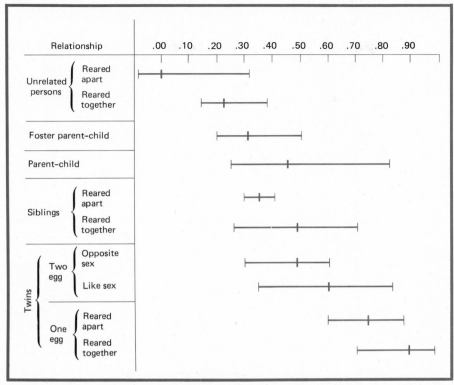

Figure 5.11 The range in correlations and the average correlation, based on 52 studies of genetic relationships and IQ scores.
Source: Erlenmeyer-Kimling & Jarvik, 1963.

The studies of unrelated persons reared apart report correlations ranging from about −.10 to .32, with the average correlation being .00. The average correlation for unrelated persons living together is about .23. As the genetic relationship changes from unrelated to that of identical twins, the size of the average correlation becomes higher. For identical twins reared apart, it is about .71. Persons such as Jensen (1973) and Shockley (1972), who indicate that heredity is the primary determinant of intelligence, base this conclusion on the fact that the greater the genetic relationship between individuals, the higher the correlation.

Figure 5.11 can also be used to support the position that environment has a considerable influence on intelligence. For example, the average correlation is higher for unrelated persons who are reared together, .23, than for unrelated persons who are reared apart, .00. It is also higher for brothers and sisters reared together, .50, than for siblings reared apart, .35, and for identical twins reared together .90, than for identical twins reared apart, .71. Nonidentical, same-sex twins have more similar environments than opposite-sex twins, and the correlations are also higher, .60 versus .48.

You may encounter studies and news stories that report a *heritability*

ratio or *heritability index*. Both the underlying theory regarding the hereditary process and the method for arriving at a numerical value, or ratio, are
too complicated to present here. However, the heritability ratio indicates
the proportion of the variable under consideration that is due to heredity.
The heritability ratio that is obtained ranges between zero and one. The
heritability ratio is 0.74 for the information summarized in Figure 5.11.

A heritability ratio is not a correlation, and it applies only to populations under clearly specified environmental conditions. It does not apply to
individuals. Jensen (1973) based his conclusions about the average difference in the intelligence of black and white school children in part on differences in heritability ratios. Kamin (1976) is representative of the scholars
who indicate that we cannot make precise estimates of the heritability of any
population.

Environmental Influence

Many environmental conditions influence intellectual development.
Nutrition, health, stimulation, the emotional and intellectual climate of the
home, and early education are important determinants (Bayley, 1970).
Given two infants with the same genes, the one receiving the better nutrition, health care, intellectual stimulation, enriched home environment, and
preschool education will score higher on an IQ test when entering the first
grade. This kind of evidence leads some scholars, for example, Hunt (1961),
Kagan (1973), and Chomsky (1976), to conclude that environment has more
influence on intelligence than heredity.

Gottesman (1963) proposed that heredity establishes the top limit
and bottom limit on intelligence. He hypothesizes that a person who has
inherited higher ability may have an IQ near 65 if raised in a greatly deprived environment, and near 180 if raised in a greatly enriched environment. On the other hand, a person who has inherited lower ability may have
an IQ near 30 if reared in a greatly deprived environment, and near 110 if
raised in a greatly enriched environment. According to this view, the possible range between the lower limit and upper limit increases as the inherited
ability increases.

The available information on genetic and environmental determinants
of intelligence indicates that a person's intelligence is dependent upon the
continual interaction of heredity and environment. The specific percentage
that heredity contributes to differences among individuals in intellectual
functioning cannot be determined. Similarly, the extent to which heredity
contributes to the differences in the average scores of blacks and whites
cannot be identified, because the differences in their environments can
neither be estimated reliably nor controlled using available research designs
and statistical methods (Hilgard, Atkinson, & Atkinson, 1979, p. 366). Thus,
the proper question to study is not how much heredity or environment influences intelligence but how both operate interactively to produce differences. Bayley (1970) offers the following advice for educators, based on
her carefully conducted longitudinal study of intellectual development that
started in infancy and continued into middle age:

The complex interaction of genetic potentials and environmental stimulation, in the context of maturing and pliable neural structures, presents a setting in which the exact expression of mental abilities may be impossible to predict. However, we have in this complex process a number of indicators of the best ways to facilitate mental growth. In essence, given the undamaged genetic potential, mental growth is best facilitated by a supportive, "warm" emotional climate, together with ample opportunities for the positive reinforcement of specific cognitive efforts and successes. (pp. 1201, 1203)

5.23 Indicate research that supports the idea that heredity is a determinant of intellectual abilities.

5.24 Indicate research that supports the idea that the environment is a determinant of intellectual abilities.

5.25 Outline your reasoned judgment regarding the interaction of heredity and environment on the development of intellectual abilities.

5.26 React to Gottesman's idea that heredity determines the lower and upper limits of intelligence.

EXCEPTIONAL CHILDREN

Learning Handicaps
Giftedness

Exceptional children are those who are considerably above or below the average of their age-group in a characteristic or behavior. It is important to recognize, however, that a child may be far below average in one or more characteristics but average or well above in others. Most special education programs that are supported with additional federal, state, and local funds under provisions of the Education for All Handicapped Children Act of 1975 are directed toward children and youth below the average in one or more characteristics. However, considerable effort has also been made in recent years to make better provisions for giftedness.

Learning Handicaps

An exceptional child with a learning handicap is one who differs from other children so much in one or more characteristics, for example, in vision or in behavior, that the child cannot profit maximally from the typical pattern of instruction provided to normally developing children. Changes must be made in what is taught or how it is taught in order to provide for exceptional children. A child is classified as exceptional on the basis of careful assessment, but increasingly children are not being labeled, for example, mentally retarded or culturally deprived. Fewer labels have resulted in part from class-action lawsuits in which minority children were alleged to have been placed in stigmatized classes for the mentally retarded on the basis of culturally biased tests (Macmillan & Meyers, 1979). Despite the negative aspects of labeling, there is a need to identify and classify children with various types of learning handicaps or giftedness so that they may participate in programs for exceptional children as defined by federal and state regulations.

Classification Schemes

Traditionally, exceptional children have been categorized into ten groups: nine have below-average characteristics, and one — gifted children — has above-average characteristics (Hewett & Forness, 1977, p. xv).

CLASSIFICATION OF EXCEPTIONAL CHILDREN

1. Children with behavior disorders.
2. Children with learning disabilities.
3. Economically disadvantaged and/or culturally different children.
4. Speech-handicapped children.
5. Mildly mentally retarded children.
6. Visually handicapped children.
7. Crippled and chronically ill children.
8. Severely emotionally disturbed children.
9. Multihandicapped children.
10. Gifted children.

Gardner (1977, pp. 106–109) has shifted from naming groups of exceptional children to classifying the characteristics of exceptional children, that is, indicating characteristics that are exceptional. This approach is intended to make identification more accurate and treatment more reliable. His three main categories of characteristics, all the subcategories of each, and the complete descriptive information for the first of each subcategory follow:

CLASSIFICATION OF EXCEPTIONAL CHARACTERISTICS

I. Learning and behavioral deficits
   A. General and specific knowledge, ability, and skill deficits
      1. Self-help and self-care behavior deficits. This category includes deficits in such areas as toileting (enuresis and encopresis), feeding, dressing, grooming, and independent traveling.
      2. Language and cognitive behavior deficits.
      3. Academic behavior deficits.
      4. Sensory and perceptual discrimination deficits.
      5. Locomotion and manual skills deficits.
      6. Self-management skills deficits.
   B. Task-related behavior deficits
      1. Deficits in prerequisite skills. This category includes those weak or absent skills prerequisite to effective learning — attention span, attending to relevant aspects of learning tasks, a reflective cognitive style, persistence, concentration, and so on.
      2. Deficits in output skills.
   C. Interpersonal (social) behavior deficits
      1. Deficits in sex-role behaviors. This category includes the excessively effeminate male and the excessively masculine female.
      2. Deficits in play and/or social interaction skills.

D. Affective behavior deficits
   1. Deficits in the types of emotional behavior expressed. This category includes the child who has difficulty in expressing such emotional reactions as *glee, happiness, laughing, affection, sadness, guilt, shame, apprehension, love,* or *anger.*
   2. Deficits in the intensity of emotional behaviors.
   3. Deficits in the appropriateness of emotional behaviors.
E. Deficits in level of motivational development
   1. Deficits in the types and amounts of incentive required for learning and performance. This category is illustrated by the child who is not influenced consistently by the types and amounts of incentive provided in a specific learning or performance situation. A classroom situation may depend upon such motivational features as task completion, parental approval, self-reinforcement, grades, and occasional teacher praise to ensure learning and performance. A child who requires large amounts of contrived teacher-provided consequences would not be successful in this environment.
   2. Deficits in the reinforcement schedule required for learning and performance.
   3. Deficits in self-managed motivational skills.
F. Deficits in age-relevant personal and social responsibility behaviors. This category includes the overly dependent child who lacks the skills to react in the absence of excessive support or direction from others.
II. Excessive behaviors
A. Excessive disruptive and nonfunctional competing behavior
   1. Excessive disruptive interpersonal behavior. This category includes such behaviors as aggression, threatening others, noncompliance, defiance, negativism, and other excessive behavior involving direct social interaction, which is of a disrupting nature.
   2. Excessive socially inappropriate behavior.
   3. Excessive nonfunctional competing behaviors.
B. Excessive affective reactions
   1. Excessive emotional reactions to external events. This category includes a variety of phobias, generalized anxieties, or oversensitivity to reprimand or other cues of rejection.
   2. Excessive emotional reactions to removal of events.
   3. Excessive emotional reactions to frustration.
   4. Excessive emotional reactions resulting from self-generated cognitive behaviors.
C. Excessive motor behaviors
   1. Excessive speech-related reactions. This category includes such speech features as stuttering and vocal intensity.
   2. Excessive activity level.
D. Excessive avoidance behaviors
   1. Excessive avoidance of tasks and activities. This category includes mobility avoidance of aversive features of various academic endeavors, competitive activities, or situations such as the classroom.
   2. Excessive avoidance of interpersonal and social contact and/or interaction.
III. Acceleration in learning and creative activities. This category includes accelerated learning and creative activities defined in terms of rate of acquisition of academic and related content, level of artistic development, and uniqueness of creative output.

Instructional Provisions

The instruction of children with handicapping learning conditions has two facets. One is to have a special education teacher instruct a child individually or as a member of a small group: the goal is to eliminate or ameliorate the handicap as quickly and as permanently as possible. The second facet, called *mainstreaming,* is to place a child in regular classes with other children as much as possible as soon as possible: the objectives are to provide the best instruction possible and to avoid stigmatizing the child.

For many years special education teachers used behavior modification techniques based on principles of conditioning almost exclusively in their work with exceptional children. Presently, they employ principles of cognitive learning along with principles of conditioning. For example, children more frequently are called on to set learning goals and to work independently, while the teachers less often provide concrete rewards and withhold items essential to satisfying a child's physiological and psychological needs, such as food, liquid, and interactions with age-mates.

There are seven steps in typical behavior modification programs. The steps follow and are related to the idea of mainstreaming to clarify the role of the special education teacher and other teachers of the child.

1. The learning problem is identified as exceptional deficit behaviors and/or excessive behaviors are observed. This is followed with a complete assessment. Psychological, educational, and medical examinations may be used in the assessment as well as teacher observations and parent reports. The kind of information that is useful in the assessment varies with the nature of the handicapping condition (see the highlighted categories of deficits and excesses).

2. The severity of the handicapping condition(s) is estimated, and the extent to which instruction from a special teacher or other therapist is required is determined. For example, the frequency of the excessive behaviors and the manner in which they are expressed determine the amount of instruction that may be required from the special teacher. In a similar way, the nature and severity of the speech deficit determine the amount of teaching required from a speech therapist.

3. The objectives of the educational program are outlined by a committee. The committee should include the parents, the regular teacher(s), and the special teacher. For many years, the objectives were stated in strictly behavioristic performance terms (see Chapter 2) and were not modified during the school year as a means of assuring accountability. Currently, the objectives are stated in more general terms and are subject to change throughout the school year, depending upon the progress of the child. Indeed, the child is aided to understand the objectives and also to set personal goals to achieve them.

4. An intervention program is planned to increase deficit behaviors, to decrease excessive behaviors, or both. The program objectives and the intervention plan are usually written and signed by the parent and a person representing the school, usually the special teacher. In some cases, the plan refers only to the objectives to be achieved by the special teacher rather than by the mainstreaming teacher(s).

5. In implementing the plan, the special teacher works out an effective reinforcement contingency program. A *reinforcement contingency* program implies that a concrete, token, or social reward will be received only immediately after a desired deficit behavior is performed or after an undesired excessive behavior ceases. The deficit behaviors to be reinforced include not only the final desired behavior but also any partial behavior in the desired direction. The child is typically taught a self-management system of contingencies.

6. The child is fully mainstreamed when deficit or excessive behaviors are corrected. The special teacher continues to contact and to work with the regular teacher(s) from whom the child receives instruction.

7. The regular teacher(s) check the child for relapses and the need for more special assistance. For example, a blind child, or one who is deficient in verbal skills, may need assistance from a special teacher in meeting a new situation after being mainstreamed for all instruction.

Some examples of behavior modification and other special education techniques follow in Table 5.11.

We should not infer from the preceding discussion that mainstreaming works effectively in all situations with all children nor that behavior modification achieves excellent results with all children who have learning handicaps. Some of the situations, however, in which mainstreaming has succeeded well are indicated in a number of studies. Goldman (1980) reports desirable results throughout a school for students with a wide variety of handicapping conditions. Masoodi and Ban (1980) describe mainstreaming techniques that were used very successfully with blind and partially seeing children. Merz (1980) outlines effective practices involving severely handicapped first-grade children. Carefully planned learning activities which required cooperation among small groups of educable mentally retarded and nonhandicapped junior high school students resulted in positive interactions among the students (Johnson, Rynders, Johnson, Schmidt, & Haider, 1979). Similarly, social acceptance of educable, mentally retarded children of grades 3, 4, and 5 by the other children was facilitated by engaging the children in small-group cooperative learning activities (Ballard, Corman, Gottlieb, & Kaufman, 1977).

Although many success stories, such as these, are reported, questions continue to be raised about the necessary conditions for effective mainstreaming. Difficulties arise when children with learning handicaps are mainstreamed before they are able to adjust to the regular classroom. Problems arise when mainstreaming teachers cannot give sufficient time and attention to the handicapped children as well as to the instruction of the other children. Semmel, Gottlieb, and Robinson (1979) report that there is not a sound empirical basis for mainstreaming and that its continuation depends upon strong moral persuasion and enforcement of relevant federal and state laws. These authors also conclude that mainstreaming will not be

TABLE 5.11 CHARACTERISTICS AND PROGRAM ELEMENTS OF EXCEPTIONAL CHILDREN

EXCEPTIONAL CHARACTERISTIC	WHAT CHILD DOES	WHAT CHILD IS EXPECTED TO DO	POSSIBLE CORRELATES	LEARNER ASSETS	PROGRAM IMPLICATIONS
Academic behavior deficits.	When reads aloud in grade-level reading materials, exhibits omissions, sound-blending errors, hesitations, substitutions, and poor use of context cues. Comprehends only 25% of reading material.	Read with fluency and 85% comprehension.	Inadequate instruction, inadequate incentive conditions, excessive negative emotionality, hearing loss.	Normal-range cognitive skills; relates well to adults; likes school.	Task analysis of reading materials, training in sound blending, use token reinforcement procedure, use easier materials, provide frequent reinforcement and social approval. Model a relaxed pleasant manner of reading
Deficits in prerequisite skills.	Attends to reading instruction for 2–3 minutes.	Attend to reading instruction for 10–15 minutes.	Excessive failure in attending to reading tasks viewed as avoidance behavior.	Attends for long period when presented easy materials.	Gradually shape attending skills by providing easy and structured performance tasks, use high-value reinforcers initially, label and praise increase in attending skills.
Excessive disruptive interpersonal behavior.	Fights with peers 3–4 times weekly, disruptive comments during class study period on average of 4–5 times daily.	No fighting, no disruptive comments.	Isolated by peer group, teased by peer group over being fat; poor self-concept behaviors.	States desire to have friends, responsive to tangible reinforcers, likes male student teacher.	Develop contingency program for appropriate classroom behavior, encourage peer group activities, use male instructor.

SOURCE: Gardner, 1977, p. 111

continued voluntarily in some schools and school districts if laws and regulations regarding the handicapped are eliminated.

Many successes are also reported for behavior modification, especially for eliminating undesired excessive behaviors and increasing desired deficit behaviors (Workman & Hector, 1978). However, Ryan (1979) makes a strong case against the use of it by classroom teachers, since the repeated use of concrete rewards tends to decrease students' intrinsic motivation.

Giftedness

Marland (1971), when Commissioner of Education, prepared a report for Congress on the status of gifted children. In the report, he defined *gifted and talented children* as those with high demonstrated achievement and/or high potential ability in any one of the following: (a) general intellectual ability, (b) specific academic aptitude, (c) creative, productive thinking, (d) leadership, (e) visual and performing arts, and (f) psychomotor skills. This definition has been very widely used since 1972, but requires some elaboration.

A *gifted student* is one who is high in general intellectual ability and in achievement in several areas such as mathematics, science, and English. An *academically talented student* is a high performer in only one broad subject field. Whereas Marland put creative and productive thinking in the same category, most persons follow Guilford's model (1967) of the structure of intellect and differentiate between divergent, or creative, thinking and convergent thinking. Both are forms of productive thinking. Educators also cannot agree whether to classify as gifted athletes, mechanics, and others who are high performers in the motor area.

The first task that teachers face is identifying the area or areas of giftedness of their students. The two main means of providing for gifted students are enrichment and acceleration.

Identification Criteria

School districts use different criteria for identifying giftedness. Obviously, when the areas included are few in number and the minimum level of performance the students must meet is high, relatively few students are identified. For example, if being talented in a subject field is defined as being in the top 2% in intellectual ability and also in achievement in the particular subject field, only a very small percentage of the student population is identified as talented in the subject field. On the other hand, if the six areas indicated by Marland are included and if the minimum level of performance is being in the top 5% of any one of the six areas, many students are identified as being gifted or talented.

Both tests and teacher observation are used in identifying gifted and talented students. Sometimes, parental judgment is used. When the identification is done annually, new students not identified in prior years are found to be gifted or talented. Accordingly, it is not uncommon for as many as 25% of the school population to be identified as having a gift or a talent.

The present author believes that it is unwise to identify and label only a small proportion of students as gifted, for example, those with an IQ of 135 or higher. The unfortunate aspect of labeling some children as gifted is the accompanying implication that the other students are not gifted. Moreover, a highly selective identification process eliminates large numbers of students, and particularly students from minority groups, who will perform with giftedness as adults. Instead of a highly selective process, the high actual or potential performance of every student should be identified, and each student should have a program designed to develop it fully. Moreover, nearly every normally developing student has at least one area of high or potentially high performance that should be identified and developed as carefully as the many high performance areas of very exceptional students. We must recognize, of course, that some schools and school districts are incapable of doing this well. In these situations, it may be wise to identify only a more select group. It would seem, however, that any school that can effectively mainstream students with learning handicaps can also make appropriate provisions for all of its high performing students in its regular program of instruction.

Enrichment

Renzulli (1977) developed an approach to teaching gifted children called the *enrichment triad model*. It is a triad inasmuch as there are three kinds of enrichment activities.

Enrichment is defined in the model as experiences that are above and beyond the regular curriculum. Included as enrichment is acquiring subject matter as rapidly as possible, regardless of the grade level of the child or the grade placement of the content. Although students may acquire the subject matter more rapidly, they are not accelerated by skipping one or more grades and thereby completing 12 school grades in less than 12 years. The model is depicted in Figure 5.12.

Before considering the three kinds of enrichment activities—general exploratory activities, group-training activities, and individual and small-group investigations of real problems—we may clarify other features of the

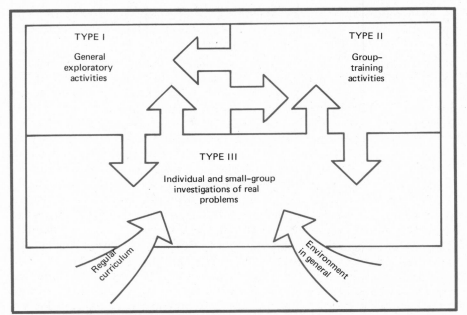

Figure 5.12 Enrichment triad model.
Source: Renzulli, 1977, p. 14.

model. First, all children, including the gifted, acquire the knowledge and skills included in the regular curriculum. These basic learnings are made interesting and exciting for all the students. Second, the model is not prescriptive with respect to the locale for learning. Students may leave the classroom and the school site for some of their learning activities. Third, the enrichment activities take into account the individual learner's specific subject-matter interests, learning styles, and other characteristics. There is no one identical program of instruction for all the gifted students of the class or grade.

We may now turn to the three kinds of enrichment activities. Renzulli indicates that the general exploratory activities should be conducted throughout the school year for all the students. The first purpose of the general exploratory activities is to bring every learner in touch with the topics and areas of study in which the student may develop a continuing interest. Accordingly, the student pursues an interest for an extended period of time rather than merely identifying and expressing it for a short period of time. Books and other instructional materials, interest centers in the classroom, resource persons, and field trips are used in arranging the exploratory enrichment activities.

The second purpose of the exploratory activities is to enable the teacher to identify relevant group-training activities for the students—the second kind of enrichment activity—and to find areas that may lead to individual and small-group investigations—the third kind. In some schools, the second and third kinds of activities are made available only to students identified as gifted or talented.

Many instructional materials for students have been designed to teach thinking processes, the group-training activities of the enrichment triad. The important task of the teacher is to identify which processes to teach, which materials and techniques to use, and when to teach them. Divergent thinking processes involving originality, fluency, flexibility, and elaboration (Guilford, 1967), and divergent production operations, such as application, analysis, synthesis, and evaluation (Bloom, 1956) should be included at some time. Although not included by Renzulli, the strategies of learning as described in Chapter 8 of this book are appropriate.

The teacher has four main responsibilities in organizing and guiding Type III enrichment activities, individual and small-group investigations of real problems. The first is to identify and focus student interest. Another is to help students develop something, such as a report or a news story, and to communicate the results of their investigative work in a realistic and meaningful way. Providing assistance to the students in carrying out their investigations, is a third responsibility. A last and very important one is to develop a laboratory-like learning environment.

The Renzulli model focuses on individual and small-group investigations of real problems as the key enrichment activities for gifted students. There is much merit and also considerable acceptance of this kind of activity. However, many other kinds of enrichment activities may also be employed. Included here are individual and small-group projects directly related to the school's curriculum. For example, students may engage in creative writing, drama, dance, and similar expressive areas. Other activities may involve research in the instructional materials center on a topic of interest or simply moving ahead or in-depth on a topic of interest. Cooperative group learning activities initiated by the students are beginning to be popular again. In general, any enrichment activity is appropriate that enables students to develop an area of their giftedness.

Acceleration

A continuing problem for gifted students is that the curriculum is graded by age and every student is required to spend one school year to complete each grade, kindergarten through grade 12. Not permitting students to learn the subject matter assigned to a higher grade unnecessarily retards the educational development of many students. Moreover, in-depth and in-breadth enrichment without any acceleration does not adequately meet the educational needs of the able student.

Accelerating able students by one grade can be accomplished in many ways and is easy to implement. The most common means are early admission to kindergarten, completing the requirements of two grades during one year or during one year and a summer session, and taking college courses for credit while in high school. The last two of these procedures were worked out in two large school districts with much success several decades ago (Klausmeier & Ripple, 1962; Klausmeier & Teel, 1964) and are still employed very effectively today in many schools.

An especially effective procedure was to identify high-ability, high-achieving grade 2 children who were in the upper half of their grade in chronological age. These students were then taught the curriculum of grade 3 that they had not yet acquired in five weeks during the summer. They entered grade 4 in the fall. This procedure resulted in the accelerated students being in the younger half of their high school class and graduating at age 17 or 18 rather than 18 or 19. Results of a first follow-up study when the children were in grade 5 showed many desirable and no undesirable effects of the acceleration (Klausmeier, 1963). The accelerates, when in grade 5, were as high in educational achievements, creativity, ethical values, attitudes toward school, and in teacher ratings of their social and emotional adjustment as the grade 5 gifted students who had not been accelerated. In a second follow-up, when the accelerated students were in junior high school, again only positive effects were found (Klausmeier, Goodwin, & Rhonda, 1968).

Stanley (1977) is engaged in a longitudinal study of students whose mathematical reasoning is very high. The students are identified as being exceptionally talented in mathematics when in grade 7 or grade 8. After identification, they are given a variety of arrangements to learn mathematics as rapidly as they can. Included are enrollment in high school and university summer-session mathematics classes, taking college courses while enrolled in junior and senior high school, and completing high school at a very young age by skipping two or more grades. One of the students in this study entered a university at age 15 and upon entry had already completed 30% of the sophomore year work. Majoring in electrical engineering, he earned eight A's and one B during his first year. Another student skipped grades 7, 9, 10, 12, and 13 and completed the baccalaureate degree a few days after his seventeenth birthday. Very high mathematical reasoning ability, high interest in mathematics, taking advanced classes with intellectual peers who may be years older, being tutored by an older talented youth and tutoring a younger one, and a great deal of self-motivated homework contribute to the very rapid progress of these youth. Stanley (1977) presents strong arguments supporting two or more years of acceleration prior to high school graduation by highly talented students. He concludes that enrichment, without any acceleration, will be injurious to the educational development of the brilliant student.

5.27 Why is there increasing reluctance to label children as being in a particular classification of exceptional children?

5.28 Return to the ten categories of exceptional children. Select those which you think are most easy to identify and those which are most difficult to identify. What do you use as the basis for making your judgments?

5.29 Return to the classification of exceptional characteristics of children. Which of the characteristics are most easy to indentify?

5.30 What is the role of the special education teacher and the regular classroom teacher in the instruction of exceptional children with handicapping conditions?

5.31 Return to the behavior modification approach to teaching children with handicapping conditions. Why is a preservice program in special education required to prepare teachers to carry out this approach?

5.32 Indicate difficulties that accompany mainstreaming exceptional children with handicapping conditions.

5.33 Indicate characteristics of a student who is gifted in (a) convergent production in an academic area, (b) divergent production in an academic area, (c) a performing art, (d) a motor area.

5.34 Some school districts use highly selective criteria and thereby identify only a small percentage of the student body as gifted, whereas other districts are much less selective. Give the pros and cons of each approach.

5.35 Evaluate Renzulli's enrichment triad model in terms of its ease of use by regular classroom teachers.

5.36 Review and Application. Recall the most important information about each of the following concepts and identify at least one possible use of the information by you as a learner, a teacher, or both:

Range of Human Differences
Differences Among Individuals
    Intellectual Abilities
    Styles of Learning
    Educational Achievements

SUMMARY

Human beings have many common needs and characteristics, but they also are different in many ways. Students of the same chronological age vary widely in general intellectual ability, primary mental abilities, and specific intellectual abilities. Differences among students in their learning abilities, styles of learning, strategies of learning, interests, and motives result in very great differences in their educational achievements. Some normally developing, rapid-learning grade 3 children achieve as high as normally developing, slow-learning grade 12 students. Moreover, a student typically does not achieve at the same level in different subject fields, such as mathematics, science, reading, foreign languages, and typing. It is not uncommon to find students who are in the upper one-fourth of their grade in one primary mental ability, such as mathematical reasoning, and in the lower one-fourth in another ability, such as word fluency or perceptual speed.

The difference in the average scores or ratings of groups of persons, such as boys and girls, social class groups, and racial and ethnic groups, is found to vary from one study to the next. Even the direction of the difference is often not the same. The age of the students at the time the study is conducted, the measures used, and the location of the study seem to be related to the results obtained. However, more studies than not report girls to be higher in verbal abilities and boys to be higher in mathematics, spatial ability, and aggressiveness. The average performance of middle social-class students is higher than that of lower social class students. The average IQ score and the average educational achievements of black school children of the same school district tend to be lower than those of whites. However, the difference in the average performance of any two groups, such as boys and girls, is very small in comparison with the wide range in the performances of the highest and lowest individuals of each group.

The relative effects of heredity and environment on each individual's development and on differences between groups have not been established with precision and accuracy. Some scholars indicate a greater impact of heredity, while others indicate a greater impact of environment. A generally accepted scientific view is that heredity and environment are in continual interaction, and the precise contribution of each cannot be determined.

Children who are considerably above or below the average of their age-group in a characteristic or behavior are designated exceptional children. However, most special education programs today are for those who are below average. There is a recent shift from labeling exceptional children mentally retarded, hyperactive, gifted, or in other terms. Instead, the behaviors are being classified, for example, deficits in specified abilities or skills, excessive behaviors in particular areas, and acceleration in learning or creativity.

Many teachers of children with learning handicaps follow behavior modification techniques based on conditioning principles and use a diagnostic-prescriptive model of instruction. However, cognitive learning principles have been employed more frequently in recent years. Children and youth with high learning and creative capabilities are offered enrichment, acceleration, or a combination of enrichment and acceleration. Mainstreaming children with learning handicaps and gifted children is generally followed, rather than placing them in special classes and special schools for all their instruction. We shall see in chap. 6 that many different approaches are used in attempting to provide for differences among students.

SUGGESTIONS FOR FURTHER READING
Dunn, R. Can students identify their own learning styles? *Educational Leadership,* 1983, *40*(5), 60–62.

Dunn, who was instrumental in conceptualizing learning styles and also in constructing a learning style inventory, indicates that most high school students can reliably identify their own learning styles. She also reports research that shows that student outcomes, including achievement and attitudes, are better when teachers take into account each student's learning style.

Dunn, R., & Dunn, K. *Teaching students through their individual learning styles. A practical approach.* Reston, Va.: Reston Publishing Co., 1978.

These authors describe 36 learning styles. Suggestions are given for designing instructional spaces and using materials and methods to take into account the different learning styles.

Farley, F. H., & Gordon, N. J. (Eds.). *Psychology and education: The state of the union.* Berkeley, Calif.: McCutchan, 1981.

Relevant chapters of this book are chap. 1, "Basic Process Individual Differences: A Biologically Based Theory of Individualization for Cognitive, Affective, and Creative Outcomes" by F. H. Farley; chap. 2, "Dimensions of Individual Differences" by T. J. Shuell; and chap. 3, "Adaptation to Individual Differences" by S. Tobias.

Fenstermacher, G. D., & Goodlad, J. I. *Individual differences and the common curriculum* (Eighty-second yearbook of the National Society for the Study of Education. Part I). Chicago: University of Chicago Press, 1983.

Four chapters describe the psychological, sociological, biological, and legal bases of individual variation, and five chapters outline both common curriculum for all students and provisions for individual differences in mathematics, natural sciences, language and literature, aesthetics and fine arts, and social studies.

Khatena, J. *Educational psychology of the gifted.* New York: Wiley, 1982.

A textbook that explains the nature of giftedness and describes means of identifying, guiding, and educating the gifted.

Khatena, J. What schooling for the gifted? *Gifted Child Quarterly,* 1983, *27*(2), 51–56.

Khatena describes four main provisions for the gifted: accelerative enrichment, the learning of intellectual processes, individualized education, and curricular programs and special projects. A comprehensive reference list is provided.

Maker, J. C. *Teaching models in education of the gifted.* Rockville, Md.: Aspen Systems Corp., 1982.

Explains the meaning of teaching models and presents ten models for educating the gifted: Bloom and Krathwohl, Bruner, Guilford, Kohlberg, Parnes, Renzulli, Taba, Taylor, Treffinger, and Williams.

Minton, H. L., & Schneider, F. W. *Differential psychology.* Monterey, Calif.: Brooks/Cole, 1980.

Differences among individuals in intelligence, achievement, special aptitudes, and personality are discussed. Sex, age, social class, and racial differences are also indicated.

Peterson, P. L. Individual differences. In H. E. Mitzel, J. H. Best, & W. Rabinowitz (Eds.), *Encyclopedia of educational research* (5th ed., Vol. 2). New York: The Free Press, 1982.

Dimensions of individual differences are identified. Considerable attention is given to the aptitude-treatment approach to providing for differences. Other areas of interest in this encyclopedia regarding individual differences are "Gifted Persons" by J. S. Renzulli and J. R. Delisle, "Handicapped Individuals" by M. C. Reynolds, "Learning Disabilities" by P. D. Weener and G. M. Senf, "Mental Retardation" by A. E. Blackhurst and R. B. Lewis, and "Special Education" by E. L. Meyen and R. Altman.

Reynolds, M. C. Classification of students with handicaps. In E. W. Gordon (Ed.), *Review of research in education* (Vol. 11). Washington, D.C.: American Educational Research Association, 1984, pp. 63–92.

A scholarly but highly readable presentation of current classification practices and suggestions for far-reaching changes. Of particular interest to "special education" and "regular classroom" teachers.

Stanley, J. C., George, W. C., & Solano, C. H. (Eds.). *The gifted and the creative: A fifty-year perspective*. Baltimore, Md.: The Johns Hopkins University Press, 1977.

This book has chapters reporting major studies of giftedness and creativity, starting with Terman's longitudinal studies of genius. The rationale and early results of Stanley's longitudinal study of mathematically talented youth that started in 1971 are presented in chaps. 5 and 6.

Sternberg, R. J., & Detterman, D. K. (Eds.). *How and how much can intelligence be increased?* Norwood, N.J.: Ablex Publishing Corporation, 1982.

Various authors report studies in which IQ scores or specific cognitive processes and skills, including self-management skills and reading comprehension, have been increased.

Webb, N. M. Sex differences in interaction and achievement in cooperative small groups. *Journal of Educational Psychology*, 1984, *76*, 33–44.

Differences between males and females in interactions and achievement were identified when the proportion of males and females in the group was not equal.

Ysseldyke, J. E., & Aigozzine, B. *Introduction to special education*. Boston: Houghton Mifflin, 1984.

An introductory textbook that presents definitions of various types of exceptionality, assessment procedures, and instructional methods.

CHAPTER 6

INSTRUCTIONAL THEORY, TECHNOLOGY, AND LEADERSHIP

MODELS OF INSTRUCTION AND SCHOOLING

INSTRUCTIONAL MEDIA AND INSTRUCTIONAL PROCESSES

USES OF COMPUTERS

INSTRUCTIONAL LEADERSHIP

Many educational psychologists are conducting research in schools to identify and test the applications of psychological theory empirically and also to extend knowledge regarding instruction and schooling. The results of this kind of research are represented in models, or mini-theories, of instruction and schooling. In general, the models focus on the improvement of education. The more important of these recent models are presented in the first part of this chapter.

Technology provides many opportunities for improving instruction. Media of instruction, such as movies, filmstrips, and books, have played an important role in instruction for many decades. These and other media are making it possible to accommodate the learning styles of students more effectively. Television has a powerful influence on student learning, and the effects of TV viewing outside school are negative as well as positive. Relating TV viewing to in-school learning is an increasingly important task. Microcomputers pose another significant challenge for instruction. Instructional media and computers are dealt with in the second and third parts of the chapter.

The potential benefits of any theory or technology to students rest on intelligent instructional leadership by teachers. Instructional leadership takes two directions. One is guiding the learning activities of students, and the other is managing teacher-student and student-student interactions in the classroom. Instructional leadership is discussed in the last part of the chapter.

MODELS OF INSTRUCTION AND SCHOOLING

Five models of instruction have emerged in recent decades. A form of schooling has also been started as an alternative to the conventional one-teacher classroom with its age-graded curriculum and class-size instruction. Two of the models of instruction, mastery learning and academic learning time, function within the conventional pattern of the one-teacher classroom and instruction of the class as a group. They do not require departure from age-grading of the curriculum. Three others, Adaptive Environments for Learning, Project PLAN, and open education also function in the one-teacher classroom, but require departing from the age-graded curriculum so that students are able to learn at their individual rates. Since the conventional pattern is the most common today, we shall examine it first to establish a referent for the five instructional models and the alternative form of schooling, Individually Guided Education.

In the typical school today, students are assigned to grades on the basis of their age. They are taught by one teacher in classes of 20 to 100 or more. The content of instruction is more similar than dissimilar for all the students in the class.

Students in some schools are assigned to classes so that each classroom group is representative of the student body of their grade in abilities, interests, ethnic and racial origin, sex, and other characteristics. Teachers in these classes typically enrich instruction in breadth and in depth for rapid learners and provide extra time and assistance to the slower learners.

Means of providing for differences among students other than by enrichment and extra time and help, while still maintaining the one-teacher, classroom-group pattern, emerged earlier in this century and persist today. In some schools, rapid learners are accelerated by one or more semesters, and slower learners are retained in a grade for one or more semesters. Separate classes and separate schools are organized for selected groups of students. Putting students of high, average, and low mental ability in different curricula of the secondary school, for example, college preparatory, general, and vocational, is still practiced.

In the conventional pattern, students are not expected to achieve at the same level. Letter grades, or other ratings that range from high to low, are used to indicate the different levels of achievement that the students attain.

Mastery Learning

The major objective of mastery learning is that all the students of a class master the same content. This is not a new idea. Washburne (1922) and Morrison (1926) developed mastery learning plans and implemented them in school settings. Their plans included arranging courses into instructional units, testing the students to identify who had achieved mastery at the end of each unit, advancing those who had achieved mastery, and giving remedial instruction to those who had not. Mastery learning was taught in methods courses for teachers and used in many schools during the 1930s. However, it was not practiced much thereafter until recently.

Carroll (1963) proposed that students can master educational tasks if the amount of time to learn and the instructional methods are varied appropriately for individual students. Thus, some students can master the same task more quickly than others following the usual classroom methods. Other students need more time as well as different methods.

Bloom (1968, 1976) used Carroll's ideas as a basis for his model of mastery learning. He argued that large numbers of students are not achieving well in conventional schools because they are not given sufficient time to learn, do not receive appropriate instruction, or both. As a result, many students are frustrated, their academic self-concepts are poor, and much of the teacher's and student's time is wasted. Many persons agree with these propositions. However, not everyone agrees with Bloom's idea that if teachers use the mastery learning approach properly differences in the amount that students learn will virtually be eliminated. For example, Arlin and Webster (1983) found that slow learners took about two and one-half times longer to achieve mastery than fast learners and that this ratio did not decrease across time. They concluded that the teacher, to give the slower students sufficient time to reach mastery, must hold back the fast learners. Anderson and Jones (1981) recognized this fact and recommended that the faster learners be provided enrichment activities.

STEPS IN IMPLEMENTING BLOOM'S MASTERY LEARNING MODEL

1. Organize a course into instructional units with clearly stated objectives for each unit.
2. Construct tests or rating scales to assess student mastery of each objective and set a criterion of mastery, for example, 90% correct on the test or a rating of 9 on a 10-point scale.
3. Use regular materials and methods to teach the class.
4. Administer a test to identify the students who have and have not achieved the objectives at the mastery level.
5. Provide corrective instruction to the students on the objectives not mastered, including giving them additional time; possibly retest them to ensure mastery. Provide enrichment activities for the students who have mastered the objectives.
6. Start all students in the next unit of instruction at the same time.

The age-graded, one-teacher classroom arrangement and teacher-directed, whole-class instruction are easily maintained by implementing Bloom's model. Students achieve the same course objectives and proceed through the age-graded curriculum at essentially the same rate. This model appeals to teaching for minimum competency in mathematics, reading, writing, and other language arts in schools where one or more of the following conditions prevail: the achievement of the majority of the students in the class is low; class size is large; many students transfer in and out of the school each year; and the teachers do not have the time, materials, skills, or other resources to adapt instruction well to differences among students in rate of learning. Elementary schools of some of our large American cities and schools in some undeveloped nations use the model extensively.

Academic Learning Time

Carroll's and Bloom's ideas on mastery learning have been incorporated in a model of instruction that focuses on the amount of time the student spends on academic learning (Fisher, Berliner, Filby, Marliave, Cahen, & Dishaw, 1980). The major objectives of this model are to get the students to spend all of the time allocated for instruction in active learning of the assigned tasks and to achieve the instructional objectives at a mastery level. Figure 6.1 depicts the model.

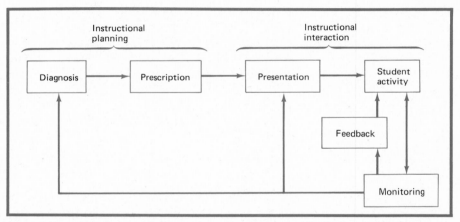

Figure 6.1 Instructional functions in the academic learning time model of classroom instruction.
Source: Fisher, Berliner, Filby, Marliave, Cahen, & Dishaw, 1980, p. 10.

The model of academic learning time is very similar to mastery learning. The difference is the focus on use of time rather than on mastery of objectives. To implement the model of academic learning time, each course is organized into smaller units of instruction that have clearly stated objectives. Before starting a unit, each student's achievement level is assessed, and related learning activities are prescribed. During the instructional sequence, the teacher uses appropriate methods to teach the subject matter of the unit. Student progress is assessed and monitored throughout the instructional sequence, not merely at the end of the unit. Students receive feedback on a daily basis during the instructional sequence, and corrective actions are taken with the students who have difficulty achieving the objectives. An attempt is made to get every student to use effectively all the time in learning that is allocated for instruction in the academic subject fields. Teacher-directed instruction of the class as a group is the primary instructional mode (Rosenshine, 1979).

The original research on academic learning time was done in one-teacher elementary classrooms in mathematics and in reading. A synthesis of the main findings follows (Fisher et al., 1980, pp. 19–22):

**RESEARCH RESULTS ON
ACADEMIC LEARNING TIME**

ACADEMIC LEARNING TIME AND STUDENT ACHIEVEMENT
The more time that teachers allocate to instruction in a particular curriculum content area, the higher the achievement in that content area.
The higher the proportion of the allocated time that students are actively engaged in learning, the higher the achievement.
The higher the proportion of time that reading or mathematics tasks are performed with high success, the higher the achievement.
An increase in the amount of time allocated to reading or math is not associated with an increase in negative attitudes toward the subject or school.

INSTRUCTIONAL PROCESSES AND CLASSROOM ENVIRONMENT
The teacher's accuracy in diagnosing student skill levels and in prescribing appropriate learning tasks is positively related to student achievement.
Substantive interaction between the student and teacher is positively related to active student participation.
Academic feedback to the student, structuring lessons, giving clear directions, and emphasizing academic goals are positively associated with student achievement.
A learning environment characterized by student responsibility for academic work and by cooperation is associated with higher achievement.

The model of academic learning time can be applied so that students not only start at appropriate points in the curricular sequence but also proceed at different rates in mastering the content of a field. When this application is made, the model is very similar to some aspects of individualized instruction, to be considered next.

Adaptive Environments for Learning

Adaptive Environments for Learning (Glaser, 1977) emerged from an earlier program started in 1964 called Individually Prescribed Instruction (IPI). The major objective of the first version of IPI in 1964 was to adapt instruction in each subject field to the rate at which each student achieved the objectives of the particular subject field (Glaser & Rosner, 1975). Mastery of objectives was required to proceed from one unit to the next. All the students achieved the same objectives in a subject field, such as math or reading, by completing essentially the same assignments, but at different speeds appropriate to the individual student. Thus, no two children of a class necessarily worked on the same objectives in math or any other subject on the same day. In a later version of IPI, teachers started giving some small-group instruction, and small groups of children worked together to achieve the same objectives. More recently, variations have been made in the instructional activities of students, and students take considerable initiative for monitoring their own progress and selecting learning activities from those that are suggested to them (Glaser, 1977). However, the essential content of each subject field that all students are to learn is still organized into a hierarchy of learning objectives that all students are to master.

The initial instructional model of IPI is depicted in Figure 6.2.

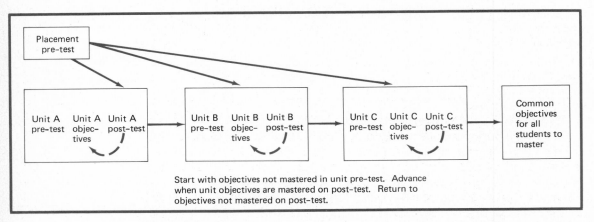

Figure 6.2 IPI model: common objectives, single activity path, individual progression based on mastery of objectives.

In IPI, the printed instructional materials and tests for each subject field are purchased by the schools and are thus available to the students and teachers who use the IPI program. The student takes a placement test and starts in the proper unit, regardless of grade in school. The student's role after being placed is to use the instructional materials and to select and carry out learning activities from the ones given. Students monitor their progress through the units by self-testing.

The primary roles of the teacher are those of a program manager and helper of individual students. The teacher makes sure that the placement testing, pretesting, posttesting, and prescription of each student's learning activities are carried out in accordance with IPI guidelines. Keeping a record of each student's mastery of objectives is another managerial activity. Clerical aides help the children and the teacher with record keeping, materials distribution, and testing. The teacher also helps individual students and may tutor individuals and teach small groups of children. In IPI, these activities are regarded as truly professional, whereas the IPI program developer, not the teacher, takes initiative for determining the content of instruction, the objectives of instruction, the materials of instruction, and the construction of the tests.

In adaptive learning, the IPI model of pretest, teach, posttest depicted in Figure 6.2 is still being followed for the objectives that all students are to master. In attaining these objectives, children are using microcomputers and are becoming competent in selecting suitable learning activities, self-testing, and self-regulation of their own learning activities. Also, in the most recent version of adaptive education, provisions are being made for elective objectives, more group instruction, and a greater variety of instructional materials. Accordingly, the learning environment is being adapted more completely to meet the educational needs of individual students.

Project PLAN

A program for learning in accordance with needs (PLAN) was developed in the 1960s (Flanagan, Shanner, Brudner, & Marker, 1975). Its major objective is to enable students to master objectives at their individual rates. It is like IPI with respect to placement testing, pretesting, post-testing, and short units of instruction with instructional objectives. However, it differs in several important ways.

First, record keeping, the scoring of the tests, and recommendations for subsequent learning activities based on the student's posttest score are done by a computer outside the school. Second, the student's textbooks and similar instructional materials are not part of PLAN. Instead, PLAN has learning guides, called Teaching-Learning Units, that are placed in the hands of the students. The Teaching-Learning Unit gives the unit objectives, lists alternative activities to achieve the objectives, and designates the textbooks and materials already available in the school to be used in completing the activities. Third, many PLAN activities are individual, but some are also for pairs, small groups, and large groups. Fourth, review of material and review of tests are systematically included in the Teaching-Learning Units. The student uses these for self-assessment of progress. Fifth, PLAN provides alternative sets of activities for different students to achieve the same objectives. The idea of alternative paths is depicted in Figure 6.3.

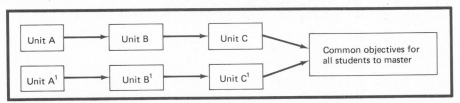

Figure 6.3 PLAN model: common objectives, alternate activity paths, individual rate of progression.

PLAN, in comparison with the first version of IPI, calls for considerably more instructional initiative and responsibility by the teacher. However, teachers who use only the PLAN Teaching-Learning Units, as those who use only IPI materials, do not share in determining the content or the objectives of their own instruction. PLAN invites teachers to delete, substitute, and add. However, when teachers do so, additional costs are involved for computer scoring and record keeping, or the teachers must do it themselves.

We have seen that two of the preceding models, mastery learning and academic learning time, call for much class-size group instruction, while Adaptive Environments for Learning and Project PLAN call for a considerable amount of one-to-one instruction. On the other hand, a common characteristic of all four models is that the objectives of instruction as well as the related instructional content are heavily determined by persons external to the school. Open education takes a very different tack.

Open Education

Open education is not the same as *open-space schooling*. Open-space schooling is an architectural plan designed to reduce building costs. Open-space schools have large spaces where hundreds of students receive most of their instruction throughout the school day. The conventional approach to education may be carried out in open-space schools as well as any innovative approach. However, open education profits from having large spaces that can accommodate 60 to 125 students, classrooms that can accommodate 20 to 40 students, small rooms for 2 to 8 students, and individual study carrels.

Open education (Walberg, 1975) has several characteristics. First, the student and the teacher together determine the learning goals, materials, and activities. Many different instructional materials are used, including those prepared by the students. Many learning activities are suggested and organized by the students. The students take initiative for arranging themselves in pairs and small groups. Talking among the students and freedom of movement are common. As much or more emphasis is placed on the student's emotional and social development as on academic learning.

The teacher's role is to respond sensitively to each student as an individual, to guide each student's total development as a person as well as a learner, and to structure the learning environment in such a way that it contributes to the student's development. The open classroom is not chaotic or disorderly, but neither is it quiet or highly structured.

Lindner and Purdom (1975) indicate that open education may be of high, medium, or low openness. In high openness, the children take much initiative for determining what they will learn and how they will proceed in their learning activities. In medium openness, the teacher and children discuss the desired learning outcomes and the activities that will be undertaken to achieve the outcomes. Accordingly, neither the outcomes nor the learning activities are determined before the teachers and children meet. However, after talking with the children, the teacher may specify both the outcomes and the activities for each child. In low openness, the teacher takes even more initiative for specifying the learning activities and desired outcomes.

Regardless of the degree of openness, there are not predetermined, identical learning outcomes for all students to achieve at the same rate. Moreover, when some students do work toward achieving the same learning outcomes, there are two or more different activity paths for attaining it, and there may be a different path for each student. The idea of varied learning outcomes and multiple activity paths is depicted in Figure 6.4.

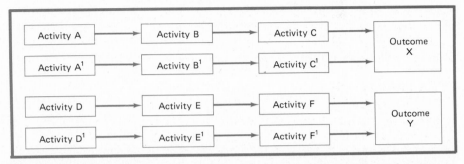

Figure 6.4 Open education model: varied outcomes, multiple activity paths, individual rate of progression.

Peterson (1979b) analyzed the results of 45 studies of open education, in which the degree of openness was not specified, and of traditional education, in which the teacher instructed the class as a group and the students worked toward achieving the same objectives. The student outcomes that Peterson found in three or more studies favoring open education and the student outcomes found in three or more studies favoring traditional education follow:

Outcomes favoring open education
Higher creativity, more favorable self-concepts, more favorable attitudes toward school, an internal locus of control, lower anxiety, and more independence.

Outcomes favoring traditional education
Higher achievement in mathematics and in reading.

Horwitz (1979) found somewhat higher educational achievement from open education than reported by Peterson, while Rosenshine (1979) reported higher achievement from directed instruction, such as occurs when the models of mastery learning and academic learning time are implemented.

Giaconia and Hedges (1982) studied only open schools. They found open-education schools that were effective in producing high creativity, positive self-concepts, and favorable attitudes toward school had four main features: emphasis on the role of the child in determining learning activities, use of diagnostic rather than norm-referenced tests, individualized instruction, and the use of manipulative materials. These four features of open schools did not produce high student achievement. To the contrary, open education schools in general were found not to be effective in producing high student achievement.

Individually Guided Education

Experience is showing that there are limitations to what one teacher can do in meeting individual students' needs in age-graded classes. Departure from this traditional approach is necessary to enable teachers to function more effectively individually and also as members of a teaching group. Individually Guided Education (IGE) was started in the 1960s and represents a major departure from conventional schooling.

IGE is a form of schooling, not a model of instruction to be implemented in a traditional school. It was developed at the elementary school level, starting in the 1960s (Klausmeier, 1975, 1977), and some features of it were adapted to the secondary school level (Klausmeier, Lipham, & Daresh, 1983). In IGE, teachers exercise a more significant role in instructional leadership in the classroom than in any other approach to education. Moreoever, IGE extends the teacher's role to advising students and to planning the educational program of the school with the school principal.

The primary aim of IGE is to arrange a complete educational program of courses and other educational activities each semester for each student. This program takes into account a student's capability for learning particular subject matter, motivational pattern, interests, and learning styles. Such a complete educational program for each student is not implemented in traditional schools today. Planning and carrying out an educational program with each student each semester involves two other changes from traditional schooling.

First, new administrative arrangements are worked out that enable teachers and counselors to engage in cooperative planning and shared decision making with the principal. At least one decision-making group is formed in the school that includes the principal and representative teachers, counselors, and, in some instances, students and parents. This arrangement enables the teachers and other persons to work with the principal in planning the school's educational programs and activities that they are responsible for carrying out.

Second, through grade 9 or 10 the teachers and students are organized into instructional and advisory groups. Each instructional and advisory group consists of 50 to 150 students and a cooperative team of two to five teachers. Each team carries out instruction in the academic subjects for the students of the unit, and each teacher of the team also advises some of the students of the unit about educational and other matters. Teachers of art, music, physical education, and similar subject fields are also organized into teams. These teachers offer instruction in their subject fields and serve as advisors to students.

A team of teachers having the same students for a considerable period of time during the day permits much flexibility in using time, materials, and space to arrange the best possible instruction for the students in the subject fields taught by the teachers of the team. When each teacher of the team also serves as an advisor to some of the students of the group, the teacher-advisor is aware of the progress and problems experienced by the advisees in the classes of all the team members. Furthermore, close and continuing contact is established between the advisor and the parents of the advisees.

Arranging the Individual
Educational Program of Each Student

In IGE elementary schools, a complete educational program in various curriculum areas is planned each semester by the student and the student's advisor. In secondary schools, a complete program of courses and other educational activities, such as intramural sports and out-of-school work experience, is planned each semester by the student and the student's advisor. The educational program lists the student's courses and other activities and indicates the student's main goals in each. The relationship of the student's characteristics to his or her complete educational program is shown in Figure 6.5.

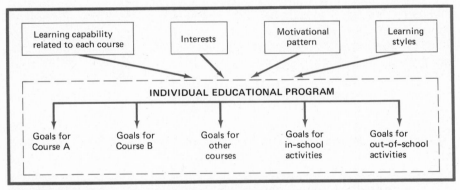

Figure 6.5 Individual educational program based on student characteristics.

As students move to successively higher levels of schooling, the differences in their individual educational programs increase. Fewer courses are required of all students, and there are more elective courses. The number of in-school activities and out-of-school activities that are supervised by the school also increases.

In developing an individual educational plan with a student, the advisor meets with the individual student before the semester begins to work out a tentative educational plan. The tentative plan lists each course, study period, cocurricular activity, and community activity—including work—for the ensuing semester. Early in the semester, the advisor again confers with the student. In this conference, the plan is prepared in written form. The plan includes the student's goals for each course and other educational activities.

Why do models of instruction in general call for adapting instruction to the educational needs and other characteristics of the individual student?

The goals are directly related to the objectives that have been established for the courses. (See Chapter 2 for a discussion of course objectives.) The student and the advisor get a copy of the student's educational plan, and it is used during the semester by the student and teachers in monitoring the student's progress.

The student's educational program is evaluated during and toward the end of the semester in terms of how well the student achieves the goals and in terms of other criteria, such as the appropriateness of each course for the student. The evaluation procedures and criteria are described in Chapter 16 of this book.

Arranging an Appropriate
Instructional Program for Each Student

For the student to have an appropriate total *educational* program, an appropriate *instructional* program must be arranged for the student in each course of the educational program. The nature of the student's instructional program varies from one course to another, depending upon the pattern of instruction followed in the particular courses. Different from the instructional models described earlier in this chapter, four patterns are possible, and the school selects which pattern to follow in each curricular area or course. The patterns are described briefly, and then guidelines for planning and implementing each student's instructional program are outlined.

Patterns for Arranging Individual Instructional Programs

Each student's instructional program in any given course is related to whether or not all the learning outcomes of the course are required of all the students and whether or not the criterion for achieving the outcomes is mastery. As in open education, alternative learning activities are provided for students to achieve the same learning outcome.

Based on the preceding considerations, four patterns of instructional programs may be arranged for individual students in their various courses (see Figure 6.6). The staff of a school, taking into account the needs and characteristics of the students, decides which of these patterns is best for each course. Depending upon the decision made, the student may have a somewhat different instructional program in each elementary curricular area or high school course.

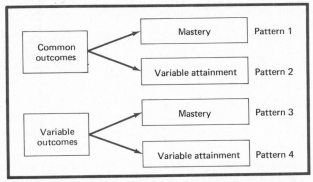

Figure 6.6 Patterns of outcomes and criteria of attainment in instructional programming for the individual student.
Source: Klausmeier, 1977, p. 61.

1. **Common outcomes, mastery criterion.** In this pattern, every individual student's program in a given course or curricular area includes the same outcomes. In addition, every student is required to achieve the outcomes to a mastery criterion. Differences in the rates at which students master the units of the course or curricular area are taken into account in three ways. First, some students complete more units than others during the same time period, such as a semester. Second, all students complete the same number of units during the semester, but they spend different amounts of time during the semester in completing the units. Third, all students complete the same number of units during the semester, but they engage in different amounts of in-depth and in-breadth enrichment activity.

2. Common outcomes, variable attainment. In this pattern, every student's instructional program includes the same outcomes. However, the students attain the outcomes to a level of achievement judged by the teacher to be adequate for each student. Therefore, any student proceeds to the next unit of instruction in the sequence if the teacher judges the student's achievement to be adequate. Rapid learners may complete more units than slower learners during a given time period, but usually complete the same number of units and engage in enrichment activities. Slower learners typically proceed through the units according to the same time schedule as other students, but master fewer outcomes.

3. Variable outcomes, mastery criterion. In this pattern, any given student's program may possibly have outcomes different from those of every other student. Typically, however, there is a core of required outcomes to be mastered by every student, and there are also some variable or elective objectives suited to each student. The outcomes included in each student's program must be achieved to a predetermined mastery level.

4. Variable outcomes, variable attainment. In this pattern, as in Pattern 3, not all students' programs include the same outcomes. However, mastery of the unit outcomes is not required of any student. This pattern also differs from Pattern 3 in that students assume much responsibility for deciding what they will learn, when they will complete the work, and how well they will achieve.

We may relate these four patterns to the models presented earlier. Individually Prescribed Instruction, Project PLAN, mastery learning, and academic learning time follow Pattern 1. Open education may follow Pattern 3 or 4, depending upon the amount of openness. In Individually Guided Education, each local elementary and secondary school staff, taking into account school district and state guidelines, has the responsibility for determining which pattern it will follow in each subject field. In IGE elementary schools, either Pattern 1 or Pattern 2 is typically followed in mathematics, reading, and spelling. Either Pattern 2 or 4 is followed in social studies, while either Pattern 3 or 4 is used in art, music, and physical education. Note, however, that any IGE school may depart from these typical patterns.

The Instructional Programming Process

A five-step sequence for arranging an instructional program for the individual student is shown in Figure 6.7. The applications of the sequence vary for different school levels and subject fields, as noted in the discussion of the four patterns.

The five steps of individual instructional programming may be elaborated as follows:

1. Preassess each student's entering achievement level, learning styles, and motivational pattern. Assessing the entering achievement level of the students is necessary when first arranging instruction to take into account the readiness of each student to learn. It is not necessary after the students

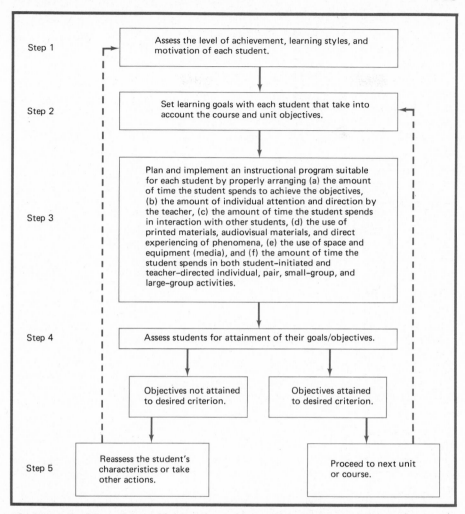

Step 1 — Assess the level of achievement, learning styles, and motivation of each student.

Step 2 — Set learning goals with each student that take into account the course and unit objectives.

Step 3 — Plan and implement an instructional program suitable for each student by properly arranging (a) the amount of time the student spends to achieve the objectives, (b) the amount of individual attention and direction by the teacher, (c) the amount of time the student spends in interaction with other students, (d) the use of printed materials, audiovisual materials, and direct experiencing of phenomena, (e) the use of space and equipment (media), and (f) the amount of time the student spends in both student–initiated and teacher–directed individual, pair, small–group, and large–group activities.

Step 4 — Assess students for attainment of their goals/objectives.

Objectives not attained to desired criterion.

Objectives attained to desired criterion.

Step 5 — Reassess the student's characteristics or take other actions.

Proceed to next unit or course.

Figure 6.7 IGE model: multiple goals, multiple activity paths, multiple criteria for progression.

have completed a first unit of instruction, since the information from the preceding unit serves this purpose. Ordinarily, only achievement testing is done before instruction begins. Learning styles, motivation, and other characteristics of the students are identified from the child's cumulative folder, or by the teacher's observations after instruction begins.

2. Set goals with each student based on the assessment. The goal that the student sets is based upon the course objectives. The objectives that the student has not yet achieved to a desired level are included in the students' goal and are used in developing the instructional plan of the student.

3. Plan and implement an instructional program in the course to enable the student to achieve the goals/objectives. This step applies when an attempt is made in the course to take into account the student's expected rate of achieving the objectives, learning styles, motivation, and other characteristics. The teacher proceeds differently with students, as a number of examples indicate.

First, more time for learning is given to the slower students than to the faster students to achieve the same goal/objective. Second, a self-motivated student is given less teacher attention and direction than an unmotivated one. Third, students who do not learn from studying by themselves spend more time in pairs or small groups interacting with other students. Fourth, the use of printed materials, audiovisual materials, and direct experiencing to learn the same content is varied to accommodate the different learning styles and interests of the students. Fifth, space and related equipment, such as the classroom itself, the instructional materials center, and the laboratory, are adapted to the different learning goals, interests, and conduct of the students. Sixth, the amount of time spent by each student in teacher-directed individual, pair, small-group, and large-group activity is varied. Similarly, time for student-initiated activities is varied. A combination of individual student activity, small-group activity, teacher-led small-group instruction, and teacher-led whole-class instruction appears to be necessary in most elementary curricular areas and high school courses. Moreover, students require a considerable amount of teacher explanation, guidance, and monitoring when abstract concepts and principles are introduced.

4. Assess each student's learning progress and achievement of goals/ objectives. This kind of assessment is essential for every unit and course. It is done during the course or unit to ensure student progress and at the end of each unit and course to determine students' achievement of their goals/ objectives.

5. If the goals/objectives are achieved to the desired level, the student proceeds to the next unit; if the goals are not attained, the teacher determines why and takes actions that are appropriate. This step is necessary only when the student must meet a minimum criterion to move on to the next unit or the next course. When the minimum criterion is mastery, the actions that are taken with early achievers and late achievers depend upon the options that are available. The early achievers may proceed to the next unit of instruction, engage in enrichment activities related to the current unit, proceed to a unit in another strand of the same curricular area, or proceed to a unit of a different curricular area. The late achiever may continue to work on the same unit, proceed to the next unit in the sequence and come back to the present one later, proceed to the next unit and try to achieve the objectives of both units simultaneously, or cease working on the particular unit temporarily.

Some schools provide these and other options for early and late achievers. However, in most schools, this amount of flexibility is not provided. Early achievers start each of the successive units at the same time as the other students. However, upon completing a unit early, they work on one or more advanced units related to the course that most students do not pursue during the semester or year, engage in enrichment activities in depth or in breadth related to the unit, or engage in independent study or other activities that may not be directly related to the unit or course. Late achievers are given more time in and out of class to achieve their goals. They set lower goals, or they proceed from one unit to the next, even though their goals are not achieved fully.

Aptitude/Treatment Interactions

Cronbach and Snow (1977) outlined a general framework, *aptitude/ treatment interactions,* for relating instructional methods to the characteristics of students. They define an *aptitude* as any characteristic of a learner that correlates positively with an outcome of learning. For example, the student's entering achievement level, learning style, intellectual ability, and motivational state are all regarded as aptitudes for learning. *Treatments* include any approach to education or instruction that is related to student outcomes of learning. The goal of research on aptitude/treatment interactions is to identify the treatments that are best for students of particular aptitudes. Individual educational programming and individual instructional programming, as indicated earlier, are educational approaches in which the aptitudes of learners are identified and the educational activities suited to each learner's aptitudes are arranged.

Progress in identifying aptitude/treatment interactions is being made but at a slow rate. For example, through experiments of short duration, students of high and low ability, high and low anxiety, and high and low achievement motivation were found to achieve differently when instruction was structured by the teacher than when structured by the students (Peterson, 1977; Peterson, 1979a). However, the results of these two studies were only partially replicated in a later study (Peterson, Janicki, & Swing, 1980).

Clark (1982) found that low-ability students like a permissive instructional method whereas high-ability students like a more structured method. The low-ability students believe that the permissive method allows them to maintain a low profile, while the high-ability students believe that the structured method makes their efforts more efficient. In general, however, low- and high-ability students achieve higher under the opposite methods—more structured for low achievers and less structured for high achievers. Accordingly, the interaction between ability level and liking of instructional method in some studies results in a negative correlation between preference for method and achievement.

Snow (1980) concluded that providing education that takes into account each learner's aptitudes is desirable and that aptitude/treatment research is designed to contribute to this approach. He indicates that no one approach to instruction will be effective for all students in all settings.

6.1 Compare mastery learning, academic learning time, Individually Prescribed Instruction, Project PLAN, and open education in terms of (a) use of placement tests, (b) common objectives for all students or different objectives for some students, (c) single or multiple learning paths to achieve the same objective, (d) student mastery of objectives or proceeding to the next unit without being required to achieve mastery, (e) student achievement of objectives at the same rate or at different rates, (f) individual student activity or whole-class instruction.

6.2 Why might open education, in contrast to Bloom's mastery learning, result in more student independence and creativity, but lower educational achievement?

6.3 Why is Individually Guided Education (IGE), in contrast to academic learning time or open education, considered to be a form of schooling rather than a model of instruction?

6.4 Describe how well your total program of courses and other educational activities in high school for any given year took into account your capability for learning the various subjects and your interests, career goals, and learning styles.

6.5 In IGE, any one of four different patterns of instructional programming may be followed in various subject fields rather than the same pattern in all subject fields. Indicate the pattern that you think should be followed in an elementary school in (a) reading, (b) mathematics, (c) social studies, and (d) art. Explain.

6.6 Compare the model of instructional programming in IGE with the model of instruction in academic learning time.

6.7 Arrange the following from highest to lowest in terms of the amount of effort required of the teacher to carry out its provisions effectively: mastery learning, traditional teaching, open education, IGE. Give reasons for your ranking.

6.8 How well can provisions be made for aptitude/treatment interactions in each of the approaches listed in the preceding question? Explain.

Matching Media and Learning Styles

Relating Sensory Modalities to Strategies of Learning

Relating Students' TV Viewing to In-School Learning

INSTRUCTIONAL MEDIA AND INSTRUCTIONAL PROCESSES

New media of instruction are continually being introduced into the instructional process. A powerful teaching procedure is to match the medium to student characteristics, such as learning style. However, habitual use of a given medium, such as television, apparently interferes with developing other learning skills such as those required for effective reading or listening (Seibert & Ullmer, 1982). Wise use of media in school, and instruction of students regarding their use of media, particularly television, are of high concern to educators.

Matching Media and Learning Styles

As we saw in Chaper 5, students typically prefer to acquire information by one sensory modality rather than by another. This preference becomes more fixed as age increases. Similarly, some students prefer to learn individually, whereas others prefer to learn as a member of a pair or a small group of peers.

Let us assume that students are to learn the process of metamorphosis (Met) of the butterfly in one class and the structural relations of the legislative, executive, and judicial branches of the federal government (Gov) in another class. Assume also that each student is identified as (1) having a preference for learning either by seeing or listening, (2) being either high or low in reading achievement, (3) being either high or low in conceptualizing ability, and (4) preferring either independent study or small-group study and discussion. Recognize, too, that sound motion pictures are excellent for showing processes and movements, such as metamorphosis, while still pictures and filmstrips work well for showing static relationships, such as government structures.

Figure 6.8 shows four students with different combinations of characteristics and indicates the media to be used with each student in learning

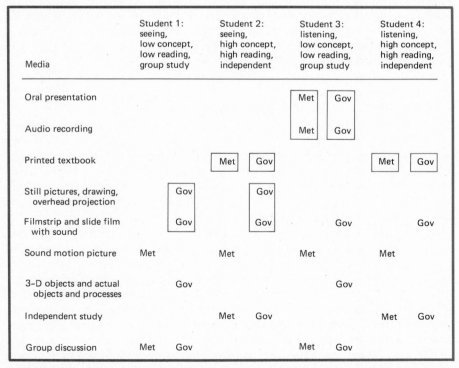

Figure 6.8 Matching student characteristics, media, and two learning outcomes: metamorphosis (Met) and government (Gov).

the concepts of metamorphosis (Met) and government (Gov). Boxes connecting two media indicate that both of the media may be equally appropriate. Study the figure carefully to see how the students, media, and outcomes are matched. Notice, for example, that the student who has a preference for seeing and for small-group discussion and is low in conceptual development and in reading can learn the concept of metamorphosis by seeing one or more sound motion pictures and engaging in group discussions.

A few generalizations can be drawn from the information in Figure 6.8. First, there are media potentially available for all kinds of learners, even the partially hearing and partially seeing who are sometimes enrolled in regular classes. Second, the audiovisual media appear to meet a greater variety of combinations of student characteristics and learning outcomes than any other single medium. This generalization, however, must be tempered by the fact that printed materials are more generally available at lower cost, as are the verbal-only and visual-only media. Third, sound motion pictures convey movement and change better than any other medium to teach process concepts such as *metamorphosis,* while graphic means can be used to show static and structural relationships better and at a lower cost than movies. Fourth, not being able to read material independently, to learn by listening, or to study independently seriously impedes the learner, since other media are usually not available except for limited and prescribed times during school hours. Moreover, the student does not develop important learning skills related to reading, listening, and independent study.

Relating Sensory
Modalities to Strategies of Learning

Salomon (1979) indicates that there is a direct relationship between the learning strategies that students develop and the media by which they acquire information. For example, students who do not learn to read materials and to listen to oral presentations also do not learn the mental skills associated with reading and listening. Salomon's conclusion is especially critical, in view of the widespread TV viewing and small amount of reading and listening done by many students.

Kerns (1981) found support for Salomon's ideas in a study conducted with grade 6 and grade 10 students. She presented the same information to the grade 6 students in a film with a sound track (bisensory modality of seeing and hearing), in an audiotape (unisensory modality of hearing), and in a visual track without sound (unisensory modality of seeing). The grade 10 students received these same versions. The grade 10 students who saw the sound film and heard the sound track recalled more information than did those who received the information by either of the two unisensory modalities; however, the grade 6 students did not. On the other hand, the students of both grades who received either of the unisensory formats produced more creative responses than did those who saw and heard the sound film.

Kerns (1981) provided two possible explanations for the better recall from viewing and hearing the sound film by the grade 10 students. First, integration of the sensory modalities increases with age. Accordingly, the grade 10 students learned better from seeing and hearing the film than did the grade 6 students. Second, increased exposure to TV and films retards students' ability to acquire and remember information by a unisensory modality such as seeing, listening, or reading. The fact that creative production was lower from viewing and hearing the sound film suggests that it did not stir the imagination. Kerns does not propose to eliminate films and TV. Instead, she suggests that after a film or TV presentation is seen, the teacher should follow up with discussion or writing activity to encourage creative production. In a follow-up of her study, Kerns found that students who first saw and heard the film and then saw the visual part without the sound track wrote excellent creative responses.

Relating Students' TV
Viewing to In-School Learning

In recent decades, TV viewing outside the school appears to have more influence on student learning and conduct than does instructional TV in the school. TV viewing outside the school will probably continue to increase, while TV instruction in school will probably decrease for two reasons. First, cable television is greatly increasing the number of commercial and instructional programs received in the home. Second, computerized games and educational programs for use with home television receivers are also increasing.

Some commercial television presents wholesome entertainment and useful information. Other programs produce undesirable effects. Either way, the effects are powerful on individual students. Regardless of the quality or content of the program, students "imitate, learn, remember, believe, and are affected by what they see on television" (Gordon, 1979, p. 60).

Undesirable Effects of TV Viewing

Violence and aggression are learned by some children and youth by watching TV. The basis for this learning is readily explained by observational learning theory (Bandura, 1977) as outlined in Chapter 4 of this book. According to this theory, children and youth view violence and aggression in cartoons and other TV programs, and they see these aggressive behaviors having desirable consequences for the heroes and heroines whom they admire. Subsequently, the children carry out the aggressive actions to achieve the same desired consequences for themselves.

There is a great deal of empirical evidence to support this theory. For example, Stein and Friedrich (1972) randomly assigned preschool children to three types of programming: (1) antisocial (*Batman* and *Superman* cartoons), (2) neutral (children's travelogue films), and (3) prosocial (*Mister Rogers' Neighborhood*). Children were observed for nine weeks while engaged in their daily nursery school activities: two weeks prior to viewing the TV programs, four weeks while viewing the programs, and three weeks of follow-up. Children became significantly more aggressive (i.e., shoving, pushing, breaking toys, etc.) after viewing *Batman* and *Superman* cartoons. Conversely, children who viewed *Mister Rogers' Neighborhood* became significantly more cooperative (helping others, sharing toys, etc.).

Early in the 1970s, Liebert, Neale, and Davidson (1973) reviewed the available research on TV and aggression and concluded:

> There is, then, a remarkable degree of convergence among all of the types of evidence that have been sought to relate violence viewing and aggressive behavior in the young: laboratory studies, correlational field studies, and naturalistic experiments all show that exposure to television can, and often does, make viewers significantly more aggressive as assessed by a great variety of indices, measures, and meanings of aggression . . . it is not television per se but only some of its present offerings that appear to have this effect. (p. 87)

Eron (1982) confirmed the prior conclusions regarding TV and aggression and also found a circular effect: television violence increases children's aggression and as children become more aggressive, they watch more television and also more violent television. Moreover, children who identify with aggressive characters and who believe that television accurately portrays life are more prone to aggressiveness than other children. Eron, Huesmann, Brice, Fischer, and Mermelstein (1983), through a three-year longitudinal study, showed that age 8-9 is a highly sensitive period during which the effects of television viewing can be especially influential on children's behavior. However, throughout the years from grade 1 through grade 5, television viewing has a cumulative effect on behavior.

In addition to increasing aggression, TV viewing affects the rate of cognitive development of some students negatively. For example, Hornik (1978) found that TV viewing, when first introduced on a widespread basis in El Salvador, had a negative effect on reading achievement and on the development of general intellectual ability during the junior high school years. The TV viewing replaced the students' participation in more stimulating intellectual activities, such as reading and interacting with people and the immediate environment. It thereby resulted in slower cognitive development.

Busch (1978) related TV viewing to reading in students of grades 2–12 in the schools of two counties in Virginia. Eighty-six percent of the third-graders preferred TV viewing to reading and watched TV about 35 hours per week. There was a slight drop in the amount of TV viewing in grades 4–6, but also a very sharp drop in parental guidance of TV viewing. Furthermore, during grades 4–6, reading achievement dropped, and lack of reading skills became obvious. TV viewing peaked in grades 7 and 8 for middle- and high-ability students, averaging about 38 hours per week. Low-ability students, however, turned even more to TV in grades 7 and 8, and 95% of them indicated that they got most of their information from TV, scarcely any from reading. In grades 9–12, high-ability students viewed TV less than they did during grades 7 and 8, whereas low-ability students with poor reading and comprehension skills continued their TV viewing. Busch (1978) concluded that TV has a very undesirable effect on the reading habits of many students, particularly the students of lower ability whose parents do not guide their TV viewing.

To clarify more specifically how TV influences cognitive development, Meringoff (1980) studied primary school children's assimilation of a story. The story was either read to an individual child who simultaneously viewed an illustrated book, or it was presented individually as a TV film. The TV group recalled more story actions and relied more on visual content for drawing inferences about story events and characters. The read-to group recalled more story vocabulary and based inferences on text content, general knowledge, and personal experiences. Thus, possible consequences of much TV viewing, even of the best programs, are that the child may develop a strong visual memory but become increasingly deficient in listening skills and in applying self-generated knowledge to reading comprehension.

Williams, Haertel, Haertel, and Walberg (1982) synthesized the available research on educational achievement and leisure-time television viewing. They concluded that the effects of television viewing up to 10 hours a week are slightly positive, but beyond 10 hours the effects are negative and increasingly more deleterious until viewing time reaches 35 to 40 hours. Beyond 35 to 40 hours, additional viewing has little effect. Another interesting conclusion was that the achievement of females and high IQ children was affected more adversely than other groups. Comstock (1982) also found an increase in television viewing to be accompanied with lower achievement in reading, mathematics, and written expression. This conclusion holds for all social classes; however, children of the lower social class view television more than those of the middle and upper social classes.

TV affects children's learning and personal development undesirably in another way. When either the children, the parents, or both are watching TV, they are not communicating ideas, feelings, and values to one another. For this reason alone, parents and educators must seriously question the wisdom of present arrangements that turn over so much responsibility for socialization of the young to an automated electronic device. Bronfenbrenner (1970) states the case well:

> And even when the parent is at home, a compelling force cuts off communication and response among the family members. Although television could, if used creatively, enrich the activities of children and families, it now only undermines them. Like the sorcerer of old, the television set casts its magic spell, freezing speech and action and turning the living into silent statues so long as the enchantment lasts. The primary danger of the television screen lies not so much in the behavior it produces

as the behavior it prevents—the talks, the games, the family festivities and arguments through which much of the child's learning takes place and his character is formed. Turning on the television set can turn off the process that transforms children into people. (p. xiv)

Positive Effects of TV Viewing

Having pointed out some negative aspects of excessive television viewing on some students, we can also identify programs with proven desirable effects such as *Sesame Street,* the *Electric Company, Mister Rogers' Neighborhood,* and *Captain Kangaroo.* The developers of these programs try to combine the most recent knowledge about learning, development, and instruction with television artistry and technology (Lesser, 1976; Palmer, 1976).

The same principles on which *Sesame Street* is based can profitably be followed in instructing children in the school:

INSTRUCTIONAL PRINCIPLES IN SESAME STREET

1. Children learn by observing and imitating; therefore, the behaviors and values to be learned by them are modeled by admired persons and television characters of different ethnic origins, sexes, and racial groups.
2. Children are easily distracted; therefore, each program focuses sharply on only a few learning outcomes.
3. Words and pictures are used to support one another, not to cancel out or interfere with one another.
4. The instruction is entertaining—fun for children and many adults.
5. Direct methods are used to teach each desired cognitive skill and item of knowledge; indirect methods are used to teach the social values of kindness, courtesy, respect for racial differences, respect for both sexes, modes of conflict resolution, justice, fair play (the models manifest these but don't verbalize them).
6. The best of human behavior is presented in interactions characterized by decency, consideration, kindness, and altruism; the unpleasant, harsh realities of the world are shown as a means of teaching conflict resolution, not as desirable forms of behavior to be observed and imitated.

Relatively little recent research has been done to identify the positive effects of instructional TV. However, earlier research by Chu and Schramm (1968) showed TV instruction in the schools to be as effective as conventional instruction in producing academic achievement. Ball and Bogatz (1970) found that watching *Sesame Street* had favorable effects on the cognitive development of 3-, 4-, and 5-year-olds. Diaz-Guerrero and Holtzman (1974) found similar effects when the program was redesigned and presented in Spanish to Mexican preschoolers. The results of their research are shown in Figure 6.9.

Liebert (1975) found positive effects of children's programs that depict prosocial behaviors of the kind mentioned earlier in connection with *Sesame Street.* In sum, many children are acquiring prosocial behavior and academic

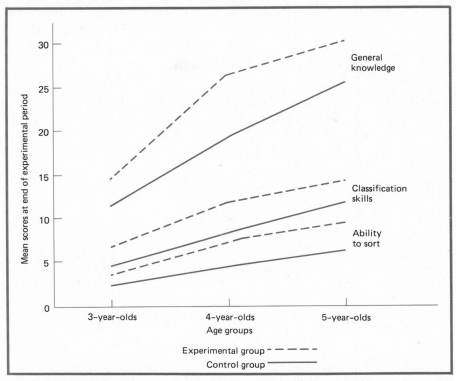

Figure 6.9 Mean scores of an experimental group of Mexican children who saw televised programs of *Plaza Sesamo* for six months and of a control group who saw noneducational television programs for the same period.
Source: Diaz-Guerrero & Holtzman, 1974.

learning from viewing educational TV that is programmed to achieve these purposes.

Guidance of TV Viewing

Gordon (1979) outlines what parents and teachers can do to ensure that TV viewing is educational. His suggestions assume that both commercial and educational TV will continue to be popular among students of school age.

He has four clear guidelines for parents. First, actively watch with the children. Second, set limits on the amount of viewing and the specific programs viewed. Third, develop criteria for evaluating the programs with the children. Fourth, send letters to the networks and to local stations, including cable TV, to influence their programming practices.

Gordon's ideas for teachers are equally succinct. First, view and discuss TV programs in class. Second, refer to programs for students to view, and discuss programs they have viewed. Third, use TV as an aid to reading and other areas of instruction by having students read or study about what they view. Fourth, be creative by relating significant educational TV programs to class work and to the personal and social development of students.

6.9 Harry prefers to learn by listening, is high in reading achievement, is high in conceptualizing ability, and prefers to study alone. Recommend media and instructional arrangements for Harry in a social studies class. Give reasons for your recommendations.

6.10 Nancy views TV a great deal, reads very little, and interacts very little with other students on academic matters. Indicate how these characteristics may influence her development of learning-to-learn skills.

6.11 Research shows many undesirable effects of TV viewing on children and youth. Indicate what parents might do so that children's TV viewing would have more positive and less negative effects.

6.12 Six instructional principles are used in developing the *Sesame Street* programs. Which of the principles do you think will be easiest for a teacher to carry out? Most difficult?

6.13 A national parent group rates TV programs in terms of their probable undesirable and desirable effects on children and youth and publishes its listing. Do you approve or disapprove of this kind of parental activity? Explain.

6.14 Gordon gives four suggestions to teachers for use of TV in class. What effects will carrying out these suggestions have on TV viewing by elementary school children? By high school students?

Administrative Record Keeping

Information Dissemination

Managing Instruction

Computer-assisted Learning

USES OF COMPUTERS

Computers are used in four main ways to facilitate learning and teaching: administrative record keeping, information dissemination, managing instruction, and teaching-learning devices. Illustrations of the first two uses and a more complete discussion of the last two follow.

Administrative Record Keeping

Waring (1981) describes the use of a microcomputer in a high school that has high student turnover. The computer records student attendance and tardiness and develops daily class lists. The information is used to increase attendance, reduce tardiness, and ensure that classes are neither too small nor too large as new students enroll in the school and others leave. The cumulative record kept by the computer is used in some cases for counseling with parents and students. The amount of record keeping and paperwork by counselors and teachers is greatly reduced.

Information Dissemination

A computerized, nationwide information system that reports results of research and other information has been set up specifically for educators. It is known as the Educational Resources Information Center (ERIC) (U.S. Government Printing Office, 1968). Persons in many locations, including local school district offices and universities, indicate on a terminal the topic about which information is desired. Sitting in the same room, they receive almost immediately a printout of pertinent titles of articles and books on the topic and an abstract of each item. Many teachers and principals use the ERIC services provided by their school district to get the most recent information regarding innovative educational practices. There may be a small charge for this service by the school district or university.

Managing Instruction

The computer performs three main functions in the management of instruction. First, it receives and stores the essential information about each instructional program that is managed by computer. For example, in computer-managed reading instruction, the computer stores the complete list of reading objectives, the list of materials and activities to achieve each objective, and in some cases the test items for each objective. Second, the computer is programmed to keep track of each student's progress on each objective. Typically, how the student achieves on each objective is inputted to the computer, based on either the teacher's judgment or a test score. At any time, the teacher can call on the computer to identify which objectives a student has and has not attempted and which the student has and has not achieved to the desired criterion. The teacher can also call on the computer to indicate all the students who are ready to start work toward any given objective or unit of instruction. Finally, the computer may be programmed to recommend instructional actions to be taken with either individual students or groups of students.

From the preceding overview, it should be clear that someone must know exactly what kind of information is to be stored in the computer and how it is to be used. The complete instructional program, including tests or other measurement procedures, must first be developed. This is called the *courseware*. Someone must also program the computer to carry out the desired storage and retrieval, including the instructional recommendations. This is called the *software*. Considerable time and effort are required to develop the courseware and software for a curricular area at one school level, such as elementary school reading.

The first widely used computer management system was PLAN (Flanagan, Shanner, Brudner, & Marker, 1975), described earlier in this chapter. PLAN has one large computer center in Iowa. Each local school using PLAN has a terminal to send and receive information by long-distance telephone.

Microcomputers located in each school building are replacing large computers outside the school building in the computer management of instruction. This arrangement enables each school staff to devise and control its own educational programs, courseware, and software and to get desired information from the computer immediately rather than by telephone. Grady and Gawronski (1983) prepared easy-to-read guidelines to aid a local school staff in selecting and using microcomputers for managing instruction and other purposes.

Computer-assisted Learning

In computer-assisted learning (CAL), the individual student interacts with the computer. Until recently CAL has not moved ahead rapidly in the schools, because the schools have had neither the computers and related equipment (hardware) nor the personnel to produce the computer course material (courseware) and to write the computer programs to guide the computer-student interactions (software). Microcomputers will undoubtedly solve the hardware problem and make easier the development of courseware and software. However, there is uncertainty about CAL because of the revolution occurring in computer hardware. Therefore, only the objectives of CAL and a brief summary of the current scene follow.

Objectives of Computer-assisted Learning

The low cost of microcomputers has put them within reach of many individuals as well as local schools. This very recent availability of low-cost microcomputers for personal use is recognized in current objectives of CAL.

Moursund (1979) identified the three major objectives of CAL in the schools. The first objective is to enable students to achieve a level of computer literacy commensurate with their level of education and also with their interest area in education. Thus, a student interested in math or science in high school requires either a higher or a different level of computer literacy than another student interested in art or English. Moursund proposes that schools include computer literacy as an educational objective for all students. Dearborn (1983) describes the functioning computer literacy program of the schools of Alexandria, Virginia. The program extends from kindergarten through grade 8. It calls for the student to learn to use the computer as a tool in the instructional process, to solve problems, and in word processing.

The second objective is to provide appropriate learning opportunities for students needing knowledge and skills in the use of the computer above the literacy level (Moursund, 1979). Complete high school courses in computer technology or units of instruction on computers in other subjects are needed to achieve this objective. As one example, Washington High School in Milwaukee, Wisconsin, has a career specialty curriculum that provides for students with three different interests in computers: those who plan to enter computer-related jobs upon high school graduation, those who intend to go to technical schools, and those who intend to go to college and major in computer science (Klausmeier, Lipham, & Daresh, 1983).

The third objective is to use computers in the teaching-learning process whenever it is educationally and economically sound (Moursund, 1979). Computerized instructional programs, appropriate instructional spaces, and computers are required to achieve this objective.

Six main problems in achieving the preceding objectives have been identified by Moursund (1979, p. 33). They are a lack of "(a) sufficient and adequate computer hardware, (b) appropriate software, (c) appropriate courseware that replaces books, course outlines, etc., (d) adequately trained teachers, (e) adequately trained school administrators, (f) adequate support from school boards, parents, and taxpayers."

Many of these problems are being resolved in Minnesota by a state educational computer consortium that was formed in 1974 (Rawitsch, 1981). The State Department of Education of Minnesota, the universities, and many local schools are consortium members. The major obstacle to solving all the problems is funding (Rawitsch, 1981).

Kulik, Bangert, and Williams (1983) summarized the research on computer-assisted learning, most of which preceded computer-assisted learning by microcomputers. They concluded that computer-assisted learning decreased the amount of time required for learning and increased student achievement on final examinations by a relatively small but consistent amount. However, the positive effects were larger for studies carried out for short periods of time than for long periods, and for disadvantaged and low aptitude students than for talented students. Better results are expected when more effective learning programs become available with the use of microcomputers (Kulik, 1983). Hall (1982), after analyzing research, theory, and practice, concluded that even though the implications of microcomputers for teaching and learning are not understood well, many persons believe microcomputers offer tremendous opportunities for improving education.

Forms of Computer-assisted Learning

There are many ways to describe the uses of computers as aids to learning in the schools. Bork and Franklin (1979), Suppes (1980), and Kulik, Bangert, and Williams (1983) have identified the main uses.

Drill and Practice

Practice is essential for learning the basic skills. Computerized instructional programs are available in mathematics and reading and enable students to practice these skills by interacting with the computer. They are used mainly with elementary school children assigned to remedial programs (Suppes, 1980). In these programs, the computer is regarded as replacing a tireless, enthusiastic human tutor who guides the practice of specific skills for 10 to 20 minutes daily until mastery is achieved.

Testing and Learning

Computers may be programmed to administer tests, to diagnose student learning difficulties, and to enable students to self-assess their learning progress (Bork & Franklin, 1979). The student initiates the testing in some cases. In others, the teacher prescribes the test items to which the student responds and which the computer scores. Usually, the computer is programmed to follow up the testing with one or more instructional sequences based on the results of the test. Increasingly, microcomputers are being used to teach students a greater variety of outcomes on an individual one-to-one basis (Hall, 1982).

Simulation

Computers are used to simulate real-world situations and events and thus to teach problem-solving strategies (Bork & Franklin, 1979). Accordingly, when students cannot go outside the school setting to learn to solve problems, the problems are simulated by the computer and brought into the school setting to be solved. Similarly, when a scientific laboratory is not available to the students, experiments are simulated by use of the computer.

6.15 Waring describes how a computer is used in a high school to increase attendance, reduce tardiness, and manage class size. Draw a mental picture of this school in terms of the number of students and their behaviors.

6.16 Find an ERIC terminal at your university and observe the kind of information persons get from it.

6.17 In computer-managed instruction, all of the objectives of the course and the activities or assignments to achieve the objectives are inputted into the computer. Each student's progress related to each course objective is inputted and then stored by the computer. The computer is programmed to provide desired information about the achievements of the individual students and groups of students. Indicate courses or subject fields that you think would be (a) most amenable and (b) least amenable to computer-managed instruction.

6.18 Why do teachers and schools prefer their own microcomputer for managing instruction to a large computer outside the building that serves many schools?

6.19 Imagine that a school calls on you to provide all the information necessary for managing instruction by computer in a course that you teach. What kinds of information would you provide?

6.20 Moursund identified three educational objectives for computer-assisted learning. Which of these objectives has highest priority if not all can be attained by a school?

6.21 Forms of computer-assisted learning include drill and practice, testing and learning, and simulation of real problems. Give an example of how each of these might be helpful to a student. Give the subject matter and grade level.

Guiding Students'
Learning Activities

Classroom Management
and Control

INSTRUCTIONAL LEADERSHIP

The instructional models and technological innovations presented in this chapter imply that effective teaching requires an ever-increasing amount of knowledge and more sophisticated teaching skills or competencies. This same conclusion may be drawn, based on the new and increasing information in the foundation areas presented in Chapters 2, 3, 4, and 5 of this book. Competencies are required in two areas: guiding students' learning activities and classroom management and control.

Guiding Students' Learning Activities

In recent years, serious attempts have been made to identify the minimum competencies that every teacher should be able to demonstrate. Other studies are being conducted to identify the competencies of effective teachers. The results from both kinds of studies merit careful consideration by both prospective and experienced teachers.

Minimum Teaching Competencies

A group of educators in Florida surveyed the research on teaching competencies (Florida Department of Education, 1982). Forty-eight generic competencies were identified. These 48 competencies were then incorporated into a questionnaire to which 5% of all certified personnel in Florida were invited to respond. The 23 competencies that follow met the criteria for inclusion as a competency that every prospective and experienced teacher should be able to demonstrate. Competencies 1–14 include knowledge and skills associated with leadership of learning activities in the cognitive domain, 15–19 include technical skills involved in leadership in the affective domain, and 20–23 include administrative skills required for effective management (Florida Department of Education, 1982, pp. 5–7).

GENERIC TEACHING COMPETENCIES

COMMUNICATION SKILLS
1. Demonstrate the ability to communicate orally information on a given topic in a coherent and logical manner.
2. Demonstrate the ability to write in a logical, easily understood style with appropriate grammar and sentence structure.
3. Demonstrate the ability to comprehend and interpret a message after listening.
4. Demonstrate the ability to read, comprehend, and interpret professional material.

BASIC KNOWLEDGE
5. Demonstrate the ability to add, subtract, multiply, and divide.
6. Demonstrate an awareness of patterns of physical and social development in students.

TECHNICAL SKILLS
7. Diagnose the entry knowledge and/or skill of students for a given set of instructional objectives using diagnostic tests, teacher observations, and student records.
8. Identify long-range goals for a given subject area.
9. Construct and sequence related short-range objectives for a given subject area.

10. Select, adapt, and/or develop instructional materials for a given set of instructional objectives and student learning needs.
11. Select, develop, and sequence related learning activities appropriate for a given set of instructional objectives and student learning needs.
12. Establish rapport with students in the classroom by using verbal and/or visual motivational devices.
13. Present directions for carrying out an instructional activity.
14. Construct or assemble a classroom test to measure student performance according to criteria based upon objectives.

AFFECTIVE DOMAIN
15. Counsel with students both individually and collectively concerning their academic needs.
16. Identify and/or demonstrate behaviors which reflect a feeling for the dignity and worth of other ethnic, cultural, linguistic, and economic groups.
17. Demonstrate instructional and social skills which assist students in developing a positive self-concept.
18. Demonstrate instructional and social skills which assist students in interacting constructively with their peers.
19. Demonstrate teaching skills which assist students in developing their own values, attitudes, and beliefs.

ADMINISTRATIVE SKILLS
20. Establish a set of classroom routines and procedures for utilization of materials and for physical movement.
21. Formulate a standard for student behavior in the classroom.
22. Identify causes of classroom misbehavior and employ a technique(s) for correcting it.
23. Identify and/or develop a system for keeping records of class and individual student progress.

Each of these generic competencies has subskills. A total of 117 have been identified. Three generic competencies and illustrative subskills follow (Florida Department of Education, 1982, pp. 5–7):

GENERIC COMPETENCIES AND SUBCOMPETENCIES

Generic Competency: Demonstrate the ability to orally communicate information on a given topic in a coherent and logical manner.

Subcompetencies
Utilizes principles of simplicity and clarity in organization of oral presentation.
Uses standard English in oral communication.
Uses vocabulary suitable to the topic and audience.

Generic Competency: Demonstrate the ability to add, subtract, multiply, and divide.

Subcompetencies
Adds, subtracts, multiplies, and divides whole numbers, decimals, and fractions.
Demonstrates the meaning and use of fractions and percents.
Represents and interprets data using charts, tables, graphs, and maps.

> **Generic Competency:** Select, adapt, and/or develop instructional materials for a given set of instructional objectives and student learning needs.
>
> **Subcompetencies**
> Determines desirable characteristics of materials based on objectives and student learning needs.
> Locates and evaluates available instructional material.
> Selects materials to assist students in mastering an objective.

These generic competencies and subskills are intended for use in guiding curriculum development in the colleges and universities of Florida that prepare teachers. A minimum competency test for administration to the teachers of Florida has also been constructed. Groups in other states are also involved in studying the minimum competencies desired of teachers.

Effective Teaching Competencies

Rosenshine (1971) reviewed the available research on effective teaching and student achievement of course content. He was able to identify only a few teacher behaviors associated with high student achievement. They included enthusiasm, achievement-oriented and businesslike behavior, well-organized lessons, and clarity of instruction. Further research has been conducted on enthusiasm and clarity of instruction.

Collins (1976, p. 2) identified eight means of expressing enthusiasm:

WAYS TO EXPRESS ENTHUSIASM

1. Rapid, uplifting, varied vocal delivery.
2. Dancing, wide-open eyes.
3. Frequent, demonstrative gestures.
4. Varied, dramatic body movements.
5. Varied, emotive facial expressions.
6. Selection of varied words, especially adjectives.
7. Ready, animated acceptance of ideas and feelings.
8. Exuberant, overall energy level.

Collins (1976) developed a program to teach enthusiasm. Prospective teachers who experienced the program demonstrated more enthusiasm than those who did not. Gillett (1980) used Collins's program in an experiment in which one group of teachers received the program and the other did not. Students of the teachers who received the program were found to be involved in learning 86% of the time, while students of the teachers who did not receive it were involved only 75% of the time.

Clarity of instruction and related teacher behaviors were studied by Cruickshank, Myers, and Moenjak (1975); Bush, Kennedy, and Cruickshank (1977); Land (1979); and Land and Smith (1979a, 1979b). The 32 teacher behaviors identified in these studies follow, with □ based on Cruickshank et al.; △ on Bush et al.; and ○ on Land and on Land and Smith (*Practical Applications of Research*, 1981, p. 3):

WAYS TO MAKE INSTRUCTION CLEAR

1. Explain the work to be done and how to do it. △
2. Ask students before they start work if they know what to do and how to do it. △○
3. Explain something; then stop so that students can think about it. △
4. Take time when explaining. △
5. Orient and prepare students for what is to follow. □○
6. Provide students with standards and rules for satisfactory performance. □
7. Specify content and share overall structure of the lectures with students. ○
8. Help students to organize materials in a meaningful way. □
9. Repeat questions and explanations if students don't understand. △○
10. Repeat and stress directions and difficult points. □○△
11. Encourage and let students ask questions. ○
12. Answer students' questions. △○
13. Provide practice time. □
14. Synthesize ideas and demonstrate real-world relevancy. □
15. Adjust teaching to the learner and the topic. □
16. Teach at a pace appropriate to the topic and students. △
17. Personalize instruction by using many teaching strategies. □
18. Continuously monitor student learning and adjust instructional strategy to the needs of the learner. ○
19. Teach in a related step-by-step manner. □○
20. Use demonstrations. □○
21. Use a variety of teaching materials. □
22. Provide illustrations and examples. □
23. Emphasize the key terms/ideas to be learned. □
24. Consistently review work as it is completed and provide students with feedback or knowledge of results. □
25. Provide an environment in which students are encouraged to process what they are learning. ○
26. Make clear transitions. ○
27. Reduce mazes. ○
28. Avoid vague terms. ○
29. Avoid filler ("uh," "ah," "um"). ○
30. Reduce nonessential content. ○
31. Communicate so that students can understand. □
32. Demonstrate a high degree of verbal fluency. □

These competencies go beyond those identified by Rosenshine (1971). They are related to achieving desired learning outcomes in the affective domain, such as favorable self-concepts and attitudes toward school, as well as to achieving subject-matter knowledge and skills.

We have seen ways of expressing enthusiasm and ways of making instruction clear—two very important techniques for guiding the learning activities of students. An equally important leadership role is gaining and maintaining control of the classroom learning environment.

Classroom Management and Control

Effective classroom management has been studied systematically only in recent times. Kounin (1970) started the modern era of research on it. He identified a number of classroom management competencies associated with high work involvement by students and freedom from deviant disruptive and withdrawal behaviors.

One competency is characterized as *with-it-ness*. Teachers "with it" are alert to student deviant behavior and stop it before it spreads to others or gets serious. A second competency is attending to more than one activity at a time. While working with an individual student or a small group, the teacher also notices what is going on throughout the room. A third competency is referred to as *smoothness* and *momentum*. The teacher keeps the lesson moving at a fast pace and shifts from one activity to another easily without interrupting the lesson or breaking into student activities. Similarly, irrelevant questions or events are not allowed to divert seat work or a teacher presentation. *Group alerting* is a fourth teacher behavior that gets good results. The teacher keeps students attentive and on their toes by questioning, choosing certain ones to recite, signaling for quiet, and similar techniques.

Recently, classroom management has been studied extensively in elementary schools and junior high schools (Emmer & Evertson, 1981; Evertson & Emmer, 1982). The competencies of effective managers have been identified, and manuals have been prepared for elementary school teachers (Evertson, Emmer, Clements, Sanford, Worsham, & Williams, 1981) and for junior high school teachers (Emmer & Evertson, 1980). Each manual lists the areas of management, one or more general prescriptions for each area, and specific guidelines for each prescription. The areas of management and the prescriptions are very similar for the two school levels, but the applications vary considerably. The five areas of management for elementary teachers and the related prescriptions follow (Evertson et al., 1981). You will notice that the prescriptions related to "planning rules and procedures" and "managing student behavior" draw heavily on operant conditioning principles:

CLASSROOM MANAGEMENT AREAS AND RELATED PRESCRIPTIONS FOR THE ELEMENTARY SCHOOL

GETTING THE CLASSROOM READY
Be certain your classroom space and materials are ready for the beginning of the school year. (p. 11)

PLANNING RULES AND PROCEDURES
Decide before the year begins what behaviors are acceptable or unacceptable in your classroom. Then think about what procedures students must follow in order to participate in class activities, to learn, and to function effectively in a school environment. Develop a list of these rules and procedures. (p. 27)

Decide ahead of time the consequences of appropriate and inappropriate behavior in your classroom, and communicate these to your students. Then be sure to follow through consistently when a child behaves appropriately or inappropriately. (p. 57)

PREPARING FOR THE FIRST FEW DAYS OF CLASS

Include in your lesson plan the sequence in which rules or procedures will be taught on each day, when and how they will be taught, and when relearning or practice will occur. Plan to teach those rules and procedures first that are needed first. Teach your rules and procedures systematically. Use (a) explanation, (b) rehearsal, (c) feedback. (p. 67)

Develop activities for the first few days of school that will involve the children readily and maintain a whole-group focus. (p. 73)

Plan strategies to deal with the potential problems that can upset your classroom organization and management. Be especially aware of things that can interfere with your monitoring or otherwise teach students bad habits. (p. 91)

MANAGING STUDENT BEHAVIOR

Monitor student behavior closely. Look for (a) students who do not follow procedures or do not finish or even start assignments, (b) violations of rules or other uncooperative or deviant behavior, (c) appropriate behavior. (p. 103)

Stop inappropriate and disruptive behavior quickly; it won't go away by itself. (p. 107)

IMPROVING INSTRUCTION

Organize instruction to provide learning activities at suitable levels for all students in your class. (p. 113)

Develop procedures that keep the children responsible for their work. (p. 127)

Be clear when you present information and give directions to your students. (p. 137)

6.22 Return to the list of 23 generic minimum teaching competencies. (a) Select the ones that you feel can be mastered by taking courses or studying independently. (b) Select the others that can be achieved only by having teaching experience in a formal or informal setting. (c) Select the competencies that this course in educational psychology can contribute to achieving.

6.23 Collins identified eight means of expressing enthusiasm. Which of them can you readily demonstrate when you desire to? Do actors and actresses learn techniques such as these?

6.24 Return to the list of ways to make instruction clear. Check the ones that your best high school teacher used. Check any that you think are not important or may not help to make instruction more effective.

6.25 Evertson and others identified five areas of classroom management in the elementary classroom and prepared prescriptions to guide teacher behavior related to each area. Check the prescriptions that you think are carried out by elementary school teachers who have few or no discipline problems.

6.26 How do the new models of instruction and education and the advances in communication and technology relate to the competencies required of the modern teacher?

6.27 Some educators propose that the prospective teacher should have a one-year paid internship as a full-time teacher, with supervision by an experienced teacher, before being certificated to teach. Do you agree or disagree with the proposal? Explain.

6.28 Review and Application. Recall the most important information about each of the following concepts and identify at least one possible use of the information by you as a learner, a teacher, or both:

Models of Instruction and Schooling
    Mastery Learning
    Academic Learning Time
    Adaptive Environments for Learning
    Project PLAN
    Open Education
    Individually Guided Education
Instructional Media and Instructional Processes
    Matching Media and Learning Styles
    Relating Sensory Modalities to Strategies of Learning
    Relating Students' TV Viewing to In-School Learning
Uses of Computers
    Administrative Record Keeping
    Information Dissemination
    Managing Instruction
    Computer-assisted Learning
Instructional Leadership
    Guiding Students' Learning Activities
    Classroom Management and Control

SUMMARY

Significant changes are occurring in education and society that require increasing knowledge and more sophisticated skills on the part of teachers. Recent models of instruction represented in mastery learning and academic learning time emphasize student mastery of the same content and teacher-directed, class-size group instruction. Individually Prescribed Instruction and Project PLAN emphasize student mastery of the same objectives but at each student's own individual rate. Open education features student participation in determining learning goals and multiple paths of learning activities to achieve the same goal. Each model has other unique features but all these models may be implemented in one-teacher classes.

Individually Guided Education (IGE) is a comprehensive form of schooling that differs from these instructional models and from conventional schooling in many ways. One objective of IGE is to humanize and personalize education and advising. A second objective is to arrange a complete educational program of courses and other educational activities for each student that takes into account the student's capability for learning particular subject matter, motivational patterns, interests, learning styles, and other characteristics. To achieve these objectives, teachers work as members of instructional teams, advise students, and share planning responsibilities with the school principal. These changed teacher roles and the change from the one-teacher classroom are essential to ensure that each student's instructional program in each course at the secondary level, and in each curriculum area at the elementary school level, has an appropriate amount of both teacher-directed and student-initiated individual, small-group, and class-size group instruction. Time for instruction, materials of instruction, and instructional methods are also adapted appropriately to each student's educational needs. Moreover, in IGE, the pattern of instruction is varied appropriately from one subject field and from one curriculum area to another. The results of research on aptitude/treatment interactions imply that teachers proceeding individually and independently cannot greatly improve instruction beyond what has been accomplished in past decades, because, with their best efforts, they are unable to provide instructional programs suited to the aptitude patterns of their individual students.

Audiovisual materials and other instructional media are being used with increasing flexibility in meeting the different learning styles and learning capabilities of students. The desirable and undesirable impact of TV on student learning and conduct is increasing. It is very probable that the particular learning mode that students use to acquire information, such as reading or TV viewing, is directly related to the life-long strategies of learning that they do and do not develop.

The use of microcomputers may contribute substantially to the improvement of instructional processes. Their possible effects on improving testing and record keeping and their use as teaching-learning devices appear to be positive. Clearly, students in school today should be educated in the use of computers. Computer applications of proven educational effectiveness and economic feasibility merit tryouts in the classroom.

The continuing innovations and the increasing knowledge about learning, development, and individual and group differences call for better preparation of prospective teachers and also extensive in-service education of experienced teachers and other educational personnel. More effective instructional leadership is called for in the guidance of student learning activities and in classroom management and control.

SUGGESTIONS FOR FURTHER READING

Arlin, M. Time variability in mastery learning. *American Educational Research Journal*, 1984, *21,* 103–120.

An investigation of the mastery learning proposition that variability among students in the amount of time required to master new tasks should decrease across time; the proposition was not upheld, indicating a need for revision of the theory.

Charles, C. M. *Elementary classroom management: A handbook for excellence in teaching.* New York: Longman, 1983.

This paperback focuses on management of the physical, social, and academic elements of the classroom. Direct teaching, facilitative teaching, and open education methods are discussed.

Comstock, G. Mass media. In H. E. Mitzel, J. H. Best, & W. Rabinowitz (Eds.), *Encyclopedia of educational research* (5th ed., Vol. 3). New York: The Free Press, 1982.

Most recent research consistently shows an inverse relationship, for all social classes, between the amount of television viewing that students do and their achievement in reading, mathematics, and written expression. However, research also shows that the lower the social class, the greater the amount of viewing.

Duke, D. L. (Ed.). *Helping teachers manage classrooms.* Washington, D.C.: Association for Supervision and Curriculum Development, 1982.

This series of articles written by different authors gives specific suggestions for effective classroom management.

Grady, M. T., & Gawronski, J. D. (Eds.). *Computers in curriculum and instruction.* Washington, D.C.: Association for Supervision and Curriculum Development, 1983.

This short handbook has concisely written selections on choosing computers, using computers, computer literacy for teachers, computer literacy for students, computer uses by subject areas, and the future of computers.

Howe, M. (Ed.). *Learning from television: Psychological and educational research.* New York: Academic Press, 1983.

Up-to-date findings on what children and adults learn from television are presented by leading researchers.

Klausmeier, H. J., Lipham, J. M., & Daresh, J. C. *The renewal and improvement of secondary education: Concepts and practices.* Lanham, Md.: University Press of America, 1983.

These authors present strategies for improving secondary education and describe the organizational arrangements that schools create to implement the strategies.

Klausmeier, H. J., Rossmiller, R., & Saily, M. (Eds.). *Individually guided elementary education: Concepts and practices.* New York: Academic Press, 1978.

Various authors describe the instructional, advisory, and organizational practices of elementary schools that utilize the IGE form of schooling.

Milavsky, J. R., Stipp, H. H., Kessler, R. C., & Rubens, R. S. *Television and aggression: A panel study.* New York: Academic Press, 1982.

This is a report of an extensive study of the effects of television violence on childhood and adolescent aggression.

Peterson, P. L., & Walberg, H. J. (Eds.). *Research on teaching: Concepts, findings, and implications.* Berkeley, Calif.: McCutchan, 1979.

Twelve essays summarize recent thinking and research on the process of teaching. Chapters 2 and 3 present contradictory conclusions regarding the effects of direct large-group instruction. Chapter 5 has a good discussion of emotional climate.

Rubenstein, E. A. Television and behavior: Research conclusions of the 1982 NIMH report and their policy implications. *American Psychologist,* 1983, *38*(7), 820–825.

Presents a summary of research conclusions and implications for national policy. There are five other interesting articles on TV in this issue.

Wang, M. C., and Lindvall, C. M. Individual differences and school learning environments. In E. W. Gordon (Ed.), *Review of research in education* (Vol. 11). Washington, D.C.: American Educational Research Association, 1984, pp. 161–225.

A clear account of the major attempts to provide for individual differences from the early 1900s to the present time.

Weil, M. L., & Murphy, J. Instruction processes. In H. E. Mitzel, J. H. Best, & W. Rabinowitz (Eds.), *Encyclopedia of educational research* (5th ed., Vol. 3). New York: The Free Press, 1982.

Six models of teaching are described: advance organizer, concept attainment, cognitive development, contingency management, self-management, and practice. Other articles pertaining to instruction in this encyclopedia are "Classroom Organization" by J. O. Bolvin, "Computer-based Education" by K. A. Hall, "Individualized Systems of Instruction" by J. A. Kulik, "Instructional Time and Learning" by H. J. Walberg and W. C. Fredrick, "Teacher Effectiveness" by D. M. Medley, and "Teaching Styles" by P. F. Kleine.

PART THREE

PRINCIPLES OF LEARNING AND TEACHING

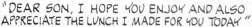

CHAPTER 7

MOTIVATION

EARLY THEORIES OF MOTIVATION

RECENT COGNITIVE THEORIES OF MOTIVATION

KINDS OF INTRINSIC MOTIVES

PRINCIPLES OF CLASSROOM MOTIVATION

Motivation is essential for learning and achievement in all fields of human endeavor. Motivation and educational achievement as reflected in grade point average are positively correlated at all levels of schooling, elementary through college (Uguroglu & Walberg, 1979). High achievement in a subject is associated with high motivation as well as high ability. Lack of motivation is associated with low achievement, regardless of level of ability. Because motivation is essential for attaining any learning outcome, this chapter on motivation is placed first in this part of the book.

Several theories of motivation have been formulated to describe and explain the motivational bases of human activity. Because of the richness and infinite variety of human behavior, there are differences in the theorists' explanations, as we shall see in the first parts of this chapter.

Theories of motivation provide a framework for understanding students' motivation, but understanding is only the beginning. Conducting the teaching-learning situation so that students will be eager to learn and will be well behaved must come next. Principles which aid teachers to achieve this objective are presented in the last part of this chapter.

EARLY THEORIES OF MOTIVATION

Psychoanalytic Theory
Association Theory
Humanistic Theory

There are three families of theories that attempt to describe and explain motivation. Each family is developed from a particular frame of reference and represents a different way of describing and explaining motivation. Therefore, they are not directly relatable to one another. However, each family is regarded by some persons as providing the best explanation of motivation. Our task as teachers is to identify what is applicable to our students and our particular situations.

A chapter or more could be given to each family of theories. The discussion in this chapter is limited to the basic concepts and principles of psychoanalytic, association, and humanistic theory. This is the chronological order in which the theories originated.

Psychoanalytic Theory

Psychoanalytic theory had widespread influence throughout the first half of this century. Some of its original concepts remain powerful today. It is a complex theory involving abnormal as well as normal behavior.

Psychoanalytic theory stems from Freud (1953), who was interested mainly in understanding and treating abnormal behavior. Two motivational concepts of original Freudian theory are homeostasis and hedonism. *Homeostasis* explains the activation, or energizing, of behavior, and *hedonism* describes the direction of activities. Homeostasis refers to the drive toward maintaining a relatively stable internal environment. Thus, when a need is experienced, such as for food, disequilibrium results. Instrumental activity is then directed toward securing food, thereby returning the organism to a state of equilibrium. Hedonism implies that pleasure and avoidance of pain are the primary end products, or goals, of activity. The person in a complete state of equilibrium is a happy person with all needs gratified.

The key energizers and controllers of behavior are the *id, ego,* and *superego.* Their interactions are depicted in Figure 7.1. The *id* is that aspect of personality and behavior governed by the instinctive drives essential for survival. Infant and childhood behavior is energized and directed by the id. The *ego* develops later and enables the individual to deal with reality with conscious awareness, for example, to delay the immediate gratification of thirst or hunger. The *superego* corresponds to conscience. It is the internal

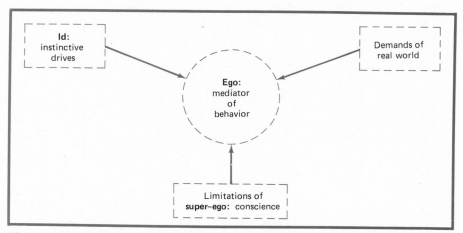

Figure 7.1 Personality-motivation structures in psychoanalytic theory.

mechanism, or value system, that directs the individual to behave in accordance with socially accepted moral behavior and to feel guilty for engaging in socially disapproved behavior.

Another major concept in Freudian theory is *unconscious motivation.* Individuals often do not understand why they behave as they do. Furthermore, in many instances, individuals are incapable of recognizing the true, underlying motives of their behavior. Their ignorance and incapability are explained by *repression,* the mental activity that consigns motives or thoughts to the unconscious as a means of avoiding dealing with them on a conscious level.

Sex and aggression are the two basic, instinctive motivational drives in Freudian theory. Freud regarded both as instinctive because they are essential for the survival of the species. The sexual drive is essential for reproduction. Aggression is essential because the environment cannot support the survival needs of an unlimited number of persons.

Since the sexual and aggressive drives are instinctual, psychoanalytic theory emphasizes early childhood experiences that influence the motivation and personality of individuals throughout their lives. During early childhood, parents typically prohibit a child from freely expressing the id-directed sexual and aggressive drives. As a result of these prohibitions, children repress these drives but retain them at the unconscious level throughout their lives. Behaviors determined by these repressed and unconscious motives are sometimes expressed in a manner destructive to the individual or to society. Thus, many apparently irrational sexual behaviors of children and adults, and also abnormal withdrawal and aggressive behaviors, are explainable only in terms of motives of which the individual is unaware.

It is interesting to note that the overriding concerns of some people today are related to sex and aggression. Monogamous marriage and family life are undergoing great change, inasmuch as immediate sexual gratification is a foremost value in life for many persons. In addition, verbal attack and lawbreaking continue unabated in the fierce struggles for power, prestige, and possessions. Murder, child abuse, rape, and incest are prevalent in American society. The high incidence of these and other destructive behaviors, seemingly related to sex and aggression, suggests why psychologists continue to be highly interested in getting a better understanding of hedonism, sexual drives, aggression, and unconscious motivation.

How is Freudian theory related to educational practice? In our schools today, different from a few decades ago, teachers do not use Freudian theory in attempting to gain a better understanding of the behavior problems of students. However, some school psychologists and some clinical psychologists and psychiatrists in mental health clinics to which students are referred rely heavily on Freudian theory.

Association Theory

Association theory was predominant throughout the first half of the century. It has waned only recently as other theories have become accepted as better explanations. Association theorists explain motivation in terms of stimulus-response relationships. In other words, they emphasize the importance of the environment in determining behavior and correspondingly deemphasize individual choice and determination.

Satisfaction and Annoyance

Edward Lee Thorndike pioneered the psychology of learning in the United States at the beginning of this century. He explained motivation for learning by the *law of effect* (Thorndike, 1898, 1911). According to this law, when a connection between a stimulus and a response is followed by a satisfying state of affairs, such as receiving a reward, the strength of the connection increases. Conversely, when a stimulus-response connection is followed by an annoying state of affairs, such as being punished, the connection is weakened. That is, when the internal connection between the particular stimulus and particular response is strengthened or weakened, the observable response to the stimulus is also strengthened or weakened.

Thorndike later recognized that punishments do not weaken responses as directly as rewards strengthen them. However, he regarded the strengthening and weakening of stimulus-response connections as occurring automatically without conscious awareness or thought.

Needs and Drives

Hull (1943, 1952), another stimulus-response associationist, replaced Thorndike's ideas about satisfaction and discomfort with *need reduction*. He also introduced the motivational concept *drive*. He defined *need* as a state of the organism that requires some kind of action to reduce, or satisfy, it. Because a need usually precedes the action, the need motivates, or drives, the activity undertaken to reduce the need. Hull regarded *drive* as a variable that intervenes between the experiencing of a need and the need-reducing activity, or *response*. The relationship of need and drive to behavior is shown in Figure 7.2. According to Hull, need is an *independent variable* that determines the *intervening variable,* or drive. Drive, combined with other intervening variables, determines behavior. In turn, reduction of the need results in satisfaction and quiescence. To illustrate, a person goes without food for a time and experiences a need for food. Hunger is the associated

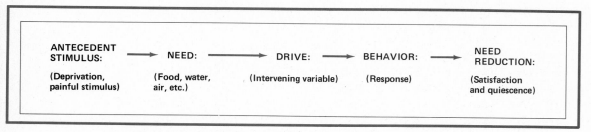

Figure 7.2 Hullian drive theory and motivation.

internal drive. The response is to seek out and eat food. Eating food gratifies the need, eliminates the drive, and is followed with satisfaction and quiescence.

Hull's early conceptualization indicated that drive is based on tissue deficit that results in states such as hunger and thirst. The tissue-based drives are called *primary drives*. Later, he accepted the idea that any internal stimulus that has sufficient intensity, for example, fear of something or desire for an incentive, can energize behavior. These drives are called *secondary,* or *learned drives.*

We observe some correspondence between Freudian and Hullian theory of motivation. According to Freud, behavior is energized by the id; according to Hull, behavior is energized by drive. Both Freud and Hull indicate that action is undertaken to satisfy needs and that satisfaction of needs is satisfying (hedonism).

Deprivation and Reinforcement

We saw in Chapter 4 that the principles of operant conditioning (Skinner, 1953) are based on animal experiments. The key motivational concepts in operant conditioning—*deprivation* and *reinforcement*—are related to operant behavior, as shown in Figure 7.3.

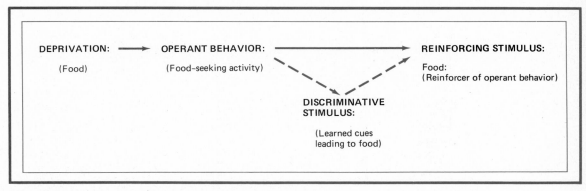

Figure 7.3 Skinnerian reinforcement theory and motivation.

Activation of the organism is related to the amount of its deprivation. Thus, to ensure activation of an animal in an experiment or training session, deprivation is carried out until the animal loses about 20 percent of its weight and becomes very active. *Operant behaviors,* or responses, that lead to a stimulus that alleviates the deprivation are strengthened by reinforcement. For example, a hungry dog jumps for the first time through a hoop to get food. Food is the initial stimulus, and getting the food is the reinforcement for the operant behavior, jumping. A reinforcement following operant behavior increases the probability that the operant behavior will be made again. In other words, the jumping behavior is strengthened each time it is followed by receiving the food. The cue or cues that the dog learns as leading to food become the *discriminative stimulus*. Accordingly, through operant conditioning, the animal trainer is able to provide the cue that will get the dog to jump through the hoop. For example, a movement of the head toward the hoop by the experimenter, but not a movement of the hand, leads to food after the dog jumps through the hoop. Nonreinforcement tends to be accompanied by extinction of a response. Thus, the dog will not continue to jump if it is never given food immediately after jumping.

The removal of a painful stimulus is also reinforcing. Removing the painful stimulus by a behavior strengthens the behavior that leads to the removal. For example, a dog walks at the side of its walker, rather than ahead, tugging at a leash that is rigged to produce pain. Walking at the side is strengthened by removal of the pain caused by the tugging.

Punishment following a behavior has a different effect than the removal of a painful stimulus. Slapping the dog after it moves ahead and tugs at a leash that is not painful is not reinforcing. It only tends to decrease the walking ahead, not to reinforce walking at the side. Accordingly, punishment should not be used, since it does not lead to reliable extinction of the behavior that it follows. Indeed, it may produce undesirable behaviors, such as avoidance and withdrawal. But more important, according to Skinner, positive reinforcers can be used reliably and effectively by an external agent, such as a teacher, to shape the behavior of students in desired directions while punishment cannot.

Operant conditioning is a form of *behavior modification*. Some teachers employ it as their primary means of maintaining classroom order and discipline. Many special education teachers make humanistic applications of Skinnerian principles of operant conditioning when working with students who have learning and behavior disabilities. *Behavior modification* is also carried out with adults in institutional settings, such as psychiatric wards and prisons. It is used in some counseling situations to change the attitudes and emotional states that impede a student's normal development. In general, conditioning principles are not used alone. Rather, modeling the desired behavior, explaining, and reasoning accompany the conditioning techniques.

In modern applications of conditioning, the deprivation of the student's basic needs is increasingly avoided, for example, withholding orange juice from a hungry 5-year-old until a desired response, such as saying a word in a particular way, is made. Stolz, Wienckowski, and Brown (1975) give a thorough account of the professional and legal aspects of behavior modification. They identify behavior modification techniques that deprive persons of their individual rights, as interpreted by the courts, and explain why they should not be used.

We have observed that association theorists emphasize deprivation, needs, drives, rewards, and reinforcement. Thought processes, such as intending, planning, and goal setting, are not used in their explanations of motivation. As we shall now see, humanistic and cognitive theorists emphasize thought processes and individual determination of behavior.

Humanistic Theory

Humanistic psychology is a personal rather than an experimental psychology. It has high intuitive appeal because the individual's normal life experiences are of primary concern. Humanists want behavior to be understood rather than to be controlled or manipulated. Phenomena such as personal choice, creativity, and self-actualization are primary interests.

Maslow (1970) and Rogers (1959) are the main proponents of humanistic psychology. In their view, one of the primary motivational forces is to be self-actualizing, that is, to grow or to be the kind of person in actuality that one is potentially capable of being. The *actualizing tendency* is regarded as an inherited characteristic of the human species. It is a tendency to develop whatever abilities, skills, and feelings one is potentially capable of by inheritance.

Full-functioning, self-actualizing adults are described as being self-aware, creative, open to experience, and self-accepting. Maslow (1970) characterizes the life experiences of these people as "challenging," "exciting," and "meaningful" rather than as "happy" and "satisfied," which are hedonistic terms. Possessing social interest and a democratic value system also characterizes the self-actualizing person.

Deficit and Growth Needs

Maslow (1970) accepts the idea that some human activity is motivated by the gratification of biological needs, but he firmly rejects the proposition that all human motivation can be explained in terms of deprivation, drive, and reinforcement. Instead, he postulates a hierarchy of needs-motives by which higher-order growth needs can control activity only after lower-order deficiency needs are gratified. In line with this idea, he outlined a hierarchy of needs-motives, as shown in Figure 7.4. The needs in the hierarchy are (1) physiological needs, (2) safety needs, (3) love and belonging needs, (4) esteem needs, (5) desires to know and understand, (6) aesthetic needs, and (7) self-actualization needs. The first four are regarded as deficiency motives, and the last three as growth motives.

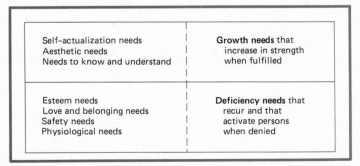

Figure 7.4 Hierarchy and prepotency of needs as a model of human motives. Source: Maslow, 1970.

1. Physiological Needs

Physiological needs include needs for oxygen, liquids, food, and rest (Maslow, 1970). These survival needs are experienced throughout the life span and are gratified on a daily basis. When experienced, they take precedence over other motives.

2. Safety Needs

Safety needs in infants and children are demonstrated by their preference for some kind of routine or rhythm rather than for disorder, by their avoidance of various forms of perceived dangerous situations, and by their withdrawal from strange and unfamiliar situations that elicit terror. Having a satisfying job is a safety need of adults.

3. Love and Belonging Needs

The love need is described as a desire or a hunger for affectionate relations with people in general and for a place in the group. The strength of this need is observed in the person who feels the absence of friends, wife or husband, children, or people more generally. Feelings of loneliness, incompleteness, being unwanted, and isolation indicate a deficiency in fulfilling this need. The child or adult whose love and belonging needs are fulfilled experiences total acceptance in a relationship with another person.

4. Esteem Needs

The need for esteem is the search for recognition as a unique and worthwhile person. Fulfillment of the esteem need is accompanied by feelings of confidence, worth, strength, and usefulness. The thwarting of this need produces feelings of inferiority, negativism, and incompetence.

5. Needs to Know and Understand

This is the first growth need. Maslow was not sure that the desires to know and understand are as clearly manifested in all human beings as are the deficiency needs. Thus, curiosity, exploration, and the desire to acquire further knowledge are more evident in some persons than in others. Where the need is strong, it is accompanied by wanting to systematize, to organize, to analyze, and to look for relationships.

6. Aesthetic Needs

Aesthetic needs, according to Maslow, are the least well understood of all needs. They are present in some individuals only and are inferred from the person's active craving for beauty. Healthy children actively seek beauty.

7. Self-Actualization Needs

The need for self-actualization is the need to be or to become the person one can be. That is, it is the tendency for persons to become in actuality what they are potentially capable of becoming. Satisfaction of this need is expressed in various careers. One person becomes a homemaker, another an athlete, another a musician, another a teacher, and so on. The persons in whom these needs have been relatively well satisfied are the healthiest in our society. Maslow indicates that self-actualization is not realized fully by young people. Young people have not fully achieved identity, personal systems of values, postromantic love relationships, satisfactory careers, and other experiences requisite for complete self-actualization. On the other hand, young people continuously grow toward self-actualization.

Maslow indicates that failure to gratify a deficiency need results in a disturbance, or *dysfunction,* while gratification remedies the dysfunction. In addition, gratification of the need being experienced most strongly at a particular time takes precedence over other needs in determining behavior. Thus, the terrified person seeks safety rather than food or esteem. Furthermore, by the principle of the *prepotency* of the needs hierarchy, continuing to experience a need lower in the hierarchy tends to inhibit behavior to gratify higher needs. For example, the hungry child does not study to gratify the needs to know and understand.

Actualizing Tendency

Rogers (1959) explains human motivation in terms of an *actualizing tendency* as follows:

> This is the inherent tendency of the organism to develop all its capacities in ways which serve to maintain or enhance the organism. It involves not only the tendency to meet what Maslow . . . terms "deficiency needs" for air, food, water, and the like, but also more generalized activities. (p. 196)

Rogers, like Maslow, assumes that self-actualization is inborn, but that it can be impeded by social constraints and unfilled needs. It can also be facilitated through environmental supports of many kinds. Rogers (1963) illustrates his perception of the growth motive and the self-actualizing tendency as follows:

> During a vacation weekend some months ago I was standing on a headland overlooking one of the rugged coves which dot the coastline of northern California. Several large rock outcroppings were at the mouth of the cove, and these received the full force of the great Pacific combers which, beating upon them, broke into mountains of spray before surging into the cliff-lined shore. As I watched the waves breaking over these large rocks in the distance, I noticed with surprise what appeared to be tiny palm trees on the rocks, no more than two or three feet high, taking the pounding of the breakers. Through my binoculars I saw that these were some type of seaweed, with a slender "trunk" topped off with a head of leaves. As one examined a specimen in the interval between the waves it seemed clear that this fragile, erect, top-heavy plant would be utterly crushed and broken by the next breaker. When the wave crunched down upon it, the trunk bent almost flat, the leaves were whipped into a single line by the torrent of water, yet the moment the wave had passed, here was the plant again, erect,

tough, resilient. It seemed incredible that it was able to take this incessant pounding hour after hour, day after night, week after week, perhaps, for all I know, year after year, and all the time nourishing itself, extending its domain, reproducing itself; in short, maintaining and enhancing itself in this position which, in our shorthand, we call growth. Here in this palmlike seaweed was the tenacity of life, the forward thrust of life, the ability to push into an incredibly hostile environment and not only hold its own, but to adapt, develop, become itself. (p. 1)

Humanistic theory has many followers in education. Many teachers use it to identify the ungratified psychological needs of students that may be preventing them from seeking to gratify the growth needs, thereby causing discipline problems, personal problems, or both. Also, self-actualization as a primary human motive is widely accepted. Many of us have no better explanation for the energizing and directing of our own daily activities.

7.1 As explained by Freudian theory, describe behaviors of adults that appear to be directed by the instinctive aggression drive at the id level and by the instinctual sex drive at the id level.

7.2 How is Skinner's explanation of motivation different from that of Thorndike?

7.3 How is Skinner's explanation of reinforcement different from that of Hull?

7.4 Sheila, a high school senior, behaves in the manner of a self-actualizing adult. Describe Sheila's behaviors.

7.5 Explain the difference between deficiency needs and growth needs in terms of how they function as motives.

7.6 Give an example of how each of the following needs functions as a motive in your own life: physiological needs, love and belonging needs, needs to know and understand, aesthetic needs.

7.7 Robert daydreams a great deal and does not spend any class time studying. Would you employ ideas from the theory of Freud, Hull, Skinner, or Maslow to identify the possible causes of Robert's behavior? Which theoretical ideas would you employ to try to change Robert's behavior? Explain.

Self-Control of Activity

Attribution of Causes of Success and Failure

RECENT COGNITIVE THEORIES OF MOTIVATION

How does thinking govern what we do? This question has been addressed only recently, but it is now of high interest to educators and psychologists. The relationship between thought processes and instrumental activities undertaken to achieve goals is one important area of interest. How individuals perceive the causes of their successes and failures and how these perceptions affect subsequent motivation and achievement is a second area (Weiner, 1979, 1980a).

Self-Control of Activity

How is your study of this chapter controlled by you? Miller and Johnson-Laird (1976) employ the theoretical construct *executive control* to account for the self-regulation of mental and motor activity. The control process *intend* is used to indicate the mental operation concerned specifically with the conscious direction of goal-directed activities. The term *plan* is used to indicate any set of internal hierarchical processes that control the order in which a sequence of goal-directed activities is performed. Thus, your intending to learn the material of this chapter directs a sequence of goal-directed activities guided by your plan for reading and studying. This overview of the conscious control of mental and instrumental motor activity is taken as the starting point for the analysis of the self-control of activity that follows.

The human being is an active, information-processing, stimulus-seeking organism, whose thoughts influence action. Thoughts, particularly in the form of intentions, have a powerful effect on the instrumental activities of a behavioral sequence (Klausmeier, 1979). The relationships between thought processes and a goal-directed sequence of instrumental motor activities and inferable mental activities are indicated in Figure 7.5.

We shall examine these relationships in an example (the numbers correspond to the parallel sequence in Figure 7.5).

1. Let us assume that a person is attending to the following situation: while planning a nature walk the person reads that there is poison ivy in the trail area. The person experiences a cognitive incongruence: wanting to take the walk but not wanting to be poisoned. The incongruence influences what the person continues to attend to and the goal the person subsequently sets.

2. Two closely related mental activities follow this incongruence: formulating a goal and intending to achieve it. The goal is to be able to identify poison ivy plants. A goal may take the form of an expectancy. An *expectancy* is an anticipated condition to be achieved, in this case, being able to recognize poison ivy. It may also take the form of an incentive, such as experiencing a feeling of success that accrues from attaining a goal. Persons set many goals in terms of both. After formulating a goal and intending to attain it, the individual either generates a plan for achieving it or retrieves a plan from memory that has been carried out earlier. Intending to carry out the plan is followed with an executive control instruction to start carrying out the instrumental activities to achieve the goal. Let us assume that in our example the plan calls for finding and studying a book to identify poison ivy. The person gets the book and starts studying it.

3. The plan for attaining the goal—studying the book until poison ivy can be identified—is used to test progress toward the goal. The intention and the plan serve to direct and sustain the goal-related activities in that, as long as the plan is not completed and the intention remains, the individual continues the instrumental activities. During this phase of the behavioral sequence, the individual tests the progress being made against the goal-achievement criterion. If the goal is not yet attained, the intention and the

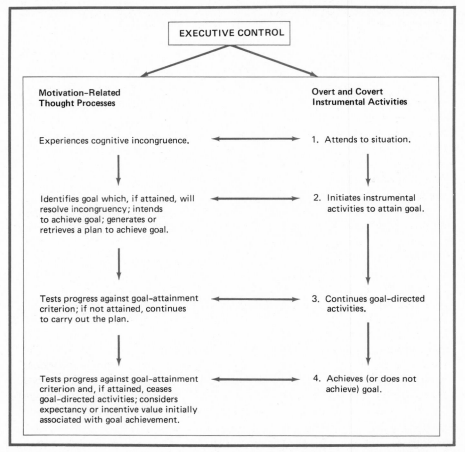

Figure 7.5 Control of instrumental goal-directed activities by motivation-related thought.

plan continue to guide the instrumental activities. In our example, the person studies the book until the criterion of being able to recognize poison ivy is met.

4. Assume that the goal is achieved: the individual has learned to identify poison ivy plants. More thought may result and influence instrumental actions. For example, if the individual feels confident of being able to recognize poison ivy, no ointment or other remedy may be purchased. If the individual is not completely confident, another plan may be generated that starts another behavioral sequence, namely, to purchase the ointment.

Many variables influence the extent to which individuals control their learning and other activities. Variables within the individual include knowledge regarding the task, plans and strategies available for completing the task, and instrumental activities available for completing the task. Thus, a young child's self-control of mental and instrumental activities is very different from an adult's. In addition, the social-psychological environment may or may not facilitate self-control. For example, a restrictive military setting permits far less self-control than school classrooms.

Attribution of Causes of Success and Failure

Weiner (1979, 1980b) formulated attribution theory that includes many powerful ideas about achievement motivation and the motivational effects of experiencing success and failure. His theory of attribution is directed mainly toward understanding how individuals explain the causes of their successes and failures and how their explanations affect their subsequent motivation to achieve. Weiner's theory extends and refines the theory of achievement motivation formulated earlier by Atkinson (1964) and McClelland, Atkinson, Clark, and Lowell (1953). These theorists explained motivation in terms of a need to experience success and to avoid failure.

According to attribution theory, persons ascribe the causes of their successes and failures to factors such as ability, effort, difficulty of task, or luck. Their motivation for similar learning tasks depends not only on whether they have experienced success or failure but also on the particular factors to which they attribute their successes or failures. The attributed causes of success and failure, for example, ability and luck, are classified by three dimensions: (1) stable from one situation to another versus unstable from one situation to another, (2) internal to the individual versus external to the individual, and (3) controllable by the individual versus uncontrollable by the individual. Eight major causes to which success and failure are attributed and the three dimensions are displayed in Table 7.1.

TABLE 7.1 ATTRIBUTION THEORY

	INTERNAL		EXTERNAL	
CONTROLLABILITY	STABLE	UNSTABLE	STABLE	UNSTABLE
Uncontrollable	Ability	Mood	Task difficulty	Luck
Controllable	Typical effort	Immediate effort	Teacher bias	Unusual help from others

SOURCE: Weiner, 1979, p. 7.

Each of the eight causes can be classified along the three dimensions. Thus, ability is regarded as being uncontrollable by the individual, internal to the individual, and stable. Luck is regarded as uncontrollable, external, and unstable. According to Weiner (1979), the *stability-instability dimension* is related primarily to the expectation of succeeding or failing on future tasks. For example, students who have experienced success on an assignment and ascribe their success to their ability (stable) rather than to luck (unstable) will expect to succeed on similar assignments. The *internality-externality dimension* is related to feelings regarding self and to persistence on tasks. To illustrate, students who have experienced failure and attribute their failure to lack of ability (internal) rather than to task difficulty (external) experience negative feelings about themselves and tend not to persist on this kind of task. The *controllability-uncontrollability dimension* is related primarily to interpersonal judgments. Thus, teachers react with anger to students who perceive themselves as not making an effort (controllable); they react with empathy or pity to one who cannot succeed because of lack of ability (uncontrollable). More explicit information follows to relate success and failure to the causes and dimensions. You will find it interesting to try to identify the causes of your own successes.

Stable-Unstable Causes

Success on a prior task attributed to one or more stable causes (high ability, typical amount of effort, task of proper difficulty, and positive teacher bias) increases motivation for similar tasks more than does prior success attributed to unstable causes (favorable mood of the student, high immediate effort, good luck, and unusual help from others). Failure on a prior task attributed to stable causes (low ability, typical effort, great difficulty of task, negative teacher bias) decreases motivation for similar tasks more than does failure attributed to unstable causes (bad mood, lack of immediate effort, bad luck, little or no help from others). In general, if either success or failure is attained and the causes of the success or failure are perceived as remaining unchanged, then subsequent success or failure will be expected with a greater degree of certainty than if the causes are perceived as unstable or changeable. Tasks on which success is expected will be performed with greater intensity than those on which failure is expected.

Internal-External Causes

Positive affect, such as high self-regard, happiness, and satisfaction, are experienced after success, while displeasure, dissatisfaction, and low self-regard are experienced after failure. These affects are experienced regardless of whether the cause of the success or failure is perceived as internal or external (Weiner, 1979). Persistence on tasks is greater when positive affect is experienced.

In addition to these feelings that are uniformly associated with success and failure, attributions of success to particular internal and external causes are associated with specific feelings. Contentment is experienced when the cause of success is attributed to effort (internal). Gratefulness and thankfulness are experienced when success is linked with other people as the cause of the success (external). Surprise, relief, and quiet are associated with luck as causing the success (external).

Affect associated with failure has a different pattern. Incompetence and resignation are felt when the cause of failure is attributed to low ability (internal). Guilt is experienced when the cause is low or little effort (internal). Anger is felt when other people are perceived as causing the failure (external). Surprise is experienced when the failure is attributed to poor luck (external).

Controllable-Uncontrollable Causes

The controllability of the causes of success and failure has been studied only very recently, and knowledge concerning it is incomplete (Weiner, 1979). However, individuals' perceptions of their ability to control or not to control the achievement of tasks determines their motivation to perform or not to perform the tasks. Persons choose tasks if they perceive that they can achieve success by their own effort or by receiving help from others (controllable). They avoid tasks where successful performance is uncontrollable by their own effort or by receiving help. Thus, a beginning swimmer avoids deep water if effort is evaluated as insufficient for ensuring success in swimming across the pool.

How are the perceptions of others regarding an individual's controllable or uncontrollable causes of failure, or need for help, related to whether or not help is given? For example, how is a teacher's reaction to failing students related to the controllable-uncontrollable causes of their failure? The schema proposed by Weiner (1980b):

CONTROLLABLE CAUSES
The opportunity to help an individual is perceived. → The need for help is attributed to the lack of effort by the individual (controllable). → Anger is experienced. → Help is not given.

UNCONTROLLABLE CAUSES
The opportunity to help an individual is perceived. → The need for help is attributed to the individual's lack of ability (uncontrollable). → Pity is experienced. → Help is given.

The research of Covington and Omelich (1979a, 1979b) and of Covington, Spratt, and Omelich (1980) supports the idea that low effort by an individual produces negative affect in others who can help the individual, while high effort produces positive affect. Prawat, Byers, and Anderson (1983) found teachers to be proudest and most satisfied when low ability students succeeded through persistent, hard effort. Moreover, the teachers felt guilty when the student stopped trying. On the other hand, the teachers became angry when high ability students, and also any other students, failed because of lack of effort.

Factors Related to the Attribution of Causation

At what age do children reliably identify the causes of their success and failures? Do the causal explanations of the same student vary from one situation to another? Can the motivation of students who expect to experience failure because of their perceived lack of ability be increased? How is helplessness learned? Let us first consider the age at which children reliably attribute the causes of their successes and failures.

Age

How well do young, school-age children comprehend attributional concepts, such as ability and failure; relate their successes and failures to the real causes; and make self-evaluative judgments, such as being of low ability? Ruble (1980) indicates that these processes are not well understood by young children. Therefore, reliable predictions about young children's achievement motivation cannot be made using attribution theory. On the other hand, students in grades 5–12 appear to understand the concepts and make the causal attributions readily (Fyans & Maehr, 1979). For example, students in these grades who believe that they achieve success because they are regularly able to do so choose activities where skill or ability can be demonstrated. Conversely, students who attribute success to luck tend to avoid tasks where skill must be demonstrated. Students in grades 5–12 who regard effort highly work consistently at tasks, not so much to achieve success, but simply to make a good effort.

It is necessary for children to be able to assess their own achievement of tasks accurately in order to interpret it as success or failure (Nicholls, 1979a). However, at age 6, there is only a small, nonsignificant correlation between children's estimate of their level of reading achievement and teachers' ratings of their reading achievement. In other words, children of age 6 do not estimate their achievement levels accurately. At age 8, correlations between children's estimates and teachers' ratings are markedly higher, and the correlations continue to increase through age 12. However, only at age 12 are effort and luck regarded by children as much less important causes of success than ability. In summary, at age 12, children estimate their achievement in reading quite accurately and attribute causes of their success and failure more realistically and in accordance with the theoretical predictions than they do at younger ages, particularly ages 6 and 8 (Nicholls, 1979a).

Although children at age 8 do not conceptualize their own ability reliably and do not attribute the causes of their successes and failures in reading realistically, second- and third-graders do understand reciprocal relationships between their own ability and effort (Cauley & Murray, 1982). The children recognized, for example, that high ability could be negated by low effort and that low ability could be compensated for with high effort. As a matter of fact, the reasoning of the 8-year-olds regarding these and other reciprocal relations was very similar to that of college students.

Situational Conditions

Do children use the same causal interpretations to explain success or failure in different situations? Equal numbers of boys and girls of grades 1,

3, and 5 were interviewed to identify what they perceived as the causes of children's success and failure in four simulated situations: an academic test, a football game, catching frogs in a pond, and finishing an art project (Frieze & Snyder, 1980). Differences in the frequencies of their causal attributions of success and failure in the four tasks were significant for each of the three grades, for each sex separately, and for mental ability above and below the median of the children of each grade. The differences are reflected in the percentages of attributions to effort, to ability, and to all other causes for all the students combined: academic test—65% effort, 15% ability, 20% all other causes; art project—27% effort, 34% ability, 39% all other causes; playing football—35% effort, 23% ability, and 42% all other causes; catching frogs—24% effort, 12% ability, and 64% all other causes including 39% task difficulty or task ease. The main conclusion of this study is that a young child's beliefs about the causes of success and failure are dependent on the child's prior experiences with the particular situation and thus vary from one situation to the next.

Attribution Modifiability

Can students who attribute failure to uncontrollable causes (lack of ability and task difficulty) rather than to controllable causes (their own effort) be taught to change their causal attributions? If so, how is this change related to performing tasks? Grade 6 boys who did not attribute failure to lack of effort were identified (Andrews & Debus, 1978). One random group of these boys received instruction designed to get them to ascribe failure to lack of effort and then to make a greater effort. This instruction, carried out by the experimenter, was successful. Furthermore, task persistence was greater, not only immediately following the instruction, but also four months later. Walden and Ramey (1983) also found that teaching kindergarten children personal control through effort produced higher achievement. In a similar vein, Bar-Tal (1978) indicated that students' attributions might be changed by teachers' pointing out the importance of effort to the students. However, for this technique to be successful, the teacher must arrange learning tasks that are suitable to each student's ability.

Feedback itself has been found to influence greater attribution to effort (Schunk, 1982). In this experiment, feedback during an assignment in the form of telling students that they were working hard had a positive effect on increasing their belief in their own ability to achieve by making a greater effort.

Learned Helplessness

How is learned helplessness related to causal attributions of success and failure? Can learned helplessness in children be counteracted? *Learned helplessness* is the belief that failure cannot be avoided (Seligman, 1975; Hiroto & Seligman, 1975; Maier & Seligman, 1976). The belief develops as students repeatedly and consistently experience feelings of failure despite expending effort and having a desire to succeed. After repeated failures, effort is drastically curtailed, self-attitudes about intellectual performance and competence become very negative, and self-esteem drops.

Thomas (1979) regards these characteristics as typical of many children who are identified as learning-disabled. They no longer believe they can achieve and take less personal responsibility for failure. They tend to attribute their failures to lack of ability rather than to lack of effort. Unfortunately, scarcely any research has been carried out in school settings to ascertain how learned helplessness can be counteracted in children with learning disabilities (Thomas, 1979).

Some characteristics of learned helplessness were found in grade 5 students not identified as having a learning disability but who were low in reading achievement (Butkowsky & Willows, 1980). The low achievers, in comparison with the average and high achievers, had low initial expectancies of success, gave up more quickly when experiencing difficulty, and attributed their failures mainly to lack of ability. They also lowered their expectations for achieving success in subsequent reading tasks. Tesiny, Lefkowitz, and Gordon (1980) found similar attribution patterns of low achievers in a study of 944 grade 4 and grade 5 students. Butkowsky and Willows speculate that teachers might use the experimental instructional technique of Andrews and Debus (1978), given earlier in this section, to help low achievers. It may be recalled that, in the experiment, students were first encouraged to attribute failure to lack of effort and then received instruction designed to get them to make a greater effort.

7.8 Relate your conscious thought processes to your motivation for learning the content of this chapter.

7.9 Have you learned any content of this chapter without intending to learn it? Explain.

7.10 How is motivation in the self-control of learning activities different from Freudian instinctive drives? From Skinnerian self-management of reinforcers?

7.11 According to attribution theory, persons attribute their successes and failures to one or more causes, each of which has three dimensions: external or internal to the individual, stable or unstable for a considerable period of time, and controllable or uncontrollable by the individual. Relate each of the following causes to these three dimensions: ability to perform a task, typical effort expended in performing tasks, difficulty of assigned task, and luck.

7.12 Bill attributes the cause of his failure to lack of ability, whereas Frank attributes his to lack of effort. Which of the two will probably have the lower expectation of achieving success in the next similar task that is assigned? Explain.

7.13 Mary attributes her repeated academic failures to lack of ability, whereas Donna attributes hers to the difficulty of the tasks. Which of the two is likely to have lower self-acceptance? Explain.

7.14 Henry fails to achieve well in several classes because of lack of effort, whereas Ed fails because of low ability. How are teachers likely to respond to Henry? To Ed?

7.15 Betty is in grade 1, and Ellen is in grade 6. Compare the two with respect to their ability (a) to estimate reliably whether they are failing or succeeding in reading and (b) to attribute the causes of their successes and failures reliably to internal versus external, stable versus unstable, and controllable versus uncontrollable causes.

7.16 Individuals learn helplessness by repeatedly trying and failing. Give examples of learned helplessness that you have observed or that you may have experienced personally.

7.17 Do you regard attribution theory as more helpful for understanding students' motivation to learn or for suggesting means of ensuring high student motivation to learn? Explain.

KINDS OF INTRINSIC MOTIVES

Interests
Competence
Curiosity

Nicholls (1979b) indicates that attributional theory is very helpful in explaining why some students try hard and achieve well and others do not. However, it does not offer many clues for motivating the many students who do not try to achieve. Ideas about intrinsic motives, though not systematically organized in a theory, provide a very promising approach to achieving optimum motivation with all students, including those of lower ability.

Interest, competence, curiosity, and self-actualization are concepts that imply intrinsic motivation. Intrinsic motivation is closely related to the idea of endogenous activity (Nicholls, 1979b). We engage in endogenous activities because they are interesting, satisfying, or fulfilling. An *endogenous activity* is undertaken as an end in itself, not as a means to an end, such as to receive a reward or to avoid failure. To illustrate, teaching is an endogenous activity for a teacher who enjoys teaching for its own sake. It is an *exogenous activity* for one who does not enjoy teaching but does it for the salary.

Interests

The term *interest* refers to a person's perception that engaging in an activity is worthwhile or enjoyable for its own sake. No reward is sought or expected from participating in the activity. The person plays a game, reads a book, or completes a project for the sake of doing it. Interests in many games and physical activities are learned in early childhood and throughout the school years. However, disinterest is also learned. For example, most children enjoy reading and arithmetic activities when they enter kindergarten or first grade, but by grade 6, disinterest is widespread.

New interests continue to develop during adolescence. For example, a biology teacher makes this new subject matter interesting to the students.

The students become interested in learning about the many new advances in the biological sciences, such as understanding heredity, and in relating them to their personal lives. Similarly, students develop an interest in a career field when placed in career exploration activities in community organizations and businesses.

Competence

Competence is regarded as an intrinsic need to deal effectively with the environment (White, 1959). In response to this need, the infant grasps and explores, crawls, and eventually walks without either external stimulation or reinforcement. Similarly, the child attends to others, listens, and learns to talk. This kind of motor and verbal activity stemming from the need for competence is not random or undirected. It is selective and persistent and enables the individual to achieve proficiency.

Competence and self-actualization, as described earlier in this chapter, serve similar roles in motivating behavior. They are present in all individuals. Finding means of enabling more persons to capitalize upon these needs in constructive ways is an important educational concern.

Curiosity

Curiosity is intrinsic in that it energizes exploratory activity without expectation of external rewards or reinforcement. Curiosity about something in the environment energizes the activity to explore it. Engaging in exploratory activity for a while reduces the curiosity that led to the particular activity. For example, walking down the street for the first time is energized by curiosity. After walking down the street and seeing what is there, the curiosity is reduced or even eliminated.

Berlyne (1960) differentiates between perceptual curiosity and epistemic curiosity. *Perceptual curiosity* involves attending to a novel item in the environment and engaging in visual, auditory, motor, or other overt activity to satisfy the curiosity. *Epistemic curiosity* is reflected in thinking about symbolic ideas; for example, a person attends to written material and tries to get the intended meaning by reading it carefully.

Maw and Maw (1964) propose that curiosity is essential for learning, creativity, and mental health. They provide the following indicators of curiosity in children (Maw & Maw, 1965): (1) children react positively to new, strange, incongruous, or mysterious elements in their environment by moving toward them, by exploring them, or by manipulating them (perceptual curiosity); (2) they exhibit a need or desire to know more about themselves and their environment (epistemic curiosity); (3) they scan new surroundings and seek new experiences; (4) they persist in examining and exploring.

Curiosity and other intrinsic motives are present not only in children but also in college students. Desire for self-improvement, desire for self-esteem, enjoyment of learning, and enjoyment of assertive interactions are four of the most common motives of students going to college (Doyle &

Moen, 1978). All of these motives are more prevalent in college students than either a desire for academic success or career preparation.

We should recognize that these intrinsic motives are present to varying degrees in all human beings, and especially in children. Accordingly, one major task of the teacher is to provide an opportunity for the expression of these motives. For example, a teacher asks students about their interests and arranges activities accordingly. Learning situations are arranged in the classroom, laboratory, or other training areas where perceptual or epistemic curiosity can be utilized. For example, giving students a choice of experiments to conduct or books to read encourages the expression of epistemic curiosity.

In addition to providing opportunity for expression of intrinsic motives, the teacher encourages the student who is low in curiosity, competence, or some other form of intrinsic motivation. As we saw earlier, students who no longer make an effort to achieve competence require remedial activities. More information on using intrinsic motives appears in the next part of this chapter.

7.18 How are your interests related to the courses you are taking now? To your long-term career goals?

7.19 Estimate the amount of effort likely to be made by different students who have a need for achieving competence at these levels: (a) high, (b) medium, and (c) low.

7.20 Describe instructional conditions that tend to increase student curiosity. To decrease it.

7.21 Assume that Teacher A is familiar only with Skinnerian theory, Teacher B only with humanistic theory, Teacher C only with attribution theory, and Teacher D only with intrinsic motivation. Assume further that the teachers try to apply ideas from these theories in their classrooms. Predict two or three things that each teacher does.

PRINCIPLES OF CLASSROOM MOTIVATION

1. Establish a learning-oriented environment.
2. Utilize students' needs and intrinsic motives.
3. Make the subject matter interesting.
4. Help each student set and attain goals.
5. Aid students to assume increasing responsibility for their learning activities.
6. Provide informative feedback and external control as necessary.

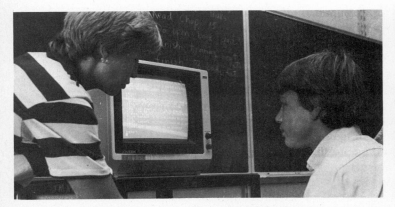

Motivation is the mainspring of human learning activity. What really turns on today's students?

Applications of these six principles must be suited to the age of the learners—nursery school through college. They must also take into account differences among learners of the same age, such as differences in their abilities, interests, and attitudes. The applications depend upon the social-psychological climate of the school and of the classroom: applications in a school where the large majority of students study reasonably hard and behave well differ from those in a school where students who attend classes regularly, study hard, and behave well are rejected by the majority. Finally, because of their differing values, capabilities, and life-styles, no two teachers will use the same applications with the same group of learners in the same situation. Therefore, as you study the principles and their illustrative applications, think about your own values regarding different approaches to motivation. Try to recall desirable and undesirable, effective and ineffective motivational techniques employed by your teachers. Identify your capabilities for self-control of your own learning activities and for creating the motivational conditions you desire as a teacher.

1. **Establish a learning-oriented environment.** A classroom that is learning oriented has several features. Students come to a learning-oriented environment intending to learn. They make a consistent, strong effort to achieve, but are free of anxiety. Students often experience success in a learning-oriented environment. Nevertheless, they may experience failure at times, not as a punishment but as a natural consequence of their lack of effort, This kind of environment requires (1) focusing student attention, (2) aiding students to establish an intention to learn, and (3) avoiding the creation of high student anxiety.

Focus student attention. Selective attending is essential for learning. Therefore, a teacher focuses students' attention on the learning activities as soon as the students enter the learning area. In this way, student curiosity becomes part of the attention-focusing process.

In social studies, attention was focused on the study of Japan in the following ways. On the first day of the unit, the students walked into an environment that was definitely Japanese. A wall map of Japan and a travel poster were in the front of the room. The bulletin boards were filled with pictures of Japan. But the most interesting things, some of the many products made in Japan, were spread out on a table. (The teacher had carefully included a number of unfamiliar objects.) Few students were in their seats when the bell rang. Most of them were still examining the products and eagerly asking the teacher about them. Instead of answering directly, the teacher asked more questions.

In addition to manipulating physical aspects of the environment, the teacher may also ask questions and encourage discussion. In an English class, a question was asked to focus attention and arouse curiosity about myths: "Where do myths come from, and why were they told in the first place?" On discussing this question, the students realized that myths were created by people not so very different from themselves. Encouraging each student to listen to and answer each question increases attention and decreases off-task activity (McKenzie & Henry, 1979).

Develop an intention to learn. Intending is the primary executive control process for the self-control of activity. For example, students intend to arrive at school on time, and they plan and carry out activities to get to school on time. Intending to get to school on time is encouraged by both parents and teachers and becomes habitual for many students at an early age. Intending to learn while at school, rather than intending to do other things, is encouraged and becomes habitual in a learning-oriented environment. For these intentions to occur, however, the school staff, parents, and students must hold the learning aspect of education in high regard. The custodial, socializing, and recreational functions are given lower priority.

Avoid producing high student anxiety. General anxiety is the anticipation of something unpleasant or painful whose source cannot be identified by the individual. In other words, the individual is apprehensive and has unpleasant feelings regarding future events but cannot pinpoint the reason for them. *Test anxiety,* on the other hand, is anxiety about test taking. Test anxiety is found in some students who desire to achieve high. A low level of anxiety encourages effort to achieve; however, high test anxiety lowers achievement (Tobias, 1979). Furthermore, test anxiety increases as achieving high on a test becomes of greater importance (Deffenbacher, 1978).

Why does high anxiety lower performance? High test-anxious persons worry about the ill effects of not doing as well as they would like to do during a test. This self-oriented worry interferes with attending to and concentrating on the test. Low test-anxious persons do not worry; they concentrate only on the test (Wine, 1980). The lower problem-solving performance by a group of college students of high test anxiety was caused by an inability to recall information from memory and also by a failure to use an appropriate problem-solving strategy (Gross & Mastenbrook, 1980). The high anxiety interfered with recalling the needed information and with being able to use a known problem-solving strategy.

Most of our knowledge about overcoming test anxiety comes from studies with college students. Teaching college students test-taking skills and how to prepare themselves psychologically for taking tests helps to eliminate the worry associated with test anxiety. However, elimination of worry and test anxiety is not enough to improve achievement, measured, for example, by course grades and grade point averages (Tryon, 1980). Rather, test anxiety is reduced and course grades are improved when students are taught more effective study habits and spend more time preparing for their tests (Culler & Holahan, 1980). Missing classes, delaying the taking of exams, and not preparing adequately are also associated with continuing high test anxiety and low achievement.

2. **Utilize students' needs and intrinsic motives.** Student activities to satisfy physiological and growth needs require wise guidance and direction so that the students learn prosocial means of satisfying their needs. Therefore, the teacher encourages students to gratify their needs through socially accepted means. A similar approach is followed with respect to intrinsic motives, such as curiosity and competence.

You recall that Maslow identified physiological, safety, love, and esteem needs as deficiency needs. When students experience one of these needs, they attempt to gratify it. Therefore, teachers relate the subject-matter content and learning activities to their students' gratification of these deficiency needs in a variety of ways. For example, the teacher points out how learning reading or math helps students prepare for work that will contribute to the satisfaction of their physiological needs. The student who is experiencing low self-esteem is encouraged to achieve higher and to interpret the classroom situation so that achieving as much as possible is accompanied with a feeling of self-esteem. The social studies teacher forms cooperative work groups to aid individual students gratify their esteem needs as well as their love and belonging needs.

Maslow regards self-actualization as a growth motive. It functions in a manner analogous to competence and the need to achieve. Giving students increasing opportunity to select more of their learning activities and to set their own standards of achievement is one means of utilizing the self-actualization need. Arranging for students to work on their own projects helps them become more self-actualizing and more competent.

As we saw, curiosity is believed to be essential for learning, creativity, and mental health. *Perceptual curiosity* is manifested by attending to novel items in the environment and exploring them. *Epistemic curiosity* is manifested in thinking about new and different symbolic ideas that are encountered. Utilizing student curiosity calls for providing instructional materials and activities that encourage each student to do some exploring, rather than engaging all students in the same activities to learn the same material.

3. Make the subject matter interesting. How is subject matter made interesting? There are many options. One is the teacher's enthusiasm for it. (Behaviors indicating enthusiasm were discussed in Chapter 6.) A second is having other persons whom the students admire indicate their interest and enthusiasm for it. Another is relating the substance to the present concerns and needs of the students. Pointing out the value of knowing the subject matter also helps. In addition, arranging for students to do attractive subject-related activities upon completing their assigned work tends to increase interest in the subject (Taffel & O'Leary, 1976).

How do instructional materials and learning activities affect interest in the subject matter? Using a variety of materials—printed, audiovisual, and three-dimensional—promotes interest in more students of a group than using a single kind of material, such as a textbook. Providing for different kinds of activities that involve doing, observing, reading, and listening produces interest in more students than does a single activity, such as having the students only listen or only read. Shifting activities during a class period of 45 minutes or longer gets better results than continuing the same activity. Enabling students to choose activities and to change from one activity to another on their own volition appeals to many students. Field trips and out-of-school activities are also helpful in creating interest.

4. Help each student set and attain goals. Goal setting is a particularly powerful motivational procedure for several reasons. Setting a goal involves an intention to achieve and thereby serves to activate learning from one day to the next. It directs the learner's activities toward the goal. It takes into account differences among students in their ability to learn and also in the amount of effort they wish to make. Goal setting allows every student the opportunity to experience success, but works only if students make an effort and do not set unattainable goals.

Effective goals are specific rather than general. *Specific goals* are exemplified by the number of exercises to be completed in a certain time. *General goals* are exemplified by encouraging students to do their best or to complete as much as they can. Students who set specific and also relatively difficult goals in spelling achieved much higher than did students who set general goals (Rosswork, 1977).

An excellent way to enable students to set goals is the use of objectives and related activities to achieve the objectives. In this approach to goal setting, unit objectives and related activities are listed and distributed to the students on the first day of the unit. The students select which of the objectives they will try to attain during a specified time interval, such as a day, week, or grading period. When the students select certain objectives and decide to try to attain them by a certain time, they are in fact setting specific goals. We should note that in some classes only objectives or only activities, rather than both, are used in goal setting. Regardless of which are used, students rarely set realistic goals without teacher guidance.

In one senior high school, students receive a list of objectives and related activities at the beginning of each unit of each course in English, math, science, and social studies (Klausmeier, Lipham, & Daresh, 1983). Mastery of a certain set of objectives in each list yields a letter grade of A, another set B, and a third set C. During the first class meeting, the students set goals in terms of the set of objectives and related letter grade they desire. The rapid learners upon completing the A objectives may elect to work on an enrichment unit for extra credit. Other students who are working on the A, B, or C objectives may experience difficulty and decide to do additional work outside the regular class period. This approach to goal setting is part of the school's regular ongoing instructional strategy and achieves excellent results in terms of high student achievement and a discipline-free, learning-oriented environment.

For goal setting to be effective, the teacher must be comfortable with this approach to student motivation and the related mode of instruction. Furthermore, the students need to be taught the goal-setting strategies for the particular course. The teacher bases these strategies on the amount of effort required by the students to achieve their goals. With a little guided practice, most elementary school students were found to be able to set their own goals (Kennedy, 1968). Furthermore, the middle- and high-achieving elementary school students who set specific goals in mathematics learned and remembered more mathematics than students of the same achievement levels who did not set goals. They also surpassed students whose goals had been set by the teacher. On the other hand, low-achieving students did better when the teacher identified and suggested goals for them. A most important conclusion from this experiment is that a teacher must exercise good judgment, based on careful observation and understanding of students, to determine the amount and kind of assistance students need in setting goals.

5. Aid students to assume increasing responsibility for their learning activities. Self-control and self-regulation of learning activities calls for students to take considerable initiative in deciding how they will learn and how much effort they will expend. Similar to goal setting, self-regulation implies voluntarily spending time and effort in learning rather than spending time and effort only to receive an external reward. The following list indicates initiatives taken by self-regulating students; non–self-regulating students need help in undertaking them (Wlodkowski, 1978, pp. 146, 147):

> Choosing learning goals that I want to accomplish.
>
> Planning how to achieve the learning goals that I have chosen.
>
> Continuing to work toward the learning goals that I have chosen and completing them.
>
> Accepting the consequences of my learning.
>
> Evaluating the results of my learning.
>
> Practicing those skills that are necessary to my learning.
>
> Checking my own progress in learning.
>
> Using my values to make choices for learning where alternatives are available.
>
> Having personal standards by which I judge the quality of my learning.
>
> Choosing challenging learning goals.
>
> Working at my own speed.
>
> Deciding how to use extra time.
>
> Asking questions when I do not understand.

Another way of considering self-control of learning activities is its relation to *personal causation,* that is, originating actions rather than being controlled or manipulated by other persons (deCharms, 1976, 1980).

In a longitudinal study of personal causation (deCharms, 1976), teachers participated in workshops to learn how to teach students to become originators of their own learning activities. The teachers learned how to teach children the following:

1. To set goals.
2. To choose activities for attaining their goals.
3. To assume personal responsibility for attaining their goals.
4. To become confident that they had the ability to attain their goals.
5. To assess their own progress.

The teachers participated in the workshops when their students were in grade 5, and they put the ideas into practice when the students were in grades 6 and 7 (deCharms, 1976). The children were of low-socioeconomic status, attending inner-city schools. Figure 7.6 gives a follow-up of the achievement test results for the children who participated in the experiment and for a control group who did not. The results are indicated in terms of the average, or mean, discrepancy in months from the average grade placement. Notice that when the experimental (trained) and control (untrained) students were in grade 5, they were close together, about six months below the mean grade placement for grade 5. However, at grades 6, 7, and 8 each, the control group, who did not receive the training in origination, continued to drop farther below the mean grade placement, while the trained group moved closer to the mean. In a yet later follow-up, a higher percentage of the trained

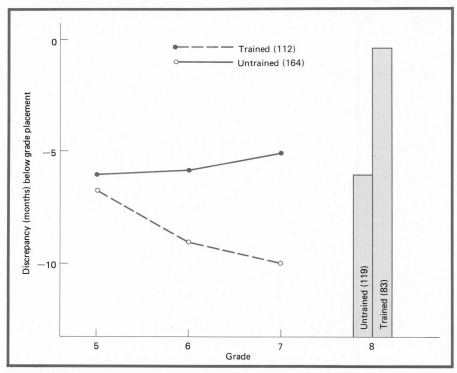

Figure 7.6 Effects of training students to originate their own motivation.
Source: deCharms, 1976, p. 144.

students were found to have graduated from high school (deCharms, 1980).

Self-control of activities is accompanied with personal causation for failure, whereas external control is not (Arlin & Whitley, 1978). Students of grades 5, 6, and 7 who perceived themselves as managing their learning activities attributed their failures in those activities to themselves. On the other hand, they attributed their failures in teacher-assigned activities to the teacher, task difficulty, or other conditions external to themselves.

Although self-control of activity is a desirable goal, not all children profit equally well from exercising control of all kinds of learning activity. For example, disabled and low-achieving readers who attributed the causes of their reading problems to themselves profited from determining the correctness of their own responses. However, the students low in internal attribution benefited more when a teacher determined the correctness of their responses (Pascarella, Pflaum, Bryan, & Pearl, 1983).

6. Provide informative feedback and external control as necessary. Students need feedback to guide goal-directed activities. The feedback may be gotten independently, as in using a dictionary to check on spelling, or it may be provided by a teacher. Forms of feedback from a teacher include oral and written comments that indicate what is correct or incorrect and appropriate or inappropriate. Feedback that stops with pointing out errors is not sufficient for many students. They also need cues as to how to overcome the errors.

Informative feedback based on knowledge of results contributes to effective learning. Social reinforcement that is accompanied with pleasant affect on the part of the learner also contributes. Recognizing effort, displaying appreciation of the student's activity, minimizing negative aspects of mistakes, and indicating confidence are a few of many social reinforcers employed by teachers to encourage continuing motivation. When related directly and immediately to a specific learning activity, they heighten intrinsic motivation for the activity (Bates, 1979).

In some situations, the use of concrete rewards and punishment appears to be necessary in order to establish or to maintain a good learning environment. Rewards are more effective than punishments. However, the effects of rewards differ greatly in cooperative and competitive situations (Ames & Ames, 1978). We shall examine the cooperative arrangements first.

When a pair of children cooperate with one another for a common reward but do not receive it, the child who causes them not to receive it is highly critical of self, loses favor in the eyes of the other child, and is regarded as incompetent and of low ability by the other child. The negative effects of not receiving a reward are more severe on the lower-performing child in this cooperative arrangement than in competitive or individualistic arrangements. Furthermore, the child who does well is also not highly regarded by self or the other child of the pair. On the other hand, when a pair of children work together cooperatively and receive a common reward, interpersonal relationships, affect, and evaluation of competence and ability are more positive than in the other arrangements. The better performer is judged to have high ability and competence, and the one of lower ability does not engage in self-criticism.

When two children who are paired together compete against one another for one reward, the loser is regarded in much the same way as the poorer performer of a pair that cooperate for a common reward but do not receive it. However, in the competitive pair, both the self-criticism by the loser and the negative evaluation of the loser by the winning competitor are less severe than they are for the low-performing member of the cooperating pair who is regarded as the cause of losing. When individuals of an entire group compete against one another, the winners and losers behave in much the same way as in the competitive pairs.

These results (Ames & Ames, 1978) demonstrate that a reward system is effective when each member of a cooperating group contributes to a learning activity and when the group receives a common reward. Interpersonal relations are smoothest and self-regard is highest in this situation.

Johnson, Johnson, and Maruyama (1983) reviewed 98 studies on the effects of individuals and small groups of varying numbers cooperating for rewards versus competing for rewards. They drew three main conclusions: (1) cooperation *without* intergroup competition promotes greater interpersonal attraction among both heterogeneous and homogeneous individuals than do interpersonal competition, individualistic efforts, and cooperation with intergroup competition; (2) cooperation *with* intergroup competition promotes greater interpersonal attraction among participants than does interpersonal competition or individualistic efforts; and (3) interpersonal competition and individualistic efforts are equally ineffective in promoting interpersonal attraction among participants.

Positive reinforcers—both concrete rewards and social reinforcers— may be used on an individual basis without encouraging either competition among individuals or groups or cooperation among members of groups. This approach requires the availability of reinforcers for all students.

An effective individual approach to reinforcement does not imply that the higher-achieving, better-behaved students get larger or more frequent reinforcers. On the contrary, the students who require most frequent reinforcers for starting work promptly are the ones habitually who do not start work promptly. They are reinforced the first time they start promptly, are promised a reinforcer for starting promptly in the future, and receive it each time they do so. As their behavior improves, the amount and frequency of reinforcement are decreased. Similarly, the students who have never read a book independently require more frequent reinforcers than the ones who read several books per week. The ones who have not yet read a book should be reinforced for just reading paragraphs and pages at first. Later, when they read a book with relative ease, they should be reinforced only for reading an entire book. Through a combination of reinforcement and reasoning with the student, improved achievement and other desired behaviors become stable.

Punishment is used only as a last resort because of its possible undesirable motivational effects. For instance, negative feelings may accrue toward the punishing person and the situation in which the punishment occurs. Also, punishment or threatened punishment does not cause the student to drop the behavior unless an alternative behavior is available. Another undesirable effect is that the punishment may actually reinforce the undesired behavior. This reinforcement occurs when the student receives peer approval for persisting in a form of behavior that is punished, and the positive effects of the peer approval outweigh the negative effects of the punishment. A final undesirable effect is that students may model the behavior of the punishing school person in the same manner as they model that of their TV heroes and heroines.

Despite potential ill effects, punishment in the form of withdrawal of a privilege until the desired performance is shown may be useful in some situations. Punishment immediately following an undesired act may be used to redirect the learner to a desired one if the desired one is available. Second, punishment may be informative. For example, getting a low grade on a paper may inform the student that the work is unacceptable and thus provide a rationale for correcting it and then getting a higher grade. Punishment may also be used to stop an undesired student activity, such as running or fighting.

We cannot ignore the serious misconduct occurring in some schools that cannot be effectively dealt with by the teacher or principal. Included here are physical attacks on students and teachers and various kinds of delinquent acts. Cooperative efforts of educators, parents, and other citizens are needed to solve these severe problems. But they should be solved. Safe schools and safe communities for students and teachers are prerequisites for creating a favorable learning environment in the school.

7.22 Indicate why teachers should carry out each of the following in their classrooms:

    a. Focusing student attention on learning activities.
    b. Developing an intention to learn in each student.
    c. Avoiding producing high anxiety in students.
    d. Utilizing students' needs and intrinsic motives.
    e. Making the subject matter interesting.
    f. Helping each student set and obtain goals.
    g. Aiding students to assume increasing responsibility for their learning activities.
    h. Providing informative feedback to the students.
    i. Exercising external control of students' behavior as necessary.

7.23 Which of the behaviors in Question 7.22 do you think would be easiest for you to implement as a teacher? Most difficult?

7.24 Return to the activities of self-regulating students. Mentally check those that you generally follow in your various courses and those that you do not.

7.25 Prepare a short presentation to make to parents about the value of goal setting by students, basing your presentation on deCharms's research.

7.26 Compare the effects of small-group cooperation, small-group competition, and individual competition on interpersonal relationships when not all individuals or groups receive a desired reward.

7.27 Explain how to arrange small-group activities and the use of a reward system to promote good interpersonal relationships among the group members.

7.28 Indicate conditions under which punishment may be the only available technique the teacher or the school may employ.

7.29 Review and Application: Recall the most important information regarding each of the following concepts, and identify at least one possible use of the information by you as a learner, a teacher, or both:

Early Theories of Motivation
    Psychoanalytic Theory
    Association Theory
    Humanistic Theory
Recent Cognitive Theories of Motivation
    Self-Control of Activity
    Attribution of Causes of Success and Failure

SUMMARY

The study of motivation is concerned with the activation, direction, and persistence of behavior. Psychoanalytic theory explains motives in terms of instinctual drives, particularly sex and aggression. Today, many persons look to this theory to explain irrational, antisocial, and hedonistic behavior.

Association theory places much emphasis on drives, reinforcement, and the control of behavior by environmental conditions and agents external to the organism. Behavior management techniques are based mainly on association theory. The use of behavior management techniques with normally developing students is declining. However, it is widely used with students who have learning disabilities and other conditions that impede learning or prosocial conduct.

Humanistic theory explains motives in terms of deficiency needs and growth needs. Self-actualization is a key construct.

Cognitive theorists forward the proposition that individuals interpret their environmental conditions and direct their behaviors in accordance with their interpretations. Goals, intentions, plans, and causal attributions of success and failure are central concepts in cognitive theory. Intrinsic motivation is a special case of cognitive theory. Here, interests, curiosity, and competence, all of which imply self-directing mechanisms, are key motivational constructs. The cognitive viewpoint toward motivation is compatible with most of the principles of learning explained throughout the next chapters.

The fact that each of many different theoretical views may be useful in explaining certain elements of motivation in human beings testifies to the changing character of the motives of the individual from infancy into adulthood, the great and rich variability among human beings, and the difficulty in finding the causes and predicting the directions of one's own behaviors or the behaviors of others. The preceding theories provide the basis for the following principles of motivation:

1. Establish a learning-oriented environment.
2. Utilize students' needs and intrinsic motives.
3. Make the subject matter interesting.
4. Help each student set and attain goals.
5. Aid students to assume increasing responsibility for their learning activities.
6. Provide informative feedback and external control as necessary.

SUGGESTIONS FOR FURTHER READING

Anderson, L. M., & Prawat, R. S. Responsibility in the classroom: A synthesis of research on teaching self-control. *Educational Leadership,* 1983, *40*(7), 62–66.

These authors summarize the research on attribution theory and indicate how teachers can use this knowledge to develop self-control in students.

Ball, S. Motivation. In H. E. Mitzel, J. H. Best, & W. Rabinowitz (Eds.), *Encyclopedia of educational research* (5th ed., Vol. 3). New York: Free Press, 1982. Pp. 1256–1267.

Outlines research, theory, and practical implications, giving major attention to attribution theory, achievement motivation, anxiety, self-esteem, and curiosity.

Keith, T. Z. Time spent on homework and high school grades: A large-sample path analysis. *Journal of Educational Psychology,* 1982, *74*(2), 248–253.

As the amount of time spent on homework increased from less than one hour per week to 10 or more hours, grades also became higher for high-, medium-, and low-ability high school students.

Marsh, H. W., Cairns, L., Relich, J., Barnes, J., & Debus, R. L. The relationship between dimensions of self-attribution and dimensions of self-concept. *Journal of Educational Psychology,* 1984, *76,* 3–32.

A series of experiments with suggestions for modifications and extensions of attribution theory.

Morgan, M. Reward-induced decrements and increments in intrinsic motivation. *Review of Educational Research,* 1984, *54,* 5–30.

A scholarly review of research and theory regarding the idea that the use of extrinsic rewards decreases intrinsic motivation.

Slavin, R. E. *Cooperative learning.* New York: Longman, 1983.

Explains cooperative learning in small groups and presents related research. Describes the positive effects on student achievement, race relations, and other variables.

CHAPTER 8

VERBAL INFORMATION

INFORMATION OF LOW MEANINGFULNESS

STRATEGIES FOR LEARNING AND REMEMBERING INFORMATION OF LOW MEANINGFULNESS

MEANINGFUL PROSE

STRATEGIES FOR COMPREHENDING PROSE

STUDY SKILLS TO IMPROVE LEARNING TEXT MATERIAL

Children acquire an amazingly large amount of verbal information before they start school. They also acquire the oral communication skills of speaking and listening. Having communication skills and a store of verbal information enables them to engage in more formal learning activities at school, including learning to read with comprehension. Gaining new knowledge by comprehending what is read is a principal means of learning in all subject fields throughout the school years. It is also important in out-of-school situations.

The first part of this chapter addresses information of low meaningfulness, such as specific facts. It then explains strategies for learning information of low meaningfulness. Much progress has been made recently in clarifying these strategies and their use in school settings.

Reading with comprehension is a very economical way of learning for many persons. Fortunately, we are gaining a much better understanding of the comprehension process. A widely accepted model for explaining the comprehension of prose, including text material, is outlined in this chapter. Afterwards, aids to learning and retention that may be incorporated directly in printed material or supplied by the teacher are presented. The chapter concludes by highlighting learning strategies for improving comprehension of prose material and study skills for increasing learning and retention of verbal information.

Notice that there are strategies for learning information of low meaningfulness, strategies for comprehending meaningful prose, and study skills for increasing learning and retention of text material. These strategies and study skills should be taught to students during the school years. Accordingly, there is no separate section on principles of teaching verbal information, since it would contain essentially the same information as the sections on the strategies and study skills.

INFORMATION OF LOW MEANINGFULNESS

Some basic information such as names and specific facts has little or no literal meaning, and some items have no logical connections. However, there are strategies that impose meaning and therefore relate items that do not have logical connections. These strategies may be employed rather than rote memorization of the material.

Names and Groups of Names

The names of nonsequenced and of sequenced groups of items are two very important kinds of verbal material of low meaningfulness. The names of the classes of the plant kingdom and of the animal kingdom exemplify names of nonsequenced items. The letters of the alphabet and the names of numerals exemplify names of sequenced items fundamental to all other verbal learning. As a matter of fact, the learning of the 26 letters of the alphabet in correct order by young children is one of the greatest feats of human learning and remembering. To the preschool child, the sounds of the letters of the alphabet are equivalent to a series of nonsense syllables to the college student.

A great deal of primary school instruction is directed toward aiding children learn the names of things. For example, children are taught the names of teachers and children, of places in and around the school, and of instructional materials. Learning names facilitates initial learning and later retention. For example, second- and fourth-grade children who were taught the names of pictures recalled about one-third more of the pictures after two months than did those who were presented the same pictures without names (Bowen, Gelabert, & Torgesen, 1978).

Specific Facts

Specific facts and technical information of all kinds have low meaningfulness. Factual information is called *knowledge* in the Bloom taxonomy (Bloom, 1956), as was indicated in Chapter 2. Several categories of information, with examples of low meaningfulness, follow:

**KINDS OF INFORMATION
OF LOW MEANINGFULNESS**

I. Knowledge of specifics
  A. People
    1. Walt Whitman was an American poet.
    2. Louis Armstrong was a jazz trumpet player.

   B. Events and dates
      1. The Protestant Reformation began in the sixteenth century.
      2. Mass polio immunization began in 1955.
   C. Places and locations
      1. Madison is the capital of Wisconsin.
      2. The northern boundary of Montana is the 49th parallel.
II. Knowledge of ways and means of dealing with specifics
   A. Conventions
      1. The subject and verb of a sentence agree in number.
      2. The driver on the right has the right-of-way at an intersection.
   B. Classifications and categories
      1. Dogs are vertebrate animals.
      2. Mercury is a kind of liquid.

This brief overview indicates the great variety of very important information of low meaningfulness that can be learned and remembered in all subject fields. Students who develop effective strategies to learn it rapidly move ahead of those who do not.

STRATEGIES FOR LEARNING AND REMEMBERING INFORMATION OF LOW MEANINGFULNESS

Rehearsal and Review

Organization

Elaboration

Mnemonic Strategies Using Visual Imagery

There are four major strategies for learning and remembering information of low meaningfulness: (1) rehearsal and review; (2) organizing items of a disconnected set into smaller, connected chunks; (3) elaboration; and (4) mnemonic (memory-aiding) devices that employ visual imagery. For effective learning and retention of a large amount of material, one or more of the last three strategies are combined with rehearsal shortly after initial learning and with later review.

These strategies relate here to verbal material of low meaningfulness. However, they can also be used by learners to study text material that contains specific information new to them. For example, the reader who is not familiar with the four preceding strategies may now pause to repeat them mentally (rehearsal) before continuing to read.

Rehearsal and Review

Rehearsal is a technical term in learning theory. It involves repeating a small amount of information immediately upon receiving it in short-term memory. Rehearsal may be covert and overt.

The immediate effect of rehearsal is to maintain the information in short-term memory for a few seconds while not attending to anything else. Rehearsing disconnected items, such as phone numbers or names and addresses, is one strategy for initially learning the information and storing it in long-term memory. Individuals who stop momentarily and deliberately rehearse new information recall more of it than those who do not (Howe & Ceci, 1979).

It cannot be assumed that children learn effective rehearsal techniques without instruction. Barclay (1979) found that no grade 6 students and very few grade 10 and grade 12 students had acquired an effective strategy for rehearsing the particular information used in the study. However, when they were taught an appropriate strategy, the students of all three grades used it on a new task without further prompting or instruction.

Review may start shortly after the initial learning or after an extended interval of time. Review has a long history of facilitating the permanent learning of difficult material and large amounts of factual material (Dansereau, 1978). Review is included in all modern study-skills programs designed to increase the permanent learning of course material. These programs recommend short review sessions distributed at different times during the semester or year rather than one long review session. The review sessions must be long enough to ensure that recall and relearning occur and yet not be so long as to become boring. The length and spacing of review sessions necessarily take into account the characteristics of the learner and the nature of the material.

Rehearsal and subsequent review accompanied with other strategies can make the learning of relatively meaningless material interesting and exciting to children. For example, preschool and kindergarten children repeatedly and with great enthusiasm sing:

> A, B, C, D, E, F, G;
> H, I, J, K, L, M, N, O, P;
> Q, R, S, and T, U, V;
> W, X, and Y and Z;
> Now I've said my ABC's;
> Tell me what you think of me.

As the different letters are sung by the group, each child holds up a large card with the respective letter in a bright color. The children enjoy repeating this kind of activity even more than once a week. On the other hand, simply repeating the ABC's or 1, 2, 3s individually or as a group is terribly boring. With boredom, attention and concentration wane, and retention is poor.

Organization

Organization has two important facets. One facet is to break down larger amounts of information into smaller amounts called *chunks*. Another is to establish connections between items that have no logical relationship. Combining these two techniques can do much to reduce the amount of rehearsal and review required for initial learning and long-term retention.

Larger amounts of information are chunked into smaller learnable units. Thus, 3129337648 is chunked into 312-933-7648. The three chunks are much more easily rehearsed and remembered than are the ten separate numerals. The amount of information in terms of the number of either separate items or chunks should not exceed the memory span—the short-term storage capacity—of the learner.

Miller (1956) indicated that short-term memory capacity is limited to seven items, plus or minus two. The items may be chunks, such as three digits grouped together, rather than separate entities, such as single digits. Seven is the average number of items that individuals can hold in short-term memory. Some persons can store more than nine items; the very young child cannot store even five. Clearly, however, exceeding any individual's short-term capacity without giving opportunity to rehearse produces poor initial learning and reduces later retention of what has been learned.

When the items to be learned have no apparent meaningful relationship or interconnections, it is appropriate to try to impose meaning and generate connections that will facilitate both immediate learning and subsequent recall. One means of imposing meaning among disconnected items is to identify categories to which smaller groups of the separate items of the list can be related (Tulving, 1972). Thus, 15 to 20 disconnected items of any taxonomy, such as the plant or animal kingdom, can be chunked together into smaller groups or classes, let us say four. Each smaller chunk of items is learned as an example of its class of things. For example, the 16 names—bear, rabbit, mink, fox; robin, wren, finch, dove; carp, bass, perch, pike; snake, lizard, turtle, alligator—are learned more readily in this related order than in random order. Moreover, if a month from today, you were asked to recall the names of the mammals, birds, fish, and reptiles given in this chapter to illustrate the idea of organizing material into related chunks, you would recall more of them than if you were simply asked to list the names of the animals given for illustration. Being given or being able to recall the names of the four classes of animals aids recall of the otherwise disconnected items.

Verbal mnemonic strategies for generating connections among separate items and chunks of items include stories, sentences, first-letter mnemonics, and rhymes (Morris, 1979). For example, Bower and Clark (1969) had students learn lists of 10 unrelated words by linking all the words of each list into a story. After all 12 lists were learned, the experimental students who had made up the stories recalled 93% of the words, while the control group remembered only 13%. Another mnemonic strategy is thinking up sentences that include each word of a list to be learned. The acronym—a first-letter mnemonic—is a popular connecting device. For example, CEDAR helps recall the Center for Educational Development and Research. The first letters of the Great Lakes—Huron, Ontario, Michigan, Erie, and Superior—form HOMES.

Rhymes help young children make connections and thereby learn important information that is remembered thereafter. "Thirty days hath September" is the beginning of the most widely known rhyme by English-speaking people. As we saw earlier, the song "A, B, C, D, E, F, G" is popular among kindergarten children. Rhymes, as well as other verbal devices mentioned here, effectively generate links among relatively disconnected items of factual information.

The preceding techniques for organizing material can be used by teachers in many different subject fields to aid students learn and remember. After students learn a technique, they can use it independently.

Elaboration

We saw that organization involves chunking, connecting, and relating items before storing them in long-term memory. *Elaboration,* on the other hand, involves adding meaning to new information by relating it to information in long-term memory. For example, students know what a reptile is. They are told that Testudinata is one of several orders of reptiles. Relating the new information about Testudinata to what they already know about reptiles increases their meaning of the term Testudinata (turtles and tortoises).

Weinstein (1978) identified the elaboration devices used by grade 9 students to gain knowledge from prose material that contained a great deal of new information. To do this, Weinstein first conducted an experiment in which students were taught to use various elaboration techniques. Favorable results were obtained. Using the results of this experiment, she conducted interviews with the students to clarify their use of the techniques. Then, she constructed an inventory that describes the techniques and their uses. Students responding to the inventory checked each technique that they used. Examples of the elaboration techniques follow (Weinstein, 1978, p. 52):

**ELABORATION TECHNIQUES
TO INCREASE MEANING**

1. Picture the main ideas or information.
2. "See" and "hear" the events in your mind.
3. Think about the purpose of or need for the material.
4. Relate the content to your experience or characteristics.
5. Think about your emotional reactions to the content.
6. Think about the ideas that you have as you read the material.
7. Relate the new ideas to what you already know.
8. Free-associate to the topics or ideas, that is, just think about the topic or ideas and see what comes to your mind.
9. Look for common sense or logical relationships in the material.

The first two elaboration techniques clearly involve visual imagery, and some of the others may also. Visual imagery is a powerful elaboration strategy that can be learned.

Mnemonic Strategies Using Visual Imagery

Learning the vocabulary of a second language, the names of the muscles of the body, and similar tasks have little inherent logical structure to aid initial learning and memory. Strategies using visual imagery have been developed to aid persons with tasks such as these. Here, the *loci*, or *place; peg*, or *hook;* and *key word mnemonics* are explained.

Loci, or Place, Strategy

Loci is the Latin word meaning "places." The *loci method* has been used since Grecian times. It works especially well for recalling a large amount of information. To use the loci method, you first memorize mental snapshots of a series of *familiar* places. These might be places in your apartment, from the front door through a hallway and living room into a kitchen. It could be the street on which you live or any other familiar place. The number of places vary from a few to 50 or more.

Your mental snapshots of the locations serve as pigeonholes for the list of items you want to learn, for example, a list of things to purchase at a bookstore. First, you convert each item of the list to a visual image. Then, locate the image of each item in a specific location of your series of mental snapshots. For example, a pencil may be pictured as unlocking the front door of the apartment, a pad of yellow paper may be pictured as shielding the hallway light, a notebook may be seen hanging in the hallway closet, and so on. Think about each item in its location for a few seconds. Once each item of the list is visualized this way in each place, it can be recalled later at the bookstore. This mnemonic is very popular with persons who perform memory exhibitions professionally.

Peg, or Hook, Strategy

The *peg,* or *hook, strategy* involves committing to memory a list of peg words rather than places with which to associate visual images. One easily memorized set of concrete peg words that is easily visualized is "One is a bun, two is a shoe, three is a tree, four is a door, five is a hive, six is sticks, seven is heaven, eight is a gate, nine is mine, ten is a hen." The words *bun, shoe, tree,* and so on form pegs that stand for the numbers. You can form visual images of a list of items to be remembered up to ten and "hang" each item on one of the ten pegs or hooks. For example, if you want to remember the bookstore list given earlier, you might form an image of a pencil stuck in a bun, a yellow pad of paper under the sole of a shoe, an open notebook draped over the limb of a tree, and so on. When you want to recall the list, you go through the peg words and retrieve the item that you put on each peg.

Excellent results have been obtained in many experiments with this set of ten peg words. Morris and Reid (1970) found that subjects who used it to learn ten nouns paired with the digits one to ten recalled twice as much as a control group who had not been taught the method. Lorayne and Lucas (1976) provide many applications of its uses. They also supply other lists of peg words.

Key Word Strategy

A final mnemonic, the *key word method,* involves using both sound and visual imagery. It is used in many experiments involving the learning of paired items, such as foreign language vocabulary (Atkinson, 1975; Hilgard, Atkinson, & Atkinson, 1979); the capitals of states, cities and their products, and famous people and their accomplishments (Levin, 1981); abstract prose that contains a great deal of factual information (Levin, Shriberg, & Berry, 1983); and other verbal information in various curriculum fields (Pressley, Levin, & Delaney, 1982).

In foreign language learning, this mnemonic involves two steps. The first step is to find a syllable of the foreign language word that sounds like an English word (the key word). The key word is the acoustic link to the foreign language word. The second step is to form a visual image associating the key word and the English equivalent of the foreign language word. This is the visual imagery link. To recall the English equivalent when given the foreign language word, the key word is retrieved first and then the visual image that links it to the English equivalent.

The key word mnemonic for two Spanish words is illustrated in Figure 8.1. *Caballo* is the Spanish word; *eye* is the key word corresponding to the pronunciation of the second syllable of *caballo;* and *horse* is the English equivalent. The visual image here is the horse kicking the eye. A visual image that shows the items in an interactive way, that is, the horse kicking the eye, especially facilitates learning (Levin, 1983). *Pato* is the second Spanish word. *Pot* is the key word that corresponds to the pronunciation of the first syllable. The image formed is a pot over the duck's head, another interactive relationship between the English equivalent and the key word. When learned this way, *pot* is recalled upon hearing the word *pato;* then, the image is recalled of the pot and the duck, and the English translation, *duck,* is recalled.

Despite the fact that this mnemonic appears to be complicated, it works effectively in certain situations to aid students in acquiring a beginning foreign language vocabulary. For example, Atkinson and Raugh (1975) taught students 120 Russian words in three sets of 40 words each. On the fourth day, the students using the key word method recalled 72% of the English vocabulary, while the control group recalled 46%. On an unannounced test six weeks later, the key word students recalled 43% of the English equivalents, and the control students 28%.

Not everyone has gotten equally excellent results. For example, Hall, Wilson, and Patterson (1981) found that college students did better in free study than using the key word method. Similarly, Fuentes (1976) found that second-year Spanish students in high school did not do better with the key word method than students without it. Levin, Pressley, McCormick, Miller, and Shriberg (1979) conducted a series of experiments to clarify

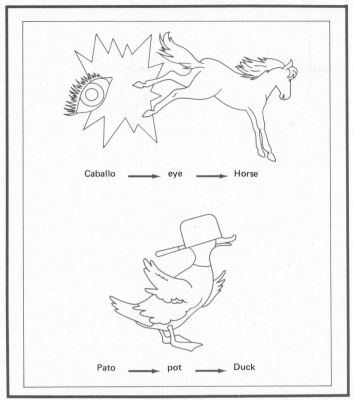

Caballo $\longrightarrow$ eye $\longrightarrow$ Horse

Pato $\longrightarrow$ pot $\longrightarrow$ Duck

Figure 8.1 Mental images used to associate spoken Spanish words with corresponding English terms. At top, *caballo* ("horse"); below, *pato* ("duck").
Source: Hilgard, Atkinson, & Atkinson, 1979, p. 239.

the conditions under which the method gets good results. Three conditions were identified. First, the students have generated neither their own learning strategies nor a beginning vocabulary in the foreign language. Second, each key word and picture for forming the visual image are supplied by the teacher to the students. Third, the teacher understands the method and carries out the related oral instruction regarding the method properly. When these conditions were met, children of grade 4 and grade 5 learned an initial vocabulary of 18 Spanish words better than control groups did. Levin et al. (1979) believe that high school students in beginning foreign language courses will profit from the key word method when appropriate adaptations of these three conditions are made. They presume that many high school students have not developed good study methods on their own.

Younger students who profit from the key word method do not independently transfer use of it from one subject field to another. Pressley and Dennis-Rounds (1980) conducted an experiment in which both 12- and 18-year-olds used the key word method to learn a list of cities paired with their products. The younger students profited more from the key word instruction than the older ones. However, without instruction, they were unable to use the method when learning a list of Latin words, while the 18-year-olds were able to use it.

Levin (1983) reviewed the research on visual imagery strategies, including the use of pictures in texts, as aids to learning and recall. Many experimenters have found the strategies to facilitate learning. However, some notable exceptions have occurred. Levin indicates that the effective use of any visual imagery strategy must be related directly to the learning task. Thus, showing a picture of a horse with the word horse on a page is not effective in aiding a child learn to decode (i.e., to read) the word *horse*. There is nothing in the picture to link it and the word. However, showing pictures of horses markedly facilitates learning the concept *horse*. Levin also noted that there are individual differences in the ability to use visual imagery strategies. People do not profit equally from instruction regarding the use of any given strategy.

Before turning to the discussion of meaningful prose, we should recognize that instruction in the use of strategies of any kind is more an art than a science. Accordingly, there are only general principles for guiding strategy instruction. Waters and Andreassen (1983) offer three principles for teaching children strategies during early and middle childhood: identify learning tasks for which the particular strategy is especially well suited; encourage children to practice the strategy; and provide verbal instruction. Verbal instruction is presumed to become more effective with increasing age. Pressley, Levin, and Bryant (1983) indicate that adolescents can be taught strategies effectively. However, many adolescents have already developed their own strategies. Accordingly, individual differences among adolescents must be given prominent attention.

Even though explicit instructional guidelines are not available, teachers should not hesitate to try out promising strategies (Peterson & Swing, 1983). The potential benefits from learning effective strategies are very great.

8.1 Give two or three examples of each of the following kinds of information of low meaningfulness: (a) names, (b) groups of names, (c) knowledge of specifics, and (d) knowledge of ways and means of dealing with specifics.

8.2 Explain how rehearsal of information facilitates its storage and subsequent retention.

8.3 Outline a rehearsal strategy and a review schedule for learning and remembering the new material in Chapters 2–6 of this book, assuming that one chapter per week is studied.

8.4 Persons vary in their ability to recall information. Do you learn better by using only this book when initially studying and later reviewing, or are you helped by preparing written notes, outlines, and summaries?

8.5 Initial learning and retention are aided by organizing large amounts of material into smaller chunks. Evaluate the conceptual structure of this chapter and its related organization into parts in terms of aiding the reader to learn and remember the main concepts. Is the number of concepts given in each set about right for you personally, or are there too many for effective rehearsal?

8.6 Give an example of the use of a story, a sentence, and a first-letter mnemonic in providing a meaningful organization for learning and recalling disconnected material.

8.7 Indicate how a rhyme facilitates (a) organization of material into chunks and (b) rehearsal of the material.

8.8 Elaboration involves adding meaning to new information by relating the new information to information already held in long-term memory. Relate this idea to the idea that instructors in educational psychology prefer that their students have some formal or informal teaching experience.

8.9 Return to Weinstein's elaboration techniques to increase meaning, and identify those which you employ while studying this chapter. Identify the kind of material to which the others apply.

8.10 Some persons use the loci, or place; peg, or hook; and key word mnemonics. Use each of these to learn some material, and decide if it is a helpful memory aid for you.

MEANINGFUL PROSE

A Model for Explaining Prose Comprehension

Within-Text Aids to Comprehension

Students gain much information by reading textbooks and similar printed material with comprehension. Despite the importance of this means of learning, the comprehension process has been studied only recently. Along with gaining a better understanding of the comprehension process, progress is being made in using aids of various kinds to facilitate the comprehension of text material. The learning strategies that students use to gain the intended meaning of text material are also being identified. This knowledge is being used to prepare more comprehensible reading material and to help students comprehend what they read.

A Model for Explaining Prose Comprehension

Kintsch and Van Dijk (1978) and Kintsch (1979) developed a model of prose comprehension to explain how persons process information as they read sentences, paragraphs, and complete passages. Their focus is on getting the gist of a complete passage as might be expressed in an abstract or summary of it. The forming of microstructures and macrostructures controlled by a goal schema is the central idea of the model, as depicted in Figure 8.2.

The terms, *microstructure* and *macrostructure*, indicate the internal representations of what is gained from reading and comprehending. A *goal schema* corresponds to the executive control of the reading comprehension process.

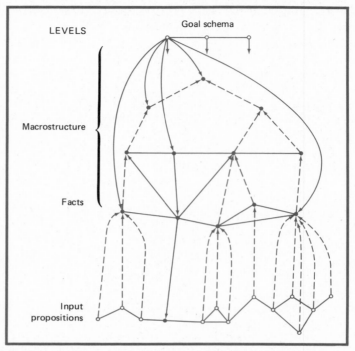

Figure 8.2 An outline for a psychological model of text comprehension.
Source: Kintsch, 1979, p. 5.

Microstructure and Macrostructure

We may gain an overview of the model by starting with the several propositions, the *microstructure,* shown at the bottom of Figure 8.2. The reader's *microstructure* of a sentence consists of one or more networks of the several propositions contained in the sentence. The networks are constructed as the sentence is being read. The reader groups related networks of propositions of one or more sentences in generating a *fact*.

The facts level is the first level of the *macrostructure*, that is, the first level at which meaning is gained that starts to get at the gist of a paragraph. Not all the facts are relevant for getting the meaning of the paragraph, that is, for constructing the macrostructure of the paragraph. Consequently, some facts are deleted, and only the relevant facts are generalized and used in constructing the next higher level of the macrostructure of the paragraph. In this way the reader forms the paragraph macrostructure, or paragraph summary.

As more paragraphs are read and comprehended, the paragraph summaries are reorganized and used in constructing the macrostructure of the entire passage. Thus, the *macrostructure* of a passage, or the meaning of it, is a hierarchically organized structure with the most important facts forming the organizational framework. The important relevant facts used in constructing the macrostructure are learned and remembered as part of the macrostructure. However, facts that are initially deleted are not automatically lost. Rather, they may be stored in long-term memory in an inactive status and later retrieved. The *goal schema,* to be discussed later, controls the entire comprehension-retention process.

We may now return to the propositional networks and facts to see how understanding the successive sentences of a paragraph proceeds in cycles. Two sentences of a paragraph will be used for illustration. The first sentence is "[The Swazi tribe] [was at war with] [a neighboring tribe]." The three groups of bracketed words correspond roughly to the three propositions of this sentence (Kintsch, 1979). These three propositions can be represented as a network consisting of nodes and relationships. The network for this sentence is depicted in Figure 8.3. The reader forms a meaning of the sentence—a microstructure—corresponding to this propositional network, as the sentence is read. Elements of it are retained in short-term memory while the next sentence is read. The actual words, that is, the *nodes,* as graphed in Figure 8.3, are not encoded as the microstructure; rather, the semantic meanings of the words and the relationships among them form the microstructure.

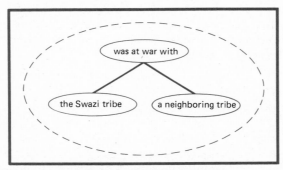

Figure 8.3 Network of propositions for the first sentence.
Source: Kintsch, 1979, p. 6.

It may be appropriate to pause to consider the relationship between a sentence and its propostions. A *proposition* is the smallest unit of information that expresses a meaning. The meaning is stored rather than the exact wording. Kintsch defines a proposition as a *relational concept* (verbs, adjectives, adverbs, prepositions, and conjunctions) and *arguments* (nouns and pronouns). The arguments of a proposition have different semantic functions, such as agent and object. The *agent* is the subject or the actor (a noun) when the relational concept is a transitive verb. If the verb is transitive, another argument is the *object* of the verb (a noun).

We may now consider the second sentence of the passage: "[Among the Swazi tribe] [were two brothers] [named] [Kakra and Gum]." The network for the sentence is shown at the bottom part of Figure 8.4. Immediately after the microstructure of this second sentence is formed, the microstructure of the first sentence, shown at the top of Figure 8.4, is retrieved from long-term memory. This, then, is the first cycle in combining the propositional networks of successive sentences of a paragraph.

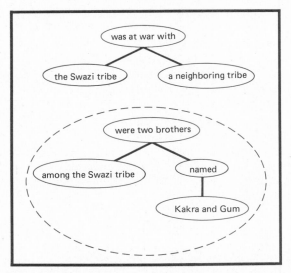

Figure 8.4 Network of propositions for the second sentence.
Source: Kintsch, 1979, p. 6.

Let us now consider the relationship among propositions, facts, and prior knowledge. The microstructures corresponding to the propositional networks are formed while reading, one microstructure for each successive sentence. Related propositions from one or more sentences that are generalized as belonging together are grouped as a *fact*. However, to establish a *fact*, the reader retrieves knowledge from long-term memory and relates the propositions inputted from the text to it. For example, if the reader has no knowledge about war, the first sentence containing the war proposition cannot be comprehended.

Let us return to the first sentence to see how relating the new knowledge with prior knowledge proceeds. The sentence indicates that the Swazi tribe was at war with a neighboring tribe. Reading this information activates in the reader's long-term memory the knowledge structure for war. For illustrative purposes, Kintsch (1979) included in the structure for war an actor, opponent, causes, and outcomes, as schematized in Figure 8.5. The Swazi tribe is inserted into this structure as the actor, and the neighboring tribe is inserted as the opponent. Since no information was presented about the causes or outcomes in the first sentence, these parts of the reader's war structure remain unfilled.

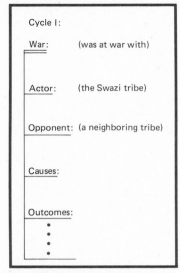

Figure 8.5 The fact analysis of the first sentence.
Source: Kintsch, 1979, p. 11.

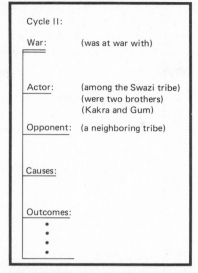

Figure 8.6 The fact analysis of the second sentence.
Source: Kintsch, 1979, p. 11.

You will recall that the second sentence included the information about the brothers, Kakra and Gum. In Figure 8.6, the network of propositions inputted from this sentence is related to the war structure established in the first sentence. Notice that the propositions are the same as those indicated earlier in the propositional network of the two sentences in Figure 8.4, except that "the Swazi tribe" of the first sentence has been deleted. The construction of a *fact* has been accomplished by grouping these propositions in terms of their relations. As successive sentences are read, only the most important propositions are retained from one sentence to the next. The others are retained in an inactive state in long-term memory. Kintsch (1979) estimates that a maximum of four propositions can be held in short-term memory and thus be available at each cycle when new propositions are being related to those already inputted. Thus, continuous relating, deleting, abstracting, and summarizing occur as successive sentences and paragraphs are read and an increasingly concise macrostructure is constructed.

Space constraints permit only a note about (1) the reader's inferring a meaning that is not provided directly in the text and (2) the reader's backtracking after having read one or more sentences.

1. When an important fact is not included in a paragraph, an inference is made in an attempt to get the intended meaning. If the inference is incorrect, misunderstanding occurs. Consider these two sentences: "Maggie ran away from home. A year later, she was found starving in San Francisco." An inference might be drawn incorrectly that Maggie, who is a dog, is a person.

2. It is possible that the first sentences of a paragraph do not contain the key fact. Despite this omission, a fact macrostructure of the sentences is constructed as the sentences are read. The key fact is then identified in a later sentence. Backtracking is now required, and the initial macrostructure must be replaced with a new one.

One or more sentences of a paragraph may contain irrelevant information. The reader must delete it from the initial macrostructure and also backtrack. Kintsch (1979) indicates that the greater the amount of inferring and backtracking required of the reader, the more difficult the material is to comprehend.

Goal Schema

We have worked upward in the model of prose comprehension (Figure 8.2) to see how meaning is gained. Gaining meaning is explained by the reader's constructing microstructures and macrostructures, including making inferences and backtracking as necessary. According to Kintsch (1979), all of these processes are controlled and monitored by a goal schema.

The *goal schema* includes the reader's purpose for reading the particular passage and also the reader's expectation of the kind of content and how it is organized. For example, if the reader's purpose is to look for specific information, a set of actions to achieve this purpose will be employed. If the purpose is to comprehend the material, the processes described thus far will be employed.

In addition to the reader's purpose for reading, a goal schema includes the reader's expectations of the substance of the material and its organization. This expectation and the reader's purpose for reading control the reader's inputting and subsequent processing of the text information. For example, your schema of an original research report probably calls for the report to have an introduction stating the research question, a description of the method, a presentation of the results, and a discussion of the results. When you read a research report and the actual schema of the report and your schema are in agreement, your schema effectively controls the processing of the information. Accordingly, your research report schema controls the reading comprehension process, starting with inputting the propositions of the first sentence. The control continues as the information of the successive sentences and paragraphs is processed and the macrostructure of the report is produced.

A comparison of the Kintsch model and other recent models of comprehension may be found in Reder (1980) and Walker and Meyer (1980). These models assume that reading is done with the purpose of comprehending and with an expectation of the kind of content to be comprehended. Similarly, the models assume that the reader is capable of recognizing the words in a passage and knows the meaning of the words.

Within-Text Aids to Comprehension

Aids to comprehension are found in some textbooks at all school levels. Some aids are inserted at the beginning of a chapter; others are placed within a chapter; still others are at the end of a chapter. Accordingly, we shall refer to the aids as *before reading, during reading,* and *after reading.* From the many studies of these aids, only those of highest importance to the college student as a learner in a new field, such as educational psychology, philosophy, or economics, will be highlighted.

Before Reading

The major kinds of aids supplied to the student in the text immediately before reading include behavioral objectives, advance organizing material, questions, and key concepts. Macdonald-Ross (1978) indicates that each of these kinds of aids, with the possible exception of behavioral objectives, is used widely with good results.

The objection to behavioral objectives, also voiced by Wittrock and Lumsdaine (1977) and expressed earlier in Chapter 2, is that in most subject fields behavioral objectives are too specific to guide comprehension effectively. Thus, detailed behavioral objectives may be more appropriate for typing and other clearly defined skills areas than for educational psychology, history, or English literature.

An *advance organizer,* as explained in Chapter 4, presents the reader, before starting to read, higher-order concepts to which to relate material encountered while reading (Ausubel, 1963, 1977). Advance organizers have proven successful in many situations with students of varying ages (Mayer, 1979). For example, an advance organizer aided college students to comprehend ideas in a textbook on computer programming (Mayer, 1980). Alexander, Frankiwiez, and Williams (1979) used advanced organizers in oral and in pictorial form with students of grades 5, 6, and 7; these organizers facilitated immediate acquisition of social studies information and also retention of it two weeks later. Lawton (1977) included rules for classifying in an advance organizer for children of age 6 and age 10. The rules helped children classify different categories of items that were included in the reading material.

An advance organizer provides the central concepts of a passage, and it may include a method for gaining the intended meaning. A schema is a kind of advance organizer; however, it provides an expectation of what is to be experienced. A schema, like an advance organizer, is a knowledge structure that is already stored in memory to which incoming information is related. Thus, persons have *schemata* (plural of *schema*) for visual experiences, such as looking at a skyscraper; for motor-skill performances, such as playing tennis; and for cognitive learning, such as reading meaningful prose. Each schema is hierarchically organized and has a slot, or *frame,* for each subschema of the complete structure. For example, the schema for reading a research report has a subschema for each part of the report, such as the methods section and the results section.

A schema may be prepared and presented to students who have not yet had an opportunity to develop it. Presenting an appropriate schema in advance of reading provides an overall structure and frames for, first, relating new information and, subsequently, integrating it. As new information is integrated into a person's existing schema, the schema itself is reorganized and changed. Anderson and his associates have found that presenting the reader with a schema prior to reading aids comprehension (Anderson, Reynolds, Schallert, & Goetz, 1977; Anderson, Spiro, & Anderson, 1978; Pichert & Anderson, 1977).

A third kind of prereading aid is the *advance question.* One kind of question calls for the reader to recall relevant information prior to reading. Another kind is to be answered while reading the new material. Frase (1971) found that advance questions that called for the reader to draw inferences from new material produced better results than advance questions that asked them to recall new information verbatim.

The last of the before-reading aids, a set of *key concepts,* gives the reader an orienting and attentional device, a structure for organizing and relating new material, and an aid to planning effective use of time. These ideas were explained in Chapter 1 and accordingly are not repeated here. Instead, part of the conceptual structure of this chapter is given (see Figure 8.7).

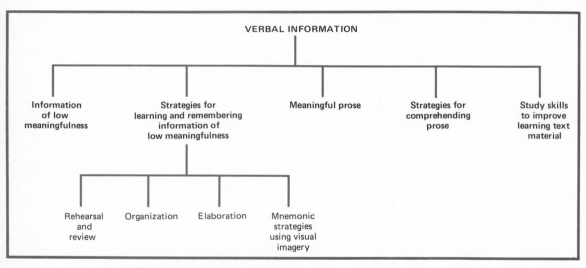

Figure 8.7 Partial conceptual structure of Chapter 8.

You notice that the complete opening-chapter structure is given but that the subordinate concepts are indicated for only one superordinate concept. Consider now the following questions that suggest how the reader might use this conceptual structure:

1. How well does a brief examination of the opening-chapter structure, followed by a few seconds of rehearsal and elaboration (a)

orient the reader to the chapter content and (b) provide the reader a structure for organizing the chapter content?

2. How well does a brief examination of the structure for "Strategies for Learning and Remembering Information of Low Meaningfulness," followed by a few seconds of elaboration and rehearsal (a) orient the reader to that part of the chapter content and (b) provide a structure for organizing that part of the chapter content?

3. How well does making a survey of the chapter that includes examining the conceptual structures at the beginning and at each main part of the chapter enable the reader to decide whether to try to complete the study of the chapter in one study session or in more than one session?

Readers may answer these questions differently, primarily because they differ in their prior knowledge of the nature of verbal information and how it is learned. Some may be able to comprehend and subsequently recall the material without taking any written notes and with little review and relearning after completing their first study of the chapter. Others will profit from activities such as making a chapter outline that includes the subconcepts for each main concept, talking with other students to clarify any concepts that are not well understood, and reviewing the chapter a few days after reading it and again a week or two later.

Within-Chapter Questions and Activities

Without getting questions before each part of a chapter or after each part (post-reading questions), readers apparently read in terms of what they think should be learned and remembered. However, Wixson (1983) found that what students recall can be controlled by the kind of post-reading question that is asked. One week after reading and then answering text-explicit, text-implicit, or schema-based questions that followed short passages, the students were retested for recall. The text-explicit group best recalled information included in the passages; the text-implicit group best recalled inferences they drew directly related to the passages; and the schema-based students best recalled schema-based information, that is, information that called for them to provide information from their knowledge store to the text information. Reynolds and Anderson (1982) asked readers a question after every four pages of a 48-page passage. They found readers to spend more time reading and more time in probing for the information called for by the questions than for other information not needed to answer the questions. These researchers conclude that readers selectively give more attention to question-relevant information and also rehearse or carry out some other information-processing strategy. The combination of greater attention and the use of a processing strategy accounts for more of the question-relevant information being learned.

Macdonald-Ross (1978) and others found that post-reading questions placed within chapters of a text and demanding recall of information are not very effective. For example, Rickards (1979) reported that post-questions that call for either recall of specific details or verbatim recall of main ideas are less effective than those that call for the reader to reorganize the detailed information in a meaningful way around the general idea contained in a passage.

Mayer (1980) found two kinds of questions to be effective in increasing comprehension and recall. One kind invites the reader to organize, apply, analyze, or evaluate the information provided in the text. The other kind calls for the reader to integrate the new material with prior knowledge and experience. You will recognize that these two kinds of questions are used throughout this book. Answering questions such as these as part of the required activities of a course has been found to improve achievement substantially (Ellis, Wulfeck, & Montague, 1980).

Questions and Activities After Reading

The primary aids to retention after reading a complete chapter or passage include questions and summaries. LaPorte and Voss (1975) compared the effectiveness of answering postquestions, of answering postquestions and receiving feedback, and of receiving a summary of the same information as called for by the questions. The postquestions plus feedback produced the best results on a one-week retention test. The postquestions group and the summary group performed less well than the postquestions plus feedback group, but better than the control group.

Rehearsal and review have been considered in connection with learning information of low meaningfulness and will not be reviewed here. However, one kind of activity, *recitation,* merits attention. In a controlled experiment, some classroom groups of grade 6 students were involved in short, daily question-and-answer recitations about what they had read and other classroom groups were not (Gall, Ward, Berliner, Cahen, Winne, Elashoff, & Stanton, 1978). The students who participated in the recitations acquired more information initially, retained more, and were more able to speak and write in response to questions.

Visual Aids

Graphics in the form of bar graphs, line drawings, and flowcharts aid learners to understand concepts and processes (Macdonald-Ross, 1977, 1978). Pictures that directly relate to the material aid the reader, especially children, to comprehend difficult ideas (Levin, 1983). The pictures make the text ideas more comprehensible, more concrete, and easier to remember. However, when pictures are used as decorative or interest-gaining devices unrelated to the content, they may hinder comprehension by providing distracting material and by making the printed material seem dull and unattractive. Placing comic strips, cartoons, and other unrelated material in the text merely for decorative purposes is also of dubious value (Macdonald-Ross, 1977).

8.11 In expository text material, a *proposition* corresponds to each meaningful unit of a sentence; a *propositional network* corresponds to the meaning of a simple sentence; and a *fact* is the main idea drawn from a complex sentence, or two or more related sentences of a paragraph. The first level of a *macrostructure,* or summary, of a paragraph is facts. Relate these ideas to those presented by Kintsch in Figure 8.2.

8.12 The individual's *goal schema* for reading particular material, as defined by Kintsch, includes the reader's purpose for reading it and the reader's expectations of the kind of content to be read and of how it is organized. Identify your own goal schema for reading a Sunday comic strip, such as *Peanuts,* and for reading a chapter of this book.

8.13 Authors try to facilitate the reader's comprehension of text material by inserting any of four kinds of material at the beginning of the chapter: behavioral objectives, an advance organizer, questions, and a conceptual structure consisting of the key concepts of the chapter. Indicate the common purposes of these before-reading aids.

8.14 Research shows that readers prefer within-chapter questions that call for application or integration rather than recall of information presented. What is your preference?

8.15 Aids inserted in texts after reading include questions and summaries. In this text, evaluate the questions and activities at the end of each part of a chapter and the summary at the end of the chapter in terms of aiding you to learn the material initially. To review the chapter after a week or more has elapsed.

8.16 Evaluate the degree to which the figures and tables in this book help you to comprehend text material initially and to recall it later.

STRATEGIES FOR COMPREHENDING PROSE

The three main strategies for learning and remembering any kind of material by reading involve organization, elaboration, and rehearsal and review. Other major considerations are intending to learn, trying to understand the writer's views, using aids to reading that are included in the material, and self-regulation of the reading process. Various individuals and groups have identified specific strategies related to specific tasks involving the preceding ideas.

A large panel of scholars and teachers identified six reading strategies that follow as essential for academic success in the first year of college (College Board, 1983). Reading specialists regard the first three strategies as comprehension strategies and the last three as study skills, or study strategies, specific to reading. However, there is not uniformity in classifying the strategies:

Children learn comprehension strategies paving the way for enjoyment and academic success.

1. Identifying and comprehending the main and subordinate ideas in a written work and summarizing the ideas in one's own words.
2. Defining unfamiliar words by decoding, using contextual clues, or by using a dictionary.
3. Separating one's personal opinions and assumptions from a writer's.
4. Recognizing different purposes and methods of writing, identifying a writer's point of view and tone, and interpreting a writer's meaning inferentially as well as literally.
5. Varying one's reading speed and method (survey, skim, review, question, and master) according to the type of material and one's purpose for reading.
6. Using the features of books and other reference materials, such as table of contents, preface, introduction, titles and subtitles, index, glossary, appendix, and bibliography.

These strategies can probably be learned by most students by the end of grade 9. Clearly, teachers should be expert in each one and should develop techniques for teaching them to students.

Camperell (1980) carried out an experiment to identify more precisely the comprehension strategies that grade 7 students employed when reading descriptive, expository material. This expository material was organized into 9 paragraphs, with a total of 55 sentences that contained 372 propositions. The propositions were identified by the same procedure used by Kintsch (1979). The passage described and explained the type of land and climate found in the Kalahari Desert in Africa. It also provided information about the life of the nomads who live in this desert.

Camperell (1980) found that the grade 7 students used nine identifiably different strategies for comprehending prose paragraphs. Most of the strategies involved two or more substrategies. The rank order of use of the strategies, from most frequently used to least frequently used, follows (Camperell, 1980, pp. 107, 108):

COMPREHENSION STRATEGIES OF GRADE 7 STUDENTS

1. Using prior knowledge to understand the material of a new paragraph by (a) relating information in the new paragraph to ideas read in previous paragraphs, (b) contrasting the ideas in a new paragraph with one's own prior knowledge and experience, and (c) comparing the ideas in a new paragraph with one's own prior knowledge and experience.
2. Using contextual information provided directly in the paragraph(s) to (a) determine the meanings of unknown words, (b) assign a specific meaning to words with multiple meanings, and (c) comprehend information that was not initially understood.
3. Identifying the important ideas of a paragraph by (a) reading all of the sentences and determining which idea is the topic of most of the sentences in a paragraph and (b) reading the first sentence and predicting the topic of most of the other sentences.
4. Identifying the important ideas of a paragraph by (a) identifying the topic of the paragraph as well as groups of ideas related to the topic and (b) dividing the ideas of a paragraph into groups of related ideas.
5. Identifying the important ideas of a paragraph on the basis of personal reactions or idiosyncratic strategies.
6. Reading a paragraph slowly to gain an understanding of the material or concentrating on the ideas of a paragraph to gain an understanding of the material.
7. Reading information in paragraphs more than once to be able to remember the information or to overcome comprehension failures.
8. Identifying sentences that give causes or effects of other information in a paragraph.
9. Noting when comprehension has or has not occurred.

Camperell (1980) also found that students above the median in reading achievement, as determined by a standardized reading achievement test, used the first four strategies more often than did those below the median. Differences in use of the other strategies were not statistically significant. Another important finding was that the students who used one or more of the strategies typically recalled more than those who did not.

Morrison (1980) administered a questionnaire to a national sample of secondary school teachers in content fields such as English, home economics, mathematics, science, and social studies. About 40% of the teachers taught grades 7 and 8, and 60% taught grades 9–12. One purpose of the study was to identify the comprehension skills that the teachers regarded as relevant to students' comprehension of reading materials used in their subject fields. Another was to identify the percentage of students whom the teachers regarded as needing help with individual skills. The skills included in the questionnaire were drawn from many sources and agreed upon by a panel of reading experts. The 14 skills follow. At the end of each skill, two numbers are given in parentheses. The first number indicates the median percentage of all the teachers who indicated that the skill is relevant. The second specifies the median percentage of the teachers who expected to offer their students help with the skill (Morrison, 1980, pp. 62, 63):

COMPREHENSION STRATEGIES DESIRED OF HIGH SCHOOL STUDENTS

1. Determining the main ideas of a paragraph (87, 64).
2. Determining the main idea of a selection (85, 68).
3. Using stated (e.g., first, next) and implied sequence clues (83, 70).
4. Analyzing relationships (e.g., cause and effect) to reach conclusions (89, 91).
5. Interpreting specialized notations (e.g., formulas, equations) (63, 93).
6. Interpreting graphic displays (e.g., maps, graphs, tables, diagrams, patterns) (79, 86).
7. Considering author's purpose (54, 84).
8. Distinguishing fact from opinion (68, 86).
9. Recognizing persuasive techniques (53, 90).
10. Questioning the relevance of information to a topic (76, 83).
11. Identifying details that support a position (79, 82).
12. Attempting to generalize from information read (86, 79).
13. Attempting to apply information gained from reading (95, 85).
14. Making use of transitional words, phrases, and clauses as bridges to join ideas (74, 76).

As one might expect, a lower percentage of the teachers of mathematics (65%), industrial arts (65%), and business education (67%) rated the comprehension skills as relevant to their reading materials. A much higher percentage of the teachers of social studies (97%), English (95%), science (89%), and home economics (78%) regarded these skills as relevant to their fields.

The extent to which children of different ages and school levels use various comprehension strategies effectively has not been catalogued.

However, Peterson, Swing, Braverman, and Buss (1982) found that fifth- and sixth-grade students used an average of 7.64 general strategies and 16.05 specific strategies to gain an understanding of mathematics exercises. The two strategies most closely related to achievement were relating prior knowledge to the present task and trying to understand the teacher's explanations.

STUDY SKILLS TO
IMPROVE LEARNING TEXT MATERIAL

In the questionnaire of secondary school teachers, Morrison (1980) found considerable variation among teachers of the different subject fields with respect to study skills. Although a lower percentage of the teachers of mathematics, home economics, and industrial arts perceived the skills as relevant to their fields, from 60–100% of the grade 9–12 teachers of every subject field regarded the following study skills as relevant to their fields (Morrison, 1980, pp. 63, 64):

STUDY SKILLS DESIRED
OF HIGH SCHOOL STUDENTS

1. Setting a purpose for reading.
2. Formulating questions relevant to purpose for reading.
3. Adjusting reading speed to type and difficulty of material.
4. Adjusting reading speed to purpose for reading.
5. Attending to organization of material.
6. Skimming material for overview.
7. Scanning material for details.
8. Taking notes in short phrases.
9. Using special features of books (e.g., table of contents, index) as appropriate.
10. Using basic references (e.g., dictionary) as needed.
11. Employing appropriate test-taking strategies.

Dansereau (1978) describes a newly developed program for teaching students study skills. The program is designed to teach students two main strategies: a study-skills strategy and a support strategy.

The six steps of the study-skills strategy are as follows: establish a mood for study, understand, recall, digest, expand, and review. MURDER is the first-letter acronym that Dansereau has generated to facilitate recall of the strategy. *Establishing a mood for study* is an element of the support strategy to be considered later. Reading for *understanding* involves using comprehension strategies, such as those indicated earlier in this chapter.

Recall implies retrieving from memory what has been studied without referral to the text. *Digesting* the material involves correcting recall as appropriate and organizing and storing the newly acquired material in long-term memory. *Expanding* on what was learned is accomplished by self-inquiry; the student is taught to find applications of what has been learned, to analyze and evaluate the new information, and to engage in other activities that go beyond the information given in the text. *Review* may be based on self-tests or tests given by the teacher.

The preceding elements of *understand, recall, digest, expand,* and *review* are similar to a method originally proposed by Robinson (1946), with which you are probably familiar: the *SQ3R method.* Its steps include surveying the material to be read, formulating questions to be answered before starting to read, reading, reciting or rehearsing after reading to answer each question, and reviewing to promote long-term retention and recall. The study skills strategy of Dansereau—understand, recall, digest, expand, and review—includes substrategies for carrying out each of the preceding steps. You will recall that Dansereau's complete program also has a support strategy.

The support strategy has three sets of substrategies: setting goals and making plans to achieve the goals, managing concentration while studying, and monitoring one's study skills and diagnosing possible difficulties. Goal setting and planning for study require establishing a mood for studying, thus the M in MURDER as indicated earlier.

I outlined a strategy in Chapter 1 similar to that of Dansereau for facilitating learning from this text. I have found that university students can readily learn the strategy and use it and that they also use many of the more specific comprehension and study-skills strategies that are indicated in the present chapter. Furthermore, I have found that university students can set realistic goals in their courses and can make plans to achieve them. However, problems with concentration in the form of not being able to get in the mood for concentrated study and not being able to cope with distractions while attempting to study occur at times for some students. Similarly, some students have had little prior experience in learning to monitor their study schedule or to diagnose their learning problems and test-taking problems. Conferring informally with other students or professors and getting assistance from a counseling center that focuses on problems of concentration are often very helpful.

8.17 Return to the nine comprehension strategies that grade 7 students employed: (a) mentally check those which you use when studying text material that contains a considerable amount of new information; (b) mentally check those that you think most students can learn by ages 10–12 if given good instruction.

8.18 Return to the 14 comprehension strategies that high school teachers desire of high school students: (a) mentally check those which you employ; (b) add others that you use.

8.19 What percentage of the college students you know use a study-skills strategy such as that proposed by Dansereau? Why do some students not employ any kind of study strategy systematically?

8.20 At which school level do you think students should seriously try to learn and use a study-skills strategy: middle school, high school, college? Give reasons.

8.21 Describe some behaviors of students who experience academic difficulty in college because of ineffective study skills. Because of poor concentration.

8.22 What relationship do you perceive between concentration and intrinsic motivation, as explained in Chapter 7?

8.23 Review and Application: Recall the most important information regarding each of the following concepts, and identify at least one possible use of the information by you as a learner, a teacher, or both:

Information of Low Meaningfulness
   Names and Groups of Names
   Specific Facts
Strategies for Learning and Remembering Information of Low
      Meaningfulness
   Rehearsal and Review
   Organization
   Elaboration
   Mnemonic Strategies Using Visual Imagery
Meaningful Prose
   A Model for Explaining Prose Comprehension
   Within-Text Aids to Comprehension
Strategies for Comprehending Prose
Study Skills to Improve Learning Text Material

SUMMARY

Much important information in many subject fields is not logically connected or inherently meaningful. However, students do not have to learn it by rote memory. Teachers, and also authors, can carefully organize the material into appropriate learning units and can establish relatedness of disconnected material before encouraging students to start learning it. Even more important, students can be taught learning strategies involving rehearsal and review, organization of material, and elaboration. Mnemonic techniques, especially those involving visual imagery, are helpful to some students.

As early as the primary grades, students who can read with independence learn a great deal by reading and studying connected discourse
in textbooks and other printed material. Recent information about how we
comprehend information presented in sentences, paragraphs, and complete
passages is providing a good foundation for identifying comprehension
strategies and teaching them to students.

Aids to improve comprehension require that the text material should
have a readily learnable and meaningfully organized conceptual structure.
Aids to make well-organized material more comprehensible are placed at
the beginning of each chapter, within the chapter, and at the end of the
chapter. These aids, when used by the student as intended, facilitate initial
comprehension and subsequent recall and application.

Students improve their initial acquisition, retention, and use of verbal
information by learning comprehension strategies and study skills. Many
effective comprehension strategies that all students should learn have been
identified recently. Present study-skills strategies include substrategies related to understanding, recalling, digesting, expanding, and reviewing. Goal
setting, establishing a mood for concentrated study, maintaining concentration while studying, and monitoring one's study contribute greatly to
effective learning of text material.

SUGGESTIONS FOR FURTHER READING

Anderson, J. R. *Cognitive psychology and its implications*. San Francisco: Freeman, 1980.

Chapter 3 presents a clear analysis of visual imagery. Chapter 4 makes
propositions and propositional networks comprehensible. Chapter 5
explains schema and prototypes.

Association for Supervision and Curriculum Development. *Teaching
thinking skills*. Washington, D.C.: Association for Supervision and Curriculum Development, 1981.

This October 1981 issue of the journal *Educational Leadership* has
several informative articles on teaching thinking skills.

Chall, J. S., & Stahl, S. A. Reading. In H. E. Mitzel, J. H. Best, & W.
Rabinowitz (Eds.), *Encyclopedia of educational research* (5th ed., Vol. 3).
New York: Free Press, 1982.

This comprehensive review of research on reading contains a short,
interesting section on comprehension.

Englert, C. S., & Hiebert, E. H. Children's developing awareness of text structure in expository materials. *Journal of Educational Psychology,* 1984, *76,* 65–74.

An experiment that found positive relationships among children's knowledge of different types of expository material, their comprehension of the material, and their reading ability.

Mayer, R. E. Aids to text comprehension. *Educational Psychologist,* 1984, *19,* 30–42.

An excellent discussion of aids to comprehension that can be used by college students; relates comprehension to information processing.

Pressley, M., & Levin, J. R. (Eds.). *Cognitive strategy research: Educational applications.* New York: Springer-Verlag, 1983.

This book presents a variety of mnemonics, general strategies, and specific strategies, including comprehension strategies, and describes classroom applications.

Rohwer, W. D. An invitation to an educational psychology of studying. *Educational Psychologist,* 1984, *19,* 1–14.

A readable interpretation of research and theory regarding study strategies; of interest to college students as learners and as teachers.

Ryan, M. P. Monitoring text comprehension: Individual differences in epistemological standards. *Journal of Educational Psychology,* 1984, *76,* 248–258.

An experiment relating the criteria that college students used in determining whether they understood chapters of their textbook to the grades they made in the course.

Short, E. J., & Ryan, E. B. Metacognitive differences between skilled and less skilled readers: Remediating deficits through story grammar and attribution training. *Journal of Educational Psychology,* 1984, *76,* 225–235.

An experiment showing dramatic positive effects of instructing children to monitor their comprehension and their effort.

CHAPTER 9

CONCEPTS AND PRINCIPLES

THE NATURE OF CONCEPTS

CONCEPT LEARNING

USING CONCEPTS

NORMATIVE DEVELOPMENT IN LEARNING AND USING CONCEPTS

INDIVIDUAL DIFFERENCES IN CONCEPT LEARNING

TEACHING CONCEPTS

Concepts are the mental tools with which we think. Having concepts enables us to understand the physical and social world and to communicate with understanding. Without having concepts with which to think, adult human beings, like infants, would be limited mainly to living in a world of sensory perceptions. The large differences among persons of the same age in intellectual functioning are closely related to the kind and number of concepts they have learned. This chapter is designed to enable you to increase your understanding of how students learn concepts and how to teach concepts effectively. Developmental trends and individual differences are also considered. Study of the chapter will help you with your present learning of concepts as well as with learning to teach others.

THE NATURE OF CONCEPTS

Concepts as Mental Constructs of the Individual

Concepts as Societally Accepted Word Meanings

Concepts as Form Classes of Words

Concrete and Abstract Concepts

Attributes of Concepts

Concepts have been studied from many different points of view. This widespread interest stems from the pervasiveness of concepts. Concepts are essential for thinking. Understanding concepts is necessary for understanding principles and for solving problems. Concepts serve as the organizing framework of every curricular area, and they are basic in all kinds of communication, including communication between teachers and their students.

Concepts as Mental Constructs of the Individual

What comes to your mind in response to these questions: What is psychology? How is psychology like sociology and cultural anthropology?

How is it different? The meaning you have of psychology and your ideas about the likenesses and differences between psychology and other behavioral sciences are your *mental construct,* or concept, of psychology. Stated more generally, a *concept* consists of a person's organized information about one or more entities—objects, events, ideas, or processes—that enables the individual to discriminate the particular entity or class of entities from other entities and also to relate it to other entities and classes of entities. Pause momentarily after each of the following words: *Pretty, swim, our, strawberry, up.* The meaning of each word and the visual images, sounds, and scents that you recall when hearing the word are your concept, or mental construct, of it. It is what you have constructed from your formal and informal learning experiences with examples of the particular concept.

Concepts as Societally Accepted Word Meanings

A concept as a public entity corresponds to the meaning of the word that names the concept. Word meanings are put into dictionaries, encyclopedias, and other books. Thus, the meanings of words compromise the societally accepted, or public, concepts of groups of persons who speak the same language. Carroll (1964) related concepts, words, and word meanings to one another in the following way. Words in a language can be thought of as a series of spoken or written entities. There are meanings for words that can be considered a standard of communicative behavior that is shared by those who speak a language. Finally, there are concepts, that is, the classes of experiences formed in individuals either independently of language processes or in close dependence on language processes. Putting the three together, Carroll (1964) stated: "A 'meaning' of a word is, therefore, a societally-standardized concept, and when we say that a word stands for or names a concept it is understood that we are speaking of concepts that are shared among the members of a speech community" (p. 187).

Return now to the first question: What is psychology? You may be uncertain whether your concept, or your meaning of psychology, is the same as that held by others. Consulting an unabridged dictionary or a psychology dictionary will help you to check your meaning.

Concepts as Form Classes of Words

Words and word phrases name concepts. Words, depending on their use in sentences, are categorized into six form classes: nominals, adjectivals, verbals, adverbials, prepositionals, and conjunctivals.

Nominals include nouns, pronouns, and noun phrases. Examples follow: nouns—chair, Americans, thought, symmetry; pronouns—she, who, themselves; noun phrases—the broken chair, the ugly duckling, a brilliant thought. Your meaning of noun, pronoun, and noun phrase is your concept of each of these subclasses of nominals.

Verbals include verbs and verb phrases. Examples follow: verbs—hit, love, throw; verb phrases—has been hit, will love, is throwing. Concepts represented by the form classes (e.g., quickly, when) *adverbials, adjectivals* (e.g., red, smooth), *prepositionals* (e.g., between, in), and *conjunctivals* (e.g., but, because) differ in many respects from one form class to another.

Concrete and Abstract Concepts

Another way of viewing concepts is whether the class of things, for example, chairs, thoughts, have examples that can be perceived. Concepts having perceptible examples are *concrete,* whereas concepts that do not have perceptible examples are *abstract.* Concrete concepts are learned more informally and earlier in life than abstract concepts. Persons typically need instruction to learn abstract concepts. Indeed, high school seniors who have not been taught the abstract concepts of English, mathematics, science, music, art, and other fields function intellectually at the level of elementary school children.

Attributes of Concepts

Some concepts are of things and are represented by *nominals.* Others are of processes and are represented by *verbals.* Still others are of qualities and are represented by *adjectivals.* All concepts, however, have certain defining attributes, including learnability, usability, clarity, generality, and power. Understanding these properties of concepts helps educators to select the concepts that should be taught.

Learnability

Some concepts are more easily learned than others. For example, concepts that have observable examples, such as *dog* and *tree,* are more easily learned than those without perceptible examples, such as *justice* and *motivation.*

Usability

Concepts vary in usability for understanding principles and for solving problems. For example, the mathematical concepts *number* and *set* are used more frequently in solving a variety of problems than the concepts *proportion* and *ratio.* Likewise, in writing, the concepts *common noun* and *proper noun* are used more often than *count noun.*

Clarity

A concept has clarity to the extent that experts agree on its meaning. Concepts that are part of the taxonomies of zoology, botany, and chemistry, for example, *animal, plant,* and *element,* have greater clarity than do many concepts in the behavioral sciences, for example, *intelligence* and *liberal.* Concepts closely related to emotions, such as *jealousy* and *anxiety,* are less clear than those that have perceptible examples. Concepts that are based on beliefs, such as *soul* and *heaven,* are even less clear. Unclear concepts are often called "fuzzy."

Generality

Many concepts are organized into taxonomies. The higher the concept in the taxonomy, the more general it is in the number of subclasses or subordinate concepts it includes: *living things* is a generic concept that is highly general; *vertebrate, mammal,* and *man* are successively less general concepts.

Power

The attribute of power refers to the extent to which a particular concept facilitates the attainment of other concepts or principles. For example, the concept *counting* is especially powerful, because understanding counting facilitates the understanding of adding and subtracting.

There is general agreement that instruction in any subject-matter field should start with the more learnable, usable, clear, general, and powerful concepts. Concepts less powerful and general, as well as factual information, can then be related to these already understood concepts and be learned more easily.

9.1 Explain the difference between a concept as an individual's mental construct and as the societally accepted meaning of the word that names the concept.

9.2 React to the statement that every word in the English language is the name of a concept.

9.3 Name two or three concrete concepts and two or three abstract concepts.

9.4 Indicate how the concepts *animal* and *spiritual* differ in learnability, usability, clarity, generality, and power.

9.5 Imagine a world in which persons do not have words that name concepts. How will they think? How will they communicate with one another?

Learning a Concept at
Four Successively
Higher Levels

Mental Processes in
Learning a Concept at
Successively Higher
Levels

Fixed Order of Learning at
Successively Higher
Levels

CONCEPT LEARNING

We marvel at the rapid physical development of children as they progress from total helplessness to complete independence. An equally remarkable progression occurs in intellectual development, although it is not equally observable. One difference between the physical and the intellectual progression is that the physical occurs primarily as a result of *maturation,* whereas the intellectual occurs primarily as a result of *learning.* As noted earlier, the learning of concepts is the foundation of intellectual progression. Remarkable progress has been made in recent years in gaining an understanding of how the same concepts are learned at increasingly higher levels of understanding and use. The mental processes that make possible the progression from one level to the next, as well as the fixed order of the progression, have been identified by recent research.

Learning a Concept at Four
Successively Higher Levels

Let us examine the four successively higher levels at which individuals learn a given concept. At each higher level of learning a concept, a person's understanding of it deepens and its use for understanding principles and for solving problems increases. The four successively higher levels at which a concept is learned—the *concrete, identity, classificatory,* and *formal* levels—are shown in Figure 9.1.

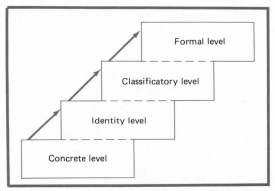

Figure 9.1 Four successively higher levels at which a concept is learned.

We may illustrate the four levels with a concrete concept, *pencil.* At some time in your early years, you saw a pencil and later were able to recognize it as the same object when you saw it in exactly the same place and position *(concrete level).* You then saw the same pencil in two different places or positions and recognized it as being the same pencil *(identity level).* After you recognized two or more different pencils at the identity level, you recognized that at least two of them were equivalent in certain ways *(classificatory level).* During this time, or shortly thereafter, you may also have learned the concepts *pen, chalk,* and *crayon* at the classificatory level. As you learned more about the class of things called *pencils,* and also about other classes of things used for writing and drawing, you could reliably identify examples of each class, call the examples by their names, and indicate some of the attributes of each class. You had learned the classificatory level of *pencil* at a higher level of understanding and use. Now consider these questions: What are the attributes of the class of things called pencils? What are the attributes of the class of things called pens? What are the common attributes of both pencils and pens (how are they alike?) and what are the critical attributes of each? (what makes them different?) If you can answer these questions, you have learned the concept of *pencil* at the *formal level.*

Try to imagine an individual's progression in the understanding and use of thousands of concepts at these four successively higher levels, and you will have an overview of the great change in intellectual functioning that occurs from infancy to maturity.

Mental Processes in Learning
a Concept at Successively Higher Levels

Certain mental processes are involved in learning a concept at each of the four successively higher levels. It is the emergence of one or more new mental operations that makes it possible to progress from one level to the next. The new mental operations do not become functional merely with neural maturation. Learning is required. Accordingly, because they do not learn, not all persons attain the formal level of many concepts. Instruction is especially important in enabling students to attain concepts at the formal level.

Concrete Level Processes

A concept is learned at the concrete level when something is attended to one or more times; discriminated from other things; and remembered; and then later is again attended to, discriminated, and recognized as the same thing. This sequence of mental processes follows:

**MENTAL OPERATIONS IN LEARNING
A CONCEPT AT THE CONCRETE LEVEL**

Attending to perceptible features of an object.
Discriminating the object from other objects.
Remembering the discriminated object (internally representing, storing, and retrieving the concrete-level representation).

For example, a young child *attends* to a clock on the wall that was experienced earlier, *discriminates* it from other objects, *represents* the clock internally, *retrieves* the earlier representation of the clock, and *recognizes* it as the same thing attended to earlier. This child has attained a concept of this particular clock at the concrete level. Recent evidence suggests that even human infants are capable of this level of conceptualizing (Bower, 1974).

Identity Level Processes

Attainment of a concept at the identity level is inferred when the individual recognizes an item as the same one previously encountered when the item is observed in a different context, when it is observed from a different spatial-temporal perspective, or when it is sensed in a different modality, such as hearing or seeing. For example, the child who recognizes the clock as the same one when it is removed from the wall of one room and placed in another room has attained the concept of that particular clock at the identity level. Similarly, the child who recognizes the family poodle whether seen from straight ahead, from the side, or from various angles has attained the concept of that particular poodle at the identity level. The sequence of mental processes follows:

**MENTAL OPERATIONS IN LEARNING
A CONCEPT AT THE IDENTITY LEVEL**

Attending to perceptible features of an object.
Discriminating the object from other objects.
Remembering the discriminated object.
Generalizing the object to be the same object when experienced in different
    contexts or modalities.
Remembering the generalized object (internally representing, storing, and re-
    trieving the identity-level representation).

Generalizing an object to be the same object when experienced in different
contexts or modalities is the new operation postulated to emerge from learning and maturation and to make possible attainment at the identity level.

    Notice that the discussion has focused on visual differences. Two
other points are now in order. First, concepts may be learned at the identity
level that are based on other sensory experiences, including hearing, touching, and smelling. Second, what is represented internally and stored for any
concept may include more than one perceptual base, for example, both seeing and hearing. Moreover, if the child also learns the name of the item, it,
too, is encoded and stored.

    Gagné (1977) treats concepts at the concrete and identity levels as
discriminations. Miller and Johnson-Laird (1976) treat concepts at these
levels as *percepts*. Piaget (1970) does not differentiate between the concrete and identity levels but refers to *object concepts*. Flavell (1977) presents a lucid account of Piaget's six phases in an infant's attainment of an
object concept during the first two years of life; object concepts are first
learned at about 18–24 months of age. However, Nelson (1974) theorized
that infants attain object concepts at 12 months of age, or even younger. We
should recognize, too, that adults meet many new and different persons for
very short time periods. They are continuoually attaining concepts of individual persons at the identity level. However, because they already have
a mature concept of *person*, their task is much easier than that of the young
child.

Classificatory Level Processes

    In order to learn a concept for the first time at the classificatory level,
at least two examples of the concept must already have been learned at the
identity level. The mental processes involved in learning a concept at this
beginning classificatory level are as follows:

**MENTAL OPERATIONS IN LEARNING
A CONCEPT AT THE CLASSIFICATORY LEVEL**

Attending to the less obvious attributes of at least two examples of the class
    of objects.
Discriminating each example from nonexamples.

Remembering the discriminated examples.
Generalizing each example experienced in different contexts or modalities to
  be the same example.
Generalizing the two examples to be equivalent (belong to the same class).
Remembering the generalization (internally representing, storing, and re-
  trieving the classificatory-level representation).

The new mental operation that makes possible attainment of concepts at the classificatory level is *generalizing* that two or more things are equivalent. Accordingly, attaining the lowest classificatory level of a concept is inferred when the individual regards at least two different examples of the same class of objects, events, or invariant relations of objects or events to be equivalent. For example, the child who treats the clock on the wall and the other one on the desk as equivalent in one or more ways has attained a concept of clock at a beginning classificatory level. At this beginning level, children seem to base their classifications on some of the intrinsic and functional attributes of the concept examples that they have experienced, but they cannot state the basis of their classifications.

Individuals attain a higher classificatory level of a concept when they can correctly identify a large number of things as examples and others as nonexamples but cannot use the defining attributes of the concept in evaluating examples and nonexamples. At this higher phase of the classificatory level, children discriminate some of the less obvious attributes of a concept and generalize correctly to a greater variety of examples, some of which are very much like nonexamples. They are also able to make the basis of their classification more explicit, but it is still incomplete.

Formal Level Processes

Persons demonstrate that they have learned a concept at the formal level when they can correctly identify examples of the concept, can give the name of the concept, can discriminate and name the defining attributes of the concept, can give a societally accepted definition of the concept, and can indicate how examples of the concept differ from examples of coordinate concepts. To attain a concept at the formal level, the individual must be capable of performing the inductive or reception operations that follow:

**MENTAL OPERATIONS IN LEARNING
A CONCEPT AT THE FORMAL LEVEL**

INDUCTIVE OPERATIONS
Hypothesizing the defining attributes and/or rules for joining the attributes.
Remembering hypotheses.
Evaluating hypotheses using examples and nonexamples.
Inferring the concept definition if the concept is already learned at the classi-
  ficatory level.
Inferring the concept if not already learned at the classificatory level.
Analyzing examples and nonexamples of the concept on the basis of the
  presence or absence of the defining attributes.

RECEPTION OPERATIONS

Assimilating information presented, including the concept name, concept definition, verbal descriptions, pictorial representations of examples and nonexamples of the concept, and actual examples and nonexamples.

Remembering the information.

Analyzing examples and nonexamples of the concept on the basis of the presence or absence of the defining attributes.

The *inductive pattern* involves formulating, remembering, and evaluating hypotheses about the attributes of the concept and then inferring the concept definition if the concept has already been attained at the classificatory level, or inferring the concept itself if it has not been learned at the classificatory level at an earlier time. A high school student encountering the concept *onomatopoeia* or *valence* for the first time illustrates the latter kind of inference. Individuals who illustrate the former kind—inference of concept definition—apparently reason in the following way. "Thing 1 is land totally surrounded by water. It is a member of one class of things. Thing 2 is land that is only partially surrounded by water. It is not a member of that class of things. Therefore, lands totally surrounded by water belong to one class, but lands only partially surrounded by water do not." The individual, from an example and a nonexample of the concept, has hypothesized a defining attribute, remembered it, evaluated the hypothesis, and is making progress toward inferring a definition of *island*.

A *meaningful reception approach* to learning is often employed in school settings to enable students to progress from merely being able to classify examples of concepts to being able to understand the concepts at a mature formal level. In expository instruction using a meaningful reception strategy, students are given the name of the concept and its defining attributes; explanations and illustrations are provided by the teacher; information may also be made available in books and visuals. The student's main task is to process and retrieve the information provided.

Much effective concept learning at the formal level involves some combination of the inductive and meaningful reception operations. It is very time-consuming for students to infer the defining attributes independently through a hypothesis-testing approach. However, to be told everything and not to do any hypothesizing typically result in lack of understanding.

It may be well to emphasize that learning a definition of a word is not learning a concept. Furthermore, verbal instruction in school settings that does not utilize examples and nonexamples of concepts leads to memorization of verbal information, not to being able to classify examples or to understand the concept.

Fixed Order of Learning at Successively Higher Levels

We have seen how the same concept is learned in a sequence from concrete level to formal level. This fixed order, or *invariant sequence*, was verified empirically in a longitudinal study (Klausmeier & Allen, 1978).

Five internal conditions of the learner were validated as necessary for attaining the last three successively higher levels of the same concept: (1) the concept has been learned at the prior level; (2) at least one new mental operation has emerged at a functioning level; (3) the operations of the prior level are performed on information of increasing quantity and complexity experienced in a greater variety of contexts; (4) the intent to attain the next higher level of the concept is present; and (5) persistence continues until the level is attained. In addition to these five internal conditions, being able to discriminate and name the defining attributes of the concept and to name the concept itself are necessary for carrying out the new operations at the formal level.

Before examining how concepts are used, we may pause to observe that most concepts are learned at all four levels, including nearly all those involving animals, plants, and inanimate objects. Many process concepts represented by verbals, for example, *swimming* and *typing,* are also learned at the four levels. Some concepts, however, have only one example. One illustration is *the earth's moon.* A concept that has only one example or that has examples of an identical form may be learned at the concrete, identity, and formal levels but not at the classificatory level. Other concepts, such as *atom, eternity,* and *soul,* do not have observable examples. These concepts are learned only at the formal level. However, the processes involved at each of these levels for these kinds of concepts are the same as those used for learning concepts at all four levels.

9.6 What can teachers observe or readily infer to ascertain that a student has learned the concept *bird* at each of four successively higher levels: concrete, identity, classificatory, formal?

9.7 How do attending, discriminating, and generalizing differ at the classificatory level and at the identity level?

9.8 Do you regard instruction as being equally important in enabling students to progress from the identity to the classificatory level and from the classificatory level to the formal level? Explain.

9.9 Recall your learning of concepts at the formal level in high school. To what extent were inductive operations and reception operations involved?

Recognizing Examples
and Nonexamples of
Concepts

Understanding
Principles

Solving Problems

Understanding
Taxonomic and Other
Hierarchical
Relationships

USING CONCEPTS

Concepts are the building blocks of intellectual development. Using concepts promotes continuously higher intellectual functioning in several ways shown in Figure 9.2.

Recognizing Examples
and Nonexamples of Concepts

Having learned a concept at the classificatory level or the formal level eliminates the need for having to learn to recognize each new example of

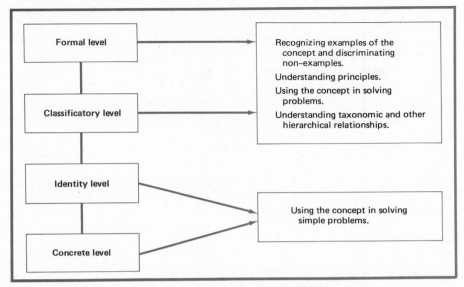

Figure 9.2 Ways of using concepts learned at successively higher levels.

the class and to discriminate each new nonexample. For instance, knowing the intrinsic and functional attributes of any particular animal, food, or color enables the individual to recognize newly encountered examples almost instantly and also to recognize other items as nonexamples. The enormous savings in time cannot be overestimated. Furthermore, when we have the name of the concept, we can communicate with others by listening, talking, reading, and writing at an amazingly rapid rate.

Understanding Principles

The term *principle* is used in a generic sense to indicate the main generalizations of a field that are accepted as true or basic. The generalizations are called *rules, laws,* or *axioms* in different fields. A *principle* may be defined formally as a relationship between two or more concepts. The concepts embedded in the principle must be understood to understand the principle. Principles, like concepts, are powerful tools of thought that are necessary for interpreting many phenomena and for solving problems.

Consider the principle that is expressed in this statement: *Water solidifies at 32°F.* Notice two things about this statement. First, it expresses a relationship among the three concepts that are italicized. *Solidifies* is a concept that expresses the relationship between *water* and *32°F.* Understanding all three concepts is necessary for understanding the principle. Second, the principle applies to a large number of situations. Whenever and wherever the temperature of water is reduced to 32°F, it changes to ice; similarly, ice melts at temperatures above 32°F.

Principles, when understood, permit one to interpret many specific situations and events. For example, knowing the axiom "All equilateral triangles are similar in shape" enables one to recognize geometric forms as equilateral triangles, regardless of such conditions as the area of the triangle and its orientation. Similarly, knowing the rule "The subject and verb of a sentence agree in number" and being able to recognize the singular and plural forms of nominals and verbals permit us to write sentences correctly. In recent years, many high school students have not been learning many basic principles of English, mathematics, science, and social studies. They function at an elementary school level as entering university freshmen.

Solving Problems

Concepts enable us to understand principles having many kinds of relationships among the concepts embedded in them. Problem solving, the most powerful ability of human beings, requires knowing the concepts and principles necessary for solving problems. Because Chapter 10 of this book deals with problem solving, this use of concepts is not discussed further here.

Understanding Taxonomic and Other Hierarchical Relationships

Some classes of things, such as those of the animal kingdom, are organized into taxonomies based on inclusive and exclusive relationships among the classes. Other classes are organized into hierarchies on the basis of other relationships, such as dependency or importance. The concepts of the taxonomy or other hierarchical relationship corresponding to the classes must be understood before the relationships among them can be learned.

Taxonomies

A taxonomy is one kind of hierarchical organization of knowledge. Having all the concepts of a taxonomy greatly extends one's understanding of a whole field of knowledge. For example, having the meaning of the concepts of the animal kingdom and understanding the relationship among them enables one to answer the following question completely and accurately: How are human beings like other animals and different from them? Having the concepts of different taxonomies, for example, those of the plant and the animal kingdoms, enables a person to relate concepts within and across the taxonomies. The vast increase in knowledge of related fields has caused authors and teachers to try to organize related concepts into taxonomies or other meaningful structures.

A partial taxonomy for geometric figures that are polygons follows in Figure 9.3. In this taxonomy, the *generic*, or most inclusive, concept is *polygon*. The *subordinate concepts* are *triangle, quadrilateral, pentagon, hexagon*, and other classes of polygons that have more than six sides. These subordinate concepts are *coordinate* to one another. That is, each subordinate concept has all the *defining attributes* of the concept superordinate to it and other defining attributes, called *critical attributes*, that are essential for defining the subordinate concept but not the *superordinate concept*. The important point here is that the meaning of every concept of a taxonomy can be

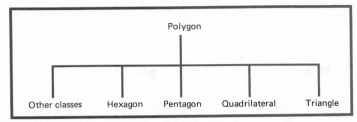

Figure 9.3 A partial taxonomy of the concept *polygon*.

stated in terms of the defining attributes of the class. To illustrate, the meaning of *polygon* can be expressed in terms of its defining attributes as a *plane, simple, closed figure with three or more straight sides*. The critical attribute of hexagon that distinguishes it from all other polygons is *six straight sides*. Accordingly, a hexagon is defined either as a polygon with six straight sides or as a plane, simple, closed figure with six straight sides.

Knowing the defining and critical attributes of the concepts included in taxonomies provides the basis for understanding and explaining important relationships among the concepts of a taxonomy. Illustrative relationships related to the concept *polygon* follow:

1. No quadrilateral is a triangle.
2. All quadrilaterals are polygons.
3. Some, but not all, polygons are triangles.
4. The sum of the triangles, quadrilaterals, and other classes of polygons is equal to the sum of all polygons.

It is easy to underestimate the importance of possessing the concepts of a taxonomy and understanding the relationships among them. Recall, for example, Guilford's structure of intellect, which, in fact, is a taxonomy. In this taxonomy, there are 120 specific abilities, each of which consists of the union of an operation, a content, and a product, the three superordinate concepts. If you have the name and meaning of each of the five operations, the four contents, and the six products and then also understand the relationship among these three superordinate concepts, you can list and define the 120 specific intellectual abilities included in the structure of intellect. On the other hand, trying to learn the name and definition of each specific ability as a separate entity would be a very formidable learning task.

Other Hierarchical Relationships

The relationships among the items of a taxonomy are hierarchical in that there are superordinate, subordinate, and coordinate concepts in taxonomies. There are other hierarchies that are not based on inclusive-exclusive relationships, for example, a hierarchy of the eight basic process concepts of science that elementary school students should learn (AAAS Commission on Science Education, 1967). The relationships among the

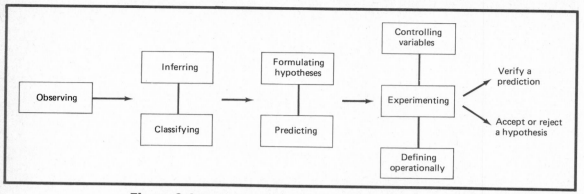

Figure 9.4 Dependency and parallel relationships among eight basic process concepts of science.

eight concepts are shown in Figure 9.4. The horizontal lines with arrows indicate a *dependency,* or prerequisite, relationship among the concepts, while the straight vertical lines indicate a *parallel* relationship. The prerequisite and parallel relationships among the eight process concepts follow (Klausmeier, Swanson, & Sipple, 1976):

> Observing is a basic process that is prerequisite for all other scientific processes.
>
> Observing is essential for inferring and classifying; however, one may infer without classifying; therefore, inferring and classifying are parallel.
>
> Inferences are used in predicting specific future events and in formulating hypotheses, that is, more generalizable statements that apply to classes of events. Predicting and hypothesizing are parallel processes; one is not dependent on the other.
>
> To test predictions or hypotheses, the scientist controls experimental variables and defines operationally as part of experimentation. Accordingly, defining operationally, controlling variables, and experimenting are related in a parallel manner. As a result of experimenting, the scientist will have the information needed to verify a prediction or to accept or reject a hypothesis.

The defining attributes of the process concepts in the preceding hierarchy differ from those of a taxonomy, because there are no superordinate, subordinate, and coordinate relationships. When the relationship among the concepts is defined in terms of prerequisites, the defining attributes of each successive concept in the hierarchy are stated in terms of the process that is prerequisite for producing it. Accordingly, the meaning of *inferring* may be expressed in terms of defining attributes as (1) relating a scientific observation to something that is known and (2) drawing a conclusion from what is observed.

We saw that the defining attributes of *polygon* are stated in terms of the observable intrinsic properties of examples of polygons. The defining attributes of *inferring* are stated in terms of an invariant relationship between the concepts *inferring* and *observing*. The defining attributes of concepts are of three kinds: intrinsic properties, functions, and invariant relations. *Intrinsic attributes* are the properties that inhere in the examples of the concept, for example, all polygons are geometric figures that have three or more straight sides. *Functional attributes* refer to what can be done with the class of things or to what it can do, for example, food is eaten, dogs bark. *Invariant relations* among examples of concepts are temporal, directional, prerequisite, etc.: *before* always precedes something that comes *later; south* is always in the opposite direction from *north; observing* is a prerequisite for *inferring*.

The meaning of a word that names a concept is best expressed in terms of the defining attributes of the concept. Miller and Johnson-Laird (1976) refer to the societally accepted meaning of a word as a *lexical concept*. In their view, having the meaning of a word enables the individual to ascertain whether an item can be labeled by the word. Having the word meaning also enables the individual to indicate the function or purpose of the item that the word names. Finally, having the meaning of a word makes it possible for the individual upon hearing the word to retrieve everything from long-term memory that the individual knows about the particular concept.

9.10 You have attained the concept *intrinsic motives* (see Chapter 7): (a) formulate one principle of classroom motivation that involves understanding the concept *intrinsic motives;* (b) give an example of how understanding the concept *intrinsic motives* helps to solve a classroom problem involving low motivation of one or more students; (c) indicate 3 or 4 other motivational concepts that can be better understood by having an understanding of the concept *intrinsic motives.*

9.11 Give a synonym for *courageous;* next, give two examples of *courageous;* and finally, give the defining attributes of *courageous.* Which is the most difficult to do? Should a teacher be able to do all three before attempting to teach the concept to students?

9.12 Give the defining attributes and the critical attributes of the concepts *evergreen tree* and *deciduous tree.* Consult an abridged dictionary if necessary.

9.13 Give the intrinsic and the functional attributes of the concept *citrus fruit.*

9.14 Refer back to the partial taxonomy for *polygon* (Figure 9.3) and to the hierarchical dependency relationships among the eight basic process concepts of science (Figure 9.4). Are the taxonomical or the dependency relationships easier for you to understand? Give possible reasons.

NORMATIVE DEVELOPMENT IN LEARNING AND USING CONCEPTS

Information that describes how normal human beings develop helps one to understand any maturing individual's current status and to predict the same individual's pattern of development across long time intervals. Pediatricians rely heavily on information concerning height, weight, coordination, and other dimensions of physical growth and health for diagnosing, predicting, and guiding an individual child's physical growth and health. Educators and others who work with children and youth need similar information about normative cognitive development so that they can diagnose, predict, and guide an individual student's cognitive learning and development. Despite this need, relatively little information about cognitive learning and development is available (Mussen, 1970; Wohlwill, 1973).

To secure this kind of information, a large longitudinal study was carried out involving four groups of students respectively enrolled in successive grades 1, 2, 3; grades 4, 5, 6; grades 7, 8, 9; and grades 10, 11, 12 (Klausmeier & Allen, 1978). Each student's performance was measured in attaining each of four concepts—*cutting tool, tree, equilateral triangle,* and *noun*—at the concrete, identity, classificatory, and formal levels. Each student's use of each concept in understanding principles of which the concept was a part, understanding taxonomic relations among the particular concept and other concepts of the taxonomy, and solving problems involving the concept and related principles was also measured. A total of 28 tests were constructed and administered to measure each student's performances, seven for each of the four concepts. The 28 tests were administered at 12-month intervals for three years to all the children, except that very difficult tests were not administered in grades 1 and 2, and very easy tests were not administered after grade 6.

Mean scores on each of the 28 measures were obtained for each group of students when in grades 1, 2, 3; grades 4, 5, 6; grades 7, 8, 9; and grades 10, 11, 12, except that very difficult tests were not administered in grades 1 and 2, and very easy ones were not administered after grade 6. Developmental curves based on the means were prepared, and differences in the performances among the students of each grade were identified.

Learning the Concrete, Identity, and Classificatory Levels

Figure 9.5 contains five developmental curves, one for the concrete level of *noun,* one for the identity level of *noun,* and one each for the classificatory level of *tree, equilateral triangle,* and *noun.* Curves are not shown for the concrete or the identity level of *cutting tool, tree,* and *equilateral triangle,* and for the classificatory level of *cutting tool,* inasmuch as the students of grade 1 had mean scores above 90 on these tests: in other words, they had already achieved full functional maturity of these three levels of these concepts.

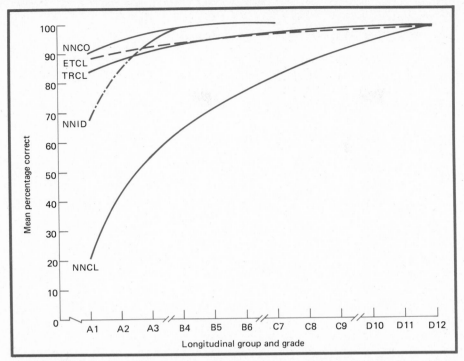

Figure 9.5 Normative development in attaining the concrete and identity levels of the concept *noun* and the classificatory level of the concepts *tree, equilateral triangle,* and *noun.*
Note: *NNCO* (concrete level of *noun*)
ETCL (classificatory level of *equilateral triangle*)
TRCL (classificatory level of *tree*)
NNID (identity level of *noun*)
NNCL (classificatory level of *noun*)

We may summarize attainment of the concrete, identity, and classificatory levels of the four concepts. The students had fully attained the concrete, identity, and classificatory levels of *cutting tool* and the concrete and identity levels of *tree* and *equilateral triangle* prior to completing grade 1. They had already made much progress toward fully attaining the classificatory level of *tree* and *equilateral triangle* in grade 1, and by grade 3, nearly full attainment of the classificatory level had occurred. The children attained the classificatory level of *noun* at a very rapid rate from grade 1 through grade 3; a less rapid rate of increase was shown thereafter, until full attainment was reached in grade 12.

Learning the Formal Level
Figure 9.6 depicts normative development related to the formal level of all four concepts. The test of the formal level for *noun* was not admin-

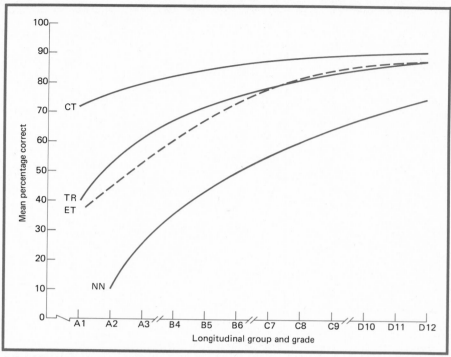

Figure 9.6 Normative development in attaining the formal level of the concepts *cutting tool (CT), tree (TR), equilateral triangle (ET),* and *noun (NN).*

istered to the students when they were in grade 1, but it was administered in grade 2; therefore, the curve for *noun* starts in grade 2.

   Two interesting conclusions may be drawn from examining the curves of the formal level. First, students understand the formal level of *cutting tool* much earlier than *noun,* while their understanding of *tree* and *equilateral triangle* is about the same and equally less than their understanding of *cutting tool* and equally more than their understanding of *noun.* Second, the rate of development is more rapid (although the level is quite low) during the primary school years; decelerates thereafter, except for *noun;* and levels off prior to reaching full functional maturity during the senior high school years.

   It should be recalled that learning the formal level of a concept is based on four capabilities: (1) being able to discriminate the defining attributes of the concept, (2) possessing the name of the concept and the names of its defining attributes, (3) understanding the definition of the concept, and (4) being able to evaluate examples and nonexamples of the concept on the basis of the presence or absence of the defining attributes. The developmental curves for *equilateral triangle* are presented in Figure 9.7 to illustrate the timing and rate for attaining these aspects of the formal level of concepts. The order of attainment from earlier to later was discriminating

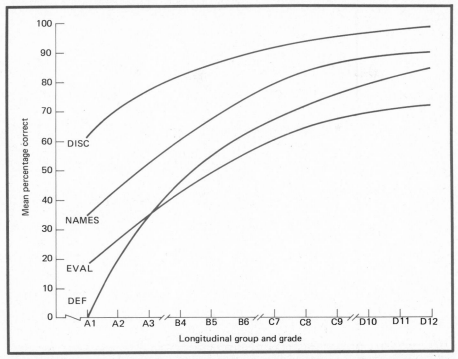

Figure 9.7 Smoothed curves for four subtests of the formal level of the concept *equilateral triangle:* discriminating defining attributes (*Disc*), acquiring names of concepts and of defining attributes (*Names*), acquiring concept definition (*Def*), and evaluating examples and nonexamples (*Eval*).

the attributes, acquiring the names, acquiring the definition, and evaluating examples and nonexamples. The rate of learning each of these items is most rapid during the primary school years and gradually decelerates thereafter. Development is not complete in grade 12. Surprisingly, the means for being able to evaluate examples and nonexamples and for having a definition of the concept name in grade 12 are only 65% and 75% respectively.

Understanding Principles

Earlier in this chapter, we saw the enormous power that principles give individuals for understanding and interacting with their physical and social environments. Figure 9.8 presents the developmental curves related to understanding principles. The curves start in the grade at which the particular test was first administered: *cutting tool,* grade 1; *tree,* grade 2; and *equilateral triangle* and *noun,* grade 3.

We see that principles, except those related to concepts that have many concrete examples in the immediate environment (e.g., *cutting tool*), are not well understood by children of primary school age. Progress in understanding principles occurs at about the same rate during the intermediate,

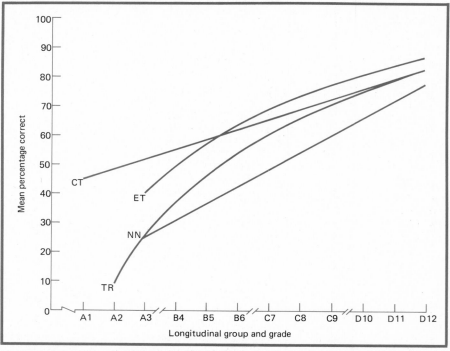

Figure 9.8 Normative development in understanding principles related to the concepts *cutting tool (CT), equilateral triangle (ET), tree (TR),* and *noun (NN).*

junior high school, and senior high school years. In grade 12, the mean achievement is still relatively low.

Understanding Taxonomic Relations

Figure 9.9 contains the developmental curves for understanding taxonomic relations. The understanding of taxonomic relations increases quite rapidly throughout the elementary school years. Students in grade 6 had from 53% to 83% correct on the tests for the four concepts. The rate of increase in understanding taxonomic relations is low during the junior and senior high school years. Students in grade 12 had mean percentages correct for the four concepts ranging from 76 to 96.

The individual's increased power to relate phenomena by understanding taxonomic relations may be inferred from four principles of taxonomic relations and examples of each that were included in the tests:

> **Relation: Some, but not all, members of a superordinate class belong to a given subclass.** Example for *cutting tool:* Some, but not all, cutting tools have a blade that is smooth.

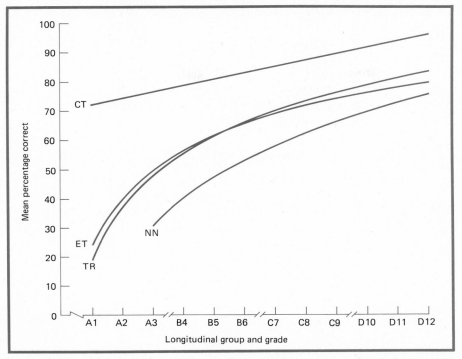

Figure 9.9 Normative development in understanding taxonomic relations of the concepts *cutting tool (CT), equilateral triangle (ET), tree (TR),* and *noun (NN).*

Relation: All members of a subclass belong to a higher class. Example for *tree:* All trees are plants.

Relation: The sum of the members of the subclasses equals the sum of the members of the superordinate class. Example for *equilateral triangle:* equilateral triangles, right triangles, and other kinds of triangles equal all triangles.

Relation: The members of one coordinate class are not members of another coordinate class. Example for *noun:* No proper nouns are common nouns.

Identifying Attributes

Earlier, we saw developmental curves for discriminating the defining attributes of various concepts. The ability to discriminate attributes is especially important at the classificatory level and is a prerequisite for learning the formal level.

A cross-sectional study was carried out specifically to learn about children's growth in the number of attributes that they attended to and used in putting things into equivalent groups, or classes (Frith & Frith, 1978). Figure 9.10 shows the mean number of attributes that groups of children at 4, 6, 8, 12, and 16 years of age identified and used in grouping 30 picture examples each of animals, human faces, and abstract drawings (Frith & Frith, 1978). Each of the 30 examples of each set had 9 attributes that could be used in forming different groupings. The examples were constructed in such a manner that 7 well-defined groupings could be formed, 2 with 5 examples each, and 5 with 4 examples each.

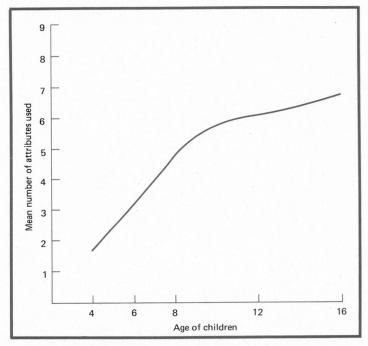

Figure 9.10 Growth in the ability to use attributes in classifying.
Source: Frith & Frith, 1978, p. 422.

As Figure 9.10 shows, the number of attributes that the children attended to and used increased markedly and consistently from a mean of 1.88 at age 4 to 6.93 at age 16. The shape of this curve bears a remarkable resemblance to the curve of discriminating defining attributes in Figure 9.7. It rises more rapidly during the early years and then progresses at a slower rate of increase during the later years.

Frith and Frith (1978) concluded that growth in classification is due to attending to and discriminating more features of things rather than to discriminating fewer features more accurately. A second interesting conclusion was that the children could not always give the names of the attributes that they used in their groupings. This was true even for the

16-year-olds. As we saw earlier, a major distinction between learning a concept at the classificatory level and the formal level is the ability not only to discriminate but also to name the defining attributes. Thus, teachers profit greatly from being able to name the attributes and then using the names in teaching the students to identify the attributes. Knowing the defining attributes of concepts is the final step in eliminating errors in classification and therefore errors in thinking and communicating.

9.15 Formulate one generalization about the rate at which the concepts *cutting tool, tree, equilateral triangle,* and *noun* are learned at the classificatory and formal levels during the successive school years. Formulate one generalization about the differences in the order in which the four different concepts develop.

9.16 Figure 9.7 shows the following order of development at grade 1 for *equilateral triangle:* being able to discriminate the attributes of the concept (60%), acquiring the names of the concept and its defining attributes (35%), evaluating examples and nonexamples (20%), and acquiring the concept definition (0%). From grade 3 onward, there was concurrent development of these four processes. Draw two or three implications of this developmental information for curriculum and instruction regarding *equilateral triangle.*

9.17 Compare the developmental curves for attaining the formal level of the four concepts (Fig. 9.6), the understanding of related principles (Fig. 9.8), and the understanding of related taxonomic relations (Fig. 9.9). Based on your comparisons, indicate the time sequence in which concepts should be taught at the formal level and the time when understanding the related principles and taxonomic relations should be taught.

INDIVIDUAL DIFFERENCES IN CONCEPT LEARNING

Age Differences

Differences Between Rapid and Slow Learners

Intraindividual Variation

The longitudinal study of concept development discussed in the preceding part of this chapter was designed to identify four areas of differences: differences among students of the same age and among students of different ages, differences in the rate at which rapid and slow learners progress across periods of time, variations in the rate at which a given individual learns concepts drawn from different subject fields, and sex differences (Klausmeier & Allen, 1978). Large differences were found in all areas except sex. Very few differences were found between boys and girls, and the few identified were inconsistent, not regularly favoring either boys or girls for any concept or for any school grade.

Age Differences

Table 9.1 gives the percentage of students of grades 1, 3, 6, 9, and 12 who had and had not fully learned the formal level of *equilateral triangle* and who did and did not fully understand the related principles. Examination of Table 9.1 reveals a wide range of differences within each grade. For

TABLE 9.1 **PERCENTAGE OF STUDENTS WHO HAD (L) AND HAD NOT LEARNED (NL) THE FORMAL LEVEL OF THE CONCEPT *EQUILATERAL TRIANGLE* AND WHO DID (U) AND DID NOT UNDERSTAND (NU) THE RELATED PRINCIPLES**

GROUP AND GRADE	FORMAL LEVEL		RELATED PRINCIPLES	
	L	NL	U	NU
A1	0	100	*	*
A3	3	97	0	100
B6	52	48	38	62
C9	75	25	51	49
D12	79	21	73	27

* Test not administered at this grade.

example, the percentages of students who had and had not fully learned the formal level were as follows: 0 and 100 for grade 1; 3 and 97 for grade 3; 52 and 48 for grade 6; 75 and 25 for grade 9; and 79 and 21 for grade 12. The comparable percentages for understanding and not understanding the related principles were 0 and 100 for grade 3; 38 and 62 for grade 6; 51 and 49 for grade 9; and 73 and 27 for grade 12 (grade 1 students were not tested for understanding the related principles).

The differences between the grades are even more dramatic. As noted in the preceding paragraph, the percentages of students who had and had not fully learned the formal level were 3 and 97 for grade 3, and 79 and 21 for grade 12. What do these percentages reveal about variation across these two widely separated grades? They indicate that 3% of the grade 3 children performed better in terms of full attainment of the formal level than 21% of the students in grade 12. Similarly, 38% of the grade 6 students fully understood the related principles, but 27% of the twelfth-graders did not.

It is difficult to visualize how to arrange instruction that would take these differences into account. To illustrate, although 52% of the grade 6 students had fully learned the formal level of *equilateral triangle,* among the 48% who had not, one would expect 21% still not to have done so in their last year of high school.

Differences Between Rapid and Slow Learners

There were 50 boys and 50 girls each in grades 1, 4, 7, and 10 who started the longitudinal study (Klausmeier & Allen, 1978). The most rapid and the least rapid learner from each of these groups—a total of eight— were identified at the end of the study by examining the performances of all the students who remained throughout the study. The performances of these eight students for the combined classificatory and formal levels of *equilateral triangle* illustrate the differences in their learning rates (see Figure 9.11). The smoothed curve represents the entire group of longitudinal students. The rates of the fast and slow learners may be compared with it.

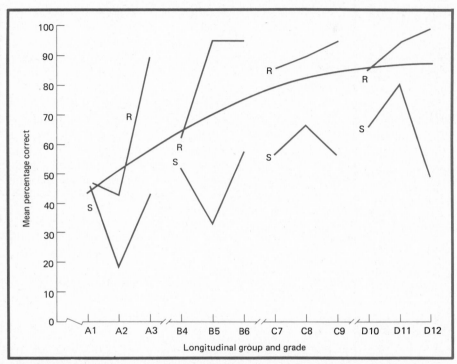

Figure 9.11 Curves of rapid (*R*) and slow (*S*) learners in attaining the combined classificatory and formal levels of the concept *equilateral triangle*.

The curves of the four rapid learners are above the smoothed curve of the group, and the increase is quite consistent from the lowest to the highest grade. The curves for the four slow developers are consistently below the curve of the group and rise and fall more than those of the rapid learners. You may notice that the differences in the percentage correct between the rapid and the slow learner of each longitudinal group is quite large.

Intraindividual Variation

Are students equally good in their understanding of concepts drawn from different subject fields? Harris and Harris (1973) analyzed the results of achievement tests consisting of 30 different concepts drawn from mathematics, science, language arts, and social studies. These tests were administered to 200 boys and 200 girls who had recently completed grade 5. The

Harrises found that most students did not achieve the concepts of all four subjects equally well.

In the longitudinal study of concept development, the achievement of the four concepts by five boys and five girls drawn randomly from the entire grade 6 group of boys and girls was examined (Klausmeier & Allen, 1978). One student scored in the top quarter of the grade 6 group for all four concept areas: *cutting tool, tree, equilateral triangle,* and *noun.* Three students had scores in two adjacent quarters, for example, the highest and the second highest quarter. Three students had scores in three adjacent quarters; either the top three quarters or the bottom three. Two students had scores in three different quarters that were not adjacent. One student had a score in all four quarters of the grade 6 group.

These results indicate that individuals vary within themselves in learning different concepts. Accordingly, cognitive growth is not unitary or global, characterized by equally high or low performance in all concepts. Therefore, we should not expect most students to attain concepts from fields such as English, mathematics, science, and social studies equally well. Only a small percentage of the students of a grade will be in either the highest quarter or the lowest quarter in all four subject fields. The large majority will be in two or three different quarters.

9.18 The difference among normally developing students of the same grade in understanding concepts and principles is very large. Some students of grades 4–6 are more advanced than other students are in grade 12. Based on your school experiences, do you think the large differences are mainly determined by hereditary differences in cognitive abilities or by lack of good instruction? Explain.

9.19 In Chapter 5, we saw that most persons are not equally high in verbal ability, numerical ability, spatial ability, inductive reasoning, and other primary mental abilities. Similar intraindividual variation is found in learning concepts. What implications do these facts have for teaching concepts from different subject fields?

Concrete Level and Identity Level

Beginning Classificatory Level

Mature Classificatory Level and Formal Level

TEACHING CONCEPTS

At what level should particular children be taught particular concepts? Three considerations are involved. First, there is an earliest time in the life of a child when the mental processes necessary to learn given concepts become functional; this earliest time is determined by learning experiences as well as by neural maturation. Second, the mental processes for learning different concepts at the same level, for example, *toy* and *time* at the classificatory level, function earlier for concrete concepts than for abstract concepts. Third, individuals continue to increase their understanding of the lower level of a concept after starting to learn the next higher level. With these three conditions in mind, a teacher can teach any student concepts at more than one level. The teacher can also help each student to progress to successively higher levels as quickly as possible, since mental processes do not emerge and become functional merely with maturation. Recall that learning is necessary for the initial functioning of mental processes. Waiting for the formal level operations to emerge as a result of neural maturation, without learning, will ensure that they do not emerge.

Concrete Level and Identity Level

Children form many concepts at the concrete and identity levels through informal experiences in the home and neighborhood prior to starting school. Despite this, students continue to learn some concepts at these levels during their elementary and high school years. For example, much learning of second languages involves experiencing and recognizing new individual words and phrases. Likewise, high school students learn to identify tiny plants or animals with the use of a microscope. Although the high school student quickly progresses to the classificatory and formal levels, initially learning to recognize the first example or two is clearly at the concrete and identity levels.

Instructional principles that help students of any age to learn concepts at the concrete and identity levels follow. As you study these principles, try to visualize young children learning to recognize their lockers for the first time or older students using a microscope to identify an amoeba for the first time.

1. Make available an actual item or a pictorial or other representation of it: inanimate object (locker), animate object (amoeba), process (a word being spoken), quality (opacity). The teacher does not necessarily supply the item. The student can identify it in the immediate classroom environment or bring it from the home or neighborhood. However, if the teacher does supply the item, it should be a typical example of its class, for example, a middle-sized dog that cannot easily be confused with any other animal (Tennyson, 1980). This example will be stored in memory and used later to learn the classificatory level.

2. Give the name of the item and aid the learner to associate the name and the item. Children may not have had the concept name in their speaking vocabularies before attending school. However, they can be expected to be able to say most of the concept names that are likely to be introduced in kindergarten and thereafter. The child's associating the name with the concept greatly facilitates learning and instruction because, when the name is learned, attention is directed to the item by speaking rather than by pointing. Furthermore, the name can be used later to get the child to retrieve the concept from memory; an example of the concept or a picture of it is no longer required.

3. Provide for immediate informative feedback after correct identification of the item and correct naming of it. Immediate feedback is very important at these levels. The elapsed time between attending to the item and recognizing it is very short. Any shifting of attention to another item prior to recognition and feedback is likely to result in failure to learn.

4. Make the item available later and determine whether the learner recognizes it. At the concrete and identity levels, it is important to present the same item that was used in the initial learning situation. Presenting a different item of the same class or an item of another class results in lack of recognition. As we saw, once the item is learned and the name associated with it, the name can be stated to cue retrieval of the concept from memory.

5. Repeat the preceding sequence (1–4) as necessary. *Sesame Street* incorporates the preceding conditions and others. In *Sesame Street*, many fundamental concepts involving numbers, the letters of the alphabet, relations such as *above* and *between*, and examples of qualities such as *red* and *soft* are taught very effectively. Examples are always given, and the name of the concept is presented orally or in written form almost simultaneously with the presentation of the example. Many delightful and different contexts are used for presenting the same item (identity level). The viewers get feedback so that they can determine whether their covert mental responses, or their overt responses, are correct or incorrect. *Sesame Street* provides for a great deal of surprise, fun, and repetition. Good classroom teaching of concepts at the concrete and identity levels does also.

Beginning Classificatory Level

Before the first grade, students learn concepts at the classificatory level for which there are many concrete examples in their immediate environment. But many concepts, such as *equilateral triangle* and *noun*, are introduced to children for the first time during the elementary grades. Still others are not introduced until high school or even in college. Principles for introducing and teaching a concept at the beginning classificatory level so that a student will be able to correctly classify a few easy examples follow. (Very few applications of the teaching principles are provided in this section of the chapter, but they are indicated in the next section. If difficulty is experienced in getting the meaning of the principles here, you may wish to return after completing your study of the next section of the chapter.)

1. Make available at least two different examples and one or two quite obvious nonexamples of the concept. For example, to teach the concept *oak tree,* present two pictures of an oak tree and one of a pine tree. Examples with defining attributes that are *salient,* that is, prominent or striking (Carnine, 1980), and also *prototypic,* that is, typical of the class (Tennyson, 1980), are needed. This procedure facilitates the student's identification of the defining attributes and thereby provides the basis for generalizing that two examples are equivalent. Nonexamples that have some of the same variable attributes as the examples, for example, same color, shape, size, use or function, are needed.

2. Aid the learner to associate the name of the concept with examples. The purpose of this procedure was indicated in the suggestion for teaching concepts at the concrete and identity levels. However, at the classificatory

Concepts are mental tools with which we think. With good instruction children learn concepts and principles at successively higher levels of understanding. Without it, they remain semi-literate throughout their lives.

level, the teacher may call on the student for the name rather than give it to the student.

3. Aid the learner to identify and name the salient defining attributes of the concept, including one or two of the critical attributes if there are coordinate concepts, such as *oak tree* and *pine tree.* You will recall that identifying the salient defining attributes of two or more examples enables the learner to see how the examples are equivalent. Being able to identify the critical attributes helps the learner to discriminate nonexamples. Let us assume that students have the names of the attributes in their speaking vocabularies. Using an inductive method, the teacher makes available two or more examples and calls on the student to identify and name the attributes. If the student cannot, the teacher points out the attributes and provides the names.

4. Aid the learner to define the concept. Being able to define a concept is not essential to learning a concept at the beginning classificatory level, but those students who can learn the definition should understand the words used in it. Memorizing a definition of a word without understanding is probably harmful and clearly a waste of time.

5. Arrange for students to recognize the concept in newly encountered examples or nonexamples. To ensure that the concept has been learned at the classificatory level, an example or two and a nonexample or two that were not used in the initial learning situation must be presented. You cannot infer that the concept has been learned at the beginning classificatory level until the student correctly identifies some examples and discriminates nonexamples that were not used in teaching the concept.

6. Provide for informative feedback. It is helpful to the student to know that an example has been identified correctly (Clark, 1971). It is even more important for a student to know when an incorrect identification has occurred and also why it is incorrect (Frayer & Klausmeier, 1971). For example, incorrectly identifying an adjective as an adverb without being corrected means that the societally accepted concept *adjective* is not being learned.

With many concepts, several years elapse between the time that children first attain a concept at the beginning classificatory level and the time at which they are capable of all the operations essential to attaining the concept at the formal level. The kind of instruction (printed instructional materials, oral instruction, and other techniques) that aids students to move from the immature to the mature phase of the classificatory level is described next.

Mature Classificatory Level and Formal Level

Carefully conducted experiments show that many students at about ages 10–12 are able to learn concepts with perceptible attributes at the formal level. However, they do not readily learn concepts at this level incidentally. For example, two lessons were prepared to teach fourth-grade students the concept *equilateral triangle* (McMurray, Bernard, & Klausmeier, 1975). Each lesson required about 35 minutes to complete. Of the two experimental groups that received the lessons, 60% and 64% attained the formal level, whereas only 7% and 11% of the two control groups had learned the concepts at this level without specific instruction. Two months later, the experimental group had maintained this higher level of attainment. A similar experiment had two lessons dealing with the concept *tree* (Klausmeier, Schilling, & Feldman, 1976). The two experimental groups of third-grade students who received the formal-level instruction performed significantly higher than the two control groups who did not receive it.

Some students at about ages 10–12 can learn some abstract concepts, but much more time is required than to learn concrete concepts (Klausmeier, 1980). For example, most of the students in grades 4 and 5 were able to learn the process concepts of science, such as *observing, predicting,* and *inferring*, at a beginning level. However, many lessons were required, and the slower-maturing students did not learn the concepts even at the classificatory level. The slower-maturing students were not able to recognize examples of these and other process concepts, even when given individual teacher attention and excellent instruction.

Students, if taught properly, continue to learn concepts at the formal level throughout the high school years, especially abstract concepts that do not have perceptible examples. Bernard (1975) prepared and used three lessons to teach high school seniors eight related concepts dealing with behavior management. The concepts were organized in a taxonomy. In this study, a control group not receiving instruction on the concepts scored 30% correct on a test measuring their knowledge; the students receiving the lessons scored 70%. In this experiment and the prior experiments, the results for the control groups indicate that relatively few concepts are learned at the formal level without instruction. However, as we saw earlier, having learned a concept at the formal level markedly facilitates the learning principles and also problem solving.

You note that, in the preceding experiments, except the one on the process concepts of science, only two or three lessons were used to teach each concept. Yet they were effective. The effectiveness is related to two facts. First, the students had already attained the concepts at the beginning classificatory level and were thus ready to learn the formal level. Second, the lessons incorporated seven principles for teaching concepts that have been tested in many different situations and found to be highly effective.

PRINCIPLES FOR TEACHING CONCEPTS AT THE MATURE CLASSIFICATORY LEVEL AND FORMAL LEVEL

1. Prepare the students to learn concepts.
2. Make available examples and nonexamples.
3. Help the learner acquire a strategy for identifying examples and nonexamples.
4. Enable the learner to acquire the names of the concepts and their defining attributes.
5. Provide for complete understanding of the concepts.
6. Provide for use of the concepts.
7. Provide for feedback.

These principles are clarified in the ensuing discussion. A variety of concrete and abstract concepts are used for illustrative purposes. To achieve continuity, the concepts *tree* and *inferring* are used more than others.

1. Prepare the students to learn concepts. Three techniques may be used to facilitate learning a set of related concepts at the mature classificatory and formal levels: (a) establish an intention to learn concepts; (b) enable the learner to identify all the concepts of the taxonomy or hierarchy that are to be learned; (c) introduce the relationships among the concepts to be learned.

   a. Establishing an intention to learn concepts, as opposed, for example, to establishing an intention to memorize a definition, activates several operations essential to attaining concepts at the mature classificatory and formal levels. First, such instructions alert the learners that they should attend to the concept examples and discriminate the attributes of the examples. Second, such instructions engage the learners in an active search for the attributes that distinguish examples from nonexamples. At the outset, then, the learner is actively engaged in searching behaviors directed toward learning the particular concepts at a higher level.

   b. Enabling the learners to become aware of the related concepts to be learned serves two purposes. First, it sets boundaries for the learning task and thus prevents confusion and unnecessary searching by the students to identify the concepts. Second, it makes it possible for the learners to identify the concepts that they already may have learned. Whether to introduce all the related concepts in a single lesson depends upon the total number included in the related group and upon their difficulty and novelty for the learners.

   c. Providing the students information about the relationships among the concepts is also helpful. For example, teaching grade 5 students the relationship between the superordinate and subordinate concepts of a particular taxonomy facilitated subsequent attainment of the concepts (Lawton & Wanska, 1979). Providing information about the relationships reduces unproductive searching behavior and eliminates possible errors.

   Preparing the students to learn a particular group of concepts by using these three techniques requires preparation on the part of the teacher. A verbal presentation combined with a film or printed material may be used effectively. Having examples available of each concept is also effective for gaining student attention and building interest. Not to be overlooked is the fact that the teacher must identify and organize the related concepts as well as the instructional materials and techniques.

   2. Make available examples and nonexamples. *Tree, herb,* and *shrub* are coordinate classes of plants. *Observing* and *inferring* are related concepts in a hierarchy of science processes. In taxonomies and hierarchies, an example of any one concept is a nonexample of all the other concepts. Learning two or more related concepts of taxonomies or hierarchies concurrently is more effective than learning them successively (Klausmeier, 1976; Tennyson, Tennyson, & Rothen, 1980).

   Teachers tend to use only the more readily available examples and nonexamples and also call on students to volunteer them. Both procedures are appropriate and can be effective, but it is wise to identify some possible examples and nonexamples prior to teaching the lessons:

Examples of *tree:* drawings, pictures, or actual trees of various classes, heights, and shapes.

Nonexamples of *tree:* drawings, pictures, or actual shrubs or herbs of various heights, classes, and shapes.

Example of *inferring:* Two children saw a footprint while they were walking on a forest trail. One of the children had observed many wild ducks in the area on past occasions. After examining the webbed footprint, the child concluded that the track was left by one of the wild ducks.

Nonexample of *inferring:* Mary saw some duck tracks on her lawn. She said, "I remember seeing ducks here before. I know that some ducks flew over here yesterday."

3. **Help the learner acquire a strategy for identifying examples and non-examples.** Having a strategy for identifying examples and nonexamples of a concept serves two purposes. It ensures that examples and nonexamples will be correctly identified. It also lessens the need for external feedback, and it may eliminate it completely.

In some situations, it is important not to err in correctly identifying something, for example, poison ivy or a stop sign. An *algorithmic strategy* may be taught to ensure accurate identification. The strategy requires the learner to know the defining attributes of the concept and to be able to examine each possible example and nonexample to identify whether every attribute is present. You will recall that an equilateral triangle has five defining attributes: three sides of equal length, three equal angles, a plane figure, a closed figure, and a simple figure. The algorithmic strategy for *equilateral triangle*—readily learned by grade 4 students—follows in Figure 9.12.

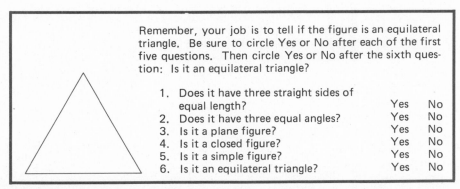

Remember, your job is to tell if the figure is an equilateral triangle. Be sure to circle Yes or No after each of the first five questions. Then circle Yes or No after the sixth question: Is it an equilateral triangle?

1. Does it have three straight sides of equal length?   Yes   No
2. Does it have three equal angles?   Yes   No
3. Is it a plane figure?   Yes   No
4. Is it a closed figure?   Yes   No
5. Is it a simple figure?   Yes   No
6. Is it an equilateral triangle?   Yes   No

Figure 9.12 Algorithmic strategy for identifying examples of *equilateral triangle*.

4. Enable the learner to acquire the names of the concepts and their attributes. You will recall that learning a concept inductively at the formal level involves inferring the concept by identifying its defining attributes from examples and nonexamples. On the other hand, meaningful reception learning involves attending to and processing information that is presented. Having the names of the defining attributes is a prerequisite for carrying out both kinds of operations.

Teachers often present a word list to students at the beginning of a unit to make sure that they can both read and understand the key words. When teaching concepts, it is important to include the words that name the defining attributes of the target concepts. Word lists with defining attributes of *tree* and *inferring* follow:

> **Vocabulary for *tree*:** tree, green plant, stem, woody stem, perennial, roots, seeds, leaves, broad leaves, needles, flowers, cones, deciduous, coniferous.

> **Vocabulary for *inferring*:** inferring, relate, observe, accurately, conclusion.

5. Provide for complete understanding of concepts. Definitions of words that name concepts are often presented in printed material and by teachers before providing the examples and nonexamples of the concept. Receiving the definition stated in terms of defining attributes eliminates students' spending time to identify the defining attributes and possibly making errors and thereby not learning the concept. Examine the three definitions that follow to see how helpful they are in learning the concepts of *tree, shrub,* and *herb* at the formal level:

> A *tree* is a kind of plant. It has roots, leaves, and seeds. It has one main stem that is woody. Trees live for many years. Trees are larger than most shrubs.
> A *shrub* is a kind of plant. It has roots, leaves, and seeds. Shrubs always have more than one main stem, and their stems are woody. Shrubs live for many years. Shrubs are smaller than most trees.
> An *herb* is a kind of plant. It has roots, leaves, and seeds. An herb may have one stem, or more than one stem. Each stem is soft or hollow on the inside. Most herbs die in the autumn at the end of the growing season, but some do not. Herbs are smaller than most shrubs.

To facilitate concept learning, definitions must be stated in terminology appropriate for the learner. Feldman and Klausmeier (1974, p. 220) found the following common-usage definition to be more effective than a technical definition with fourth-graders, whereas the technical definition was more effective with eighth-graders:

Common-usage definition

An *equilateral triangle* is a figure with three sides that are equal in length.

Technical definition

An *equilateral triangle* is a figure with three straight sides of equal length. It is plane, closed, and simple.

We should recognize that the defining attributes of many concepts are not given in the definitions of words contained in dictionaries. Definitions of words given in dictionaries are usually synonyms, examples, or uses of the words in context. These have limited value in determining the defining attributes of concepts (Markle, 1975). The teacher must use authoritative printed material in arriving at the defining attributes of most concepts.

6. **Provide for use of the concepts.** Concepts learned at the formal level are used in understanding principles, in understanding taxonomic and other hierarchical relationships, and in solving problems. The time at which students may be ready to use their concepts in these ways is related to many conditions, including how the particular subject matter is organized and the sequence of teaching that is being followed. Even though the students might not use the concepts immediately in all these ways, it is well for the teacher to know some uses of the particular concepts that the students are learning. Illustrative principles and problem-solving exercises for *tree* and *inferring* follow:

Illustrative principles involving *tree*

1. The water and minerals that a tree needs to grow and make food are collected by its roots.
2. Water, minerals, and organic materials are transported by the tree's trunk.
3. The food that a tree uses is usually produced by its leaves.
4. The seeds of a tree are formed from special cells in the tree's flowers.
5. New trees develop from seeds.
6. To grow and produce food, a tree requires air, light, water, and minerals.

Illustrative principles involving *inferring*

1. Making more accurate and reliable scientific observations permits the drawing of more accurate and reliable inferences.
2. Inferences based on two or more scientific observations are more reliable than those based on a single observation.
3. Quantitative observations allow more precision and accuracy in drawing inferences than do qualitative observations.
4. Scientific observing and inferring are essential for predicting the outcomes of scientific events.

Illustrative problem for *tree*

Suppose that it is spring. You want to find an apple tree that will grow many seeds. You can pick one of many trees growing in an orchard. Which tree would you choose?

Illustrative problem for *inferring*

A kitchen baster full of water was put into a beaker of water and squeezed. What *inference* can you make from this experiment shown in Figure 9.13?

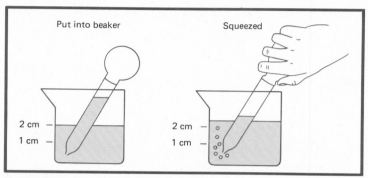

Figure 9.13 Illustrative problem for *inferring*.

7. **Provide for feedback.** At the formal level, as at the classificatory level, students need feedback to ensure that they do not incorrectly classify examples as nonexamples or vice versa. How much of the feedback must be provided externally depends in part on the strategies the students have learned for identifying examples and nonexamples and for checking their own understanding.

Students also profit from external feedback that aids them to recognize if they have fully learned the concept. For example, students who were informed that they had not attained mastery continued to work for a longer period of time than those who were not informed (Tennyson, 1980). Moreover, they performed much better on a test measuring their understanding of the concepts.

9.20 Compare the five principles for teaching concepts at the concrete and identity levels with the six principles for teaching concepts at the beginning classificatory level. What are the main differences? How are these differences related to the mental operations necessary for learning a concept at the identity level and at the classificatory level?

9.21 Check the preceding principles with your observations of the teaching of concepts in *Sesame Street* or *Electric Company*.

9.22 Seven principles for teaching concepts at the mature classificatory level and the formal level were given. Based on your high school and college experience, indicate the two or three principles that were most frequently carried out and the two or three that were least frequently carried out.

9.23 Arrange four concepts — *intelligence, principle, question,* and *table* — from easiest to most difficult to teach in terms of (a) making available examples and nonexamples to students, (b) enabling students to acquire the meaning in terms of defining attributes, and (c) providing opportunities to use the concepts.

9.24 Refer back to your answers to Question 9.23: (a) Why does the instructor in educational psychology have more difficulty in making concepts clear than the instructor in English composition or biology? (b) Why do the learning tasks in educational psychology require the students to take more initiative for finding applications of the concepts?

9.25 Review and Application: Recall the most important information regarding each of the following concepts, and identify at least one possible use of the information by you as a learner, a teacher, or both:

The Nature of Concepts
    Concepts as Mental Constructs of the Individual
    Concepts as Societally Accepted Word Meanings
    Concepts as Form Classes of Words
    Concrete and Abstract Concepts
    Attributes of Concepts
Concept Learning
    Learning a Concept at Four Successively Higher Levels
    Mental Processes in Learning a Concept at Successively Higher Levels
    Fixed Order of Learning a Concept at Successively Higher Levels
Using Concepts
    Recognizing Examples and Nonexamples of Concepts
    Understanding Principles
    Solving Problems
    Understanding Taxonomic and Other Hierarchical Relationships
Normative Development in Learning and Using Concepts
    Learning the Concrete, Identity, and Classificatory Levels
    Learning the Formal Level
    Understanding Principles
    Understanding Taxonomic Relations
    Identifying Attributes
Individual Differences in Concept Learning
    Age Differences
    Differences Between Rapid and Slow Learners
    Intraindividual Variation
Teaching Concepts
    Concrete Level and Identity Level
    Beginning Classificatory Level
    Mature Classificatory Level and Formal Level

SUMMARY

Concepts are essential for thinking. The words representing concepts are used in our verbal communications. Unless we share the same meanings of the words, that is, have the same societally accepted concepts, we do not understand one another.

Concepts vary in learnability, usability, clarity, generality, and power. Instruction should start with the concepts that are most learnable, usable, clear, general, and powerful.

A given concept is attained at four successively higher levels: concrete, identity, classificatory, and formal. Mental processes, such as generalizing and hypothesizing, emerge with learning and maturation and make it possible to learn a concept at the successively higher levels.

Persons attain the four successively higher levels of a concept in a fixed order. Furthermore, with the attainment of the successively higher levels, the ability to use concepts in understanding superordinate-subordinate relations, in understanding principles, and in solving problems follows in an orderly manner. Having the name of a concept and the names of its defining attributes markedly helps students learn concepts at the classificatory and formal levels and also helps them use the concepts.

Students of the same age vary greatly in understanding concepts, understanding principles, and solving problems. Some students in grade 3 are equal to others in grade 12. In addition, the same individual of any age typically varies in understanding the concepts and principles of different subject fields, such as English, mathematics, and science.

Principles for teaching concepts vary according to the level of concept attainment desired of the student. From grade 4 on, a considerable amount of instruction is directed toward student attainment of the mature classificatory level and the formal level. Principles for teaching these levels are as follows:

1. Prepare the students to learn concepts.
2. Make available examples and nonexamples.
3. Help the learner acquire a strategy for identifying examples and nonexamples.
4. Enable the learner to acquire the names of the concepts and their defining attributes.
5. Provide for complete understanding of the concepts.
6. Provide for use of the concepts.
7. Provide for feedback.

Teachers require excellent instructional materials and time for planning to put the preceding principles into effect. A combination of appropriate materials and good teaching produces large gains in students' conceptual learning and development.

SUGGESTIONS FOR FURTHER READING

Klausmeier, H. J. *Learning and teaching concepts: A strategy for testing applications of theory.* New York: Academic Press, 1980.

The original report of a longitudinal study conducted in the intermediate grades to validate the classroom applications of the theory of concept learning and development explained in this chapter. The applications appear in this chapter in the principles for teaching concepts.

Klausmeier, H. J., & Allen, P. *Cognitive development of children and youth: A longitudinal study*. New York: Academic Press, 1978.

The original report of a longitudinal study conducted in grades 1–12 to validate the theory of cognitive learning and development. Chapter 2 explains the design of the study; chaps. 3–5 present the theory; and chaps. 6–8 give the results.

Park, O. Example comparison strategy versus attribute identification strategy in concept learning. *American Educational Research Journal*, 1984, *21*, 145–162.

An experiment to ascertain whether initial learning and retention are facilitated equally well by presenting prototype examples and aiding students in identifying the attributes of the prototype, or by presenting examples and non-examples and aiding the students to learn the defining attributes of the concept. The findings suggest using a combination of the two strategies.

Tennyson, R. D., Youngers, J., & Suebsonthi, P. Concept learning by children using instructional presentation forms for prototype formation and classification-skill development. *Journal of Educational Psychology*, 1983, *75*(2), 280–291.

These authors make clear the value of presenting examples of concepts and questioning students regarding whether a presented instance is or is not an example of the concept.

Weil, M. L., & Murphy, J. Instruction processes. In H. E. Mitzel, J. H. Best, & W. Rabinowitz (Eds.), *Encyclopedia of educational research* (5th ed., Vol. 3). New York: Free Press, 1982. Pp. 890–917.

The authors discuss six most well-researched or most widely used teaching strategies: advance organizer (Ausubel and others), concept attainment (Klausmeier and others), cognitive development (Piaget and others), contingency management (Bandura, Skinner, and others), self-management (Bandura, Skinner, and others), and basic practice, or direct instruction (Rosenshine and others).

PEANUTS CARTOON COPYRIGHT BY FIELD ENTERPRISES, INC., 1982

CHAPTER 10

PROBLEM SOLVING AND CREATIVITY

THE NATURE OF
PROBLEM SOLVING

DEVELOPMENTAL
TRENDS AND
INDIVIDUAL
DIFFERENCES IN
CONVERGENT PROBLEM
SOLVING

PRINCIPLES FOR
FOSTERING CONVERGENT
PROBLEM SOLVING

THE NATURE OF
CREATIVITY

PRINCIPLES FOR
FOSTERING CREATIVITY

Problem solving enables individuals and groups to adapt to the physical environment and to change it. This is possible as each generation learns to solve problems. The solutions to some problems are achieved by *convergent problem solving*—the finding of correct solutions and answers. But every generation also encounters problems for which new solutions are needed—solutions found by *creative,* or *divergent, problem solving.*

Every human being is capable of learning to solve problems and to be creative. Furthermore, the college years are especially opportune for reaching out and extending one's abilities. As a teacher, being able to model problem solving and creative processes may be as important as being able to teach the processes directly. Your study of this chapter will aid you to increase your understanding of problem solving, creativity, and related instructional processes.

THE NATURE OF PROBLEM SOLVING

Models of Problem
Solving

Problem Solving by
Small Groups

What is a problem? We are confronted with a problem when we encounter a situation and we try to respond but do not have immediately available the substantive information, specific methods, or general plan to reach a solution. At times, we experience unsolvable problems for which we either do not have one or more of these means available or do not have the capability for applying and using them.

The preceding ideas about a problem apply to both convergent and creative, or divergent, problem solving. In *convergent problem solving*, as contrasted with creative problem solving, people attempt to reach solutions which are correct or generally accepted as appropriate or correct. You can readily infer the characteristics of a problem requiring convergent solution by trying this one: rearrange the five letters *g a n r e* to make a word (not a proper noun); then rearrange them differently to make a second word. Give yourself time to get at least one of the words. Now do some introspecting. Did you understand the problem? Did you accept it as one to try to solve? How did you go about trying to identify the words? Do you have a general plan for doing anagrams? Do you have specific strategies? Do you have the essential prior word knowledge, that is, the pronunciation and spelling of *anger* and *range*?

In *creative*, or *divergent*, *problem solving* people attempt to reach solutions that are novel or unconventional for the problem solver. A practice exercise used to encourage creative thinking follows: "List different ways for using a brick." There is no one correct or generally accepted answer; rather, there are many answers. Persons who produce many different uses are regarded as fluent. Producing categories of different uses indicates flexibility. Coming up with remote uses is one indicator of originality.

We have given simple illustrations of problems and of the difference between convergent and divergent problem solving. In this part of the chapter, our interest is problem solving generally. Subsequent parts discuss teaching convergent problem solving and encouraging creativity, a special kind of problem solving.

Models of Problem Solving

Psychologists are keenly interested in gaining a better understanding of problem solving. Many decades ago, they attempted to identify the sequential activities involved in problem solving. To generate their sequences, they analyzed problem-solving tasks, observed persons involved in problem solving, and formulated the *sequences,* or steps, involved in solving problems. Recent approaches involve more sophisticated methods. We shall now examine some of the classical approaches to problem solving that either persist today or are antecedents of more recent approaches.

Classical Models

Four models that indicate the sequence of operations involved in solving problems are given in Table 10.1. Examine them to see if one or another is more closely related to your problem-solving experiences and to your major field of interest. You readily see many likenesses among the sequences and a few differences. The differences probably arise because of the different interests of the persons formulating the sequences.

Rossman (1931) was particularly concerned with clarifying what was involved in the *invention* of something. He regarded invention as based on a problem-solving sequence similar to that identified by others. However,

**TABLE 10.1 FOUR CLASSICAL
PROBLEM-SOLVING SEQUENCES**

ROSSMAN (1931)	DEWEY (1933)	GUILFORD (1959), MERRIFIELD ET AL. (1960)	POLYA (1945)
Observation of need or difficulty	Experiencing a difficulty	Preparation	
Formulation of problem	Locating and defining the problem	Analysis and problem identification	Understanding the problem
Gathering of information			Working out connections between the known and unknown, including a plan of solution
Formulation of possible solutions	Mentally elaborating the problem and suggesting possible hypotheses	Production	Carrying out the plan
Analysis and testing of solutions	Testing hypotheses	Verification	Examining the solution
Formulation of new ideas		Reapplication	
Testing and accepting new ideas			

his last two steps suggest that the first solution is not acceptable but instead leads to the formulation and testing of more ideas.

Dewey (1933) was interested in describing *reflective thinking*. He tried to explain *purposive mental activity,* activity by which we arrive at reasoned conclusions. His ideas are still very popular in the behavioral and social sciences.

Merrifield, Guilford, Christensen, and Frick (1960) were interested in identifying the different abilities involved in solving problems. Their sequence is based on Guilford's *structure of intellect* (1967). Later in this chapter, we shall see refinements of this sequence.

Polya (1945) was particularly interested in problem solving in mathematics. His sequence is still applied widely by persons in engineering, mathematics, science, and other fields where problem-solving exercises are an integral part of the curriculum (Tuma & Reif, 1980).

Cognitive Information-processing Model

Guilford (1967) wrote a book in which he combined the problem-solving sequence presented in Table 10.1 with other ideas related to the structure of intellect. The resulting model of problem solving is shown in Figure 10.1.

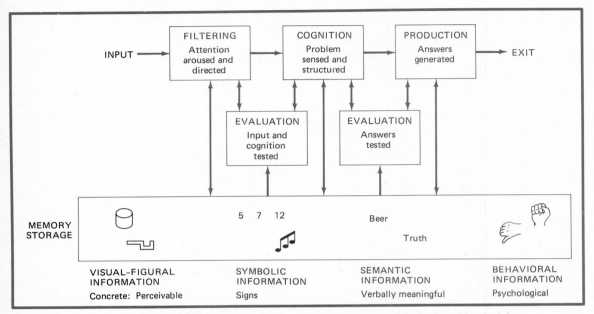

Figure 10.1 Guilford's information-processing model of problem solving.
Source: Guilford, 1967, p. 315.

Before studying the model, recognize that the five mental operations of Guilford's structure of intellect are *cognition, convergent production, divergent production, evaluation,* and *memory.* Guilford regards these operations as sufficient for all problem solving. Note also that information that is learned may be *figural, symbolic, semantic,* or *behavioral.* Learned information in these four areas is stored in memory and must be retrieved from memory to solve problems (see the bottom of Figure 10.1).

Guilford's model has five main phases, the first four of which follow: input of information from the external or internal environment, filtering the information (arousing and directing attention), cognition (sensing a problem and structuring it), and production (generating answers). At each phase, information is retrieved from memory storage and is used both in relating new and old information and in evaluating the outcome of each phase of the processing. The fifth phase of the model involves verifying (evaluating) the final answer. If the answer is verified, the problem-solving process ceases. If the answer is not verified, the five-phase cycle begins anew.

The Guilford model indicates neither control of the problem-solving operations nor a general problem-solving plan or program. We may now add these to the Guilford model from the *cognitive information-processing* point of view that pervades this book. The completed model is shown in Figure 10.2. Executive control is the theoretical construct that indicates the control of motivation and the information-processing operations. The goals, intentions, or expectancies of the individual triggered by executive control start the problem-solving process. An intention to continue to work on the problem until it is solved provides the continuing motivation for the problem solver's activities. Executive control also directs the problem-solving operations, from attending to the environment through verification of the solutions.

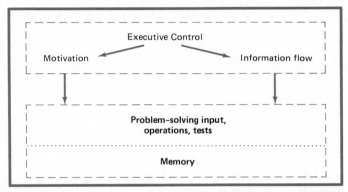

Figure 10.2 A cognitive information-processing model of problem solving.

Computer Simulation Model

A computer receives information, processes it, and outputs the results. A *program,* or plan, controls the processing. Persons who use computers to study problem solving generate programs that computers use to solve problems. These researchers are trying to identify the programs and specific mental processes that human beings use. The researchers use the computer because the programs and processes of human beings cannot be observed directly.

A most significant outcome of computer simulation of problem solving is called the *General Problem Solver.* Successive versions of the General Problem Solver are described by Ernst and Newell (1969) and Newell and Simon (1972). The General Problem Solver deals with a variety of problems, such as solving word puzzles, proving trigonometric identities, and applying rules of logic.

The General Problem Solver is far too technical to explain and illustrate here. However, the field of computer simulation is growing rapidly. Mayer (1977) evaluates the computer simulation of problem solving and of other learning outcomes, such as concept attainment, as offering a breakthrough in the psychology of thinking. He indicates, however, that computer simulation also has certain basic drawbacks. One is that the human-machine analogy, the description of mental operations as computer operations, is not a perfect analogy. Another drawback is a flaw in the logic of computer simulation. Although a computer program may simulate human thinking behavior, this does not mean it simulates the underlying cognitive processes.

Science Model

Reif and Heller (1982) formulated a three-phase model for solving problems in the sciences: describe and analyze the problem initially, search for its solution, and assess the solution. They carefully delineated the several subprocesses for each phase. For example, the search for the solution involves organizing the known and desired information, identifying subproblems, identifying a method for solving a chosen subproblem, and applying the method in solving the subproblem. This cycle is continued until the subproblems are solved.

Another very important element of the science model is having the knowledge that is essential for solving each specific problem or class of problems. Every problem requires knowledge of particular concepts and principles and the ability to apply the knowledge to the problem. Missing this knowledge, or not having the ability to apply it, the student cannot use the model in solving problems.

Reif and Heller (1982) indicate that their model, though applied by them to physics problems, is usable in any scientific domain. Moreover, they propose that students should be taught this scientific problem-solving method directly, not only the processes but also how to gain and structure relevant knowledge.

Problem Solving by Small Groups

Much problem solving is done by small groups in school and at home. Even more is called for than at present if the quality of learning and teaching in school and of family life is to be improved. Research on small group problem solving is providing sound information on making small group problem solving more effective and more enjoyable.

Effectiveness of Initial
Learning and Transfer by Small Groups

In three classical studies, the average achievements of groups of four who worked together were found to be higher than the average of individuals who worked alone (Hudgins, 1960; Klausmeier, Wiersma, & Harris, 1963; Wegner & Zeaman, 1956). In two of the three experiments, those who had initially learned as members of quartets performed less well later working alone than those who had initially learned working alone. In the third experiment, there was no difference between those who initially worked in quartets or those who worked alone (Hudgins, 1960).

Why is the average performance of small groups superior to the av-

Convergent problem solving enables individuals and groups to find solutions that are accepted as correct. Divergent problem solving leads in different directions to solutions that are novel to the individual and in some cases to society in general. To what extent should the school teach both kinds?

erage performance of individuals in initial learning situations? During initial learning, members of small groups *collectively* arrive at an understanding of the problem more quickly by interacting with one another than individuals working alone. They secure information more rapidly and apply it more effectively. They bring a larger variety of methods to bear on the solution, pose more solutions, and verify the solutions more reliably.

Effects of Group
Composition and Within-Group Activity

The preceding studies did not investigate the composition of the groups in terms of the ability of the members or the activities of the members and their interactions with one another. Accordingly, the question may be raised with respect to how the composition of the group, the amount of activity, and the kind of activity by small-group members influence their performance. Webb (1980) made a careful analysis of the activities of grade 11 students in solving mathematical problems. Groups of four were compared with individuals. The groups consisted of either high-ability, medium-ability, low-ability, or mixed-ability students. Each mixed-ability group had one high-ability, one low-ability, and two medium-ability students. Ability of the students was based on the results of aptitude and achievement tests. The students in each group did not know one another. The groups were instructed to help each other solve the problems, to ask questions of one another, and to explain how to solve the problems to any member who was confused. The groups, and also those working individually, had access to written hints that provided a step-by-step solution to each problem.

Webb (1980) found that those individual students who participated actively in trying to solve the problems got the correct solutions. The written hints aided them in the absence of assistance from a group member. The individual students who did not participate actively did not get the answers. Some members of groups did not interact with other members, but they got the correct solutions using the same processes as the individual workers. Webb concluded that individual or group work is not the primary consideration in determining the effectiveness of initial problem solving. Rather, activity or inactivity is.

Webb identified additional factors within the different groups that influence whether or not the members participate actively: the composition of the group, the perceived status and role of the members of the group, and motivation.

The largest number of noninteracting students—those who did not participate in the group work—was in mixed-ability groups. In the mixed-ability groups, most of the interaction was between the high-ability and the low-ability members. The high-ability students generally helped those of low ability. The median-ability students often experienced difficulty. However, unless they were assertive in asking for help, they were left out of the group interaction. Webb felt that the inactivity of the medium-ability students was due to lack of confidence in their ability and their feelings of low status. The lack of confidence and the feelings of low status were due to the behavior of the high-ability students. The high-ability students usually assumed responsibility for leading the activities, provided explanations to the low-ability students, and ignored the students of average ability.

The medium-ability students in the uniform medium-ability groups interacted frequently. They asked questions of one another. Those who had learned noted and corrected the errors of others and gave explanations. In this grouping, medium-ability students did not experience the low status or lack of confidence felt by the medium-ability students in the mixed-ability groups (Webb, 1980).

In both the uniformly high-ability and low-ability groups there was little interaction and group effort. Webb (1980) concluded that members of the high-ability groups probably thought that raising questions, correcting, and explaining were unnecessary. The members of the low-ability groups probably thought that no one was capable of correcting errors or explaining. Both the uniformly high- and low-ability groups tended to rush through the problems without attending to other members' lack of understanding or inability to solve the problems.

Webb (1982) carried out a similar experiment in junior high school classes. She found three kinds of student interaction to be related to achievement: receiving no explanation in response to a question or error or only a correct answer without explanation was negatively related to achievement; both giving explanations and receiving explanations were positively related to achievement. Not receiving an explanation or only a correct answer without an explanation was the most powerful predictor of achievement. Another finding was that high ability students in mixed-ability groups achieved highest while medium-ability and low-ability students achieved lower and at the same level. Webb and Cullian (1983) got these same results in a follow-up study of the same students three months later.

In a study conducted with grade 5 students, Swing and Peterson (1982) found that task-related interaction in mixed-ability groups of four children enhanced achievement and retention of high- and low-ability students but not of middle-ability students. Based on all of these studies, we conclude that medium-ability students do not fare well in mixed ability groups.

Before proceeding further, we should recognize that the students in these experiments were not rewarded for working together or for individual work. As we shall see, outcomes of group problem solving are related to a reward system as well as to the composition and interactions of the group members.

Outcomes of Cooperative Small-Group Activities

Johnson, Skon, and Johnson (1980) indicate that small groups can be arranged so that the members either cooperate or compete for rewards. *Cooperation* among members of small groups is arranged by having one person's achievement of his or her goals result in other members' achieving their goals. *Competition* among members of small groups is arranged by having one person's achievement of his or her goals result in other members not achieving theirs. In individual work, the goal achievement of one person is not directly related to that of others.

Johnson, Skon, and Johnson (1980) report that cooperative effort for which all group members are rewarded equally produces higher achievement than group members competing for rewards or individuals competing who are not members of small groups. Three factors account for the higher achievement. First, the cooperative groups develop superior problem-solving strategies. Second, medium- and low-ability students profit from their interactions with the high-ability students. Third, the incentive for achievement is increased by peer support and encouragement.

The Johnsons arrived at their conclusions through practical research conducted in school settings. A relatively simple teaching technique of assigning students to work together on regular classroom tasks was used. The outcome of cooperative and competitive group activity was a project or product to which all members contributed; however, the rewards were manipulated.

Another pioneering research group used specially devised programs for teaching cooperative problem solving in small groups (Slavin, 1980). In this research, recognition and rewards were manipulated systematically. Furthermore, the studies were typically done in desegregated schools where the desired outcomes included high achievement, positive race relations, mutual concern, and self-esteem.

To what extent are higher achievement and other desired outcomes attained through use of these specially devised programs and other cooperative-group techniques? Slavin (1980, pp. 337–338) states:

> Presently, the research on cooperative learning in classrooms justifies the following conclusions:
>
> 1. For academic achievement, cooperative learning techniques are no worse than traditional techniques, and in most cases they are significantly better.
> 2. For low level learning outcomes, such as knowledge, calculation, and application of principles, cooperative learning techniques appear to be more effective than traditional techniques to the degree that they use:
>   a. A structured, focused, schedule of instruction;
>   b. Individual accountability for performance among team members;
>   c. A well-defined group reward system, including rewards or recognition for successful groups.
> 3. For high level cognitive learning outcomes, such as identifying concepts, analysis of problems, judgment, and evaluation, less structured cooperative techniques that involve high student autonomy and participation in decision-making may be more effective than traditional individualistic techniques.
> 4. Cooperative learning techniques have strong and consistent effects on relationships between black, white, and Mexican-American students.
> 5. Cooperative learning techniques have fairly consistent positive effects on mutual concern among students regardless of the specific structure used.
> 6. There is some indication that cooperative learning techniques can improve students' self-esteem.
> 7. Students in classes using cooperative learning generally report greater liking of school than do traditionally taught students.

10.1 State a problem that you have recently solved by convergent thinking and another one by divergent thinking.

10.2 Which of the four classical sequences of problem solving, described respectively by Rossman, Dewey, Guilford, and Polya, would a mathematician or physicist probably endorse? A social scientist?

10.3 Guilford's information-processing model of problem solving is shown in Figure 10.1. In solving the problem of rearranging the letters *g a n r e* to make a word, relate your mental activities to the model.

10.4 Explain the functions of executive control in problem solving.

10.5 Research shows that small groups solve problems in less time than individuals working alone, but that transfer is not always better for persons who learn in small groups but later work alone. Describe what must occur in small-group learning to secure high transfer to working alone.

10.6 Webb found that the composition of small groups in terms of the ability level of the members—all high, all low, all medium, and mixed—was related to how effectively the members worked with one another and to their feelings toward one another. Relate the findings of Webb's experiment to your own experiences in small groups.

10.7 Using the conclusions of Johnson, Skon, and Johnson, and of Slavin, explain how small-group work should be arranged to yield (a) high student achievement and (b) good interpersonal relations among students of different racial and ethnic backgrounds.

10.8 (a) Some students have a strong preference for working individually rather than as a member of a small group. (b) Students with high ability for learning a given task can learn it in less time working individually than being a member of a mixed-ability group. Give some pro and con arguments for having (a) and (b) students engage in small-group problem-solving activities with other students of different ability levels.

DEVELOPMENTAL TRENDS AND INDIVIDUAL DIFFERENCES IN CONVERGENT PROBLEM SOLVING

Developmental Trends in Convergent Problem Solving

Individual Differences in Convergent Problem Solving

One problem faced by teachers is that they do not have reliable norms for estimating children's growth in problem-solving skills during the school years. Having such information can be as helpful to the teacher in understanding an individual student's pattern of growth as having weight and height curves is to the physician or school nurse. Similarly, accurate information about the range of individual differences can be used effectively in understanding and guiding students.

Developmental Trends in Convergent Problem Solving

Klausmeier and Allen (1978) conducted a longitudinal study—discussed at length in Chapter 9—dealing with the cognitive development of children of school age. The children were tested on many aspects of cognitive development, including their ability to solve problems. The children received four sets of problem-solving items. Each item involved solving a problem that required use of one of the following concepts and related principles: *cutting tool, tree, equilateral triangle,* and *noun.*

Figure 10.3 gives the developmental curves for solving problems related to each of the four concepts. Two points related to the curves need clarification. First, the curves for *equilateral triangle* and *noun* start at grade 3, because these were the grades at which the tests were first administered. Second, a mean percentage below 20 is not considered an indicator of true problem-solving ability, because students can get about 20% correct by guessing.

We observe in Figure 10.3 that the ability to solve problems involving *cutting tool* increases rapidly between grades 1 and 2, and at a gradually decelerating rate thereafter through grade 12. Problem solving involving

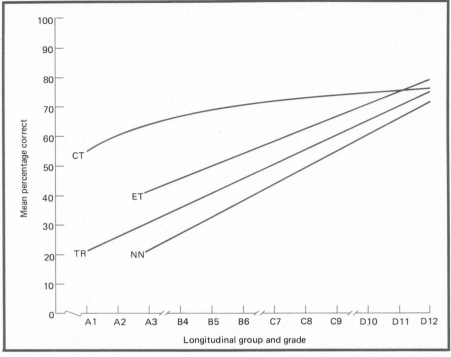

Figure 10.3 Normative development in solving problems related to the concepts *cutting tool (CT), equilateral triangle (ET), tree (TR), noun (NN).*

the other concepts shows a uniform rate of increase from the primary school years through grade 12.

Two other important conclusions may be drawn. First, the level of problem-solving performance is quite low throughout the school years. We cannot tell whether students are not taught problem-solving skills effectively or whether the ability develops slowly even with effective instruction. Second, the ability to solve problems involving the use of concrete concepts and related principles, that is, *cutting tool,* develops much earlier than the ability to solve problems involving abstract concepts, that is, *noun.*

Individual Differences in
Convergent Problem Solving

Information that follows from our study (Klausmeier & Allen, 1978) shows how students of school age vary in convergent problem solving. The hardest problem for *equilateral triangle* is given; after the problem, the percentage of children of grades 3, 6, and 9 who got the correct solution is given. This information, drawn from the first year of the study, enables you to see the percentage the students of each grade who got the problem correct and the percentage of the younger children who got the same items correct in comparison with the percentage of the older students.

Line v bisects the upper angle of this equilateral triangle. Suppose that side z is 2 inches long. Line w would then be:
a. 1 inch.
b. 2 inches.
c. 3 inches.
d. It is impossible to tell without measuring.
e. I don't know.

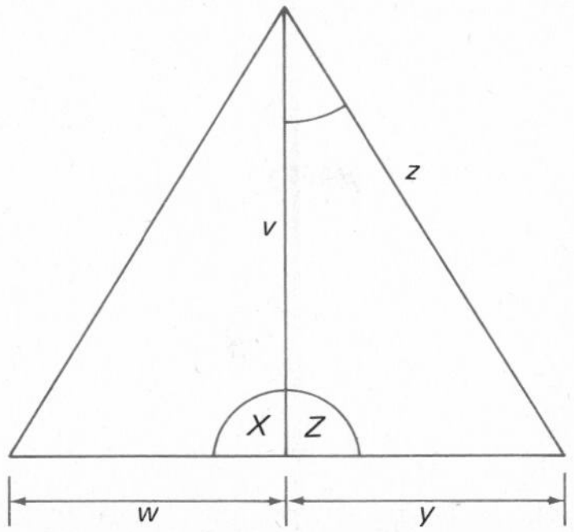

Figure 10.4 Hardest problem related to the concept *equilateral triangle.*

Figure 10.4 depicts the problem. The percentages of students solving the problem were: 10 (grade 3), 17 (grade 6), 37 (grade 9). Notice that while 10% of the grade 3 students solved the problem, 63% of the grade 9 students did not.

The preceding individual differences in problem solving are representative of the problem-solving ability found in various subject fields. How may the differences among children of the same grade and between grades be accounted for? Scandura (1981) presents an explanation in terms of three levels of problem solving: naive, neophyte, and expert.

Naive problem solvers have relatively little generalized knowledge that enables them to understand spoken or written problems and relatively few generalized strategies for solving different classes of problems. Accordingly, upon encountering a problem the naive problem solver must engage in much initial learning. The nature of the problem, the explanation of the problem, and the strategies to be employed represent new learning experiences. Two other attributes characterize naive problem solvers: relatively little memory capacity and low capability for applying their knowledge (executive control).

The neophyte has more knowledge regarding the problem domain and a greater number and variety of generalized problem-solving procedures, or strategies. Memory capacity is greater and executive control is more advanced. Having more knowledge, more problem solving procedures, and advanced executive control, neophytes are able to identify which procedures may apply to a particular problem and to apply the procedures one after another. Neophytes solve the same problems with greater speed and accuracy, and they solve more difficult problems with less trial and error than the naive persons.

The expert problem solver has a larger store of generalized knowledge, more and higher-order generalized procedures, greater memory capacity and memory retrieval, and more advanced executive control. Moreover, the expert has organized the knowledge and procedures into a hierarchical structure. Separate items of knowledge and individual procedures are not retrieved from memory one at a time and applied. Rather, the more advanced executive control enables the expert to retrieve the relevant knowledge items and procedures without much search and to apply them quickly to solving the problem. The expert solver completes the same problems with greater speed and accuracy than the neophyte and is able to solve more difficult problems.

Schoenfeld and Herrmann (1982) provide support for the preceding explanation. In their study, students' perceptions of the structure of mathematical problems were examined before and after a month-long intensive course in mathematical problem solving. The students' perceptions were compared with experts' perceptions. At the beginning of the course, the students perceived the problems on the basis of their surface structure (i.e., words or objects given in the problem statement). After the course, the students perceived the problems more like the experts in terms of principles and procedures relevant for solving the problems. Thus, the students' criteria for problem perception shifted as their knowledge of the principles and procedures became more richly structured.

10.9 In a longitudinal study, the problem-solving proficiency of students was found to be lowest for problems involving the concept *noun,* at an intermediate level for *tree* and *equilateral triangle,* and highest for *cutting tool.* Indicate possible reasons for this finding.

10.10 The differences in problem-solving performances among normally developing students are very great. Explain causes of these differences, using Scandura's ideas.

10.11 Marietta, grade 9, does not solve verbal or mathematical problems well, but she is sociable and physically able. Should her teachers make a determined effort to increase her proficiency in problem solving, or should they accept the possibility that she will never become proficient in problem solving and focus their instruction on building her strengths? Explain.

PRINCIPLES FOR FOSTERING CONVERGENT PROBLEM SOLVING

1. Analyze the problem.
2. Recall or generate a plan for solving the problem.
3. Recall prior information or gain new information.
4. Produce a solution.
5. Verify the problem-solving processes and the solution.
6. Secure feedback and assistance.

These principles are based on the research and theory in the preceding sections of this chapter. The principles considered together may be regarded as a general plan for guiding one's own problem solving and for guiding the teaching of both subject-matter content and problem-solving skills rather than the teaching of problem-solving skills only. The applications of this plan will necessarily vary from one problem area to another, such as making new friends and solving trigonometry problems, and also from one level of schooling to another, such as primary and high school.

1. Analyze the problem. Teaching students to analyze a problem comes at the beginning of the problem-solving sequence. Analysis of a problem by the student involves identifying the knowns, or *givens*, becoming aware of the desired outcome, and determining how to proceed from the givens to the desired outcome. Accepting the problem as one to be solved and estimating one's capabilities for solving it are also part of the analysis.

It is essential for the teacher to analyze the problem in order to teach students how to analyze it. Or, with more mature students, the teacher and students may analyze together. One very important aspect of this analysis by the teacher is to take into account both the learner's ability to perform the analysis and to solve the problem. The kindergarten teacher necessarily proceeds very differently from the college professor.

2. Recall or generate a plan for solving the problem. A problem-solving plan that includes a *program,* or general overview, of how to proceed and specific strategies and skills appropriate for solving the particular problems is called a *hierarchical plan* (Miller, Galanter, & Pribram, 1960). Having a plan to guide thought and action makes problem solving rational rather than blind trial and error. Teachers aid learners solve particular problems by encouraging them to recall a plan that has already been learned, to generate a refined or new plan, or to combine these into a new plan.

Aiding students to recall plans may be made explicit in many ways. For example, the teacher may ask the class: "What do we already know about how to solve problems like this?" Or, individuals may be called upon to describe their approaches.

Refining a plan or generating a new one is at the heart of increasing students' problem-solving capabilities. Either is accomplished by teaching the students to incorporate elements of an already-learned plan into a new plan that meets the requirements for solving the more complex or more advanced problem. For instance, students who already have a plan for getting the meaning of a paragraph can be taught how to incorporate this plan in a plan for getting the gist of a story of five or ten paragraphs. Expository techniques, discovery methods, and combinations of these are used to teach students how to refine a plan or to generate a new one.

Expository techniques, patterned after meaningful reception learning, include demonstrations by the teacher or a student and oral, written, or filmed explanations. Discovery calls for the students to generate their own plans. Whole-class and small-group discussion led by teacher are commonly used in a guided discovery approach. In general, an approach guided by the teacher gets better results in less time with more students than does independent discovery by the students.

In addition to the general plan for broad groups of problems, specific strategies are usually required for classes of problems and even for specific sets of problems within a class of problems. Techniques for aiding students to recall relevant strategies and to refine existing strategies or generate new ones are similar to those for the general plan.

3. Recall prior information or gain new information. To solve particular problems, students need three kinds of information: factual information, concepts, and principles. The teacher helps students secure needed information by instructing them in retrieving information from long-term memory and in identifying and using various sources of information.

Students not yet having learned the concepts or principles necessary for solving the problem poses a real dilemma for the teacher. The decision whether to defer the problem-solving activity in favor of teaching the concepts or principles must be made. The amount of time required to learn the concepts or principles and the ability of the learner to acquire them are primary factors to be taken into account. As we saw in Chapter 9, many grade 6 children attain concepts and principles before some grade 12 students (Klausmeier & Allen, 1978). We also found that with the best instruction designed to help each student achieve mastery, some slow-developing students at the end of grade 5 could not attain the basic process concepts of science sufficiently well to solve science problems that other students solve early in grade 4 (Klausmeier, 1980).

4. Produce a solution. The teacher's role in aiding learners to produce correct solutions is accomplished by encouraging them to recall or develop a general problem-solving plan and specific strategies that are applicable to the particular class of problems. The teacher encourages hesitant learners who are fearful about making mistakes to produce their solutions as soon as they are reasonably confident of their correctness. On the other hand, students who arrive at solutions with little reflective thought or without checking their answers may be encouraged to take time to think and to check. In this regard Greer and Blank (1977) found that an impulsive cognitive style was not related to the strategies that students used in solving problems, but it was related to the time spent by the students prior to offering a solution. Instruction to increase the amount of time the students spent in thinking before offering a solution was found to be effective in improving performance.

5. Verify the problem-solving processes and the solution. Earlier in Figure 10.1, we saw that Guilford's information-processing model of problem solving involves *input, filtering, cognition, production,* and *evaluation, or verification.* Guilford calls for verification not only after an answer is produced but also at each step of the problem-solving sequence. The verification process is illustrated for you with the following division exercise: $414 \div \frac{2}{3}$. Regarding input and filtering, is sufficient information provided for you to identify the problem? Regarding cognition, do you understand the problem? Regarding producing the solution, do you have a plan and specific strategies for solving the problem? Regarding the solution, is your answer correct? How do you determine whether it is? This kind of continuous verification of the processes is required for effective problem solving.

6. Secure feedback and assistance. Feedback and overcoming difficulties identified by the feedback are required throughout a problem-solving sequence. With some problems, students are able to secure feedback and to overcome difficulties independently. With other problems, they require assistance in gaining feedback, overcoming difficulties, or both.

The assistance may be given directly. For example, the teacher observes the students as they conduct an experiment. The teacher confirms correct procedures, points out errors, and helps students who cannot proceed independently. Assistance may also be indirect, as when the teacher demonstrates and models the correct procedures prior to students starting to solve the problem.

The importance of the teacher as a model in providing assistance to students is suggested by social learning theory (Bandura, 1977). Regarding problem solving, Zimmerman and Blotner (1979) arranged for the same adult to model a difficult problem-solving situation to two groups of second-grade children. The adult either did not persist in trying to solve the problem and quit after 30 seconds or persisted for 15 minutes. The successful modeling was accompanied with "There, I did it" and the not successful with "I cannot do it; I give up." The children who observed the persisting model persisted longer in their subsequent attempts to solve problems than those who observed the unsuccessful, low-persisting performance.

10.12 In teaching convergent problem solving, indicate why the teacher should teach the learner to use the following strategy:

a. Analyze the problem.
b. Recall or generate a plan for solving the problem.
c. Recall prior information or gain new information.
d. Produce a solution.
e. Verify the problem-solving process and the solution.
f. Secure feedback and assistance.

10.13 Which of the preceding six steps are most difficult for you personally to implement when faced with a problem?

10.14 Refer back to the problem, "Rearrange the letters *g a n r e* to make a word." Which do you think is more difficult for teachers: (a) to make clear to students the nature of the problem? (b) to identify and verbalize a plan for solving the problem? (c) to communicate the plan to the students? Explain.

10.15 Based on your own school experiences, identify a class in which you were taught plans, or strategies, for solving the problems encountered in learning the course material. Describe the best features of the class.

THE NATURE OF CREATIVITY

Although *creativity* is a widely used term, it is not defined in the same way by scholars who study creativity. Over two decades ago, 25 definitions of creativity had already appeared, most of them stressing the role of originality (Morgan, 1953). MacKinnon (1962) emphasized the adaptiveness of creativity as well as its originality:

> True creativeness fulfills at least three conditions. It involves a response or an idea that is novel or at the very least statistically infrequent. But novelty or originality of thought and action, while a necessary aspect of creativity is not sufficient . . . it must to some extent be adaptive, to, or of, reality. It must serve to solve a problem, fit a situation, or accomplish some recognizable goal. And, thirdly, true creativeness involves a sustaining of the original insight, an evaluation and elaboration of it, a developing of it to the full. (p. 485)

Barron (1969), one of the pioneers in the study of highly creative adults, pointed to the outstanding contributions of creative persons to society:

> All of us are both creatures and creators, but we vary both in our quality as a creation and in our power to create.
>
> Great original thoughts or ideas are those which are not only new to the person who thinks them but new to almost everyone. These rare contributions are creative in perhaps a stronger sense of the term; they not only are the results of a creative act, but they themselves in turn create new conditions of human existence. The theory of relativity was such a creative act; so was the invention of the wheel. Both resulted in new forms of power, and human life was changed thereby.
>
> Creative power of an outstanding order is marked by the voluminous production of acts which can claim a notable degree of originality, and the occasional productions of acts of radical originality. (p. 19)

Davis (1981), a modern scholar, views creativity as a pervasive aspect of one's life-style and defines creativity in very global terms:

> Creative thinking is much more than using your imagination to crank out lots of new ideas. Creative thinking is a lifestyle, a personality trait, a way of perceiving the world, a way of interacting with other people, and a way of living and growing. Living creatively is developing your talents, tapping your unused potential, and becoming what you are capable of becoming. Being creative is exploring new places and new ideas. Being creative is developing a sensitivity to problems of others and problems of humankind. And being creative is using your imagination to crank out lots of new ideas to solve those problems. (p. 2)

Models of Creative Problem Solving

Figure 10.1 presented a cognitive information-processing model of problem solving and focused on convergent production of answers. The model can be modified to focus on divergent production of creative outcomes. There are other models that are applicable to all areas of creativity, two of which are shown in Table 10.2.

TABLE 10.2 SEQUENCES IN CREATIVE PROBLEM SOLVING

PARNES, NOLLER, AND BIONDI (1977)	FELDHUSEN AND GUTHRIE (1979)
Fact Finding	Problem Generation *Processes:* fluency, flexibility, originality, deferred judgment, evaluation
	Problem Clarification *Processes:* analysis, evaluation
Problem Finding	Problem Identification *Processes:* synthesis
Idea Finding	Idea Finding *Processes:* fluency, flexibility, analysis, originality, deferred judgment
Solution Finding	Synthesizing a Solution *Processes:* synthesis, elaboration, evaluation
Acceptance Finding	Implementation *Processes:* synthesis, evaluation, originality, flexibility

---

The model of Parnes, Noller, and Biondi (1977) draws on information from many sources and also on a wealth of experience in teaching creative problem solving. It stresses the idea of seeking and finding, moving into many possible directions. It is explained more fully in a training manual, *Guide to Creative Action* (Parnes, Noller, & Biondi, 1977).

The model of Feldhusen and Guthrie (1979) is based on a factor analysis of test performances as well as other research. It, too, is used in teaching creative problem solving to students, including teachers and other school personnel enrolled in university courses. Most of the processes involved in carrying out each step are related to Guilford's ideas (1967) regarding divergent production and evaluation.

Mansfield and Busse (1982) outline a five-phase model of the creative process in scientific fields: (1) selection of a problem that is important and potentially soluble, (2) extended effort to solve the problem, (3) setting constraints on solution of the problem, (4) changing the constraints through a restructuring process, and (5) verification and elaboration of the results. These steps bear some resemblance to those of Guilford and Merrifield presented earlier in this chapter.

Abilities Related to Creativity

Divergent Production Abilities

Guilford (1959, 1967) identified 24 specific abilities related to creativity. The 24 abilities involve the divergent production of 6 products—units, classes, relations, systems, transformations, and implications—related to four contents—figural, symbolic, semantic, and behavioral. Divergent production of the products essentially involves four suboperations, or processes—fluency, flexibility, originality, and elaboration. These processes are universally acknowledged to be associated with creativity. Examples of these four processes, related intellectual operations, products, and types of task (test item) used to measure each process are depicted in Table 10.3. Before examining Table 10.3, be aware that most studies of creativity call for students to produce responses to test items rather than to produce something as part of their school work.

TABLE 10.3 DIVERGENT PRODUCTION PROCESSES

PROCESS	INTELLECTUAL OPERATION	PRODUCT	TYPE OF TASK USED TO MEASURE PROCESS
Ideational fluency	Divergent production	Units	Write names of things fitting broad classes, for example, things that are white and edible.
Semantic spontaneous flexibility	Divergent production	Classes	List uses for a wooden lead pencil.
Originality	Divergent production	Transformations	Write titles for a short story *(clever)*. Give remote (distant in time, in space, or in sequence of events) consequences for a specified event *(remote)*.
Semantic elaboration	Divergent production	Implications	Add detailed operations needed to make a briefly outlined plan succeed.

In the task involving divergent production of units in Table 10.3, a *fluent* individual comes up with many names of white, edible things rather than a limited number. For example, the young child who says "milk," "bread," "cake," "flour," and "mashed potato" scores higher on the task than the one who gives only the first two.

Spontaneous flexibility implies that, without instruction, the individual produces responses that indicate a readiness to modify things and ideas from the manner in which they are commonly experienced. For example, a child who indicates that a lead pencil may be used to hold a window up and to write words is considered more flexible than the one who merely indicates it is used for writing.

Originality involves the production of products that are judged *clever* or *remote*. Guilford (1967) prepared a test that utilizes this short story:

> A man had a wife who had been injured and was unable to speak. He found a surgeon who restored her power of speech. Then the man's peace was shattered by his wife's incessant talking. He solved the problem by having the doctor perform an operation on him so that, although she talked endlessly, he was unable to hear a thing she said. (p. 156)

Here are nonclever titles for the story: "A Man and His Wife," "Medicine Triumphs," and "Never Satisfied." Titles that Guilford regards as clever include "My Quiet Wife," "Operation: Peace of Mind," and "Yack, Yack, Hack."

Remoteness implies products that are rarely produced. In one objective method of determining remoteness, the frequency of the responses of a group is tallied. The responses made the fewest times are considered the most remote. For example, the least frequently given titles to the prior story are evaluated as the most remote.

Elaboration involves expanding products in greater detail and at a higher level of analysis. For example, given a drawing of an electric light bulb and asked to name groups of people or occupations that it could symbolize, a person might respond "electrician," "teacher," "gifted student," or "communications." These responses are considered to involve a higher level of analysis of the situation (use of light bulbs) and to arrive at an implication.

We shall not elaborate further on the preceding processes, except to note that all of them require a person to *produce* something rather than to recognize something as being a correct or appropriate response or product. A student's response is not scored on the usual right or wrong basis. Rather, to measure *fluency,* the number of responses is simply counted. *Originality* is determined by rating the cleverness and remoteness of a student's responses. The number of different categories of responses determines *flexibility*.

Notice that only *semantic content* is involved in the preceding tasks. As you are aware, painters, sculptors, and architects typically express themselves in *figural content*. Statesmen, salesmen, and many others express their creative ideas in *behavioral content*. The same four divergent production processes underlie creative performances in these content areas.

College students can improve their creative abilities. Reese, Treffinger, Parnes, and Kaltsounis (1976) reported the results of a two-year, four-semester course in creative problem solving. Each semester emphasized a different aspect of creativity. The effects were measured with tests reflecting Guilford's *structure of intellect*. The course had no effect on the memory or evaluation operations in the structure of intellect, but significantly improved divergent production and cognition.

In a totally different setting, Goor and Rapoport (1977) found that the use of small-group creativity games in a summer camp for disadvantaged children produced improvement on a variety of tests of divergent production. Furthermore, the effects persisted through a four-month follow-up that was conducted. In this study, each small group of children had a leader who structured instruction to include the management of peer reinforcement and self-reinforcement of creativity. Accordingly, these authors emphasize the importance of structured instruction that is intense and includes both peer reinforcement and self-reinforcement.

Other Abilities and Creativity

What is the relationship of ideational fluency, spontaneous flexibility, and divergent problem solving to educational achievement? Houtz and Speedie (1978) found that scores on tests of divergent thinking correlated low with measures of educational achievement. Accordingly, students high or low on a test of divergent thinking were not also high or low in educational achievement.

What is the relationship between general intellectual ability (IQ) and creativity? In one study of children with IQs from very low to very high, moderately positive correlations were found between IQ and measures of divergent thinking (Ripple & May, 1962). In another study, the *average* creativity scores of children of low IQ were found to be lower than the *average* creativity scores of children of average and high IQ (Klausmeier & Wiersma, 1965).

Although researchers have found moderately positive correlations between divergent thinking and IQ, these correlations are not high enough to justify using only intelligence tests to identify students high in creativity (MacKinnon, 1962; May, 1961; Torrance, 1965). Students with high IQ scores vary markedly in creativity, and highly creative students vary markedly in IQ scores. This fact has been clearly stated: "It is commonly observed that many children who are very high in intelligence as measured by IQ are not concomitantly high in such other intellectual functions as creativity, and many children who are high in creativity are not concomitantly high in intelligence, as measured by IQ" (Getzels & Jackson, 1962, p. 3). Here is a similar point of view: "The best conclusion at present is that intelligence, as measured, accounts for only a minor portion of the variation in creative performance and, by itself, is by no means an adequate measure of creativity" (Taylor & Holland, 1962, pp. 93–94).

A longitudinal study of creative adolescents, still in progress, indicates the comparative value of creativity tests, intelligence tests, and educational achievement tests in predicting subsequent creative production (Torrance, 1977). The students, enrolled in grades 7–12, were administered the Torrance Tests of Creative Thinking (Torrance, 1966b), an intelligence test, and a test of educational achievement. A follow-up was conducted 12 years later. The *combined* measures of creative thinking, obtained in 1959, yielded a higher correlation (.51) with creative achievements twelve years later in 1971 than either the intelligence test or the educational achievement test *singly*. Moreover, the correlations for the tests of originality, fluency, and flexibility singly with creative achievements were higher than the correlations for either intelligence or educational achievement with creative achievements.

Creativity test scores do not correlate high with course grades (Taylor, Smith, & Ghiselin, 1963), nor do ratings of creativity by teachers and scores on creativity tests (Holland, 1959; Klausmeier, Harris, & Ethnathios, 1962; Yamamoto, 1963). Taking this fact into account, as well as recognizing that high creativity does not correlate high with mental ability, National Merit Scholarship administrators have made 25 scholarships available each year to candidates who cannot qualify for scholarships on the basis of their high school grades or IQ test scores, but who manifest a high level of creative ability in the sciences or arts. The following creative activities were considered in making the scholarship awards (Barron, 1969, pp. 129–130):

HIGH SCHOOL CREATIVITY SCALES

CREATIVE SCIENCE SCALE
1. Presenting an original paper at a scientific meeting sponsored by a professional society.
2. Winning a prize or award in a scientific talent search.
3. Constructing scientific apparatus on own initiative.
4. Inventing a patentable device.
5. Having a scientific paper published in a science journal.

CREATIVE ARTS SCALE
1. Winning one or more speech contests.
2. Having poems, stories, or articles published in a public newspaper or magazine or in a state or national high school anthology.
3. Winning a prize or an award in an art competition (sculpture, ceramics, painting, and so forth).
4. Receiving the highest rating in a state music contest.
5. Receiving one of the highest ratings in a national music contest.
6. Composing music that is performed at least once in public.
7. Arranging music for a public performance.
8. Having at least a minor role in plays (not high school or church-sponsored).
9. Having leads in high school or church-sponsored plays.
10. Winning a literary award or prize for creative writing.
11. Having a cartoon published in a public newspaper or magazine.

Personality Variables Related to Creativity
Earlier we saw that certain processes, such as originality and flexibility, correlate positively and moderately high with creative production. Certain personality variables have also been identified as correlating posi-

tively with creativity. At the same time, certain personality variables are deterrents to creativity.

Correlates of Creative Production

Barron (1969) studied creativity and personality variables in living writers, mathematicians, architects, and scientists. Highly creative individuals in these groups were compared with others who had an equal amount of education but were judged by their contemporaries to be less creative (Barron, 1969, p. 70):

**PERSONALITY TRAITS
OF CREATIVE INDIVIDUALS**

1. Genuinely values intellectual and cognitive matters.
2. Values own independence and autonomy.
3. Is verbally fluent; can express ideas well.
4. Enjoys esthetic impressions; is esthetically reactive.
5. Is productive; gets things done.
6. Is concerned with philosphical problems, for example, religion, values, the meaning of life.
7. Has high aspiration level of self.
8. Has a wide range of interests.
9. Thinks and associates to ideas in unusual ways; has unconventional thought processes.
10. Is an interesting, arresting person.
11. Appears straightforward, forthright, candid in dealings with others.
12. Behaves in an ethically consistent manner; has consistent personal standards.

The preceding characteristics of creative individuals may be related to the interests, activities, and hobbies of high-creative and low-creative women musicians during their childhood, adolescent, and college years. Trollinger (1983) found that the high-creative females consistently chose solitary activities while the majority of the low-creative females chose activities involving social interaction. The high-creative females chose reading more frequently than the low. Finally, the high-creative females consistently engaged in creative activities, such as writing, that could be pursued alone.

Teachers are interested in helping children to become creative adults. But they do not expect children to produce creative products of the kind Barron's adults did. Rather, school-age children will produce ideas and things novel to them, if properly instructed, and will gradually develop the abilities and personality traits essential for more mature levels of creativity.

Deterrents to Creative Production

Simberg (1971) identified perceptual, cultural, and emotional "blocks" to creativity. They are probably more prevalent in adults and adolescents than in children. Those pertaining to perceptual and emotional areas are particularly interesting. You may wish to estimate whether any of them may be slowing your creative productivity.

DETERRENTS TO CREATIVITY

A. Perceptual blocks
  1. Difficulty in isolating the problem.
  2. Difficulty caused by narrowing the problem too much.
  3. Inability to define terms.
  4. Failure to use all of the senses in observing.
  5. Difficulty in seeing remote relationships.
  6. Difficulty in not investigating the obvious.
  7. Failure to distinguish between cause and effect.
B. Emotional blocks
  1. Fear of making a mistake or making a fool of oneself.
  2. Grabbing the first idea that comes along.
  3. Rigidity of thinking.
  4. Overmotivation to succeed quickly.
  5. Pathological desire for security.
  6. Fear of supervisors and distrust of colleagues and subordinates.
  7. Lack of drive in carrying a problem through to completion and testing.
  8. Lack of drive in putting a solution to work.

10.16 Compare the definitions of creativity by (a) MacKinnon, (b) Barron, and (c) Davis, and identify the one most like your ideas about creativity.

10.17 Compare the models of creative problem solving developed by Parnes, Noller, and Biondi and by Feldhusen and Guthrie.

10.18 Relate the steps of the preceding models to Rossman's problem-solving model.

10.19 Give an example of fluency and nonfluency, flexibility and inflexibility, originality and unoriginality, and elaboration and nonelaboration.

10.20 All the items of IQ tests are scored either right or wrong. How is this fact related to the fact that correlations between IQ and creativity are not high?

10.21 Return to Barron's personality traits of creative individuals. Mentally check each one that you think the classroom teacher should manifest and also one or more that, if manifested, might lead to difficulty for the teacher.

10.22 Most of us are not as creative as we might be. Return to the perceptual and the emotional blocks to creativity identified by Simberg. Check the perceptual and the emotional blocks that slow down your creative efforts. Which of these can you eliminate independently?

10.23 Indicate one or two things teachers can do to help their students prevent or eliminate each emotional block identified by Simberg.

PRINCIPLES FOR FOSTERING CREATIVITY

1. Provide for variety in instructional materials and forms of student expression.
2. Develop favorable attitudes toward creative achievement.
3. Encourage continuing creative expression.
4. Foster productivity.
5. Provide assistance and feedback.

Creative problem solving is a kind of more general problem solving. Accordingly, the plan for teaching convergent problem solving presented earlier in this chapter serves as a model for teaching creative problem solving, except that divergent processes and outcomes are substituted for convergent processes and outcomes. The preceding principles for fostering creativity go beyond the general problem-solving plan and take into account personality and other variables that have been identified as closely related to creative achievement.

1. Provide for variety in instructional materials and forms of student expression. Fluency, originality, flexibility, and elaboration in producing products are the main divergent production processes. These processes underlie creativity in the figural, symbolic, semantic, and behavioral content areas. We want all students to have an opportunity to develop their creativity in these areas. Therefore, it is essential to have instructional materials related to each kind of content and also to encourage students to generate products, including forms of expression, appropriate for each content.

For example, young children may express themselves *behaviorally* in spontaneous play, *symbolically* in singing with other children, and *figurally* in finger painting and other activities. Later, a TV drama, poem, or painting is produced by the elementary and high school student. These different forms of creative production require instructional materials that go beyond the usual books, published creativity programs, and audiovisual equipment.

How effective are published materials in teaching creativity? Mansfield, Busse, and Krepelka (1978) reviewed the research on five published creativity programs. In general, the developers of the programs regard the results as providing strong support for their programs. However, Mansfield, Busse, and Krepelka are uncertain about how well performance on creativity tests taken in school predicts later real-life creative accomplishments. Thus, it seems advisable to continue to identify local materials and activities for teaching creativity in addition to those available in published form.

The idea that provisions should be made for creative expression in different forms is widely accepted. Torrance (1977) forwards this proposition in connection with culturally different students, including disadvantaged black students. Torrance identified 17 "creative positives" of these students—areas conducive to creativity in which they surpass the majority and the advantaged:

**CREATIVITY STRENGTHS OF
CULTURALLY DISADVANTAGED STUDENTS**

1. Ability to express and communicate feelings and emotions through creative writing, music, creative movement, interpersonal relations, etc.
2. Ability to improvise with commonplace materials.
3. Articulateness in role playing, sociodrama, and storytelling.
4. Enjoyment of and ability in the visual arts—drawing, painting, sculpture, etc.
5. Enjoyment of and ability in creative movement, dance, dramatics, etc.
6. Enjoyment of and ability in music, rhythm, etc.
7. Expressiveness of speech, richness of imagery, colorfulness of language, etc.
8. Fluency and flexibility in nonverbal media (figural, motor, etc.).
9. Enjoyment of and skills in small-group activities.
10. Responsiveness to the concrete.
11. Responsiveness to the kinesthetic.
12. Expressiveness of gestures, "body language," etc., and ability to "read body language" and nonverbal communication.
13. Humor and ability to create surprise.
14. Originality of ideas in problem solving.
15. Problem centeredness and persistence in problem solving.
16. Emotional responsiveness and responsiveness to emotion.
17. Quickness of physical and emotional warm-up.

2. Develop favorable attitudes toward creative achievement. Creativity has strong affective components: open-mindedness and receptivity to new ideas, valuing creativity in society and personal development, and interests and motives of a creative person (Davis & Bull, 1978). Davis and Bull believe that these affective aspects of creativity are learned more readily than some abilities, such as producing original products. Furthermore, they found that these affective components were strengthened in a university course on creativity.

How may attitudes such as these be communicated to children? Davis (1973), with the assistance of a writer, artists, and others, developed a delightful book that many children enjoy. It is called *Imagination Express: Saturday Subway Ride*. The first page, which follows, illustrates how the desired affective aspects of creativity are made explicit to a child:

> Let me tell you about last Saturday.
> I took a ride on a new super subway that travels a fast circle from Kansas City to Pittsburgh to Dublin to Tokyo to Santa Monica and back.
> What's wrong?
> You say there's no such subway, and you're about to close the book and stare out the window?
> Well, maybe you're wrong. Maybe I zipped around the world on an underground thought, a daydream, a nightdream, or a superfastspecialfivecityidea.
> That's what this book is all about.
> Ideas.
> You say my subway ride is just a wild idea and pretty silly?
> Well, what about flying? People said that men flying around in machines

was a wild idea and pretty silly. Then the Wright brothers took off and ZIP!

People once thought that TV was just a wild idea and probably wouldn't work—and bicycles, too, and life insurance and polio vaccine.

A wild idea is something that people find hard to accept because it's new and sounds strange and looks funny and maybe it's light green suede and smells of paprika. Anyway, it's something people haven't thought about before, and that makes them afraid.

Some people only feel safe with old, comfortable, tired-out ideas. I guess those people never learned to stretch their minds.

That's what this book is all about, too—learning to stretch your mind, learning to reach out for big, new, different, and even wild ideas.

Why?

So you can solve problems and create new things and improve old things and have more fun. Ideas are good anywhere, anytime, in any climate and even underwater.

Now, you've gotten me way off the subway track. Let's get back to last Saturday. (p. 7)

Torrance (1965) made several suggestions for establishing a classroom climate favorable for creative expression. Recognizing that the suggestions might seem obvious, he indicated that most teachers do not practice them. The suggestions follow (Torrance, 1965, p. 43):

1. Be respectful of unusual questions.
2. Be respectful of imaginative, creative ideas.
3. Show your pupils that their ideas have value.
4. Occasionally have pupils do something "for practice" without the threat of evaluation.
5. Tie in evaluation with causes and consequences.

3. Encourage continuing creative expression. The intellectual activities of poets and artists during four quarters of a creative enterprise are shown in Figure 10.5. Notice that the poets and artists spend a great deal of time in early preparation. Then there is a considerable increase in the time given to formulation of their ideas. As preparation falls off, revision increases markedly. There are, of course, wide differences in the total length of time required to bring forth the poem or the painting. Some are produced in a day; others take months. Indeed, some novelists start and complete a work in less than a year, while others spend five or more years from the time they have ideas until the novel is finished.

The amount of time and effort for a creative achievement varies with the developmental level of the learner and the nature of the goal. For example, kindergarten children do a finger painting in a few minutes, wash their hands, and go to some other activity. If given a blank sheet of paper and crayon, the primary school child fills the page with something in a relatively short time and is ready for another activity. Such spontaneous expressions are to be highly encouraged.

Many larger high schools sponsor art exhibits of students' work; arrange programs which include musical compositions by the students; produce small volumes of student poetry and other literary work; print students'

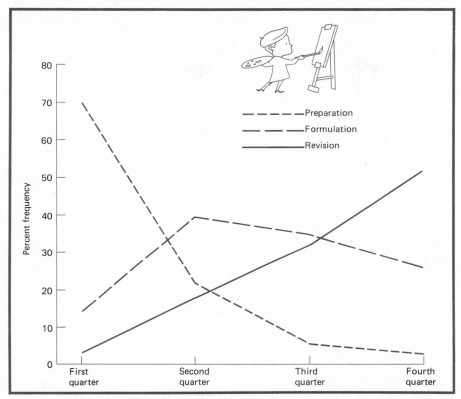

Figure 10.5 Intellectual activities of poets and artists during four quarters of a creative enterprise.
Source: Johnson, 1955, p. 30.

short poems, short stories, and essays in the newspaper; and stage students' plays. These are a few of the useful means for encouraging student creativity and for opening up opportunities for them to continue to produce after they finish school. These practices are in harmony with the ideas of encouraging creativity on a continuing basis.

4. **Foster productivity.** Girls in a modern dance class profit from discussing and practicing different dances before they bring a polished performance to a larger group. Students write several essays, stories, or biographies before identifying their best ones for a school publication. We recognize, too, that adult poets, composers, and artists produce a large number of works, many of which are not brought to the public, or at least are not well received. Accordingly, we should encourage learners to transform their creative ideas into tangible products. Clearly, productivity is needed that goes beyond having creative ideas and talking about them.

5. **Provide assistance and feedback.** It might be assumed that creative achievement occurs without giving students assistance and providing feed-

back. Too much direction and critical evaluation do hinder creativity. However, teaching students creative problem-solving methods and specific techniques for generating novel ideas is essential for fostering students' creative abilities. Similarly, providing feedback, offering constructive criticism, and ensuring desired consequences of creative learning activities contributes a great deal to student growth in creativity.

You are probably familiar with a number of techniques that are designed to increase creative productivity. These techniques—brainstorming, attribute testing, idea checklists, and others—are included in published creativity programs. Explanations of them are given by Davis (1981) and Maker (1982).

There are many opportunities for teachers to foster creativity. It is not difficult, but flexibility and originality on the part of the teacher are required, as may be seen in the following example:

EXAMPLE OF TEACHING CREATIVITY

When I first told my classes (high school English) about April 23, the anniversary of William Shakespeare's birth, I gave each class the following list of projects from which they could choose. They were asked to identify a project that interested them most and have it ready for April 23, which would be set aside for our celebration. The projects could be done individually or in small groups:

1. Dramatizing a scene from *Macbeth.*
2. Making a bulletin board display.
3. Writing a poem in commemoration of Shakespeare.
4. Drawing a character or scene from *Macbeth.*
5. Designing a costume for one of the characters.
6. Constructing or drawing a model of the Globe Theatre.
7. Writing a report on some aspect of Shakespeare.
8. Giving an oral report.
9. Making a diorama of a scene from *Macbeth.*
10. Memorizing a speech and presenting it before the class.
11. Presenting a panel discussion.

The foregoing list was suggestive. When presenting it to the classes I told the students not to feel restricted to the list. I wanted them to feel free to carry out their own ideas.

Flexibility on my part was even more important after the students had selected their projects. Some students asked for specific directions. For instance, students giving written or oral reports wished to know if they had to be a specific length. Those dramatizing passages wondered if they could select any speech, or if I required a certain number of lines. The four groups that worked on bulletin board displays asked if there were requirements which they had to meet. I set no specifications of this kind. In the case of reports I merely said that they should be well developed. I had learned that if you require written work to be 500 words long, for example, the students spend most of their time counting the words.

Three of the students wrote poems. I had, of course, told the classes that I would give them all of the help that I could, and these three students sought help often. One of them brought four poems in after school and wanted my advice as to which was the best and should be read on April 23. I talked with him about different poets' ideas about what they wrote, and he decided which one was the best for him. He told me that he enjoyed writing poetry very much but just never had much occasion to do so. I suggested that he submit his poem to *Patterns in Print,* a publication of student work. It was accepted and will appear in this year's edition. The critical point is that without much encouragement he continued to write until he was satisfied with his poem.

Two days before the deadline one of the students brought in a model of the Globe Theatre which she had made out of sugar cubes. A tremendous amount of time and talent was involved in its construction. The most rewarding aspect of this situation was that she rarely volunteered in class and had not appeared to be interested in English.

10.24 Recall one of your classes in which student creativity was strongly encouraged. Indicate one or two things that the teacher did in the class related to each of the following five principles for fostering creativity:

a. Provide for variety in instructional materials and forms of student expression.
b. Develop favorable attitudes toward creative achievement.
c. Encourage continuing creative expressions.
d. Foster productivity.
e. Provide assistance and feedback.

10.25 Which of the five principles for fostering creativity do you think would be easiest for a teacher to implement? Most difficult? Explain.

10.26 Return to Torrance's five suggestions for establishing a classroom climate favorable for creative expression. Indicate one or two things you would do as a teacher to carry out each suggestion.

10.27 Some college students are low in creativity. Based on your experiences, do you think these students are lacking in creative ideas or in producing products related to the ideas?

10.28 Review and Application: Recall the most important information regarding each of the following concepts, and identify at least one possible use of the information by you as a learner, a teacher, or both:

The Nature of Problem Solving
   Models of Problem Solving
   Problem Solving by Small Groups
Developmental Trends and Individual Differences in Convergent Problem Solving
   Developmental Trends in Convergent Problem Solving
   Individual Differences in Convergent Problem Solving
Principles for Fostering Convergent Problem Solving
The Nature of Creativity
   Models of Creative Problem Solving
   Abilities Related to Creativity
   Personality Variables Related to Creativity
Principles for Fostering Creativity

SUMMARY

Convergent problem solving is directed toward finding solutions that can be evaluated as correct or appropriate. *Divergent problem solving* is directed toward producing a variety of solutions that go in new and different directions. Creative solutions cannot be evaluated as right or wrong.

Classical models of problem solving typically included five or six steps that started with identifying the problem and ended with verifying the solution. More recently, the steps have been analyzed in more detail with the intent of identifying the specific mental processes involved at each step of the problem-solving sequence.

Problem solving by small groups is of specific interest from the standpoint of its effects on achievement and interpersonal relations. Small-group members who cooperate achieve higher than individuals who work alone. However, activity on the part of each small-group member is essential for individual learning as well as for high achievement by the group. Interpersonal relations among small-group members are favorable when they cooperate and each member experiences a desired consequence of the group effort. When several small groups compete and only one group wins and is rewarded, interpersonal relations are very poor among the members of the losing groups. The outcomes of small-group activities in terms of achievement and interpersonal relations among members of groups depend upon many variables, most of which skillful, knowledgeable teachers can control.

The ability to solve problems develops slowly but continuously throughout the school years. The rate of development varies widely among normally developing students. Moreover, the same student varies in the ability to solve problems from different subject fields, such as English, mathematics, and science.

The nature of problems in different subject fields, such as art, English, mathematics, music, and sociology varies greatly. Plans for solving the problems in these and other areas must be suited to the nature of the problem. A general plan that can be adapted to different kinds of problems has the following steps, or phases:

1. Analyze the problem.
2. Recall or generate a plan for solving the problem.
3. Recall prior information or gain new information.
4. Produce a solution.
5. Verify the problem-solving process and the solution.
6. Secure feedback and assistance.

Creativity is increasingly regarded as a pervasive aspect of a person's life-style. In fact, it appears that adults typically approach most of the problems they encounter with either a divergent style or a convergent style. Models for teaching creativity and for becoming more creative personally are similar to those for convergent problem solving but emphasize divergent production processes rather than convergent production processes.

The desired outcomes of creativity instruction include favorable attitudes toward creativity, freedom from emotional blocks, and greater originality, flexibility, and fluency. These outcomes are achieved when ideas such as the following are practiced:

1. Provide for variety in instructional materials and forms of student expression.
2. Develop favorable attitudes toward creative achievement.
3. Encourage continuing creative expression.
4. Foster productivity.
5. Provide assistance and feedback.

SUGGESTIONS FOR FURTHER READING

Bransford, J. D., & Stein, B. S. *The ideal problem solver: A guide to improving thinking, learning, and creativity.* New York: W. H. Freeman, 1984.

Presents a model of problem solving with suggestions for improving problem-solving skills, memory, intelligent criticism, and communication.

Davis, G. A. *Creativity is forever.* Cross Plains, Wis.: Badger Press, 1981.

Davis defines creativity, summarizes major studies, describes techniques for encouraging creativity, and reviews creativity tests. The last chapter is directed toward increasing individual creativity.

Maker, J. C. *Teaching models in education of the gifted.* Rockville, Md.: Aspens Systems Corp., 1982.

Presents models of convergent and divergent problem solving and instructional applications for gifted students.

Mansfield, R. S., & Busse, T. V. Creativity. In H. E. Mitzel, J. H. Best, & W. Rabinowitz (Eds.), *Encyclopedia of educational research* (5th ed., Vol. 1). New York: Free Press, 1982. Pp. 385–394.

A scholarly discussion of the difference between real-life creativity and tested creativity. The question posed by the authors is how well real-life creativity is being educated.

Mayer, R. E. *Thinking, problem solving, cognition.* New York: W. H. Freeman, 1983.

Explains human thinking, problem solving, and cognition from an information-processing point of view.

CHAPTER 11

MOTOR AND VOCAL SKILLS

MOTOR AND PERCEPTUAL BASES OF SKILLS

CHARACTERISTICS OF SKILL LEARNING

A MODEL TO EXPLAIN MOTOR LEARNING

NORMATIVE DEVELOPMENT AND INDIVIDUAL DIFFERENCES IN MOTOR ABILITIES

PRINCIPLES FOR TEACHING MOTOR AND VOCAL SKILLS

The importance of psychomotor skills in society and in our personal lives is easily underestimated. We tend to think of the great advances in art, architecture, medicine, science, and other fields almost exclusively in terms of intellectual abilities. However, the people making these advances use their psychomotor as well as their intellectual abilities continuously. Furthermore, millions of people still make their livelihood through skilled work. Persons in white-collar jobs are happier and more effective as they maintain mental and physical fitness through a regular program of exercise.

Many skills can be acquired initially during the elementary and high school years. Skill improvement can continue through most of the life span. In this regard, students who go on to college have more opportunity to develop new skills and to improve partially developed skills than their peers who do not go on to school. In fact, skills can be improved more during college than during any later time in life.

Our main interests in this chapter are the learning, long-term development, and teaching of motor and vocal skills. Study of this chapter will help you to gain a better understanding of skill learning and to improve your own skills and your teaching of skills to others.

MOTOR AND PERCEPTUAL BASES OF SKILLS

A clear differentiation between a motor ability and a psychomotor skill will make the study of this chapter more meaningful. A *motor ability* involves a muscular operation or movement combined with a part or parts of the body. For example, finger dexterity, trunk flexibility, and limb strength are motor abilities. These abilities are partly a product of learning and partly a product of the innate structure of the individual. Abilities develop at different rates in growing human beings and change with maturation and learning.

A *psychomotor skill* is a coordinated set of muscular actions that are guided by conscious mental activity and used in performing a task. For example, handwriting, typing, and playing the piano are psychomotor skills. Performing a psychomotor skill involves motor activity and also perception of external and sometimes internal conditions.

Skills vary in the amount of motor and perceptual involvement, as shown in Figure 11.1. Skills with high motor and low perceptual involvement include walking, dancing, running, swimming, bicycling, and gymnastics. Skills with a considerable amount of both perceptual and motor involvement include playing a musical instrument by note and taking dictation in shorthand. In performing these skills, individuals see or hear the stimuli that, in turn, guide their motor responses. Some skills have low motor and high perceptual involvement. In silent reading, the motor component is low, but includes focusing the eyes from left to right across the page, moving from top to bottom as successive lines are read, and grouping the words to achieve a fast rate. However, the main component of reading silently is cognitive, that is, recognizing words and associating meanings with them. The relative amount of perceptual and motor activity involved in performing a skill influences the activities involved in learning and teaching the skill. In this chapter, we are concerned with skills high in the motor component and intermediate in the perceptual component.

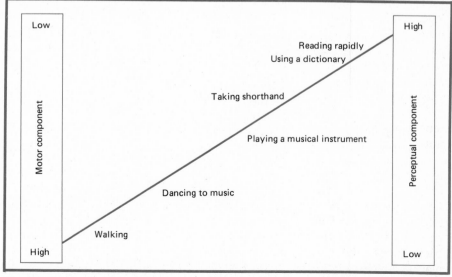

Figure 11.1 Relative amount of motor and perceptual involvement for different skills.

> 11.1 Do you have a better understanding of your own motor abilities or your psychomotor skills? Explain.
>
> 11.2 Figure 11.1 gives skills that vary in the relative amount of perceptual and motor involvement. For each example given, provide a different skill.
>
> 11.3 Identify two or three psychomotor skills in which you are proficient, and one or two in which you are weak. Identify a few conditions in and out of school that contributed to your present proficiencies and weaknesses.

CHARACTERISTICS OF SKILL LEARNING

Deliberate Control Shifts to Automatic Control

Less Obvious and Fewer Cues Guide Movements

Feedback Becomes More Rapid

Movement Patterns Become More Coordinated

Performance Becomes Increasingly Stable

There are two distinct theoretical perspectives regarding the learning of skills. The *S–R, stimulus-response, theory* indicates that skilled performance results from chaining separately learned and discrete S–R units. For example, the foreign language words or phrases learned one at a time as discrete responses are chained into speaking sentences; separate notes and phrases are chained in learning to play a musical instrument.

S–R theory does not include the learning of plans or strategies as part of skill learning. Rather, practice of the skill eventually leads to automatic performance of it. Learning a skill based on this theory involves a great amount of repetitive activity without learning a strategy, or plan, for performing the skill.

A more recent approach to skill learning is based on cognitive information-processing theory (Kaye, 1979; Lee & Magill, 1983; Posner & Keele, 1973; Singer & Gerson, 1979). Researchers indicate that a hierarchical motor program, not a chain of S–R units, is acquired internally. The motor program includes both a model of the skill and a plan for carrying it out. The internal model, such as of handwriting or typing, is a hierarchical organization of the skill that includes the total skill and its subskills. Similarly, the plan includes an overall strategy for performing the skill and strategies for the subskills. Thus, as you start to write, your movements are guided by a global plan of writing and subplans for writing letters and words. You check what you write against your internalized model of writing. You are not executing a series of chained S–R responses, inasmuch as many sentences and paragraphs are particular combinations of words that you have not written before.

Your internalized model of the skilled performance that you desire to demonstrate and your plan for performing it may be in the form of visual or aural images, verbal descriptions, or a combination of images and descriptions. For example, your internalized handwriting model and handwriting plan are visual, whereas your speaking model and speaking plan are aural. In cognitive information-processing theory, the internal mechanism for retrieving both the model and the plan from memory and for activating the plan is called executive control. Chapter 4 of this book explains executive control and other information-processing concepts.

In learning a skill, movements improve with practice guided by the skill program. The model and the plan also change during the course of learning the skill. Thus, instruction based on this theoretical approach requires the teacher to be able to communicate the program to the learner, to analyze the skill into its components, to diagnose the learner's performance, and to guide practice accordingly.

A dramatic example of learning to perform a skill after first acquiring an internal model is illustrated in the Suzuki method of teaching violin playing. This method was developed in Japan many years ago (Pronko, 1969). In the Suzuki method, a single selection of music is played to a baby only a few months old. The same piece of music (expertly executed and recorded) is played repeatedly over several months until the baby recognizes it. Then another piece is selected and played until the baby recognizes it. As the baby grows, other musical selections are gradually added until age 3 or 4, when the child gets music lessons. At this age the child is taught not to read music but to play by ear, producing sounds that match the auditory models stored in memory since infancy. Corrections in the child's patterns of movements are made until the internal standard is matched. As skill develops, the child becomes able to play excellently. Finally, at the age of 5 or 6, the child is taught to read music.

The Suzuki technique, according to reports, produces extremely capable musicians. As Posner and Keele (1973) point out, the Suzuki method probably has strong motivational effects which may in part account for its success. However, the method does illustrate the training technique of first incorporating performance models in memory which can then be matched through feedback and correction of actual movements.

We shall now examine the main changes that occur from earlier to later performing of a skill. As you read, think of a skill you perform best and identify where you are on the continuum of each item that is presented.

Deliberate Control Shifts to Automatic Control

Miller, Galanter, and Pribram (1960) led the departure from the S–R explanation of skill learning. They emphasized the importance of mental activity and conscious control of movements. In the early phase, movements are slow and unsure, each one controlled by an internal plan that is partially incorporated in verbal statements as well as visual images. Beginning golfers, for example, think about how to grip the club, including the placement of the fingers and the thumbs. They covertly verbalize such things as "grasp the club firmly in the left hand, have both thumbs pointing down the shaft, and put the right small finger on the left index finger." In the later phase, the actions are rapid and precise, a series of movements controlled by a plan that is not verbalized in any detail as the movements are carried out. The skilled golfer takes a club from the bag and grasps it with little or no verbalization or thought about how to do so. The plan that has been learned for grasping the club may be thought of as a part of a *program* that controls the sequence by which the movements are carried out.

Extending the ideas of Miller et al., Posner and Keele (1973) described the acquisition of *central motor programs.* Their view is that first a mental *template,* or model of performance, is established. This can result from watching an accomplished performer carry out the skill, by mentally practicing a skill after being given verbal instructions, or both.

After the template is established, the learner begins to execute movements. The feedback from the movements is compared to the template which has been stored in memory. If a discrepancy occurs, the movements are altered by changing the instructions to the muscles, and the results (feedback) are again compared to the mental standard. After enough practice, the program (i.e., the sequence of movements conforming to the standard template) is securely established, and performance is no longer dependent upon voluntary control or upon continuous attention to feedback. Extensive practice guided by a program brings a person to the point where the actions involved in the performance of a skill become automatic.

Automaticity of movements in the performance of skills is required to attain high proficiency in the skill. For, as the skill becomes more and more automatic and very little conscious attention is given to performing the movements, the individual can increasingly attend to other elements of the environment (Stelmach & Larish, 1980). For example, when a player's dribbling of a basketball is automatic, he or she can be more aware of and attend to the other players' actions on the court, the coach's instructions, etc. The highly skilled performance enables the individual to give conscious attention only to the game strategies and other nonmovement considerations.

Less Obvious and
Fewer Cues Guide Movements

Imagine that you are walking from one place to another. As you walk, you see such things as the sidewalk, a brick wall, a sign, etc. Besides seeing things ahead and to the side, you hear sounds, particularly from behind you. These are the *extrinsic visual and auditory cues* that guide your walking. There are also continuous *internal kinesthetic cues* from the muscles and joints. These tell you that you are moving and in what direction you are going.

In the early stages of skill development, persons learn which *cues* to respond to as well as the movements they have not performed before. The more obvious cues are noted and responded to first. Later, the less obvious cues that are needed for excellent performance are noted. Thus, beginning golfers, when putting, may notice only the distance from the ball to the cup, the slant of the green in an uphill or downhill direction, and their gripping of the putter. Later, they will attend to many less obvious cues, including the length of the grass, the direction in which the grass has been mowed, the softness of the green, any slight indentations in the green, and also slight variations in the positions of their hands, body, and feet.

Skilled individuals respond to fewer cues as well as to less obvious ones. They carry out a sequence of movements guided by a single cue rather than have each movement guided by a separate cue. For example, piano students beginning to play a particular selection need to look at the music constantly. After they have learned to play it well, they need only occasionally glance at the music. An experience common to most of us is parking an automobile. Recall the many cues to which you responded in your first attempts to park the car in a parallel parking space. Compare them with your present use of cues. With increasing skill, you use fewer cues and less obvious ones that you were unaware of as a beginner.

Feedback Becomes More Rapid

The beginning typist looks at the paper or stops momentarily to think whether a certain letter or word has been completed properly. In contrast, the skilled typist realizes without visual input or any slowing down that the word is completed and the next one is called for. Both the beginner and the accomplished typist utilize feedback, but the role of feedback is somewhat different in the two cases, as a number of researchers have demonstrated.

Lashley (1951) analyzed the finger movements of the skilled pianist and concluded that the succession of movements is much faster than can be accounted for in kinesthetic feedback loops; therefore, sensory control of the movements seems to be ruled out. Later, Pew (1966) was able to demonstrate that feedback-dependent movements occurred in the early practice of an experimental task and that later control by a motor program occurred as skill was gained. He noted that as skill increased, the motor program controlled the ongoing sequences of movements rather than each movement as a separate unit. The skilled performer made groups of rapid movement sequences and only sampled feedback over longer time intervals, occasionally pausing and making a correction of a discrete movement.

More recently, using cameras and other equipment, Glencross (1975) was able to show that response-produced feedback could not be used in rapid hand cranking, that is, making rapid circular movements with the arms, because it would always be out of phase with the ongoing cranking movements. After summarizing all the research, Glencross (1977) explained the changing role of feedback in terms of a two-state control system. During the early stages of skill acquisition, movements are monitored almost continuously through the use of feedback. As increasing competence is acquired, longer sequences of actions are combined into increasingly larger action units. Simultaneously, the sequences and units are integrated into hierarchical patterns, and the action units are carried out with very little or no feedback.

We readily infer from this explanation why the instructor of skilled performers in golf, tennis, music, and other areas must videotape the expert's movements to identify and correct possible difficulties. Along similar lines, we can see how it is possible for the expert quarterback or symphony conductor to pay relatively little attention to the motor aspects of the performance and to concentrate totally on other elements of the situation.

Movement Patterns Become More Coordinated

The change from an unskilled to a highly skilled performance is accompanied by a change from slow and inaccurate movements to rapid and accurate ones that occur at precisely the right times. For example, there are many muscular movements and mental operations involved in such an apparently simple task as writing a sentence legibly. Those who are skilled in writing do not hesitate about whether or not to capitalize words, how to punctuate, how to join letters within a word, or how to start and end words. As they write, making rapid changes in vertical, horizontal, and circular movements, an observer sees only a continuous series of smooth movements coming at exactly the right times, with no jerks or stops.

The skilled typist not only integrates movement patterns and feedback operations into a program to reproduce individual words quickly, but also perceives a relatively long series of words in one visual fixation of the page. One fixation of five or six words provides all the cues needed to reproduce the words. Furthermore, little or no conscious thought is given to such motor acts as striking the letter keys, the space bar, or the shift key. Similarly, as the expert typist types material heard through a tape recorder, the auditory cues available through listening and the production of successive words and other symbols provide the continuous steady cues essential to rapid production of evenly typed copy with few or no errors.

Practice, is, of course, essential to building coordinated movement patterns. But practice alone, even when supported by reinforcement, is not as effective as practice that is guided by a program.

Performance Becomes Increasingly Stable

As a skill is learned to higher perfection, it becomes increasingly stable and is performed well under a variety of changing conditions. Stability of performance under changing conditions is observed in individual athletic championships and in group sports before large audiences. On television and on stage, star actors and musicians, including teenagers, perform superbly under potentially distracting circumstances, such as bright lights, noise, and unpredictable audience behaviors. In addition, they often perform at top level, despite physical ailments and psychological problems that tend to incapacitate the less skilled person.

Fitts (1964, 1965) identified three phases in skill learning that may readily be related to the five characteristics of a skilled performance (deliberate control shifts to automatic control, less obvious and fewer cues guide movements, feedback becomes more rapid, movement patterns become more coordinated, performance becomes increasingly stable). The learning of a skill begins with a *cognitive phase,* usually of relatively short duration, during which the learner thinks about how to perform the skill. During this phase, a motor program is learned. Observing skilled performances is usually involved in learning the program. The skilled performance that is observed may be accompanied with a verbal description by the skilled performer. Other activities of this stage include becoming aware of the movements that are required to perform the skill. There is relatively little practice during this phase.

During the *intermediate,* or *organizing, phase,* there is more practice and the receptor-effector-feedback operations become more highly organized. There is less conscious, deliberate guidance of the movements. Less attention is given to specific movements. Cues that are less obvious are differentiated, and feedback and correction become more rapid and less conscious. Speed and coordination improve.

In the *perfecting phase,* performance is even less consciously directed. Control is of larger sequences of movements that replace the single and intermediate units of the earlier phases. Eventually the skill is performed at an automatic level. Throughout this phase, there is much practice of the entire skill, but there is also diagnosis followed with practice of any movements that might contribute to better performance of the skill.

11.4 Trace the learning of any skill in which you are proficient in terms of the following:

a. Deliberate control shifts to automatic control.
b. Less obvious and fewer cues guide actions.
c. Feedback becomes more rapid.
d. Movements become more coordinated.
e. Stability under a variety of conditions increases.

11.5 For any skill that you perform with proficiency, describe your central motor program, that is, your model of the performance and your plan for performing it.

11.6 How would a teacher applying the cognitive information-processing explanation of skill learning proceed with the learner in the beginning phase of teaching a skill?

11.7 Compare writing your name and parking a car parallel to the curb. Indicate which of these two skills, compared to the other, requires more or less of the following:

a. Conscious control of movements.
b. Use of obvious cues to guide your actions.
c. Speed of feedback and correction.
d. Coordination of movements with vision.
e. Stability of the skill under stressful conditions.

11.8 Compare the child's learning to speak the parents' language and the Suzuki method of learning to play a musical instrument.

11.9 What differences in cues and other conditions might contribute to some basketball players having higher free-throw percentages on the home court than away from home?

An internal program consisting of a model of the performance and a plan for carrying it out underlies the smooth performance of motor and vocal skills. How well do students learn the programs merely by practicing the skills?

A MODEL TO EXPLAIN MOTOR LEARNING

In the first part of this chapter, we saw five ways in which behavior changes as higher proficiency in performing a skill is achieved. The changes are reflected in both motor behaviors and mental structures and processes. Singer and Gerson (1979) outlined a model for relating cognitive information-processing theory of learning, as described earlier in Chapter 4, to the learning of motor skills. The model is shown in Figure 11.2.

Two elements of this model differ slightly from the general model presented in Chapter 4. They merit attention because they take into account

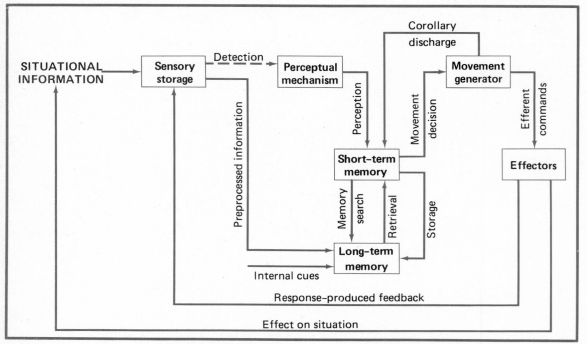

Figure 11.2 A cognitive information-processing model of motor learning.
Source: Singer & Gerson, 1979, p. 218.

various aspects of motor learning that are not provided for in the general model. First, some information is sensed very rapidly and is transmitted directly as preprocessed information from sensory storage to long-term memory rather than transmitted to short-term memory and processed. This occurs as proficiency in a skill increases and the learner responds automatically to external cues. Second, response-produced feedback from the effectors (muscles and glands) is transmitted directly to sensory storage. This, too, is essential for making very rapid reactions to cues, such as occurs without conscious awareness when returning a tennis volley, typing very rapidly from a record, or carrying on a conversation.

     We saw earlier in this chapter that the S–R theory of skill learning is being replaced by cognitive information-processing theory. Accordingly, increasing attention is being given by learners as well as by teachers to understanding the internal mechanisms and processes that are involved in learning psychomotor skills. Related to the model of motor learning in Figure 11-2, Singer and Gerson (1979) identified the relationships among the information-processing mechanisms, the cognitive processes that may be activated by the learner, and their functions as shown in Table 11.1.

TABLE 11.1 RELATIONSHIPS AMONG INFORMATION-PROCESSING MECHANISMS, COGNITIVE PROCESSES, AND MOTOR ACTIVITIES

MECHANISMS	COGNITIVE PROCESSES	FUNCTIONS AND PURPOSES
1. Sensory storage*	Receive. Transmit.	Briefly hold information. Forward it to long-term storage for memory contact or directly to perceptual mechanism.
2. Perceptual mechanism	Detect. Alert. Selectively attend. Recognize. Transmit.	Realize existence of signal. Anticipate. Filter. Analyze features. Match (present cues with stored information). Make meaning of information. Forward information to short-term storage for action.
3. Short-term storage	Rehearse and process information temporarily. Compare. Transform. Appraise situation. Select programs from long-term storage. Plan program execution. Transmit information.	Retain information for immediate use and decision making. Retrieve information from long-term storage for analysis, decision making, and attributions following feedback. Organize (chunk). Make more functional space available. Provide additional meaning. Form performance and goal expectancies. Establish emotional state. Transmit programs to movement generator. Determine parameters (location, speed, direction, timing, amplitude, force, effort) in which program is to operate. Transfer information to long-term storage to establish learning.
4. Long-term storage	Store information permanently.	Make information available for future use, establish pertinence, aid in anticipation, expectancies, and perception.

(Continued on next page)

TABLE 11.1 *(Continued)*

MECHANISMS	COGNITIVE PROCESSES	FUNCTIONS AND PURPOSES
5. Movement generator	Initiate program for motor behavior.	Cue appropriate musculature to execute within response parameters.
	Initiate corollary discharge.	Alert sensory center of the brain, anticipate movement.
6. Effectors	Receive command.	Execute observable performance.
	Activate feedback sources.	Provide information for future usage (comparison, recognition) by making it available for long-term storage.
		Provide information to peripheral organs to help regulate ongoing behavior, to adapt behavior to situational demands.
		Provide information to influence arousal and attitudinal states.

* Cognitive processes do not directly influence storage but can affect orientation to stimuli.
SOURCE: Singer & Gerson, 1979, pp. 224–225.

11.10 Return to the model of motor learning of Singer and Gerson (Figure 11.2), and trace the flow of information from reading the following command until it is performed: "Write the last name of the current president of the United States."

11.11 What is first searched for and retrieved from long-term memory in carrying out the motor activity in Question 11.10? What is searched for later?

11.12 Return to the relationships among information-processing mechanisms, cognitive processes, and motor activities as specified by Singer and Gerson (Table 11.1). Identify the cognitive processes that you did and did not engage in from the time you read the command in Question 11.10 until you completed the writing.

11.13 How does being able to relate a motor performance to specific cognitive processes aid in the diagnosis of learner difficulties?

Strength

Reaction Time

Balance

Flexibility

Sex Differences

NORMATIVE DEVELOPMENT AND INDIVIDUAL DIFFERENCES IN MOTOR ABILITIES

Fleishman (1964) identified 25 motor abilities. Combinations of these abilities are used in performing many different skills. The names and definitions of a few of the 25 abilities follow in Table 11.2:

TABLE 11.2 BASIC MOTOR ABILITIES

ABILITY	DEFINITION

Static strength
  Trunk emphasis
  Arm-hand-shoulder emphasis
	Ability to exert maximum force against objects, even for a brief period.

Dynamic flexibility	Ability to make repeated, rapid, flexible movements recovering from strain effectively.
Gross body equilibrium	Ability to maintain equilibrium when depending on nonvisual cues, for example, vestibular and kinesthetic cues.
Gross body coordination	Ability to coordinate the simultaneous actions of different parts of the body while making gross bodily movements.
Balance Visual cues	Ability to maintain balance with the eyes open and the feet in various positions.

Speed of limb movement
  Arm
  Leg
	Ability to move the arm or leg quickly where accuracy is not required.

Reaction time	Ability to respond quickly to a stimulus.
Finger dexterity	Ability to make skillful, controlled manipulations of tiny objects involving use of the fingers.

Strength

Strength of grip is measured with a hand dynamometer, an instrument that one squeezes with the preferred hand. It correlates higher with vitality than any other measure of strength, such as of the arms or the trunk. Children of the same age who have a stronger grip are able to mobilize their strength more effectively than those with a weaker grip. This difference seems to carry over to mental tasks. Mentally retarded children do not seem to be able to mobilize their energies for either physical or mental tasks as well as bright children (Klausmeier, Check, & Feldhusen, 1960).

Figure 11.3 shows growth curves in strength of grip for boys and girls, ages 6–18. These curves are based on averages for many individuals; each individual's curve is not so smooth. The same is true of other curves presented in this section.

Figure 11.3 indicates that boys on the average are stronger than girls at all ages, 6–18. For both sexes, a steady increase in strength occurs with age, with the rate of increase about the same for boys and girls until age 13. At that age, the curve rises quite sharply for boys. It continues to rise for girls after age 13, but at a decelerating rate.

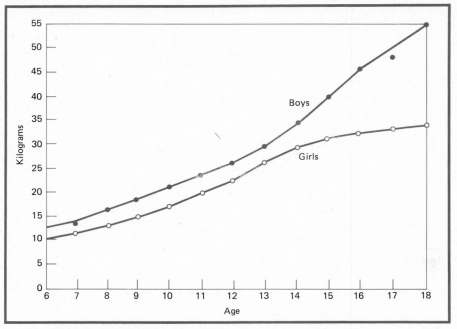

Figure 11.3 Growth curve for strength of grip.
Source: Jones, 1944, p. 103.

Reaction Time

Reaction time is the time elapsing between the presentation of a stimulus and the beginning of the response to the stimulus. Reaction time is important in many activities. Many critical situations — braking an automobile to avoid a crash, piloting an airplane in turbulent weather conditions, responding to a starter's signal in an athletic contest — require a quick motor response. Other tasks demanding rapid reactions to successive stimuli include playing a musical instrument, typing, and dancing.

Fairweather and Hutt (1978) studied the reaction time of boys and girls of ages 5–11. In this study, the child had to choose between reacting to two stimuli. The girls consistently exhibited faster reaction times than the boys. Both boys and girls improved with age.

Figure 11.4 shows changes in measures of reaction time with age. The measures are digital (finger) reaction and foot reaction. Both involve measuring the time between the presentation of a stimulus and movement of the finger or foot. Although the curves are somewhat different, the general pattern is a sharp decrease (.320–.240) in digital and foot reaction time from age 8 until the 20s, maintenance of about the same time (.240) through the 40s, and a sharp increase starting in the 50s. The figure shows that, during the school years, reaction time improves rapidly.

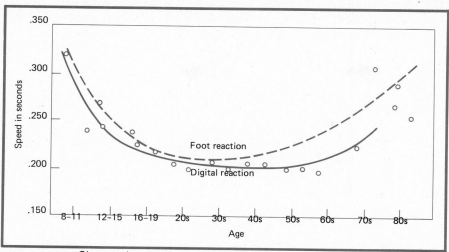

Figure 11.4 Changes in reaction time with age.
Source: Miles, 1931, p. 631.

Balance

We know that young children have difficulty maintaining their balance when learning to walk. What happens as they grow older? In Table 11.3, balance scores from 0 to 6 (lowest possible score to highest possible score) are indicated, and the frequency of the boys and girls of each age group who made each score are given. Table 11.3 shows a consistent rise in the mean, or average, balance scores for both boys and girls from ages 4–6 until 11–12. The increase in the averages for boys is from 0.1 for ages 4–6 to 3.8 for ages 11–12. The increase for girls is from 0.5 for ages 4–6 to 2.5 for ages 11–12. The gradual falling off from ages 12–13 onward is somewhat more apparent for the girls than the boys. However, in the study that Table 11.3 summarizes (Cron & Pronko, 1957), girls at age 13 and older appeared more

TABLE 11.3 BALANCE SCORES BY SEX AND AGE

AGE GROUPS	NUMBER	BOYS' SCORES								GIRLS' SCORES								TOTALS
		0	1	2	3	4	5	6	AVERAGE	0	1	2	3	4	5	6	AVERAGE	AVERAGE
13–15	54	3	2	2	8	11	2	7	3.7	1	7	4	5	2	0	0	2.0	3.1
12–13	57	2	1	7	4	12	6	4	3.6	2	6	2	7	3	0	1	2.3	3.1
11–12	52	0	3	4	8	7	6	6	3.8	2	3	3	5	3	2	0	2.5	3.3
10–11	62	3	9	6	5	7	8	3	3.0	2	5	4	6	0	4	0	2.4	2.8
9–10	64	2	8	7	7	5	4	3	2.8	5	4	7	7	4	1	0	2.1	2.5
8– 9	80	7	11	8	9	11	2	2	2.5	7	6	6	5	4	2	0	2.0	2.3
7– 8	61	12	10	9	7	0	4	0	1.6	5	3	3	3	3	2	0	2.1	1.8
6– 7	48	17	11	7	1	0	1	0	0.9	3	2	3	2	1	0	0	1.6	1.1
4– 6	23	10	1	0	0	0	0	0	0.1	9	1	2	0	0	0	0	0.5	0.3

SOURCE: Cron & Pronko, 1957, p. 35.

self-conscious than both younger girls and boys while performing the balance task. Therefore, the results for the older girls are questionable. It is interesting, too, that up through ages 7–8, the girls had better balance than the boys; thereafter, the boys were consistently better than the girls.

Flexibility

Extent flexibility is the ability to extend or stretch the whole body or parts of it as far as possible in various directions. *Dynamic flexibility* also involves the ability to extend and stretch; however, the criterion is not the extent or distance of maximum movement, but the rapidity of repeated movements. Figure 11.5 shows growth curves for boys and girls for the two abilities.

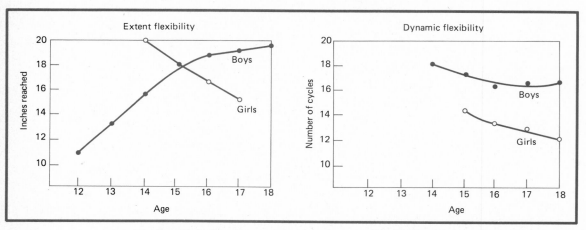

Figure 11.5 Developmental curves for extent flexibility and dynamic flexibility in boys and girls.
Source: Fleishman, 1964, pp. 122, 124. © 1964. Reprinted by permission of Prentice-Hall, Inc.

These curves are interesting because of the difference between boys and girls. Boys are consistently higher than girls in dynamic flexibility; boys have already peaked at age 14 and girls at age 15. Extent flexibility in boys increases at a rapid rate from ages 12 to 15 and then at a decelerating rate from ages 15 to 18. An opposite pattern holds for girls, who show an actual decrease from ages 14 to 17. Accordingly, girls at age 14 have reached their maximum capability for bending, twisting, and other movements that require flexibility, whereas boys continue to gain in extent flexibility till age 18. It is possible that this difference is partially responsible for the masterful performances in gymnastics by girls at a younger age than boys.

Sex Differences

We have seen differences between males and females in their rate of development and also in their mean performances. The more rapidly rising curve for girls than boys in early life probably reflects heredity, since girls mature physically earlier than boys. The girls' earlier decelerating rate of growth in an area such as strength probably reflects lack of practice or use, as well as earlier physical maturation. Boys' superiority in strength at all ages is probably determined by heredity. However, the average difference between boys and girls may decrease as more girls engage in running, weight lifting, and other strength-building exercises. Girls' faster reaction time early in life is also probably hereditary.

The differences among members of the same sex are far greater than the small differences between the means of boys and girls, as we saw in the balance scores in Table 11.3. Although not shown in Figures 11.3 and 11.4, many girls of any age excel many boys of the same age in strength, while many boys are better than many girls in reaction time.

11.14 Examine Table 11.3, and identify the years that the boys and the girls had balance scores ranging from 0 to 5 or 0 to 6 (0 lowest score possible, 6 highest score possible). Compare this range with the difference between the means of the boys and the girls for the same years.

11.15 Table 11.3 shows that 4% of the boys of ages 8–9 and 20% of the boys of ages 13–15 made perfect balance (6) scores. On the other hand, 14% of the boys of ages 8–9 and about 9% ages 13–15 scored 0. Similar patterns prevail for psychomotor skills. Does this information imply that instruction in the same skill should be geared according to each boy's level of performance or according to chronological age? Explain.

11.16 The average score on different motor tests made by groups of students of various ages have been reported, and others can be obtained readily in any school. Suppose a teacher sets as a goal of bringing as many students as possible close to the average score. Is this teacher acting wisely or unwisely? Explain.

11.17 The psychomotor abilities of females will probably continue to develop later in life as equal opportunity for physical education continues to expand. Which of the following do you think will show the greatest and least increase as girls engage in more physical activities during the high school and college years: strength, running speed, finger dexterity, eye-hand coordination? Explain.

PRINCIPLES FOR TEACHING MOTOR AND VOCAL SKILLS

1. Analyze the skill and the learner's characteristics.
2. Aid the learner to acquire a model of the skill.
3. Aid the learner to acquire a plan for performing the skill.
4. Arrange for appropriate practice.
5. Provide feedback and correct inadequate movements.
6. Encourage independent learning.

The principles for teaching skills indicate external conditions that facilitate skill learning. They reflect a synthesis of the prior information in this chapter. New information, including examples of implementing the principles, is also presented.

    1. Analyze the skill and the learner's characteristics   As we saw earlier in this chapter, skills are organized hierarchically. Knowledge of the skill hierarchy to be taught, that is, the whole skill and its subskills, and of how it is learned are essential for planning and carrying out instruction. This same knowledge is needed in assessing where the student is in terms of being able to perform the skill. Typically, the student's readiness and ability to profit from guided practice are assessed by observing the student performing the skill.

    In the first example that follows, the analysis of writing is considered from the standpoint of being left-handed. In the second example, a child's ability to speak is analyzed.

    Handwriting. How is handwriting different for left-handed and right-handed children? In most situations, the source of the light is from the left. This arrangement is suitable for right-handers, but not for left-handers. Because we are taught to write from left to right on a page, the left-handed child is continuously covering what has just been written, whereas the right-hander can see immediately what has been written. Printed models of handwriting are for right-handed persons. The downward slant of letters is to the left. These models are appropriate for right-handers, but left-handed children normally slant the letters straight down or toward the right so that they can see what has been written before it is covered by the left hand moving to the right across the page. Suppose that a teacher has a left-handed child in class. What sort of an analysis of the skill in relation to left-handed children's ability to write should be made before instruction begins? Without careful analysis, it is possible that the teacher might insist that the left-handed children use precisely the same slant and spacing of letters as the right-handers and do nothing to make other needed arrangements for seating and lighting.

    Speech correction. A speech therapist's account of her first meeting with a student follows:

> The objectives of my first meeting with Sarah were:
>
> 1. to discover how she produced the "s" sound;
> 2. to determine how her production of the sound differed from the correct production of the sound;
> 3. to determine the ways in which her means of production of the sound should be changed; and
> 4. to determine her abilities to correctly evaluate her production of the sound, to discriminate between correct and incorrect sounds, and to identify the differences between them.
>
> To accomplish the first objective . . . I watched her, listened to her, asked her to describe the tactual and kinesthetic elements of the sounds she produced, and tried to duplicate her production of the sound.

To accomplish the second and third objectives I reviewed in my mind the correct means of producing the sound and compared her means of production to this mental model. I tried to determine which elements of her production were incorrect and the ways in which these elements were wrong. At this point I formed tentative judgments about how these incorrect elements should be changed.

To accomplish the fourth objective I presented her with a variety of tasks. To begin with I had to produce the sound and then ask her to tell whether or not she thought her own subsequent production was correct. I then presented her with a series of discrimination tasks. These required her to discriminate between correct and incorrect sounds when I made them, to point out differences between correct and incorrect sounds, to compare her production of the sound to my productions, and to try to point out differences between the productions made by her and by me. . . . She performed these tasks . . . with her unaided hearing, with an auditory training unit, with a tape recorder, with a mirror, with face-to-face contact, and with various combinations of these methods.

My evaluation showed that she was substituting the voiceless "th" sound, for the "s" sound. Her tongue was protruding between her teeth. In order to produce the sound correctly she would have to learn to place her tongue in the proper position behind her teeth. Regarding her feelings toward her production of the sound and her ability to discriminate between correct and incorrect sounds, I discovered that she knew her production was incorrect and had already learned to recognize the auditory and visual differences between correct and incorrect sounds. She knew that she was not supposed to protrude her tongue, but she did not know the proper placement for it. When she tried to produce the sound with her tongue behind her teeth, she failed to groove it properly and she blocked the air stream from coming out of the center of her mouth.

As a result of my evaluation I formed the following plan of action:

1. to teach her to analyze more fully the various aspects of my correct and incorrect productions of the "s" sound;
2. to teach her to analyze more fully the various aspects of her production of the sound;
3. to teach her to compare the various aspects of her productions with those of my correct productions; and
4. to try to teach her to modify the incorrect aspects of her productions so she could learn to say the sound correctly.

2. **Aid the learner to acquire a model of the skill.** Live demonstrations by the teacher and filmed demonstrations of a skill provide an overview of the skill to be learned and a model to be imitated. The music teacher provides both when singing the melody through before having the children sing. In professional and collegiate football, the coaching team comprises backfield, line, defensive, and offensive coaches—as many as seven or eight different specialists. Each coach demonstrates, explains, and teaches the particular skills involved in playing a particular position.

Viewing a model performing a task gives learners an opportunity to construct an internal model to match in their own performances. They continue movements which match the model and try to correct movements that deviate from it. Videotaping is helpful in this regard. Students can learn much by observing themselves in action. However, explanation and guidance from the teacher are also helpful, especially to beginners.

Although students learn much from observing, a word of caution concerning the use of models is warranted. Teachers of creative dance and creative writing demonstrate what creativity means to them. These demonstrations simply illustrate to the students what creativity or appropriate expression is for the demonstrator. Similarly, in art instruction, technical skills may be demonstrated. When the students are to develop their own art products, however, the teacher helps the student with technical skills as necessary, but leaves ideas, composition, and color to the student.

It is relatively easy for a music teacher to provide models to a group. One teacher indicates how it may be done:

> The second time the students met, they listened to two recordings of "Revolutionary Tea," one by Burl Ives and the other by a group of children. The children compared the enunciation on the recordings and found that it was easier for one person than for a group to tell a story in song. The recording of "Revolutionary Tea" made by the children was musically correct, but some parts of the song were difficult to understand. The students suggested ways of improving the enunciation on the children's recording and then tried the suggestions themselves.

3. Aid the learner to acquire a plan for performing the skill. It has been established that having a plan for performing a skill, such as parallel parking or playing a musical composition, facilitates achieving a skilled performance. It is not perfectly clear, however, how the plans of individuals for carrying out the same skill vary, or how well skilled performers can verbalize their plans. Similarly, knowledge is incomplete about when to teach a plan and when to help learners develop their own plans.

Singer (1977) indicated that when the purpose is to teach the highest level of a particular skill, a carefully guided method based on a clearly outlined plan is appropriate. However, when the movements to be learned are to be transferred and used in a number of different skills in a variety of situations, the learners should take more initiative for constructing their own plans. In the latter case, teachers should guide less and permit learners to exercise more initiative.

In a classic experiment that has had lasting impact on teaching skills in physical education classes, Davies (1945) showed the value of aiding students in learning plans for archery. She divided her students into two groups. The experimental group, called the *tuition group*, was given verbal instruction throughout the course in how to shoot a bow and arrow. In this instruction, the experimenter told the students what she thought was necessary for them to understand the nature of the skill and how to become proficient in it. The *control group* was given only the necessary equipment and minimum safety instructions and then left to practice on their own. Each group met for 18 class sessions during a three-month period. Differences favoring the tuition group became apparent early in the semester and increased as practice progressed. At the end of the semester, the tuition group performed much better than the control group. The control group members tended to acquire inefficient methods and to stay with the methods during successive class periods.

Davies concluded that verbal directions and explanations by a teacher help learners to improve their learning of skills in at least three ways. First, the verbal instruction directs the students' attention to more adequate techniques than those they have acquired on their own. Second, it promotes insight into the factors related to successful performance of the task. Third, it gives the learners a feeling of security and confidence in relinquishing a familiar mode of behavior and seeking one that is better.

Waterland (1956) achieved similar excellent results with verbal instruction that included teaching a plan for bowling. The students practiced the plan mentally and subsequently bowled much better than those who were not taught the plan and did not practice mentally.

4. Arrange for appropriate practice. Practice is necessary for increasing proficiency in any skill. Considerable research has been carried out on effective practice for different kinds of skills.

Four conditions of effective practice may be inferred from cumulative research on the practice of skills that are composed of subskills, for example, handwriting, playing a musical instrument, typing, and bowling. First, there should be some practice of the whole skill at the outset rather than only practice of each individual movement or part and gradually building up to the whole skill. For example, the student should type words rather than only letters, and should roll the bowling ball down the lane rather than practice walking and swinging the arm. Second, as skill increases, a greater portion of each practice session should be directed toward the subskills that are necessary for achieving proficiency in the whole skill. Third, the skill should be practiced as nearly as possible under the same conditions under which it will be carried out. For example, students should type their class assignments rather than nonsense syllables from a typing workbook. Fourth, the practice should be distributed over a larger number of short sessions rather than massed over a smaller number of long sessions.

West (1983) provides a very readable account of acquiring typewriting skills. Since many college students can improve their personal typing skills, a few of West's ideas follow.

> After a small amount of practice at a new key, never use nonsense syllables for any purpose at any time; to attain initial keyboard proficiency, use alphabetic sentences or a set of about 30 short words that contain the entire alphabet.
> For early untimed practice to gain speed or accuracy, use a variety of materials; do not repeat lines of material.
> After gaining initial keyboard proficiency, carry out separate practice for increasing speed and for increasing accuracy. Emphasize increasing speed more than accuracy when being accurate is not critical.
> Start production typing early; use personal typing activities (correspondence, manuscripts, tables, etc.) rather than practice exercises from manuals.

Keep records of speed and accuracy as a means of measuring progress and experiencing success.

Distribute rather than mass practice to increase speed or accuracy.

Arrange for immediate feedback as a means of identifying and correcting errors.

Analyze (or have an expert analyze) your typing performance periodically to ascertain possible deficiencies in speed or accuracy that can be eliminated; identify means for eliminating the deficiencies.

West (1983) indicated that it is too early to decide whether acquiring proficiency in the use of a word processor can be guided by the same principles as gaining typing proficiency. However, the word processor is an advanced typewriting system that automates the editing and storing of text. Presumably, the typing part of word processing is carried out in the same way as on a typewriter.

The length and distribution of practice sessions in general, not in typing only, are important. Excellent results are achieved when the practice sessions are long enough to bring about improvement and when the time between sessions is long enough to overcome fatigue, but not so long that forgetting occurs. In most secondary schools, class periods in all subject fields are of the same length, and teachers cannot control this length. In any subject where skills are taught, the teacher should raise questions such as these: Within a period of this length, what is the best arrangement of active practice and rest? What can the students be learning profitably when they are not engaged in active practice?

In the elementary school, teachers have more opportunities to control time arrangements. The elementary teacher has better opportunity to experiment with a variety of practice and rest arrangements. In the fourth grade, for example, experimenting can be done to ascertain whether children learn to spell as efficiently with 15 minutes of active practice on alternate days as with 15 minutes daily. When cursive handwriting is introduced, a test can be made to find whether 20 minutes of practice in four 5-minute sessions during one day achieve the same or better results than 20 minutes all at once.

5. Provide feedback and correct inadequate movements. Knowledge of results is one of the most powerful variables in skill learning. There is no improvement without such knowledge; there is deterioration after its withdrawal. Feedback is required to give the students knowledge of results. In many skills, students themselves can directly observe the results of their actions. In others, they cannot, so the teacher should provide information.

Progress in many skills is quite easily measured. Furthermore, there are interesting ways in which a teacher can provide the learners with knowledge of their progress. Information can be given verbally in such simple statements as "correct" or "incorrect." A verbal analysis can be given of the student's performance, and the results of performance tests of all sorts can be incorporated in charts or given to the student directly.

Generally, incorrect responses or poor movements should be corrected. A primary determiner of the efficiency with which pupils acquire any skill is the quality of the help given when inadequate movements are made. When individuals perform a movement incorrectly and receive no feedback to the contrary, they tend to repeat it.

How often should knowledge of results be made available? When should errors be corrected? How can this be done with a group? In a few concise statements, a music teacher working with a class on enunciation answers these questions:

> I provided feedback in several ways. The students could usually tell by the expression on my face whether or not their words were clear. Each time they finished a verse or the whole song I mentioned at least one part that they performed well and told them why it was good. The group was small enough so that as they left the room I would point to each student for a particular contribution to the group singing.
>
> I also served as a guide when the students were having difficulty. On the word "ask," some students added the "s" sound to the "a" too soon. I corrected their enunciation by suggesting that the "s" be minimized and that the students focus their attention on the "k." Several students who were correctly singing "ask" demonstrated for the group by singing the second verse of the song.

How often should knowledge of results be made available to children who cannot evaluate the adequacy of their own responses? When should errors be corrected? How does a teacher working with one child at a time proceed? A speech therapist used the following methods:

> In the early stages of therapy, I verbally evaluated each of Sarah's responses. Instead of merely labeling a response as correct or incorrect, I told her why it was right or wrong, gave her suggestions for the correction of inadequate responses, and informed her of progress toward or regression from the correct response. With the help of such mechanical aids as a mirror, an auditory training unit, and a tape recorder, I tried to help her to understand fully the basis of my evaluations.

6. **Encourage independent learning.** Skills are taught in school so that learners can use them independently in their many activities outside school. In addition to guiding and monitoring active practice in school, the teacher should encourage group discussion among peers and self-analysis, so that each learner acquires increasing independence in improving his or her performances. Indeed, persons do not acquire a high degree of skill when they remain dependent on someone else for guiding and monitoring their activities.

Self-assessment and independence in learning are easier to achieve in a one-to-one situation than in a group setting. Some ingenious procedures used by a speech therapist with one of her students to encourage self-assessment follow:

> Throughout corrective therapy I tried to teach Sarah to diagnose her own responses. Although I assumed the initial responsibility for the diagnosing, I did so in such a way as to prepare her for making her own.

I helped her to analyze the various aspects of the correct production of the "s" sound and helped her to learn to compare her productions to this model. I introduced the use of the tape recorder to help her to hear her errors. When she was able to do well at discrimination tasks, I helped her to analyze her responses by asking questions in such a way that she would be able to arrive at the correct conclusions. When I felt that she was capable of analyzing her own responses, I let her try to do so. If she made errors, I helped her to correct them by again asking appropriate questions.

Sarah eventually reached the point where she was able to correctly analyze her own responses and to modify her incorrect productions of the sound without my help. She was then able to do much practicing of the sound outside of the actual speech class.

It is more difficult for a teacher to help individual students in a group of 25 to 30 diagnose their performances. Observe how a music teacher proceeded:

I encouraged independent evaluation throughout the process of learning the song. For example, each student had a chance to comment on the tape recordings that the students made. They were encouraged to be critical, but to offer positive suggestions or to ask for help when a section did not satisfy them. The students' self-appraisals were responded to by me and the members of the class as time and other conditions permitted.

11.18 Describe a plan for learning a skill, and indicate how you would attempt to teach it to students.

11.19 Four principles of effective practice of skills that are composed of subskills, such as typing and playing a musical instrument, were presented. Indicate how you might apply these principles in improving your proficiency in a skill.

11.20 Assume you are teaching handwriting at the elementary school level or personal typing at the high school level. There are 25 students in the class. Indicate how you would provide feedback and correct inadequate performances.

11.21 Using a skill in which you are proficient, describe how any or all of the six teaching principles were implemented by your teacher.

11.22 Indicate the extent to which your high proficiency in a skill results from high quality instruction, individual ability, or individual effort? Explain.

11.23 Review and Application: Recall the most important information regarding each of the following concepts, and identify at least one possible use of the information by you as a learner, a teacher, or both:

Motor and Perceptual Bases of Skills
Characteristics of Skill Learning
   Deliberate Control Shifts to Automatic Control
   Less Obvious and Fewer Cues Guide Movements
   Feedback Becomes More Rapid
   Movement Patterns Become More Coordinated
   Performance Becomes Increasingly Stable
A Model to Explain Motor Learning

SUMMARY

Psychomotor skills and physical fitness are important to persons of all ages. We are all happier and more effective when we maintain our mental and physical fitness through motor activities.

The skills we attain vary in the amount of motor and perceptual involvement. Walking, for example, is high in the motor and low in the perceptual component, whereas reading is high in the perceptual and low in the motor component.

The change from a lower to a higher level of proficiency in performing skills is accompanied by control of movements shifting from deliberate to automatic, less obvious and fewer cues guiding actions, more rapid feedback and correction, better coordination of movements, and more stable performance under changing conditions. The learning of a skill has three phases during which these attributes of a skilled performance emerge: a beginning cognitive phase, an intermediate organizing phase, and a final perfecting phase. As proficiency increases, there is less thinking about how to perform the movements.

Teachers can help students become more proficient in performing skills by (1) analyzing the skill and the learner's capabilities for performing it, (2) aiding the learner to acquire a model of the skill, (3) aiding the learner to acquire a plan for performing the skill, (4) arranging for appropriate practice, (5) providing feedback and correcting inadequate movements, and (6) encouraging independent learning.

SUGGESTIONS FOR FURTHER READING

Cheska, A. T., & Marsh, R. R. Physical development. In H. E. Mitzel, J. H. Best, & W. Rabinowitz (Eds.), *Encyclopedia of educational research* (5th ed., Vol. 3). New York: Free Press, 1982. Pp. 1416–1421.

A readable account of physical and motor development. Other articles in this encyclopedia related to psychomotor skills are business education, health education, music education, motor skills development, sex differences, and speech communication.

Singer, R. N., & Gerson, R. F. Learning strategies, cognitive processes, and motor learning. In H. F. O'Neil, Jr. & C. D. Spielberger (Eds.), *Cognitive and affective learning strategies*. New York: Academic Press, 1979. Pp. 215–247.

A model of information processing and motor behavior is presented; cognitive and motor processes and their relationships are explained.

GARFIELD CARTOON COPYRIGHT BY UNITED FEATURES SYNDICATE, 1982

CHAPTER 12

ATTITUDES AND VALUES

CHARACTERISTICS OF ATTITUDES

MEANS OF LEARNING ATTITUDES

DEVELOPMENTAL TRENDS IN ATTITUDE DEVELOPMENT

MORAL DEVELOPMENT

PRINCIPLES FOR FOSTERING ATTITUDE LEARNING

Attitudes influence how well students learn and how they behave. Accordingly, teachers aid students in learning the attitudes that facilitate subject matter learning and that promote healthy interpersonal relations among students and adults. Teaching attitudes is especially important today, since many students do not have favorable attitudes toward school.

Study of the first part of this chapter will enable you to increase your understanding of the nature of attitudes, of how they are learned, of changes in attitudes during childhood and adolescence, and of moral development. Fortunately, there is renewed interest in these areas, and very interesting studies have been completed recently. In the last part of the chapter, principles for fostering attitude learning are given.

CHARACTERISTICS OF ATTITUDES

Attitudes Influence Approach and Avoidance Behaviors

Attitudes Are Based on Feelings and Information

Attitudes May Become Stronger or May Change Direction

Attitudes Vary in Significance to the Individual and Society

Attitudes and values are alike in that they are learned, emotionally toned predispositions to react in a consistent way toward persons, objects, and ideas. Attitudes and values are also different in several ways. *Attitudes* change more rapidly and are of lesser significance to the individual. Thus, a person's attitudes toward certain musical compositions may change, but the person's valuing of music remains constant.

The conditions for learning attitudes and values are much the same. Most of the discussion in this chapter is in terms of attitudes, but when particular authors are cited, their usage is followed.

Our attitudes and values vary in their influence on our approach and avoidance behaviors, their relative amount of affective and cognitive content, their permanence, and their significance to ourselves and society. This variability among attitudes is shown in Figure 12.1.

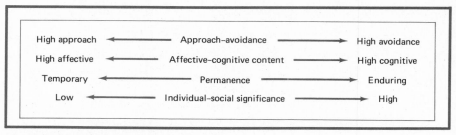

Figure 12.1 Characteristics of attitudes.

Attitudes Influence
Approach and Avoidance Behaviors

Attitudes and values are very important in daily life because they determine the direction of many activities. If individuals have a favorable attitude toward something, they *approach* it, or are supportive of it. Conversely, an unfavorable attitude leads to *avoidance* or conflict. For example, high school students with favorable attitudes toward mathematics take elective courses in mathematics. Those with negative attitudes complete only the required courses and manifest their dislike of the subject matter while taking the courses.

Attitudes Are Based on Feelings and Information

The *affective component* of an attitude refers to the emotions one associates with an object, person, event, or idea. That is, something is pleasing or displeasing; it is liked or disliked.

The *cognitive component* corresponds to a person's knowledge about an entity, such as New York City, or about a class of entities, such as all big cities. Although a distinction is made between *affect* and *cognition,* it does not imply that feeling is not a conscious mental experience. For this reason, some persons refer to affect as the "hot" aspect of cognition and to thinking as the "cold" aspect.

Figure 12.2 shows the relative weighting of the *affective* (feeling, emotional) and *cognitive* (informational) components of attitudes. As the figure indicates, weighting may vary from very high to very low for both the affective and the cognitive components. Consider the three examples of attitude objects named in the figure. Attitude A is based largely on emotional experiences and weakly on informational experiences with religions of various denominations. Attitude B is based about equally on informational and emotional experiences with group work. Attitude C is largely based on informational experiences, with relatively few emotional experiences.

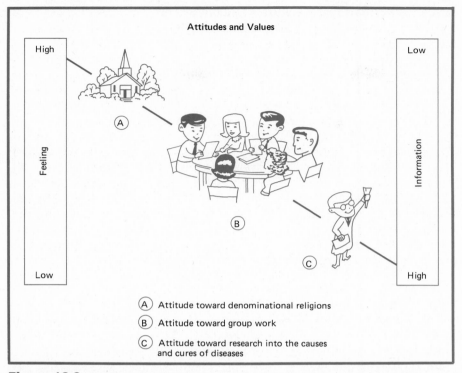

Attitudes and Values

(A) Attitude toward denominational religions

(B) Attitude toward group work

(C) Attitude toward research into the causes and cures of diseases

Figure 12.2 Relative weighting of the feeling and informational components of attitudes.

In general, commercial advertising uses the A approach, while schools use the C approach. The advertisers, of course, want individuals to acquire a favorable attitude toward a product, so they present their products in a most pleasant emotional setting with carefully selected favorable information only. On the other hand, teachers usually present much pro and con information with less consideration of affect.

Attitudes May Become
Stronger or May Change Direction

Some attitudes are learned initially, become stronger, and endure. Others are learned, but are later modified. Moreover, which ones endure and which are modified vary from one individual to another and from one group to another. In this regard, our attitudes are less permanent than our understanding of concepts and of principles.

You can probably recall some attitudes that you learned in childhood that have endured. They may be favorable attitudes toward members of your family or teachers, toward physical activities, or toward ideas such as justice and fair play. You can also recall other attitudes that have changed during the years or that were dropped entirely. The attitudes that you have integrated into your value system and that no longer change are internalized and permanent.

Some attitudes of groups of people, like those of individuals, persist, and others change. You can probably identify some attitudes of your parents' generation that are like those of your generation. Conversely, marked shifts occur in many Americans' attitudes toward a given country as international tensions and conflicts emerge and then get resolved.

In our profession, student teaching is regarded as a very important part of teacher preparation. Do the attitudes of student teachers toward education change during student teaching? Mahan and Lacefield (1978) examined the effects of a year-long student-teaching experience in which each student teacher had two successive supervising teachers. Marked changes occurred in the attitudes of the student teacher regarding the nature of knowledge, learning, learners, and the school when these attitudes differed initially from those of the supervising teacher. The change was consistently in the direction of the attitudes of the supervising teachers.

Attitudes Vary in Significance to the Individual and Society

Some attitudes are of higher significance to the individual than others. Attitudes toward other persons are typically of high significance to the individual. For example, students who feel that other students are friendly and helpful approach them with openness and warmth. These students express their emotional dependency freely and feel favorably toward themselves. On the other hand, students who feel that other students are unfriendly probably experience isolation or rejection and lose most avenues for the interchange of feelings and ideas.

Attitudes and values vary in their importance to differently organized segments of society, such as the community, state, and nation, and therefore can cause problems. As an example, differences in the values among groups of parents of a community result in failure to agree upon the attitudes and values that students should learn in school. Differences between groups of educators, for example, between administrators and teachers regarding rules to be enforced in the school, also reflect important value differences.

Sperry (1977) presents a strong argument for giving greater attention to values. He states that a person's values, and also those of society in the aggregate, directly and constantly shape actions and decisions. All decisions, in his opinion, boil down to a choice among alternatives of what is most valued. His ideas merit serious consideration by educators. Related to society at large he concludes:

> As a social problem, human values can be rated above more tangible concerns like poverty, pollution, and overpopulation on the grounds (a) that these more concrete conditions are all man-made and are very largely

products of human values, (b) that they are not correctable on any long-term basis without effecting changes in the underlying human values involved, and further, (c) that the strategic way to remedy such conditions is to try to actively correct the social value priorities in advance, rather than waiting for the corrective changes to be forced by worsening external conditions. Otherwise, we are destined to live continuously on the margins of tolerability, because it is not until things threaten to become intolerable that the voting majority gets around to changing its established values. (pp. 237–238)

12.1 How is your attitude toward daily exercise different from your concept of daily exercise?

12.2 Analyze your attitudes toward recreational reading and toward denominational religion in terms of their approach-avoidance effects, affective-cognitive content, permanence, individual significance, and social significance.

12.3 Sperry proposes that value change is essential for solving problems such as poverty and pollution. Relate this idea to the fact that discipline retains its position as the foremost problem of the schools from year to year.

MEANS OF LEARNING ATTITUDES

Observing and Imitating

Receiving Reinforcement

Gaining Verbal Information

Attitudes may be initially learned and subsequently modified in several ways. One way is by observing and imitating others. A second is through being conditioned by others. A third is by gaining verbal information. However, how affect relates to cognition is of crucial importance to attitude learning and to learning more generally. We shall examine this area before looking at the modes of attitude learning.

Assume that you turn your head and see a person whom you have never seen before. In the very short period of time after you see the person, which sequence of operations occurs? Is it a series of (a) thinking operations that result in recognition of the stimulus as a person, (b) followed with affect, or feeling, and then (c) forming a judgment, such as "This is something to avoid or not to avoid"? Or do affect and judgment come first followed by the cognitions that result in recognition of the stimulus as a person? Similarly, imagine that you hear these words addressed to you: "Hello, who are you?" Which comes first? Is it the feeling of avoidance or of approach that you derive from the tone of the voice, or is it the meaning of the words? The answers to these questions are of great importance in getting a better understanding of initial attitude learning. They are even more important in understanding how almost instantaneous favorable and unfavorable affect, based on an existing attitude toward any particular learning task, may be related to the subsequent learning of it.

In Figure 12.3, Zajonc (1980) summarizes three possible temporal sequences of internal events involved in recognizing something that is

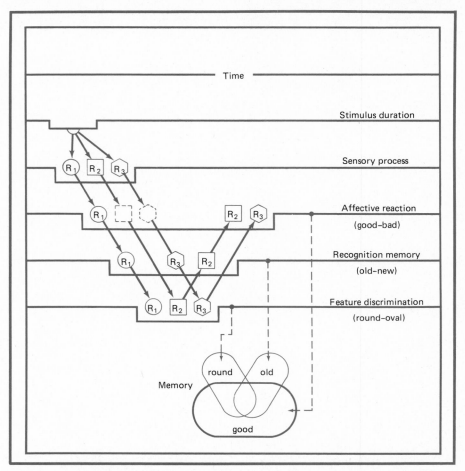

Figure 12.3 Alternative timing sequences for affective reaction, object recognition, and feature discrimination.
Source: Zajonc, 1980, p. 170.

sensed and in discriminating the features of something that is sensed. Notice in the figure that the *recognition* is of something as either *old* (experienced before) or *new* (not experienced before), while the *discrimination* is of a feature of something as either *round* or *oval*. The *affective judgment* that is made is *good* or *bad*. Turning to the temporal sequences, we see that a stimulus is experienced for a fixed time interval. The stimulus triggers the sensory process and the subsequent *affective reaction*, *recognition* (memory), and *feature discrimination*. The breaks in the horizontal lines indicate the range in the onset times of each of the preceding, not the range in the ending time. In the three sequences shown, R_1, R_2, and R_3, the sensory process has the earliest onset time.

In sequence R_1, the affective reaction of good or bad is regarded as strong and salient. It is experienced first and dominates the ensuing recognition as old or new and the feature discrimination as round or oval. The research of Zajonc supports this sequence. However, other research supports the view that, although the affective reaction comes first and is dominant, discriminating the features of something precedes recognition of it. For example, a racetrack is recognized as a racetrack after features of it are discriminated.

Sequences R_2 and R_3 are much alike with regard to the cognition-affect sequence and are widely accepted but probably incorrectly, according to Zajonc. In these sequences, the affective reaction is aroused, but it is regarded as so weak that it does not significantly influence the subsequent "cold" cognitions. In R_2, feature discrimination follows the weak affective reactions, then comes recognition, and finally the affective reaction of good or bad. In R_3, recognition precedes feature discrimination and is followed with the affective reaction of good or bad. As indicated in Figure 12.3, the outcomes of the experiences are stored in memory, regardless of the particular sequence.

Zajonc (1980) argues that not only is affect the first stage of an organism's reaction to stimuli, but affect is also the first element retrieved from memory. Thus, when persons recall an event, a person, a name, in fact, anything whatsoever, the affect experienced at the time of the original learning is the first element to emerge during the retrieval process.

Zajonc points out other aspects of affect. One is that it is inescapable; it functions at the unconscious, as well as at the conscious level. Thus, we seem to be unable to avoid an affective reaction at the time of first experiencing an event and again when retrieving the event from memory. Second, affective judgments tend to be unchanging over a short period of time. We more readily accept the fact that we can be wrong about matters of cognition, such as the number of objects seen, than about our affective reactions, such as liking or disliking what was seen. We tend to trust and not to question our affective reactions as much as our cognitions. Third, affective judgments implicate the self. "I don't like mathematics as well as reading" applies to the individual, not to the object of the individual's affective reaction. Finally, affective reactions are difficult to verbalize. We have an emotional reaction to a stranger almost instantaneously and automatically. However, we can neither verbalize the feeling well nor explain why we experience it.

Before proceeding further, recall the two different views regarding the affect-cognition sequence given in Figure 12.3. What may contribute to these different interpretations? Human beings vary greatly in the intensity of their affective reactions to the same thing, such as seeing a snake or hearing a command from another person. Also, the intensity of the same individual's reactions varies greatly from one situation to another. Thus, the view of cognition followed by affective judgment may apply to some situations where low affect is experienced, while the affect-cognition sequence may hold in situations when intense affect is experienced.

Observing and Imitating

Recall from Chapter 4 that much social learning occurs through observing models (Bandura, 1977). *Observational learning* works in three ways. First, observing a model's behavior enables observers to acquire the behavior of the model that has not previously been learned. Second, observing a model's behavior may either strengthen or weaken already learned behavior of the observer. In some cases, the observer has already learned the behavior, but it has been inhibited. Punished behavior seen in a model further inhibits the behavior that was already learned. On the other hand, rewarded behavior of a model disinhibits a behavior an observer has already learned. Third, observing a model may have the effect of eliciting behavior that has not been performed recently.

Attitudes may be learned by observing a model; they also influence whether behavior that is observed is imitated. A positive attitude may be formed for the first time as the observer reacts favorably to a model or a model's behavior. It is strengthened if the model's behavior is rewarded in the presence of the observer. Assume that the observer has already formed a favorable attitude toward a particular model or to a class of models represented by a particular model. In this case, an approach reaction precedes the thinking operations that result in imitation of the modeled behavior. However, if a negative attitude toward the model or the behavior has already been learned, it is unlikely that the behavior of the model will be attended to and reproduced.

Receiving Reinforcement

As you remember from your study of operant conditioning, responses (operants) are strengthened through reinforcement. Scholars disagree in their explanations of why reinforcements have a strengthening effect, not that reinforcements have an effect. Similarly, both on philosophical and psychological bases, they do not agree on the extent to which reinforcements should be used.

At the present time, principles of operant conditioning continue to be used appropriately in school settings to change negative attitudes and to eliminate emotional reactions that impede normal development. Use of conditioning principles is usually accompanied by reasoning and other forms of physical and verbal guidance.

As an illustration of reinforcement, four groups of university students were given high praise or no praise on their assignments (McMillan, 1977). The assignments required either much or little effort. The students who received high praise and completed high-effort assignments formed more positive attitudes toward the subject matter of the assignment and the assignment itself than did the other three groups. McMillan (1976) reviewed other studies and found a positive relationship between students' attitudes toward a specific subject and achievement in that subject; however, a non-significant relationship was found between attitudes toward school generally and overall scholastic achievement. Marjoribanks (1976) also found specific subject field attitudes to be positively correlated with achievement in the particular subject fields.

Gaining Verbal Information

As we have seen, information that affects attitudes is gained by observing the behaviors of others and by interacting verbally with them. Other means of gaining information are by listening and by reading. How does gaining different kinds of information influence attitude learning?

Simms (1978) did two experiments to answer this question. The first was a short laboratory experiment. The second was conducted in a university classroom setting and ran for three and one-half weeks. The same information was given in printed form to the students in the laboratory experiment and by oral lectures to the students in the university class-room experiment. The results were essentially the same in both experiments. Only the specifics from the university classroom experiment follow.

The descriptive information was derived from biographies and historical accounts of eight outstanding women. The information was prepared to be of high, medium, or low favorableness for each of these eight women. Each experimental group of students listened to one of six different combinations of information of high, medium, and low favorableness. They received no feedback or rewards from the lecturer. After each series of lectures was completed, the students responded to a rating scale measuring the admirability of the women presented in the lectures. The score obtained was inferred to be a measure of the respondent's attitudes toward the women presented.

Figure 12.4 gives the mean judgments of the students regarding the admirability of the women described in the six different sequences and combinations. It is seen that receiving only information of high favorableness (HHHH) regarding a woman resulted in the highest mean rating of admirability and receiving only information of low favorableness (LLLL) resulted in the lowest. The other four combinations were in-between. Simms concluded that teachers can influence the attitudes of their students by presenting them with information of different degrees of favorableness.

Ashby and Wittmaier (1978) found that receiving different kinds of verbal information influenced girls' attitudes toward female roles. They presented stories orally to fourth-grade girls. Some girls heard two stories with women in traditional female roles, and other girls heard two stories with women in nontraditional roles. The girls who heard the nontraditional stories rated traditionally male jobs as more appropriate for females than did the girls who heard the traditional stories.

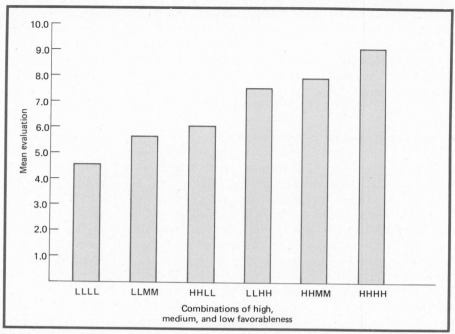

Figure 12.4 Mean ratings of admirability based on six sequences of information of low, medium, and high favorableness.
Source: Simms, 1978, p. 743.

12.4 Zajonc indicates that judgments of liking and disliking are made on the basis of affect without intervening thought. How does this influence the acceptance or rejection of ideas and people?

12.5 Compare Zajonc's ideas about the sequence of sensory process, affective reaction, and feature discrimination with those of other psychologists.

12.6 Do you agree or disagree with Zajonc (a) that affect is inescapable? (b) that we trust our affective reactions more than our cognitions? Give personal examples that support or fail to support Zajonc's views.

12.7 Bandura explains how behaviors are learned through observing and imitating a model (see Chapter 4). Describe how attitudes are learned through observation and imitation.

12.8 A popular TV person influences many adolescents' attitudes regarding clothing, heterosexual behavior, etc. Explain how this influence is generated.

12.9 Teacher A regularly praises students upon completing difficult assignments, while Teacher B accepts the assignments without comment. In which class do you predict more positive student attitudes toward the subject matter? Why?

12.10 Simms found that providing information of high favorableness about a person produced more favorable attitudes than providing information of low favorableness. What does this suggest about influencing attitudes?

12.11 Which do you regard as most influential in shaping your attitudes at present: (a) information that you gain by reading, (b) information that you gain by observing others, including by TV viewing, (c) information that you gain by interacting with peers, (d) self-reinforcement and reinforcement from others?

**DEVELOPMENTAL TRENDS
IN ATTITUDE DEVELOPMENT**

Childhood

Adolescence

Childhood

Estvan and Estvan (1959) found that some attitudes of children remain stable from first grade to sixth grade while others change. For example, negative attitudes toward lower-status living were acquired before the children reached first grade and remained relatively unchanged through the sixth grade. On the other hand, the children's attitudes toward upper-status living throughout the first six years of school became increasingly favorable.

Flanders, Morrison, and Brode (1968) identified significant changes in children's attitudes toward school over a four-month period. There was a significant reduction of positive pupil attitudes toward (1) teacher attractiveness, (2) fairness of rewards and punishments, (3) teacher competence, and (4) interest in schoolwork. Two factors were correlated with these observed changes in attitude. Students who believed that successes and failures are caused by forces beyond their own control had a greater negative shift in attitude than children who believed that successes and failures are self-determined and a product of their own behaviors. Also, in classrooms of teachers who provided less praise and encouragement, there was greater loss of positive attitudes than in classrooms of teachers who provided more praise and encouragement.

Children's knowledge about their emotions, one of the elements of attitudes, increases with age during the elementary school years (Taylor & Harris, 1983). For example, both normal and maladjusted boys know that a negative emotion gradually wanes in intensity over time. They also know that differences between people in their level of distress persists across time and that an emotionally charged episode, especially a happy one, is more memorable than a neutral one. However, throughout the elementary school years, they remain relatively ignorant regarding voluntary control strategies that can be brought to bear on the display and experiencing of emotions. It is probable that they are equally ignorant of strategies for modifying attitudes.

We note a final feature of attitudes. Children do not respond to an

attitude stated as an abstract principle in the same way they respond to
concrete examples of the principle. Zellman (1975) had a "select" group
of children of grade 3–grade 6 and an "unselected" group of grade 5–
grade 9 respond to abstract principles and concrete examples of the principles. The select children came from better residential homes, and the
other group was unselected as to type of home. Acceptance of the abstract
principles was relatively high for both groups, as shown in Figure 12.5.

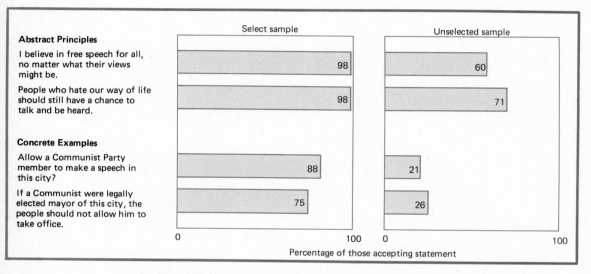

Figure 12.5 Reactions of students to abstract value statements and to concrete applic-
tions of the values.
Source: Zellman & Sears, 1971, p. 118. Copyright 1971 by the American Psychological Association, Reprinted by permission.

The drop in acceptance, especially for the unselected group, was very
marked from the abstract principles to the concrete examples. Zellman
and Sears (1971) explain why the difference occurs:

> Attitudes regarding free speech for dissenting or nonconforming political
> groups are acquired by a socialization process wholly different from that
> involved in the acquisition of the abstract principle of free speech. In brief,
> the abstract belief in "free speech for all" simply mimics the dominant adult
> political norm; it is learned as a slogan bearing no concrete implications. In
> contrast, most children's attitudes toward rights of free expression for
> specific dissenting political groups depend more upon their attitudes toward
> the groups than upon their acceptance of the general principle of free
> speech. Children do not deduce from an abstract principle to concrete
> situations, and there is no evidence that free speech in concrete situations
> is taught as a dominant norm of the adult political world. (pp. 122–123)

Adolescence

During early adolescence, influence on children shifts from adults in
the home, school, and neighborhood to peers. Personal and social factors

become more important; indeed, they attain their maximum influence during the junior and senior high school years. During these years, young adolescents experience the greatest conflict regarding who they are and where they belong in the world. Many adolescents experience a conflict between identification with the role of the child (from which they are emerging) and the role of the adult (which they are beginning to assume), a conflict they resolve through greater involvement with their peers.

Peer Groups and Friendship Patterns

The *peer group* is of great importance to the adolescent. It can be a source of difficulty as well as a boon to healthy attitude development. In a study of over 3000 adolescents, Schwartz, Puntil, and Simon (1977) found the major cause of delinquency to be related to peer pressure and peer norms. These researchers conclude that illegal, destructive, and other behaviors offensive to the community typically occur in the absence of adults and in the presence of one or more peers. When adults are not present, some adolescents appear to undergo a personality change. This personality change becomes an invisible, but powerful, barrier separating the adolescent from adults. The invisible barrier is formed, according to these researchers, for two reasons. First, adults avoid involvement in the lives of adolescents. Second, the adolescents skillfully hide from adults, including parents, how they behave with their peers.

Similarity in attitudes and values plays an important role in friendships among high school students (Kandel, 1973). Being of the same age, sex, and ethnicity were found to be three highly significant factors in the formation of friendships. Another factor was the use of marijuana. Students who abstained from using it had as closest friends others who also abstained, whereas those who used it were more likely to have friends who did also.

It may come as a surprise that the use of marijuana is so critical in friendship formation. However, each generation of adolescents has a few important areas of dissent from the adult control group. These become a basis for friendships and peer group information.

Horan and Williams (1982) found a means of counteracting negative peer influence. In this study, counselors taught junior high school students to be assertive. The students observed assertive behavior of peers related to the use and non-use of alcohol and tobacco and practiced being assertive. This education resulted in a significant decrease in stated willingness to use alcohol and marijuana and in verbal assertiveness against their use. Three years after the original study, the educated students were using alcohol and marijuana less than control students and were also more assertive against the use of these drugs.

Parental and Adolescent Attitudes

How wide is the difference in attitudes between adolescents and their parents? Lerner, Karson, Meisels, and Knapp (1975) studied the views of adolescents and their parents regarding 36 topics of current interest, including abortion, drugs, politics, parental control, sexual activity, and women. In this study, the adolescents indicated how they thought their parents would respond, and the parents anticipated the responses of their children. The adolescents overestimated the difference between themselves and their parents, whereas the parents underestimated the differences. Apparently, the desire of adolescents for independence is related to their overestimating the differences, whereas the desire of the parents to maintain a close relationship with their children leads to underestimating the differences.

Cheating Behavior

Cheating reappears as an important concern from one generation to the next (Bushway & Nash, 1977). Using crib notes during an exam, copying answers from another student, giving another student answers or completed assignments, and evading rules are common examples of cheating. Behaviors like these can be traced across the centuries. For example, Brickman (1961) indicates that in ancient China, civil service examinations were given in individual cubicles to prevent the examinees from cheating and the examinees were searched before they entered the cubicles. The death penalty was in effect for cheating for both the examinee and examiner, but some cheating still occurred. Apparently, then as now, the value of self-preservation and self-gain is stronger than fair play for some people. And many persons feel they will not get caught, or, if they do, the punishment will not be too severe.

When does cheating begin? Schab (1969) found the greatest incidence in grade 1, the second greatest in grade 8, and the third greatest in grade 7. Thus, before the high school years, many students have already started cheating.

Shepherd (1966) reported that 96% of high school and college students admitted cheating on school tests at some time. Why do so many high school students cheat? Schab (1969) indicated that pressure to get grades to gain admission to college or to maintain an existing grade point average is one factor. Montor (1971) concluded that students cheat because they do not understand why cheating is wrong. Cornehlsen (1965) studied 200 high school seniors and found that 33% of the girls and 55% of the boys felt that cheating was justified when the student's success or survival was in jeopardy. Bushway and Nash (1977) conclude that the time has arrived for a greater emphasis on the prevention, rather than on the causation of cheating. They recommend that future research focus on strategies that prevent or reduce cheating.

Part-Time Work and Attitudes

Steinberg, Greenberger, Garduque, Ruggiero, and Vaux (1982) examined the effects of part-time employment on the attitudes and other behaviors of adolescents who were attending high school full time. Working contributed to the personal development of the students; they became more punctual and dependable at work. However, they became less involved in productive social activities and relationships, such as with members of the family and classmates. They also used cigarettes and marijuana more. They developed cynical attitudes toward work and accepted unethical work practices. Accordingly, these authors doubt the value of attempting to integrate young adolescents into the work place as a means of enhancing their personal and social development.

12.12 Some attitudes of school children change during the elementary school years, while other attitudes become more fixed from grade 1 to grade 6. Account for this in terms of the learning of attitudes described earlier in this chapter.

12.13 Identify an abstract principle that many children will probably accept and a concrete example of it that fewer will accept. What does this imply for teaching?

12.14 The major cause of delinquency has been found to be related to peer pressure and peer norms. Brainstorm activities that will result in adolescents spending more time with both younger children and adults and less time with peers.

12.15 Why do many parents avoid involvement in the lives of their adolescent children?

12.16 How does the separation of advising and teaching in high schools discourage adult-student interactions on matters of high personal importance to the student?

12.17 Brainstorm some means of preventing cheating.

MORAL DEVELOPMENT

Stages of Moral Development

Individual Differences in Moral Development

Learning Moral Values

The development of morality is a primary concern of teachers, parents, and others who are responsible for the education and socialization of the young. One of the most ambitious attempts to explain moral development is that of Kohlberg (1973). He explains moral development in terms of the changing value orientations and the related moral reasoning of the maturing individual. Kohlberg proposes that the moral behavior of a person is determined primarily by the person's reasoning about what is and what is not moral.

Stages of Moral Development

Figure 12.6 outlines Kohlberg's six stages of moral reasoning. Before proceeding further, notice that there is very little overlapping of the stages, the theory being that persons apply the same moral orientation in all situations. Many psychologists disagree with this premise. They find that persons use different orientations, or stages of moral reasoning, in different situa-

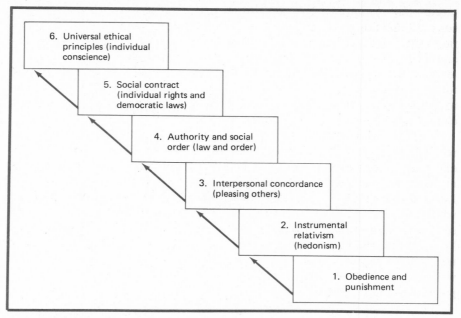

Figure 12.6 Stages of moral development.
Source: Kohlberg, 1973.

tions. But there is also much agreement that the six stages depict a general progression from early childhood to adulthood quite reliably. Furthermore, the successive stages provide a sensible framework for the guidance of moral development.

Kohlberg regards stages 1 and 2 as a *preconventional level* of moral development. At this level, children respond to cultural rules and labels of good and bad and right and wrong. However, they interpret these labels in terms either of the hedonistic consequences of action (punishment, reward, exchange of favors) or in terms of the physical power of those who enunciate the rules and labels. In other words, children base their actions on the reasoning that punishment or reward will follow the actions.

Stages 3 and 4 are regarded by Kohlberg as the *conventional level* of moral development. At this level, maintaining the expectations of the individual's family, group, or nation is perceived as valuable in its own right, regardless of immediate and obvious consequences. The attitude is more than conformity to personal expectations and social order. It includes maintaining, supporting, and justifying the social order and identifying with persons involved in it. The conventional level differs from the preconventional level in that children perceive the role and desires of others as well as their own. Rightness, wrongness, and other values, as recognized by others, are applied by the individuals to their own actions.

Stages 5 and 6 are regarded by Kohlberg as successively higher levels of *autonomous, principled behavior*. At these levels, individuals define their moral values and principles apart from the authority of the groups or persons holding these principles and apart from the individual's own identification with these groups. The individual's internalized values concerning right and wrong shape decisions that guide actions. Persons at these levels may lead protests to get rid of laws and regulations that they regard as not good for the welfare of the social unit. Similarly, they may initiate legal actions to get rid of unfair practices. They work to elect government officials to change laws and regulations.

There is considerable evidence that differences in the levels of moral reasoning are positively but not perfectly related to moral behavior. For example, more disruptive junior high school students, in comparison with nondisruptive students, were found to be at Level 4 and fewer were at Level 5 (Geiger & Turiel, 1983). One year later, the disruptive students who were found to be no longer disruptive demonstrated Level 5 moral reasoning. Weiss (1982) found that 16- and 18-year olds who understood higher levels of moral reasoning scored relatively high on a moral reasoning test and arrived at decisions on moral bases. Students who understood less well scored lower and arrived at their decisions on prudential bases (appropriate for the particular circumstances) rather than on moral bases.

Individual Differences in Moral Development

Kohlberg found considerable variation in the stages of moral development represented by boys of age 10 and higher. At age 10, most boys are in stages 1, 2, and 3, but a few are in stage 4. By age 13, about equal numbers of boys are in stages 2, 3, and 4; however, there are a few in stages 1 and 5. At age 16, about equally large numbers are in stages 3, 4, and 5; however, smaller numbers are also in stages 1, 2, and 6. You can see in Table 12.1 that at age 10, the most frequently given responses correspond to stage 1 (the obedience and punishment orientation); at age 13, they corre-

TABLE 12.1 RANK ORDER OF NUMBER OF MORAL STATEMENTS BY MORAL DEVELOPMENT STAGE AND BY DIFFERENT AGE-GROUPS OF BOYS (1 = MOST FREQUENT RESPONSES. 3 = LEAST FREQUENT RESPONSES)

	RANKS BY AGE-GROUP		
MORAL DEVELOPMENT STAGE	10 YEARS	13 YEARS	16 YEARS
6			
5			1
4		2	2
3	3	1	3
2	2	3	
1	1		

SOURCE: Kohlberg, 1973, p. 9.

spond to stage 3 (the good boy–nice girl orientation); and at age 16 they correspond to stage 5 (the social contract, legalistic orientation).

Because of this large variability, it is clear that one cannot infer much about the stage of moral development from the age of the individual. This variability among boys of the same age is not critical to instruction about moral values, as we shall see. Some teachers put children of about the same age in small groups to discuss situations involving moral values; the children in the lower stages then learn the interpretations of those in the higher stages.

Learning Moral Values

Kohlberg does not want students told the moral values they should learn. Rather, he would have a child learn moral values from participating in teacher-led discussions in which there are some classmates at the same stage as the individual and others at the next higher stage or two. His thesis is that the person in a given stage will reject the lower stage and will then learn both the values and the reasoning of persons at the next higher stage.

To aid teachers with this process, moral dilemmas have been prepared that may be presented to the students. One of these dilemmas is now paraphrased, and children's reasoning that is representative of each stage is presented:

SIX STAGES OF REACTION TO A MORAL DILEMMA

SITUATION

A woman was near death. There was one drug that might save her. The drug was expensive, $2000 for a small dose that cost the druggist only $200. Heinz, the woman's husband, could raise only $1000. He told the druggist his wife was dying, but the druggist would not sell the drug to Heinz. Heinz broke into the man's store and stole the drug for his wife. Should Heinz have done this? Was it right or wrong? Why? (Other questions involving morality are also raised.)

REACTIONS

Stage 1: No. Stealing is wrong. Heinz should be put in jail.
Stage 2: No. Stealing is wrong. He should have been able to get the money.
Stage 3: No. It was partly wrong to steal. He wouldn't like it if someone broke into his store. Dishonor would be brought to his family.
Stage 4: No. He should have kept trying to get more money. He shouldn't let his wife die either.
Stage 5: It was wrong legally for Heinz to steal the money, but it would be more wrong for him to let his wife die.
Stage 6: Yes. It was legally wrong but morally right. The moral duty to save a life is more important than the legal duty not to steal.

The Kohlberg approach does not require the teacher to commit himself or herself to any particular values. Moreover, it makes it possible to turn student conflicts involving different moral values into fruitful learning experiences.

Another approach to teaching and learning values is called *values clarification*. Values clarification was described initially in a book by Raths, Harmin, and Simon (1966). In a later book, Simon and Clark (1975) presented a refined version of the goals of values clarification and the instructional process. The goals of values clarification are to learn a valuing process and to apply the process to value-laden situations. In theory, learning the process will help students experience positive values in their own lives and act more constructively in social situations. The process consists of a variety of suggested activities to help students learn the valuing process and build personal values. The activities are to be carried out in a supportive, nonjudgmental classroom environment.

Lockwood (1978) analyzed the research related to values clarification and to teaching moral reasoning with moral dilemmas based on Kohlberg's ideas. He found that persons applying Kohlberg's ideas consistently had as their desired outcome getting students to reach a higher level of moral reasoning. On the other hand, those applying the values clarification process apparently expected different kinds of outcomes, such as an increase in self-esteem, self-concept, or personal adjustment; a change in value priorities; and improved classroom behavior.

Lockwood's conclusions regarding moral reasoning follow:

> The direct discussion approach generally produces significant development in moral reasoning. . . . While this approach appears to produce consistent development in group mean scores, not all subjects advance consistently. . . . Some subjects advance substantially whereas others remain at their pretest position. . . . A second observation about the effects of the direct discussion approach is that, on the average, the obtained mean developmental increases are in the Stage Two to Stage Three range. (p. 358)

Lockwood's conclusions regarding values clarifications follow:

> It should not be claimed, on the basis of the research reviewed, that values clarification has a demonstrated impact on students' self-esteem, self-concept, or personal adjustment. . . . There is no evidence that values clarification has a systematic, demonstrated impact on students' values. . . . Although no enduring effect can be claimed, values clarification, on the basis of teachers' perceptions and a measure of observable behavior, appears to positively affect students' classroom behavior. . . . It is not warranted to claim that values clarification positively affects the interpersonal relationships of students or that it contributes to reduced drug usage. (p. 344)

Not all persons agree that either of the preceding approaches is highly effective for learning and teaching moral values. As we saw earlier in this chapter, more direct approaches, such as modeling and information giving, can be used in which the particular attitudes to be learned are presented to the students. After the presentations, there is a sound basis for discussion and reasoning.

12.18 According to Kohlberg's theory, is it possible for persons to proceed from stage 2 (hedonism) to stage 5 (individual rights and democratic laws) without experiencing stages 3 and 4? Cite instances where persons persistently violate laws and unwritten moral codes but demand all constitutional rights for themselves.

12.19 Kohlberg reported stage 1 as being most common for boys at age 10, stage 3 at age 13, and stage 5 at age 16. What kind of moral behavior, therefore, should teachers expect of the boys who are in these stages at these ages?

12.20 A student cheats on exams but never steals property from others. Discuss whether these contradictory behaviors can be explained by Kohlberg's idea that moral reasoning is the primary determinant of moral behavior.

12.21 Relate Kohlberg's recommended method for teaching moral values to the learning of attitudes by observing models and by gaining new information.

12.22 Kohlberg's recommended method of teaching implies that describing and explaining moral and immoral behavior in terms of consequences on self and others are ineffective in teaching morality. Do you agree? Explain.

PRINCIPLES FOR FOSTERING ATTITUDE LEARNING

1. Identify the attitudes to be taught.
2. Provide for pleasant emotional experiences.
3. Provide exemplary models.
4. Extend informative experiences.
5. Use small-group instructional techniques.
6. Encourage deliberate attitude change.

---

1. Identify the attitudes to be taught. Our society continues to change rapidly, and the attitudes of its citizens do also. As a result, we cannot be sure which attitudes students have learned in either their homes or neighborhoods. Accordingly, we cannot expect students to come to our classes either knowing or accepting the attitudes that are necessary for a good learning environment. At the same time, we do know that the more time students spend in active learning, the higher they will achieve. It would seem reasonable, therefore, to identify the attitudes that underlie desirable

New attitudes are learned and the intensity and approach-avoidance dimensions of existing attitudes are changeable. What techniques can teachers use to aid students in developing strong, positive attitudes toward self, classmates, and schooling?

student classroom behaviors. The following list of student behaviors indicative of underlying attitudes is intended as a beginning point for an individual teacher's consideration; it can also be used by an entire school staff. The student

1. Likes the subject matter.
2. Likes the teacher or teachers.
3. Likes classmates.

4. Works well independently.
5. Works well with others.
6. Is courteous to others.
7. Starts work promptly.
8. Works throughout the class period.
9. Takes good care of own property.
10. Takes good care of others and public property.
11. Accepts the teacher as the classroom leader.
12. Behaves well and reasons with the teacher and classmates about desirable conduct.

As we saw earlier in Chapter 2, one important educational objective is to go beyond teaching attitudes and aid students in acquiring a value system. Despite the importance given to this objective at the verbal level, schools typically have not tried to determine the values to be taught to students. A noteworthy statement of values that could be used has been formulated by Rokeach (1973). He identified 18 terminal values that he considers as being widely accepted by Americans. He regards values as determining a person's attitudes toward specific objects, people, and activities. His list merits serious consideration by educators as a starting point for ranking their own values and for identifying values to teach students.

A comfortable life	Inner harmony
An exciting life	Mature love
A sense of accomplishment	National security
A world at peace	Pleasure
A world of beauty	Salvation
Equality	Self-respect
Family security	Social recognition
Freedom	True friendship
Happiness	Wisdom

Before proceeding to the next principle, we should recall Kohlberg's approach to the teaching of moral values. He proposes that students should not be taught any specific moral values. Instead, they should learn successively higher levels of moral reasoning by interacting with others who reason at the higher levels. This approach is accepted as constructive; however, it is not regarded as sufficient for enabling many students to identify and learn prosocial attitudes and values. A more direct approach as indicated in this and the next principles is needed.

2. Provide for pleasant emotional experiences. Earlier in this chapter we saw that persons involuntarily and instantaneously make favorable and unfavorable judgments about persons and situations, based on affect or feeling. Furthermore, this affective aspect of prior experiences is rapidly retrieved from memory when making judgments in new situations. Thus, learned affect tends to carry over from one situation to another. It would seem reasonable, therefore, to try to encourage liking for the teacher and liking for the subject matter. Two of many means of producing desirable affect are encouraging and praising the student for trying and ensuring that the student experiences success on academic tasks. We should recognize, however, that a child's achieving success by adult standards, e.g., letter grades, teacher comments, produces negative affect if the child does not accept the adult standard (Bryant, 1983).

Besides striving for pleasant affect, wise teachers also try to prevent high anxiety in their students. Why should high anxiety be avoided? Sieber, O'Neil, and Tobias (1977) found that high student anxiety interfered with learning at three times: at the time attention is first directed to the learning situation; after information has been received and is being processed; and later when information is being used, such as during an examination. Tobias (1979) does not recommend that teachers use clinical procedures to reduce the anxiety of highly anxious students. Rather, high anxiety is to be recognized and prevented wherever possible. Striving students with a history of academic failure or a lack of sound study or coping skills respond to high academic demands with high anxiety more than students who have experienced successes and have learned to cope with high demands. Thus, differential, but realistic, teacher expectations are required in order not to produce high anxiety and yet to encourage reasonable effort.

Might we use fear to teach attitudes regarding potentially dangerous situations? We are all aware of the potential dangers of cigarette smoking, careless driving, and venereal disease. How can people be taught to avoid these? What is the effect of inducing fear? Rogers and Mewborn (1976) identified the effects of fear appeals, giving persons information regarding the probability of each danger occurring, and providing recommended protective and preventative measures, or coping behaviors, to avoid the potential dangers. The participants in the experiment were three groups of college students. The participants in the smoking study had to have been smoking at least ten cigarettes daily during the past year. Those in the safe driving study had to have a valid driver's license. Those in the venereal disease study had to show no allergy to penicillin. One result of the experiment was that arousing fear in the students did not influence their intentions to avoid the potential dangers. However, providing information regarding coping behaviors, that is, protective and preventative measures, did influence their intentions. The main finding of Rogers and Mewborn (1976) was as follows:

> Regardless of what the threatened event was, or how anxious it was, or how likely it was to occur, the stronger the belief that a coping response could avert a danger, the more strongly people intended to adopt the communicator's recommendations. . . . The data indicated that the efficacy component acted

upon intentions, not by making the threat seem less severe or less likely to occur but by directly strengthening beliefs in the ability to cope with danger when it is confronted. (p. 59)

3. Provide exemplary models. The importance of exemplary *identifying figures* on the observer's attitudes is well illustrated in modern advertising, especially television commercials. A favorite technique is to have the product endorsed by someone with wide-ranging, popular appeal, who becomes an *identifying figure* to observe and imitate. A similar technique is to associate prestige with the product: "Scientists have found . . .," "Four out of five doctors recommend . . . ." Some appeals are so personal that buyers purchase the product to feel better and become like whoever does the endorsing or recommending. *Sesame Street* uses popular identifying figures—males and females, blacks and whites—who appeal to children and parents of all social classes and regions of the country.

Schools have not been nearly as successful as TV in providing exemplary models for two reasons: Too many teachers have not regarded themselves as identifying figures for their students and the reading materials do not provide exemplary models that appeal to many students. Some of the terms students use to describe admired teachers are *enthusiastic, friendly, cheerful, sociable, interesting, knowledgeable,* and *businesslike.* Students see their admired teachers as ones who are competent as teachers and who have high regard for the students. Finally, the more the teacher's behaviors are perceived as bringing desirable consequences to the teacher, the more probable it is that the student will try to match the teachers' behaviors and will accept the implied attitudes and values.

Instructional materials may not provide an adequate range of identifying models. The basic textbooks and library books, including fiction and biography, are often inadequate for many students, because the possible identifying characters are too unrealistic to serve as exemplary models. Also, a disproportionate amount of school literature is not representative of the family and home situations from which many children come or of the occupations and successes they will achieve as adults. Reading material requires continuous examination in terms of the attitudes and values that are presented. For example, how many models are representative of black culture and views? Oriental? native American? lower social class? female?

4. Extend informative experiences. Getting information about the object of the attitude facilitates initial attitude acquisition. It may also result in attitude change. The means of acquiring information include direct experiences with persons, ideas, and objects; reading books and other materials; listening to the radio; watching television; and seeing sound movie films.

One possible difficulty in arranging direct experiences with the attitude objects is that unpleasant emotions may be experienced and unfavorable information gathered. Having children from residential or rural areas visit the section of a city where a minority group is concentrated may result in even less favorable and more prejudiced attitudes toward that group. Similarly, taking children from large cities into a rural area may not result in more favorable attitudes toward life in the country.

New information does not always have the same effect on individuals. When the distance is small between individual's attitudes and information presented to them, they judge the information as fair and factual. However, with increasing distance between individual's attitudes and information presented, the favorable judgment is sharply reduced, and the information is perceived as propagandistic and unfair (Hovland, Harvey & Sherif, 1957).

Recently, textbook publishers have tried to reduce sex role stereotyping to encourage the positive portrayal of females and to increase the number of female characters in children's books. Scott and Feldman-Summers (1979) found support for these actions in terms of eliminating sexist attitudes. Reading about female characters engaged in nontraditional female activities increased elementary school children's perceptions of the number of girls who can engage in these same activities. However, it did not affect their perceptions of other activities not portrayed in the stories.

5. **Use small-group instructional techniques.** Four group techniques for attitude modification that almost any teacher may use are (1) receiving and discussing information in groups; (2) group decision making; (3) role playing; and (4) cooperative small-group activity to reduce prejudice.

Receiving and discussing information in groups. The experience of listening to the radio or watching television is different if done in groups than if done alone. Group listening is more effective than solitary listening, particularly if the majority of the group is favorable to what is being presented. It is less effective, however, if a majority of the group is opposed to the content of the presentation. A study by Mitnick and McGinnies (1958) supports this assertion and also provides a bridge between individual and group reception of a communication and group decision making resulting from discussion. These investigators assessed the effects on high school students of a film on racial tolerance. Students who scored high, middle, and low in white ethnocentrism were identified and were then, on a stratified random basis, assigned to one of three groups. One group saw the film — unfavorable to white ethnocentrism — but did not discuss it; another group saw and discussed the film; the control group neither saw nor discussed the film.

Viewing the test film significantly reduced prejudice in highly prejudiced students in the film-alone condition. In the film-discussion condition, the effects of the film on these students were much smaller. Apparently, the discussion tended to counteract the effect of the film on them. Examination of the transcripts of the discussion revealed that the highly prejudiced students spent most of the discussion time expressing their antiblack attitudes, thus reinforcing their attitudes and counteracting the film. The low-prejudiced students, in contrast, tended to examine the general problem of group prejudice raised by the film, thus reinforcing the effects of the film on them.

Two further findings are of interest. The stability of the attitude change one month later was greater for the film-discussion group than for the film-alone group. The latter had regressed significantly toward their original attitudes.

Group decision making. When individuals share in making a decision, they tend to behave in accordance with that decision to a greater extent than when they do not take an active part. This effect is related to the fact that small groups permit relatively free discussion. It is possible for attitudes and behaviors to be changed by the give-and-take in discussion, by the reinforcing and negating of expressions by the members, and by the emotional commitment involved in decision making.

Role playing. Various forms of role playing are employed in school situations. Unrehearsed dramatization dealing with a social or psychological problem is usually the method chosen. In unrehearsed role playing, there is none of the memorizing of lines or coaching that is essential to ordinary dramatic presentations.

Role playing is generally preceded by informal class discussion of a recently experienced problem or other event. Students then carry out roles by dramatizing such behavioral characteristics as shyness, aggressiveness, good manners, prejudice, and courtesy. They may also carry out roles drawn from novels, short stories, newspaper stories, and plays which the class has studied. As the students portray different roles, they express their feelings as well as present information, thus combining emotional and informational experiences that are related to their underlying attitudes.

There are some precautions connected with role playing. A teacher should not put students in highly uncomfortable roles. For example, it would be unfortunate to have a shy child try to play the role of either a shy, withdrawn child or a boisterous, aggressive one. The best procedure is to discuss the role-playing situation and the characters or roles with the whole class and then to ask for volunteers. Needless to say, the teacher should know the children well before trying role playing.

Cooperative small-group activity to reduce prejudice. One of the continuing concerns in our society is racial and ethnic prejudice. Cook (1978) analyzes the *contact hypothesis* as a means of eliminating prejudice. This hypothesis, as initially stated, was that if members of hostile groups come to know each other through personal contact, mutual understanding and liking will follow and neutralize the negative relationships that formerly existed. Cook (1978) states the current contact hypothesis as follows:

> Attitude change favorable to a disliked group will result from equal status contact with stereotype-disconfirming persons from that group, provided that the contact is cooperative and of such a nature as to reveal the individual

characteristics of the person contacted and that it takes place in a situation characterized by social norms favoring equality and equalitarian association among the participating groups. (pp. 97–98)

Notice that the prejudiced and disliked members of the group are of equal status. The group members toward whom the hostility is directed are *stereotype-disconfirming persons*. That is, they dress, speak, and act like the prejudiced but liked group members, not the disliked. The basis of the group association is achieving a group goal cooperatively. This means that each group member contributes his or her share to achieving a group goal. Finally, the situation is structured deliberately to favor equality among individuals and groups, rather than inequality or discrimination. Cook (1978) did a series of in-depth, sustained experiments to test the hypothesis. When all the conditions were put into effect over an extended period of time, 40% of strongly prejudiced white, female college students changed their attitudes toward black, female college students.

Slavin (1979) studied biracial learning teams in desegregated junior high schools. One hundred seventy whites and 124 blacks participated as the experimental group. Five teachers—two blacks and three whites—carried out the biracial teaming arrangements in their classes. Each student team had four or five members who represented a cross section of the class; and they worked cooperatively to achieve a team goal. Cross-racial friendships among the experimental groups were found to increase after a ten-week period. In a follow-up nine months later, the experimental students made three times more cross-racial choices for friends than did the control students. Slavin concludes that these choices, based on sociometric tests, reflect a real change in the students' attitudes.

Johnson, Johnson, and Maruyama (1983) analyzed 98 studies to identify conditions under which proximity and interaction in small groups in school settings, such as in desegregated schools and mainstreamed classrooms, led to positive relationships between ethnically diverse students, handicapped and nonhandicapped students, and homogeneous students. Cooperation to achieve a common goal by members of both heterogeneous and homogeneous groups, without competition among the small groups, promoted greater interpersonal attraction than did interpersonal competition by group members, individualistic efforts, and cooperation among group members with competition among the groups. The greater interpersonal attraction included more positive interactions among group members, stronger feelings of psychological acceptance and safety, more realistic views of self and group members, more feelings of success, and increased expectations of favorable future interactions with group members, regardless of their heterogeneity. Cooperation among small group members, with competition among the groups, promoted greater interpersonal attraction among the group members than did interpersonal competition or individualistic efforts. When small group members competed for rewards, oppositional interaction occurred that was accompanied by feelings of psychological rejection, stereotyping, feelings of failure, and expectations of distasteful and unpleasant future interactions with heterogeneous classmates.

Learning situations must be arranged deliberately in the school setting to influence student attitudes positively. As we have seen, cooperative small-group activities provide some of the best opportunities for learning and practicing many prosocial attitudes and related behaviors. Furthermore, best results accrue when members of small groups perceive themselves as being of equal status. Teacher skill in arranging small group work is needed for many students to receive status and not to be rejected.

6. Encourage deliberate attitude change. The process of deliberately changing one's own attitudes, such as a negative attitude toward persons of another race or a negative attitude toward reading, involves a change in affect, cognition, or both. To change the attitude, one must first recognize the presence of the attitude. The undesirable effects of the attitude on self or others may then be analyzed. Reading to gain new information about the attitude object and the problems caused by the undesired attitude may be helpful. Another way of gaining information is talking and working with persons who hold the desired attitude, as is possible in small-group cooperative projects.

The preceding techniques are often effective in deliberately changing an attitude. Moreover, some persons are able to discontinue undesired actions or to initiate desired actions upon recognizing the nature of their own attitudes, even though they cannot completely change their feelings. Human relations programs in teacher education designed to eliminate discrimination by teachers against children on bases such as race, sex, and age assume that persons can learn not to discriminate.

12.23 Twelve behaviors indicative of desired student attitudes and 18 values were given. Select any that you think should not be fostered, and add others.

12.24 Assume that "working well with other students" is a desirable behavior. Indicate one or two things that a teacher can do to implement each of the following principles for teaching it:

    a. Provide for pleasant emotional experiences
    b. Provide exemplary models
    c. Extend informative experiences
    d. Use small-group instructional techniques
        (1) Receiving and discussing information in groups
        (2) Group decision making
        (3) Role playing
        (4) Cooperative small-group activity to reduce prejudice

12.25 Which of the four preceding principles do you regard as easiest for a teacher to implement? Most difficult? Explain.

12.26 Indicate the characteristics of the members of small groups and the kinds of small-group processes that contribute to reducing prejudice among the group members.

12.27 Discuss whether it is possible for a teacher to hold a prejudice, to recognize it, and then not to discriminate?

12.28 Review and Application: Recall the most important information regarding each of the following concepts, and identify at least one possible use of the information by you as a learner, a teacher, or both:

Characteristics of Attitudes
 Attitudes Influence Approach and Avoidance Behaviors
 Attitudes Are Based on Feelings and Information
 Attitudes May Become Stronger or May Change Direction
 Attitudes Vary in Significance to the Individual and Society
Means of Learning Attitudes
 Observing and Imitating
 Receiving Reinforcement
 Gaining Verbal Information
Developmental Trends in Attitude Development
 Childhood
 Adolescence
Moral Development
 Stages of Moral Development
 Individual Differences in Moral Development
 Learning Moral Values
Principles for Fostering Attitude Learning

SUMMARY

Attitudes are learned, emotionally toned predispositions to behave in a consistent way toward persons, objects, and ideas. Attitudes have both an affective component and an informational component. Attitudes are learned in different ways, including by observing others, by conditioning, and by gaining information by reading and other means. Much attitude learning occurs in small-group arrangements and by viewing TV.

Some attitudes are learned during the early elementary school years and become stronger with increasing years of schooling; others become weaker in intensity; and still others change in direction. Early adolescence is marked by a considerable change in attitudes toward self, adults, and peers. Many enduring attitudes and values are learned prior to high school graduation.

Kohlberg indicates that moral reasoning, based on attitudes and values regarding what is right and wrong, influences moral behavior. He proposes that moral reasoning develops in six stages and that all individuals go through the same stages. In his view, children learn the successively higher levels of moral reasoning by discussing moral issues with other persons who are at the next higher stage of moral reasoning. He states that as students interact with persons at a higher level about the reasons for reacting in a particular way to a situation, they accept the higher level and start to reason accordingly.

It is appropriate for a school staff and parents to identify the attitudes and values that they desire students to learn. When the attitudes are identified and agreed upon, attempts can be made to teach the attitudes. In the instructional process, appropriate adaptations of the following principles can be made for different age groups:

1. Identify the attitudes to be taught.
2. Provide for pleasant emotional experiences.
3. Provide exemplary models.
4. Extend informative experiences.
5. Use small-group instructional techniques.
6. Encourage deliberate attitude change.

SUGGESTIONS FOR FURTHER READING

Aronson, E. *The social animal* (4th ed.). New York: W. H. Freeman, 1984.

A highly readable interpretation of the attitudinal bases of normal and abnormal human interaction. Includes race relations and prejudice, advertising, sex, aggression and violence, ethics, television, and many other current topics.

Combs, A. W. Affective education or none at all. *Educational Leadership*, 1982, *39*(7), 494–497.

An excellent account of the relationship between affective learning and learning in general. (There are other excellent articles on affective education in this issue of this journal.)

Davis, E. D. Should the school teach values? *Phi Delta Kappan*, 1984, *65*, 358–360.

Discusses the responsibility of the school to teach civic values, for example, self-respect and responsibility, rather than particular religious beliefs.

Enright, R. D., Lapsley, D. K., & Levy, Jr., V. M. Moral education strategies. In M. Pressley & J. R. Levin (Eds.), *Cognitive strategy research: Educational applications.* New York: Springer-Verlag, 1983. Pp. 43–83.

The authors explain five strategies for teaching moral education based on Kohlberg's ideas, and evaluate the usability and effectiveness of the strategies at different levels of schooling.

Irwin, D. M. Moral development. In H. E. Mitzel, J. H. Best, & W. Rabinowitz (Eds.), *Encyclopedia of educational research* (5th ed., Vol. 3). New York: Free Press, 1982. Pp. 1237–1241.

Presents an overview of the theories of Piaget, Kohlberg, and Turiel on moral development. Another article in this *Encyclopedia,* "Moral education," by H. C. Johnson, Jr., summarizes research and theory on moral education.

Mischel, W. *Introduction to personality* (3rd ed.), New York: Holt, Rinehart and Winston, 1981.

Chapter 16 deals with anxiety and stress and chap. 18, self-control. Other means of coping are explained in other chapters.

Reimer, J., Paolitto, D. P., & Hersh, R. H. *Promoting moral growth: From Piaget to Kohlberg.* New York: Longman, 1983.

Colleagues of Kohlberg explain his approach to moral development and moral education.

Steinberg, L., Blinde, P. L., & Chan, K. S. Dropping out among minority youth. *Review of Educational Research,* 1984, *54,* 113–132.

A readable review of the research regarding the relatively high dropout rate of bilingual students, particularly those of Hispanic backgrounds.

CHAPTER 13

PERSONALITY INTEGRATION AND CLASSROOM DISCIPLINE

BASES OF PERSONALITY INTEGRATION

PRINCIPLES FOR FOSTERING PERSONALITY INTEGRATION

ENCOURAGING DISCIPLINED BEHAVIOR

Personality integration refers to adjustment to the environment that is characterized by a positive self-concept, self-control, ethical behavior, social responsibility, and other attributes beneficial to the individual and society. Personality integration changes, since the self-concept, ethical behavior, and other attributes of personality integration are learned throughout the school year. Accordingly, teachers have a powerful influence on their students' present and future personality integration.

This chapter is designed to increase your understanding of personality integration and how to foster it. Classroom discipline is considered in the context of promoting personality integration.

BASES OF PERSONALITY INTEGRATION

Good Health

Reasonable Achievements

Positive Self-Concept

Adequate Modes of Coping

Secure Family Environment

Let us consider the difference between personality and personality integration. Consider a definition of *personality* by an eminent scholar in the field: "the dynamic organization within the individual of those psychophysical systems that determine his unique adjustment to his environment" (Allport, 1955, p. 48). A similar definition is offered by Johnson and Medinus (1965): "the distinct and unique organization of traits in an individual as reflected in how he reacts to himself and others and in how they react to him, and also in how he meets frustrations and conflicts — that is, how he adjusts to his environment" (p. 444). These views focus on the individual's adjustment but are neutral with respect to the desirable or undesirable effects of the individual's actions on others, that is, the prosocial, altruistic behaviors or the delinquent behaviors of the individual.

Different from the neutral aspect of personality, *personality integration* implies self-control of conduct, ethical behavior, social responsibility, and concern for others. It includes individual self-realization and need gratification, but not at the expense of thwarting or denying the self-realization and need gratification of others.

Kanfer (1979) captures the sharp conflict between gratification of individual needs and social responsibility that has recently arisen in our society:

> The combination of social and personal controls that has existed for two
> centuries in the United States seems to have been adequate to maintain a
> strong and cohesive society. But the last decade has seen increasing
> strains in the maintenance of a socialization process that yields both
> personal satisfactions and communal involvement. Harmon (1977) believes
> that there are sufficient signs of strain in the western social paradigm to
> herald a profound transformation in western society. He listed the following
> items as indicators of a coming change in cultural values: (a) a decreased
> sense of community, (b) an increased sense of alienation and purpose-
> lessness, (c) an increased frequency of personal disorders and mental
> illness, (d) an increased rate of violent crime, (e) an increased frequency
> and severity of social destruction, (f) an increased use of police to control
> behavior, (g) an increased public acceptance of hedonistic behaviors
> (particularly sexual) and lax public morality, and (h) an increased interest
> in noninstitutionalized religious activities. Taken together, they reflect a
> tendency toward decreased social cohesion and increased self-concern
> and personal autonomy. (p. 234)

Kanfer poses the question as to whether our society can survive so much hedonism and lack of social responsibility and social cohesion. He proposes the development of *altruism,* that is, individual self-control in the service of others. Altruism is a very critical aspect of personality integration, as we shall see in the ensuing discussion of five conditions that contribute to personality integration.

Good Health

Physical and mental health are essential for full self-realization. Both the school and the home traditionally have attempted to promote good health in children. In recent decades, however, health problems that pose serious problems for the home and school have emerged. New cooperative means for resolving them are required.

The increased sexual activity of young students has increased veneral diseases and pregnancies. Both pose serious difficulties for an increasing number of students. Cousins (1979) regards the increasing number of children born to young unmarried women as a most serious social problem. He states that about 600,000 teenagers become mothers each year and that more than 10,000 are 14 years of age or younger. Moreover, many of these teenagers have additional children to receive the added welfare payments given for each family member. The Population Resource Center has estimated that the cost for the first 10 years of life of each child born to a teenager will be $18,710, more than $8 billion for the entire group. Cousins further indicates that the catastrophic economic cost is the minor part of the problem. The social, moral, and psychological impact on the life of the children and the parents is even far more serious.

In addition to the pregnancies among girls, large numbers of students, starting as early as age 10 to 12, are using drugs with disastrous ill effects on health and academic learning. Hilgard, Atkinson, and Atkinson (1979) provide an easy-to-read-summary of the effects of psychoactive drugs. Included as psychoactive drugs are the depressants, alcohol and heroin; the stimulants, amphetamines and cocaine; and the hallucinogens, LSD and marijuana. They conclude their summary as follows:

> In concluding this discussion, several aspects of drugs and their effects on consciousness are worth noting. First, the range of subjective experiences following the use of drugs is very wide, both in response to a particular drug and in the same person's response to different drugs. Some experiences are highly pleasurable, while others represent frightening dissociations. Second, the objective changes in behavior, such as the effects on fatigue or aggression, are also highly variable, dependent on dosage, and in many instances unpredictable. Finally, the social setting in which the drug is taken may influence the user's experiences and behavior. That the results may endure — and reappear as flashbacks — shows that the influences on brain processes may be profound. What is most evident is that, in resorting to drugs, individuals relinquish some of their normal controls by assigning control to a chemical agent. (pp. 176–177)

A new and interesting area of research related to health is sleep. Taub and Berger (1976) studied the effects of extending sleep beyond the habitual amount, reducing it, and advancing and delaying the beginning of the sleeping period. Both advancing and delaying the habitual sleeping period by three hours resulted in impaired performance, as reflected by reaction time and missed signals on an auditory task and by errors on an addition task. A reduced amount of sleep and an extended amount had similar, but somewhat less consistent, effects on the three measures. Taub and Berger conclude that our optimal level of performance is highly dependent upon the maintenance of an established temporal rhythm of sleep and wakefulness.

Reasonable Achievements

Being extremely deficient in one or more of the psychomotor skills that are common to other children of about the same age may constitute a serious block to achieving personality integration. It may lead children to perceive themselves in an unfavorable way, and they may later show withdrawal or aggressive behavior. Similarly, it may prevent the usual give-and-take social relationships in play and recreational activities that other children normally experience. Children much less proficient than others in various psychomotor skills can learn to adapt, but they need help from the teacher.

As psychomotor skills affect personality integration, so do academic achievement and lack of it. Children and youth of low academic achievement are usually less well accepted in the classroom than those of low psychomotor abilities. Perhaps other students tend to equate academic achievement with worth as a human being. Because of this unfavorable reaction from others, the children of low academic achievement may experience relatively severe adjustment problems. They may have difficulty in accepting themselves, especially if they feel that their teacher and classmates do not accept them. It is not surprising, therefore, that anxiety and emotional disturbance are higher in children of low and average academic ability than in children of high abilities (Feldhusen & Klausmeier, 1962).

Positive Self-Concept

The *general self-concept* is the complete set of perceptions persons have of themselves. An *individual's self-concept* includes awareness of what the individual is and how well the individual performs and achieves. A person's self-concept may range from high to low in positiveness. A positive self-concept contributes to personality integration.

Self-esteem refers to how one feels about one's self and is more emotionally toned than the self-concept. There is a positive relationship between the self-concept and self-esteem, but it is not perfect. For example, a student may be low-achieving and have a positive academic self-concept but may not have high academic self-esteem. High self-esteem is also regarded as contributing to personality integration.

Both the self-concept and self-esteem are measured by specially constructed inventories, and separate scores are obtained for each one. Questions dealing with how positively students rate their academic abilities or their physical appearance are used to measure the self-concept. Questions involving how good students feel about their academic abilities or their physical appearance are used to measure self-esteem. In most tests, the higher the score, the more positive is the self-concept and the higher is the self-esteem.

Organization of the Self-Concept

Shavelson, Hubner, and Stanton (1976) identified how the self-concept is organized. The hierarchical nature of its organization is shown in Figure 13.1. The *general self-concept*— also referred to simply as the *self-concept*— and the academic, social, emotional, and physical self-concepts are frequently used in studies of the self-concept. Marsh, Smith, Barnes, and Butler (1983) extended the structure shown in Figure 13.1 to include 10 self-concepts as follows: (1) physical abilities, (2) physical appearance, (3) peers, (4) relationships with parents, (5) reading, (6) mathematics, (7) all school subjects, (8) total nonacademic self-concept, (9) total academic self-concept, and (10) total self-concept. The total nonacademic self-concept consists of the sum of 1–4, the total academic self-concept the sum of 5–7, and the total self-concept the sum of 1–7. The correlations among the first seven

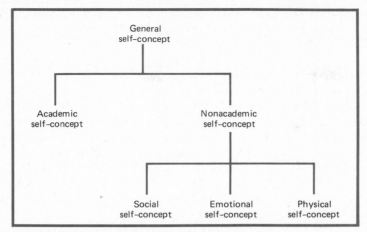

Figure 13.1 Hierarchical organization of the self-concept.
Source: Shavelson, Hubner, & Stanton, 1976, p. 413.

concepts are all relatively low, indicating that individuals vary considerably in the positiveness of their different self-concepts.

Self-Concept, Achievement, and Other Behavior

Hansford and Hattie (1982) reviewed 128 studies of self-measure and various achievement and performance measures. The self-measures were mainly self-concept and self-esteem measures. Correlations from $-.77$ to .96 were found between the self-measures and the performance/achievement measures; however, the average correlation was positive and low, ranging from .21 to .26. Variables related to the size and direction of the correlations included grade level, low and high socioeconomic status, ethnic group, low and high ability, the self-test employed in the study, and the nature and type of achievement measure. Based on these findings, we should recognize that the extent to which students' self-concepts are related to their achievements varies tremendously from one situation to another.

In a carefully conducted longitudinal study of six months duration, academic self-concepts were found to correlate relatively high with school achievement while nonacademic self-concepts did not (Marsh et al., 1983). In this study, three kinds of academic self-concepts and four kinds of nonacademic self-concepts were measured. Reading self-concept was found to correlate highest with mathematics and total academic achievement, and low with nonacademic self-concepts. Conversely, nonacademic self-concepts did not correlate positively with any area of academic achievement. Based on these findings as well as the earlier review, we see the importance of relating specific self-concepts to specific areas of achievement.

Shepard (1979) found self-acceptance to be closely related to one's nonacademic self-concept. She also indicates that persons who are nonacceptant of themselves are likely to experience poor mental health. More-over, persons who are nonacceptant of self are also inclined not to accept others.

Development of the Self-Concept

Larned and Muller (1979) carried out a cross-sectional study of 1471 boys and girls enrolled in grades 1–9, all the children of two New Mexico rural school districts. About 45% of the children were of Mexican-American extraction. Four areas of self-concept and self-esteem were measured. The four areas were physical maturity, peer relations, academic success, and adaptiveness to school.

What happened to the positiveness of the self-concept developmentally in the four different areas? Did it increase, remain stable, or decline? Similarly, what was the progression for self-esteem? Did it rise, remain steady, or fall? Figure 13.2 depicts the means for the self-concept and for self-esteem in the four areas for the boys and girls in grades 1–9.

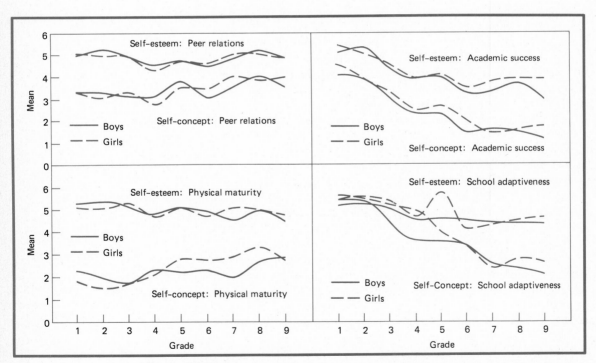

Figure 13.2 Mean self-concept and mean self-esteem of boys and girls related to peer relations, academic success, physical maturity, and school adaptiveness.

A few of the more interesting developmental trends, as well as all the sex differences, are summarized as follows:

1. The changes in the *peer relations self-concept* and *peer relations*

self-esteem were relatively small, from grade to grade. The differences in the means for the boys and girls were not significant at any grade level.

2. There was a gradual but slight rise in the positiveness of the *physical maturity self-concept* from grades 2 through 8. The differences between the means of the boys and girls were not statistically significant at any grade level. There was a very slight downward trend in *physical maturity self-esteem* across the grades. The differences in the means for boys and girls were not significant at any grade level.

3. The *academic success self-concept* of the boys and girls decreased sharply across the grades. However, the differences in the means of the boys and girls were not significant at any grade level. *Academic success self-esteem* followed a similarly decreasing pattern, and the differences between the means of the boys and girls were not significant at any grade level.

4. The *school adaptiveness self-concept* of the boys and girls decreased sharply across the grades. The means of the girls were significantly higher than the means of the boys in grades 3 and 4. The *school adaptiveness self-esteem* also decreased across the grades until grade 7, but not so sharply as self-concept. The differences in the means of the boys and girls were not significant at any grade level.

In their study, Larned and Muller found that academic self-esteem and school adaptiveness self-esteem decreased markedly from the primary grades through grade 6 and then stabilized during grades 7–9, while peer relations self-esteem remained stable or increased throughout grades 1–9. McCarthy and Hoge (1982) found that global self-esteem, which is not heavily weighted by academic self-esteem, gradually but consistently increased from grade 7 through grade 12. Fortunately, students become more acceptant of themselves and of others as they approach physical, social, and emotional maturity.

Adequate Modes of Coping

Coping refers mainly to intrapersonal and interpersonal relationships. The need to cope arises when individuals cannot achieve their goals because of the actual or perceived behaviors and goals of others, including peers, teachers, and parents. One positive means of coping is to modify one's goals and behaviors and to continue the goal-directed efforts. Another is to try to change others' goals and behaviors through discussion and other peaceful means. When these do not work, other means are employed. The usual modes employed by students are withdrawal and aggression.

Withdrawal and Avoidance

In the school setting, absenteeism is one means of withdrawing from an unwanted situation. Daydreaming and not engaging in task-oriented behaviors are others. These forms of *withdrawal* are not highly disruptive to other classmates. Moreover, they usually do not interfere directly with the teacher's instructional role. They can, however, have serious consequences for the individual student if they are used repeatedly and become the primary means of coping with school situations. Obviously, the absentee and day-dreamer do not learn subject matter. Withdrawing students may also acquire an habitual escape mechanism and may not experience healthy social interactions.

Habitual withdrawal and avoidance are detrimental to personality integration. Nevertheless, occasional withdrawal and avoidance are widely used means of adjusting. In fact, permitting withdrawal or avoidance achieves better results in some school situations than forcing a student to participate. The girl who feels that her appearance will be pitied or disapproved by classmates should not be forced to speak or recite. The shy child should not be called upon to play the role of a heroine. Many psychologically frustrating situations for students can be handled in the same way as physically dangerous situations. The wise teacher permits avoidance of personality-damaging situations until the child has knowledge and skills to cope with them.

Aggression and Related Behaviors

Aggression, as used here, implies hostility directed against a perceived source of frustration—usually another person. Aggressive reactions are hostile attacks with the purpose of removing or injuring the source of frustration. Physical aggression is often observed in smaller children. One child takes a toy from another, and hitting, biting, scratching, gouging, or hair-pulling ensues. In older children and adults, aggression generally takes the form of verbal attacks, but there is much physical aggression also.

Figure 13.3 shows a sequence of aggression and counteraggression between two individuals. It is based on a frustration-aggression paradigm initially formulated by Dollard, Doob, Miller, Mowrer, and Sears (1939). Bill, frustrated by Henry (see *A*), attacks him (see *B*). Henry strikes back *(C)*. Bill retaliates more strongly *(D)*, but Henry overpowers him *(E)*. Bill, in turn, may withdraw or acquiesce outwardly, or both boys may reinterpret their attitudes toward themselves and the situation and return to a status similar to that preceding the frustrating situation.

Berkowitz (1962) modified the original frustration-aggression hypothesis by introducing anger as a variable intervening between frustration and aggression. Subsequently Rule and Nesdale (1974) supported the view that having a goal blocked produces frustration, which, in turn, is accompanied by anger and followed by aggression. In addition to goal blocking and a feeling of frustration, attack and insult by the goal blocker also have been shown to arouse anger. Berkowitz (1983) elaborated his earlier ideas regarding anger as an intervening variable between frustration and aggression. He concluded that anger is not an automatic response, that frustration can be followed with flight as well as with anger. This is because thought processes and memories markedly influence reactions to aggression.

Most aggression has negative effects on the individuals involved and on society generally. Prosocial aggression, however, does not, since it is aggression used in a socially approved way to achieve goals that are ac-

Figure 13.3 Sequence of frustration, aggression, and counteraggression.

ceptable to the moral standards of the group. Prosocial aggressive actions, for example, a policeman forcibly taking a firearm from a student, are performed to prevent threatened persons from being injured. The aggressive actions are undertaken to reach a goal that contributes to the welfare of helpless or nonaggressive individuals or a group of persons. Anger is not the motivating force for the aggressive actions.

Aggressive reactions may be verbal as well as physical. In fact, verbal interactions typically precede physical attack. During the verbal interchange, there is increased emotional arousal, intensified anger, and less control of rational thinking processes. The implication of this sequence for teacher-student interactions and the teacher's role in controlling students' angry interactions can hardly be overemphasized.

Secure Family Environment

Family life continues to change rapidly, and the school is expected to take on more functions formerly performed by the family. As this trend continues, the family and the home per se appear less effective in fostering the personality integration of the child. More cooperative efforts between the home and the school appear to be needed. In this section of the chapter, we shall examine some key studies associated with the family environment and its impact on various aspects of the child's development.

Effects of Divorce

Hetherington (1979) indicates that 40% of the current marriages of young adults are expected to end in divorce and that 50% of the children born in the 1970s will spend some time living in a single-parent family. What is the impact of current divorces on children? Hetherington's main findings are now summarized:

1. Almost all children experience the transition of divorce as painful even though divorce may be the best solution to a destructive family environment. Children's most common early responses to divorce are anger, fear, depression, and guilt. After the first year following divorce, tension reduction and an increased sense of well-being emerge. Most children cope with and adapt to the short-term crisis of the divorce within a few years. When the crisis is compounded by multiple stresses and continual adversity, developmental disruptions may occur.

2. There is wide variability in the quality and intensity of children's responses to divorce and the subsequent single-parent household. Some children manifest severe disruptions in development. Other children seem to sail through a turbulent divorce and stressful aftermath and emerge as competent, well-functioning individuals. Children who have histories of maladjustment prior to the divorce tend to respond with long-lasting emotional disturbance after the divorce.

3. The impact of marital discord and divorce is more pervasive and enduring for boys than for girls. Family discord escalates in the year following divorce. During the first year following divorce, boys show more problems than children in discordant nuclear families.

Hetherington (1979) summarizes her own research and that of others on the effects of divorce on children:

> A conflict-ridden intact family is more deleterious to family members than is a stable home in which parents are divorced. An inaccessible, rejecting, or hostile parent in a nuclear family is more detrimental to the development of the child than is the absence of a parent. Divorce is often a positive solution to destructive family functioning; however, most children experience divorce as a difficult transition, and life in a single-parent family can be viewed as a high-risk situation for parents and children. This is not to say that single-parent families cannot or do not serve as effective settings for the development of competent, stable, happy children, but the additional stresses and the lack of support systems confronted by divorced families impose additional burdens on their members.

Most research has viewed the single-parent family as a pathogenic family and has failed to focus on how positive family functioning and support systems can facilitate the development of social, emotional, and intellectual competence in children in single-parent families. Neither the gloom-and-doom approach nor the political stance of refusing to recognize that many single-parent families headed by mothers have problems other than financial difficulties is likely to be productive. We need more research and applied programs oriented toward the identification and facilitation of patterns of family functioning, as well as support systems that help families to cope with changes and stress associated with divorce and that help to make single-parent families the basis of a satisfying and fulfilling life-style. (p. 857)

Sex-Role Socialization

Historically, the father's role was that of breadwinner and the mother's that of homemaker (Bernard, 1981). Boys and girls had teachers who modeled these roles, and the same roles were portrayed in instructional materials. Thus, most boys and girls readily learned their sex roles.

Smaller family size, the employment of many married women, and the unemployment of men have changed but not clarified the roles of males and females. Lack of agreement and accompanying confusion between the father and mother at home and among teachers at school regarding adult sex roles are common. Bernard (1981) views the changing sex roles of adults as presenting many unresolved and continuing problems in sex-role socialization of children.

Increasing absence of the father is one aspect of the changing role of males and females. What is the effect of the absence of the father on sex-typed behavior in male children? Boys without their true father (as opposed to stepfather or foster father) present in the home were rated by their teachers as more masculine, aggressive, disobedient, and independent than boys with fathers present (Santrock, 1977). Boys from divorced homes were more aggressive than boys from widowed homes. Boys were rated by their teachers as less disobedient when the father's absence occurred later in their development. Lamb (1979) indicates that the negative effects of the father's absence because of work are similar to those for divorce and death. Deviant or deficient sex-role development tends to be found in some boys raised without fathers.

Family Climate and Educational Development

Mize and Klausmeier (1977) identified factors within the student, within the school, and within the family that contribute to very rapid and very slow cognitive development of children during the elementary school years, grades 1–6, and during the secondary school years, grades 7–12. The cumulative effects of the factors for the elementary school years and secondary school years were identified when the students were in grade 6 and grade 12, respectively. Because they are interrelated, the contributions of the three kinds of factors are shown in Table 13.1.

TABLE 13.1 VARIABLES DISCRIMINATING AND NOT DISCRIMINATING BETWEEN RAPID AND SLOW DEVELOPERS IN GRADE 6 AND GRADE 12

VARIABLES	SIXTH GRADE	TWELFTH GRADE
SELF		
IQ score	Yes	Yes
Self-esteem	Yes	Yes
Internalized responsibility for learning	No	No
Attitudes toward school	Yes	Yes
Attitudes toward curriculum	Yes	Yes
Achievement motivation	Yes	Yes
Self-directedness of behavior	Yes	Yes
Peer relations	No	Yes
Attitudes toward parents–home	No	Yes
SCHOOL/EDUCATION		
Absenteeism[a]	Yes	Yes
Grades (A–F)	Yes	Yes
Curriculum (courses taken)	No	Yes
School involvement–activities	No	Yes
Extracurricular activities:		
TV viewing[a]	No	Yes
Reading	Yes	Yes
Sports	No	No
Hobbies	Yes	Yes
School structure[b]	No	No
Classroom structure[b]	No	No
Home–school interaction	No	Yes
Rapport with teachers	No	Yes
HOME/FAMILY		
Demographic:		
Socioeconomic status of parents	Yes	Yes
Marital status of parents	No	No
Number of children in family	No	No
Parental attitudes		
toward school–education	Yes	Yes
Parental expectations for child	Yes	Yes
Parental involvement with child	No	Yes
Parental supervision–control of child	No	Yes
Intellectual climate of home	Yes	Yes
Child's home responsibilities	No	No
Parental child-rearing attitudes	No	No

[a] Only these two variables were higher for the slow developers.
[b] The rapid and slow developers went to the same schools and had their instruction in the same or similar classroom arrangements; therefore, no difference in these variables should be expected.
SOURCE: Mize & Klausmeier, 1977, p. 220.

Eight of the 31 variables did not differentiate between the rapid and slow developers of either grade 6 or grade 12. Fourteen did for the students of both grades. Nine variables discriminated between the rapid and slow developers of grade 12, but not of grade 6. More variables discriminating at the secondary school level is interpreted as follows. The self-concept, school-education, and home-family variables associated with rapid and slow cognitive development had become more stable by grade 12 and also more sharply differentiated than they were by grade 6. The grade 6 students were still developing cognitively and socially, and some of their attitudes and behaviors related to self, school, and family had not yet crystallized and been integrated. For example, grade 6 students whose rate of cognitive development was slow nevertheless had peer relationships, attitudes toward parents and home, involvement in school activities, and rapport with teachers similar to those of the rapid developers.

The relationship of the various variables to rapid and slow cognitive development at grade 12 may be summarized succinctly. The rapid developers had higher IQ scores, higher self-esteem, and more favorable attitudes toward the curriculum and school. Their achievement motivation and self-directedness of behavior were higher. Their relations with peers and attitudes toward home and parents were better. They attended school more regularly, made higher grades, took more college preparatory courses, and participated in more school activities. They read more, watched TV less, and had more education-related hobbies. There was more home-school interaction, and the students had better rapport with their teachers. More often the students came from upper-middle-class or middle-class homes characterized by a good intellectual climate. The parents had higher aspirations and expectations for their child, were more involved with their child, held more positive attitudes toward school and education, and were more concerned and actively interested in their child's school, teachers, and curriculum.

13.1 Why might individual need gratification and self-realization not result in personality integration?

12.2 Differentiate between personality development and the development of personality integration.

13.3 Estimate the probable effects of a venereal disease, giving birth to a child without being married, or the habitual use of drugs or alcohol on the personality integration of a student 12–18 years old. Is the school justified in carrying out educational programs to prevent these conditions? Is the school justified in not providing such programs?

13.4 Indicate two or three teacher behaviors that encourage acceptance of a low-achieving student by other students. Indicate teacher behaviors that encourage lack of acceptance.

13.5 The self-concept ranges in positiveness from high to low. Using a scale of high, medium, and low, rate yourself with regard to your academic self-concept, social self-concept, emotional self-concept, and physical self-concept. Are you equally positive in all four?

13.6 Bill has negative academic, social, and physical self-concepts, although he achieves above average, is not rejected by other students, and is of average height, weight, and physical prowess. Why might Bill have developed these negative self-concepts?

13.7 Compare the developmental trends related to the four self-concept areas found by Larned and Muller: physical maturity, peer relations, academic success, and adaptiveness to school.

13.8 Larned and Muller reported a continuing drop in the academic self-concept and in the academic self-esteem of students from grade 1 to grade 9. Indicate conditions in the schools that might have contributed to this drop.

13.9 Based on your own experiences and your associations with other students, do you think the majority of students have a lower academic self-concept during the junior high school years than during the elementary school years? Explain.

13.10 Withdrawal and aggression are widely used modes of coping. Give an instance when each one is appropriately used and when each one is inappropriately used.

13.11 Patterns of family living continue to change. For example, divorce and single-parent families are common. How may a divorce affect a child's personality integration adversely? How may a single-parent family interfere with sex-role socialization?

13.12 Return to Table 13.1. Compare the home/family variables of slow developers at grade 6 and at grade 12. Which of the self variables and the school/education variables do you think might be related to the home/family variables?

PRINCIPLES FOR FOSTERING PERSONALITY INTEGRATION

1. Maintain an orderly learning environment.
2. Help students set and attain realistic achievement goals.
3. Aid students to develop positive self-concepts.
4. Encourage the attainment of prosocial behaviors.
5. Aid students to develop self-control.

1. Maintain an orderly learning environment. An orderly learning environment has several features that all of us have probably experienced. Students arrive at class on time, start working immediately, and remain actively engaged in learning activities throughout the learning session. To

Schools that care make a real effort to aid students in developing a positive self-concept, self-discipline, ethical conduct, and social responsibility.

attain this kind of learning environment, the teacher must ensure that there are suitable learning activities for each student, that reasonable standards of conduct are understood and followed by the students, and that the availability of materials and the teacher's methods promote effective use of time by all the students. In many schools, many teachers establish an orderly learning environment by planning carefully in advance of teaching and then exercising firm democratic classroom leadership. Some teachers in the same schools are less successful. The less successful teachers do not arrange appropriate learning activities for the students, do not make standards clear, and they may be wishy-washy or autocratic in their leadership.

We have come to realize recently that in some schools even the best teachers have difficulty in establishing a good learning environment. In these schools many of the students are disruptive, are not interested in being educated, and are immune to the rewards and punishments that teaches control as individuals. As is indicated in the following discussion, only a schoolwide effort can modify this kind of school.

Rutter, Maughan, Mortimore, Ouston, and Smith (1979) studied inner-city secondary schools of London. They reported that some of these secondary schools were perceived by the students and the staff as more favorable environments for student learning and prosocial behavior than others. In the better schools, three kinds of conditions were observed. First, the teachers made it clear to the students, in a variety of ways, that they expected them to do well academically and to behave well. The principal supported the teachers in implementing these expectations, and the students appeared to accept them. Second, the teachers modeled desired outcomes in their own classrooms, such as starting classes and learning activities promptly, continuing until the end of the class period, showing enthusiasm for what they were doing, and not being absent. Third, the teachers provided feedback and reinforced the students' desired behaviors and achievements. In the secondary schools where this kind of environment was pervasive, in comparison with those in which it was not, the students attended school more regularly, spent more class time in actively learning, achieved higher, behaved better, and were less frequently apprehended by the police as delinquents. Edmonds (1982) reported similar conclusions regarding American schools.

2. **Help students set and attain realistic achievement goals.** Some persons still believe that students ought to experience failure in school, regardless of high effort, as preparation for meeting similar failure in adult life. However, the evidence is clear that productive, happy adults have a backlog of school successes and that repeated successes do not lead to an inflated opinion of self or undue self-centeredness. Teachers help students experience success by working with them in setting realistic goals in their classes (Klausmeier, Lipham, & Daresh, 1983). When this is done, achievement clearly increases.

As we saw earlier in this chapter, academic achievement is positively related to the academic self-concept but not to the nonacademic self-concept. Accordingly, it appears unwise to focus attention and instruction on building the child's nonacademic self-concept for an extended period of time prior to teaching academic concepts and skills.

In this regard, Calysn and Kenny (1977) compared the effects of self-enhancement and skills-development approaches to instruction at the high school level. They found that the skills-development approach that was accompanied with student success on academic learning tasks improved students' self-concepts. At the same time, the self-enhancement model of instruction did not produce either high achievement or positive self-concepts. Similarly, Scheirer and Kraut (1979) concluded that a positive change in the self-concept is more likely to be an outcome of increased achievement rather than an intervening variable, or condition, necessary for better achievement to occur. Thus, helping the student to achieve at an appropriate level promotes achievement, and it also contributes to the formation of a positive self-concept.

3. **Aid students to develop positive self-concepts.** Positive self-concept formation and self-esteem may not precede or cause higher educational

achievement. However, having positive academic and nonacademic self-concepts is an essential element of healthy personality integration.

Aiding students to achieve as well as they can is highly desirable, but more than this is required. Both the teacher and other students must convey to the student that they accept the student academically. If their acceptance is not felt, the student may not perceive himself or herself positively. Recognition and approval are equally helpful in the social and physical areas. As Rogers, Smith, and Coleman (1978) indicate, students must receive positive feedback and perceive others as acceptant of them in order to form positive self-concepts.

4. Encourage the attainment of prosocial behaviors. Aronson, Bridgeman, and Geffner (1978) emphasize two variables that contribute to the attainment of prosocial behavior. The first is the development and enhancement of the student's self-esteem. The second is the development of productive interpersonal relations, including liking others, reducing prejudice, and being able to take the perspective of another person. In a similar vein, Rushton (1976) calls for the development of *altruistic behavior,* that is, behavior carried out for the benefit of others.

How are these kinds of values and behaviors developed? Aronson et al. (1978) indicate that students learn prosocial behaviors and values in small-group activities that teach cooperation. Rushton (1976) reports that observation of models is a primary means of learning altruistic behaviors. Role playing following observation of a model has a further facilitative effect. Peterson's research (1983) shows that altruism increases during the elementary school years. She indicates further that the increase is due to two main factors: increased competency in performing helping tasks and increased acceptance of responsibility for helping. Teaching children to become more competent and encouraging them to assume responsibility for helping increases their altruistic behaviors.

Clark (1980) favors teaching empathy as a prosocial value. He defines *empathy* as the ability to feel the experiences, needs, aspirations, frustrations, joys, sorrows, anxieties, hurt, or hunger of others as if they were one's own. Clark's ideas regarding the importance of empathy merit serious attention:

> The inability of human beings with power to understand the legitimate needs and aspirations of other human beings—the inability of human beings to understand that their fellow human beings share their anxieties, their frailties, their posturing, their desire to make the most out of the limited interval of conscious and evaluative life—this lack of simple expanded empathy is in the eyes of this observer the basis of social tensions, conflicts, violence, terrorism, and war. . . . The survival of the human species now appears to depend upon a universal increase in functional empathy. Trained human intelligence must now dedicate itself to the attainment of this goal. (p. 190)

5. Aid students to develop self-control. As we saw in Chapter 4, the behavior of others can in some situations be controlled through the application of operant conditioning principles. Moreover, when humanely applied, results favorable to the individual are being achieved. However, inhumane applications have been made. As a consequence, behavior modification practices based on conditioning principles have come under increased scrutiny (Stolz, Wienckowski, & Brown, 1975). The application of painful stimuli procedures to change behavior, as well as the taking away or withholding of necessities, has been interpreted by the courts as depriving individuals of their rights as citizens (Stolz et al., 1975). In accordance with this judgment, withholding juice and snacks and isolating children from other children until desired behaviors are performed have been outlawed in nursery schools of Wisconsin.

With the decline in behavior modification practices, a strategy is emerging to help students understand principles of social interaction and to develop self-control. Mischel (1979) suggests that quite early in life, students learn plans and specific strategies to guide their social interactions. These plans and strategies are verbalized by the child and take the form of self-instructions that control or monitor increasingly complex behavior. Mischel illustrates this formulation and use of plans by an 11-year-old:

> If I had to teach a plan to someone who grew up in the jungle—like a plan to work on a project at 10 A.M. tomorrow—I'd tell him what to say to himself to make it easier at the start for him. Like "if I do this *plan* on time I'll get a reward and the teacher will like me and I'll be proud." But for myself, I know all that already, so I don't have to say it to myself— Besides, it would take too long to say, and my mind doesn't have the time for all that, so I just remember that stuff about why I should do it real quick without saying it—It's like a method that I know already in math; once you have the method you don't have to say every little step. (p. 749)

How to teach children self-control is being investigated. For example, Wang and Stiles (1976) carried out a study in an ongoing classroom setting. Second-grade children in the experimental group were taught a self-scheduling system that involved their understanding possible learning activities, selecting which ones to carry out, and working out a self-schedule. These experimental children, in comparison with the control group, took a greater amount of responsibility for deciding their learning tasks and scheduling their time to work on the tasks. This approach to instruction was effective in increasing the students' self-control of learning activities, and it also led to completion of more learning activities.

Illustrative of another approach to teaching young children self-control is that of Toner, Moore, and Ashley (1978). They had first- and second-grade boys serve as self-controlling models for other children in a temptation situation. The boys who modeled the rules to their peers learned the rules and also self-control in following the rules. The authors concluded that this kind of modeling for peers is an effective, nonpunitive technique for increasing young children's self-control.

Kohler (1981) identified many kinds of school activities that have provided youth opportunity to learn responsibility and self-control. Some of the most interesting high school activities follow (pp. 427–428):

Mathematics. Students in a computer class in Denver, Colorado, designed and executed a program that placed commuters in car pools. Young people in Maine had to master computation skills in order to design and build a boat.

Home Economics. Students in Colorado run their own food service center called Munchies, Inc. In day-care centers all over the U.S., young people learn about parenting by planning activities and caring for younger children.

History. Students in Georgia dug up archeological materials from an area that was about to be bulldozed for construction. Students from many parts of the country have preserved the oral history and traditions of their regions in magazines such as *Foxfire*.

English. Students in St. Paul wrote and distributed a handbook with consumer information for teenagers.

Social Studies. In Philadelphia young people undertake internships in various social agencies. In California teenagers provide therapy and companionship for patients at a state mental hospital.

General. In all subject areas students are motivated to learn when they are responsible for teaching younger students.

13.13 Indicate why each of the following principles for fostering personality integration should be implemented:

a. Maintain an orderly learning environment.
b. Help students set and attain realistic achievement goals.
c. Aid students to develop positive self-concepts.
d. Encourage the attainment of prosocial behaviors.
e. Aid students to develop self-control.

13.14 Indicate which of the preceding principles is easiest for a teacher to implement and which is most difficult.

13.15 Calysn and Kenny found that teaching students basic skills as a means of enhancing their self-concepts was more effective than developing self-concepts and then teaching basic skills. Relate this finding to conditions in the school that probably lead to a lowering of a student's academic self-concept.

13.16 Describe a few specific activities that teachers can employ to foster prosocial behavior in their students.

13.17 How may self-control of learning activities and conduct be taught effectively?

ENCOURAGING DISCIPLINED BEHAVIOR

How is classroom discipline related to classroom learning generally? Effective classroom discipline is not possible under poorly guided learning conditions. Desirable learning conditions were presented in Chapters 7–12. Discipline problems arise much less frequently where these desirable conditions are operative. Fostering personality integration furthers self-discipline in students, as was indicated earlier in this chapter. Thus, classroom discipline methods should be directed toward fostering the personality integration of the individual student as well as toward creating a good learning environment for all students.

The desired goal of classroom discipline methods is that students exercise self-control of their learning activities and conduct. Some students in some situations exercise self-control that is conducive to an excellent learning environment for all the students. However, in most sitations it is necessary to exercise external control of the conduct of some students. In this part of the chapter, our concern is with identifying the bases of discipline problems and actively fostering disciplined conduct in the classroom and school.

Recognizing Extent and Types of Discipline Problems

Discipline problems have become very serious in our schools. In 1980, Gallup's annual poll of the public's attitude toward school ranked discipline as the major problem (Gallup, 1980). Regarding the most serious kinds of misconduct, the public believed (1) that parents, rather than the courts, should deal with school truancy; (2) that the schools, rather than the courts, should deal with fighting in school, using drugs or alcohol on school property, striking a teacher, or stealing clothing or money from other students; and (3) that the courts should deal with vandalism of school property and bringing weapons to school. A later poll (Gallup, 1983) showed discipline still to be the major problem in our schools. In this poll, the first four reasons given for lack of discipline in the school were as follows: lack of discipline in the home (72% of the respondents), lack of respect for law and authority throughout society (54%), students who are constant trouble-makers can't be removed from school (42%), and some teachers are not trained properly to deal with discipline problems (42%). From these two polls we see that the public no longer regards ineffective teachers as the major cause of discipline problems and that the home and the courts, rather than the school, must deal with some of the problems.

Teachers participating in a national poll of the National Education Association in 1980 indicated that discipline was a major problem for them (*Phi Delta Kappan*, 1980). Fifty-four percent of the teachers reported that student behavior interfered with their teaching. The teachers felt that they could not independently control many of the serious behavior problems. They indicated that the schools' written discipline policies were clear but were not consistently applied (67%), were not strict enough (51%), and were not sufficiently comprehensive (58%).

Literally hundreds of different classroom disturbances and student behavior problems may be characterized as discipline problems. Kooi and Schutz (1965) consolidated the most frequent types of classroom disturbances of the 1960s into five categories. The categories and examples of each follow:

1. Physical aggression: hitting, pushing, bullying.
2. Peer affinity: whispering, moving without permission.
3. Attention seeking: passing notes, making wisecracks.
4. Challenge to authority: disobedience, protesting amount of work.
5. Critical dissension: making criticisms that are not constructive.

To this earlier list must be added the very serious current problems of physical attack on students and teachers, truancy, vandalism, stealing, bringing weapons to school, and using drugs and alcohol on school property. Unfortunately, preventive programs thus far have failed to reduce the use of alcohol and drugs by youth (Nathan, 1983), and most schools have no positive means of dealing effectively with alcohol and drug use. Suspension, however, is rapidly increasing.

Identifying Environmental Factors That Influence Student Conduct

The environments of students influence their behavior in school. Environmental factors often cited as influences upon student behavior include (1) the family situation, (2) the peer group, (3) television viewing, (4) the social-psychological climate of the school, and (5) teacher behaviors.

Family Situation

Earlier in this chapter home conditions were shown to be related to personality integration. Unfavorable aspects of the family situation were discussed in relation to divorce, sex-role socialization, and parental attitudes toward the education of their children. In connection with school discipline, teachers most often cited irresponsible parents and unsatisfactory home conditions as the two factors that influence misbehavior in public schools ("Discipline," *Today's Education,* September/October, 1976). Swick (1980) reported malnutrition, lack of sleep, child abuse and neglect, excessive television viewing, and violence to be the main home conditions associated with lack of school discipline. As was indicated earlier, the public believes that lack of discipline in the home and lack of respect for law and order throughout society are the two main causes of lack of discipline in the school (Gallup, 1983).

Peer Group

The family, in many cases, is no longer the student's psychological home. As parents spend less and less time with their children—either out of necessity or choice—their influence is often weakened. As a result, the peer group and the media dominate the behavior of millions of young people attending schools throughout the country.

Peer group influences are often the cause of delinquent, aggressive, and violent student behavior (Feldhusen, 1978). The peer group that causes the most severe behavior problems is the gang. The crime rate in school is reported to be proportional to gang presence and crime activity in the school area (National Institute of Education, 1977). Gangs are the chief cause of fear among students and teachers in many large city schools, because gang members who attend school are often armed (Neill, 1978). For the students in peer groups that engage in frequent misbehavior or delinquency, the most effective way to resist further misbehavior or delinquency is to terminate their association with these groups (Knight & West, 1975).

Television Viewing

The influence of television on students has become more evident. Most American students spend more hours watching TV than they spend in school. According to Postman, who was interviewed in *U.S. News & World Report* ("TV's 'disastrous' impact on children," January 19, 1981, p. 43), "Between the ages of 6 and 18, the average child spends roughly 15,000 to 16,000 hours in front of a television set, whereas school consumes no more than 13,000 hours." This fact represents a difference of more than two school years. Television is everywhere, and it affects not only the attitudes and values of young people, but also their behavior.

Television teaches children to behave in socially acceptable ways; but it also causes problems. As was indicated earlier in Chapter 6, Eron (1982) and Eron, Heusmann, Brice, Fischer, and Mermelstein (1983) concluded that many boys and girls who view violence and aggression in television shows learn to behave with violence and aggression. Busch (1978) and Hornik (1978) propose that students who view television many hours daily do not learn reading and listening skills. Not having these skills, they are unable to perform many of the learning tasks of the typical classroom and thus experience discipline problems.

Social-Psychological Climate of the School

The family, peers, and television viewing can be viewed as factors outside the school that influence student behavior. Does the school climate itself affect student behaviors? Each school is a social system with a unique social-psychological environment and has been viewed in recent years as a major cause of its own problems. Duke (1978) reported the following conditions as contributing to a school environment that fosters student misbehavior and discipline problems (Duke, 1978, p. 427):

1. Grossly inadequate vocational guidance.
2. Too many harmful teachers.
3. Lack of individualized instruction.
4. Inadequate curriculum.
5. Lack of personal support.
6. Too few alternative ways to learn.

Although the preceding conditions contribute to discipline problems, they should not be overemphasized, as Duke (1978) states:

> In thinking about the various arguments implicating the school system in the genesis of behavior problems, one fact stands out. As the focus for blame becomes more diffuse, the quality of supporting evidence decreases. Fewer efforts to blame the school system are based on controlled investigations involving carefully selected samples than are the studies that single out family background, peer group, or teacher variables. A greater tendency also exists for critics of the school system to make sweeping statements condemning factors that are very difficult to define or measure. (pp. 427–428)

How school size affects student behavior is an important, easily measurable factor of school environment. Larger schools have more violence, crime, and vandalism than smaller schools (National Institute of Education, 1977). Large schools, particularly in urban areas, compress thousands of youth into a small space, are hard to manage, are impersonal, and facilitate delinquent peer associations. In schools with populations of 3000 or more, students easily become anonymous and can drop out emotionally and/or academically without being noticed (Tewel & Chalfin, 1980).

Teacher Behaviors

Teachers whose classrooms are disorganized, whose intructional units are poorly planned, and whose attitudes toward students are negative have a degrading effect on student self-concepts. These teachers are, in fact, fostering discipline problems (Swick, 1980). A comprehensive review of research concerning teacher-related variables and student misbehavior indicated a number of teacher characteristics to be associated with student misconduct (Kauffman, 1977). These included insensitivity to the student's individuality, inappropriate expectations for the students, inconsistent classroom management, instruction in nonfunctional skills, and harsh methods of controlling student behaviors.

Fostering Disciplined Conduct

We have seen that many discipline problems cannot be solved by teachers working independently. However, problems that are directly attributable to teacher influence should be eliminated. Techniques of classroom management have been developed and the use of punishment and modeling has been refined to aid teachers in fostering disciplined student conduct.

Specific Management Techniques

How teachers manage their classrooms is crucial to developing positive student self-concepts and discipline. Fortunately, two books have been published recently that contain many useful, practical suggestions for teachers (Kohut & Range, 1979; Swick, 1980). A synthesis of their most important suggestions follows. Note that many practices are preventive in nature.

SUGGESTIONS FOR
FOSTERING CLASSROOM DISCIPLINE

1. *Learn school policies.* Know what the school expects from both the teacher and students concerning discipline.
2. *Establish a few classroom rules or guidelines.* These should be fair and reasonable, and their rationale should be explained to the students. Don't have a long list of do's and don'ts.
3. *Discuss expectations.* Explain the purposes and goals of the class and the obligations of both the students and the teacher to make the learning experience successful.
4. *Learn names.* Learn the names of the students as quickly as possible. Initially, a seating chart may be necessary. Calling a student by name early in the year gives the student a sense of well-being that he or she is more than just a student in your class. Furthermore, students will perceive that you are well-organized and in control.
5. *Overplan lessons.* For the first few weeks, overplanning lessons will impress upon students that the entire class period will be used constructively. Students' expectations of how you value the time spent with them, as well as of your control of the learning situation, are often established very early. By your model, students will determine the values and expectations you desire.
6. *Set a positive example.* Teachers who are cynical, unmotivated, and unorganized are asking for behavior problems. The teacher who is well organized, listens to students, and portrays interest and concern in active learning has fewer behavior problems than less involved teachers.
7. *Invite students to succeed.* Give students verbal and nonverbal attention. When students who are becoming behavior problems begin to receive positive messages from the teacher on a continuous basis, their behavior problems diminish. This is a practice which is easier said than done. However, the cycle of negative messages–negative behavior–negative messages should be replaced with a positive approach if the teacher wants to see positive behavior.
8. *Be firm and consistent.* This does not mean harshness. Firm and consistent teachers can also be friendly, caring, loving, supportive, and warm with students. Misbehavior in students is usually not a negative reaction to the teacher personally, but is caused by many other factors, including the students' perception of the role as "teacher." Firmness and consistency in discipline provide an environment where all students can expect fairness and can have a feeling of security concerning behavior expectations.

   Although a firm handling of students who misbehave often will be forceful and require negative expressions, positive responses are most effective in dealing with and solving discipline problems. The following example indicates how a firm response can be positively handled: "Paul, you must not feel well today! You know pushing is not your way of doing things. You spend some time alone until you can act more like the Paul I know" (Swick, 1980). Note how the teacher's response to Paul indicates what was done wrong, that Paul can behave better, and that the purpose of the punishment was given.
9. *Restore order when a problem occurs.* When serious misconduct occurs in class, the other students will judge the teacher by the way the misbehavior is handled. The restoration of classroom order is the first priority. Minor problems may be handled by ignoring them or by simply stating to the student what the misbehavior was and reminding the student of

the preferred behavior; for example, "Lisa, stop writing notes and get to work on our assignment."

10. *Avoid emotional outbursts.* Avoid arguing with the student in front of the class, making the punishment personal, being sarcastic, or making threats that cannot be fulfilled. If the situation is tense, the use of humor can often be the best course of action to defuse the situation. Relax the other students and thwart an offending student's challenge to your authority. At times, removal of a student from the classroom may be the best method of restoring classroom order. Other students feel more comfortable when they know the teacher is in control of the class.

11. *Handle your own problems whenever possible.* Students behave better in classrooms where they know the teacher really is in control and does not always search for the principal to handle problems. Although some situations may require outside help, try to handle misbehavior yourself whenever possible.

12. *Help students understand the negative consequences of their misbehavior.* The sooner students perceive their behavior is hurting themselves and their classmates, including their peers' negative reactions toward them, the greater the chances that the misbehavior will diminish. Help students understand that positive individual behavior is much more conducive to making the whole class successful than misbehavior.

13. *Schedule conferences when necessary.* If initial efforts to control student behavior fail, an individual teacher-pupil conference allows the teacher to get to know the student better, to identify possible causes of the misbehavior, and to plan solutions to the problem. Parents can provide the teacher with information that can be useful in understanding the student's problem. Parents can also suggest what actions might be most effective and speak to their child about the classroom problem. When parents and teachers are communicating with each other, behavior problems are more likely to be solved than if this contact does not exist. Prior to scheduling or speaking with parents, it is often useful to get the input of other teachers, guidance counselors, the school psychologist, and the principal concerning their experiences with the particular student and the parents.

In recent years, there is increasing interest in reasoning with students as a means of securing compliance with the teachers' suggestions. The reasons for complying change from one age group to the next in a manner similar to moral reasoning, discussed in Chapter 12. For example, Kuczynski (1983) found that 9- and 10-year-olds complied most when they were aware that not complying would result in unfavorable consequences to others. They complied less and about equally when simply told to comply and when aware that not complying would result in unfavorable consequences to themselves.

Use of Punishment

In Chapter 4, we saw that punishment is not as effective as positive reinforcement in controlling behavior and that in some situations punishment has negative consequences. At times, however, because a student engages in disruptive behavior that is not immediately controllable with reinforcements, punishment is used to get the student to desist. Moreover, if the punishment is accompanied with reasoning, the student may develop self-discipline and self-control.

Early, sharp punishment immediately following misconduct produces more self-control than mild, deferred punishment (Cheyne & Walters, 1969; LaVoie, 1974; Parke, 1969). If the punishment is accompanied by a rationale, however, the effects upon self-control are longer-lasting. To be effective, justifications, or *rationales,* that accompany punishment must be at a level students can readily understand.

Research concerning punishment rationales and self-control was summarized by Pressley (1979): "Rationales which emphasize the property rights and feelings of others become increasingly effective with increasing age. These rationales require more cognitive sophistication to understand than either simple prohibitions or rationales emphasizing physical consequences" (p. 341). Thus, rationales for punishment which emphasize how the offenders' actions harmed other people are more effective in bringing about self-control in adolescents than in children of elementary school age. On the other hand, rationales that emphasize the negative consequences to the misbehaving individual are more effective with elementary school children.

Modeling Self-disciplined Behaviors

We saw in Chapter 4 and in this chapter that much learning occurs through observing a model. Students can learn self-control and socially constructive attitudes and conduct if they have appropriate models.

One of the chief ways teachers maintain control of their classrooms is by maintaining control of themselves. The teacher who is liked by students and whose behavior is in control can be sure that some students will also learn self-control.

Some teachers consciously interact with students verbally and nonverbally while the students are working and indicate support and concern for the students. Other teachers sit at their desks and are perceived by the students as lazy and uninterested. Both kinds of teacher behaviors may be imitated by the students.

In conclusion, one of the best ways that teachers can be very effective in developing positive self-control in students is by creating and maintaining a classroom environment that is not beset by disciplinary problems. Studying the principles of personality integration, self-concept development, and some of the factors that contribute to student problems will assist you in understanding student behaviors. Learning the classroom management procedures described in this chapter and in Chapter 6 will enable you to minimize your role as a disciplinarian and maximize it as a teacher.

13.18 The goals of classroom discipline are creating a favorable learning environment for all students and fostering the personality integration of each student. Is one of these possible without the other? Explain.

13.19 The public seems to agree that the school, rather than the courts or other agencies, should deal with fighting in school, using drugs or alcohol on school property, striking a teacher, and stealing from other students. Who in the school should deal with these acts when they occur?

13.20 Summarize the main characteristics of the student and family conditions associated with discipline problems in school.

13.21 Delinquent behavior is often associated with peer group, gang activities. Why do teachers and parents hesitate to break up gangs?

13.22 Indicate what teachers might do in the classroom to lessen the undesirable effects of TV viewing on student behavior.

13.23 Give a concrete example of each of the six conditions of the school that foster student misbehavior:

a. Grossly inadequate vocational guidance.
b. Too many harmful teachers.
c. Lack of individualized instruction.
d. Inadequate curriculum.
e. Lack of personal support.
f. Too few alternative ways to learn.

13.24 Draw up a list of teacher characteristics and teaching methods that foster discipline problems.

13.25 Return to the 13 management techniques for fostering discipline. Estimate your ability to carry each one out successfully, given classes of normally developing students who are not excessively aggressive or withdrawn.

13.26 Prepare ideas to present to a student to accompany a punishment for a serious misbehavior. State the misbehavior, indicate the punishment, and give the age of the student.

13.27 Describe ways that a teacher may model a favorable environment for learning.

13.28 Review and Application. Recall the most important information regarding each of the following concepts, and identify at least one possible use of the information by you as a learner, a teacher, or both:

Bases of Personality Integration
   Good Health
   Reasonable Achievements
   Positive Self-Concept
   Adequate Modes of Adjustment
   Secure Family Environment
Principles for Fostering Personality Integration
Encouraging Disciplined Behavior
   Recognizing Types of Discipline Problems
   Identifying Environmental Factors That Influence Student Conduct
   Fostering Disciplined Conduct

SUMMARY

Personality integration is reflected in a healthy self-concept, self-control, ethical behavior, and social responsibility. Good physical and mental health, achievement in line with ability, a healthy self-concept, and appropriate modes of coping with frustrating situations are basic to personality integration. Family life, as well as schooling, contributes greatly to personality integration. The negative effects on children of a poor home situation are widespread and serious. Understanding the child's emotional problems arising from the home situation and responding to the child with empathy are increasingly important concerns of teachers.

Personality integration may be fostered by applying the following principles appropriately at different school levels:

1. Maintain an orderly learning environment.
2. Help students set and attain realistic achievement goals.
3. Aid students to develop positive self-concepts.
4. Encourage the attainment of prosocial behaviors.
5. Aid students to develop self-control.

Fostering the personality integration of students and maintaining discipline are very closely related. The desired goal of classroom discipline methods is that students exercise increasing self-control of their activities and behave in an orderly manner. Despite this goal, lack of discipline is regarded by the public and by many teachers as the foremost problem of education.

The kinds and frequency of discipline problems are well documented. Similarly, conditions related to discipline problems of individual students and conditions related to the home, the peer group, TV viewing, and the school environment itself are quite well understood. In many schools, most discipline problems can be overcome by a consistent schoolwide effort that involves cooperation by the school staff—including administrators and counselors—and by more enlightened and skillful classroom control by individual teachers.

SUGGESTIONS FOR FURTHER READING

Charles, C. M. *Building classroom discipline*. New York: Longman, 1981.

This paperback presents seven widely used models of discipline and indicates how to develop an integrated approach that includes preventive, corrective, and supportive techniques.

Duke, D. D. (Ed.). *Helping teachers manage classrooms*. Washington, D.C.: Association for Supervision and Curriculum Development, 1983.

Focuses on improving discipline with emphasis on classroom management techniques and special problems of teachers and students. Chapter 7 presents a strong case for teaching self-discipline and explains how to proceed.

Etzioni, A. The role of self-discipline. *Phi Delta Kappan*, 1982, *64*(3), 184–187.

Etzioni relates discipline to character development. Students learn self-discipline, including the making of wise decisions, in carefully structured situations, rather than in authoritarian or permissive situations.

Gallup, G. H. The 15th annual Gallup Poll of the public's attitudes toward the public schools. *Phi Delta Kappan*, 1983, *65*(1), 33–47.

The top four problems of the schools indicated by the persons who participated in the 1983 poll were lack of discipline (25%), use of drugs (18%), poor curriculum/poor standards (14%), and lack of proper financial support (13%).

Kounin, J. S. *Discipline and group management in classrooms*. New York: Holt, Rinehart and Winston, 1970.

This book presents the practical suggestions of a keen observer of classroom situations.

Mischel, W. Convergences and challenges in the search for consistency. *American Psychologist*, 1984, *39*, 351–364.

A scholarly interpretation of how the study of personality has changed in recent years and why the conclusions drawn regarding the consistency of a person's behavior have become more tentative. Special attention is given to children's learning to delay gratification of needs.

Rubenstein, E. A. Television and behavior: Research conclusions of the 1982 NIMH report and their policy implications. *American Psychologist*, 1983, *30*(7), 820–825.

Presents the many undesirable effects of a large amount of uncritical, unsupervised television viewing on children and youth.

Scott-Jones, D. Family influences on cognitive development and school achievement. In E. W. Gordon (Ed.), *Review of Research in Education* (Vol. 11). Washington, D.C.: American Educational Research Association, 1984, pp. 259–304.

An update of research and theory regarding the impact of the family on the children's cognitive development and school achievement.

Wayson, W. W., & Lasley, T. J. Climates for excellence: Schools that foster self-discipline. *Phi Delta Kappan*, 1984, *65*, 419–421.

These authors present principles for building self-discipline, based on their extensive research.

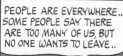

CHAPTER 14

RETENTION AND TRANSFER

FEATURES OF LONG-TERM MEMORY

FACTORS AFFECTING RETENTION AND FORGETTING

METAMEMORY

BASES OF TRANSFER OF LEARNING

PRINCIPLES FOR FOSTERING RETENTION AND TRANSFER

This chapter completes the sequence of securing high motivation for learning (Chapter 7), making the initial learning of different outcomes effective (Chapters 8–13), and ensuring retention and transfer of what has been learned. The chapter starts with an explanation of how information is stored in long-term memory and how it is subsequently retrieved after extended periods of time. The factors that improve retention and retard forgetting are identified. Next to be discussed is *metamemory*, that is, understanding one's own memory system and strategies for remembering. We then move to a consideration of transferring what we have recently learned to performing new tasks. Knowledge about retention, transfer, and instruction is applied to teaching for retention and transfer in the last part of the chapter. Much of the information throughout the chapter should be helpful in understanding and possibly improving one's own retention.

FEATURES OF LONG-TERM MEMORY

Storing Different Kinds of Information

Encoding Information for Long-Term Storage

Retrieving Information from Long-Term Memory

It is convenient to separate *long-term memory* from the *sensory register* and *short-term memory* for discussion purposes. However, in the initial learning of any outcome, they are closely related. Therefore, it is appropriate to review the information-processing sequence presented in Chapter 4. The phases and processes of the sequence are depicted in Figure 14.1.

We may now examine long-term memory more analytically, starting with the storage process. There are two different dimensions of storage. One

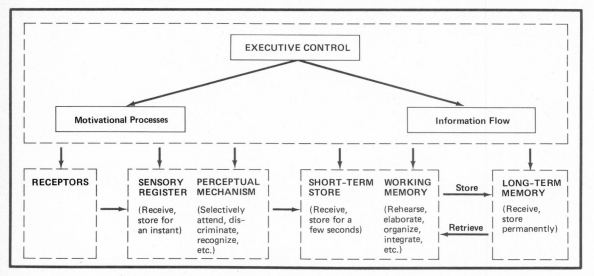

Figure 14.1 Information-processing model of retention.

is the *kind of stores,* also referred to as *type of memory,* and the other is the *form of encoding.* These are depicted in Figure 14.2.

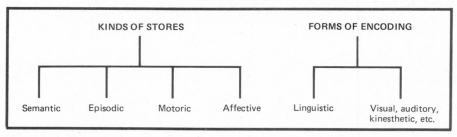

Figure 14.2 Storage process in long-term memory.

Storing Different Kinds of Information

The four kinds of stores were discussed in Chapter 4 and are reviewed briefly here. *Semantic memory* (Tulving, 1972) includes the meanings gained from using and understanding language. Specific factual information and the meanings of concepts, principles, and theories, as discussed in previous chapters, are regarded as semantic content. Verbal information about procedures, such as the rules of grammar, and strategies of learning discussed in Chapter 8, are also forms of semantic content.

Episodic memory is our permanent record of events that we have personally experienced (Tulving, 1972). Episodic memory is illustrated by remembering your first day at school or remembering that you saw five topics listed under the title of this chapter.

The retention of motoric actions parallels that of semantic and episodic content (Singer, 1978). Internal motor programs control our movements used in skilled verbal or motor performances, as was indicated in Chapter 11. Motor programs that include a model of the skill and plans for performing it are held in a *motoric store*.

Knowledge is fragmentary regarding memory of the affect, or feeling, that accompanies an experience and that leads to good-bad, approach-avoidance, and similar judgments. As we saw in Chapter 12, Zajonc (1980) proposes that affect is stored during initial learning and is retrieved at the time the event or other experience is recalled. The retrieval from *affective memory* is typically involuntary. Thus, we involuntarily experience fright as a greatly feared object comes into view.

Retrieving and relating two or more kinds of content are common and facilitate initial learning. For example, in the early phase of skill learning, both motoric information and semantic information are retrieved from memory and guide the performance of the skill. Similarly, episodic content and feeling are retrieved when recalling an episode, for example, the marriage of a close friend.

Encoding Information for Long-term Storage

Encoding occurs as a function of holding and processing information in working memory. Both a sufficient amount of time (Pezdek & Miceli, 1982) and effective processing strategies are required for new information to be encoded and stored in long-term memory (Masson & Miller, 1983).

In what form is information encoded and subsequently stored in long-term memory? Present assumptions are that it is encoded linguistically and also in different kinds of images. Some aspects of an episode that we have experienced, for example, eating breakfast this morning, may be stored and recalled in the form of visual images. For example, describing a cup used at breakfast is guided by the visual image of it that is retrieved from long-term memory. Sounds that we attend to are encoded and stored aurally. Thus, we recognize a person whom we hear on the telephone by retrieving the sound of the person's voice. Movement patterns are stored kinesthetically. You will recall the visual, auditory, and other images are encoded and stored in a transformed neural form, not as exact replications of what is experienced.

Linguistic encoding takes place when we gain information from activities involving words. We are able to organize, store, and retrieve vast amounts of information linguistically. In this regard, Miller and Johnson-Laird (1976) indicate that if we have the meaning of a word, hearing the word will help us to retrieve the meaning of the word and the meaning of all other words related to it. Pause momentarily to recall as much as you can regarding short-term memory. Do you recall anything in addition to information expressed in words?

Being able to relate and retrieve information from different memory stores, such as semantic and motoric, greatly increases our capability for learning. Being able to relate the linguistic and the imaginal codes does also. As we saw in Chapter 8, the key word method in foreign language learning involves linking a sound of the foreign language word *(linguistic code)* with a key word, thus providing an auditory link between the two. Then a visual image *(visual code)* is formed of the key word and the English equivalent, thus forming a visual link between these two words.

Interaction between two codes usually has a strengthening effect, but it sometimes has a weakening effect on one of them. Loftus, Miller, and Burns (1978) presented to college students a series of slides depicting an automobile-pedestrian accident. Groups of the students were then verbally presented one of three kinds of information: consistent, misleading, or irrelevant. The misleading information produced the least accurate recall of the accident. Apparently it weakened the visual image store. Furthermore, it had a greater impact when introduced just prior to the final recall test rather than immediately after viewing the slides.

Some persons are more able than others to store and retrieve visual images. The same is true for the other modes of encoding. The differences in modes of encoding may be reflected in students' preferences for learning by different sensory modalities. Thus, some prefer to learn by listening and reading, some by seeing, and some by doing. Similarly, interest in careers such as art, music, athletics, and teaching English may be related to encoding capabilities.

Retrieving Information from Long-term Memory

Retrieval of information is quite simple when we can ask ourselves a question and recall the desired information. When we cannot recall something that we are sure we once knew, there are a few search strategies to help us (Morris, 1979). One strategy for searching long-term memory involves mentally recreating the context in which the initial learning occurred (Watkins, Ho, & Tulving, 1976). Thus, if you can recall the classroom or other place where you met a person, it may help you to recall the person's name. Similarly, if you can recall the classroom setting on the day a professor lectured, it may help you recall information presented in the lecture.

Another strategy involving context is to try to reconstruct an event or episode. For example, if people misplace reading glasses, they try to reconstruct the situation from the time of last using the glasses. An attempt is made to remember when the glasses were last used, what was being read, and so on. Lindsay and Norman (1972) describe a systematic reconstruction strategy. Consider this question: "What were you doing on Monday afternoon in the second week of December two years ago?" The question is broken down into more specific questions, such as "Where was I two years ago?" "What happened about two weeks before Christmas?" "What happened about two weeks after Thanksgiving?" From these questions, more specific questions are generated. Eventually, a detailed timetable is reconstructed, and a great deal of information is recalled.

Two other search strategies have been identified. One involves the alphabet. If a name is to be recalled, we may go through the alphabet systematically in the expectation that the first letter of the name will trigger the complete name.

Tulving (1968) demonstrated how having the name of a concept facilitates retrieving examples of the concept. High school students were told to learn and remember a list of words. The words represented things of various categories, for example, things found on a farm (wheat, tractor); substances for flavoring food (sugar, cloves); and musical instruments (drum, flute). Half the students, after being presented the list, were asked to recall all the words they remembered. The other half were given the category names as *retrieval cues* and were asked to recall all the words belonging to each category. This form of cuing greatly facilitated recall. Tulving recommended teaching students this strategy by having them identify key concepts when learning initially. Recalling the key concepts then facilitates subsequent retrieval of the related information.

Children progressively become more adept in searching their memories, but young children of primary school age profit from receiving instructions to guide their search (Kobasigawa, 1977). Six- and eight-year-olds were shown cue cards to aid their recall of items related to each cue. Without instruction as to how to use the cue cards, the 6-year-olds performed less well. With instruction, there were no differences between the two age-groups.

14.1 Indicate the role of executive control and describe the flow of information between working memory and long-term memory as you recall the phases and the processes involved in the information-processing sequence.

14.2 Give an example of what is stored in each kind of long-term memory: semantic, episodic, motoric, and affective.

14.3 Give an example of each kind of encoding: linguistic, visual, auditory, olfactory, and kinesthetic.

14.4 Give one example of information pertaining to this course in Ed. Psych. that you might retrieve by using each of the following search and retrieval strategies: (a) recreating the context in which initial learning took place, (b) reconstructing an event or episode, (c) using the alphabet, and (d) using concepts.

FACTORS AFFECTING RETENTION AND FORGETTING

Type of Learning Outcome

Conditions of Initial Learning

Interference and Reorganization

The type of learning outcome has a powerful relationship to retention. For example, motor skills are remembered much better than technical information. The conditions of initial learning, such as learning with meaning and intending to remember, greatly affect long-term storage and subsequent retrieval. Interference of new learning with what has already been learned and reorganization of information while retrieving it both play important roles in retention and forgetting. Since these factors have been considered in different contexts in Chapters 7–13, they are only highlighted here.

Type of Learning Outcome

Figure 14.3 shows curves of retention for three types of outcomes — ideas, facts, and nonsense syllables. Ideas, corresponding to concepts and principles, are remembered for long periods of time. Many concepts learned at a beginning level in early childhood — such as *number, animal,* and *plant* — become stronger and remain strong throughout one's life. On the other hand, factual information, such as the names of the countries of the world or the dates of historical events, is forgotten quite rapidly if it is not used. Nonsense syllables and bits of information of low meaningfulness are forgotten almost immediately.

Differential retention of different types of learning outcomes has been identified at various school levels. Highlights of a classical report by Sterrett and Davis (1954, pp. 455–466) follow:

RETENTION OF SCHOOL SUBJECT MATTER

ELEMENTARY SCHOOL
Reading achievement increased during the summer vacation.
Knowledge of specific arithmetic facts decreased during the summer more rapidly than knowledge of fundamental arithmetic operations.

SECONDARY SCHOOL
Loss in mathematics knowledge ranged from 10% during the summer to 33% during the school year.
Loss in scientific knowledge was much higher for technical terms than for general information and applications of factual information. Seniors' scores fell 42% three months after completing an advanced chemistry course. Five years after high school graduation, college students were able to recall about 19% of the informational material of high school chemistry.

COLLEGE
Loss in college science courses varied from 50% after a four-month interval to 94% after one year. The loss was greater for technical information than for principles and their applications.
Retention was higher after four years for required subjects, such as history and English, than for electives, such as physics, chemistry, and Latin.

Notice that reading achievement increased during the summer. Skills, including verbal skills, typically are not forgotten. Furthermore, many elementary school children read during the summer. Those who already have some independence in reading improve without instruction. Students of all school ages tend not to use mathematical or any other kind of technical information outside of the classroom setting. Much of this kind of information is forgotten shortly after a course is completed.

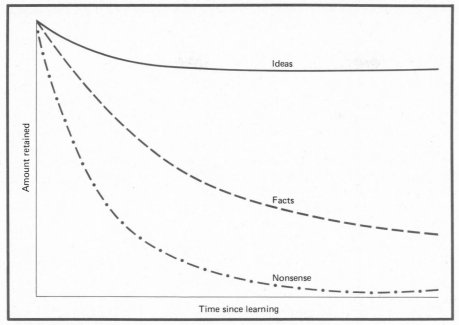

Figure 14.3 Retention curves for different classes of material.
Source: Deese & Hulse, 1967, p. 383.

Conditions of Initial Learning

The stage for long-term retention is set at the time of initial learning. Learning with meaning, intending to remember, and organizing the material to be remembered are three of the most critical conditions of initial learning.

Learning with Meaning

Learning with meaning leads to better retention than memorizing without understanding. In a classical experiment, children of similar characteristics were taught subtraction by a meaningful method and by a mechanical method (Brownell & Moser, 1949). Those taught by the meaningful method learned the meaning of place value and how to apply it when doing subtraction exercises involving borrowing. The other group was taught a mechanical method and then drilled on exercises that required borrowing. Those who were taught the mechanical method made more rapid progress in the first few days because the meaningful method required more time to learn. At the end of 15 days, however, they were already dropping behind those taught by the meaningful method. More important, when a new learning situation was arranged, those who had been taught understanding of the subtraction process performed far better than those who had not.

When a heterogeneous group of children is given the same material to learn, it is invariably not meaningful for some. The result is that they forget it. But when the material is matched in difficulty to each child's achievement level, there is no difference in retention among children of low, average, and high intelligence. In one study of this effect, children were pretested and then taught a series of ten subtraction items immediately above the level of difficulty at which each had performed correctly in the pretest. Each child was taught each item in as meaningful a way as possible and then given an acquisition test. A five-minute interpolated activity followed the acquisition test. As Figure 14.4 shows, after this interpolated activity, the retention scores of two groups went up slightly. When the same test was repeated seven weeks later, the percentage of retention was nearly the same for all three IQ groups: about 90% of what each group had retained five minutes after initial learning activity was completed. Similar results were obtained with the same children in counting and addition (Feldhusen & Klausmeier, 1959; Klausmeier & Check, 1962).

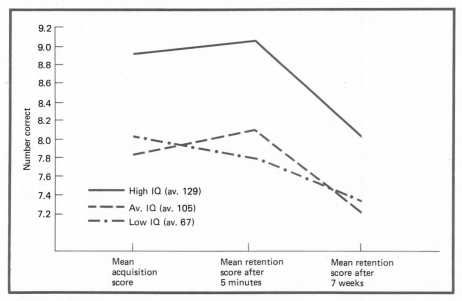

Figure 14.4 Retention in subtraction by children of low, average, and high intelligence.
Source: Klausmeier, Feldhusen, & Check, 1959, p. 69.

Intending to Remember

Intending to remember facilitates initial acquisition and recall regardless of the type of material and the meaningfulness of the learning activity. Students with an intention to remember at the time of initial learning attend to the learning task more intently and process the information more thoroughly. They then recall it better later. To illustrate, undergraduates in an educational psychology course studied a passage on the history of drug addiction (Ausubel, Schpoont, & Cukier, 1957). The control group was instructed to read the passage at normal speed, to use the rest of the period to study the facts and ideas, and to be prepared for a test that would immediately follow their reading and study. This acquisition test was administered. Fourteen days later, they were given an unannounced retention test. The same procedure was used with the experimental group, with one exception. They were told immediately after completing the acquisition test that another test on the material would be given in 14 days. The scores of the two groups were not significantly different on the acquisition test. However, the experimental group, that is, the group told at the time of the acquisition test that it would be retested in 14 days, scored *lower* than the control group on the retention test. Thus, intent to remember established at the time of initial learning facilitates retention. Intent to remember introduced after initial learning does not improve retention.

Organization

Organization involves actively relating and connecting information. Two familiar external organizational frameworks for large amounts of information are taxonomies and other hierarchical arrangements. Topical and chronological outlines are other organizational frameworks that are used widely in textbooks and other instructional materials. This textbook uses conceptual structures, as explained in Chapters 1 and 8. Using these structures to relate what you already know with the new text information improves initial learning. In turn, the key concepts of the structures that you recall provide the cues for searching long-term memory and retrieving all the information you have regarding the concepts. As you organize your existing knowledge and then reorganize it based on the new information, you construct an increasingly powerful and usable structure of knowledge.

Lange (1978) indicates that students encode and store meaningfully organized units of material in the same manner in which they initially perceive the organization of the material. He found that students readily accepted key words and the accompanying visuals for learning a foreign language. Lange indicates that students profit from instruction that helps them organize. Furthermore, they learn how to organize by observing exemplary organizational frameworks.

Interference and Reorganization

A child spells a word correctly on a test but cannot recall the correct spelling the next day in a writing activity. A college senior cannot recall content learned at the beginning of the semester on a final exam. What may produce forgetting of this kind?

Interference

That learning new material may interfere with the recall of what has been learned earlier has been long-established. This kind of interference is called *retroactive inhibition*. Retroactive inhibition sharply reduces the retention of relatively meaningless material and to a lesser extent reduces the retention of meaningful prose.

In a series of experiments (Bower, 1974; Thorndyke & Hayes-Roth, 1979), the main characters and theme in two successive prose passages were held constant, but the details regarding the names of the characters, their occupations, dates of events, and so on, were deliberately changed in the second passage. Study of the second passage increased the recall of the main characters and theme of the two passages, but it weakened the recall of the detailed information of the first paragraph. Thus, whether later learning interfered with or facilitated the recall of earlier information depended on the particular information that was presented in the second passage.

Anderson (1980) explains retroactive inhibition as failure to activate semantic networks of information in long-term memory. Thus, something is learned at a rudimentary level once. Accordingly, the internally represented network of it is very weak and becomes even weaker as competing information is stored. Later, this internal network cannot be retrieved.

Two practical suggestions may be made about retroactive inhibition. The first is to avoid learning the kind of material that interferes with recalling earlier material. The second is to practice and review the earlier material to strengthen the semantic network.

Reorganization

Reorganizing material during the retrieval process may result in failure to recall even when no interference occurs. Consider an example of reorganization during retrieval. A student learns to spell *accommodate* correctly as part of the organized program of spelling instruction. Later in the day, the student uses the word in writing a story. The student then writes *accomodate*. In the retrieval process, an incorrect spelling has been reorganized and accepted as correct.

A slightly different viewpoint about retrieval failure is embodied in the *subsumption theory* discussed in Chapter 4 (Ausubel, 1963). You may recall that, according to this theory, specific items of information are related to a more inclusive concept at the time of initial learning. Both the specific items and the concept are remembered for a while. With the passage of time and lack of use, the specific items cannot be retrieved from memory, because each specific item can no longer be dissociated from the more inclusive concept. To illustrate, a child learns to recognize a particular red ball, red crayon, and red pencil when initially learning the concept *red*. A year later, however, the child cannot recall any of the specific items that were involved in initially learning the concept.

14.5 Indicate the main learning outcomes of this chapter that you should focus on learning, using long-term retention as your selection criterion.

14.6 Indicate why meaningful learning results in better long-term retention than the verbatim memorizing of material.

14.7 How is your retention of the main ideas of this chapter affected by what you intend to remember?

14.8 How does having a conceptual structure before starting to study facilitate initial learning and subsequent search and retrieval?

14.9 How do persons learn effective organizational frameworks for storing and subsequently retrieving information?

14.10 Explain how interference, reorganization, and subsumption produce forgetting.

METAMEMORY

Thus far in this chapter, the nature of long-term memory, various strategies for retrieving information, and factors affecting storage and retrieval have been indicated. Knowing about memory and being able to monitor one's own strategies for remembering are designated by the term *metamemory*. The concept of metamemory applies to all aspects of the memory system, not merely long-term memory, and is one aspect of metacognition that was discussed in Chapter 4 (Flavell, 1971). Metamemory is a new and very promising field of study.

Flavell and Wellman (1977) defined an individual's *metamemory schema* as the internal representation of one's knowledge about memory and the memory requirements of a task. The person's metamemory schema determines how well he or she will be able to retrieve what has been learned. An individual's probable memory performance related to any given learning task depends on the individual's knowledge of the characteristics of the items to be learned and the demands of the task, on the individual's memory characteristics, and on the individual's memory strategies relevant to the task—all shown in Figure 14.5 (Flavell & Wellman, 1977, p. 23).

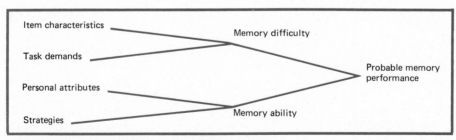

Figure 14.5 An individual's metamemory schema.
Source: Flavell & Wellman, 1977, p. 23.

We may consider each part of the schema in more detail. Regarding item characteristics, the difficulty of recalling the items depends in part upon the number and kind of items. For example, the items may be few or many, and they may or may not be meaningfully related. The difficulty also depends in part on the demands of the task, such as recognizing the items from a list that is given versus recalling them, or reciting a passage verbatim versus recalling the main ideas.

Memory performance on a particular task is related to the individual's personal attributes that are relevant to information retrieval. A person's knowledge regarding the human memory system in general may range from very little to fairly complete. Similarly, recognition of one's own ability to recall the particular task information may be poor to excellent.

Finally, how well a person remembers is related to the person's strategies for remembering a particular task. The person may have effective strategies or none at all.

The powerful idea underlying metamemory is that individuals can learn the requirements of learning tasks, memory strategies, and use of the strategies. It is helpful, of course, for teachers to know memory strategies and to be able to identify the strategies that students may be able to learn. Many strategies related to learning and remembering information of low meaningfulness and to learning and remembering meaningful prose material were described in Chapter 8. Retrieval strategies were described earlier in this chapter.

14.11 Your metamemory consists of your knowledge about memory processes, your knowledge of your capability for remembering different kinds of tasks, your knowledge of memory strategies for storing and for retrieving information, and your knowledge of which strategies to employ in particular situations. Describe your metamemory for remembering the content of this chapter.

14.12 Assume that a week from now you will want to draw Figure 14.5, including the lines and words, depicting the factors influencing memory performance. Estimate the difficulty of this task for you, and outline the strategies you will use to ensure recall.

14.13 Identify what you have learned about memory in this chapter and Chapter 8 to increase your ability to recall.

Similarity of Task Information

Similarity of Information-processing Requirements

BASES OF TRANSFER OF LEARNING

We want students to be able to use initially learned outcomes to learn more advanced outcomes in school and to deal with situations out of school with more effectiveness or other desired consequences. The use of learned outcomes to facilitate learning in other situations is referred to as *transfer of learning.*

Transfer of learning may be positive or negative. *Negative transfer* occurs when learning one outcome interferes with learning a second one (*proactive inhibition*). Thus, learning to spell *believe* may interfere later with learning to spell *bereave* and *receive*. *Positive transfer* occurs when an outcome learned in one situation is remembered and applied to a new situation. For example, learning the rule that "*i* follows *e* except after *c*" facilitates the subsequent spelling of words containing *ei* and *ie*.

Transfer may be lateral or vertical. Through *lateral transfer*, individuals are able to perform a different but similar task of about the same level of complexity as that which they have learned. For example, children learn to recognize new words in a reading class; this achievement helps them recognize new words of about the same difficulty in a social studies text. Through *vertical transfer*, a person is able to learn similar but more advanced material. Here information and skills acquired in one situation facilitate learning new information or skills in the same subject field. For example, learning the concepts *square, rhombus,* and *quadrilateral* enables one to understand the principle that quadrilaterals vary according to the length and parallelism of the sides.

Some persons (e.g., Mayer, 1975; Royer, 1979) make a distinction between near and far transfer. Related to education, *near transfer* refers to the transfer from one school-learned outcome to another. *Far transfer* applies to transfer from the educational setting to the out-of-school world.

Teachers are concerned with securing positive transfer inside and outside the school setting. Teachers and educational policymakers explicitly or implicitly act on a theory or combination of theories of transfer in making decisions concerning what to teach. Two main groups of theories have emerged historically (Klausmeier & Davis, 1969; Ripple & Drinkwater, 1982; Royer, 1979). The first group is based on the similarity of the information between the initial learning task and the transfer task. The second takes similarity of the information into account but also includes the strategies of learning and abilities that may be involved in the two situations.

Similarity of Task Information

Identical-Elements Theory
The identical-elements theory of transfer was formulated by Thorndike (1913). It assumes that elements present in the initial learning situation must also be present in the new situation for transfer to occur. The identical elements are presumed to be specific facts and skills. Thus, after students have mastered an addition fact, for example, 7 + 3, they can use it in learning to solve new problems in which the same fact appears. After they have learned to write a few letters of the alphabet, they can use this skill in learning to write words that include the letters. These are examples of vertical transfer in the educational setting. The theory also points to a practical way to help students with transfer to out-of-school situations, namely, teaching knowledge and skills in school that are identical to those encountered outside the school.

The application of these ideas had profound effects on the curriculum in the first half of this century. For example, the natural sciences were brought into the high school curriculum. Modern foreign languages came in on a widespread basis as replacements for Greek and Latin. Vocational education in its many varieties was started as part of the regular high school curriculum. In elementary education, the idea of identical elements led to identifying the English words and the arithmetic facts most widely used by adults. For example, letters written by adults were examined, and the frequency with which various words appeared was noted. The most frequently used words were given the highest priority for inclusion in reading and other elementary school textbooks. Much emphasis was also given to the specific facts and specific skills in arithmetic that adults used frequently.

Along with emphasis on specifics, drill to achieve mastery was encouraged. It is not surprising that all this emphasis on specific facts and drill virtually shunted concepts, principles, and relationships aside with the result that they were not given enough attention. Current instructional programs that are based on detailed behavioristic objectives also do not give proper attention to principles, problem solving, creativity, and other higher-level outcomes.

Generalization Theory

Generalization theory holds that principles are learned and that these principles facilitate learning novel tasks that are similar. In a classical experiment dealing with generalization (Judd, 1908), two groups of boys threw a small dart at a target placed under water. Refraction was explained to one group before starting, but the other group was given no explanation of the principle. Both groups began their practice with the target placed under 12 inches of water; the same amount of practice was required for both groups to reach the same results. At this point, knowledge of the principle appeared to be of no value. Then the task was changed, but only by reducing the depth of the water. The difference between the performance of the two groups was striking in that the boys who understood the principle now learned to perform the task much more efficiently than those who did not. It was not the identical elements in the two situations that facilitated the new learning but understanding the principle of refraction.

This experiment by Judd was replicated as nearly as possible much later by Hendrickson and Schroeder (1941). The replication confirmed the results of Judd as follows: (1) understanding the principle facilitated positive transfer, (2) understanding the principle also facilitated the original learning, and (3) the completeness of the theoretical information had a direct effect on both initial learning and transfer: the more complete the information, the better the results.

The examples just given deal with the initial learning and transfer of a psychomotor skill. It has also been shown that understanding of principles facilitates initial learning and transfer in the cognitive domain (Klausmeier, Harris, & Wiersma, 1964; Wittrock, 1963).

Generalization theory provides a more sensible basis for curriculum development and teaching practices than identical-elements theory. When the teacher is freed from attempting to teach a large number of specific facts and skills, concepts and principles can be taught. Long-term projects, problem-solving activities, and class discussions replace the drill on specific facts and skills.

Transposition Theory

The theory of transposition goes further than that of generalization in that the entire pattern of means-ends relationships is proposed as the basis of transfer. For example, after persons recognize "The Star-Spangled Banner" in the key of F, they readily recognize it when it is transposed into the key of G.

Applied to Judd's dart-throwing experiment, transposition theory implies that it is not only the principle but the individual's perception of the relationships among the principle, the angle of the dart, the depth of the water, and the placement of the target that facilitates transfer. Transposition theory applied to arithmetic means that the specific facts and skills of addition, even the principle underlying addition, do not provide an adequate basis for transfer of learning. Instead, the understanding of the relationships among the facts, processes, and principles facilitates the learning of the new arithmetic tasks. The more extensive the knowledge of relationships gained during initial learning, the greater the transfer (Johnson & Zara, 1960).

Similarity of
Information-processing Requirements

The ability theory of transfer introduced here is based on the similarity of the information-processing requirements of two tasks. It takes into account the cognitive processes and strategies, as well as the substantive information, that are involved in performing similar tasks (see Figure 14.6).

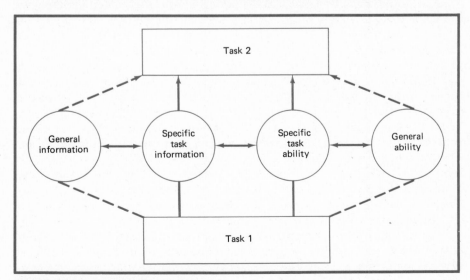

Figure 14.6 Ability theory of transfer.

Keys to better retention include making the initial learning meaningful and thorough and teaching students strategies for remembering.

According to this theory, facilitation of learning a second task depends upon four factors. One of these is the recall of the specific substantive information, facts, concepts, and principles of the first task. The second is the use of a specific ability or abilities acquired from study or practice of the first task. In addition, there may be a general ability that is not specific to the initial task but that is developed to a higher level through practice of the first task; this general ability facilitates learning the second task. Finally, general information not specific to the first task may be learned that facilitates learning the second task. Thus, the first two factors are necessary and sufficient for positive transfer, and the last two, if present, facilitate learning the second task.

Assume that children know the subtraction facts involving units and teens, that is, $1 - 1 = 0$ through $18 - 9 = 9$. They have just completed learning to perform a two-place subtraction task that involves borrowing, or *regrouping*: $22 - 6 = 16$. They now are given a second exercise: $23 - 6 = ?$ The second exercise requires understanding a specific concept and a specific ability that were learned in performing the first task. Without breaking down the first task into all the task-specific information and abilities, we see that it involves understanding the concept of place value and also the ability to perform a subtraction strategy for regrouping, that is, to perform the operations $12 - 6$ and $1 - 0$ to get 17. This ability, acquired in performing the first task, will lead to a quick performance of the second task if the learner perceives the similarity between the two tasks; has the subtraction fact, $13 - 6$; understands the concept of place value; and can use the subtraction strategy acquired through performing the first subtraction exercise. Moreover, if the specific ability to perform the subtraction strategy is strengthened by completing the two exercises, a general ability may emerge that can be applied in solving all regrouping exercises. This illustration involves a relatively simple learning task. Abilities, however, related to all kinds of verbal and motor tasks are involved in transfer of learning.

We may return to the idea of strategies for performing tasks. A general strategy is learned through performing a variety of similar tasks rather than a set of identical tasks. In a series of experiments, different but similar tasks of about the same level of difficulty were given to subjects (Harlow, 1949). At first, there was little improvement in performance, but suddenly improvement was very rapid in terms of fewer errors and less time. The term *learning-to-learn* was given to this phenomenon. It is essentially a learning strategy. Learning-to-learn has been identified for other learning outcomes. For example, we observed it in numerous experiments on concept learning (Klausmeier, Ghatala, & Frayer, 1974).

As we saw earlier in this chapter, research concerning the memory strategies that children learn incidentally and that they can learn intentionally is moving ahead rapidly. Similar interest about children's transfer strategies is also beginning (Gagné & White, 1978; Royer, 1979).

14.14 Give an example of each: positive, negative, vertical, lateral, near, and far transfer.

14.15 Explain the likenesses and differences among the following theories of transfer; identical-elements, generalization, and transposition.

14.16 Give an application of the ability theory of transfer.

14.17 Positive transfer results either in learning a new task more efficiently or in performing a task more effectively without further learning. Give one or two examples of each of these.

PRINCIPLES FOR FOSTERING RETENTION AND TRANSFER

1. Foster intent to remember.
2. Make the initial learning meaningful and thorough.
3. Help the student learn retrieval strategies.
4. Provide for transfer.
5. Encourage self-regulation of retention and transfer.

1. Foster intent to remember. An intention to remember should be established before students start a learning sequence, not after it is completed. One technique for accomplishing this is for the teacher to tell the students why they should try to remember by indicating what will occur at the end of the learning sequence. For example, they may be tested or called upon to give a report indicating what they have learned. The teacher may indicate a reward they will receive if they remember or point out other desired consequences of being able to remember. Finally, the teacher may suggest that they should try to remember because they will use what they learn in a school or out-of-school situation.

A second technique is to discuss with the students reasons for trying to remember and then to teach a strategy for learning well and remembering. Students typically will come up with many reasons for trying to remember, including the ones in the preceding paragraph. Since learning strategies were described in Chapter 8 and will be mentioned later in this chapter, they are not discussed further here.

2. Make the initial learning meaningful and thorough. When initial learning is meaningful and thorough, it can be retrieved from memory better than when it is not meaningful or thorough. Three easily applied techniques contribute powerfully to making original learning meaningful and thorough.

First, select the most meaningful learning outcomes. For example, given the opportunity to teach factual information or understanding and applications of concepts, focus on the understanding and applications of the concepts. Include only the factual information that is necessary for learning to understand and apply the concepts.

Second, organize larger amounts of information into smaller chunks. Student progress in learning one or more chunks should be possible during each learning session. The difficulty of the chunks necessarily takes into account the students' capability to learn the material.

Third, teach the students strategies for getting meaning as was emphasized in Chapter 8. One effective strategy for use with inherently meaningful material is relating the various elements of the new material; a second strategy is relating the new material to what is already known. An effective means of relating the elements of new material is to identify the major concept, principle, or process and then connect the detailed or technical information to it. The meaningful way of learning subtraction discussed earlier in this chapter followed this strategy. Getting the gist of a paragraph or longer passage does also. Relating new material to what one already knows simply requires pausing when reading or gaining information by other means, recalling what one already knows, and connecting the new and the old. These strategies, as the one to be mentioned in the next paragraph, are taught to students in the same way as other skills, mainly by explanation, demonstration, and guided practice.

Corno (1980) developed a highly successful experimental program for teaching grade 3 children strategies for learning and remembering called *memory support strategies*. Eight lessons of about 30 minutes each were prepared for use by the children with a minimal amount of adult supervision. In this experiment involving 840 children, the children's parents taught the skills using specially prepared lessons. The children were taught eight skills, or strategies. Four of the strategies correspond to techniques that teachers use to "structure" instruction in their classes. The strategies are stating goals, marking important points, summarizing, and reviewing. The children were also taught four techniques that teachers use to promote "sharing," that is, demands for the children to participate. The four participation strategies were asking questions, volunteering, answering when called on, and talking about lesson material in class. The application of these strategies by the children was directed mainly to instruction in reading.

The children who received the eight memory support lessons achieved higher in reading and vocabulary development than those who did not. They also gained knowledge about teachers' structuring techniques and demands for participation. The children had retained this knowledge at the time of a retention test four months after receiving the instruction. Corno (1980) concluded that grade 3 children can learn and then use these and other strategies that will increase their independence in achieving and remembering classroom learning outcomes.

Students at times must learn information that does not have inherent meaning and is not logically related. With this kind of learning, the teacher's task is to aid the students learn and use strategies that impose meaning and generate connections. The strategies include rehearsal, elaboration, overlearning, review, and the formal mnemonic devices presented in Chapter 8. In teaching the use of any strategy, it is important to give the learner sufficient time to process information when applying it to any given situation. For example, Pezdek and Miceli (1982) found that third-grade children could integrate pictorial and verbal information when given 15 seconds for the integration; however, they could not hold and integrate the two sources of information in short term memory when given only 8 seconds.

3. Help the Student Learn Retrieval Strategies. When an item cannot be recalled immediately, a strategy is needed to search long-term memory to locate it. We cannot assume that students have learned search strategies. When they have not, it is appropriate to teach them the strategies.

A number of retrieval strategies are available. One strategy involves going through the letters of the alphabet to aid in recalling names. Reconstructing the context in which the initial learning occurred is another useful strategy. It is especially helpful when searching for any kind of episodic information. A third strategy involves trying to recall the context of the initial learning situation in order to identify a search cue. Organizational cues facilitate retrieval: if material was organized during the initial learning, having any item of the organization provides a cue for retrieving all items of the organization. For example, having the superordinate concept *memory system* helps to retrieve the concepts *sensory register, short-term memory,* and *long-term memory.* Similarly, the term *working memory* provides a cue for recalling the processes that are carried out in working memory.

Grimmett (1983) found that some 5-year-olds and all 10-year-olds effectively used two sets of concepts *nice, nasty;* and *big, little* as cues for recalling specific animal names without instruction in how to do so. On the other hand, Buss, Yussen, Mathews, Miller, and Rembold (1983) found that second-graders required instruction regarding how to sequence the ideas in a story in order to recall the story when the story sentences were presented in a scrambled order. Thus, teachers must try to identify the kind of retrieval strategies that their students have and have not learned.

4. Provide for transfer. Factual information, concepts and principles, problem-solving skills, and information-processing strategies learned in one situation facilitate learning in other situations. As we move from factual information to strategies, the possibilities for positive transfer increase. Moreover, the more thoroughly something is learned initially, the more likely it will both facilitate subsequent higher-order learning and be applied to other situations.

The beneficial transfer effects of prerequisite knowledge on the subsequent learning of higher-order tasks is documented in many studies. For example, Klausmeier and Allen (1978) found that students who had attained concepts at the classificatory or formal level could use the concepts in understanding principles and also in solving problems. Further, the higher the level of understanding the concept, the more effective was the use of it. On the other hand, children of the same grades who had not attained the concepts were unable to understand the principles or to solve the related problems. The implication is that, if we want students to understand principles and solve problems that involve concepts, we should make sure that the students have attained the essential concepts.

Applying what has been learned should not be assumed to be automatic. Rather, students profit from engaging in activities that are directed specifically to ensure transfer. Application questions and application activities may be arranged for this purpose. For example, at the end of each main part of a chapter in this book, there are questions inviting you to relate the content to some aspect of your current situation as a learner or to some aspect of your professional life as an educator. These questions are included to foster transfer.

Other activities can also be arranged to provide for transfer. For example, prospective M.D.'s, teachers, and nurses observe the practices of experienced persons. They also engage in some of the practices themselves. In their observation and practice, they apply knowledge and skills gained earlier at the verbal level.

Regardless of the kind of learning outcome, transfer is encouraged by using a number of different learning tasks, rather than by repetition of a single task. This conclusion applies across all school levels. In this regard, Eisenberger, Masterson, and McDermitt (1982) found that college women who were given three different kinds of learning tasks subsequently produced a higher quality essay than did those who were given only one.

5. Encourage self-regulation of retention and transfer. Becoming self-directive with respect to retention and transfer necessarily involves self-direction of initial learning. An example of a strategy for increasing student self-directed study follows.

The PQ4R self-directed learning strategy was developed by Thomas and Robinson (1972) and is still used widely. It starts with a preview of the text chapter by reading the headings or other indicators of the main concepts. On the basis of the preview, students formulate questions to answer. The questions are usually directed at either the meaning or applications of the concepts given in the chapter headings identified in the preview. Questions such as these are illustrative: "What is meant by an intention to remember?" "How can I get my students to establish an intention to remember?" Then, part of the chapter is read to answer the question. While reading to answer the question, the student reflects by trying to think of examples, to understand, or to relate it to an earlier part of the chapter or book. After finishing a part of the chapter, the student recites mentally or overtly, trying to answer the questions that were raised. Upon completing the chapter, the student reviews, trying to recall the main points, the questions, and their answers. The student's use of the PQ4R strategy is guided by the goal of comprehending and recalling the text information. The PQ4R method itself is a strategy for achieving this goal.

The application of the PQ4R and similar strategies to elementary and high school situations calls for understanding what students are capable of learning and which strategies are appropriate for different kinds of learning tasks. Creativity is also required, since guidelines for teaching the strategies to younger students have not been established.

14.18 Which one of the following principles of retention and transfer do you think is easiest for a teacher to implement? Most difficult? Why?

a. Foster intent to remember.
b. Make the initial learning meaningful and thorough.
c. Help the student learn retrieval strategies.
d. Provide for transfer.
e. Encourage self-regulation of retention and transfer.

14.19 Indicate why each of the principles of retention and transfer should be implemented rather than left to the student's initiative.

14.20 Recall a class in which the principles of retention and transfer were implemented least often or least well. What information do you recall from the class? Compare the class with another one in which the principles were implemented effectively.

14.21 Suggest one or two ways in which you would foster student intent to remember.

14.22 Outline the retrieval strategies that you understand and could teach students to use.

14.23 Give examples of what you are doing to ensure transfer from this course to your activities either as a learner or as a teacher.

14.24 At what school level do you think students could learn to use the PQ4R study-skills strategy? Justify your choice.

14.25 Review and Application: Recall the most important information regarding each of the following concepts, and identify at least one possible use of the information by you as a learner, a teacher, or both:

Features of Long-term Memory
　Storing Different Kinds of Information
　Encoding Information for Long-term Storage
　Retrieving Information from Long-term Storage
Factors Affecting Retention and Forgetting
　Type of Learning Outcome
　Conditions of Initial Learning
　Interference and Reorganization
Metamemory
Bases of Transfer of Learning
　Similarity of Task Information
　Similarity of Information-processing Requirements
Principles for Fostering Retention and Transfer

SUMMARY

Information is held in long-term memory in one of four stores: semantic, episodic, affective, or motoric. Accordingly, we are able to recall meanings, episodes, feelings, and motor programs. One form in which information is encoded and subsequently stored is linguistic. Other forms consist of visual images and neural representations related to the other sensory modalities: auditory, olfactory, and kinesthetic. Semantic information is encoded linguistically, whereas episodes, motor programs, and feelings typically involve a combination of linguistic and other modes of encoding.

Retrieving information involves finding the desired information in long-term store and activating it. Much information can be retrieved by raising a question or using some other means of accessing and searching long-term memory. A most powerful strategy for retrieving information that cannot be recalled readily is to reconstruct mentally the context in which the initial learning or episode occurred. Other mental search strategies include the use of the first letter of the alphabet and the use of concepts.

How well information can be retrieved after extended time intervals is heavily dependent upon the type of learning outcome and the conditions of initial learning. Skills and concepts are remembered much better than technical information or information learned initially by rote. Intending to remember at the time of initial learning, learning with meaning, and organizing material into a semantic network markedly facilitate long-term retention. Reorganization of information when recalling it and interference of new, related information with information learned earlier impede retention.

Metamemory refers to the individual's understanding of the memory system and the means of facilitating retention. How well an individual will recall depends upon the nature of the information to be recalled, the individual's capacity to recall, and the person's strategies for remembering and recalling.

Transfer of learning between two tasks is explained either in terms of the similarity between the tasks in substance or in terms of the similarity between the tasks in information-processing requirements. An ability theory explains transfer in terms of the information-processing requirements. According to this view, the individual perceives the relationships between the tasks and is able to apply the information and abilities used in the first task to learning the second task.

Retention and transfer are fostered by applying the following principles:

1. Foster intent to remember.
2. Make the initial learning meaningful and thorough.
3. Help the student learn retrieval strategies.
4. Provide for transfer.
5. Encourage student self-regulation of retention and transfer.

SUGGESTIONS FOR FURTHER READING

Anderson, J. R. *Cognitive psychology and its implications.* San Francisco: Freeman, 1980.

Chapter 6 has a good account of long-term memory, retention, and forgetting.

Ghatala, E. S. Developmental changes in incidental memory as a function of meaningfulness and encoding condition. *Developmental Psychology,* 1984, *20,* 208–211.

An experiment comparing the effects of an acoustic strategy (a word that rhymed with the given word) with a semantic strategy (a meaning of the word).

Howe, M. J. A., & Ceci, S. J. Educational implications of memory research. In M. M. Gruneberg & P. E. Morris (Eds.), *Applied problems in memory.* New York: Academic Press, 1979. Pp. 59–94.

Individual differences in memory are described and ways of increasing the ability to remember are presented.

Hunter, I. M. L. Memory in everyday life. In M. M. Gruneberg & P. E. Morris (Eds.), *Applied problems in memory*. New York: Academic Press, 1979. Pp. 1–24.

The importance of memory in everyday affairs is described and memory techniques in non-literate cultures are described.

Kail, R. *The development of memory in children* (2nd ed.). New York: W. H. Freeman, 1984.

Describes the development of memory, metamemory, and mnemonic strategies.

Loftus, E. *Memory*. Reading, Mass.: Addison-Wesley, 1980.

Chapter 2 of this popular book describes the sensory, short-term, and long-term phases of information processing.

Ripple, R. E., & Drinkwater, D. J. Transfer of learning. In H. E. Mitzel, J. H. Best, & W. Rabinowitz (Eds.), *Encyclopedia of educational research* (5th ed., Vol. 4). New York: Free Press, 1982. Pp. 1947–1955.

Reviews research on transfer with the focus on transfer in the educational setting. "Cognition and Memory" by F. B. Murray & L. Mosberg is another article in this *Encyclopedia* of interest to retention and transfer.

Siegel, L. S., & Lindner, B. A. Short-term memory processes in children with reading and arithmetic disabilities. *Developmental Psychology*, 1984, *20*, 200–207.

An experiment to identify differences in coding processes and in short-term memory between children with learning disabilities and normal children.

PART FOUR

MEASURE-MENT AND EVALUATION

CHAPTER 15
EDUCATIONAL MEASUREMENT

ATTRIBUTES OF
GOOD MEASUREMENT

NORM-REFERENCED
AND OTHER
PUBLISHED TESTS

CRITERION-REFERENCED
ACHIEVEMENT TESTING

MEASURING
PSYCHOMOTOR SKILLS

TEACHER-DEVELOPED
MEASUREMENT
TECHNIQUES

We all recognize the importance of accurate measuring at the gasoline pump, the grocery store, the bank, and other places. Measurement is even more important in educational settings, where decisions are made daily that directly affect how individual human beings learn and how they feel. Accordingly, measurement tools used in the school, such as tests and rating scales, should be valid and reliable.

It is important for teachers to be able to interpret the results of published educational achievement, mental ability, creativity, and other tests. Being able to use the results of criterion-referenced tests in planning and carrying out instruction is becoming increasingly critical as this kind of test is used more widely. Skill in developing paper-and-pencil tests and other measurement techniques for use in the classroom contributes directly to measuring and enhancing student progress in learning.

Two points merit attention before proceeding to the main discussion of educational measurement. First, the whole field of educational testing is undergoing critical analysis, and many arguments are appearing in the mass media as well as in professional books and articles regarding the kinds of tests to use and not to use. A full chapter could easily be devoted to summarizing the pros and cons of intelligence testing, criterion-referenced testing, or even essay examinations. The many arguments on each kind of testing are not presented in this chapter. Rather, some uses, misuses, and limitations of each main kind of test are presented.

Second, a considerable knowledge of statistics and of the substance of the area being tested, that is, achievement, intelligence, creativity, is neces-

Lewis Madison Terman (1877–1956), president of the American Psychological Association in 1923. Terman became prominent with his revision and extension of the Binet-Simon intelligence scale (known as the Stanford-Binet), which was published as *The Measurement of Intelligence* (1916). This test and other tests based on it have had a great influence on education, including ability grouping and the diagnosis of giftedness and mental retardation.

Louis Leon Thurstone (1887–1965), president of the American Psychological Association in 1933. Thurstone rejected the idea of general intelligence and, through factor analysis, identified a number of primary mental abilities, including number, word meaning, spatial, and inductive reasoning. Tests of the primary mental abilities are used widely in vocational guidance in secondary schools and in employment agencies.

Distinguished contributors to educational and psychological measurement.

sary to become an expert in measurement and test construction. In this chapter, scarcely any information will be provided regarding the substantive area of any kind of test, or of statistics. Rather, the focus is on explaining different kinds of tests and their uses by teachers. For the person who desires to attain more proficiency in measurement, there is an appendix devoted entirely to statistical terminology and research methods. In addition, the books listed at the end of this chapter provide more complete treatments of educational measurement.

Validity
Reliability
Usability

ATTRIBUTES OF GOOD MEASUREMENT

Tests are used for many purposes. One purpose is to assess a student's capability for learning particular subject matter. Another is to measure the

Joy Paul Guilford (1897–   ), president of the American Psychological Association in 1950. Guilford is best known for his formulation of a structure of intellect that includes 120 specific abilities. This approach to intelligence includes divergent, or creative, thinking abilities. Modern programs of gifted, talented, and creative education use Guilford's ideas regarding creative abilities.

Lee Joseph Cronbach (1916–   ), president of the American Psychological Association in 1957. Cronbach is a leader in the field of measurement, including aptitude/treatment interactions. The first edition of his *Essentials of Psychological Testing* was published in 1949. It and the later editions have contributed materially to better test construction.

student's progress during a learning sequence and to use the results to provide feedback to the student. A third purpose is to measure achievement at the end of a unit of instruction; a school grade; or a level of schooling, such as elementary or high school. To achieve any of these purposes well, a test must have high validity, reliability, and usability. The term *test* is used in this chapter to indicate any instrument, such as a test or questionnaire, and also any procedure, such as observing or interviewing, that is used to get quantitative or qualitative information regarding any area of student performance.

Validity

Validity is a term used to relate the properties of a test to the purpose of testing. A test may be valid for one purpose but not for another. The three main purposes of testing in the school are to answer three questions: (1) How well do the items of the test sample all the content that the test claims to represent *(content validity)?* (2) How well do the test scores predict present or future performance of the students *(predictive validity)?* (3) How relatable are the scores on the test to the theoretical ideas, or constructs, that the test is said to measure *(construct validity)?* The two types of validity that teachers are most concerned with are content and predictive validity. These will be discussed after a short note regarding construct validity.

A test is *construct-valid* to the extent that the scores on the test are relatable to theoretical ideas, or constructs (Cronbach, 1970). For example, a test of anxiety has high construct validity to the extent that scores on it are relatable to the constructs included in theoretical explanations of anxiety. Similarly, a test of reading comprehension has high construct validity if the test scores can be related directly to how well students understand what they read in textbooks and other printed material. Accordingly, determining the construct validity of tests is of more concern to theorists and experimenters than it is to practitioners. Procedures described by Cronbach (1970) for ensuring that a test has high construct validity require considerable knowledge of the substantive area being tested as well as statistical knowledge.

Content Validity

The items included in a final examination in a course cannot directly measure the students' knowledge of all the content, because of the time constraint. Instead, the items should be a carefully selected sample of the entire content. Based on a student's achievement of the sample of the content measured by the test, the teacher infers how well the student has learned all the content. The more nearly a test samples all the content, rather than only part of it, the higher is the content validity of the test. Educators want all of their achievement tests, questionnaires, rating scales, and other measurement techniques to have high content validity.

Assume that there are two objectives of an educational psychology course. One objective is that the students comprehend the concepts presented in the textbook. Another is that the students be able to apply the concepts. Let us assume further that the concepts of all the chapters are regarded as of equal importance. The logical way for an instructor to proceed in constructing a content-valid test is to list all the concepts. After they are listed, the number of items to be included in the test is decided. The instructor includes an equal number of concepts from each chapter on which to base one or more comprehension items and one or more application items. In this way, an equal proportion of all the concepts of each chapter is tested.

Test publishers who construct educational achievement tests that are intended for use in classrooms throughout the nation try to determine the content that is taught in all the classrooms in order to sample it properly. How this is done may be illustrated with standardized educational achievement tests, such as in reading, mathematics, science, or other school subjects.

The authors of a test make a thorough analysis of the textbooks that are most widely used in a subject. They also examine courses of study and the research literature pertaining to children's concepts and learning experiences at successive ages or grades. Using these analyses, the authors prepare detailed outlines of the content to be covered in each test at each grade. These outlines specify the relative proportion of content to be devoted to the various skills and understandings within each subject. Thus, each outline serves as the blueprint of each test that ultimately emerges. After this blueprint is formulated, the authors consult specialists and teachers in each subject regarding the test items.

As we see, care is taken by test publishers to prepare achievement tests that are *content-valid.* However, it cannot be assumed that any standardized achievement test is content-valid for a particular school, inasmuch as the school may have taught a different content. Therefore, the staff of a school must examine the test to see if the items actually test the content they teach.

Predictive Validity

Which objectives of this course is this student ready to achieve with a reasonable amount of effort? How well will this student in first-year French perform next year in second-year French? For what kind of career should this student prepare? When using test scores to answer these questions, we are concerned with the predictive validity of the scores.

A most important area of prediction in education is achievement from one year to the next and from one school level to the next in a given subject field. A student's standardized achievement test score in a given subject field has quite high validity for predicting the student's achievement level in the same subject the next year. The grades made by the student in a subject are also useful in predicting the student's subsequent achievement in the same subject.

Reliability

Reliability refers to the accuracy of a measurement. Reliable test scores give true estimates of a student's present status. For example, reliable scores from the subtests of a reading readiness test administered early in the first grade give an accurate estimate of each child's present reading status. If the subtests also have high predictive validity, the teacher can use the test scores in predicting how each child will achieve during the semester. Accordingly, the test scores, along with teacher observation, may be used in deciding what is appropriate instruction for each child.

Test scores are neither totally reliable nor totally unreliable. They range in reliability from high to low. Four conditions contribute to low test reliability. If these conditions can be avoided, the teacher can secure reliable measures of student achievement. First, a test may be unreliable because of poorly constructed items that do not discriminate between students who know the content being tested and those who do not. That is, a student who knows particular subject matter answers items incorrectly as well as the one who does not know it.

The length of a test also can contribute to low reliability. Suppose 300 words in spelling have been taught during the year, and a test is constructed to measure spelling achievement. Five words are a totally inadequate sample of the total. More reliable scores are obtained with a longer test of 25–50 items. Of course, a test can be made so long that students become tired or bored and respond unreliably.

A third contributor to low reliability is inaccurate and inconsistent scoring. For example, an objective test item may be scored incorrectly. As another example, the answers to an essay question may not be rated, or graded, consistently. Accordingly, two equally good answers to a question are assigned different ratings.

Insufficient time for the student to complete an achievement test lowers its reliability. Accordingly, a test score is not a reliable measure of the achievement of those students who needed more time to complete it.

Usability

In addition to validity and reliability, a number of practical matters dealing with usability must be considered, particularly when published tests are being purchased. *Usability* refers to the following matters: (1) the amount of time required to administer a test; (2) the amount of preparation or education required to administer and interpret a test; (3) the amount of time required to score a test; (4) the ease of interpreting the test results after the scores are obtained; (5) the cost; and (6) the mechanical makeup of a test. Test publishers usually provide information in a test manual about the validity, reliability, and usability of their test. Statistical terms of the kind included in the appendix of this book are often used in the manuals in describing the properties of the test.

The best source of information about many different tests is the *Mental Measurements Yearbook*. Successive editions have been published periodically since 1938. This yearbook gives descriptive information about the validity, reliability, and usability of many published tests. Critical reviews and a bibliography of articles and books are included for many tests.

15.1 Explain why a social studies test administered in the last year of elementary school might have high content validity but low predictive validity for the first grade of middle school or junior high school.

15.2 A mental ability test must be reliable to have predictive validity; however, high reliability is not sufficient for ensuring predictive validity. Explain.

15.3 Teachers examined a 60-item achievement test before administering it. They deleted 10 items that did not measure what they taught. Estimate the probable effect of this deletion on (a) the content validity of the test, (b) the predictive validity of the test, and (c) the reliability of the test. Explain.

NORM-REFERENCED AND OTHER PUBLISHED TESTS

One kind of widely used published test measures educational achievement. Another measures mental ability. Other published tests have been constructed to measure creativity, learning styles, attitudes, and self-concepts. The results of these tests aid teachers and counselors in securing a better understanding of individual students and in planning their education. These are the main types of published tests used in education, but there are others. Textbooks in educational measurement, including those listed in the "Suggestions for Further Reading" at the end of this chapter, provide information about the tests discussed in this chapter and about other tests, including interest and personality tests.

Norm-referenced Tests of Educational Achievement

Dwyer (1982) defines achievement testing as the assessment of the outcomes of formal instruction in the cognitive-domain areas, such as English, mathematics, and reading. Instruction is considered as subject matter that is taught and that students are expected to learn. Creativity, moral behavior, motivation, and similar domains are not included. Similarly, intelligence and aptitude are not regarded as achievement. There are two main kinds of achievement tests: norm-referenced and criterion-referenced tests. Criterion-referenced tests are discussed later in this chapter.

Norm-referenced educational achievement tests are also referred to as *standardized educational achievement tests*. They are designed to measure the extent to which students have achieved the content typically taught in various subject fields. There are separate tests for different subjects, such as reading and arithmetic at the elementary school level and chemistry and American history at the high school level. There are also complete batteries of achievement tests that have subbatteries for the primary grades, intermediate grades, middle school or junior high school, and senior high school. The batteries at the lower school levels typically include tests of reading, language arts, mathematics, and study skills. Those for the high school often include English, mathematics, social studies, and science. Standardized educational achievement tests are used to measure student achievement during a school year and over a period of years. They cannot be used to measure the day-to-day progress of students nor the learning outcomes that are unique to a classroom or a school. For these purposes, locally constructed tests, including criterion-referenced tests, are used. Three main features of standardized tests are now considered.

Interpretation of Raw Scores

Norm-referenced educational achievement tests are usually administered to groups of students. Answer sheets are generally used from grade 2 on. The answer sheets are sent to the test publisher for scoring. The publisher scores the answer sheets by computer and returns a computer printout of the test results that gives each student's name, *raw score* in each area tested, and one or more equivalent *derived scores*. The *derived scores* are based on the scores of the students who participated in standardizing, or norming, the test. The derived scores, as we shall now see, are necessary to interpret a raw score.

Publishers provide tables of norms, as well as computer printouts, for interpreting raw scores. By use of these tables, *raw scores* typically can be related to any of four kinds of *derived scores:* a standard score, a percentile rank, a stanine score, and a grade equivalent. Figure 15.1 shows how these scores are related, except for grade equivalent.

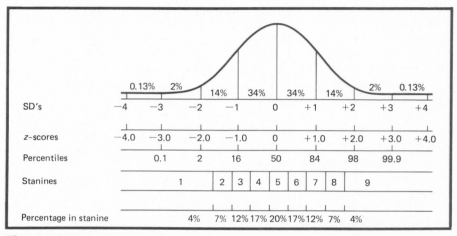

Figure 15.1 SD's, z-scores, percentiles, and stanines in a normal distribution.

The *normal curve* is presented at the top of the figure. Notice how it is divided into *standard deviation units,* SD's, from the mean. (A standard deviation unit indicates how much each score departs from the mean of all the scores.) Sixty-eight percent of the scores fall between +1 SD and −1 SD of the mean, and 96% between +2 SD and −2 SD. About 2% are above +2 SD, and 2% below −2 SD. Thus, a raw score that is exactly 1 SD above the mean can be expressed as a z-score of +1, a percentile rank of 84, and a stanine of 7.

A *z-score* is a kind of standard score. (A raw score is changed to a standard score by subtracting it from the mean and dividing the remainder by the standard deviation unit.) *Standard scores* are expressed not only in whole numbers, such as −3.0, but also in fractional parts, such as −3.1. Test publishers increasingly provide tables of standard-score norms that enable any raw score to be changed to a standard score. The standard scores of two different achievement tests are more nearly comparable than are any other derived scores, such as percentile ranks. Thus, a raw score equivalent to a +1 z-score on two different achievement tests of reading is interpreted as meaning the student achieved at the same level on the two tests.

As shown in Figure 15.1, *percentile ranks* range from 0.1 to 99.9. A raw score equivalent to a percentile rank of 2 means that 2% of all the students of the norming group scored below it. Stated differently, it means that this student's score is above 2% of the scores of the norming group and below 98%. A percentile rank of 50 means that 50% of the norming group scored below it.

Stanine scores are also a kind of standard score and range from 1 to 9. Stanine scores are not divided further into fractional parts. Stanine 5 is exactly in the middle of the distribution and includes 10% of the cases on either side of the mean as depicted in Figure 15.1. The other stanines are evenly distributed on either side of stanine 5 and include from 4% to 17% of the cases. Notice that all raw scores are changed to only 9 stanine scores. A difference of two stanines is assumed to represent a significant difference in performance.

Raw scores can also be converted to *grade equivalents*. For example, a grade equivalent of 9.1 is equal to the average of the scores made by ninth-grade students of the norming group in the first month of the ninth grade. A grade equivalent of 3.5 is equivalent to the average of the scores made by third-grade norming students in the fifth month of the third grade.

Grade equivalents are the least informative of derived scores and the most likely to be misinterpreted. Thus, a grade equivalent of 9.1 in mathematics made by a grade 6 student does not mean that the student can perform in mathematics as well as the typical beginning grade 9 student. It means instead that this student got as many items correct as the average number correct for beginning grade 9 students. The items gotten correct by the grade 6 student may not be the same items that the typical grade 9 student gets correct.

Profile of Achievements

Figure 15.2 gives Frank Smith's raw scores on the Comprehensive Tests of Basic Skills and the equivalent percentile ranks. These percentile ranks are also plotted in profile form. Notice that a raw score of 19 in reading comprehension is equivalent to a percentile rank of 53, while a raw score of 18 in spelling is equivalent to a percentile rank of 75.

How might we summarize Frank's profile? Frank's achievement level is equivalent to the 59th percentile rank in total reading, the 70th percentile rank in total language, and the 39th percentile rank in total arithmetic. Assume that this is a content-valid achievement test for this school. We would assess Frank's achievement as considerably lower in arithmetic than in language. If the teacher's judgment about Frank's achievements supports these test results, we would infer that the teacher should study Frank further to determine what might be contributing to his relatively low achievement in mathematics. Possibly he could be aided in achieving higher in math.

We are often interested in how teachers' ratings of students' educational achievements compare with test results. Teachers' ratings of their

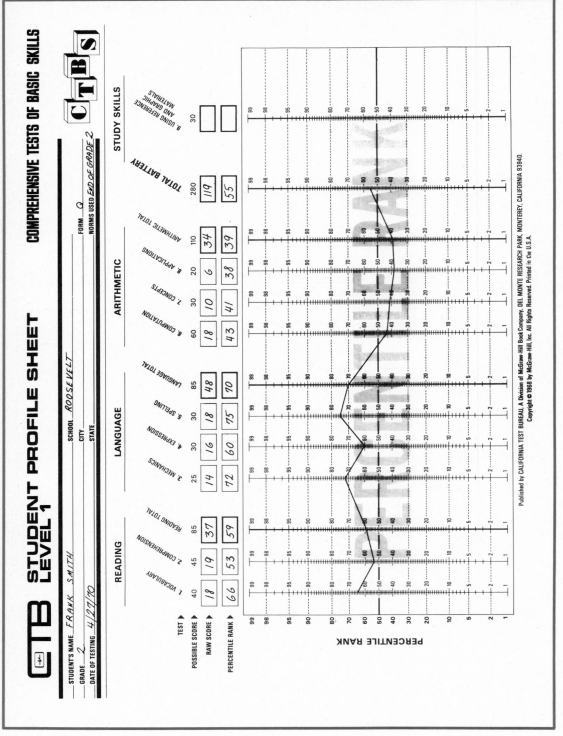

Figure 15.2 Profile of performance of Frank Smith as a second-grader on the Comprehensive Tests of Basic Skills (1968).

students' achievement in English and mathematics were found to correlate quite high but far from perfectly with the students' standardized achievement test scores (Pedulla, Airasian, & Madaus, 1980). The correlations would have been higher, except that the teachers included persistence, attention span, motivation, and classroom participation in their ratings of achievement.

Item Quality

Standardized achievement tests are among the better sources to which a teacher can turn to find examples of well-constructed achievement test items and also concise directions to the students regarding how to proceed in responding to test times. The directions and items given in Figure 15.3 are taken from the Study Skills Test of the Stanford Achievement Test. Study them carefully to see if you might improve them in any way. Also, do you think all students attending school today should at some time learn the skills necessary to answer the questions?

TEST 8: Social Studies (Continued)   *Part B: Study Skills*

DIRECTIONS: Look at each graph or map and read the questions that go with it. Decide which of the answers given is *best*. Then fill in the answer space which has the same number as the answer you have chosen.

Use the table below in answering questions 46–50

The Great Lakes

Name of Lake	Area in Square Miles	Length in Miles	Maximum Depth in Feet	Eleva-tion in Feet
Erie	9,940	241	210	572
Huron	23,010	206	750	581
Michigan	22,400	321	923	581
Ontario	7,540	193	778	246
Superior	31,820	383	1,302	622

46 The deepest lake is —
 1 Huron   3 Ontario
 2 Michigan   4 Superior
 46 ○○○○ (1 2 3 4)

47 What is the length in miles of Lake Ontario?
 5 7540   6 193   7 778   8 246
 47 ○○○○ (5 6 7 8)

48 The lake with the greatest elevation is also —
 1 smaller than Lake Erie
 2 more shallow than Lake Michigan
 3 shorter than Lake Huron
 4 the largest, the longest, and the deepest
 48 ○○○○ (1 2 3 4)

49 How many lakes have a greater elevation than Lake Huron?
 5 none   6 one   7 two   8 three
 49 ○○○○ (5 6 7 8)

50 How many lakes are both deeper and larger in area than Lake Michigan?
 1 none   2 one   3 two   4 three
 50 ○○○○ (1 2 3 4)

Figure 15.3 Sample questions from the Stanford Achievement Test, Form W, Intermediate 1.
Source: Kelley, Madden, Gardner, & Rudman, 1964.

Status of Norm-referenced Achievement Tests

The Gallup Poll (Gallup, 1983) showed 75 percent of the public favoring the use of national achievement tests so that the achievement of students in local schools could be compared with students in other communities. Only 17% were opposed and 8% indicated they didn't know. In another survey, educational achievement tests were regarded as very useful by 36% of parents with children attending public schools and somewhat useful by 45% (Educational Testing Service, 1980a). Two percent had no opinion, while 17% regarded them as not too useful. The opinions of nonwhite parents were very similar to those of white parents.

Despite this widespread support, there is debate in some school districts regarding the continued use of norm-referenced educational achievement tests. Three conditions are responsible for the debate. First, in many schools, the results have not been used to arrange more desirable instructional conditions for individual students. For example, even though one student scores at the 80th percentile in science and another at the 20th, both are treated as if they are equally ready to learn the same science subject matter. Second, the quality of instruction in a classroom, school, or school district has been evaluated unfairly on the basis of students' test scores. For example, the mean, or average, educational achievement of the students of each school of a district or a state is reported without indicating the differences among the schools in the mental ability, home environment, motivation, and similar characteristics of each student population. Finally, norm-referenced educational achievements are being replaced in some schools with criterion-referenced achievement tests, because criterion-referenced tests have greater content validity than the norm-referenced tests. Criterion-referenced testing is explained later in this chapter.

Tests of Mental Abilities and Special Aptitudes
The terms *mental ability, intellectual ability,* and *general intelligence* are used synonymously by different test publishers and also by educators. Some mental ability tests are administered individually to one student at a time, while others are administered to students in groups. Special aptitude tests measure capabilities related to particular subjects and career fields. Social intelligence is an emerging field of testing (Ford & Tisak, 1983).

Individual Tests of Intelligence
Two widely used individual intelligence tests are the Revised Stanford-Binet Intelligence Scale (Terman & Merrill, 1960) and the Wechsler Intelligence Scale for Children (Wechsler, 1949, 1974). Each of these tests is administered by a skilled examiner to individuals, rather than to groups. Given skilled test administrators, these tests are more reliable measures of general intellectual ability than mental ability tests administered to groups.

The Revised Stanford-Binet Intelligence Scale is now discussed in some detail. This scale, first standardized in 1916, has set the pattern for intelligence testing from 1916 to the present time. It is used to test the mental development of persons from age 2 through adulthood. As shown in Figure 15.4, there is a test for each 6-month interval from ages 2 through 4, and one for each 12-month interval from ages 5 through 14. There are four tests for older persons (Average Adult, Superior Adult I, Superior Adult II, Superior Adult III).

The test for each age has six subtests. The examiner administers the tests and identifies the age at which the person passes all six subtests. This process continues upward to the age at which no subtest is passed. For each

RECORD FORM — Form L-M Stanford-Binet Intelligence Scale

Name............................... Sex........... Date of test............... Year Month Day
Address.. Birthdate...............
School............... Grade........... Examiner........... Age...............
Parent.. [From............... Agency.......]
Birthplace............... of father............... of mother...............
Occupation of father............... of mother...............

CA
MA
IQ

TEST SUMMARY

Yrs.   Mos.

II
II-6
III
III-6
IV
IV-6
V
VI
VII
VIII
IX
X
XI
XII
XIII
XIV
AA
SA I
SA II
SA III

Total
MA Score
Testing time

FACTORS AFFECTING TEST PERFORMANCE
OVERALL RATING OF CONDITIONS

	Optimal	Good	Average	Detrimental	Seriously detrimental	
Attention						
a) Absorbed by task						Easily distracted
Reactions During Test Performance						
a) Normal activity level						Hyperactive or depressed
b) Initiates activity						Waits to be told
c) Quick to respond						Urging needed
Emotional Independence						
a) Socially confident						Shy, reserved, reticent
b) Realistically self-confident						Distrusts own ability or overconfident
c) Comfortable in adult company						Ill-at-ease
d) Assured						Anxious about success
Problem Solving Behavior						
a) Persistent						Gives up easily or can't give up
b) Reacts to failure realistically						Withdrawing, hostile, or denying
c) Eager to continue						Seeks to terminate
d) Challenged by hard tasks						Prefers only easy tasks
Independence of Examiner Support						
a) Needs minimum of commendation						Needs constant praise and encouragement

Was it hard to establish a positive relationship with this person?...............

Figure 15.4 Record Booklet—Form L-M, Stanford-Binet Intelligence Scale.
Source: Terman & Merrill, 1960.

test passed, the person is awarded 2 months of mental age. For example, if an 8-year-old passes all six subtests for age 8, a mental age of 96 months is recorded. For each of the six subtests at each age passed thereafter, an additional 2 months of age is recorded. The total mental age (MA) is computed by adding. The MA that is obtained is then divided by the subject's actual chronological age (CA) and multiplied by 100. The resulting score is the IQ. The 8-year-old with an MA of 96 months has an IQ of 100 ($\frac{96}{96} \times 100$). The Revised Stanford-Binet, like all intelligence tests since then, has been constructed so that the average IQ is 100. However, not all tests, including the Revised Stanford-Binet, get an average IQ of exactly 100 for each age.

The Revised Stanford-Binet Intelligence Scale is based on the assumption that intelligence is an overall or general intellectual ability. The items in the test, therefore, are constructed to include a wide variety of cognitive processes, including memory, verbal reasoning, mathematical reasoning, and vocabulary. Accordingly, scores from the Revised Stanford-Binet correlate positively with educational achievement in mathematics, science, language arts, and social studies.

The three Wechsler Intelligence Scales are for three different age-groups: 4–6, 6–16, and 16–75. The Revised Wechsler Intelligence Scale for Children (WISC-R) is used with children of ages 6–16. Because the WISC-R is administered much like the Revised Stanford-Binet, we shall deal only with its substance.

The WISC-R consists of six verbal and six performance tests. The six verbal tests are information, comprehension, arithmetic, similarities, vocabulary, and digit span. The six performance tests are picture completion, picture arrangement, block design, object assembly, coding, and mazes. The performance tests require little use of language. Concerning the 1974 WISC-R, Wechsler says:

> The revised WISC, like the Scale it succeeds, has been designed and organized as a test of general intelligence. Its author believes that general intelligence exists; that it is possible to measure it objectively; and that, by so doing, one can obtain a meaningful and useful index of a subject's mental capacity. He also believes that the much challenged and berated IQ, in spite of its liability to misinterpretation and misuse, is a scientifically sound and useful measure, and for this reason he has retained the IQ as an essential aspect of the revised Scale. (p. 111)

The WISC-R Verbal IQ correlates higher with achievement in academic subjects than the Performance IQ. Large differences between Verbal IQ and Performance IQ are found occasionally in some children. It is possible that a pupil with a markedly higher Performance IQ may have a language problem and that one with a markedly higher Verbal IQ may have an emotional problem. A profile of the verbal and performance test scores can be plotted. Some clinicians find such a profile useful in the diagnosis of brain injury, personality disorders, and learning disabilities. For this reason, the WISC-R is used widely by clinical and school psychologists.

Reynolds and Jensen (1983) compared the scores of 270 black and 270 white children who were part of the national sample used in revising the WISC. The children of the two groups were matched on age, sex, and full-scale WISC-R IQ. Small but significant differences were found between the black and white children. Blacks exceeded whites on memory; whites exceeded blacks on performance (mainly spatial visualization); and there was no difference on verbal ability.

Either the Stanford-Binet or the WISC-R is used as one of several procedures in identifying children who function intellectually at a very low level and in diagnosing children who may have learning disabilities of any kind. They very likely will continue to be used in securing this kind of diagnostic information, because we do not have better means for making these judgments.

Misuse of these intelligence tests has occurred. As one example, children administered the test only once have been categorized and treated for the rest of their school lives as if their IQs were unchangeable. In addition, some children from intellectually impoverished backgrounds have been improperly categorized as mentally retarded and then educated as if they were mentally retarded.

Group Tests of General Intellectual Ability

Group tests of general intellectual ability are also referred to as *scholastic aptitude, academic aptitude,* and *mental ability tests.* They are used more extensively after the first grade than individual mental ability tests. One advantage of group tests is that they do not require specially educated examiners. Furthermore, the scores of group tests correlate about as high with educational achievement in academic subjects as do those of the Stanford-Binet and Wechsler tests.

Two types of items are used in group tests of intellectual ability. One type measures outcomes that, supposedly, all pupils have had an equal opportunity to learn. The other type is intended to measure outcomes that no student has had an opportunity to learn.

Two practice items from the Lorge-Thorndike Intelligence Tests, Levels A–H, Form 1 (Lorge, Thorndike, & Hagan, 1964) follow in Figure 15.5. They give an idea of the type of item used in group tests of intelligence for elementary school pupils. Notice that the first one measures vocabulary and the next one measures mathematical reasoning.

Group tests of intellectual ability are timed. Answer sheets are usually used, and scoring is usually done by computer by the test publisher. Proper administration requires that the students taking the test understand the directions, do their best, and be in good physical and emotional health. These same conditions are essential for any group test.

Why are group intellectual ability tests used so widely? First, the ability test is economical in terms of student and teacher time. It can be administered in the same amount of time as an educational achievement test in one subject field. Second, it gives a better estimate of the student's ability

PAGE 4

1

1V   A-H

For each exercise in this test you are to read the word in dark type at the beginning of that exercise. Then, from the five words that follow you are to choose the word that has the same meaning or most nearly the same meaning as the word in dark type. Look at sample exercise 0.

0. loud   **A** quick   **B** noisy   **C** hard   **D** heavy   **E** weak

The word which has most nearly the same meaning as **loud** is **noisy**. The letter in front of **noisy** is **B**, so on your answer sheet make a heavy black pencil mark in the **B** answer space for exercise 0.

Do all the exercises in this test the same way. Try every exercise in your section of the test.

PAGE **13**

3

1V   A-H

In this test you are to work some arithmetic problems. After each problem are four possible answers and a fifth choice, "none of these," meaning that the correct answer is not given.

Work each problem and compare your answer with the four possible answers. If the correct answer is given, fill in the space on the answer sheet that has the same letter as the right answer. If the correct answer is not given, fill in the space on the answer sheet that has the same letter as "none of these." Look at sample exercise 0.

0. If candy costs a cent a piece, how much will nine pieces cost?
    A 1¢   **B** 7¢   **C** 8¢   **D** 9¢   **E** none of these

The correct answer is 9¢. The letter in front of 9¢ is **D** so on your answer sheet make a heavy black pencil mark in the **D** answer space for exercise 0.
Now look at sample exercise 00.

00. Mrs. Jones bought a pound of potatoes for 10¢ and a pound of spinach for 15¢. How much did she spend?
    F 5¢   **G** 10¢   **H** 15¢   **J** 20¢   **K** none of these

The correct answer is 25¢. The answers at **F, G, H**, and **J** are wrong, so you would choose "none of these" as your correct answer. The letter in front of "none of these" is **K** so on your answer sheet make a heavy black pencil mark in the **K** answer space for exercise 00.

Do all the exercises in this test the same way. Try every exercise in your section of the test.

Figure 15.5 Practice items from Lorge-Thorndike Intelligence Tests.

related to all academic subject fields than any single educational achievement test.

Despite their widespread use, two flagrant misuses of group ability tests have occurred. First, students have been placed in "ability" groups, or educational "tracks," based solely on a mental ability score and have been kept in the same track thereafter. Second, a cutoff score on a group ability test has been used as the sole basis for selecting students to receive special education provisions. For example, an IQ of 85 is used to identify "slow learners," and 130 "gifted students." These practices are unfair to students who have little opportunity to learn at school and in their homes.

During the late 1960s and early 1970s, some opposition to intellectual ability testing arose because of these and other misuses of the test results. The misuses and proper uses of ability testing are discussed by Cronbach (1975) and by Cleary, Humphreys, Kendrick, and Wesman (1975). More recently, Green (1978) indicates that the lower mean scores of minority groups reflect the educational disadvantages experienced by them and that the test results can be helpful in preventing further discrimination against them.

Until recently, minority groups were not included in the process of standardizing mental ability tests, but they now are. The differences in the usefulness of the tests for predicting the educational achievements of students of different ethnic, racial, and socioeconomic groups are being studied. For example, Oakland (1978) found that correlations between mental ability and reading and mathematics achievement in the elementary grades were slightly higher for white than for black children. Two explanations were offered for this finding. First, the lower correlations may result from education having a different effect on the achievements of black children than on white children; and second, the difference may be real, that is, unaffected by education (Oakland, 1978).

With the high attention given in recent years to admission standards both at the graduate and undergraduate levels, many students are being coached in test taking. Swinton and Powers (1983) reported that special preparation resulted in significantly higher scores on the analytic subtest of the Graduate Record Examination. Sesnowitz, Bernhardt, and Kanin (1982) indicated that commercial test preparation courses significantly increased Scholastic Aptitude Test scores. Bangert-Drowns, Kulik, and Kulik (1983) surveyed the literature on coaching, or special preparation. They found the average increase from coaching to be about 15 points on the Scholastic Aptitude Test, about 6 IQ points on other intellectual ability tests, and 2–3 months on the grade-equivalent scale of standardized achievement tests. Moreover, the gains were greater when students (1) were given a pretest prior to coaching, (2) practiced on tests identical to the criterion tests, and (3) practiced on a regular schedule for longer periods of time. These findings support earlier research on the effects of teaching students test-taking skills related to specific tests.

Special Aptitude Tests

Psychologists and others continue to try to identify the aptitudes that correlate higher than general intellectual ability with success in different careers. Tests that have high predictive value for this purpose are very useful to students and their parents when deciding which high school courses to take. They are also helpful to adults who are uncertain about jobs in which they may be most effective.

The General Aptitude Test Battery (GATB) is the foremost aptitude test battery in use today. It was developed by the U.S. Employment Service and is used in employment offices throughout the nation to identify occupations that individuals are best suited for. It is also available to nonprofit organizations, such as high schools and colleges. Counselors use it to help students decide on careers. It measures the following areas: general intelligence, verbal ability, numerical ability, spatial ability, perceptual ability, aiming ability, speed, finger dexterity, manual dexterity, and reasoning.

Rarely are other aptitude tests found that measure the motor areas and that relate the results of the tests to success in various occupations.

Social Intelligence

Guilford (1967) proposed the idea of social intelligence. Its main feature is the ability to adapt to social situations. Ford and Tisak (1983) administered six measures of social intelligence and four measures of academic intelligence to adolescents. Subsequent factor analyses revealed a distinct social intelligence factor. Based upon this finding, these scholars propose that there is a marked difference between intellectual and social competence and that educational programs directed toward the development of social competence are justifiable.

Creativity Tests

In recent years, a number of tests designed to measure creative abilities have been published. One test follows for illustrative purposes.

The Torrance Tests of Creative Thinking (Torrance, 1966a) are intended for use from kindergarten through graduate school. The test items measure divergent thinking rather than convergent thinking. Students' responses to the various test items are not scored for correctness. Rather, each item is scored for one or more of the following divergent thinking abilities: fluency, flexibility, originality, and elaboration. These are the main attributes of creative production included in Guilford's structure of intellect (Guilford, 1967). Representative items of the Torrance test follow:

TEST ITEMS TO MEASURE CREATIVITY

Ask-and-Guess. Given a sketch, the student is told to (1) ask all the questions needed to know exactly what is happening in the drawing, (2) guess as many causes as possible for the action in the picture, and (3) guess possible consequences of what is taking place in the picture.

Product Improvement. This item presents a picture of a stuffed animal and allows students ten minutes to list "the cleverest, most interesting, and unusual ways" they can think of for changing the toy to make it more fun to play with as a toy, regardless of cost.

Unusual Uses. The student is given ten minutes to list "interesting and unusual uses" for a common object, such as a tin can or a cardboard box.

Just Suppose. Here the student is asked to guess what would happen if a certain situation occurred. This is an example: "Just suppose clouds had strings attached to them which hang to earth. What would happen?" Five minutes are allowed for the test.

All types of creativity tests have lower reliability than is desired. The construct validity of originality tests is reasonably well established (Milgram, 1983); however, their validity for predicting creativity in real-life situations has not been established. Thus, creativity tests should *not* be used as the sole basis for selecting a student for a particular curriculum or a kind of instruction that other students do not receive nor should they be used as a basis for deciding upon a career. Rather, creativity test results are helpful in understanding the creative aspect of a student's development and in arranging instruction that is designed to develop the creativity of every student.

Caution is necessary in administering creativity tests. In a carefully conducted study, somewhat different results were obtained with grade 6 students when creativity tests were administered under (1) an untimed, gamelike condition, (2) a conventional, testlike condition on one day, and (3) a conventional testlike condition on two adjacent days (Hattie, 1980). Most reliable results were achieved under the conventional one-day testlike condition.

Learning Style Inventories

Do you prefer a bright light or a dim light when studying? Do you persist until tasks are finished, or do you fail to complete many things that you start? Do you prefer working alone or studying with other persons? Do you prefer to learn by reading or by seeing an instructional film? The answers to these and similar questions indicate learning styles.

As we saw in Chapter 5, where learning styles were discussed, Dunn and Dunn (1978) have identified 36 different learning styles related to four areas as follows:

Environment: Sound, light, temperature, room design.
Emotional: Motivation, persistence, responsibility, structure.
Sociological: Peers, self, pair, team, adult, varied.
Physical: Perceptual, intake, time, mobility.

An inventory has been developed to measure the learning styles related to each of the four areas (Dunn, Dunn, & Price, 1983). A computer-generated learning style profile is prepared for each student, and recommendations are given concerning how to arrange the environment for the student (Dunn & Dunn, 1978). Groups of students with similar profiles are also identified by computer, and recommendations for the groups are made available to the school. A few computer-generated recommendations for different learning styles follow (Dunn, Dunn, & Price, 1984):

RECOMMENDATIONS FOR ACCOMMODATING LEARNING STYLES

NEEDS WARM RATHER THAN COOL ENVIRONMENT WHEN STUDYING

Create den area near sources of heat (radiators) or on inside walls away from doors and windows; permit wearing of sweaters, etc.

TEACHER-MOTIVATED RATHER THAN SELF-MOTIVATED

Establish den area near teacher; praise often; incorporate reporting to teacher into prescription; include in small-group instructional techniques when teacher is involved.

RESPONSIBLE RATHER THAN NOT RESPONSIBLE FOR COMPLETING ASSIGNMENTS
Begin by designing short-term prescriptions; as they are successfully completed, gradually increase their length, being certain to keep them on the student's level of functional ability.

HAS AUDITORY PREFERENCES RATHER THAN VISUAL OR OTHER PREFERENCES
Use tapes, records, radio, television, instructional packages (if adult-oriented, use adult voices; if peer-oriented, use peer voices); require activities that involve talking, listening, and repeating what is heard; use instructional packages.

FUNCTIONS BEST IN LATE MORNING RATHER THAN AT OTHER TIMES DURING THE DAY AND EVENING
Permit student to self-schedule; if not possible, teach student's most difficult subject(s) in the late morning.

Dunn (1983) reports that students achieve higher when their learning styles are accommodated. Despite this finding, teachers should give careful consideration to all the possible effects of accommodating each student's present styles. One consideration is which styles to try to accommodate and which to change, if possible. This decision may be different for a child of age 8 and an adolescent of age 16. For example, if a child of age 8 prefers to study math at night but not during school hours, should the teacher try to change the preference? Should the teacher accommodate the style of a 16-year-old adolescent who prefers to learn science by watching films and listening to recordings to reading about it? If another prefers to study seriously only when preparing for tests, what should be done? The author has found that some parents of elementary school children want teachers to permit their children to lounge about on the carpet when studying, rather than to require them to sit at a desk, and also to allow them to move about the room freely, rather than to stay at a desk or table. Other parents do not want these conditions for their children; they desire more "discipline." Teachers, too, are divided on matters such as these.

A second decision is to ascertain which styles can and cannot be provided for in terms of available space and instructional materials. For example, should a lounging area be established in every classroom?

A third decision is to determine which styles can be accommodated with a reasonable amount of time and effort. For instance, it is possible that a large amount of effort to accommodate the different times of day elementary school children prefer to study may not pay large dividends.

Attitude and Self-Concept Inventories

Students' attitudes influence how they respond to their instruction, subject matter, and many other aspects of their school life, as was explained in Chapter 12. The students' self-concepts are related to how they conduct themselves in and out of school, as was indicated in Chapter 13. A number of tests, usually called *inventories,* have been published for measuring students' attitudes and self-concepts. The ones which follow are from the uncopyrighted collections of the Instructional Objectives Exchange (IOX). This organization produces many lists of objectives and related test items that local schools may use.

Attitude Toward School

The IOX *Attitude Toward School* will be used to illustrate an attitude inventory. It has separate tests for the primary, intermediate, and secondary school levels (Instructional Objectives Exchange, 1972). For each level, there is a direct self-report inventory and an inferential self-report inventory. To guide teacher observations, there is also a list of student behaviors indicative of student attitudes.

What is a *direct self-report inventory?* It is a test with questions that indicate the exact intent of the questions, for example, Do you like your classmates? It is easy to fake the expected answer, namely, a favorable attitude, to this kind of question. What is an *inferential self-report inventory?* It has questions that camouflage the intent of the questions. Answers to inferential questions are not so readily faked. The IOX recommends that students should not be asked to identify themselves by giving their names on either the direct or inferential inventory. Not revealing their identity is intended to ensure honest responding. Answer sheets may be used with the direct and inferential inventories. Thus, they may be scored by machine or by hand.

The IOX attitude inventories are designed to measure the student's attitudes toward six dimensions of their schooling as follows:

SIX DIMENSIONS OF STUDENT ATTITUDES

Attitudes Toward Teachers: The student's subjective feelings about teacher behaviors related to mode of instruction, authority and control, and interpersonal relationships with the student.

Attitudes Toward the School's Social Structure and Climate: The student's attitude toward the school as a social center, a rule-making and rule-enforcing entity, and an opportunity for extracurricular activities.

Attitudes Toward School Subjects: The student's attitudes toward the commonly taught school subjects.

Attitudes Toward Learning: The student's attitude toward the learning experience (independent of attitude toward school, teachers, and subjects) as reflected in intellectual curiosity, willingness to study, volunteering, interest in problem solving, etc.

Attitudes Toward Peers: The student's feelings regarding the structure and climate of relationships within the peer group, rather than toward particular individuals within that group.

General Attitudes Toward School: The student's orientation toward schooling in general, rather than toward the particular school the student is attending.

Examples of direct questioning, inferential questioning, and observation used in the IOX inventories follow. The direct questions are from the senior high school inventory; the inferential questions are from the intermediate level; and the observation schedule is from the primary level and the intermediate level (Instructional Objectives Exchange, 1972).

THREE MEANS OF MEASURING ATTITUDES

DIRECT QUESTIONS, ATTITUDES TOWARD PEERS, SENIOR HIGH SCHOOL (The student is to respond to each item with *strongly agree, agree, disagree,* or *strongly disagree*)
I enjoy working on class projects with other students.
School is a good place for making friends.
There are many closed groups of students here.

INFERENTIAL QUESTIONS, ATTITUDES TOWARD PEERS, INTERMEDIATE LEVEL
You are going to write a true story about yourself and the pupils at your school. You want the story to be realistic. The following list contains things that might be true about the pupils at your school. Fill in the space labeled *A* on the answer sheet if the sentence is one you would include, or *B* if you would not include it:
    If a new pupil came to my school, he could make friends easily.
    I feel like a part of a group at school.
    Most of the pupils at school aren't much fun.

OBSERVATIONAL INDICATORS, COMPLIANCE WITH SCHOOL RULES, PRIMARY AND INTERMEDIATE LEVELS (The rule that is violated is implied)
Fighting with another child in the classroom or on the playground.
Using inappropriate language.
Disrupting classroom activities.
Damaging school property.

Self-Concept

The IOX self-concept test parallels that of the IOX attitude test. There are direct self-report and inferential self-report inventories and observational indicators for the primary, intermediate, and secondary school levels. Four dimensions of the self-concept are measured: family, peer, scholastic, and general. The following direct self-report items imply the student's own attitudes toward self:

MEASURING THE SELF-CONCEPT

PRIMARY LEVEL, FAMILY (Item to be read to the children and marked *yes* or *no* on a specially prepared answer sheet)
Do you often get into trouble at home?
Are you an important person in your family?
Do members of your family pick on you?

INTERMEDIATE LEVEL, PEER (To be read by the student and checked *true* or *untrue*)
Other children are interested in me.
I should get along better with other children than I do.
I am popular with kids my own age.

SECONDARY LEVEL, SCHOLASTIC (To be checked *strongly agree, agree, disagree,* or *strongly disagree*)
School work is fairly easy for me.
I sometimes feel upset when I'm at school.
Getting good grades is fairly important to me.

SECONDARY LEVEL, GENERAL
I am satisfied to be just what I am.
I often let other people have their way.
I often do things that I'm sorry for later.

15.4 Think of published tests as providing information of very high, high, some, little, or no value in arranging high-quality education for individual students. Assign one of the preceding ratings to each of the following kinds of published tests: educational achievement, mental ability, creativity, learning styles, attitudes, self-concept. Explain the reasons for your ratings.

15.5 How are tests of general intellectual ability, special aptitude, and creativity alike in terms of the uses to be made of the test results? How are they different?

15.6 Individually administered intelligence tests are much more expensive to administer than group IQ tests. Why do you think individual tests are still administered?

15.7 Here are the learning styles of two elementary school children:

Mary needs quiet, prefers a desk or chair when studying, is self-motivated, prefers to study alone, has an auditory preference, and prefers not to move about when studying.

Sue prefers sound, such as background music; prefers lounging on the floor when studying; has low motivation for studying; prefers learning with several peers; has a visual preference, and likes to move about frequently when studying:

Indicate which of the styles you think teachers should try to accommodate and which of the styles teachers should try to change before Mary and Sue complete elementary school. Indicate why.

15.8 Self-concept and attitudes toward school may be measured by direct questioning, inferential questioning, and observation. What are some advantages and limitations of each of these approaches?

15.9 The results of published tests may be used advantageously or misused. Indicate one or two ways in which results from each of the following tests (a) may be used advantageously and (b) may be misused: educational achievement in reading, general intellectual ability, aptitude for careers, creativity, learning styles, attitudes toward teacher authority, academic self-concept.

Domain-referenced Testing

Objective-referenced Testing

Minimum Competency Testing

CRITERION-REFERENCED ACHIEVEMENT TESTING

Criterion-referenced achievement testing has emerged in two distinct ways (Nitko, 1980). One way is concerned with organizing the content that is to be learned and tested. This approach involves formulating content domains and constructing *domain-referenced tests*. The other emphasizes the criterion, or standard, that is established for passing a test. Persons following this approach have focused on instructional objectives and constructing *objective-referenced tests*. Minimum competency tests are objective-referenced and are used to determine whether students have acquired a minimum level of desired knowledge and skills.

Domain-referenced Testing

A *domain* refers to a closely related area of knowledge or skills. A *knowledge domain* might consist of the classes of the animal kingdom. A *skill domain* might be adding whole numbers. Usually the domain is defined narrowly, such as adding whole numbers. The whole field of addition as a domain is too broad, since it includes whole numbers, common fractions, and decimal fractions and can be learned only over a period of many years.

Subject matter experts identify the domains of knowledge and skill of a particular subject field. The tasks of each domain are arranged either in a logical order or in terms of the difficulty of learning them. Related tests are constructed to measure the amount of knowledge from none to complete and to measure a skill from no proficiency to a perfect performance.

What is the criterion of acceptable performance for a particular student in domain-referenced testing? After a domain is specified, a test is constructed to measure the achievement of each task of the domain. For example, ten tests are constructed if there are ten tasks in the domain, one to measure the achievement of each task. An acceptable performance by a beginning student might be passing the test of the easiest task. Passing all ten tests is necessary for demonstrating mastery of the domain. Thus, the criterion of acceptable performance established by the teacher varies for the same individual from one time to another, for example, from the beginning to the end of a semester.

Domain-referenced testing does not require the use of norms for interpreting a student's test scores as does standardized educational achievement testing. Instead, an individual's score or performance is referenced to the tasks of the domain. Assume, for example, that the domain is counting by fives to 100. A child's being able to count to 25 can be *referenced,* or related, to this domain, regardless of how other students achieve. Moreover, anyone, including a student, parent, or teacher, can interpret the individual's present level of achievement in relation to mastery of the complete domain.

Many local school districts, state education agencies, and test publishers are currently organizing subject fields into domains of knowledge and skills. They are also constructing tests for each task of the domain.

These tests are then being used in local schools to chart the course of each individual student's progress. Microcomputers, as well as teachers and teacher aides, keep track of each student's progress.

Although domain-referenced testing is relatively recent, there is a possibility that it will become the primary means of measuring student achievement. Much depends on how well the subject matter domains can be delineated, the extent to which local schools accept and teach the domains, and the availability of low-cost tests and record-keeping procedures for charting the progress of individual students.

We should recognize that domain-referenced testing does not automatically ensure that teachers will have content-valid tests. The tests will have high content validity only if teachers accept the domains without modification and teach the recommended content.

Objective-referenced Testing

Objective-referenced testing is also domain-referenced if the instructional objectives are related directly to a clearly specified domain of knowledge or skills. In the early years of objective-referenced testing, instructional objectives were often written without first having specified the domain. Even today, some teachers write instructional objectives without being aware of the complete domain of knowledge or skills to which their objectives are related.

In objective-referenced testing, the objectives of instruction are specified, and one or more test items are constructed to measure the achievement of each objective. Assume that a test of 12 items is constructed for each objective. A cutoff score, such as 85% correct, is used as the criterion for determining whether the student has mastered the objective. In typical objective-based instruction, a student must achieve the established criterion in order to proceed to the next objective of the instructional sequence.

An interesting question regarding objective-referenced testing is how well students respond to not being compared with others. University students who were told that their achievements would be evaluated in comparison with other students achieved higher on the same test than those who were told they would be evaluated in terms of the percentage of test items they answered correctly (Crocker & Benson, 1976). It is not known whether elementary and high school students would respond like the university students.

Minimum Competency Testing

Minimum competency tests are usually objective-referenced and may also be domain-referenced. Minimum competency tests in reading, mathematics, and language arts are being used in many school districts and throughout many states. In some school districts, students are not promoted from one grade to the next or from one school level to the next, or they are not awarded a high school diploma until they achieve a certain cutoff score on the relevant minimum competency tests. In 1978, most states had already started minimum competency testing in reading and in other subject fields or were planning to do so (Chall, 1979).

Oregon was the first state to pass a minimum competency law. The school district of Portland, Oregon, constructed its own locally developed minimum competency tests in reading, mathematics, and language usage for grades 3–8 to meet the provisions of the Oregon law. The criteria that the testing program was designed to meet are as follows:

> It should help students become competent beginning as early as the third grade rather than denying diplomas to students who had arrived at the late stages of their secondary education without acquiring required competencies.
> It should focus on basic skills competencies initially since these were the first competencies in which students were to be certified under the State mandate and since these were the highest priorities of the school system.
> It should assist teachers, parents and students in instructional decision making by giving clear, accurate and unbiased information about student performance on specific major competencies and goals within the local curriculum leading to further diagnosis and prescription in areas in which a student's progress toward meeting district graduation competencies appeared unsatisfactory.
> It should assist administrators, board members and citizens in administrative and policy decision making by giving clear, accurate and unbiased information about how Portland schools are doing in comparison with others and whether performance levels within the District are heading upward, remaining constant, or decreasing over time.
> It should give every student a chance to be measured at his or her individual functional level and thus avoid discouraging some students while failing to challenge others.
> There should be as little testing as possible and each test required should be short enough to be administered in approximately one 50 minute period. (Hathaway, 1980, pp. 345–346)

The tests in reading, mathematics, and language usage were constructed to measure major competencies, along with the subcompetencies that were selected by teachers. Three major competencies in reading, mathematics, and language usage follow to indicate the nature of the competencies (Hathaway, 1980, pp. 347–348):

MAJOR COMPETENCIES IN READING, MATHEMATICS, AND LANGUAGE USAGE

READING COMPETENCIES, GRADES 3–8
1. The student can interpret meanings of commonly used words: context clues; synonyms, antonyms; structure components; multiple meanings.
2. The student can comprehend the literal meanings or explicit content of written materials: recall of details; interpreting directions; sequence of details; classification of facts; recall of stated main idea.
3. The student can interpret implied and related meanings from the content and presentation of written materials: drawing inferences; recognizing cause and effect; prediction of events; summary and synthesis.

MATHEMATICS COMPETENCIES, GRADES 4–8
1. The student can add whole numbers.
2. The student can subtract whole numbers.
3. The student can multiply whole numbers.

LANGUAGE USAGE COMPETENCIES, GRADES 3–8
1. The student can recognize and use fundamental sentence and paragraph structures.
2. The student can use basic grammar correctly.
3. The student can punctuate correctly.

There are tests to measure each student's attainment of each competency. The tests are administered in the fall and in the spring. The results of the fall testing are used by the teacher to determine where to focus the instruction for each child, while the results of the spring testing are used to assess each student's progress during the year.

Using the fall testing, the teacher knows whether the criterion for each minimum competency has been met and also whether it has not been met. If it has not been met, a further indication is given of how far the student is behind in terms of completing all the minimum competencies by the end of grade 8, provided there is no change in the rate at which the student passes the tests. The teacher is then expected to do further diagnostic work and, if the problem is confirmed, to take remedial measures. This use of the results is intended to ensure good instruction for every student and also completion of the minimum competencies required for high school graduation not later than the end of grade 8.

The achievements of the students of each teacher are summarized and are made available to the teacher and the principal. If it appears that the students of a given teacher are not achieving as well as they should be, the teacher and the principal try to ascertain the causes and then remedy the situation. In addition to the preceding uses of the test results, the achievements of the students of each school are summarized and compared with the achievements of all the students of the Portland School District. School district officials can then identify any school that is experiencing more difficulties than other schools and try to work with the school staff in improving the situation. Moreover, the achievements of the students of each school and of the entire district are compared from year to year. This kind of information is used in improving the curriculum of the school district from year to year.

From the preceding, we see how competency-based testing is intended to help the individual students of a school district achieve the minimum competencies in reading, mathematics, and language usage that have been established for high school graduation. The program is arranged in such a way that the individual teacher, each principal, and the district officials all have key responsibilities in designing the program and making it work effectively. Moreover, the parents are involved through a program of parent-teacher conferences. This kind of approach appears to hold more promise than state programs of minimum competency testing that focus only on meeting minimum competencies during the high school years.

15.10 Outline the information that would be needed before starting to construct each of the following kinds of tests: domain-referenced, objective-referenced, and minimum competency tests.

15.11 A minimum level of achievement or performance on a criterion-referenced test, such as 85% correct, is established for retaining a student in a unit of instruction; a grade in school; or a level of schooling, such as middle school. Give two or three arguments for and against not advancing a student (exclude one with learning handicaps) (a) from one short instructional sequence to another, (b) from one grade in school to the next, and (c) from one level of schooling to another, such as elementary school to middle school.

MEASURING PSYCHOMOTOR SKILLS

A relatively small number of motor abilities, including speed, accuracy, strength, endurance, and coordination, underlie the performance of many different psychomotor skills. These abilities are measured by *performance tests*. Teachers of different subject fields are interested in measuring one or more of these abilities of their students.

Speed may be measured in terms of the amount accomplished during a fixed time period, such as the number of words typed per minute, or in terms of the time needed to perform a task, such as the time for running the 100-yard dash. *Accuracy* in these two examples may be measured by a simple count of errors or by distance off target. *Strength* is inferred from the lifting of weights or the pressure applied to a scale. *Endurance* is estimated by observing performance either across a time interval, such as during the first and last minutes of a speed test of typing, or in a physically demanding activity, such as running 1000 yards. *Coordination* is rated by directly observing an individual's performance, such as throwing a baseball or playing the violin, or by rating a product, such as a paragraph of handwriting or a page of shorthand.

There are not many published tests in the psychomotor domain. The General Aptitude Test Battery, however, has tests of motor coordination, finger dexterity, and manual dexterity.

The Youth Fitness Test was developed by the American Association for Health, Physical Education, and Recreation (1965). It is the first test of physical fitness for which national norms have been developed. Appropriate for students in grade 5 through college, the battery includes subtests that measure different aspects of fitness, including strength, speed, coordination, and endurance. Figure 15.6 indicates one measurement of running speed.

3 shuttle run
BOYS AND GIRLS

EQUIPMENT

Two blocks of wood, 2 inches × 2 inches × 4 inches, and stopwatch. Pupils should wear sneakers or run barefooted.

DESCRIPTION

Two parallel lines are marked on the floor 30 feet apart. The width of a regulation volleyball court serves as a suitable area. Place the blocks of wood behind one of the lines as indicated in FIGURE 7. The pupil starts from behind the other line. On the signal "Ready? Go!" the pupil runs to the blocks, picks one up, runs back to the starting line, and *places* the block behind the line; he then runs back and picks up the second block, which he carries back across the starting line. If the scorer has two stopwatches or one with a split-second timer, it is preferable to have two pupils running at the same time. To eliminate the necessity of returning the blocks after each race, start the races alternately, first from behind one line and then from behind the other.

RULES

Allow two trials with some rest between.

SCORING

Record the time of the better of the two trials to the nearest tenth of a second.

30 ft

Figure 15.6 Example of a psychomotor test.
Source: American Association for Health, Physical Education, and Recreation, 1965, p. 19.

15.12 Compare the administration of a performance test, such as in typing or the shuttle run, and of a paper-and-pencil educational achievement test in terms of (a) the instructions given to the students, (b) the testing equipment and materials required, and (c) the scoring of the test.

15.13 Apply the concepts of predictive validity, reliability, and usability to performance testing.

Objective Tests

Essay Tests

Work Samples

Teacher Observation

TEACHER-DEVELOPED MEASUREMENT TECHNIQUES

Excellent instruction requires frequent measurement of each student's achievement to determine the student's progress in learning and to provide feedback. To achieve these purposes, teachers use objective tests, essay tests, work samples, and observation. Skill in constructing tests and using other measurement techniques requires practice. The purpose here is to provide an overview of various kinds of test items and measurement techniques. Detailed instructions for constructing test items are provided in the textbooks included in the "Suggestions for Further Reading" at the end of this chapter.

Objective Tests

The principal types of objective test items are (1) alternate-choice, (2) multiple-choice, (3) matching, and (4) completion. Most students of educational psychology have responded to many items of these types. However, they may not have written any. Consideration of the strengths and weaknesses of each type may prove helpful in deciding the kind of item to construct.

Alternate-Choice Items

Alternate-choice items (*True/False, Yes/No,* etc.) require the student to select one of two choices as correct. Some strengths of alternate-choice items are that they may be adapted to testing in many classes, they test a great deal of material in a short amount of time, and they are easily scored. Weaknesses of these items are that guessing is encouraged, the learner is presented with a wrong as well as a right response, and constructing alternate-choice items in which either choice is always correct is difficult. When some of the items in the test are usually true and others are always true, the student is faced with the problem of deciding whether a usually true item should be marked *True* or *False*.

Hopkins and Stanley (1981) make the following suggestions for constructing true/false items (pp. 251–253):

SUGGESTIONS FOR CONSTRUCTING TRUE/FALSE ITEMS

1. Avoid using specific determiners as clues.
2. Avoid a disproportionate number of either true or false statements.

3. Avoid the exact wording of the textbook.
4. Avoid trick statements.
5. Limit each statement to the exact point to be tested.
6. Avoid excess use of negative words and phrases.
7. Avoid ambiguous words and statements.
8. Avoid complex vocabulary and language and unnecessarily complex sentence structure.
9. Require the simplest possible method for indicating the response.
10. Use true/false items only for points that lend themselves unambiguously to this kind of item.

Multiple-Choice Items

Multiple-choice items require the student to select one of three, four, or five choices as correct or better than the others. The multiple-choice item is used widely in published tests, because it is adaptable to measuring such outcomes as the understanding of concepts, the ability to apply information, and the ability to evaluate. Multiple-choice items are more difficult to construct than alternate-choice ones.

Gronlund (1981) provides suggestions for constructing multiple-choice items and gives examples of poor and better construction. The suggestions and some of the examples follow (pp. 189–197):

SUGGESTIONS FOR CONSTRUCTING MULTIPLE-CHOICE ITEMS

1. The stem of the item should be meaningful by itself and should present a definite problem.
   Poor: South America
   A is a flat, arid country.
   B imports coffee from the United States.
   C has a larger population than the United States.
   Ⓓ was settled mainly by colonists from Spain.

   Better: Most of South America was settled by colonists from
   A England.
   B France.
   C Holland.
   Ⓓ Spain.

2. The item stem should include as much of the item as possible and should be free of irrelevant material.
   Poor: Most of South America was settled by colonists from Spain. How would you account for the large number of Spanish colonists settling there?
   A They were adventurous.
   Ⓑ They were in search of wealth.
   C They wanted lower taxes.
   D They were seeking religious freedom.

Better: Why did Spanish colonists settle most of South America?
  A They were adventurous.
  Ⓑ They were in search of wealth.
  C They wanted lower taxes.
  D They were seeking religious freedom.

Best: Spanish colonists settled most of South America in search of
  A adventure.
  Ⓑ wealth.
  C lower taxes.
  D religious freedom.

3. Use a negatively stated item stem only when significant learning out-comes require it.
Poor: Which one of the following is not a safe driving practice on icy roads?
  A Accelerating slowly.
  Ⓑ Jamming on the brakes.
  C Holding the wheel firmly.
  D Slowing down gradually.

Better: All of the following are safe driving practices on icy roads EXCEPT
  A accelerating slowly.
  Ⓑ jamming on the brakes.
  C holding the wheel firmly.
  D slowing down gradually.

4. All of the alternatives should be grammatically consistent with the stem of the item.
Poor: An electric transformer can be used
  A for storing up electricity.
  Ⓑ to increase the voltage of alternating current.
  C it converts electrical energy into mechanical energy.
  D alternating current is changed to direct current.

Better: An electric transformer can be used to
  A store up electricity.
  Ⓑ increase the voltage of alternating current.
  C convert electrical energy into mechanical energy.
  D change alternating current to direct current.

5. An item should contain only one correct or clearly best answer.
Poor: Which one of the following is the best source of heat for home use?
  A Coal.
  B Electricity.
  C Gas.
  D Oil.

Better: In the midwestern part of the United States, which one of the fol-lowing is the most economical source of heat for home use?
  Ⓐ Coal.
  B Electricity.
  C Gas.
  D Oil.

6. Items used to measure understanding should contain some novelty, but not too much novelty.

7. All distracters should be plausible.
   Poor: Who discovered the North Pole?
   - A Christopher Columbus.
   - B Ferdinand Magellan.
   - Ⓒ Robert Peary.
   - D Marco Polo.

   Better: Who discovered the North Pole?
   - A Roald Amundsen.
   - B Richard Byrd.
   - Ⓒ Robert Peary.
   - D Robert Scott.

8. Verbal associations between the stem and the correct answer should be avoided.
   Poor: Which one of the following agencies should you contact to find out about a tornado warning in your locality?
   - A State Farm Bureau.
   - Ⓑ Local Radio Station.
   - C United States Post Office.
   - D United States Weather Bureau.

   Better: Which one of the following agencies should you contact to find out about a tornado warning in your locality?
   - A Local Farm Bureau.
   - Ⓑ Nearest Radio Station.
   - C Local Post Office.
   - D United States Weather Bureau.

9. The relative length of the alternatives should not provide a clue to the answer.
   Poor: What is the major purpose of the United Nations?
   - Ⓐ To maintain peace among the peoples of the world.
   - B To establish international law.
   - C To provide military control.
   - D To form new governments.

   Better: What is the major purpose of the United Nations?
   - Ⓐ To maintain peace among the peoples of the world.
   - B To develop a new system of international law.
   - C To provide military control of nations that have recently attained their independence.
   - D To establish and maintain democratic forms of government in newly formed nations.

10. The correct answer should appear in each of the alternative positions approximately an equal number of times, but in random order.

11. Use special alternatives such as "None of the above" or "All of the above" sparingly.

Matching Items

Matching items call for pairing an item in the first column with a word or phrase in the second column. The content domain of each group of items to be matched should be related. For example, if you wish to test association of synonyms and association of men and events, use two sets of items: the first to deal with synonyms and the second to deal with men and events. Generally, matching items measure only whether the association has been made and whether the student recognizes it. Matching items do not usually measure the extent to which meaning has been established.

Gronlund (1981) makes six suggestions for constructing matching items (pp. 172–175):

SUGGESTIONS FOR CONSTRUCTING MATCHING ITEMS

1. Use only homogeneous material in a single matching exercise.
2. Include an unequal number of responses and premises, and instruct the pupil that responses may be used once, more than once, or not at all.
3. Keep the list of items to be matched brief and place the shorter responses on the right.
4. Arrange the list of responses in logical order.
5. Indicate in the directions the basis for matching the responses and premises.
6. Place all of the items for one matching exercise on the same page.

Gronlund (1981) offers the following as an example of a well-constructed matching item (p. 174):

Directions: On the line to the left of each historical event in *Column A*, write the letter from *Column B* which identifies the time period during which the event occurred. Each date in *Column B* may be used once, more than once, or not at all.

Column A		*Column B*	
B	1. Boston Tea Party	A	1765–1769
A	2. Repeal of the Stamp Act	B	1770–1774
E	3. Enactment of the Northwest Ordinance	C	1775–1779
C	4. Battle of Lexington	D	1780–1784
A	5. Enactment of Townshend Acts	E	1785–1789
B	6. First Continental Congress		
E	7. United States Constitution drawn up		

Completion Items

Completion items are those in which words or phrases have been omitted in sentences. To facilitate scoring of completion tests, consecutive numbers may be placed in the blanks, with instructions that the answers corresponding to the numbers be placed in the left margin. The weakness of this kind of item is that it measures recall, not comprehension, application, analysis, and other high-level cognitive skills.

Essay Tests

An essay test item may be responded to in a few minutes, during a class period, or over an even longer period of time. Essay tests are sometimes preferred to objective tests because they are less time-consuming to construct. Nevertheless, they require considerably more time to grade. Another possible advantage is that essay tests motivate the student to study materials for the purpose of understanding concepts, principles, and generalizations, rather than memorizing facts. Most important, however, essay tests are useful for measuring the students' ability to express themselves clearly in writing, to recall and organize relatively large amounts of material, and to evaluate.

One problem with essay tests is that content validity is low when only a few items can be included in a test. An even more critical problem is that the subjective nature of the scoring may lead to low reliability. Thus, two students who perform equally well on a given essay test may be assigned a different rating or letter grade.

The grading of essay tests may be improved by following these suggestions (Hopkins & Stanley, 1981, p. 233):

SUGGESTIONS FOR GRADING ESSAY QUESTIONS

1. Before scoring any papers, review the material in the textbook that covers the questions, and also the lecture notes on the subject.
2. Make a list of the main points that should be discussed in every answer.
3. Read over a sampling of the papers to obtain a general idea of the quality of answer that may be expected.
4. Score one question through all of the papers before evaluating another question.
5. Read the answer through once and then check it over for factual details.
6. More than one reader is always desirable and should be employed when practicable.

Work Samples

The written work of students is often read and rated. For instance, a student's ability to solve simultaneous equations with two unknowns may be assessed by examining the exercises that the student has completed. Likewise, the teacher may assess a student's skill in expressing thoughts in complete sentences by selecting a written social studies report and judging sentence structure. Either complete assignments or portions of assignments may be selected for evaluating students' progress.

Teacher Observation

Observation of students' verbal and overt actions is the principal measurement technique used to facilitate and evaluate student learning in many different situations, for example, conducting an experiment, hitting a baseball, giving a talk, conversing in a foreign language, or making a map. Furthermore, teachers are capable of arriving at quite reliable judgments about many characteristics of an individual student from their daily observations. For example, kindergarten and primary school teachers, without any special instruction or guidance, rated their students from 1 to 5 on a number of characteristics (Stevenson, Parker, Wilkinson, Hegion, & Fish, 1976). The combined ratings of certain characteristics were found to be good predictors of each student's achievement the following year in reading and arithmetic as measured by standardized tests. The ratings of the student characteristics that correlated high with later tested achievement in arithmetic, reading, or both were as follows (Stevenson et al., 1976, p. 509):

Effective Learning: "Catches on" quickly; assimilates new material easily; readily grasps new principles; seems to understand explanations easily.

Following Instructions: Unusually skillful in remembering and following instructions.

Retaining Information: Superior memory for details and content.

Vocabulary: High-level vocabulary; always uses precise words; conveys abstractions.

From this study, we cannot infer how well teachers who have students for only one class period daily may be able to rate these and other characteristics. Similarly, it is not known that the same high relationship between these ratings and achievement would be found with older students. It is assumed, however, that teachers of all school levels in all subject fields can learn to observe their students' behaviors and arrive at sound judgments regarding their achievements and other characteristics.

15.14 Identify two or more specific learning outcomes that can readily be measured by (a) objective tests, (b) essay tests, (c) work samples, and (d) classroom observation.

15.15 Compare multiple-choice items with true/false and essay items with respect to (a) the kind of learning outcome that can be measured, (b) the amount of time required to construct the item, and (c) the reliability of the test scores.

15.16 Teachers observe and mentally rate their students on what the students says and does in class. Would you expect the ratings of high school teachers or elementary school teachers to be more accurate with respect to students' (a) subject matter achievement, (b) capability or aptitude for learning the subject matter, (c) creativity, (d) attitudes toward the class and the teacher's methods, and (e) academic self-concept? Explain.

15.17 Why might parents want a published test of educational achievement, intellectual ability, learning style, and self-concept to be used to supplement a teacher's judgments in these areas regarding their child?

15.18 Write (a) four true/false items, (b) two multiple-choice items, (c) a set of four matching items, and (d) two essay questions to measure student achievement of the content of this chapter related to teacher-developed measurement techniques. Using the Bloom taxonomy, indicate what each item is designed to measure.

15.19 Review and Application. Recall the most important information regarding each of the following concepts, and identify at least one possible use of the information by you as a learner, a teacher, or both:

> Attributes of Good Measurement
>> Validity
>> Reliability
>> Usability
> Norm-referenced and Other Published Tests
>> Norm-referenced Tests of Educational Achievement
>> Tests of Mental Abilities and Special Aptitudes
>> Creativity Tests
>> Learning Style Inventories
>> Attitude and Self-Concept Inventories
> Criterion-referenced Achievement Testing
>> Domain-referenced Testing
>> Objective-referenced Testing
>> Minimum Competency Testing
> Measuring Psychomotor Skills
> Teacher-developed Measurement Techniques
>> Objective Tests
>> Essay Tests
>> Work Samples
>> Teacher Observation

SUMMARY

Valid, reliable, and usable tests are needed in instruction and evaluation. High validity is desired to ensure that the test items sample the content being taught and that the test scores are useful in predicting how well students will achieve. High reliability ensures that a test measures students' performances consistently and accurately. Usable tests ensure that time and money are spent wisely in testing.

Many published tests are available to measure educational achievement, mental ability, creativity, learning styles, attitudes, self-concepts, and other student characteristics and performances. Norm-referenced educational achievement tests measure the outcomes of learning in specific curriculum areas, such as reading, mathematics, and science. The scores that students make on these tests are interpreted by using appropriate national norms.

The Wechsler Intelligence Scale for Children and the Revised Stanford-Binet Intelligence Scale are administered to individuals. Other intelligence tests commonly used in the schools are administered to groups of students. Tests of general intellectual ability are used to predict how students will achieve in academic subject fields, such as science and mathematics. Specific aptitude tests are used to predict achievement in a particular field, such as music and art. The results of published tests of creativity, learning styles, attitudes, and self-concept aid teachers to get a more complete understanding of the individual student and to arrange instruction accordingly. Performance tests are used for assessing the achievement of verbal, motor, and vocal skills.

Criterion-referenced tests may be published or locally constructed. They are used to measure the attainment of closely related domains of achievement or skill. Each test measures a particular task or objective of the domain. A criterion is established to determine when the student masters each task or objective of the domain.

Teacher-developed tests and procedures are essential for ensuring student progress in learning. The four main kinds of tests and procedures are paper-and-pencil tests, performance tests, ratings of students' work samples, and observation of student performances. High validity and reliability are as critical for teacher-made tests as they are for published tests. The construction of valid, reliable tests by teachers requires thorough knowledge of the content that is taught and skill in constructing the tests.

SUGGESTIONS FOR FURTHER READING

Bloom, B. S., Hastings, J. T., & Madaus, G. F. *Handbook on formative and summative evaluation of student learning.* New York: McGraw-Hill, 1971.

This practical handbook provides many examples of excellent test items for measuring knowledge and comprehension in chap. 7, application and analysis in chap. 8, synthesis and evaluation in chap. 9, and affective outcomes in chap. 10. Chapters 13–23 provide models and examples of test items for different school levels and various subject fields: preschool in chaps. 13 and 14, language arts in chap. 15, social studies in chap. 16, art in chap. 17, science in chap. 18, mathematics in chap. 19, literature in chap. 20, writing in chap. 21, second languages in chap. 22, and industrial arts in chap. 23.

Boehm, A. E., & Weinberg, R. A. *The classroom observer: A guide to developing observation skills.* New York: Teachers College Press, 1977.

A short, practical guide for making observations in the preschool and elementary school.

Cartwright, C., & Cartwright, P. G. *Developing observation skills.* (2nd ed.). New York: McGraw-Hill, 1984.

Explains observation procedures and gives many examples of observation reports.

Dwyer, C. A. Achievement testing. In H. E. Mitzel, J. H. Best, & W. Rabinowitz (Eds.), *Encyclopedia of educational research* (5th ed., Vol. 1). New York: Free Press, 1982. Pp. 12–22.

Presents a good description of achievement tests, types of items, and uses of test results.

Gronlund, N. E. *Measurement and evaluation in teaching* (4th ed.). New York: Macmillan, 1981.

Chapters 5–10 of this practical book deal with the construction of classroom tests, including objective, interpretive, and essay tests. Observational techniques are explained in chap. 16, and peer appraisal and self-report inventories in chap. 17.

Hopkins, K. D., & Stanley, J. C. *Educational and psychological measurement* (6th ed.). Englewood Cliffs, N.J.: Prentice-Hall, 1981.

Most of this book is devoted to constructing tests. Chapter 7 deals with principles of constructing achievement tests; chap. 8, essay tests; chap. 9, objective tests; and chap. 10, affective and noncognitive objectives. Chapter 13 explains standardized tests for measuring scholastic aptitude; chap. 14, educational achievement; and chap. 15, interests, personality, and social areas.

Sternberg, R. J. What should intelligence tests test? Implications of a triarchic theory of intelligence for intelligence testing. *Educational Researcher*, 1984, *13*, 5–15.

A scholarly analysis of present IQ testing and how it would change if the triarchic theory was implemented.

CHAPTER 16

EVALUATION OF STUDENT LEARNING AND EDUCATIONAL PROGRAMS

MEASUREMENT DEVICES USED IN EVALUATION

EVALUATING STUDENT PROGRESS AND THE EFFECTIVENESS OF A COURSE

EVALUATING EACH STUDENT'S TOTAL EDUCATIONAL PROGRAM AND REPORTING TO PARENTS

EVALUATING ELEMENTS OF A SCHOOL'S EDUCATIONAL PROGRAM

EVALUATING EDUCATIONAL MATERIALS AND PROCESSES

Carefully conducted evaluation provides the basis for making wise decisions in four critical areas of education. Evaluation is essential for determining whether a student is making as much progress in a course as might be expected. It is also carried out when planning a student's total educational program, and again at the end of the semester when determining how appropriate the program was for the student. Determining how well a program area of the school, such as reading or health education, meets the educational needs of the student body requires evaluation. Evaluation is also necessary for determining the effectiveness and usability of instructional materials and educative processes. Skill in evaluation in these four areas contributes to more effective student learning, a higher quality of teaching, and continuous improvement in the quality of education. Since evaluation requires the use of quantitative and qualitative information, we shall review the kinds of measurement devices used in evaluation prior to considering the four areas of evaluation.

MEASUREMENT DEVICES USED IN EVALUATION

The demands for reliable measurement as a means of improving the quality of education became increasingly strong and persuasive in the early 1980s. For example, the National Commission on Excellence in Education (1983) stated that schools, colleges, and universities should adopt more rigorous standards of academic performance and that standardized tests of achievement should be administered toward the end of each level of schooling to determine how well students have met the academic standards. Ebel (1982), reflecting national opinion, proposed that (a) no instructional program should be continued in the absence of evidence of its effectiveness, (b) school systems should publish the results of systematic public assessments of student achievement annually, and (c) each teacher should submit evidence periodically of the achievement of his or her students.

Thus far we have used the terms measurement, assessment, and evaluation. While these processes are closely related, they are also different. Educational *measurement* involves getting information about a variable such as student achievement, and assigning a numeral or a letter grade to it. For example, we measure students' achievement in mathematics by administering a standardized educational achievement test and scoring it.

Assessment involves measuring and interpreting the measurement. Thus, we interpret each student's score on the achievement test in terms such as *above or below the mean, equivalent to a certain percentile rank,* or in some other way. In this assessment, no value judgment is made about the goodness or adequacy of the student's achievement.

Evaluation involves making value judgments using quantitative information, qualitative information, or both. Typically, evaluation calls for establishing criteria of effectiveness, appropriateness, or some other desired consequence and for relating the quantitative and qualitative information to the criteria. For example, the student with a percentile rank of 30 on a mathematics achievement test is evaluated as not achieving as well as might be expected in terms of the student's ability to achieve, based on a percentile rank of 60 on a test of mathematical reasoning ability. In this case, the criterion established is to achieve at a level near, or at, the ability level.

We shall deal with criteria for evaluating in more detail in later sections of this chapter. At this point, nine kinds of frequently used measurement devices described in Chapter 15 are related to various purposes for securing the measurements, as shown in Table 16.1. Not all of the devices are necessarily used in any one school. It is assumed that the reader is familiar with the measurement devices. Therefore, only relationships between the main kinds of measures and their purposes are indicated.

Norm-referenced intellectual ability tests are used in some schools to get an estimate of each student's capability for learning academic subject matter. On the other hand, norm-referenced and criterion-referenced educational achievement tests are used to determine the knowledge and skills the student has already acquired in the particular subject fields, such as reading, mathematics, or chemistry, and to estimate how well the student will continue to learn the subject matter. Locally constructed educational achievement tests also are applicable only to the specific subject fields for which the tests are constructed.

Published criterion-referenced tests, locally constructed tests, and the teacher's own measurement devices are used to measure each student's achievement level prior to starting an instructional sequence, such as a unit or course, and also at the end of the sequence. The students' progress during the instructional sequence is measured by the same techniques.

TABLE 16.1 FREQUENTLY USED MEASUREMENT DEVICES AND THEIR PURPOSES

MEASUREMENT DEVICE	ABILITY TO LEARN SUBJECT MATTER	LEVEL OF ACHIEVEMENT AT BEGINNING AND AT END OF COURSE	LEARNING PROGRESS DURING UNIT OR COURSE	LEARNING STYLE, COGNITIVE STYLE	MOTIVATIONAL STATE OR PATTERN, INCLUDING INTERESTS AND CAREER GOALS	SELF-CONCEPT	RELATIONS WITH PEERS	ATTITUDES TOWARD SCHOOL, TEACHERS, SUBJECTS, ETC.
Standardized norm-referenced intellectual ability or other aptitude test	x							
Standardized norm-referenced educational achievement test in particular subject matter	x							
Published criterion-referenced test in particular subject matter	x	x	x					
Locally constructed criterion-referenced test in particular subject matter	x	x	x					
Published inventory or questionnaire				x	x	x	x	x
Locally constructed inventory or questionnaire				x	x	x	x	x
Teacher-made paper-and-pencil test or teacher-developed test of performance		x	x	x				
Teacher and/or student rating of work sample		x	x	x				
Teacher observation		x	x	x	x	x	x	x

Published inventories and questionnaires are used in some schools to assess each student's learning styles, motivation, self-concept, relations with peers, and other areas of the affective domain. Locally constructed inventories and questionnaires replace the published ones in many schools so as to reflect the interest of the local school staff. Teacher observation is used to secure the information desired by a particular teacher or group of teachers.

Notice that teacher-made tests, teacher ratings of samples of student work, and teacher observation achieve many important purposes of measurement. They are equally effective in carrying out evaluation in each of the four areas that follow.

16.1 Compare the uses of published tests, locally constructed tests, and teacher measurement procedures in measuring student abilities and achievements.

> 16.2 Compare the uses of published inventories, locally constructed inventories, and teacher observation in measuring student characteristics in the affective domain.

EVALUATING STUDENT PROGRESS AND THE EFFECTIVENESS OF A COURSE

Teaching and evaluating are closely related. This relationship will be clarified first, as we examine the times for gathering the information that is used in evaluating student progress in a course or unit of instruction. Then, the continuing relationship between evaluation and instruction will be discussed, and criteria of evaluation will be presented.

Coordinating the Timing and Purposes of Evaluation

Let us assume that the teacher wishes to aid the students make progress toward achieving their individual learning goals and simultaneously to evaluate the effectiveness of each unit of instruction and the entire course. Three times at which evaluation information may be helpful and the purpose of securing it at each time follow in Table 16.2. For illustrative purposes, the timing and purposes of evaluation are related to a unit of instruction rather than to a semester course; however, a course can be substituted for a unit.

TABLE 16.2 EVALUATION OF EACH STUDENT'S PROGRESS DURING THE UNIT AND OF THE EFFECTIVENESS OF THE UNIT

TIMING	PURPOSE
1. At the beginning of the unit.	a. To plan an appropriate instructional program for each student.
2. During the unit.	a. To provide feedback to the student to facilitate learning and to the teacher to facilitate instruction.
3. At the end of the unit.	a. To determine whether the student has attained the learning goals.
	b. To decide the student's next learning activities.
	c. To evaluate the student's instructional program.
	d. To evaluate the effectiveness of the unit for all students.
	e. To improve the unit the next time it is offered.

To evaluate each student's progress during a unit of instruction and the appropriateness of each student's instructional program, evaluative information concerning each student is needed at three times. The first time is either prior to starting the course or soon after the course begins. This early information is used to plan an appropriate instructional program for the student and for the student to set goals, as was indicated in the sequence of purposeful learning outlined in Chapter 4. Three useful kinds of information to have at the beginning of a unit are each student's level of achievement related to the content of the particular unit, the student's learning styles, and the student's interests.

The second time to obtain evaluative information is during each unit to ascertain each student's progress and to provide feedback to the student and to the teacher, or to the teachers in a teaching team. The student should receive the results of the evaluation immediately. When tests and work samples are used for this purpose, they must necessarily be scored by the student or teacher, and the results be made immediately available to the student.

The third time evaluative information is needed is at the end of the unit to ascertain each student's achievement of learning goals, to evaluate the appropriateness of each student's instructional program, and to evaluate the effectiveness of the unit for all the students enrolled in it. Information from this end-of-unit evaluation is used in developing the student's instructional program for the next unit and in improving instruction for all students. Unit instruction is interpreted broadly here to include allocation of time, space and equipment, instructional materials, instructional activities, and the teacher's methods.

Relating Evaluation
to Instruction

Individual instructional programming was explained in Chapter 6. We saw that the individual instructional programs of the students of a class vary from one situation to another in terms of the objectives to be achieved by the different students, the instructional materials to be used, and the learning activities to be undertaken. At one extreme, the programs of all the students include the same objectives, and only the time to achieve the objectives varies from one student to another. Some high school elective courses, such as calculus or fourth-year Spanish, are of this kind. At the other extreme, each student's program has objectives and activities that differ from those of every other student. Independent study is representative of this extreme. Most courses have some objectives that are required of all students and other objectives that are for only certain students. Accordingly, the instructional programs of the students in these courses are alike with respect to the required objectives and different with respect to the elective objectives.

Regardless of the particular pattern of arranging instruction appropriately for individual students, evaluation must be directly related to instruction. We shall now walk through a five-step sequence of instruction and evaluation to make clear the relationship between them.

1. Assess the learning capability and other characteristics of each student. Assessing each student's learning capability is essential if each student is to have learning objectives of an appropriate level of difficulty. Assessing the learning styles and interests of each student is necessary if learning activities are to be arranged that appropriately take into account each student's learning styles and interests. The assessment of learning capabilities, interests, and learning styles may be carried out by giving tests at the beginning of the unit, by referring back to earlier units, by observation during the early days of instruction, or by some combination of these.

A criterion-referenced test is often used when the placement of each student depends upon the student's entering achievement level, that is, upon what the student already knows. The test may be published or locally constructed. Whether it is published or locally constructed, the teacher must have some way of relating the students' scores to their placement. For example, placement in two or more different groups may be possible. Thus, one school may place students in four different groups in algebra in grade 9, based on students' scores on a test or on their grades in grade 8 mathematics. For example, there may be a pre-Algebra group, a regular Algebra 1 group, an advanced Algebra 1 group, and a regular Algebra 2 group. Within each group, further arrangements may be made to take into account learning styles and interests. As another example, a four-person elementary school teaching team may place 100 children in 8 different reading groups, with each group working on a different set of reading skills. Within each group, interests and learning styles are accommodated through use of materials and individual, small-group, and whole-group activities.

2. Aid the students set goals in terms of the unit objectives. Unit objectives that each student has not achieved are included in the student's learning goals, and related instructional plans are made to achieve the objectives. The goals/objectives of the student provide the primary basis for evaluating the students' progress during the unit and their goal attainment at the end of the unit.

3. Plan and carry out an instructional program appropriate for each student. Arranging an instructional program so that each student achieves individual learning goals is accomplished in different ways. We saw how students may be placed differently at the beginning of a course or school year. Other ways are now indicated. One way is to vary the amount of time that different students take to achieve the same objectives. Another is to arrange for students to use the same amount of time, but to work on different unit objectives. These procedures take into account differences among students in their capability for learning the unit material. The use of printed materials, audiovisual materials, and three-dimensional objects may be varied for some of the students, especially to take into account differences in their learning styles. The amount of teacher-directed whole-class, small-group, and individual assignments may be modified for different students. Similarly, the amount of student-initiated small-group and individual activity may be varied for the students. These latter procedures take into account differences in interests, learning styles, and motivation patterns.

As instruction proceeds during the unit, student progress is assessed and evaluated. Evaluation of each student's progress may involve use of any or all of three criteria. First, is the student making progress as expected toward achieving his or her goals? Second, is the student's rate of progress appropriate in terms of the student's capability for achieving the particular goals/objectives? Finally, is the student making a reasonable amount of progress in terms of the amount of effort expended? Answering these questions implies making judgments about each student's rate of progress, that is, evaluating individual progress.

4. Assess the student's attainment of goals/objectives. Assessment is needed before the end of each unit to identify the students who achieve their goals/objectives before the end of a scheduled time period. Students who achieve their goals early are given enrichment activities, or they start the next unit of the course and are thereby accelerated.

Practical considerations in many schools require each unit of instruction to be completed by the students at a specified time. Therefore, the majority of students are assessed for attainment of the unit goals/objectives on or near the last day of the unit.

5. Evaluate the students' goal achievement and take actions accordingly. Students who achieve their goals/objectives at the specified time progress to the next unit. A student who does not attain his or her goals/objectives to a desired level is studied to ascertain the appropriateness of the goal along with the readiness of the student to attain it. After this determination, actions are taken, such as holding the student back or advancing the student with other students and giving the student additional time and help.

Establishing Evaluation Criteria

The information obtained during the unit and in the final assessment regarding the students' attainment of their learning goals is used in evaluating the appropriateness of the instructional program of each student. It is also used for evaluating the effectiveness of the unit materials, activities, and methods.

Four criteria commonly used for evaluating the *appropriateness* of the instructional program of the individual student are as follows. First, did the student achieve his or her learning goals? Second, was the program, including objectives, time allocation, materials, and activities, appropriate for the student in terms of the student's capability for achieving the goals? Third, did the program appropriately take into account the student's interests, learning styles, and other characteristics? Fourth, was the program appropriate in terms of the amount of effort required by the student?

One or more of the following four criteria are commonly used for evaluating the *effectiveness* of the unit for all the students. First, was the content of appropriate difficulty levels in terms of the students' differing capabilities for learning it? Second, were the time allocations, equipment, instructional materials, learning activities, and teaching methods effective in aiding the students to achieve their learning goals/course objectives? Third, were the instructional materials, learning activities, and teaching methods suitable to the students in terms of their learning styles and interests? Fourth, were the effects of the unit desirable in terms of the students' attitudes, self-concepts, and other outcomes in the affective domain?

You will recall from the timing and purposes of evaluation discussed earlier that teachers make these evaluative judgments during the instructional sequence in order to make their instruction effective. The judgments are summarized toward the end of the course. Thus, it is entirely appropriate for teachers to consider with their students the evaluation criteria that the teachers are using. A simple rating form for reading follows to illustrate the kind of value judgments that a student might make:

STUDENT RATING OF INSTRUCTION

Directions: Below you will find questions about reading. Place a check next to the group of words that describes how you feel about reading.

1. In reading

_____ I did as well as I possibly could have.

_____ I did about as well as I could have.

_____ I didn't do as well as I could have.

_____ I didn't do nearly as well as I could have.

2. Reading was

_____ very hard for me.

_____ hard for me.

_____ easy for me.

_____ very easy for me.

3. Reading was

_____ very interesting to me.

_____ interesting to me.

_____ uninteresting to me.

_____ very uninteresting to me.

4. In reading,

_____ I would rather have spent more time learning by myself.

_____ I would rather have spent more time learning with another student.

_____ I would rather have spent more time learning with a small group of students.

_____ I would rather have spent more time learning with the whole class.

_____ everything was about right.

5. I think what I learned in reading is

_____ very useful to me.

_____ useful to me.

_____ not useful to me.

16.3 Identify the kind of information teachers should have regarding each student (a) before starting to teach the course, (b) during the course, and (c) at the end of the course. Indicate how they should use each kind.

16.4 Five purposes of evaluation at the end of a course or unit were listed in Table 16.2. Based on your experiences as a learner, which purposes did your teachers achieve most regularly?

16.5 Four criteria for evaluating the appropriateness of the instructional program of a student were given. Evaluate these criteria in terms of whether other criteria should be added to them.

16.6 Four criteria for evaluating the effectiveness of a unit or course were given. Based on your experience as a learner, which of the criteria were least frequently met by your teachers?

EVALUATING EACH STUDENT'S TOTAL EDUCATIONAL PROGRAM AND REPORTING TO PARENTS

Coordinating the Timing and Purposes of Evaluation

Relating Evaluation to Advising and Teaching

Establishing Evaluation Criteria

Reporting Student Progress and Grading

The educational program of a student for a semester or year includes all the organized course activities and all the informal learning experiences for which the school assumes supervision. Student's educational programs are more alike in the elementary school than in the high school in terms of the subject matter that is included in all the students' programs. Electives and cocurricular activities typically are not found in the elementary grades. Despite this difference, the learning activities of no two elementary school children are identical, even during a week, when a serious attempt is made to take into account differences among students in their capability for learning particular subject matter, their learning styles, interests, motivational patterns, and other characteristics. In this part of the chapter, the times at which evaluation of the student's individual educational program is conducted and the related purposes of the evaluation are given first. This discussion is followed with a strategy for evaluating individual student's programs and reporting to parents.

Coordinating the Timing and Purposes of Evaluation

The timing and purposes of evaluating each student's total educational program of course work and other activities parallel those for evaluating the student's instructional program in each course, as shown in Table 16.3.

The purposes identified in Table 16.3 are assumed to be readily understood and are not explained further, except in connection with the role of the student in the evaluation process and with the role of the teacher as an advisor. Students learn to set goals and to monitor their progress with some success even in the primary grades. As students mature and acquire more sophisticated goal-setting and other learning strategies, they assume increasing responsibility for evaluation of their own progress. However, even college students profit from wise guidance and assistance in evaluation from an advisor.

In the elementary school, the teacher serves as an advisor to each student of a classroom group of about 25. For each student at the secondary level to receive adequate guidance, each teacher serves as an advisor to about 20 students and takes responsibility for planning, monitoring, and evaluating the educational program of each advisee in all courses and other activities. The high school counselor has a very important role in this approach to evaluation, since each counselor typically aids a group of teachers in their advisory roles. In the strategy that follows, the teachers serve as advisors.

Relating Evaluation to Advising and Teaching

The strategy that follows resulted from cooperative research carried out by local high schools and the author (Klausmeier, 1983). In these schools, each teacher serves as an advisor to about 20 students. As an advisor, the teacher takes primary responsibility for planning, monitoring, and evaluating each advisee's program.

1. Develop an educational plan for the semester with the student and the parents. An educational plan is worked out in a conference with the student and the parents in the semester prior to the start of the next one or at the beginning of the semester. The plan has three main elements. First, it lists the courses, extracurricular activities, study periods, and other educational activities in which the student will engage in the school and community. Second, the kinds of materials and activities that will be helpful in accommodating the student's prior school work, learning capabilities,

TABLE 16.3 EVALUATION OF EACH STUDENT'S TOTAL EDUCATIONAL PROGRAM

TIMING	PURPOSES
1. Prior to assigning the high school student to particular courses or the elementary school child to activities and objectives within each program area, for example, language arts, social studies.	a. To plan an appropriate total educational program for and with each individual student and the student's parents each semester.
2. During the semester and year (at least twice per semester).	a. To provide feedback to the student relative to each course or program area. b. To monitor the student's progress; to identify possible difficulties the student may be experiencing and their causes; and to take appropriate actions with the students, including making changes in the program.
3. At the end of each semester.	a. To determine the extent to which the student has achieved individual goals in all courses or program areas. b. To determine how suitable the various elements of the total program were for the student in terms of the criteria that were established. c. To provide the information for planning the student's next educational program (i.e., of the student who continues in the same school). d. To identify courses and other curricular elements that might need improvement.

motivation, learning styles, interests, and other characteristics are noted. Third, the student sets tentative goals in broad terms, such as the number of units to be completed in each course, the letter grade expected, and the amount of effort to be made. How explicitly the goals are set varies with the maturity of the students, the nature of the subject matter, and many other local conditions. Changes that will improve the program are made in the plan throughout the semester.

2. Monitor the student's progress related to each program element. The educational plan is prepared early in the semester and is necessarily global and tentative. The present discussion assumes that the actual program experienced by the student, rather than the plan worked out earlier, serves as the basis of the monitoring process.

The three important points to consider here are the involvement of the student, the frequency of the monitoring, and the necessity to monitor all the elements of the student's educational program. The student participates directly in the monitoring. Individual conferences are held in which the student and the advisor supply the information necessary to assess the student's progress. Problems related to each course and any other element of the educational program are identified and resolved.

Each local school determines the frequency of the monitoring conferences. One of two conferences each semester is sufficient for most students. (In some situations, a final evaluation conference and the first planning conference for the ensuing semester are combined.)

3. Evaluate the student's semester program. Evaluating the student's attainment of his or her goals in each course is based on the statement of the goals included in the student's educational plan or on goals subsequently formulated. Evaluative information regarding the student's achievements in each course and in other non-course activities is compiled. In an individual conference, the student and the advisor compare the two and evaluate the achievement in terms such as above, at, or below the expected level.

To evaluate the appropriateness of each student's program, one necessary consideration is how the student achieved in relation to the student's capability for learning the particular subject matter. Other considerations are how the course activities and materials related to the student's general interests (and to older students' career interests), to learning styles, and to motivational characteristics. Another criterion involves whether the student, the advisor, and parents regard each element of the program, and the program in its totality, as worthwhile to the student at the present time, in the future, or both.

As students gain experience in goal setting, planning, and evaluation, they take greater initiative in all aspects of the goal setting-planning-monitoring-evaluation sequence. The advisor holds conferences with individual students and also with groups of advisees to teach the student these processes.

Establishing Evaluation Criteria

The goals of the student provide one criterion for evaluating elements of the student's program. Other criteria include suitability of the program elements in terms of the student's capability for learning the particular subject matter, the amount of effort made, and other characteristics of the student. These criteria were discussed in connection with evaluating the instructional program. The scale that follows is used in middle schools and high schools and serves as a basis for discussion between the advisor and the student:

FORM FOR OBTAINING STUDENT OPINION OF A COMPLETED EDUCATIONAL PROGRAM

Directions: Think about all your courses and other educational activities during last semester. Then check each item. I am also checking the items. You and I will discuss these ratings in a conference. No other person will see them.

1. Some courses require a great deal of work and effort, and others require very little. Your courses required

   _____ far too much.

   _____ too much.

   _____ about the right amount.

   _____ too little.

   _____ far too little.

2. Some things are more worthwhile doing than others. The assignments and activities in your courses

   _____ were very worthwhile.

   _____ did not have much value.

   _____ did not have any value.

3. Some assignments and activities are more difficult than others. Most of the assignments and activities in your courses were

   _____ far too difficult.

   _____ too difficult.

   _____ of about the right difficulty.

   _____ too easy.

   _____ far too easy.

4. Some assignments and activities are more interesting than others. Most of the assignments and activities in your courses were

   _____ very interesting.

   _____ moderately interesting.

   _____ of some interest.

   _____ not at all interesting.

5. School should help you learn English, math, social studies, science, and many other things. Your courses and other activities were

_____ very helpful.

_____ moderately helpful.

_____ of some help.

_____ not at all helpful.

6. School should help you make friends and get along with other students. Your courses and other activities were

_____ very helpful.

_____ moderately helpful.

_____ of some help.

_____ not at all helpful.

7. School should help you become a good citizen. Your courses and other activities were

_____ very helpful.

_____ moderately helpful.

_____ of some help.

_____ not at all helpful.

The process of working out an educational plan with each student, monitoring each student's progress, and evaluating the student's completed program is time-consuming. Not all schools are able to work out the necessary arrangements. Two alternatives are possible. One alternative is to carry out the three-step sequence with only some of the students. For example, teacher-advisors can carry out the sequence with only half of their advisees and a different half each semester. A second alternative is to do only the evaluation, not the planning or the monitoring. This evaluation also may be for only a part of the students. A typical, but ineffective, approach is for a guidance counselor or assistant principal to schedule the courses of the students and to gather evaluation information informally or to ignore it completely. Evaluation that does not involve the teachers of the students has generally failed to provide useful feedback to the students or the teachers.

Reporting Student Progress and Grading

In a nationwide survey (National Education Association, 1971), teachers were asked to indicate the methods that they use for reporting pupil progress to parents. The results follow in Table 16.4:

TABLE 16.4 METHODS OF REPORTING STUDENT PROGRESS

METHOD OF REPORTING	ELEMENTARY	SECONDARY
Parent-teacher conferences	84.2%	54.4%
Classified scale of letter grades	55.9	79.4
Formal letter or written paragraph	26.0	21.1
Descriptive word grade	29.2	10.0
Percentage grade	4.4	13.7
Pass-fail	7.3	9.3
Classified scale of numbers	6.7	7.8
Dual marking system	4.0	4.9

SOURCE: National Education Association, 1971, pp. 81–82.

Notice that the percentages add up to more than 100%. Many schools use more than one method, producing this effect.

Regardless of the form of reporting, evaluating a student's progress provides the information for preparing progress reports. The ensuing discussion focuses on reporting to parents and on report cards.

Parent-Teacher Conferences

Parent-teacher conferences continue to replace report cards with letter grades sent to parents. One kind of reporting form for use in teacher-parent-child conferences is criterion-referenced. It lists the learning tasks and indicates those that have and have not been mastered. This kind of report form is used increasingly in the elementary grades and will undoubtedly become more prevalent in secondary schools as minimum competency testing becomes more widespread. An example of this kind of reporting form is shown in Figure 16.1. This particular form is for mathematics. The child colors each appropriate entry to indicate ability to perform the task. The parent, child, and teacher can then talk about the child's progress. Similar forms are used in other curricular areas. While conducting a conference reporting progress in curricular areas, other topics may also be discussed, such as the child's interests; work habits; relationships with other children in the classroom, on the playground, and in other groups; relationships with teachers and other staff members; and possible behavioral, health, emotional, and learning problems.

Most parents are eager to provide information that will aid the teacher in providing effective instruction to their child. For example, the parents give information about the child's interests, reaction to school, personal relationships with members of the family and neighborhood friends, home responsibilities, health, and any particular problems.

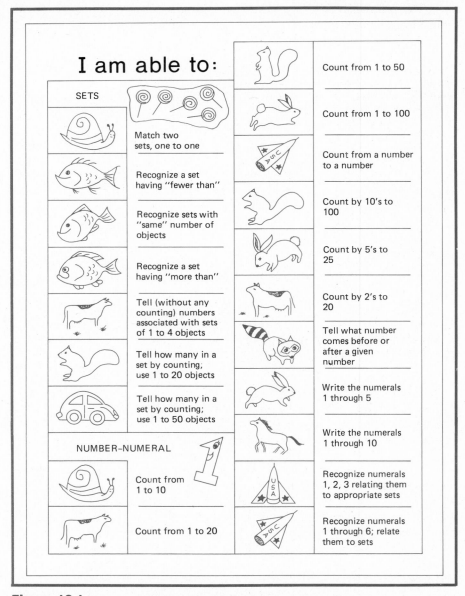

Figure 16.1 First page of skill folder in elementary mathematics.

The following tips for conducting a successful conference are drawn from several publications of the National Education Association (1969):

SUGGESTIONS FOR CONDUCTING PARENT-TEACHER CONFERENCES

1. Accept the parent's feelings and attitudes. This does not mean that you approve or disapprove of them; you merely accept the fact that they are there.
2. Develop real interaction. To obtain helpful information about the child, ask leading questions rather than those which may be answered with Yes or No. It is better to ask, "How does Johnny feel about school?" than, "Does Johnny like school?"
3. Talk parent talk, not pedagese. Don't say "peer group"; say "children of the same age." Don't drop a word curtain between you and the parent.
4. Remember what you can and can't say. Find out beforehand what information you're not supposed to give to parents. In some districts, for example, a child's IQ is not revealed.
5. Don't be tempted into unethical conduct. No matter how you feel about the teacher Johnny had last year, don't join in when parents criticize that teacher. Keep them to the subject, which is How can we help Johnny now?
6. Avoid direct comparisons of the child with other children. Encourage the parent not to compare one child with another, especially a brother or sister.
7. Avoid open or implied criticism of the parents.
8. Listen thoughtfully to criticism of the school, and plan later visits for parents who are critical of the school program.
9. Be honest. Low test scores should be honestly, but tactfully, explained.
10. Avoid the expression of judgments or opinions unless asked for.
11. Suggest several possible remedies for problems, and let the parents choose which they will try. Encourage the parents to suggest their own remedies for any problem that has appeared. If the problem is too complex for the school, be ready to suggest other sources of help.

Before moving to report cards, we should recognize that criterion-referenced evaluation of student progress may be used in report cards as well as in teacher-parent conferences. However, the conferences give the teacher the opportunity to explain the domain and the criteria used, as well as to receive parent comments and to respond to questions. Moreover, samples of the child's work may be brought to the conferences.

Report Cards

A report card is presented in Figure 16.2 to illustrate norm-referenced evaluation of student progress and to show how the evaluation of student achievement is kept separate from the evaluation of other student behaviors. A report card such as this may also serve as a basis of discussion in a parent-teacher conference.

The citizenship behaviors and the work habits are checked only if the teacher thinks the child can and should improve. The teacher enters a check if a conference with the parents is desired. Even though the citizenship

Report of.. Grade...........

Good citizenship and good work habits are necessary for satisfactory school progress.

The items checked suggest ways in which your child can and should improve:

CITIZENSHIP	Report Periods			
	1	2	3	4
Being self reliant...............				
Working well with others..........				
Playing well with others..........				
Observing rules of safety.				
Practicing good health habits........				
Showing regard for property.........				
Respecting rightful authority.........				
Showing courtesy to others.........				

WORK HABITS	Report Periods			
	1	2	3	4
Working carefully and accurately.........				
Getting to work promptly.........				
Completing work promptly.........				
Using spare time to advantage.........				
Listening to and following directions......				
Sharing in group planning.........				
A conference with parent is desired (Call school for an appointment)......				

SCHOOL SUBJECTS

√—Indicates how your child compares with other children of this grade level. X—Losing position (little or no progress)

Effort: S—Satisfactory; U—Unsatisfactory; I—Improving

	1st Report Period					2nd Report Period					3rd Report Period					4th Report Period				
	Above Grade Level	At Grade Level	Below Grade Level	Effort		Above Level Grade	At Grade Level	Below Grade Level	Effort		Above Grade Level	At Grade Level	Below Grade Level	Effort		Above Grade Level	At Grade Level	Below Grade Level	Effort	
				S I U					S I U					S I U					S I U	
Reading...........																				
Language...........																				
Spelling...........																				
Writing...........																				
Social Studies........																				
Science...........																				
Arithmetic........																				
Music...........																				
Art...........																				
Physical Education																				

Attendance	Days Present	Days Absent	Times Tardy	Days Present	Days Absent	Times Tardy	Days Present	Days Absent	Times Tardy	Days Present	Days Absent	Times Tardy

TOTALS FOR THE YEAR

Parent's Signature			

Figure 16.2 Elementary school report card.

behaviors and work habits may not be checked often, they indicate the school's objectives to the student and the parents. Effort is checked as satisfactory, unsatisfactory, or improving and, accordingly, is kept separate from achievement. The child's achievement in each subject field is checked on a norm-referenced, or comparative, basis with other children of the same grade. Notice that the teacher is required to evaluate the child's achievement as above, at, or below grade level. Both school and school district information are used in making this judgment.

As we saw earlier regarding the different ways of reporting, high schools use letter grades more and conferences less than elementary schools. Letter grades may be based on either absolute or relative standards. For example, one high school employs absolute standards in certain courses by indicating the different sets of objectives that the students must master in order to receive a grade of A, B, C, or D. In other courses, the letter grades are based on how well the student achieves in relation to other students. For example, a test is given toward the end of the grading period, and letter grades are assigned to students according to their ranks on the test. Some teachers rarely give grades lower than C, while others give a considerable number of F's.

16.7 Compare the timing and purposes of evaluating a student's instructional program in a course and a student's complete educational program.

16.8 Compare the ease with which a high school teacher who has 20 advisees and an elementary school teacher who has 25 advisees can evaluate the educational programs of their advisees.

16.9 Why is evaluating the student's complete educational program needed even when evaluation of the student's instructional program in each course is conducted well?

16.10 What do you perceive to be the advantages of using both a report card and a parent-teacher conference for reporting student progress?

16.11 Some persons argue for abolishing letter grades, and others argue for retaining them. Identify as many pro and con arguments as you can.

EVALUATING ELEMENTS OF A SCHOOL'S EDUCATIONAL PROGRAM

Developing an Evaluation Strategy

Establishing Evaluation Criteria

Illustrative Program Evaluation

The evaluation of a program area of a school, such as its mathematics program or its program for students with learning disabilities, may be planned and carried out internally by the school staff, or it may be conducted by one or more persons who are not local staff members. The focus here is on internal evaluation that is carried out for the purpose of continuously improving the quality of education in the local school. Accordingly, it is planned and carried out by the local school staff, not by external evaluators. A local school improvement committee, consisting of representative teachers, counselors or school psychologists, and administrators assume responsibility for planning and conducting the evaluation. This kind of evaluation is ongoing and continues from one year to the next.

Developing an Evaluation Strategy

In the preceding sections, we saw the kind of student information that is used in evaluating the instructional program of each student and in evaluating each student's total educational program. Some of the same student information can be used in evaluating a program area, such as reading or career education.

Planning the Evaluation

Evaluating the effectiveness of a number of program areas on an annual basis requires careful planning to ensure that the results will be used continuously to improve the quality of education. Three major areas of decision making are involved during a planning period. The first kind of decision making is to identify the purposes of the evaluation, the program areas to be evaluated, and the students to be involved. Usually, the students are all those enrolled in each grade of the school. The second kind is to identify the information-gathering tools and procedures and to outline the means of analyzing and summarizing the information. The third kind of decision making indicates the kinds of evaluation judgments to be made and the kinds of actions to be taken based on the judgments. Planning the evaluation process is necessary each year, although getting started the first year is more time-consuming.

First-Year Evaluation

During the first year of implementing the plan, the information on each group of students in each program area included in the evaluation is gathered, processed, and summarized. The summarized data are interpreted and related to the evaluative criteria. Then evaluative judgments are made.

The first year is the baseline year. Accordingly, the performances of the students enrolled in each grade of the school are the baseline performances. The performances of each successive group of students of each grade, each year thereafter, can be compared with those of the groups of the baseline year.

Using the first-year evaluation, groups of staff members, such as the primary school teachers or the high school English teachers, set goals in the program area of interest. The goals are set for each group of students that continues into the next grade of the school and for the new group that enters the lowest grade of the school. The goals are set in terms of student outcomes, such as achievement, attitudes, and self-concepts. The goals to be achieved by each successive group of students entering a grade necessarily take into account their capability for learning the particular subject matter.

Second-Year Evaluation

During the second year of evaluation, the goals set by the staff toward the end of the first year (or at the beginning of the second year) are used to monitor student attainment of the goals. Thus, the second-year evaluation requires five main kinds of activities. First, the information is gathered, processed, and summarized. Second, the attainment of the goals by each grade group of students is evaluated. Third, the program areas for each grade group are evaluated in terms of effectiveness, appropriateness, and value. Fourth, the evaluative results for all the groups and program areas are summarized and interpreted. Fifth, using the evaluative results, the staff sets goals for each group of students in each area of interest for the next year and plans the improvements that are necessary to achieve the goals.

Establishing Evaluation Criteria

This cycle of planning the evaluation; gathering, analyzing, and interpreting information; evaluating; setting goals and planning changes to achieve the goals; and carrying out the plans is continued from one year to the next. The effectiveness of each program area is typically evaluated on the basis of three criteria. First, how well did the group of students achieve the goals set for it? Second, did the students perform as well as could be expected in terms of their capability for learning the particular subject matter? Third, did the program have unintended negative effects, for example, less favorable attitudes toward school or a decrease in attendance?

Illustrative Program Evaluation

The implementation of this evaluation strategy in a middle school from 1981 through 1984 follows. The same school and many other schools are currently using the same strategy. Accordingly, the strategy is described as it is being implemented at the present time.

Data Gathered and Analysis of Data

1. Program Areas: English, mathematics, reading.
2. Student Groups: All the students of each grade 7 and grade 8.
3. Measurement Devices, Schedule of Administration, and Data Analysis.
   3.1 Standardized Achievement Test Battery. 9 scores: word knowledge, reading, total reading, language, spelling, math computation, math concepts, math problem solving, total math. Administered annually in the spring to all the students of grade 7 and grade 8.
   3.2 Mental Ability Test. 1 score. Administered when the students are in grade 7.

      The scores of the grade 7 and grade 8 students on each standardized achievement test and the ability test are ranked from lowest to highest (10 rankings, 1 for each test), and the 10th, 25th, 50th, 75th, and 90th percentile ranks are computed for each test. For each grade 7 and grade 8 group of students, the national percentile ranks corresponding to each of the five preceding local percentile ranks for each test are derived, using appropriate test manuals and statistical techniques. Each of the five local percentile ranks is compared annually with the corresponding national percentile ranks to see if it is higher or lower. This information is summarized annually in tables for each grade 7 and grade 8.
   3.3 Locally Constructed Minimum Competency Test in Mathematics. 1 score. Administered annually in the fall and spring

to all the students of each grade 7 and grade 8. The test is scored in terms of percentage correct.

The scores of the students of each grade 7 and grade 8 are ranked from highest to lowest, and the percentages corresponding to the 10th, 25th, 50th, 75th, and 90th percentile ranks of each grade 7 and grade 8 are obtained. This information is tabled annually for grades 7 and 8.

3.4 Published Student Attitudes Questionnaire. 7 scores: three scores are for the teacher's mode of instruction, authority and control, and interpersonal relationships with students; the other four scores indicate attitudes toward learning, social structure and climate, peer relations, and attitudes toward school in general. Administered annually in the spring to all grade 7 and grade 8 students.

3.5 Published Self-Appraisal Inventory. A total of 4 self-concept scores: general self, peer, family, and scholastic. Administered in the fall to all students of grade 7 and grade 8. In accordance with generally accepted procedures, the students do not give their names on the answer sheets for the attitudes and self-appraisal inventory. However, they indicate their grade in school.

For each grade 7 and grade 8, the mean for each subtest of the student attitude questionnaire and the self-appraisal inventory is computed, and the mean is related to the published definition of the mean rating that was obtained. This information is tabled annually for each grade 7 and grade 8. It cannot be related to any other information on an individual student, since the students do not identify themselves on the answer sheets.

Annual Goal Setting by Staff

Each year the school's improvement committee examines all the information that is gathered. It then sets goals to be achieved during the ensuing year. For example, if the tested achievement is substantially lower in grade 7 reading than in grade 7 math, and if the test results are supported by teacher judgments, a goal is set to raise the achievement in grade 7 reading the following year. Similarly, if the 75th percentile rank of the grade 8 students in mathematics is considerably lower than the mental ability rank, a goal is set to raise the achievement level of the students of higher mental ability whose achievement levels are below their ability level. Similar goal setting is done regarding the affective measures and school attendance. Plans are laid to achieve each goal, and the plans are then implemented.

Results

The mean national percentile ranks for language, mathematics, reading, and spelling follow, in Table 16.5, for the baseline year 1977–78 and for 1980–81 for the grade 7 and grade 8 students (the average *mean* mental ability percentile rank for the grade 7 students for the two years was 36, and for grade 8 it was 38):

TABLE 16.5 **SELECTED MEAN NATIONAL PERCENTILE RANKS FOR 1977–78 AND 1980–81**

	MATHEMATICS		LANGUAGE		READING		SPELLING	
	1977–78	1980–81	1977–78	1980–81	1977–78	1980–81	1977–78	1980–81
Grade 7	30	44	30	42	34	34	40	48
Grade 8	32	42	30	34	30	35	32	39

The above results show the considerable improvement that occurred from 1977–78 to 1980–81 in each area for each grade, except for grade 7 reading. Notice that the grade 7 percentile ranks in math, language, and reading were considerably above the mean mental ability rank in 1980–81, whereas they were considerably below it in 1977–78.

16.12 Evaluating the educational programs of a school necessarily continues from one year to the next. Identify as many reasons as you can that support this point of view.

16.13 Teachers who serve on a school's improvement committee require time to attend meetings of the committee and also to do related committee work. Prepare a presentation to be made to parents or school-board members to justify an appropriate amount of released time for these teachers from teaching, advising, or other activities.

16.14 Explain how evaluation information gathered annually enables teachers to set realistic goals for groups of students to achieve in program areas of interest.

16.15 Three criteria for evaluating the effectiveness of a program area are given. Rate each criterion in terms of whether you think it would be highly endorsed, endorsed, not endorsed, or resisted by the majority of parents; by teachers. Give reasons for your ratings.

16.16 Four kinds of information are gathered annually in the middle school cited for illustrative purposes. Indicate any other information that should be gathered to evaluate these same programmatic areas and any of the four kinds of information that should not be. Provide a rationale for your additions and deletions.

16.17 The illustrative school did not evaluate other curricular programs, because of the amount of time already required of the students for testing and of the staff for conducting the evaluation. Outline a plan for alternate-year evaluations so that other curricular areas can be evaluated without increasing the amount of time required.

EVALUATING EDUCATIONAL
MATERIALS AND PROCESSES

New instructional materials for students are continually being developed. Similarly, new or refined educative processes are being developed, for example, methods of teaching, administrative arrangements, teacher-advising arrangements, and means of reporting to parents. We may use the word *products* to refer to educative processes as well as instructional materials.

New educational products are often evaluated systematically in three phases. The timing and related purposes of each phase of the evaluation follows in Table 16.6:

TABLE 16.6 FORMATIVE, SUMMATIVE, AND USER EVALUATION OF PRODUCTS

TIMING	PURPOSE
While the product is being developed *(formative evaluation)*.	To ensure that the product achieves its intended goals.
Immediately prior to release and national distribution *(summative evaluation)*.	To evaluate the overall effectiveness of the product.
Prior to adoption *(user evaluation)*.	To determine the effectiveness and usability of the product in the particular school, school district, or state.

The phases described in Table 16.6 should not be regarded as clearly separated in time. Rather, each subsequent phase can start a year or two before the final results of the preceding phase are fully analyzed and reported. Thus, local schools can start their user evaluation of the product before the results of the summative evaluation are in final published form.

Conducting Formative Evaluation

As the term implies, *formative evaluation* is concerned with ensuring the effectiveness of a product as it is being formed or developed. The criteria for evaluating the product are stated in terms of its effects on the intended users. Thus, the criteria for a curricular program are stated in terms of its effects on the students who use it.

There are three main tasks in the development of a product and the related formative evaluation. A reading readiness program called the Pre-Reading Skills Program, which was developed and evaluated by Venezky and Pittelman (1978), is used to illustrate formative evaluation. The program includes material for use by the children and the teacher, criterion-referenced tests, and a record-keeping and management system.

The first step in developing and formatively evaluating a product is to describe the persons, or *target group,* for whom the product is intended and also the situation in which it will be used. The target group for the Pre-Reading Skills Program is English-speaking children enrolled in kindergarten who are not yet able to profit from formal instruction in reading. The Pre-Reading Skills Program is intended for use in regular kindergarten classrooms. (A program was later developed for Spanish-speaking children.)

Second, the goals, or objectives, of the product are indicated in terms of what it is intended to accomplish. The goal of the Pre-Reading Skills Program is to aid the children learn prereading skills, including two sound skills — sound matching and sound blending — and three visual skills — attending to letter order, attending to letter orientation, and attending to word detail. There are subskills for each major skill.

Third, the product is developed, and its effectiveness throughout the development is evaluated. In the development of the Pre-Reading Skills Program, instructional activities to teach the skills were developed and pilot-tested in three kindergarten classrooms in the spring of 1971. A first version of the complete program was developed during the summer of 1971 and used by 16 teachers during the 1971–72 school year. Based on the information gained, the program was revised in the summer of 1972, and the revision was evaluated during the 1972–73 school year in terms of how well the children learned. An in-service education program for teachers was developed in the summer of 1972 and evaluated during the 1972–73 school year. Based on the 1972–73 evaluation, minor revisions were made in the program materials. A large-scale tryout of the program materials and the in-service program for teachers was conducted in 1973–74. The formative evaluation focused on how well the children learned and retained the skills during kindergarten and on their retention of the skills from the spring of the kindergarten year to grade 1 in the fall. The first commercial edition of the program was published in 1974 (Venezky, Pittelman, Kamm, & Leslie, 1974), and a bilingual edition was published four years later (Venezky, Pittelman, Felker, Higgins, & Chicone, 1978).

Conducting Summative Evaluation

After each component has been developed and evaluated, the completed program is tried out in classrooms representative of the kind in which it is intended for use. In this way, the effectiveness of the complete program is determined. The ease of using it and the cost per pupil of the materials are also ascertained.

Both formative and *summative evaluation* rely on a number of measuring devices. Tests may be designed specifically to measure how well the target group achieves the intended goals. Questionnaires may be used to get the opinions of students and teachers regarding the worthwhileness and effectiveness of the product. Observations and teacher self-reports may be obtained to ascertain the usability and other features of the product.

We now consider a high school course, Project Physics, to illustrate a more comprehensive summative evaluation than was conducted for the Pre-Reading Skills Program. The two main purposes of the project were to develop teaching methods and instructional materials and media suitable for different students, especially the scientifically disadvantaged, and for different conditions of instruction, especially those less than optimal (Walberg & Welch, 1972).

The course was pilot-tested and formatively evaluated for two years before the summative evaluation. In preparation for the summative evaluation, 57 physics teachers were selected randomly from a nationwide population of physics teachers to teach either Project Physics or the course each was already teaching. Both these groups were acquainted with their roles during the summer before teaching the courses in the ensuing school year.

A large battery of achievement tests in physics was administered to the students of all the teachers. Six instruments to measure the students' attainment of affective objectives were also administered. Special studies were made of teacher behaviors and enrollment trends in schools where Project Physics was taught. The College Board's Advanced Placement Test in physics and the New York Regents' examination in physics, both standardized tests, were administered to the two groups of students.

The main results were that Project Physics students achieved as high as, or significantly higher than, the control students. Further, the Project Physics groups were significantly higher in their perceived image of physics; in their attitudes toward and interest in science, especially physics; and in their desire to learn more about the subject. The evaluators concluded that the course materials were successful in meeting the objectives, as originally set forth, and that the course was likely to be effective in raising physics enrollments.

Conducting User Evaluation

User evaluation before final adoption may be illustrated with instructional materials. A two-phase evaluation sequence is followed. First, the published instructional materials, related tests, and suggestions to teachers are tried out for a year or two in a small number of classrooms or schools rather than in all the classrooms and schools of the school district or state. Second, if the evaluation warrants an adoption throughout the district or state, continuing, but less intensive, evaluation is carried out to make sure that the materials and procedures work well in all the classrooms. The continuing evaluation is conducted because some materials and other educative processes that work well in the schools in residential or suburban areas of a school district or state do not work well in inner-city schools, and vice-versa. For example, teacher advising differs greatly in a school with an annual student turnover of 75% from a school with a turnover of 10%.

Questions to be considered in the user evaluation prior to district or state adoption include the following:

1. Is the product equally usable and effective for all kinds of intended users, for example, learners of varying ability levels, the different schools of the district or state?

2. Does the product have undesired effects, for example, generation of unfavorable teacher or student self-concepts, as well as the desired effects?
3. How much added effort on the part of the teachers, counselors, or administrators is involved in preparing to use the product and in actually using it?
4. Do the users have the technical capability, the time, and the monetary resources for conducting the user evaluation?

An earlier part of this chapter was devoted to the evaluation of educational programs of the local school by the local school staff. The same kind of technical capability and planning and evaluation strategy indicated there is applicable to user evaluation of new products.

A final note is in order regarding the evaluation of large-scale federally funded and state-funded programs, such as minimum competency testing, programs for preschool children, and programs for bilingual students. The results of the evaluation of state and national programs such as these are used to determine state and federal policies, including the funding of new programs and the funding of continuing programs by the federal and state governments. Accordingly, the results of national evaluations of these programs influence not only educational practices but also other social conditions of the target populations..

The national evaluation of federally funded programs was studied by Cronbach and associates (1980). Immediate reform was urged, and new and better ways of conducting the national evaluations were suggested. Continuing evaluation of the kind suggested throughout this chapter was proposed as a means of improving programs, rather than conducting a one-time summative evaluation to determine whether to continue or discontinue the programs.

16.18 Compare the purposes of formative evaluation and summative evaluation, using the development of a set of instructional films as an example.

16.19 Give two or three reasons why the product developer (a) should be the summative evaluator of the product and (b) should not be.

16.20 Three questions to be considered in user evaluation deal with usability of the product by different kinds of intended users of a school district or state, the possible undesired effects of the product as well as desired effects, and the amount of effort required to use the product. Explain why the potential user should address each of these concerns before adopting the product throughout a district or state.

16.21 Five areas of evaluation are described in this chapter: student progress in courses, individual students' instructional programs in courses, individual students' complete educational programs of courses, other elements of a school's educational programs, and educational products. Arrange these in order from highest priority to lowest priority in terms of (a) facilitating student learning and (b) the continuous improvement of education. Explain your priorities.

16.22 Review and Application. Recall the most important information regarding each of the following concepts, and identify at least one possible use of the information by you as a learner, a teacher, or both:

Measurement Devices Used in Evaluation
Evaluating Student Progress and the Effectiveness of a Course
    Coordinating the Timing and Purposes of Evaluation
    Relating Evaluation to Instruction
    Establishing Evaluation Criteria
Evaluating Each Student's Total Educational Program and Reporting to Parents
    Coordinating the Timing and Purposes of Evaluation
    Relating Evaluation to Advising and Teaching
    Establishing Evaluation Criteria
    Reporting Student Progress and Grading
Evaluating Elements of a School's Educational Program
    Developing an Evaluation Strategy
    Establishing Evaluation Criteria
    Illustrative Program Evaluation
Evaluating Educational Materials and Processes
    Conducting Formative Evaluation
    Conducting Summative Evaluation
    Conducting User Evaluation

SUMMARY

Evaluation is necessary for facilitating student learning and teaching and for continuously improving the educative process. Many different kinds of measurement devices are used in gathering information for use in evaluation. Locally constructed tests and teacher-developed procedures are used to achieve most of the purposes of evaluation. However, published norm-referenced and published criterion-referenced tests also serve useful purposes.

The foremost role of teachers in evaluation is evaluating the progress of their students and the effectiveness of their courses. The same information that is gathered at the beginning of a unit or course, during the course, and at the end of a course to evaluate each student's progress can also be used to evaluate each student's instructional program and the effectiveness of the course for all the students enrolled in it.

The timing and purposes of evaluating each student's complete educational program parallel those for evaluating each student's instructional program in each course. The same information regarding student progress is used. The planning, monitoring, and evaluation of each student's educational program requires that teachers serve as educational advisors to small groups of students.

Evaluating elements of a school's total educational program, such as its various curricular areas or its provisions for children with handicapping conditions, contributes effectively to the continual improvement of educa-

WHAT'S RIGHT WITH THE SCHOOLS?
The Making of a Journalist

NORMAN COUSINS

Norman Cousins has been called "America's Nuclear Age version of the classic Renaissance Man." His knowledge ranges broadly across human concerns from science and art to politics and war. He is the author of a bestseller, *Anatomy of an Illness,* and was formerly owner and editor of the Saturday Review.

In my first year of high school I had a biology teacher who seemed like a character out of a Dickens novel. He was one of the least ambiguous personalities I have ever known. When he had a suggestion to make, he invested the enterprise with total personal commitment. It was difficult to remain uninfluenced in his presence.

One day he told the class about a national essay contest on the evils of alcohol, sponsored by the Women's Christian Temperance Union. It was his ambition to have one of his students win the award. The WCTU, he felt, was doing God's work, and he wanted to help.

I took up the challenge, and for the next three weeks the WCTU dominated my life. I made a special trip from my home in New Jersey to the New York Public Library and filled hundreds of cards with notes on that old devil alcohol. I diagrammed the actions of liquor on its malevolent course through the frail human body. I dutifully observed its effect on the heart, the stomach, the pancreas, and the liver. I was conscientiously horrified at the way it ravaged the blood vessels of the brain and converted the delicate brain-cell tissue into a malfunctioning shambles. I became totally convinced that I was dealing with history's ultimate evil.

I set down all of these terrifying impressions with a missionary zeal. My biology teacher was overjoyed. He put his arms around me and said, "I think we have done it."

And we had. The essay won first place, which took the form of a check for $25. That award caused me to make two definite decisions about my future: (1) I would not drink, and (2) I would become a writer—there was probably more gold in them thar hills.

SOURCE: *Phi Delta Kappan* 1980, *62*(1). Back cover page.

WHAT'S RIGHT WITH THE SCHOOLS?
Professional Support in Defying Convention

ROSALYN S. YALOW

Rosalyn S. Yalow is head of the Department of Clinical Sciences, Albert Einstein College of Medicine, Montefiore Medical Center, New York City. A mere outline of her distinguished career in science and medicine fills half a column in *Who's Who*. She is perhaps best known to the general public as winner of the Nobel Prize for medicine and physiology in 1977. Her determination to pursue a career not generally open to women earlier in this century has been an inspiration to many talented young women of today.

By seventh grade I was committed to mathematics. A great chemistry teacher at Walton High School, Mr. Mondzak, excited my interest in chemistry, but when I went to Hunter, the college for women in New York City's college system (now the City University of New York), my interest was diverted to physics, especially by Professors Herbert N. Otis and Duane Rolier. In the late Thirties when I was in college, physics, and in particular nuclear physics, was the most exciting field in the world.

I was excited about achieving a career in physics. My family, being more practical, thought the most desirable position for me would be as an elementary school teacher. Furthermore, it seemed most unlikely that good graduate schools would accept and offer financial support for a woman in physics. However, my physics professors encouraged me and I persisted. As I entered the last half of my senior year at Hunter in September 1940, I was offered what seemed like a good opportunity. Since I could type, another of my physics professors, Jerrold Zacharias, now at the Massachusetts Institute of Technology, obtained a part-time position for me as a secretary to Rudolf Schoenheimer, a leading biochemist at Columbia University's College of Physicians and Surgeons. This position was supposed to provide an entree for me into graduate courses, via the back door, but I had to agree to take stenography. On my graduation from Hunter in January 1941, I went to business school. Fortunately, I did not stay there too long. In mid-February I received an offer of a teaching assistantship in physics at the University of Illinois, the most prestigious of the schools to which I had applied. It was an achievement beyond belief. I tore up my stenography books, stayed on as secretary until June, and during the summer took two tuition-free physics courses under government auspices at New York University. In September I left for the University of Illinois where I received my Ph.D. in physics in 1945.

SOURCE: *Phi Delta Kappan,* 1980, *62*(3), p. 233.

tion in the local school. Teachers have key roles in this kind of evaluation. Representative teachers serve on a school committee that plans and monitors the evaluation and related goal setting. In this way, teachers share in determining the purposes of the evaluation, the specific tests to be used, the scheduling of the tests, interpreting the information, setting goals, and making the changes necessary to achieve the goals.

Formative evaluation is conducted while a new or refined product is being developed to ensure that the product achieves its objectives with its intended target group. Summative evaluation is carried out to get a final estimate of the effectiveness, usability, and cost of the completed product. User evaluation is conducted before adopting the product throughout a school district or state to ensure that the product is effective and usable in the different school situations of the district or state. User evaluation is necessary because each school is unique in terms of its student body, staff, physical plant, and other characteristics.

SUGGESTIONS FOR FURTHER READING

Bloom, B. S., Hastings, J. T., & Madaus, G. F. *Handbook on formative and summative evaluation of student learning.* New York: McGraw-Hill, 1971.

This is the most practical and complete handbook available. Chapters 4, 5, and 6 deal with summative evaluation of student learning, evaluation for placement and diagnosis of students, and formative evaluation of student learning, respectively.

Brooks, D. M., & Van Cleaf, D. W. *Pupil evaluation in the classroom: An all level guide to practice.* Lanham, Md.: University Press of America, 1983.

Provides teachers strategies for evaluating academic achievement and social behavior. It is written specifically for teachers rather than test specialists.

Hopkins, K. D., & Stanley, J. C. *Educational and psychological measurement* (6th ed.). Englewood Cliffs, N.J.: Prentice-Hall, 1981.

Chapter 12 of this measurement textbook is focused on grading and reporting. Do's and don'ts of parent conferences are included.

Joint Committee on Standards for Educational Evaluation. *Standards for evaluation of educational programs, projects, and materials.* New York: McGraw-Hill, 1981.

Standards are presented for conducting evaluations and for analyzing information and reporting conclusions.

Klausmeier, H. J., Lipham, J. M., & Daresh, J. C. *The renewal and improvement of secondary education: Concepts and practices.* Lanham, Md.: University Press of America, 1983.

In chaps. 2 and 3, Klausmeier describes individual educational programming and individual instructional programming; in chap. 7 he explains how to evaluate instructional programs, educational programs, and elements of the schools' total educational program; in chap. 13 he gives the results of schools' putting the recommended evaluation techniques into practice.

Klausmeier, H. J., Rossmiller, R. A., & Saily, M. (Eds.), *Individually guided elementary education: Concepts and practices.* New York: Academic Press, 1977.

Chapters 4, 5, and 6 describe the evaluation of three sets of curriculum materials: elementary school mathematics (T. Romberg), pre-reading (R. Venezky and S. Pittleman), and elementary school reading (W. Otto).

Natriello, G., & Dornbusch, S. *Teacher evaluative standards and student effort.* New York: Longman, 1984.

Examines the relationship between teachers' standards and student achievement; outlines evaluation techniques to improve student performance.

Sax, G. *Principles of educational and psychological measurement and evaluation* (2nd ed.). Belmont, Calif.: Wadsworth, 1980.

Chapter 17 of this textbook explains evaluating student progress and reporting pupil progress; chap. 18 describes program evaluation.

APPENDIX

STATISTICS

BRANCHES OF STATISTICS AND KINDS OF MEASUREMENT SCALES

TABULATING AND GRAPHING DATA

MEASURES OF LOCATION AND VARIABILITY

MEASURES OF RELATIONSHIP

INTERPRETATION OF TEST SCORES

SAMPLING AND EXPERIMENTAL PROCEDURES

Knowledge of statistics is used by educators in four ways. It aids them in conducting their own research. It also enables them to understand reports of research. With the widespread use of calculators and microcomputers, teachers are using statistics increasingly to summarize information related to their students' achievement and other characteristics. Finally, knowledge of statistics aids educators in understanding the characteristics of tests and in interpreting norm-referenced and criterion-referenced tests.

The term *statistics* is used in three ways. It indicates a bit of numerical information—for example, 200 students are enrolled in grade 9, the median salary of the teachers of city A is $22,000. Statistics also refers to a body of theoretical information used in describing a distribution of scores and drawing inferences based on a comparison of two or more distributions of scores. Finally, the term is used to indicate a method for describing or comparing distributions of scores. For example, the mean is a statistic used in describing a distribution of scores, while analysis of variance is a statistic used in determining the extent to which a difference found among two or more distributions of scores is due to chance factors. Most of this appendix presents and explains statistical methods.

A person does not have to be able to compute the statistic used in a study in order to understand the results of the study. It is helpful, however, to understand (1) branches of statistics and kinds of measurement scales, (2) tabulating and graphing data, (3) measures of location and variability, (4) measures of relationship, (5) statistics and the interpretation of scores, and (6) sampling and experimental procedures. These concepts are explained in the remainder of this appendix.

TABLE A.1 DATA GATHERED ON 46 FIFTH GRADERS

STUDENT NUMBER	SEX	AGE IN MONTHS	IQ	IQ RANK	WORD MEANING	PARAGRAPH MEANING	SPELLING	WORD STUDY SKILLS	LANGUAGE	ARITHMETIC COMPUTATION	ARITHMETIC CONCEPTS	ARITHMETIC APPLICATION	SOCIAL STUDIES	SCIENCE
(1)	(2)	(3)	(4)	(5)	(6)	(7)	(8)	(9)	(10)	(11)	(12)	(13)	(14)	(15)
1	M	122	137	1.0	73	80	80	68	77	64	63	69	86	85
2	F	131	114	15.5	51	57	66	62	62	59	65	69	70	60
3	M	124	118	11.0	52	43	46	70	53	52	52	55	81	60
4	M	136	98	34.5	49	40	39	39	28	33	50	34	46	52
5	F	137	119	9.0	52	52	60	62	56	46	46	41	42	44
6	M	128	106	24.0	52	59	36	67	92	40	52	44	62	36
7	F	127	113	17.0	67	72	53	73	29	52	43	47	54	56
8	M	129	99	33.0	32	24	53	34	43	33	39	41	45	38
9	M	129	106	24.0	47	50	46	48	57	45	48	49	64	75
10	F	126	108	19.5	49	67	54	57	32	52	57	58	58	56
11	F	125	107	21.5	27	36	45	40	27	44	36	38	45	39
12	M	134	82	44.0	27	34	29	29	34	33	27	42	39	45
13	F	117	94	39.0	42	42	46	62	44	46	57	46	37	42
14	F	133	103	27.0	42	50	49	57	27	44	41	49	50	42
15	F	120	65	46.0	27	32	32	20	48	16	33	32	35	29
16	F	128	101	29.5	44	48	38	34	64	50	48	53	56	56
17	F	120	96	37.5	56	61	66	63	27	60	71	85	64	65
18	M	129	105	26.0	49	23	38	24	65	29	50	51	64	57
19	M	125	115	14.0	56	80	64	62	65	40	65	55	95	95
20	M	122	106	24.0	52	43	39	48	37	36	59	44	50	46

	Sex													
21	M	122	117	12.0	56	61	66	63	64	60	71	85	64	65
22	F	128	107	21.5	67	50	66	48	70	43	55	49	54	65
23	M	127	86	42.0	33	32	42	20	29	41	29	47	40	38
24	M	133	119	9.0	56	57	45	57	53	49	61	61	62	85
25	F	135	89	41.0	37	36	37	39	27	45	45	41	39	40
26	M	131	120	7.0	67	77	66	73	95	59	85	72	95	85
27	F	120	97	36.0	30	48	43	30	32	49	39	44	45	50
28	M	123	98	34.5	46	37	39	20	36	41	41	46	51	58
29	F	123	101	29.5	35	41	52	42	50	38	36	42	51	47
30	M	123	72	45.0	26	21	30	18	22	36	29	29	32	28
31	F	133	100	31.5	44	48	41	33	40	40	46	34	40	46
32	F	126	129	3.0	70	65	66	71	70	41	54	49	67	56
33	F	130	128	4.0	73	84	95	85	92	57	68	85	64	72
34	M	129	96	37.5	39	39	53	57	34	40	50	39	43	43
35	M	130	84	43.0	36	30	35	24	32	43	36	34	39	32
36	M	127	114	15.5	41	47	48	42	37	46	55	51	60	58
37	F	123	102	28.0	44	39	47	58	34	46	29	42	41	42
38	F	130	125	5.0	57	67	88	85	66	58	63	69	81	75
39	M	120	116	13.0	46	49	64	58	50	45	55	49	95	63
40	F	123	132	2.0	75	80	68	76	80	52	52	51	74	81
41	F	132	100	31.5	54	70	71	90	80	56	61	75	56	69
42	F	120	124	6.0	70	61	66	85	95	52	68	53	70	58
43	M	125	119	9.0	56	52	49	63	51	56	76	61	58	56
44	F	130	108	19.5	49	57	52	70	57	43	55	47	52	42
45	F	120	91	40.0	44	48	46	57	41	44	21	46	45	51
46	M	121	110	18.0	59	65	58	53	61	43	68	61	74	91
$\overline{X}$		127	106		4.9	5.2	5.2	5.3	5.1	4.6	5.1	5.1	5.7	5.6
s		4.98	15.1		1.3	1.6	1.5	2.0	2.1	.94	1.4	1.4	1.7	1.7

NOTE: All scores in columns 6–15 can be changed to grade equivalents by inserting a decimal point between the two digits as has been done for $\overline{X}$ and s.

Students who have already had a course in statistics merely need to scan this appendix to identify any concepts that may be new to them. Students with little previous work in statistics will find that they must read slowly. Also, there are many introductory statistics textbooks including those listed at the end of this appendix that may be consulted for more information.

BRANCHES OF STATISTICS AND KINDS OF MEASUREMENT SCALES

There are two basic branches of statistics and several different types of measurement scales. *Descriptive statistics* are used in summarizing bodies of numerical information, such as the test scores of a high school senior class or the salaries of the teachers of a school district. *Inferential statistics* are used by the researcher to draw inferences or conclusions about a population based on an analysis of the measurements of a sample of the population. For example, we can infer whether the third-grade boys and girls of a state achieve at the same level in mathematics computation by properly drawing a sample of the boys and a sample of the girls of the state, getting a reliable achievement test score on each boy and girl included in the samples, and statistically analyzing the scores. The statistics discussed throughout this appendix are either descriptive or inferential.

We now turn to three different kinds of measurement scales and will examine actual data to classify them. Table A.1 presents 13 different measurements that were made on 46 fifth-grade students. These measurements are scaled in three different ways.

1. Nominal scale. A nominal scale indicates descriptive categories, for example, gender (male and female) and achievement (pass and fail). Nominal information is summarized by counting the number of instances of each category; for example, Table A.1 shows that there are 22 males and 24 females in the group of 46 fifth graders.[1]
2. Ordinal scale. Measurements can be ranked from highest to lowest; this kind of scale is called ordinal. An ordinal scale is found in column (5) of Table A.1, where each pupil's rank in IQ is listed. The numbers in this column indicate each individual's position in the group, with 1 designating the highest IQ. Note that ties are handled by averaging the ranks involved: Pupils 2 and 36, who tied for fifteenth and sixteenth place, are both assigned a rank of 15.5.
3. Interval scale. The variables in columns (3) and (4) and columns (6) through (15) of Table A.1 are scaled in intervals of equal units expressed in numbers, for example, age in months and IQ in

---

[1] Table A.1 is referred to so often throughout this appendix that you might find it convenient to duplicate it and examine it whenever it is referred to.

numerical scores. Interval measurement is more precise than rank-order measurement. To illustrate, an IQ score of 110 is not only higher than one of 100, it is 10 points higher; similarly, it is 20 points higher than one of 90. On an ordinal scale the rank order of the three highest IQs, whether 110, 100, and 90 or 110, 109, and 80, is 1, 2, 3.

TABULATING AND GRAPHING DATA

Frequency Distribution Table

Cumulative Distribution

Histogram

Frequency Polygon

Table A.1 presents information about 46 individuals, but it is difficult to form an impression of the group on any variable or to relate any individual's performance to that of the group simply by inspecting the scores. A means of capturing the essence of the data is a tabular or a graphic representation. Several procedures are now considered.

Frequency Distribution Table

The frequency of occurrence of the values of variables may be summarized and presented in a frequency distribution table. Table A.2, based on Table A.1, gives the frequencies of the males and females. Note that the variable (sex) is included in the title of the table and that the categories (male and female) are listed in the table. Two often-used symbols appear: f, indicating the frequency for each category, and N, the total number of cases in the group.

TABLE A.2 FREQUENCY DISTRIBUTION ACCORDING TO SEX

SEX	f
Male	22
Female	24
	$N = 46$

Two-way tables are frequently used for summarizing two categories of information. By assigning a label of "at or above average" or "below average" to each child's IQ and then ascertaining the number of males and females in each category, we can present the relationship of IQ to sex for this particular group in tabular form, as in Table A.3. Note that the subtotals or marginal frequencies (22, 24, and 25, 21) are the sums of the two rows and two columns of entries, respectively, and that the total frequency (46), the sum of all the entries, appears in the lower right-hand corner of the table.

When interval data, such as the test scores of individuals, are tabulated,

**TABLE A.3 FREQUENCY
DISTRIBUTION ACCORDING TO SEX AND IQ**

| | IQ | | |
SEX	AT OR ABOVE AVERAGE	BELOW AVERAGE	TOTAL
Male	13	9	22
Female	12	12	24
Total	25	21	46

the number of different scores is often large, making it desirable to group the scores into class intervals as shown in Table A.4. Consider the column of IQ scores in Table A.1, where the 46 scores range from 65 to 137. When the IQ scores in column 4 of Table A.1 are grouped into class intervals as has been done in Table A.4 (the other columns are included to explain other concepts), the information is more easily understood.

TABLE A.4 FREQUENCY DISTRIBUTION OF IQS

CLASS INTERVAL	f	CUMU-LATIVE f	CUMU-LATIVE (%)	REAL LIMITS OF CLASS INTERVAL	MIDPOINT OF CLASS INTERVAL
133–137	1	46	100.0	132.5–137.5	135
128–132	3	45	97.8	127.5–132.5	130
123–127	2	42	91.3	122.5–127.5	125
118–122	5	40	87.0	117.5–122.5	120
113–117	6	35	76.1	112.5–117.5	115
108–112	3	29	63.0	107.5–112.5	110
103–107	7	26	56.5	102.5–107.5	105
98–102	8	19	41.3	97.5–102.5	100
93– 97	4	11	23.9	92.5– 97.5	95
88– 92	2	7	15.2	87.5– 92.5	90
83– 87	2	5	10.9	82.5– 87.5	85
78– 82	1	3	6.5	77.5– 82.5	80
73– 77	0	2	4.3	72.5– 77.5	75
68– 72	1	2	4.3	67.5– 72.5	70
63– 67	1	1	2.2	62.5– 67.5	65

The first step in developing the frequency distribution in Table A.4 was to determine the size of the class interval. A class interval of 5 was chosen. The size of the class interval is indicated by the number of scores included in the interval. For instance, the interval 98–102 includes the scores 98, 99, 100, 101, and 102. An interval with the whole number limits of 98 and 102 — its *class* limits — may also be interpreted as extending from 97.5 to 102.5 — its *real* limits. These real limits are shown in the fifth column of Table A.4.

Once the class intervals are established, it is a simple matter to record and tally the individual scores as has been done in the second column of Table A.4. The accuracy of the frequencies may be checked by comparing the sum of the frequencies in the frequency table with the number of scores in the original list.

Cumulative Distribution

In some situations it may be of interest to know the number of individuals whose scores lie within and below a particular class interval. This information is supplied in Table A.4 in the column labeled "cumulative f." At a glance one can tell how many children (11) have IQs of 97 or below. The cumulative frequency is obtained by adding the entries in the frequency column, starting with the lowest class interval. For instance, the cumulative frequency (5) for the interval 83–87 is the sum of the frequency for that interval (2) and the frequencies for all intervals below it (1, 0, 1, 1).

Sometimes the cumulative frequency information is converted into percentage. This is accomplished by dividing the cumulative frequency by the total number of individuals. For example, the cumulative frequency through the 83–87 class interval is 5, which is 10.9 percent of 46 (that is, 5/46).

Histogram

The IQ frequencies in Table A.4 may be graphically displayed in a histogram as in Figure A.1. The vertical axis of the histogram is marked off

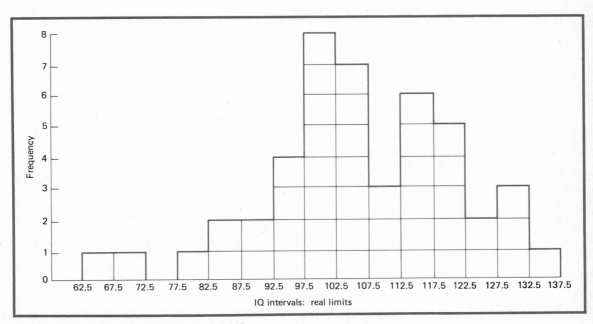

Figure A.1 Histogram of 46 fifth graders' IQs.

in frequency units. The horizontal axis is marked off in real limits, but it could be done in class intervals. In effect, each individual's score is represented by a small square; 46 such squares are enclosed by the heavy lines that form the shape of the histogram. Notice that the units on each axis of the graph are labeled and that the histogram is given a title to aid the reader in interpreting the information.

Frequency Polygon

A histogram is useful for portraying one distribution of scores, but not for comparing two or more distributions since one histogram cannot be superimposed on another and interpreted readily. The frequency polygon is more appropriate for graphing two or more distributions.

The frequency polygon is similar to the histogram in construction; however, the shape of the frequency polygon is determined by connecting the midpoints of each class interval as shown in Figure A.2.

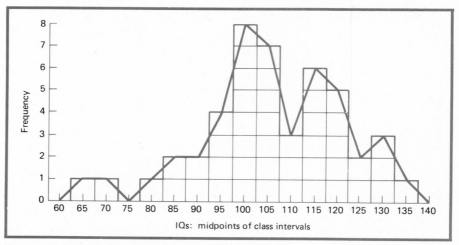

Figure A.2 Frequency polygon of IQs superimposed on histogram.

Measures of
Central Tendency

Partition Values

Measures of Variability

MEASURES OF LOCATION AND VARIABILITY

In the previous pages we have examined one kind of descriptive statistics that is used in summarizing and displaying information. Two other kinds will now be explained—namely, measures of location and measures of variability. Measures of location include measures of central tendency and partition values.

Measures of Central Tendency

Three measures of central tendency are the mean, median, and mode. Each is an indicator of the typical characteristic or performance of a group.

Mean

The mean is the arithmetic average of a set of scores. It is calculated by adding all the scores and dividing the total by the number of scores. Suppose you wished to find the mean of these five scores: 11, 10, 6, 5, and 3. Their sum, 35, divided by the number of scores, 5, yields a mean of 7. For ungrouped data like these and like those presented in Table A.1, the formula for computing the mean is given in Computing Guide 1.

COMPUTING GUIDE 1
COMPUTING THE MEAN OF UNGROUPED DATA

Let: $\bar{X}$ = the mean
Σ = the sum of
X = each score
N = the number of cases

Formula: $\bar{X} = \dfrac{\Sigma X}{N}$

Example: Find the mean of the 46 IQ scores shown in Table A.1.
Step 1: Add the 46 IQs; determine that $\Sigma X = 4876$.
Step 2: Substitute numbers in the formula and perform the indicated operations.

$$\bar{X} = \frac{4876}{46} = 106.0$$

NOTE: $\bar{X}$ is read as "X bar"; Σ is read as "sigma."

This formula has been programmed into some microcomputers and into some hand calculators. After the scores are entered, the mean button or switch is pressed, the calculation is performed by the machine, and the mean is outputted by the machine. Since computers and calculators are so readily available, data are rarely grouped into class intervals for computing the mean.

Median

The median is the point in a distribution on each side of which there is an equal number of cases. If there is an odd number of cases, the median is the middle score. For example, given the scores 10, 8, 6, 5, and 1, the median is 6 as two cases lie above it and two below it. If there is an even number of total cases, the median is the point that lies midway between the two middle-most scores. Given the scores 3, 6, 8, and 12, the median is 7.

The computation of the median for grouped data is more complicated, but it can readily be accomplished. Rather than providing a technical description for computing the median, we present the steps in nontechnical language in Computing Guide 2.

COMPUTING GUIDE 2
COMPUTING THE MEDIAN OF GROUPED DATA

Example: Find the median of the 46 IQ scores as grouped in Table A.4:

Step 1: Find the interval in which the midpoint lies by multiplying the number of cases *(N)* by .5: $(46 \times .5 = 23)$.

Step 2: Determine the real limits of the interval containing the median by counting up 23 scores from the lower end of scores. Checking the cumulative frequency column in Table A.4, the 23rd score lies in the interval with real limits of 102.5 to 107.5.

Step 3: Add to the lower real limit (102.5) a value determined by multiplying the size of the class interval (5) by 4/7. The cumulative *f* to 102.5 is 19. $23 - 19 = 4$. We need 4 of the 7 in the $102.5 - 107.5$ interval to reach the midpoint (23) of the distribution.

Therefore:

$$\text{median} = 102.5 + \frac{4}{7} \times 5$$
$$102.5 + 2.9 = 105.4$$

Notice that half the cases, 23, are found in or below the interval with real limits of 102.5 to 107.5. Since 19 cases fall below 102.5 and there are 7 cases in the interval 102.5–107.5, we need to go through $\frac{4}{7}$ of the interval to reach 23. Observe that for this grouped data the median is 105.4, quite close to the mean of 106.0 for the same ungrouped data.

Mode

The mode is the most frequently occurring score in an ungrouped distribution of scores. In a grouped distribution it is the midpoint of the class interval that includes the greatest number of scores. In Table A.1 there are two modes in the distribution of IQ: 106 and 119 both occur three times. A distribution having two modes is called *bimodal*. When the grouped IQ data in Table A.4 are considered, the mode is 100 inasmuch as eight IQs occur in the interval that has a midpoint of 100.

Relationship Among Mean, Median, and Mode

The mean is affected by all scores in the distribution. When the distribution of the scores is near symmetric, that is, without extreme scores on either end, the mean is an accurate indicator of central tendency. If a distribution is nonsymmetric, the median is a better indicator of central tendency.

Classroom data may be either symmetric or nonsymmetric. On standardized achievement tests, large numbers of students of a grade typically do not get either very high or very low scores, so the distribution is symmetric. In this situation the mean is an appropriate statistic to use.

Teachers often construct their own tests, and many students obtain perfect or near perfect scores and few obtain low scores. When scores are clustered at one end of the distribution, the median score is the preferred indicator of central tendency.

The mode is not useful with a small number of cases; however, when large numbers of scores are involved and there is a heavy concentration of scores in one class interval, the mode may be the most appropriate statistic.

Partition Values

Quartiles and percentiles are points in a distribution that divide the distribution into quarters and hundredths, respectively. Any score in a distribution can be located in relation to these points. Quartiles and percentiles are computed in a manner analogous to the median. (The median is a measure of location as well as a measure of central tendency.)

Q_1, the first quartile, is the point below which one-fourth of the scores of a distribution are located; Q_3 is the point below which three-fourths lie; similarly, P_{85} is the point below which 85 percent of the scores are located. From this brief account we can see that the median $= Q_2$ (second quartile) $= P_{50}$ (fiftieth percentile). Keep in mind that a partition value is a point in a distribution and is not necessarily equal to any score of the distribution.

As we shall see later, test publishers typically convert the raw scores that students make on IQ and achievement tests to percentile scores to enable the educator to ascertain how a particular student has scored in relation to the national sample used in standardizing the test. The mean score of any group can also be converted to an equivalent percentile score. One often sees newspaper accounts of the mean percentile scores in reading and other subject fields for the students of one or more grades of each school district.

Measures of Variability

To describe a set of data, a measure of central tendency is not sufficient; a measure of the variability, spread, or dispersion of the scores is also needed. Measures of variability include the range, variance, and standard deviation.

Range

The range is the simplest measure of variability. It is the difference between the highest and lowest real limits in the distribution. For example, the range of IQ calculated from Table A.1 is $137 - 65 + 1 = 73$, or $137.5 - 64.5 = 73$. The 1 is added in the first computation because the real limits are not used, as they are in the second computation. As a statistic, the range has the drawback of taking into account only the two extreme scores or measures; however, reporting both the mean and the range provides more useful information than either one alone. Both statistics can readily be obtained from any distribution of scores.

Variance and Standard Deviation

The variance and the standard deviation are widely used in describing the way in which scores are dispersed about the mean. The variance (s^2) is defined as the average of the squares of the deviations of the scores from their mean; the standard deviation (s) is simply the square root of the variance. The size or value of s^2 and s tells us how homogeneous a group is on a given variable, for example, how homogeneous a ninth-grade class is in algebra achievement. Given a mean of 50, a class with an s of 2 is far more homogeneous than one with an s of 10.

Consider a simple case of six scores: 0, 4, 6, 6, 8, and 12. The sum of these scores is 36, and the mean is $36 \div 6 = 6$. The next steps in calculating the variance are to subtract each score from the mean, square the resulting deviation, and sum these squared deviations. In this case,

SCORES	DEVIATION SCORES = SCORES − MEAN	SQUARED DEVIATION SCORES
0	$0 - 6 = -6$	$(-6)^2 = 36$
4	$4 - 6 = -2$	$(-2)^2 = 4$
6	$6 - 6 = 0$	$0^2 = 0$
6	$6 - 6 = 0$	$0^2 = 0$
8	$8 - 6 = 2$	$2^2 = 4$
12	$12 - 6 = 6$	$6^2 = \underline{36}$
	Sum of the squared deviations $= 80$	

Notice that the sum of the deviation scores equals zero; this will always be the case if the calculations are correct. The next step in computing the variance is to find the average of the squared deviation scores. This is accomplished by dividing the sum of the squared deviations by the number of cases less one ($N - 1$). Thus,

$$s^2 = \frac{\text{sum of the squared deviations}}{N - 1}$$

$$= \frac{80}{6 - 1} = \frac{80}{5} = 16$$

The standard deviation is then computed by taking the square root of the variance:

$$s = \sqrt{s^2} = \sqrt{16} = 4$$

The standard deviation, in this case 4, is expressed in units comparable to the original set of scores; it is a measure of the dispersion or spread of the scores about the mean. It is seldom necessary to change raw scores to deviation scores because of the availability of desk calculators and rapid electronic computers which permit computing variance, standard deviation, and many other measures without first computing the deviation scores.

Computing Guide 3 gives the formula (in raw score units) and the procedure for computing the variance and the standard deviation.

COMPUTING GUIDE 3
COMPUTING THE VARIANCE AND THE STANDARD
DEVIATION OF UNGROUPED DATA

Let: s^2 = the variance
        s = the standard deviation
        N = the number of cases
        ΣX^2 = the square of each score, subsequently added together
        $(\Sigma X)^2$ = the sum of all scores, subsequently squared

Formula: $s^2 = \dfrac{1}{N-1}\left[\Sigma X^2 - \dfrac{(\Sigma X)^2}{N}\right]$

$s = \sqrt{s^2}$

Example: Find the variance and standard deviation of the 46 IQ scores in Table A.1.

Step 1: Add all the scores; determine that $\Sigma X = 4876$.

Step 2: Square all scores and add them; determine that $\Sigma X^2 = 527{,}104$.

Step 3: Substitute numbers in the formula and perform the indicated operations:

$$s^2 = \frac{1}{46-1}\left[527{,}104 - \frac{(4876)^2}{46}\right]$$

$$= \frac{1}{45}(527{,}104 - 516{,}856) = 227.73$$

Step 4: Take the square root of s^2 to determine s:

$$s = \sqrt{227.73} = 15.09$$

Recall that in raw score form, without grouping the data into a frequency table, the $\bar{X} = \Sigma X/N$. Recognize that no new symbols are used in the formula for variance and standard deviation.

MEASURES OF RELATIONSHIP

Product-Moment
Correlation

Rank-Order
Correlation

The relation between two variables, or two measurements, involving the same individuals is expressed as a correlation coefficient. One purpose of knowing the relationship is so that each individual's performance on one variable can be used in predicting the same individual's performance on the other variable—for example, in predicting mathematics achievement from reading achievement or in predicting freshmen college grades from an academic aptitude test score in the senior year of high school. Another purpose of the correlational method is to predict future performance in a given area based on present performance in the same area—for example, reading achievement in grade 4 from reading achievement in grade 3. The higher the correlation coefficient between any two sets of measurements, the more accurately the predictions can be made. The two main kinds of correlation coefficient are the product-moment and the rank order.

Product-Moment Correlation

The product-moment coefficient of correlation, designated by the symbol r, is a widely employed statistic. It is computed to ascertain the relationship between two sets of measurements (variables) on the same individuals or on the same variable between pairs of individuals. The r can range from -1.00 for a perfect inverse linear relationship to $+1.00$ for a perfect direct relationship. We now consider the interpretation of a correlation coefficient.

1. A correlation of $+1.00$ indicates a perfect positive relationship between two variables. If during each year of school attendance the number of words that students recognized at sight increased by a constant number, then years of schooling and word recognition would correlate perfectly, $+1.00$. Correlations of $+1.00$ are rarely found in education or in any behavioral science.

2. A correlation of -1.00 indicates a perfect negative relationship between two variables. If the resale value of textbooks decreased by a constant amount with each year of use, then the correlation between years of use and resale value would be -1.00.

3. A correlation of .00 indicates no relationship. A .00 correlation is expected between the weight of college freshmen males or females and their standardized reading achievement test scores.

4. A correlation between .00 and $+1.00$ or between .00 and -1.00 indicates an imperfect relationship. The higher the absolute value, that is, the closer the correlation is to $+1.00$ or -1.00, the greater the degree of relationship and the more accurately one can make predictions. Thus, one can more accurately predict that students who do well in reading will also do well in science if the correlation between reading and science achievement is .60 rather than .40. Similarly, one can predict more reliably the resale value of textbooks three years later if the correlation is $-.80$ rather than $-.50$.

5. A correlation is not a percentage; therefore, a correlation of .90 cannot be interpreted as indicating a relationship twice as high as .45 or three times as high as .30. Squaring a correlation coefficient, however, does indicate in percentage the extent to which two or more sets of values are related, that is, have something in common. Thus, $.50^2 = .25$ indicates that 25 percent of what is measured can be considered common to the two sets of measurements. The relationship indicated by the first three correlation values mentioned above can be assessed by considering them as being $.90^2 = 81$ percent in common, $.45^2 = 20$ percent in common, and $.30^2 = 9$ percent in common. There is a greater difference be-

tween correlations than their numerical values seem to indicate, and this difference is better shown by the values of their squares than by the value of the correlation coefficients.

6. The extent to which a correlation coefficient of any given value is a relationship of importance depends on the nature of the variables that are correlated. A correlation of .60 between reading achievement and social studies achievement might not be considered by school people to be of any particular importance to the students or the teachers; however, a correlation of .60 between the amount of schooling completed and lifetime earnings would be judged to be very important. Here we are discussing the importance represented by correlations of the same value. The statistical significance of a correlation coefficient can be determined and the level of significance interpreted in the same manner as for other tests of significance.

7. Although two sets of scores may correlate positively, we cannot infer that one causes the other. For example, the length of shoes that children wear from ages 6 to 12 correlates positively with the number of words they spell correctly during the same years; so also does the number of permanent teeth and arithmetic achievement. Obviously, longer shoes do not cause better spelling, nor do more permanent teeth cause higher arithmetic performance; rather, changes in all four variables from year to year are mainly attributable to an underlying variable, namely maturation.

The size of the sample must be taken into account in interpreting correlation coefficients. For example, a correlation of .20 may indicate a small but reliable relationship between two variables if the N is above 100, but it may be merely a chance fluctuation from zero, not indicative of any relationship, if the N is small, for example, 10 or fewer.

The meaning of correlation coefficients may be made more clear by constructing a scattergram, a table on which the two scores of each individual are plotted. Figure A.3 shows three scattergrams in which r equals .89, .51 and $-.03$. The number of individuals having scores at or between the values given on the Y axis and the X axis are indicated. For example, in the scattergram where $r = .89$ three individuals have scores at or between 2.0 and 2.9 on both variables while five have scores at or between 3.0 and 3.9 on both variables.

The extent of the relationship implied by each r may be estimated by observing the extent to which the cases cluster along the dotted diagonal line extending from the lower left corner to the upper right corner of each scattergram. Only six of the 46 sets of scores lie more than one measurement unit from the diagonal where $r = .89$, whereas most of them do where $r = -.03$.

There are several formulas for computing a product-moment correlation. Ordinarily, raw scores are used in conjunction with a calculator or

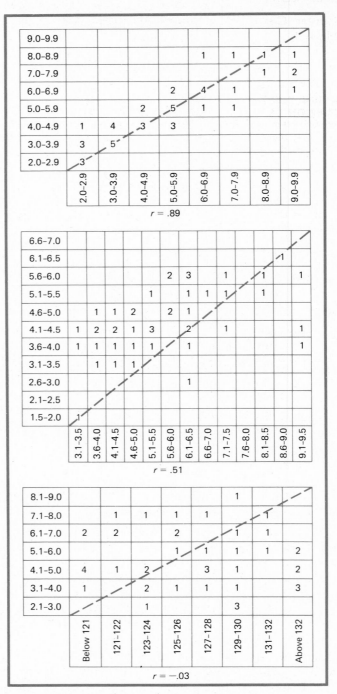

Figure A.3 Scattergrams depicting $r = .89, .51, -.03$.

microcomputer. Computing Guide 4 gives the procedure using raw scores from Table A.1.

COMPUTING GUIDE 4
COMPUTING THE PRODUCT-MOMENT COEFFICIENT OF CORRELATION BETWEEN TWO VARIABLES

Let: r = the product-moment correlation coefficient
          N = the number of cases
     ΣXY = the sum of the cross products (a cross product is each person's X score multiplied by his Y score)
    $\Sigma X \Sigma Y$ = the sum of all the X scores multiplied by the sum of all the Y scores
      ΣX^2 = the square of each X score, subsequently added together
    $(\Sigma X)^2$ = the sum of all the X scores, squared
      ΣY^2 = the square of each Y score, subsequently added together
    $(\Sigma Y)^2$ = the sum of all the Y scores, squared

Formula: $r = \dfrac{N\Sigma XY - \Sigma X \Sigma Y}{\sqrt{[N\Sigma X^2 - (\Sigma X)^2][N\Sigma Y^2 - (\Sigma Y)^2]}}$

Example: Compute the product-moment correlation between paragraph meaning (X) and language scores (Y) for the 46 children in Table A.1.
     Step 1: Add all the raw scores for X; add all the raw scores for Y. Determine that $\Sigma X = 2354$; $\Sigma Y = 2350$.
     Step 2: Square all X scores and add the products; square all Y scores and add the products. Determine that $\Sigma X^2 = 132{,}218$; $\Sigma Y^2 = 139{,}008$.
     Step 3: Multiply X by Y for each child; add these to determine that $\Sigma XY = 133{,}538$.
     Step 4: Substitute numbers in the formula and perform the indicated operations:

$$r = \frac{(46 \times 133538) - (2354 \times 2350)}{\sqrt{[(46 \times 132218) - (2354)^2][(46 \times 139008) - (2350)^2]}}$$

$$= \frac{610{,}848}{\sqrt{540{,}712 \times 871{,}868}} = \frac{610{,}848}{686{,}607} = .89$$

Rank-Order Correlation

The product-moment correlation indicates the relationship between two interval variables. It is also possible to calculate a correlation between measurements expressed as ranks. Students of a class or school are often ranked from highest to lowest on test scores or other characteristics. When a group is ranked on any two characteristics, the rank-order correlation (rho) between the two sets of rank can be ascertained.

In Table A.5 the word meaning and language scores for a random sample of 23 students from Table A.1 are reported in columns (2) and (3). (Only 23 are used for convenience in illustrating the procedure.) These scores are converted to ranks from 1 to 23 in columns (4) and (5).

**TABLE A.5 DATA ON A RANDOM
SAMPLE OF 23 FIFTH GRADERS FOR
COMPUTING RANK-ORDER CORRELATION**

STUDENT NUMBER	WORD MEANING	LANGUAGE	WORD MEANING RANK	LANGUAGE RANK	d	d^2
(1)	(2)	(3)	(4)	(5)	(6)	(7)
1	73	77	1.5	5.0	−3.5	12.25
3	52	53	9.5	9.5	0.0	0.0
7	67	92	4.5	3.5	1.0	1.0
8	32	29	20.0	19.0	1.0	1.0
9	47	43	13.0	13.0	0.0	0.0
10	49	57	11.5	8.0	3.5	12.25
12	27	27	22.0	21.0	1.0	1.0
14	42	44	16.0	12.0	4.0	16.0
17	56	64	7.0	6.5	0.5	0.25
18	49	27	11.5	21.0	−9.5	90.25
20	52	37	9.5	14.0	−4.5	20.25
21	56	64	7.0	6.5	0.5	0.25
24	56	53	7.0	9.5	−2.5	6.25
25	37	27	18.0	21.0	−3.0	9.0
26	67	95	4.5	1.5	3.0	9.0
27	30	32	21.0	17.5	3.5	12.25
28	46	36	14.5	15.0	−0.5	0.25
30	26	22	23.0	23.0	0.0	0.0
33	73	92	1.5	3.5	−2.0	4.0
34	39	34	17.0	16.0	1.0	1.0
35	36	32	19.0	17.5	1.5	2.25
39	46	50	14.5	11.0	3.5	12.25
42	70	95	3.0	1.5	1.5	2.25
					$\Sigma d = 0.0$	$\Sigma d^2 = 213.00$

Computing Guide 5 gives the procedure for calculating the rank-order correlation, including the handling of identical scores. As noted in the computing guide, a rank-order correlation of .90 is found.

**COMPUTING GUIDE 5
COMPUTING THE RANK-ORDER COEFFICIENT OF
CORRELATION BETWEEN TWO VARIABLES**

Let: Rho = the rank correlation coefficient
  N = the number of cases
  Σd^2 = the differences in rank for each pair of scores, squared and subsequently summed

Formula: $Rho = 1 - \dfrac{6\Sigma d^2}{N(N^2 - 1)}$

Example: Compute the rank-order correlation between word meaning (X) and language scores (Y) for the 23 children in Table A.5.
  Step 1: Rank separately each set of scores, giving 1 to the highest, and so on. Tied scores take the mean of the ranks assigned to them as a common rank.

Step 2: Subtract to find the difference in rank (d) for each pair of scores (see column 6, Table A.5).
Step 3: Square each difference in rank to obtain d^2 (see column 7, Table A.5).
Step 4: Sum these d^2; find that $\Sigma d^2 = 213$ (see column 7, Table A.5).
Step 5: Substitute numbers in the formula and perform the indicated operations:

$$Rho = 1 - \frac{6(213)}{23(529 - 1)} = 1 - .10 = .90$$

Often teachers are called upon to interpret the scores that students make on standardized, norm-referenced tests. Understanding what is meant by a normal distribution aids this interpretation.

The Normal Distribution

The normal distribution, illustrated in Figure A.4, is a theoretical distribution that is symmetric about the mean. Sometimes referred to as the bell-shaped curve, it has characteristics that are of great importance for interpreting test scores and other information.

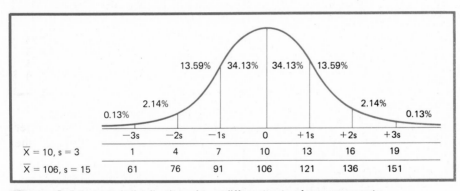

Figure A.4 A normal distribution of two different sets of measurements.

The idea of normality applies to the shape or form of the distribution, but not to the values of the distribution, such as the mean and the standard deviation. As is shown in Figure A.4, one normal distribution of scores may have a mean of 10 and a standard deviation of 3 and another a mean of 106 and a standard deviation of 15; in fact, both the mean and standard deviation can be of any value.

For any amount of deviation from the mean that is expressed in standard deviation units, a normal probability table can be used to ascertain the proportion of the total area under the normal curve up to that deviation or between the mean and that amount of deviation. For example, about 34 percent of the area lies on each side of the mean up to the point that is one standard deviation from the mean; thus about 68 percent of the area lies between $+1\sigma$ and -1σ, as can be seen in Figure A.4. The area between $+2\sigma$ and -2σ includes 95 percent of the total area; thus, only about 5 percent of the area lies beyond $+$ or -2 standard deviation units. Moreover, 99.7 percent of the area of the probability curve lies between $+3\sigma$ and -3σ. The percent of the test scores of a distribution, if normally distributed, coincides with the percent of the area under various parts of the normal curve. Most IQ tests have been constructed to have a mean of 100 and a standard deviation of 15. Accordingly, approximately 68 percent of all IQ scores fall between 85 and 115 while only three-tenths of 1 percent fall below 55 and above 145.

Standard Scores

Earlier we saw that changing raw scores to percentile scores makes it possible to compare how an individual has performed on several tests. We can also change a set of raw scores to standard scores, sometimes called sigma scores or z-scores, to make scores on different tests comparable and thereby interpretable. A standard score is derived by dividing the deviation score (the difference between the raw score and the group mean) by the standard deviation for the particular set of test scores; that is,

$$\text{standard score} = \frac{\text{individual raw score} - \text{group mean}}{\text{standard deviation of group scores}}$$

Because raw scores fall below or above the mean, standard scores may be negative or positive. Also, most standard scores fall within the range of $+3$ to -3 standard deviation units, just as almost all the area under the normal curve falls between these points. The sum of any complete set of standard scores is always zero.

Stanine Scores

Stanine scores are based on a normal distribution and are widely used in reporting test results. The following statements about stanines can be understood by consulting Figure A.5. There are only nine stanine scores, each a whole number from 1 to 9. Each stanine is equivalent to half a standard deviation unit except at either extreme. (Notice in Figure A.5 that standard deviation is indicated by σ rather than s.) The extreme stanines, 1 and 9, include all the scores beyond $\pm1.75\sigma$, while stanines 2 through 8 include all the scores between $\pm1.75\sigma$.

Test publishers typically change each raw score to a stanine score, as well as to a percentile score, and report all three scores. The chief advantage in using stanine scores rather than point scores, such as percentile scores, is that small differences between scores are not given undue attention. As has been noted in Chapter 15, errors of measurement are found in all test scores. These errors are minimized through conversion of raw scores to stanines, whereas they are maintained in the point scores. The disadvantage of stanine scores in comparison with percentile scores is

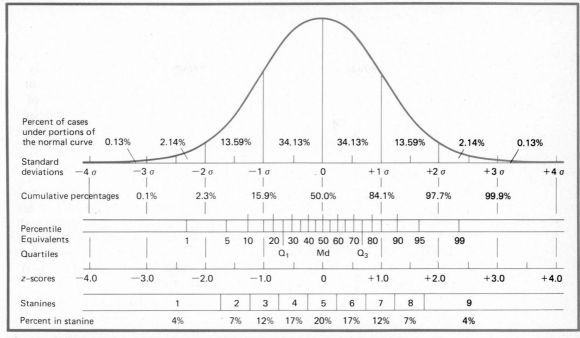

Figure A.5 The relationship of some derived scores to the normal distribution.

that preciseness is lost. For example, the stanine scores of 4, 5, and 6 include the percentile scores that range from 23 to 77.

Various kinds of derived scores that have been explained in the preceding pages are shown in Figure A.5. Since they are based on a normal curve, they can readily be compared. For example, a score that falls one standard deviation unit above the mean is equivalent to a cumulative percentage of 84.1, a percentile score of 84, and a z-score of $+1.0$. It is in the fourth quartile, which includes the top 25 percent of all scores, and is equivalent to a stanine 7 score. We should pause to recognize that teachers and other educators must understand percentile scores, stanine scores, mean, median, and standard deviation to interpret standardized, norm-referenced test scores.

SAMPLING AND EXPERIMENTAL PROCEDURES

Sampling Procedures

Hypothesis Testing

Statistical Significance of Differences

In Chapter 1 we presented information relating to the methods used in educational research, including controlled experimentation. Here we present concepts relating to inferential statistics that are helpful in understanding reports of various kinds of studies. Procedures frequently used in controlled experiments dealing with either learning or instruction are explained and illustrated with specific examples.

Sampling Procedures

A population for a research study is the total number of all the possible individuals from which one or more samples is selected. In a small study the population of interest may be all the 9-year-old children of a certain school. On the other hand, in the National Assessment of Educational Progress the population is all the 9-year-old children of the 50 states.

In many studies, conclusions are drawn about the entire population, based on data gathered on a sample of the population. A sample, rather than the whole population, is studied to save time and money. Simple random sampling and stratified random sampling are the two main types of sampling.

Simple Random Sampling

In simple random sampling, each member of the population has an equal chance of being included in the sample and every possible combination of members of the population has the same chance of being included. For example, if the entire population of 17-year-old girls in a city is 5000 and a sample of 500 is desired, each of the 5000 must have an equal chance of being drawn into the sample of 500. Any possible combination of 500 therefore has an equal chance to be included in the sample that is actually drawn.

Stratified Random Sampling

In this type of sampling, the population is divided into subgroups, called strata, on the basis of one or more characteristics. In educational research two variables frequently used in stratification are achievement level and sex. A teaching method in mathematics might be hypothesized to be differentially effective for boys and girls, and for children of above- and below-average achievement. The experimenter would then want to have random samples of pupils of all possible combinations of these variables: high-achieving boys, high-achieving girls, low-achieving boys, and low-achieving girls. After identifying all the children in these four groupings, each child would be assigned a number, and using a table of random numbers, the experimenter would draw from each group the desired number of children.

Hypothesis Testing

Hypotheses are stated in either of two forms: directional or null. The *directional hypothesis* states the experimenter's best judgment about the direction of the outcomes of the experiment, while the *null hypothesis* specifies no direction or no relationship. Suppose that we wish to answer this question: Do individual conferences of 10 minutes duration during which pupils set goals pertaining to mathematics objectives affect the number of objectives the pupils attain? We could state the possible outcomes of the experiment in terms of either the null hypothesis or a directional hypothesis:

There is no difference in the number of mathematics objectives attained by pupils who have a weekly 10-minute goal-setting conference and by those who do not.

The pupils who have a weekly 10-minute goal-setting conference will attain more mathematics objectives than those who do not.

In the following pages various experimental designs for carrying out this experiment on goal setting are given along with the related tests of statistical significance. You will see that there are several methods of conducting an experiment given the same samples of the same population of students. Moreover, there are different tests of statistical significance.

Statistical Significance of Differences

The statistical significance of the difference between or among mean scores obtained in an experiment is derived to determine the extent to which the difference is due to chance. Levels of significance widely used for rejecting the null hypothesis are .05 and .01. The .05 level is interpreted to mean that the probability is 5 in 100 that a difference this large would have occurred by chance; the probability that it would not have occurred by chance is 95 in 100. The lesser the probability of occurring by chance, for example, 1 in 100, the more likely it is that the obtained difference is a real or true difference resulting from the manipulated variable, also referred to as the experimental treatment.

Various tests of statistical significance may be made to compare the scores of groups. Commonly used tests are the t-distribution for confidence intervals, the t-test, the F-test, and chi-square. Each of the last three yields a single number, or value, which can be compared with values reported in a statistical table. The values in the table can, in turn, be used in determining the probability that the difference is due to chance.

The *t*-Distribution for Confidence Intervals

Table A.6 gives the data collected in an experiment designed to answer the goal-setting question. At the outset of the experiment, two groups of 50 pupils each were selected randomly from all the third graders of a school district. One group of 50 served as the experimental group that participated in setting goals, the other 50 as the control group. The goal-setting procedure was then carried out. Each child of the experimental group participated once a week in a goal-setting conference with his or her teacher. In the conference the teacher and child identified and talked about the number of mathematics objectives that the child had mastered during the prior week, and the child set a goal in terms of number of objectives to be mastered during the next week.

Each week data were gathered regarding the number of objectives that each child attained, the *dependent variable* in this experiment. The mean number of objectives mastered throughout the course of the experiment by the children of the experimental and control groups is presented in Table A.7, as are the standard errors of the means. The standard error of the mean

TABLE A.6 **NUMBER OF OBJECTIVES ATTAINED BY TWO GROUPS BEFORE (BASELINE) AND DURING AN EXPERIMENT USING GOAL-SETTING PROCEDURES**

EXPERIMENTAL GROUP		CONTROL GROUP	
BASELINE PERIOD	EXPERIMENTAL PERIOD	BASELINE PERIOD	EXPERIMENTAL PERIOD
7	7	17	17
30	22	23	20
26	12	19	13
24	23	33	22
28	19	24	24
39	21	21	17
22	16	26	15
22	22	30	20
25	17	31	15
30	18	15	15
18	13	21	19
32	20	16	8
23	22	13	2
21	14	24	8
20	17	15	12
16	15	20	8
18	10	21	20
29	23	23	16
33	24	21	14
27	18	19	8
16	24	33	21
22	18	25	13
24	17	26	13
22	22	22	11
26	19	25	16
10	10	20	11
11	19	17	13
16	10	22	14
20	18	28	14
15	16	14	7
21	19	7	4
24	20	20	11
5	14	14	17
16	18	17	7
14	16	8	0
15	23	19	14
15	16	29	9
26	18	20	7
20	26	22	5
14	20	10	3
7	11	12	3
19	28	9	14
14	24	14	15
14	16	10	13
10	7	10	14

(Continued on page 559)

TABLE A.6 (Continued)

EXPERIMENTAL GROUP		CONTROL GROUP	
BASELINE PERIOD	EXPERIMENTAL PERIOD	BASELINE PERIOD	EXPERIMENTAL PERIOD
30	24	22	6
16	25	22	11
8	12	12	17
19	23	14	3
9	9	25	8

(S.E.) is simply the estimated standard deviation of the sampling distribution of the mean, and it indicates how the mean might have fluctuated from its reported value had a different sample been drawn.

TABLE A.7 MEANS AND STANDARD DEVIATIONS (s) FOR EXPERIMENTAL AND CONTROL GROUPS

GROUP	$\overline{X}$	s	S.E.	99 PERCENT CONFIDENCE INTERVAL
Experimental	17.90	5.09	.727	15.95–19.85
Control	12.34	5.68	.811	10.17–14.51

In the last column in Table A.7 the 99 percent confidence intervals for the means are specified. These intervals are interpreted to mean that data similar to those collected would 99 percent of the time come from a population whose mean lay within the interval. We conclude that the goal-setting conferences resulted in making the two groups drawn from a single population different since the 99 percent confidence intervals for the experimental group and the control group do not overlap.

The t-Test

The t-Test is also a method for testing the significance of the difference between two means. The formula for arriving at a t-ratio is as follows:

$$t = \frac{\overline{X_1} - \overline{X_2}}{\sqrt{\left(\frac{\Sigma d_1^2 + \Sigma d_2^2}{N1 + N2 - 2}\right)\left(\frac{N1 + N2}{N1\ N2}\right)}}$$

where $\overline{X}$ = mean
d^2 = the sum of the deviations of each score from the mean squared
N = the number of cases

The *t*-ratio obtained is used to enter an appropriate *t*-distribution table, using the proper degrees of freedom. The *t*-value obtained for the preceding data is 5.1, $p \leq .01$. This *t*-value leads to the same conclusion as that obtained using the preceding 99 percent confidence interval.

Analysis of Variance and the *F*-Test

The *t*-Test is appropriate only for comparing two sets of measurements. Analysis of variance (ANOVA) is a procedure for testing the differences among two or more sets of measurements. Analysis of variance might be used when either simple random sampling or stratified random sampling has been employed to assign individuals to three or more groups.

A more sophisticated approach to the question about the effectiveness of the goal-setting conference might have taken into account the achievement level of the children in mathematics. One might have hypothesized that the goal-setting procedure would affect high and low achievers differentially, with the low achievers profiting more than the high achievers.

The way to test this hypothesis is to stratify the total population of third graders into above- and below-average achievers in mathematics and then draw 25 above-average and 25 below-average achievers randomly for the experimental group and equal numbers for the control group. The experimental design in Figure A.6 might be used. The two dimensions of the figure represent the two experimental variables — treatment and achievement level. Notice that the design gives the *N* in each cell, and that the total *N* has not changed from the preceding experiment.

	Treatment	
	Experimental	Control
Above average	*N* = 25	*N* = 25
Below average	*N* = 25	*N* = 25

Achievement level

Figure A.6 Experimental design for an experiment testing the effectiveness of a goal-setting procedure for above- and below-average achievers in mathematics.

The results of conducting the experiment in this manner and computing the analysis of variance (ANOVA) to determine the effects of being above average or below average in achievement and of setting goals or not setting goals (treatment) are given in Table A.8. These two effects are called *main effects*. The statistic calculated for each effect is *F*. When the effect is significant, it is noted by a *p*-value. The *p* values of .01 for achievement group and of .001 for treatment indicate that the experimental group differs from the control group in the number of objectives attained and that the above-average achievers differ from the below-average achievers in the same way. Although not shown in Table A.7, the children of above-average entering achievement and those who set goals attained more objectives during the experiment. The interaction term provides an answer to the question as to whether the goal-setting treatment was equally effective for the above-average and below-average achievers. Because it does not meet the significance level of .01 set in advance, the null hypothesis is not rejected, meaning that we cannot conclude that the goal-setting conferences affects above- and below-average achievers differently; however, since a p value of .05 was obtained, the interaction deserves further study.

TABLE A.8 ANALYSIS OF VARIANCE OF NUMBER OF OBJECTIVES ATTAINED

SOURCE	df	MEAN SQUARE	F	p
Achievement group	1	219.04	8.50	<.01
Treatment	1	772.84	29.99	<.001
Interaction	1	158.76	6.16	<.05
Error	96	25.77		

To complete the discussion of the entries in Table A.8, we see that the error term used in computing F is simply the numerical value obtained when the mean square for any effect is divided by the mean square for error, that is, $219.04 \div 25.77 = 8.50$. Likewise, degrees of freedom (df) are used in the calculations.

Analysis of Covariance and the F-Test

Let us continue hypothesizing about the goal-setting procedure by suggesting that the number of objectives attained during the course of the experiment might be related to each pupil's previous attainment of objectives. In this case, data might be collected before the experiment begins to identify the number of objectives attained by the children during a baseline period.

An analysis taking into account both a premeasure and a dependent measure on each child is known as an analysis of covariance. The premeasure in our example is the number of objectives each child attained during the baseline period, and it is called the covariate. In effect, the final scores on the dependent variable are adjusted on the basis of the relationship between this covariate and the dependent measure. The preexperimental differences among the children are first controlled, and then an analysis of variance is performed. The F-test is utilized, and results are reported for an analysis of covariance in the same manner as for an analysis of variance. Probability values based on analysis of covariance are interpreted in the same way as for analysis of variance. We should note before proceeding that a measure different from the dependent measure is typically used in analysis of covariance.

Chi-Square

The preceding analyses are most often used in conjunction with interval data. Tests of significance for other kinds of data have also been developed. The most commonly used statistical procedure for nominal data, chi-square, is discussed here.

Suppose in conjunction with a study of reading, pupils were asked the following two questions:

1. Did you read a book last week?
2. Did you see either of your parents reading a book last week?

Each of the pairs of responses for 100 students can be tallied in a two-way table like the one in Figure A.7. Applying the chi-square test to these frequencies, it is found that the chances are less than 1 in 1000 that the two variables are independent. In other words, whether the parent is seen reading or not is closely associated with whether the child read a book that week.

		Child reads?	
		Yes	No
Parents read?	Yes	42	8
	No	19	31

Figure A.7 Two-way table of frequencies for computing chi-square test.

The chi-square test is not difficult to compute, and the probability values obtained are interpreted in the same manner as for any other test of significance. As noted earlier, chi-square tests are performed on nominal data; the other tests of significance discussed in this section are performed only on interval data.

SUGGESTIONS FOR FURTHER READING

Borg, W. R., & Gall, M. D. *Educational research: An introduction* (4th ed.). New York: Longman, 1983.

Explains how to conduct many different kinds of educational research and how to interpret research reports.

Chase, C. I. *Elementary statistical procedures* (3rd ed.). New York: McGraw-Hill, 1984.

Includes all the concepts discussed in this appendix.

Glass, G. V., & Stanley, J. C. *Statistical methods applied to education* (2nd ed.). Englewood Cliffs, N.J.: Prentice-Hall, 1982.

An introductory text of an intermediate level of difficulty.

Hinkle, D. E., Wiersma, W., & Jurs, S. G. *Basic behavioral statistics.* Boston: Houghton Mifflin, 1982.

An easy introductory text that starts with teaching the basic mathematics needed for computing simple statistics.

Isaac, S., & Michael, W. B. *Handbook in research and evaluation* (2nd ed.). San Diego, CA.: Edits Publishers, 1981.

Chap. 3 is an excellent readable summary of research methods.

REFERENCES

Alexander, L., Frankiewicz, R. G., & Williams, R. E. Facilitation of learning and retention of oral instruction using advance and post organizers. *Journal of Educational Psychology*, 1979, *71*, 701–707.

Allport, G. W. *Becoming.* New Haven, Conn.: Yale University Press, 1955.

American Association for the Advancement of Science Commission on Science Education. *Science—A process approach.* Washington, D.C.: American Association for the Advancement of Science–Xerox, 1967.

American Association for Health, Physical Education, and Recreation. *Youth fitness test manual.* Washington, D.C.: American Association for Health, Physical Education, and Recreation, 1965.

Ames, C., & Ames, R. The thrill of victory and the agony of defeat: Children's self and interpersonal evaluations in competitive and noncompetitive learning environments. *Journal of Research and Development in Education*, 1978, *12*, 79–87.

Anderson, J. R. *Cognitive psychology and its implications.* San Francisco: Freeman, 1980.

Anderson, L. W., & Jones, B. F. Designing instructional strategies which facilitate learning for mastery. *Educational Psychologist*, 1981, *16*, 121–138.

Anderson, R. C., Pichert, J. W., & Shirey, L. L. Effects of the reader's schema at different points in time. *Journal of Educational Psychology*, 1983, *75*, 271–279.

Anderson, R. C., Reynolds, R. E., Schallert, D. L., & Goetz, E. T. Frameworks for comprehending discourse. *American Educational Research Journal*, 1977, *14*, 367–381.

Anderson, R. C., Spiro, R. J., & Anderson, M. C. Schemata as scaffolding for the representation of information in connected discourse. *American Educational Research Journal*, 1978, *15*, 433–440.

Andrews, G. R., & Debus, R. L. Persistence and the causal perception of failure: Modifying cognitive attributions. *Journal of Educational Psychology*, 1978, *70*, 154–166.

Arlin, M., & Webster, J. Time costs of mastery learning. *Journal of Educational Psychology*, 1983, *75*, 187–195.

Arlin, M., & Whitley, T. W. Perceptions of self-managed learning opportunities and academic locus of control: A causal interpretation. *Journal of Educational Psychology*, 1978, *70*, 988–992.

Arnstine, D. G. The language and values of programmed instruction (Part II). *The Educational Forum*, 1964, *28*, 337–346.

Aronson, E., Bridgeman, D. L., & Geffner, R. Interdependent interactions and prosocial behavior. *Journal of Research and Development in Education*, 1978, *12*, 16–27.

Ashby, M. S., & Wittmaier, B. C. Attitude changes in children after exposure to stories about women in traditional or nontraditional occupations. *Journal of Educational Psychology*, 1978, *70*, 945–949.

Atkin, J. M. Behavioral objectives in curriculum design: A cautionary note. *The Science Teacher*, 1968, *35*, 27–30.

Atkinson, J. W. *An introduction to motivation*. Princeton, N.J.: Van Nostrand, 1964.

Atkinson, R. C. Mnemotechnics in second language learning. *American Psychologist*, 1975, *30*, 821–828.

Atkinson, R. C., & Raugh, M. R. An application of the mnemonic keyword method to the acquisition of a Russian vocabulary. *Journal of Experimental Psychology: Human Learning and Memory*, 1975, *104*, 126–133.

Atkinson, R. C., & Shiffrin, R. M. The control of short-term memory. *Scientific American*, 1971, *224*, 82–90.

Ausubel, D. P. *The Psychology of meaningful verbal learning*. New York: Grune & Stratton, 1963.

Ausubel, D. P. The facilitation of meaningful verbal learning in the classroom. *Educational Psychologist*, 1977, *12*, 162–178.

Ausubel, D. P., Novak, J. D., & Hanesian, H. *Educational psychology: A cognitive view* (2nd ed.). New York: Holt, Rinehart and Winston, 1978.

Ausubel, D. P., Schpoont, S. H., & Cukier, L. The influence of intention on the retention of school materials. *Journal of Educational Psychology*, 1957, *48*, 87–92.

Backman, M. E. Patterns of mental abilities: Ethnic, socioeconomic, and sex differences. *American Educational Research Journal*, 1972, *9*, 1–12.

Ball, S., & Bogatz, G. A. *The first year of Sesame Street: An evaluation*. Princeton, N.J.: Educational Testing Service, 1970.

Ballard, M., Corman, L., Gottlieb, J., & Kaufman, M. J. Improving the social status of mainstreamed retarded children. *Journal of Educational Psychology*, 1977, *69*, 605–611.

Bandura, A. *Social learning theory*. Englewood Cliffs, N.J.: Prentice-Hall, 1977.

Bandura, A. Self-efficacy mechanism in human agency. *American Psychologist*, 1982, *37*, 122–147.

Bandura, A., Ross, D., & Ross, S. A. Imitation of film-mediated aggressive models. *Journal of Abnormal and Social Psychology*, 1963, *66*, 3–11.

Bangert-Drowns, R. L., Kulik, J. A., & Kulik, C. C. Synthesis of research on the effects of coaching for aptitude and admissions tests. *Educational Leadership*, 1983–1984, *41*(4), 80–82.

Bank, B. J., Biddle, B. J., & Good, T. L. Sex roles, classroom instruction, and reading achievement. *Journal of Educational Psychology*, 1980, *72*, 119–132.

Barclay, C. B. The executive control of mnemonic activity. *Journal of Experimental Child Psychology*, 1979, *27*, 262–276.

Barron, F. *Creative person and creative process*. New York: Holt, Rinehart and Winston, 1969.

Bar-Tal, D. Attributional analysis of achievement-related behavior. *Review of Educational Research*, 1978, *48*, 259–271.

Bates, J. A. Extrinsic reward and intrinsic motivation: A review with implications for the classroom. *Review of Educational Research,* 1979, *49,* 557–576.

Bayley, N. Development of mental abilities. In P. H. Mussen (Ed.), *Carmichael's manual of child psychology* (Vol. 1). New York: Wiley, 1970.

Berkowitz, L. *Aggression: A social psychological analysis.* New York: McGraw-Hill, 1962.

Berkowitz, L. Aversively stimulated aggression: Some parallels and differences in research with animals and humans. *American Psychologist,* 1983, *38,* 1135–1144.

Berlyne, D. E. *Conflict, arousal, and curiosity.* New York: McGraw-Hill, 1960.

Bernard, J. The good-provider role: Its rise and fall. *American Psychologist,* 1981, *36,* 1–12.

Bernard, M. E. *The effect of advance organizers and within-text questions on the learning of a taxonomy of concepts* (Tech. Rep. No. 357). Madison: Wisconsin Center for Education Research, 1975.

Block, J. H. Issues, problems, and pitfalls in assessing sex differences: A critical review of the *Psychology of sex differences. Merrill-Palmer Quarterly,* 1976, *22,* 283–308.

Bloom, B. S. (Ed.). *Taxonomy of educational objectives. Handbook I: Cognitive domain.* New York: McKay, 1956.

Bloom, B. S. Learning for mastery. *Evaluation Comment* 1(2). Los Angeles: Center for the Study of Evaluation of Instructional Programs, University of California, 1968.

Bloom, B. S. *Human characteristics and school learning.* New York: McGraw-Hill, 1976.

Blount, N. S., Klausmeier, H. J., Johnson, S. L., Fredrick, W. C., & Ramsay, J. G. *The effectiveness of programed materials in English syntax and the relationship of selected variables to the learning of concepts* (Tech. Rep. No. 17). Madison: Wisconsin Center for Education Research, 1967.

Bork, A., & Franklin, S. D. The role of personal computer systems in education. *AEDS Journal,* 1979, *13,* 17–30.

Bowen, C., Gelabert, T., & Torgesen, J. Memorization processes involved in performance on the visual-sequential memory subtest of the Illinois Test of Psycholinguistic Abilities. *Journal of Educational Psychology,* 1978, *70,* 887–893.

Bower, G. H. Selective facilitation and interference in retention of prose. *Journal of Educational Psychology,* 1979, *66,* 1–8.

Bower, G. H., & Clark, M. C. Narrative stories as mediators for serial learning. *Psychonomic Science,* 1969, *14,* 181–182.

Bower, G. H., & Hilgard, E. R. *Theories of learning* (5th ed.). Englewood Cliffs, N.J.: Prentice-Hall, 1981.

Bradley, L. A., & Bradley, G. W. The academic achievement of black students in desegrated schools: A critical review. *Review of Educational Research,* 1977, *47,* 399–449.

Brainerd, C. J. *Structures of thought in middle-childhood: Recent research on Piaget's concrete-operational groupements.* Paper presented at the Third Annual Meeting on Structural Learning, Philadelphia, 1972.

Brainerd, C. J. The stage question in cognitive-developmental theory. *Behavioral and Brain Sciences,* 1978, *2,* 173–213.

Brickman, W. W. Ethics, examinations and education. *School and Society,* 1961, *89,* 412–415.

Bronfenbrenner, U. *Two worlds of childhood: U.S. and U.S.S.R.* New York: Simon & Schuster, 1970.

Brooks, L. W., Dansereau, D. F., Spurlin, J. E., & Holley, C. D. Effects of headings on text processing. *Journal of Educational Psychology,* 1983, *75,* 292–302.

Brownell, W. A., & Moser, H. E. *Meaningful versus mechanical learning: A study in grade III subtraction* (Duke University Studies in Education, No. 8). Durham, N.C.: Duke University Press, 1949.

Bruner, J. S., Olver, R. R., Greenfield, P. M., et al. *Studies in cognitive growth: A collaboration at the center of cognitive studies.* New York: Wiley, 1966.

Bryant, B. K. Context of success, affective arousal, and generosity: The neglected role of negative affect in success experience. *American Educational Research Journal,* 1983, *20,* 553–562.

Burt, C., Jones, E., Miller, E., & Moodie, W. *How the mind works.* New York: Appleton-Century-Crofts, 1934.

Busch, J. S., Television's effects on reading: A case study. *Phi Delta Kappan,* 1978, *59,* 668–671.

Bush, A., Kennedy, J., & Cruickshank, D. An empirical investigation of teacher clarity. *Journal of Teacher Education,* 1977, *28,* 53–58.

Bushway, A., & Nash, W. R. School cheating behavior. *Review of Educational Research,* 1977, *47,* 623–632.

Buss, R. R., Yussen, S. R., Mathews, S. R., II, Miller, G. E., & Rembold, K. L. Development of children's use of a story schema to retrieve information. *Developmental Psychology,* 1983, *19,* 22–28.

Butkowsky, I. S., & Willows, D. M. Cognitive-motivational characteristics of children varying in reading ability: Evidence for learned helplessness in poor readers. *Journal of Educational Psychology,* 1980, *72,* 408–422.

Calsyn, R. J., & Kenny, D. A. Self-concept of ability and perceived evaluation of others: Cause or effect of academic achievement? *Journal of Educational Psychology,* 1977, *69,* 136–145.

Camperell, K. *Identification of seventh-grade students' insights about the strategies they used to study and understand an expository text* (Tech. Report No. 566). Madison: Wisconsin Center for Education Research, 1980.

Cardinal principles of secondary education. Washington, D.C.: Department of Interior, Bureau of Education, Bulletin No. 35, 1918.

Carnine, D. Three procedures for presenting minimally different positive and negative instances. *Journal of Educational Psychology,* 1980, *72,* 452–456.

Carroll, J. B. A model of school learning. *Teachers College Record,* 1963, *64,* 723–733.

Carroll, J. B. Words, meanings, and concepts. *Harvard Educational Review,* 1964, *34,* 178–202.

Carroll, J. B. Ability and task difficulty in cognitive psychology. *Educational Researcher,* 1981, *10,* 11–21.

Case, R. Intellectual development: A systematic reinterpretation. In F. H. Farley & N. J. Gordon (Eds.), *Psychology and education: The state of the union.* Berkeley, Calif.: McCutchan, 1981.

Cattell, R. B. The structure of intelligence in relation to the nature/nurture controversy. In R. Cancro (Ed.), *Intelligence: Genetic and environmental influences.* New York: Grune & Stratton, 1971.

Cauley, K. M., & Murray, F. B. Structure of children's reasoning about attitudes of school success and failure. *American Educational Research Journal,* 1982, *19,* 473–480.

Chall, J. S. Minimum competency in reading: An informal survey of the states. *Phi Delta Kappan,* 1979, *60,* 351–352.

Cheyne, J. A., & Walters, R. H. Intensity of punishment, timing of punishment, and cognitive structure as determinants of response inhibition. *Journal of Genetic Psychology,* 1969, *7,* 231–244.

Chomsky, N. The fallacy of Richard Herrnstein's IQ. In N. J. Block & G. Dworkin (Eds.), *The IQ controversy.* New York: Pantheon, 1976.

Chu, G. C., & Schramm, W. *Learning from television.* Washington, D.C.: National Association of Educational Broadcasters, 1968.

Clark, D. C. Teaching concepts in the classroom: A set of prescriptions derived from experimental research. *Journal of Educational Psychology Monograph*, 1971, *62*, 253–278.

Clark, K. B. Empathy: A neglected topic in psychological research. *American Psychologist*, 1980, *35*, 187–190.

Clark, R. E. Antagonism between achievement and enjoyment in ATI studies. *Educational Psychologist*, 1982, *17*, 92–101.

Cleary, T. A., Humphreys, L. G., Kendrick, S. A., & Wesman, A. Educational uses of tests with disadvantaged students. *American Psychologist*, 1975, *30*, 15–41.

College Board. *Academic preparation for college: What students need to know and be able to do*. New York: Office of Academic Affairs, The College Board, 1983.

Collins, M. L. The effects of training for enthusiasm on the enthusiasm displayed by preservice elementary teachers. Unpublished doctoral dissertation. Syracuse, N.Y.: Syracuse University, 1976.

Combs, A. W. Affective education or none at all. *Educational Leadership*, 1982, *39*(7), 494–497.

Comprehensive Tests of Basic Skills. *Bulletin of Technical Data, Form Q, No. 1*, California Test Bureau. New York: McGraw-Hill, 1968.

Comstock, G. Mass media. In H. E. Mitzel, H. H. Best, & W. Rabinowitz (Eds.), *Encyclopedia of educational research* (5th ed., Vol. 3). New York: Free Press, 1982.

Cook, S. W. Interpersonal and attitudinal outcomes in cooperating interracial groups. *Journal of Research and Development in Education*, 1978, *12*, 97–113.

Cornehlsen, V. H. Cheating attitudes and practices in a suburban high school. *Journal of the National Association of Women Deans and Counselors*, 1965, *28*, 106–109.

Corno, L. Individual and class level effects of parent-assisted instruction in classroom memory support strategies. *Journal of Educational Psychology*, 1980, *72*, 278–292.

Cousins, N. Unwed mothers in America. *Saturday Review*, December 1979, *6*, 8.

Covington, M. V., & Omelich, C. L. Effort: The double-edged sword in school achievement. *Journal of Educational Psychology*, 1979a, *71*, 169–182.

Covington, M. V., & Omelich, C. L. It's best to be able and virtuous too: Student and teacher evaluative responses to successful effort. *Journal of Educational Psychology*, 1979b, *71*, 688–700.

Covington, M. V., Spratt, M. F., & Omelich, C. L. Is effort enough, or does diligence count too? Student and teacher reactions to effort stability in failure. *Journal of Educational Psychology*, 1980, *72*, 717–729.

Crocker, L., & Benson, J. Achievement, guessing, and risk-taking behavior under norm-referenced and criterion-referenced testing conditions. *American Educational Research Journal*, 1976, *13*, 207–215.

Cron, G. W., & Pronko, N. H. Development of the sense of balance in school children. *Journal of Educational Research*, 1957, *51*, 33–37.

Cronbach, L. J. *Essentials of psychological testing* (3rd ed.). New York: Harper & Row, 1970.

Cronbach, L. J. Five decades of public controversy over mental testing. *American Psychologist*, 1975, *30*, 1–14.

Cronbach, L. J., & Associates. *Toward reform of program evaluation*. San Francisco: Jossey-Bass, 1980.

Cronbach, L. J., & Snow, R. E. *Aptitudes and instructional methods*. New York: Irvington, 1977.

Cruickshank, D. R., Myers, B., & Moenjak, T. *Statements of clear teacher behaviors provided by 1,009 students in grades 6–9*. Unpublished manuscript. Columbus, Ohio: College of Education, Ohio State University, 1975.

Culler, R. E., & Holahan, C. J. Test anxiety and academic performance: The effects of study-related behaviors. *Journal of Educational Psychology,* 1980, *72,* 16–20.

Dansereau, D. The development of a learning strategies curriculum. In H. F. O'Neil, Jr. (Ed.), *Learning strategies.* New York: Academic Press, 1978.

Davies, D. R. The effect of tuition upon the process of learning a complex motor skill. *Journal of Educational Psychology,* 1945, *36,* 352–365.

Davis, G. A. *Imagination express: Saturday subway ride.* Buffalo, N.Y.: D.O.K. Publishers, 1973.

Davis, G. A. *Creativity is forever.* Madison, Wisc.: Badger Press, 1981.

Davis, G. A., & Bull, K. S. Strengthening affective components of creativity in a college course. *Journal of Educational Psychology,* 1978, *70,* 833–836.

Dearborn, D. E. Computer literacy. *Educational Leadership,* 1983, *41*(1) 32–34.

de Charms, R. *Enhancing motivation: Change in the classroom.* New York: Irvington Publishers, 1976.

de Charms, R. The origins of competence and achievement motivation in personal causation. In L. J. Fyans (Ed.), *Achievement motivation: Recent trends and theory.* New York: Plenum, 1980.

Deese, J., & Hulse, S. H. *The psychology of learning.* (3rd ed.). New York: McGraw-Hill, 1967.

Deffenbacher, J. L. Worry, emotionality, and task-generated interference in test anxiety: An empirical test of attentional theory. *Journal of Educational Psychology,* 1978, *70,* 248–254.

Dewey, J. *How we think.* New York: Heath, 1933.

Diaz-Guerrero, R., & Holtzman, W. H. Learning by televised "Plaza Sesamo" in Mexico. *Journal of Educational Psychology,* 1974, *66,* 632–643.

Discipline. *Today's Education,* September/October 1976, *65,* 20.

Doherty, V. W., & Hathaway, W. E. *K-12: Course goals in second language* (Tri-County Goal Development Project). Portland, Ore.: Commercial-Educational Distributing Services, 1973.

Doherty, V. W., & Hathaway, W. E. *K-12: Course goals in health education* (Tri-County Goal Development Project). Portland, Ore.: Commercial-Educational Distributing Services, 1974a.

Doherty, V. W., & Hathaway, W. E. *K-12: Course goals in music* (Tri-County Goal Development Project). Portland, Ore.: Commercial-Educational Distributing Services, 1974b.

Doherty, V. W., & Hathaway, W. E. *K-12: Course goals in physical education* (Tri-County Goal Development Project). Portland, Ore.: Commercial-Educational Distributing Services, 1974c.

Doherty, V. W., & Peters, L. B. *K-12: Program goals and subject matter taxonomies for course goals in art, biological and physical sciences, business education, health education, home economics, industrial education, language arts, mathematics, music, physical education, second language, social science, and career education* (Tri-County Goal Development Project). Portland, Ore.: Commercial-Educational Distributing Services, 1978.

Dollard, J., Doob, L. W., Miller, N. E., Mowrer, O. H., & Sears, R. R. *Frustration and aggression.* New Haven, Conn.: Yale University Press, 1939.

Doyle, K. O., & Moen, R. E. Toward the definition of a domain of academic motivation. *Journal of Educational Psychology,* 1978, *70,* 231–236.

Duke, D. L. The etiology of student misbehavior and the depersonalization of blame. *Review of Educational Research,* 1978, *48,* 415–437.

Dunn, R. Can students identify their own learning styles? *Educational Leadership,* 1983, *40*(5), 60–62.

Dunn, R., & Dunn, K. *Teaching students through their individual learning styles: A practical approach.* Reston, Va.: Reston Publishing Co., 1978.

Dunn, R., Dunn, K., & Price, G. E. *Learning style inventory.* P. O. Box 3271, Lawrence, Kansas, 1983.

Dunn, R., Dunn, K., & Price, G. E. *Learning style inventory research manual.* P. O. Box 3271, Lawrence, Kansas, 1984.

Dwyer, C. A. Achievement testing. In H. E. Mitzel, J. H. Best, & W. Rabinowitz (Eds.), *Encyclopedia of educational research* (5th ed., Vol. 1). New York: Free Press, 1982.

Ebel, R. L. Intelligence: A skeptical view. *Journal of Research and Development in Education,* 1979, *12,* 14–21.

Ebel, R. L. Three radical proposals for strengthening education. *Phi Delta Kappan,* 1982, *63,* 375–378.

Edmonds, R. R. Programs of school improvement: An overview. *Educational Leadership,* 1982, *40*(3), 4–11.

Educational Testing Service. Four out of five parents believe tests are useful. *Examiner.* Princeton, N.J.: Educational Testing Service, 1980a.

Educational Testing Service. *National college-bound seniors.* Princeton, N.J.: Educational Testing Service, 1980b.

Eisenberger, R., Masterson, F. A., & McDermitt, M. Effects of task variety on generalized effort. *Journal of Educational Psychology,* 1982, *74,* 499–505.

Eisner, E. W. Educational objectives: Help or hindrance. *School Review,* 1967, *75,* 251–282.

Ellis, J. A., Konoske, P. J., Wulfeck, W. H., II, & Montague, W. E. Comparative effects of adjunct postquestions and instructions on learning from text. *Journal of Educational Psychology,* 1982, *74,* 860–867.

Ellis, J. A., Wulfeck, W. H., II, & Montague, W. E. The effect of adjunct and test question similarity on study behavior and learning in a training course. *American Educational Research Journal,* 1980, *17,* 449–457.

Emmer, E. T., & Evertson, C. M. *Organizing and managing the junior high school.* Austin, Tex.: Research and Development Center for Teacher Education, 1980.

Emmer, E. T., & Evertson, C. M. Synthesis of research on classroom management. *Educational Leadership,* 1981, *38*(4), 342–347.

Erlenmeyer-Kimling, L., & Jarvik, L. F. Genetics and intelligence: A review. *Science,* 1963, *142,* 1477–1479.

Ernst, G. W., & Newell, A. *GPS: A case study in generality and problem-solving.* New York: Academic Press, 1969.

Eron, L. D. Parent-child interaction, television violence, and aggression of children. *American Psychologist,* 1982, *37,* 197–211.

Eron, L. D., Huesmann, L. R., Brice, P., Fischer, P., & Mermelstein, R. Age trends in the development of aggression, sex typing, and related television habits. *Developmental Psychology,* 1983, *19,* 71–77.

Estvan, F. J., & Estvan, E. W. *The child's world: His social perception.* New York: Putnam, 1959.

Evertson, C. M., & Emmer, E. T. Effective management at the beginning of the school year in junior high classes. *Journal of Educational Psychology,* 1982, *74,* 485–498.

Evertson, C. M., Emmer, E. T., Clements, B. S., Sanford, J. P., Worsham, M. E., & Williams, E. L. *Organizing and managing the elementary school classroom.* Austin, Tex.: Research and Development Center for Teacher Education, 1981.

Fairweather, H., & Hutt, S. J. On the rate of gain of information in children. *Journal of Experimental Child Psychology,* 1978, *26,* 216–229.

Feldhusen, J. F. Behavior problems in secondary schools. *Journal of Research and Development in Education,* 1978, *4,* 17–28.

Felhusen, J. F., & Guthrie, V. A. Models of problem solving processes and abilities. *Journal of Research and Development in Education,* 1979, *12,* 22–32.

Feldhusen, J. F., & Klausmeier, H. J. Achievement in counting and addition. *Elementary School Journal,* 1959, *59,* 388–393.

Feldhusen, J. F., & Klausmeier, H. J. Anxiety, intelligence and achievement in children of low, average, and high intelligence. *Child Development*, 1962, *33*, 403–409.

Feldman, C. F., & Toulmin, S. Logic and the theory of mind. In W. J. Arnold (Ed.), *Nebraska symposium on motivation 1975: Conceptual foundations of psychology*. Lincoln: University of Nebraska Press, 1976.

Feldman, K. V., & Klausmeier, H. J. Effects of two kinds of definition on the concept attainment of fourth and eighth graders. *Journal of Educational Research*, 1974, *67*, 219–223.

Fennema, E., & Sherman, J. Sex-related differences in mathematics achievement and related factors: A further study. *Journal for Research in Mathematics Education*, 1978, *9*, 189–203.

Fisher, C. W., Berliner, D. C., Filby, N. N., Marliave, R., Cahen, L. S., & Dishaw, M. M. Teaching behaviors, academic learning time, and student achievement: An overview. In C. Denham & A. Lieberman (Eds.), *Time to learn*. Washington, D.C.: National Institute of Education, 1980.

Fitts, P. M. Perceptual motor skill learning. In A. W. Melton (Ed.), *Categories of human learning*. New York: Academic Press, 1964.

Fitts, P. M. Factors in complex skill training. In R. Glaser (Ed.), *Training research and education*. New York: Wiley, 1965.

Flanagan, J. C., Shanner, W. M., Brudner, H. J., & Marker, R. W. An individualized instructional system: PLAN. In H. Talmage (Ed.), *Systems of individualized education*. Berkeley, Calif.: McCutchan, 1975.

Flanders, N. A., Morrison, B., & Brode, E. Changes in pupil attitudes during the school year. *Journal of Educational Psychology*, 1968, *50*, 334–338.

Flavell, J. H. Stage-related properties of cognitive development. *Cognitive Psychology*, 1971, *2*, 421–453.

Flavell, J. H. *Cognitive development*. Englewood Cliffs, N.J.: Prentice-Hall, 1977.

Flavell, J. H. Metacognition and cognitive monitoring. *American Psychologist*, 1979, *34*, 906–911.

Flavell, J. H., & Wellman, H. M. Metamemory. In R. V. Kail & J. W. Hagen (Eds.), *Perspectives on the development of memory and cognition*. Hillsdale, N.J.: Erlbaum, 1977.

Fleishman, E. A. *The structure and measurement of physical fitness*. Englewood Cliffs, N.J.: Prentice-Hall, 1964.

Florida Department of Education. *Florida Teacher Certification Examination* (Registration Bulletin). Tallahassee: State of Florida, Department of Education, 1982.

Ford, M. E., & Tisak, M. S. A further search for social intelligence. *Journal of Educational Psychology*, 1983, *75*, 196–206.

Frase, L. T. Effect of incentive variables and type of adjunct questions upon text learning. *Journal of Educational Psychology*, 1971, *62*, 371–375.

Frayer, D. A., & Klausmeier, H. J. *Variables in concept learning: Task variables* (Theoretical Paper No. 28). Madison: Wisconsin Center for Education Research, 1971.

Freud, S. *The interpretation of dreams* (Vol. 4, Freud's complete psychological works). London: Hogarth Press, 1953.

Frieze, I. H., & Snyder, H. N. Children's beliefs about the causes of success and failure in school settings. *Journal of Educational Psychology*, 1980, *72*, 186–196.

Frith, C. D., & Frith, U. Feature selection and classification: A developmental study. *Journal of Experimental Child Psychology*, 1978, *25*, 413–428.

Fuentes, E. J. *An investigation into the use of imagery and generativity in learning a foreign language vocabulary*. Unpublished doctoral dissertation, Stanford University, 1976.

Fulkerson, K. F., Furr, S., & Brown, D. Expectations and achievement among third-, sixth-, and ninth-grade black and white males and females. *Developmental Psychology,* 1983, *19,* 231–236.

Furst, E. J. Bloom's taxonomy of educational objectives for the cognitive domain: Philosophical and educational issues. *Review of Educational Research,* 1981, *51,* 441–453.

Fyans, L. J., Jr., & Maehr, M. L. Attributional style, task selection, and achievement. *Journal of Educational Psychology,* 1979, *71,* 499–507.

Gagne, R. M. Curriculum research and the promotion of learning. In R. W. Tyler, R. M. Gagne, & M. Scriven (Eds.), *Perspectives of curriculum evaluation* (AERA Monograph Series on Curriculum Evaluation: Monograph No. 1). Chicago: Rand McNally, 1967.

Gagne, R. M. *The conditions of learning* (3rd ed.). New York: Holt, Rinehart and Winston, 1977.

Gagne, R. M., & White, R. T. Memory structures and learning outcomes. *Journal of Educational Psychology,* 1978, *48,* 187–222.

Gall, M. D., Ward, B. A., Berliner, D. C., Cahen, L. S., Winne, P. H., Elashoff, J. D., & Stanton, G. C. Effects of questioning techniques and recitation on student learning. *American Educational Research Journal,* 1978, *15,* 175–199.

Gallup, G. H. The 12th annual Gallup Poll of the public's attitudes toward the public schools. *Phi Delta Kappan,* 1980, *62,* 33–46.

Gallup, G. H. The 15th annual Gallup Poll of the public's attitudes toward the public schools. *Phi Delta Kappan,* 1983, *65,* 33–47.

Gardner, W. I. *Learning and behavior characteristics of exceptional children and youth.* Boston: Allyn & Bacon, 1977.

Geiger, K. M., & Turiel, E. Disruptive school behavior and concepts of social convention in early adolescence. *Journal of Educational Psychology,* 1983, *75,* 677–685.

Gettinger, M., & White, M. A. Which is the stronger correlate of school learning? Time to learn or measured intelligence? *Journal of Educational Psychology,* 1979, *71,* 405–412.

Gettinger, M., & White, M. A. Evaluating curriculum to fit with class ability. *Journal of Educational Psychology,* 1980, *72,* 338–344.

Getzels, J. W., & Jackson, P. W. *Creativity and intelligence: Explorations with gifted students.* New York: Wiley, 1962.

Giaconia, R. M., & Hedges, L. V. Identifying features of effective open education. *Review of Educational Research,* 1982, *52,* 579–602.

Gillett, M. H. *Effects of teacher enthusiasm on at-task behavior of students in elementary classes.* Unpublished doctoral dissertation, University of Oregon, 1980.

Glaser, R. *Objectives and evaluation: An individualized system.* Pittsburgh, Pa.: Learning Research and Development Center, 1967.

Glaser, R. *Adaptive education: Individual diversity and learning.* New York: Holt, Rinehart and Winston, 1977.

Glaser, R., & Rosner, J. Adaptive environments for learning: Curriculum aspects. In H. Talmage (Ed.), *Systems of individualized education.* Berkeley, Calif.: McCutchan, 1975.

Glencross, D. J. The effects of changes in task conditions on the temporal organization of a repetitive speed skill. *Ergonomics,* 1975, *18,* 17–28.

Glencross, D. J. Control of skilled movements. *Psychological Bulletin,* 1977, *84,* 14–29.

Goldman, N. Mainstreaming procedures at an exemplary school. *Phi Delta Kappan,* 1980, *62,* 263.

Goor, A., & Rapoport, T. Enhancing creativity in an informal educational framework. *Journal of Educational Psychology,* 1977, *69,* 636–643.

Gordon, N. J. Television and learning. In H. J. Walberg (Ed.), *Educational environments and effects.* Berkeley, Calif.: McCutchan, 1979.

Gottesman, I. I. Genetic aspects of intelligent behavior. In N. Ellis (Ed.), *Handbook of mental deficiency: Psychological theory and research*. New York: McGraw-Hill, 1963.

Grady, M. T., & Gawronski, J. D. (Eds.). *Computers in curriculum and instruction*. Washington, D.C.: Association for Supervision and Curriculum Development, 1983.

Green, B. F. In defense of measurement. *American Psychologist*, 1978, *33*, 664–679.

Greer, R. N., & Blank, S. S. Cognitive style, conceptual tempo, and problem solving: Modification through programmed instruction. *American Educational Research Journal*, 1977, *14*, 295–315.

Grimmett, S. A. Processing of multiple codes in memory by 5- and 10-year-olds. *Developmental Psychology*, 1983, *19*, 3–8.

Gronlund, N. E. *Measurement and evaluation in teaching* (4th ed.). New York: Macmillan, 1981.

Gross, T. E., & Mastenbrook, M. Examination of the effects of state anxiety on problem-solving efficiency under high and low memory conditions. *Journal of Educational Psychology*, 1980, *72*, 605–609.

Guilford, J. P. Three faces of intellect. *American Psychologist*, 1959, *14*, 469–479.

Guilford, J. P., & Hoepfner, R. *Structure-of-intellect factors and their tests*. Report of the psychological laboratory, No. 36. Los Angeles: University of Southern California Press, 1966.

Guilford, J. P. *The nature of human intelligence*. New York: McGraw-Hill, 1967.

Guilford, J. P. Intelligence isn't what it used to be: What to do about it? *Journal of Educational Research and Development*, 1979, *12*, 33–46.

Hale, G. A., & Alderman, L. B. Children's selective attention with variation in amount of stimulus exposure. *Journal of Experimental Child Psychology*, 1978, *26*, 320–327.

Hall, J. W., Wilson, K. P., & Patterson, R. J. Mnemotechnics: Some limitations of the mnemonic keyword method for the study of foreign language vocabulary. *Journal of Educational Psychology*, 1981, *73*, 345–357.

Hall, K. A. Computer-based education. In H. E. Mitzel, J. H. Best, & W. Rabinowitz (Eds.), *Encyclopedia of educational research* (5th ed., Vol. 1). New York: Free Press, 1982.

Haller, E. J., & Davis, S. A. Does socioeconomic status bias the assignment of elementary students to reading groups? *American Educational Research Journal*, 1980, *17*, 409–418.

Hansford, B. V., & Hattie, J. A. The relationship between self and achievement/performance measures. *Review of Educational Research*, 1982, *52*, 123–142.

Harlow, H. F. The formation of learning sets. *Psychological Review*, 1949, *56*, 51–65.

Harmon, W. W. The coming transformation. *Futurist*, 1977, *11*, 5–12; 106–112.

Harris, M. L., & Harris, C. W. *A structure of concept attainment abilities*. Madison: Wisconsin Center for Education Research, 1973.

Hathaway, W. E. A school-district-developed, Rasch-based approach to minimum competency achievement testing. In R. M. Jaeger & C. K. Tittle (Eds.), *Minimum competency achievement testing: Motives, models, measures, and consequences*. Berkeley, Calif.: McCutchan, 1980.

Hattie, J. A. Should creativity tests be administered under testlike conditions? An empirical study of three alternative conditions. *Journal of Educational Psychology*, 1980, *72*, 87–98.

Havighurst, R. J. *Human development and education*, New York: Longman, 1953.

Havighurst, R. J. *Developmental tasks and education* (3rd ed.). New York: Longman, 1972.

Hendrickson, G., & Schroeder, W. H. Transfer of training in learning to hit a submerged target. *Journal of Educational Psychology*, 1941, *32*, 205–213.

Hennessy, J. J., & Merrifield, P. R. A comparison of the factor structures of mental abilities in four ethnic groups. *Journal of Educational Psychology,* 1976, *68,* 754–759.

Hennessy, J. J., & Merrifield, P. R. Ethnicity and sex distinctions in patterns of aptitude factor scores in a sample of urban high school seniors. *American Educational Research Journal,* 1978, *15,* 385–389.

Hetherington, E. M. Divorce: A child's perspective. *American Psychologist,* 1979, *34,* 851–858.

Hewett, F. M., & Forness, S. R. *Education of exceptional learners* (2nd ed.). Boston: Allyn & Bacon, 1977.

Hilgard, E. R., Atkinson, R. L., & Atkinson, R. C. *Introduction to psychology* (7th ed.), New York: Harcourt Brace Jovanovich, 1979.

Hiroto, D. S., & Seligman, M. E. Generality of learned helplessness in man. *Journal of Personality and Social Psychology,* 1975, *31,* 311–327.

Hodgkinson, H. L. What's STILL right with education. *Phi Delta Kappan,* 1982, *64,* 231–235.

Hoepfner, R., Guilford, J. P., & Bradley, P. A. *Identification of transformation abilities in the structure of intellect model.* Los Angeles: Psychological Laboratory, University of Southern California, 1968.

Hoffman, K. I., Guilford, J. P., Hoepfner, R., & Doherty, W. J. *A factor analysis of the figural-cognition and figural-evaluation abilities.* Los Angeles: Psychological Laboratory, University of Southern California, 1968.

Holland, J. L. Some limitations of teacher ratings as predictors of creativity. *Journal of Educational Psychology,* 1959, *50,* 219–223.

Hopkins, K. D., & Stanley, J. C. *Educational and psychological measurement and evaluation* (6th ed.). Englewood Cliffs, N.J.: Prentice-Hall, 1981.

Hooper, F. H., Brainerd, C. J., & Sipple, T. S. *A representative series of Piagetian concrete operations tasks* (Theoretical Paper No. 57). Madison: Wisconsin Center for Education Research, 1975.

Horan, J. J., & Williams, J. M. Longitudinal study of assertion training as a drug abuse strategy. *American Educational Research Journal,* 1982, *19,* 341–351.

Hornik, R. C. Television access and the slowing of cognitive growth. *American Educational Research Journal,* 1978, *15,* 1–15.

Horwitz, R. A. Psychological effects of the "open classroom." *Review of Educational Research,* 1979, *49,* 71–86.

Houtz, J. C., & Speedie, S. M. Processes underlying divergent thinking and problem solving. *Journal of Educational Psychology,* 1978, *70,* 848–854.

Hovland, C. I., Harvey, O. J., & Sherif, M. Assimilation and contrast effects in reactions to communication and attitude change. *Journal of Abnormal and Social Psychology,* 1957, *55,* 244–252.

Howe, M. J. A., & Ceci, S. J. Educational implications of memory research. In M. M. Gruneberg & P. E. Morris (Eds.), *Applied problems in memory.* New York: Academic Press, 1979.

Hudgins, B. B. Effects of group experience on individual problem solving. *Journal of Educational Psychology,* 1960, *51,* 37–42.

Hull, C. L. *Principles of behavior.* New York: Appleton-Century-Crofts, 1943.

Hull, C. L. *A behavior system.* New Haven, Conn.: Yale University Press, 1952.

Hunt, J. M. *Intelligence and experience.* New York: Ronald Press, 1961.

Hyman, H. H., & Wright, C. R. *Education's lasting influence on values.* Chicago: University of Chicago Press, 1979.

Hyman, H. H., Wright, C. R., & Reed, J. S. *The enduring effects of education.* Chicago: University of Chicago Press, 1975.

Instructional Objectives Exchange. *Attitude toward school: Grades K-12.* Los Angeles: Instructional Objectives Exchange, 1972.

Jensen, A. R. *Educability and group differences.* New York: Harper & Row, 1973.

Johnson, D. M. *The psychology of thought and judgment.* New York: Harper & Row, 1955.

Johnson, D. W., Johnson, R. T., & Maruyama, G. Interdependence and interpersonal attraction among heterogeneous and homogeneous individuals: A theoretical formulation and a meta-analysis of the research. *Review of Educational Research,* 1983, *53,* 5–54.

Johnson, D. W., Skon, L., & Johnson, R. Effects of cooperative, competitive, and individualistic conditions on children's individualistic problem-solving performance. *American Educational Research Journal,* 1980, *17,* 83–93.

Johnson, R., Rynders, J., Johnson, D. W., Schmidt, B., & Haider, S. Interaction between handicapped and nonhandicapped teenagers as a function of situational goal structuring: Implication for mainstreaming. *American Educational Research Journal,* 1979, *16,* 161–167.

Johnson, R. C., & Medinus, G. R. *Child psychology: Behavior and development.* New York: Wiley, 1965.

Johnson, R. C., & Zara, R. C. Relational learning in young children. *Journal of Comparative and Physiological Psychology,* 1960, *53,* 594–597.

Jones, H. E. The development of physical abilities. In National Society for the Study of Education. *Adolescence. 43rd Yearbook. Part I.* (Vol. 43). Chicago: University of Chicago Press, 1944.

Judd, C. H. The relation of special training to general intelligence. *Educational Review,* 1908, *36,* 28–42.

Kagan, J. A developmental approach to conceptual growth. In H. J. Klausmeier & C. W. Harris (Eds.), *Analyses of concept learning.* New York: Academic Press, 1966.

Kagan, J. What is intelligence? *Social Policy,* 1973, *4,* 88–94.

Kamin, L. J. Heredity, intelligence, politics, and psychology. In N. J. Block & G. Dworkin (Eds.), *The IQ controversy.* New York: Pantheon, 1976.

Kandel, D. Adolescent marihuana use: Role of parents and peers. *Science,* 1973, *181,* 1067–1070.

Kanfer, F. H. Personal control, social control, and altruism: Can society survive the age of individualism. *American Psychologist,* 1979, *34,* 231–239.

Kauffman, J. M. *Characteristics of children's behavior disorders.* Columbus, Ohio: Merrill, 1977.

Kaye, K. The development of skills. In G. J. Whitehurst & B. J. Zimmerman (Eds.), *The functions of language and cognition.* New York: Academic Press, 1979.

Kearney, N. C. *Elementary school objectives.* New York: Russell Sage Foundation, 1953.

Kelley, T. L., Madden, R., Gardner, E. F., & Rudman, H. C. *Stanford Achievement Test, Intermediate II Battery, Form W.* New York: Harcourt Brace Jovanovich, 1964.

Kennedy, B. J. *Motivational effects of individual conferences and goal setting on performance and attitudes in arithmetic* (Tech. Report No. 61). Madison: Wisconsin Center for Education Research, 1968.

Kerns, T. Y. Television: A bisensory bombardment that stifles children's creativity. *Phi Delta Kappan,* 1981, *62,* 456–457.

Kibler, R. J., Barker, L. L., & Miles, D. T. *Behavioral objectives and instruction.* Boston: Allyn & Bacon, 1970.

Kintsch, W. On modeling comprehension. *Educational Psychologist,* 1979, *14,* 3–14.

Kintsch, W., & van Dijk, T. A. Towards a model of text comprehension and production. *Psychological Review,* 1978, *85,* 363–394.

Klausmeier, H. J. Effects of accelerating bright older elementary pupils: A follow up. *Journal of Educational Psychology,* 1963, *54,* 165–171.

Klausmeier, H. J. IGE: An alternative form of schooling. In H. Talmage (Ed.), *Systems of individualized education.* Berkeley, Calif.: McCutchan, 1975.

Klausmeier, H. J. Instructional design and the teaching of concepts. In J. R. Levin & V. L. Allen (Eds.), *Cognitive learning in children: Theories and strategies*. New York: Academic Press, 1976.

Klausmeier, H. J. Origin and overview of IGE. In H. J. Klausmeier, R. A. Rossmiller, & M. Saily (Eds.), *Individually guided elementary education: Concepts and practices*. New York: Academic Press, 1977.

Klausmeier, H. J. Introduction. In H. J. Klausmeier & Associates, *Cognitive learning and development: Information-processing and Piagetian perspectives*. Cambridge, Mass.: Ballinger, 1979.

Klausmeier, H. J. *Learning and teaching concepts: A strategy for testing applications of theory*. New York: Academic Press, 1980.

Klausmeier, H. J. Research-based educational improvement. In H. J. Klausmeier, J. M. Lipham, & J. C. Daresh (Eds.), *The renewal and improvement of secondary education: Concepts and practices*. Lanham, Md.: University Press of America, 1983.

Klausmeier, H. J., & Allen, P. S. *Cognitive development of children and youth: A longitudinal study*. New York: Academic Press, 1978.

Klausmeier, H. J., & Associates. *Cognitive learning and development: Information-processing and Piagetian perspectives*. Cambridge, Mass.: Ballinger, 1979.

Klausmeier, H. J., & Check, J. Retention and transfer in children of low, average, and high intelligence. *Journal of Educational Research*, 1962, *55*, 319–322.

Klausmeier, H. J., Check, J., & Feldhusen, J. Relationships among physical, mental, achievement, and personality measures in children of low, average, and high intelligence at 125 months of age. *American Journal of Mental Deficiency*, 1960, *65*, 69–78.

Klausmeier, H. J., & Davis, J. K. Transfer of learning. In R. L. Ebel (Ed.), *Encyclopedia of educational research*. New York: Macmillan, 1969.

Klausmeier, H. J., Feldhusen, J., & Check, J. *An analysis of learning efficiency in arithmetic of mentally retarded children in comparison with children of average and high intelligence*. U.S. Office of Education Cooperative Research Project No. 153. Madison: University of Wisconsin, 1959.

Klausmeier, H. J., Ghatala, E. S., & Frayer, D. A. *Conceptual learning and development: A cognitive view*. New York: Academic Press, 1974.

Klausmeier, H. J., Goodwin, W., & Rhonda, T. Effects of accelerating bright, older elementary pupils — A second follow-up. *Journal of Educational Psychology*, 1968, *59*, 53–58.

Klausmeier, H. J., Harris, C. W., & Ethnathios, Z. Relationships between divergent thinking abilities and teacher ratings of high school students. *Journal of Educational Psychology*, 1962, *53*, 72–75.

Klausmeier, H. J., Harris, C. W., & Wiersma, W. *Strategies of learning and efficiency of concept attainment by individuals and groups*. U.S. Office of Education Cooperative Research Project No. 1442. Madison: University of Wisconsin, 1964.

Klausmeier, H. J., Lipham, J. M., & Daresh, J. C. *The renewal and improvement of secondary education: Concepts and practices*. Lanham, Md.: University Press of America, 1983.

Klausmeier, H. J., & Ripple, R. E. Effects of accelerating bright older pupils from second to fourth grade. *Journal of Educational Psychology*, 1962, *53*, 93–100.

Klausmeier, H. J., Schilling, J. M., & Feldman, K. V. *The effectiveness of experimental lessons in accelerating children's attainment of the concept tree* (Tech. Report No. 372). Madison: Wisconsin Center for Education Research, 1976.

Klausmeier, H. J., & Sipple, T. S. Factor structure of the Piagetian stage of concrete operations. *Contemporary Educational Psychology*, 1982, *7*, 161–180.

Klausmeier, H. J., Swanson, J. E., & Sipple, T. S. *The analysis of nine process concepts in elementary science* (Tech. Report No. 428). Madison: Wisconsin Center for Education Research, 1976.

Klausmeier, H. J., & Teel, D. A research-based program for gifted children. *Education*, 1964, *85*, 131–136.

Klausmeier, H. J., & Wiersma, W. The effects of IQ level and sex on divergent thinking of seventh grade pupils of low, average, and high IQ. *Journal of Educational Research*, 1965, *58*, 300–302.

Klausmeier, H. J., Wiersma, W., & Harris, C. W. Efficiency of initial learning and transfer by individuals, pairs, and quads. *Journal of Educational Psychology*, 1963, *54*, 160–164.

Knight, B. J., & West, D. J. Temporary and continuing delinquency. *British Journal of Criminology*, 1975, *15*, 43–50.

Kobasigawa, A. Retrieval strategies in the development of memory. In R. V. Kail, Jr., & J. W. Hagen (Eds.), *Perspectives on the development of memory and cognition.* Hillsdale, N. J.: Wiley, 1977.

Kohlberg, L. The contribution of developmental psychology to education: Examples from moral education. *Educational Psychologist*, 1973, *10*, 2–14.

Kohler, M. C. Developing responsible youth through youth participation. *Phi Delta Kappan*, 1981, *62*, 426–428.

Kohut, S., Jr., & Range, D. G. *Classroom discipline: Case studies and viewpoints.* Washington, D.C.: National Education Association, 1979.

Kooi, B., & Schutz, R. A factor analysis of classroom disturbance intercorrelations. *American Educational Research Journal*, 1965, *2*, 37–40.

Kounin, J. S. *Discipline and group management in classrooms.* New York: Holt, Rinehart and Winston, 1970.

Krathwohl, D. R., Bloom, B. S., & Masia, B. B. *Taxonomy of objectives: The classification of educational goals. Handbook II: Affective domain.* New York: McKay, 1964.

Kuczynski, L. Reasoning, prohibitions, and motivations for compliance. *Developmental Psychology*, 1983, *19*, 126–134.

Kulik, J. A. Synthesis of research on computer-based instruction. *Educational Leadership*, 1983, *41*(1), 19–21.

Kulik, J. A., Bangert, R. L., & Williams, G. W. Effects of computer-based teaching on secondary school students. *Journal of Educational Psychology*, 1983, *75*, 19–26.

Lamb, M. E. Paternal influences and the father's role: A personal perspective. *American Psychologist*, 1979, *34*, 938–943.

Land, M. L. Low-inference variables of teacher clarity: Effects on student concept learning. *Journal of Educational Psychology*, 1979, *71*, 795–798.

Land, M. L., & Smith, L. R. Effect of a teacher clarity variable on student achievement. *Journal of Educational Research*, 1979a, *72*, 196–197.

Land, M. L., & Smith, L. R. The effect of low inference teacher clarity inhibitors on student achievement. *Journal of Teacher Education*, 1979b, *30*, 55–57.

Lange, G. Organization-related processes in children's recall. In P. A. Ornstein (Ed.), *Memory development in children.* Hillsdale, N.J.: Erlbaum, 1978.

LaPorte, R. E., & Voss, J. F. Retention of prose materials as a function of post-acquisition testing. *Journal of Educational Psychology*, 1975, *67*, 259–266.

Larned, D. T., & Muller, D. Development of self-concept in grades one through nine. *Journal of Psychology*, 1979, *102*, 143–155.

Lashley, K. S. The problem of serial order in behavior. In L. A. Jeffress (Ed.), *Cerebral mechanisms in behavior: The Hixon symposium.* New York: Wiley, 1951.

LaVoie, J. C. Aversive, cognitive, and parental determinants of punishment generalization in adolescent males. *Journal of Genetic Psychology*, 1974, *124*, 29–39.

Lawton, J. T. The use of advance organizers in the learning and retention of logical operations and social studies concepts. *American Educational Research Journal*, 1977, *14*, 25–43.

Lawton, J. T., & Wanska, S. K. The effects of different types of advance organizers on classification learning. *American Educational Research Journal,* 1979, *16,* 223–239.

Lee, T. D., & Magill, R. A. The locus of contextual interference in motor skill acquisition. *Journal of Experimental Psychology,* 1983, *9,* 730–746.

Lerner, R. M., Karson, M., Meisels, M., & Knapp, J. R. Actual and perceived attitudes of late adolescents and their parents: The phenomenon of the generation gaps. *Journal of Genetic Psychology,* 1975, *126,* 195–207.

Lesser, G. S. Applications of psychology to television programming: Formulation of program objectives. *American Psychologist,* 1976, *31,* 135–136.

Lesser, G. S., Fifer, G., & Clark, D. H. Mental abilities of children from different social-class and cultural groups. *Monographs of the Society for Research in Child Development,* 1965, *30*(4, Serial No. 102).

Levin, J. R. The mnemonic '80s: Keywords in the classroom. *Educational Psychologist,* 1981, *16,* 65–82.

Levin, J. R. Pictorial strategies for school learning: Practical illustrations. In M. Pressley & J. R. Levin (Eds.), *Cognitive strategy research: Educational applications.* New York: Springer-Verlag, 1983.

Levin, J. R., Pressley, M., McCormick, C. B., Miller, G. E., & Shriberg, L. K. Assessing the classroom potential of the keyword method. *Journal of Educational Psychology,* 1979, *71,* 583–594.

Levin, J. R., Shriberg, L. K., & Berry, J. K. A concrete strategy for remembering abstract prose. *American Educational Research Journal,* 1983, *20,* 277–290.

Liebert, R. M. Positive social learning. *Journal of Communication,* 1975, *25,* 90–97.

Liebert, R. M., Neal, J. M., & Davidson, E. S. *The early window: Effects of television on children and youth.* New York: Pergamon Press, 1973.

Linder, R., & Purdom, D. Four dimensions of openness in classroom activities. *Elementary School Journal,* 1975, *76,* 147–150.

Lindsay, P. H., & Norman, D. A. *Human information processing: An introduction to psychology.* New York: Academic Press, 1972.

Lockwood, A. L. The effects of value clarification and moral development curricula on school-age subjects: A critical review of recent research. *Review of Educational Research,* 1978, *48,* 325–364.

Loftus, E. F., & Loftus, G. R. On the permanence of stored information in the human brain. *American Psychologist,* 1980, *35,* 409–420.

Loftus, E. F., Miller, D. G., & Burns, H. J. Semantic integration of verbal information into visual memory. *Journal of Experimental Psychology: Human Learning and Memory,* 1978, *4,* 19–31.

Loman, N. L., & Mayer, R. E. Signaling techniques that increase the understandability of expository prose. *Journal of Educational Psychology,* 1983, *75,* 402–412.

Lorayne, H., & Lucas, J. *The memory book.* New York: Ballantine Books, 1979.

Lorge, I., Thorndike, R. L., & Hagan, E. *Lorge-Thorndike Intelligence Test, Form 1, Levels A-H.* Boston: Houghton Mifflin, 1964.

Luiten, J., Ames, W., & Ackerson, G. A meta-analysis of the effects of advance organizers on learning and retention. *American Educational Research Journal,* 1980, *17,* 211–218.

Maccoby, E. E. Sex differences in intellectual functioning. In E. E. Maccoby (Ed.), *The development of sex differences.* Stanford, Calif.: Stanford University Press, 1966.

Maccoby, E. E., & Jacklin, C. N. *The psychology of sex differences.* Stanford, Calif.: Stanford University Press, 1974.

Macdonald-Ross, M. Graphics in text. In L. S. Shulman (Ed.), *Review of research in education* (Vol. 5). Itasca, Ill.: F. E. Peacock, 1977.

Macdonald-Ross, M. Language in texts. In L. S. Shulman (Ed.), *Review of research in education* (Vol. 6). Washington, D.C.: American Educational Research Association, 1978.

MacKinnon, D. W. The nature and nurture of creative talent. *American Psychologist,* 1962, *17,* 484–495.

Macmillan, D. L., & Meyers, C. E. Educational labeling of handicapped learners. In D. C. Berliner (Ed.), *Review of research in education* (Vol. 7). Washington, D.C.: American Educational Research Association, 1979.

Madaus, G. F., Airasian, P. W., & Kellagan, T. *School effectiveness: A reassessment of the evidence.* New York: McGraw-Hill, 1980.

Mager, R. F. *Developing attitudes toward instruction.* Palo Alto, Calif.: Fearon, 1968.

Mahan, J. M., & Lacefield, W. Educational attitude changes during year-long student teaching. *Journal of Experimental Education,* 1978, *46,* 4–15.

Maier, S. F., & Seligman, M. E. Learned helplessness: Theory and evidence. *Journal of Experimental Psychology: General,* 1976, *105,* 3–46.

Maker, J. C. *Teaching models in education of the gifted.* Rockville, Md.: Aspen Systems Corp., 1982.

Mansfield, R. S., & Busse, T. V. Creativity. In H. E. Mitzel, J. H. Best, & W. Rabinowitz (Eds.), *Encyclopedia of educational research* (5th ed., Vol. 1). New York: Free Press, 1982.

Mansfield, R. S., Busse, T. V., & Krepelka, E. J. The effectiveness of creativity training. *Review of Educational Research,* 1978, *48,* 517–536.

Marjoribanks, K. School attitudes, cognitive ability, and academic achievement. *Journal of Educational Psychology,* 1976, *68,* 653–660.

Markle, S. M. They teach concepts, don't they? *Educational Researcher,* 1975, *4*(6), 3–9.

Marland, S. P., Jr. *Education of the gifted and talented.* Washington, D.C.: U.S. Government Printing Office, 1971.

Marsh, H. W., Smith, I. D., Barnes, J., & Butler, S. Self-concept: Reliability, stability, dimensionality, validity, and the measurement of change. *Journal of Educational Psychology,* 1983, *75,* 772–790.

Maslow, A. H. *Motivation and personality* (2nd ed.). New York: Harper & Row, 1970.

Masoodi, B., & Ban, J. R. Teaching the visually handicapped in regular classes. *Educational Leadership,* 1980, *37*(4), 351–355.

Masson, M. E. J., & Miller, J. Working memory and individual differences in comprehension and memory of text. *Journal of Educational Psychology,* 1983, *75,* 314–318.

Maw, W. H., & Maw, E. W. *An exploratory investigation into the measurement of curiosity in elementary school children* (U.S. Office of Education Cooperative Research Project No. 801). Washington, D.C.: U.S. Government Printing Office, 1964.

Maw, W. H., & Maw, E. W. Differences in preference for investigatory activities by school children who differ in curiosity level. *Psychology in the Schools,* 1965, *2,* 263–266.

May, F. B. *Creative thinking: A factorial study of seventh-grade children.* Unpublished doctoral dissertation. Madison: University of Wisconsin, 1961.

Mayer, R. E. Information processing variables in learning to solve problems. *Review of Educational Research,* 1975, *45,* 525–541.

Mayer, R. E. *Thinking and problem solving: An introduction to human cognition and learning.* Glenview, Ill.: Scott, Foresman, 1977.

Mayer, R. E. Can advance organizers influence meaningful learning? *Review of Educational Research,* 1979, *49,* 371–383.

Mayer, R. E. Elaboration techniques that increase the meaningfulness of technical text: An experimental test of the learning strategy hypothesis. *Journal of Educational Psychology*, 1980, *72*, 770–784.

Mayer, R. E. Can you repeat that? Qualitative effects of repetition and advance organizers on learning from science prose. *Journal of Educational Psychology*, 1983, *75*, 40–49.

McCarthy, J. D., & Hoge, D. R. Analysis of age effects in longitudinal studies of adolescent self-esteem. *Developmental Psychology*, 1982, *18*, 372–379.

McClelland, D. C., Atkinson, J. W., Clark, R. A., & Lowell, E. L. *The achievement motive*. New York: Appleton-Century-Crofts, 1953.

McKenzie, G. R., & Henry, M. Effects of testlike events on on-task behavior, test anxiety, and achievement in a classroom rule-learning task. *Journal of Educational Psychology*, 1979, *71*, 370–374.

McMillan, J. H. Factors affecting the development of pupil attitudes toward school subjects. *Psychology in the Schools*, 1976, *13*, 322–325.

McMillan, J. H. The effect of effort and feedback on the formation of student attitudes. *American Educational Research Journal*, 1977, *14*, 317–330.

McMurray, N. E., Bernard, M. E., & Klausmeier, H. J. *An instructional design for accelerating children's concept learning* (Tech. Report No. 321). Madison: Wisconsin Center for Education Research, 1975.

Melton, R. F. Resolution of conflicting claims concerning the effect of behavioral objectives on student learning. *Review of Educational Research*, 1978, *48*, 291–302.

Meringoff, L. K. Inference of the medium on children's story apprehension. *Journal of Educational Psychology*, 1980, *72*, 240–249.

Merrifield, P. R., Guilford, J. P., Christensen, P. R., & Frick, J. W. *A factor-analytic study of problem-solving abilities* (Report of the psychological laboratory No. 22). Los Angeles: University of Southern California Press, 1960.

Merz, C. Mainstreaming as a natural experience. *Educational Leadership*, 1980, *37*(4), 438–440.

Messe, L. A., Crano, W. D., Messe, S. R., & Rice, W. Evaluation of the predictive validity of tests of mental ability for classroom performance in elementary grades. *Journal of Educational Psychology*, 1979, *71*, 233–241.

Messick, S. Potential uses of noncognitive measurement in education. *Journal of Educational Psychology*, 1979, *71*, 281–292.

Messick, S., & Associates. *Individuality in learning*. San Francisco: Jossey-Bass, 1976.

Miles, W. R. Measures of certain human abilities throughout the life span. *Proceedings of the National Academy of Science*, 1931, *17*, 627–633.

Milgram, R. M. Validation of ideational fluency measures of original thinking in children. *Journal of Educational Psychology*, 1983, *75*, 619–624.

Miller, G. A. The magical number seven plus or minus two: Some limits on our capacity for processing information. *Psychological Review*, 1956, *63*, 81–97.

Miller, G. A., Galanter, E., & Pribram, K. H. *Plans and the structure of behavior*. New York: Holt, Rinehart and Winston, 1960.

Miller, G. A., & Johnson-Laird, P. N. *Language and perception*. Cambridge, Mass.: Harvard University Press, 1976.

Minton, H. L., & Schneider, F. W. *Differential psychology*. Monterey, Calif.: Brooks Cole, 1980.

Mischel, W. On the interface of cognition and personality: Beyond the person-situation debate. *American Psychologist*, 1979, *34*, 740–754.

Mitnick, L. L., & McGinnies, E. Influencing ethnocentrism in small discussion groups through a film communication. *Journal of Abnormal and Social Psychology*, 1958, *56*, 82–90.

Mize, G. K., & Klausmeier, H. J. *Factors contributing to rapid and slow cognitive development among elementary and high school children* (Working Paper No. 201). Madison: Wisconsin Center for Education Research, 1977.

Montor, K. Cheating in high school. *School and Society*, 1971, *99*, 96–98.

Morgan, D. N. Creativity today. *Journal of Aesthetics and Art Criticism*, 1953, *12*, 1–24.

Morris, P. E. Strategies for learning and recall. In M. M. Gruneberg & P. E. Morris (Eds.), *Applied problems in memory*. New York: Academic Press, 1979.

Morris, P. E., & Reid, R. L. Repeated use of mnemonic imagery. *Psychonomic Science*, 1970, *20*, 337–338.

Morrison, B. *The identification of reading skills essential for learning in seven content areas at postelementary levels* (Tech. Report No. 528). Madison: Wisconsin Center for Education Research, 1980.

Morrison, H. C. *The practice of teaching in the secondary school*. Chicago: University of Chicago Press, 1926.

Moursund, D. Microcomputers will not solve the computers-in-education problem. *AEDS Journal*, 1979, *13*, 31–39.

Mussen, P. H. (Ed.). *Carmichael's manual of child psychology* (Vol. 1, 3rd ed.). New York: Wiley, 1970.

Nathan, P. E. Failures in prevention: Why we can't prevent the devastating effects of alcoholism and drug abuse. *American Psychologist*, 1983, *38*, 459–467.

National Assessment of Educational Progress. *National assessment of educational progress: Citizenship objectives for 1974–75 assessment*. Denver, Colo.: National Assessment Office, 1972a.

National Assessment of Educational Progress. *National assessment of educational progress: Science objectives for 1972–73 assessment*. Denver, Colo.: National Assessment Office, 1972b.

National Commission on Excellence in Education. A nation at risk: The imperative for educational reform. *The Chronicle of Higher Education*, 1983, *26*, 11–16.

National Education Association. Reporting pupil progress. *NEA Research Bulletin*, 1969, pp. 75–76.

National Education Association. Reporting pupil progress to parents. *NEA Research Bulletin*, 1971, pp. 81–82.

National Institute of Education. *Violent schools—safe schools*. Washington, D.C.: U.S. Department of Health, Education, and Welfare, 1977.

Neill, S. B. Violence and vandalism: Dimensions and correctives. *Phi Delta Kappan*, 1978, *59*, 302–307.

Nelson, G. K., & Klausmeier, H. J. Classificatory behaviors of low socioeconomic status children. *Journal of Educational Psychology*, 1974, *66*, 432–438.

Nelson, K. Concept, word, and sentence: Interrelations in acquisition and development. *Psychological Review*, 1974, *81*, 267–285.

Newell, A., & Simon, H. A. *Human problem solving*. Englewood Cliffs, N.J.: Prentice-Hall, 1972.

Nicholls, J. G. Development of perception of own attainment and causal attributions for success and failure in reading. *Journal of Educational Psychology*, 1979a, *71*, 94–99.

Nicholls, J. G. Quality and equality in intellectual development: The role of motivation in education. *American Psychologist*, 1979b, *34*, 1071–1084.

Nitko, A. Distinguishing the many varieties of criterion-referenced tests. *Review of Educational Research*, 1980, *50*, 461–485.

Oakland, T. Predictive validity of readiness tests for middle and lower socioeconomic status Anglo, black, and Mexican American children. *Journal of Educational Psychology*, 1978, *70*, 574–582.

Pallas, A. M., & Alexander, K. L. Sex differences in quantitative SAT performance: New evidence on the differential coursework hypothesis. *American Educational Research Journal*, 1983, *20*, 165–182.

Palmer, E. L. Applications of psychology to television programming: Program execution. *American Psychologist*, 1976, *31*, 137–138.

Parke, R. D. Effectiveness of punishment as an interaction of intensity, timing, agent nurturance and cognitive structuring. *Child Development*, 1969, *40*, 213–236.

Parnes, S. J., Noller, R. B., & Biondi, A. M. *Guide to creative action*. New York: Scribner, 1977.

Pascarella, E. T., Pflaum, S. W., Bryan, T. H., & Pearl, R. A. Interaction of internal attribution for effort and teacher response mode in reading instruction: A replication note. *American Educational Research Journal*, 1983, *20*, 269–276.

Paulsen, K., & Johnson, M. Sex role attitudes and mathematical ability in 4th-, 8th-, and 11th-grade students from a high socioeconomic area. *Developmental Psychology*, 1983, *19*, 210–214.

Pedulla, J. J., Airasian, P. W., & Madaus, G. F. Do teacher ratings and standardized test results of students yield the same information? *American Educational Research Journal*, 1980, *17*, 303–307.

Peters, L., & Doherty, J. *K-12: Course goals in social science* (Vol. 1, Tri-County Development Project). Portland, Ore.: Commercial Educational Distributing Services, 1976.

Peterson, L. Influence of age, task competence, and responsibility focus on children's altruism. *Developmental Psychology*, 1983, *19*, 141–148.

Peterson, P. L. Interactive effects of student anxiety, achievement orientation, and teacher behavior on student achievement and attitude. *Journal of Educational Psychology*, 1977, *69*, 779–792.

Peterson, P. L. Aptitude X treatment interaction effects of teacher structuring and student participation in college instruction. *Journal of Educational Psychology*, 1979a, *71*, 521–533.

Peterson, P. L. Direct instruction reconsidered. In P. L. Peterson & H. J. Walberg (Eds.), *Research on teaching: Concepts, findings, and implications*. Berkeley, Calif.: McCutchan, 1979b.

Peterson, P. L., Janicki, T., & Swing, S. R. Aptitude treatment interaction effects of three social studies teaching approaches. *American Educational Research Journal*, 1980, *17*, 339–360.

Peterson, P. L., & Swing, S. R. Problems in classroom implementation of cognitive strategy instruction. In M. Pressley & J. R. Levin (Eds.), *Cognitive strategy research: Educational applications*. New York: Springer-Verlag, 1983.

Peterson, P. L., Swing, S. R., Braverman, M. T., & Buss, R. Students' aptitudes and their reports of cognitive processes during direct instruction. *Journal of Educational Psychology*, 1982, *74*, 535–547.

Pew, R. W. Acquisition of hierarchical control over the temporal organization of a skill. *Journal of Experimental Psychology*, 1966, *71*, 764–771.

Pezdek, K., & Miceli, L. Life-span differences in memory integration as a function of processing time. *Developmental Psychology*, 1982, *18*, 485–490.

Phi Delta Kappan. NEA survey investigates teacher attitudes, practices. *Phi Delta Kappan*, 1980, *62*, 49–50.

Piaget, J. Piaget's theory. In P. H. Mussen (Ed.), *Carmichael's manual of child psychology* (Vol. 1, 3rd ed.). New York: Wiley, 1970.

Pichert, J. W., & Anderson, R. C. Taking different perspectives on a story. *Journal of Educational Psychology*, 1977, *69*, 309–315.

Polya, G. *How to solve it*. Princeton, N.J.: Princeton University, 1945.

Popham, W. J. Instruction and objectives. In W. J. Popham, E. W. Eisner, H. J. Sullivan, & L. L. Tyler (Eds.). *Instructional objectives. American Educational Research Association Monograph Series on Curriculum Evaluation*. Chicago: Rand McNally, 1969.

Posner, M. I., & Keele, S. W. Skill learning. In R. M. W. Travers (Ed.), *Second handbook of research on teaching*. Skokie, Ill.: Rand McNally, 1973.

Practical Applications of Research. Newsletter of Phi Delta Kappa's Center on Evaluation, Development, and Research. Bloomington, Ind.: *Phi Delta Kappan*, 1981, 3.

Prawat, R. S., Byers, J. L., & Anderson, A. H. An attributional analysis of teachers' affective reactions to student success and failure. *American Educational Research Journal*, 1983, *20*, 137–152.

Prescott, G. A., Balow, I. H., Hogan, T. P., & Farr, R. C. *Metropolitan Achievement Tests. Primary 2. Forms JS and KS. Teacher's Manual for Administering and Interpreting*. New York: Psychological Corporation, 1978.

Pressley, M. Increasing children's self-control through cognitive interventions. *Review of Educational Research*, 1979, *49*, 319–370.

Pressley, M., & Dennis-Rounds, J. Transfer of a mnemonic keyword strategy at two age levels. *Journal of Educational Psychology*, 1980, *72*, 575–582.

Pressley, M., Levin, J. R., & Bryant, S. L. Memory strategy instruction during adolescence: When is explicit instruction needed? In M. Pressley & J. R. Levin (Eds.), *Cognitive strategy research: Psychological foundations*. New York: Springer-Verlag, 1983.

Pressley, M., Levin, J. R., & Delaney, H. D. The mnemonic keyword method. *Review of Educational Research*, 1982, *52*, 61–91.

Pronko, N. H. On learning to play the violin at the age of four without tears. *Psychology Today*, 1969, *2*, 52–53; 66.

Purkey, S. C., & Smith, M. S. Synthesis of research on effective schools. *Educational Leadership*, 1982, *40*(3), 64–69

Raths, L., Harmin, M., & Simon, S. *Values and teaching*. Columbus, Ohio: Merrill, 1966.

Rawitsch, D. G. Implanting the computer in the classroom: Minnesota's successful statewide program. *Phi Delta Kappan*, 1981, 453–454.

Reder, L. M. The role of elaboration in the comprehension and retention of prose: A critical review. *Review of Educational Research*, 1980, *50*, 5–53.

Redfield, D. L., & Rosseau, E. W. A meta-analysis of experimental research on teacher questioning behavior. *Review of Educational Research*, 1981, *51*, 237–245.

Reese, H. W., Treffinger, D. J., Parnes, S. J., & Kaltsounis, G. Effects of a creative studies program on structure-of-intellect factors. *Journal of Educational Psychology*, 1976, *68*, 401–410.

Rehberg, R., & Rosenthal, E. *Class and merit in the American high school*. New York: Longman, 1978.

Reif, F., & Heller, J. I. Knowledge structure and problem solving in physics. *Educational Psychologist*, 1982, *17*, 102–127.

Renzulli, J. S. *The enrichment triad model: A guide for developing defensible programs for the gifted and talented*. Wethersfield, Conn.: Creative Learning Press, 1977.

Rest, J. R., Davison, M. L., & Robbins, S. Age trends in judging moral issues: A review of cross-sectional, longitudinal, and sequential studies of the Defining Issues Test. *Child Development*, 1978, *49*, 263–279.

Reynolds, C. R., & Jensen, A. R. WISC-R Subscale patterns of abilities of blacks and whites matched on full scale IQ. *Journal of Educational Psychology*, 1983, *75*, 207–214.

Reynolds, R. E., & Anderson, R. C. Influence of questions on the allocation of attention during reading. *Journal of Educational Psychology*, 1982, *74*, 623–632.

Rickards, J. P. Adjunct postquestions in text: A critical review of methods and processes. *Review of Educational Research*, 1979, *49*, 181–196.

Ripple, R. E., & Drinkwater, D. J. Transfer of learning. In H. E. Mitzel, J. H. Best, & W. Rabinowitz (Eds.), *Encyclopedia of educational research* (5th ed., Vol. 4). New York: Free Press, 1982.

Ripple, R. E., & May, F. B. Caution in comparing creativity and IQ. *Psychological Reports*, 1962, *10*, 229–230.

Robinson, F. P. *Effective study*. New York: Harper & Row, 1946.

Rogers, C. R. Actualizing tendency in relation to "motives" and to consciousness. In M. R. Jones (Ed.), *Nebraska symposium on motivation*. Lincoln: University of Nebraska Press, 1963.

Rogers, C. R., Smith, M. D., & Coleman, J. Social comparison in the classroom: The relationship between academic achievement and self-concept. *Journal of Educational Psychology*, 1978, *70*, 50–57.

Rogers, R. W., & Mewborn, C. R. Fear appeals and attitude change: Effects of a threat's noxiousness, probability of occurrence, and the efficacy of coping responses. *Journal of Personality and Social Psychology*, 1976, *34*, 54–61.

Rosenshine, B. *Teaching behaviour and student achievement*. London: National Foundation for Educational Research in England and Wales, 1971.

Rosenshine, B. Content, time, and direct instruction. In P. L. Peterson & H. J. Walberg (Eds.), *Research on teaching: Concepts, findings, and implications*. Berkeley, Calif.: McCutchan, 1979.

Rossman, J. *The psychology of the inventor*. Washington, D.C.: Inventors, 1931.

Rosswork, S. G. Goal setting: The effects on an academic task with varying magnitudes of incentive. *Journal of Educational Psychology*, 1977, *69*, 710–715.

Royer, J. M. Theories of transfer of learning. *Educational Psychologist*, 1979, *14*, 53–69.

Ruble, D. N. A developmental perspective on theories of achievement motivation. In L. J. Fyans (Ed.), *Achievement motivation: Recent trends in theory and research*. New York: Plenum Press, 1980.

Rule, B. G., & Nesdale, A. R. Differing functions of aggression. *Journal of Personality*, 1974, *42*, 467–481.

Rushton, J. P. Socialization and the altruistic behavior of children. *Psychological Bulletin*, 1976, *83*, 898–913.

Rutter, M., Maughan, B., Mortimore, P., Ouston, J., & Smith, A. *Fifteen thousand hours: Secondary schools and their effects on children*. Cambridge, Mass.: Harvard University Press, 1979.

Ryan, B. A. A case against behavior modification in the ordinary classroom. *Journal of School Psychology*, 1979, *17*, 131–136.

Salomon, G. Media and symbol systems as related to cognition and learning. *Journal of Educational Psychology*, 1979, *71*, 131–148.

Sanders, N. M. *Classroom questions: What kinds?* New York: Harper & Row, 1965.

Santrock, J. W. Effects of father absence on sex-typed behaviors in male children: Reason for the absence and age of onset of the absence. *Journal of Genetic Psychology*, 1977, *130*, 3–10.

Scandura, J. M. Problem solving in schools and beyond: Transitions from the naive to the neophyte to the master. *Educational Psychologist*, 1981, *16*, 139–150.

Schab, F. Cheating in high school: Differences between the sexes. *Journal of the National Association of Women Deans and Counselors*, 1969, *33*, 39–42.

Scheirer, M. A., & Kraut, R. E. Increasing educational achievement via self-concept change. *Review of Educational Research*, 1979, *49*, 131–150.

Schoenfeld, A. H., & Herrmann, D. J. Problem perception and knowledge structure in expert and novice mathematical problem solvers. *Journal of Experimental Psychology: Learning, Memory, and Cognition*, 1982, *8*, 484–494.

Schunk, D. H. Effects of effort attributional feedback on children's perceived self-efficacy and achievement. *Journal of Educational Psychology*, 1982, *74*, 548–556.

Schwartz, G., Puntil, J. E., & Simon, W. *Summary and policy implications of the youth and society in Illinois reports.* Chicago: Department of Mental Health, Institute for Juvenile Research, 1977.

Science Research Associates. *Iowa Tests of Educational Development. Rights Keys, Norms, and Conversion Tables* (1974 ed.). Chicago: Science Research Associates, 1974.

Scott, K. P., & Feldman-Summers, S. Children's reactions to textbook stories in which females are portrayed in traditionally male roles. *Journal of Educational Psychology,* 1979, *71,* 396–402.

Seibert, W. F., & Ullmer, E. J. Media use in education. In H. E. Mitzel, J. H. Best, & W. Rabinowitz (Eds.), *Encyclopedia of educational research* (5th ed., Vol. 3). New York: Free Press, 1982.

Seligman, M. E. *Helplessness.* San Francisco: Freeman, 1975.

Semmel, M. I., Gottlieb, J., & Robinson, N. M. Mainstreaming: Perspectives on educating handicapped children in the public school. In D. C. Berliner (Ed.), *Review of research in education* (Vol. 7). Washington, D.C.: American Educational Research Association, 1979.

Sesnowitz, M., Bernhardt, K. L., & Kanin, D. M. An analysis of the impact of commercial test preparation courses on SAT scores. *American Educational Research Journal,* 1982, *19,* 429–441.

Shane, H. G. *Curriculum change toward the 21st century.* Washington, D.C.: National Education Association, 1977.

Shavelson, R. J., Hubner, J. J., & Stanton, G. C. Self-concept: Validation of construct interpretations. *Review of Educational Research,* 1976, *46,* 407–441.

Shepard, L. A. Self-acceptance: The evaluative component of the self-concept construct. *American Educational Research Journal,* 1979, *16,* 139–160.

Shepherd, J. The Look youth survey. *Look,* 1966, 44–49.

Sherman, J. Mathematics, spatial visualization, and related factors: Changes in girls and boys, grades 8–11. *Journal of Educational Psychology,* 1980, *72,* 476–482.

Sherman, J., & Fennema, E. The study of mathematics by high school girls and boys: Related variables. *American Educational Research Journal,* 1977, *14,* 159–168.

Shiffrin, R. M., & Atkinson, R. C. Storage and retrieval processes in long-term memory. *Psychological Review,* 1969, *76,* 179–193.

Shockley, W. Dysgenics, geneticity, and raceology: A challenge to the intellectual responsibility of educators. *Phi Delta Kappan,* 1972, *53,* 297–307.

Sieber, J. E., O'Neil, H. F., Jr., & Tobias, S. *Anxiety, learning, and instruction.* Hillsdale, N.J.: Erlbaum, 1977.

Siegler, R. S. When do children learn: The relationship between existing knowledge and learning. *Educational Psychologist,* 1980, *15,* 135–150.

Siegler, R. S. Five generalizations about cognitive development. *American Psychologist,* 1983, *38,* 263–277.

Simberg, A. L. Obstacles to creative thinking. In G. A. Davis & J. A. Scott (Eds.), *Training creative thinking.* New York: Holt, Rinehart and Winston, 1971.

Simms, E. Averaging model of information integration theory applied in the classroom. *Journal of Educational Psychology,* 1978, *70,* 740–744.

Simon, S. B., & Clark, J. *More values clarification.* San Diego, Calif.: Pennant Press, 1975.

Singer, R. N. To err or not to err: A question for the instruction of psychomotor skills. *Review of Educational Research,* 1977, *47,* 479–498.

Singer, R. N. Motor skills and learner strategies. In H. F. O'Neil, Jr. (Ed.), *Learning strategies.* New York: Academic Press, 1978.

Singer, R. N., & Gerson, R. F. Learning strategies, cognitive processes, and motor learning. In H. F. O'Neil, Jr., & C. D. Spielberger (Eds.), *Cognitive and affective learning strategies.* New York: Academic Press, 1979.

Sipple, T. S., Allen, P. S., & Klausmeier, H. J. *Supplementary tabular information to accompany Cognitive development of children and youth: A longitudinal study, by H. J. Klausmeier and P. S. Allen, Academic Press, 1978; and Cognitive learning and development: Information-processing and Piagetian perspectives, by H. J. Klausmeier and Associates,* Ballinger, 1979 (Tech. Report No. 495). Madison: Wisconsin Center for Education Research, 1979.

Sipple, T. S., & Klausmeier, H. J. *Correlation matrices and factor loadings involving twenty-nine tasks derived from Piagetian theory* (Project Paper). Madison: Wisconsin Center for Education Research, 1981.

Skinner, B. F. *The behavior of organisms.* New York: Appleton-Century-Crofts, 1938.

Skinner, B. F. *Science and human behavior.* New York: Macmillan, 1953.

Slavin, R. E. Effects of biracial learning teams on cross-racial friendships. *Journal of Educational Psychology,* 1979, *71,* 381–387.

Slavin, R. E. Cooperative learning. *Review of Educational Research,* 1980, *50,* 315–342.

Smedslund, J. Piaget's psychology in practice. *British Journal of Educational Psychology,* 1977, *47,* 1–6.

Snow, R. E. Aptitude, learner control, and adaptive instruction. *Educational Psychologist,* 1980, *15,* 151–158.

Sperling, G. The information available in brief visual presentations. *Psychological Monographs,* 1960, *74,* No. 6 (Whole No. 498).

Sperry, R. W. Bridging science and values: A unifying view of mind and brain. *American Psychologist,* 1977, *32,* 237–245.

Stanley, J. C. Rationale of the study of mathematically precocious youth (SMPY) during its first five years of promoting educational acceleration. In J. C. Stanley, W. C. George, & C. H. Solano (Eds.), *The gifted and the creative: A fifty-year perspective.* Baltimore, Md.: The Johns Hopkins University Press, 1977.

Stein, A., & Friedrich, L. K. Television content and young children's behavior. In J. P. Murray, E. A. Rubinstein, & G. A. Comstock (Eds.), *Television and social behavior.* 2 vols. Washington, D.C.: Television and Social Learning, U.S. Government Printing Office, 1972.

Steinberg, L. D., Greenberger, E., Garduque, L., Ruggiero, M., & Vaux, A. Effects of working on adolescent development. *Developmental Psychology,* 1982, *18,* 385–395.

Stelmach, G. E., & Larish, D. D. A new perspective on motor skill automation. *Research Quarterly,* 1980, *51,* 141–157.

Sternberg, R. J. The nature of mental abilities. *American Psychologist,* 1979, *34,* 214–230.

Sternberg, R. J., & Detterman, D. K. (Eds.). *How and how much can intelligence be increased?* Norwood, N.J.: Ablex Publishing Corporation, 1982.

Sterrett, M. D., & Davis, R. A. The permanence of school learning: A review of studies. *Educational Administration and Supervision,* 1954, *40,* 449–460.

Stevenson, H. W., Parker, T., Wilkinson, A., Hegion, A., & Fish, E. Predictive value of teachers' ratings of young children. *Journal of Educational Psychology,* 1976, *68,* 507–517.

Stolz, S. B., Wienckowski, L. A., & Brown, B. S. Behavior modification: A perspective on critical issues. *American Psychologist,* 1975, *30,* 1027–1048.

Suppes, P. The future of computers in education. In R. Taylor (Ed.), *The computer in the school: Tutor, tool, tutee.* New York: Columbia University, Teachers College Press, 1980.

Swick, K. J. *Disruptive student behavior in the classroom.* Washington, D.C.: National Education Association, 1980.

Swing, S. R., & Peterson, P. L. The relationship of student ability and small-group interaction to student achievement. *American Educational Research Journal*, 1982, *19*, 259–274.

Swinton, S. S., & Powers, D. E. A study of the effects of special preparation on GRE analytical scores and item types. *Journal of Educational Psychology*, 1983, *75*, 104–115.

Taffel, S. J., & O'Leary K. D. Reinforcing math with more math: Choosing special academic activities as a reward for academic performance. *Journal of Educational Psychology*, 1976, *68*, 579–587.

Taub, J. M., & Berger, R. R. The effects of changing the phase and duration of sleep. *Journal of Experimental Psychology: Human Perception and Performance*, 1976, *2*, 30–41.

Taylor, C. W., & Holland, J. L. Development and application of tests of creativity. *Review of Educational Research*, 1962, *32*, 91–102.

Taylor, C. W., Smith, W. R., & Ghiselin, B. The creative and other contributions of one sample of research scientists. In C. W. Taylor & F. Barron (Eds.), *Scientific creativity: Its recognition and development*. New York: Wiley, 1963.

Taylor, D. A., & Harris. P. L. Knowledge of the link between emotion and memory among normal and maladjusted boys. *Developmental Psychology*, 1983, *19*, 832–838.

Tennyson, C. L., Tennyson, R. D., & Rothen, W. Content structure and instructional control strategies as design variables in concept acquisition. *Journal of Educational Psychology*, 1980, *72*, 499–505.

Tennyson, R. D. Instructional control strategies and content structure as design variables in concept acquisition using computer-based instruction. *Journal of Educational Psychology*, 1980, *72*, 525–532.

Terman, L. M. *The measurement of intelligence*. Boston: Houghton Mifflin, 1916.

Terman, L. M., & Merrill, M. A. *Measuring intelligence*. Boston: Houghton Mifflin, 1937.

Terman, L. M., & Merrill, M. A. *Revised Stanford-Binet Intelligence Scales*. Boston: Houghton Mifflin, 1960.

Tesiny, E. P., Lefkowitz, M. M., & Gordon, N. H. Childhood depression, locus of control, and school achievement. *Journal of Educational Psychology*, 1980, *72*, 506–510.

Tewel, K. J., & Chalfin, F. Close encounters in the classroom: A technique for combatting irresponsibility among today's high school youngsters. *Phi Delta Kappan*, 1980, *62*, 56–58.

Thomas, A. Learned helplessness and expectancy factors: Implications for research in learning disabilities. *Review of Educational Research*, 1979, *49*, 208–221.

Thomas, E. L., & Robinson, H. A. *Improving reading in every class: A sourcebook for teachers*. Boston: Allyn & Bacon, 1972.

Thorndike, E. L. Animal intelligence. *Psychological Review*, 1898, Monograph Supplement 2, 8.

Thorndike, E. L. *Animal intelligence*. New York: Macmillan, 1911.

Thorndike, E. L. *The psychology of learning: Educational psychology* (Vol. 2). New York: Columbia University, Teachers College Press, 1913.

Thorndike, E. L. *The measurement of intelligence*. New York: Columbia University, Teachers College Press, 1926.

Thorndyke, P. W., & Hayes-Roth, B. The use of schemata in the acquisition and transfer of knowledge. *Cognitive Psychology*, 1979, *11*, 82–106.

Thurstone, L. L. Primary mental abilities. *Psychometric Monographs*, 1938, No. 1.

Thurstone, L. L. *The differential growth of mental abilities*. Chapel Hill, N.C.: Psychometric Laboratory, University of North Carolina, 1955.

Thurstone, L. L., & Thurstone, T. G. *SRA Primary Mental Abilities*. Chicago: Science Research Associates, 1963.

Tobias, S. Anxiety research in educational psychology. *Journal of Educational Psychology,* 1979, *71,* 573–582.

Tolman, E. C. *Purposive behavior in animals and men.* Berkeley, Calif.: University of California Press, 1949.

Toner, I. J., Moore, L. P., & Ashley, P. K. The effect of serving as a model of self-control on subsequent resistance to deviation in children. *Journal of Experimental Child Psychology,* 1978, *26,* 85–91.

Torrance, E. P. *Rewarding creative behavior: Experiments in classroom creativity.* Englewood Cliffs, N.J.: Prentice-Hall, 1965.

Torrance. E. P. *Torrance Tests of Creative Thinking.* Princeton, N.J.: Personnel Press, 1966a.

Torrance, E. P. *Torrance Tests of Creative Thinking: Technical-norms manual.* Lexington, Mass.: Personnel Press, 1966b.

Torrance, E. P. Creatively gifted and disadvantaged gifted students. In J. C. Stanley, W. C. George, & C. H. Solano (Eds.), *The gifted and the creative: A fifty-year perspective.* Baltimore, Md.: The Johns Hopkins University Press, 1977.

Trollinger, L. M. Interests, activities and hobbies of high and low creative women musicians during childhood, adolescent and college years. *Gifted Child Quarterly,* 1983, *27,* 94–97.

Tryon, G. S. The measurement and treatment of test anxiety. *Review of Educational Research,* 1980, *50,* 343–372.

Tulving, E. Organized retention and cued recall. In H. J. Klausmeier & G. T. O'Hearn (Eds.), *Research and development toward the improvement of education.* Madison, Wis.: Dembar Educational Research Services, 1968.

Tulving, E. Episodic and semantic memory. In E. Tulving & W. Donaldson (Eds.), *Organization of memory.* New York: Academic Press, 1972.

Tuma, D. T., & Reif, F. (Eds.), *Problem solving and education: Issues in teaching and research.* Hillsdale, N.J.: Erlbaum, 1980.

TV's "disastrous" impact on children. *U.S. News & World Report,* January 19, 1981.

Uguroglu, M. E., & Walberg, H. Motivation and achievement: A quantitative synthesis. *American Educational Research Journal,* 1979, *16,* 375–389.

U.S. Government Printing Office. *How to use ERIC* (GOP 0-310-154). Washington, D.C.: U.S. Government Printing Office, 1968.

Venezky, R. L., & Pittelman, S. D. *PRS: A pre-reading skills program for Individually Guided Education.* In H. J. Klausmeier, R. A. Rossmiller, & M. Saily (Eds.), *Individually Guided Education: Concepts and practices.* New York: Academic Press, 1978.

Venezky, R. L., Pittelman, S. D., Felker, M. P., Higgins, S. L., & Chicone, S. K. *PRS vocabulary segment.* Chicago: Encyclopedia Britannica, 1978.

Venezky, R. L., Pittelman, S. D., Kamm, M. R., and Leslie, R. C. *Prereading skills program.* Chicago: Encyclopedia Britannica, 1974.

Verplanck, W. S. The operant conditioning of human motor behavior. *Psychological Bulletin,* 1956, *53,* 70–83.

Walberg, H. J. Psychological theories of educational individualization. In H. Talmage (Ed.), *Systems of individualized education.* Berkeley, Calif.: McCutchan, 1975.

Walberg, H. J., & Fredrick, W. Instructional time and learning. In H. E. Mitzel, J. H. Best, & W. Rabinowitz (Eds.), *Encyclopedia of educational research* (5th ed., Vol. 2). New York: Free Press, 1982.

Walberg, H. J., & Welch, W. E. A national experiment in curriculum evaluation. *American Educational Research Journal,* 1972, *9,* 373–384.

Walden, T. A., & Ramey, C. T. Locus of control and academic achievement: Results from a preschool intervention program. *Journal of Educational Psychology,* 1983, *75,* 347–358.

Walker, C. H., & Meyer, J. F. Integrating information from text. *Review of Educational Research,* 1980, *50,* 421–437.

Wang, M. C., & Stiles, B. An investigation of children's concept of self-responsibility for their school learning. *American Educational Research Journal,* 1976, *13,* 159–179.

Waring, M. G. Personalizing the high school via computer. *Phi Delta Kappan,* 1981, *62,* 455.

Warner, W. L., Havighurst, R. J., & Loeb, M. B. *Who shall be educated?* New Haven, Conn.: Yale University Press, 1944.

Washburne, C. W. Educational measurements as a key to individualizing instruction and promotions. *Journal of Educational Research,* 1922, *5,* 195–206.

Waterland, J. C. *The effect of mental practice combined with kinesthetic perception when the practice precedes each overt performance of a motor skill.* Unpublished master's thesis, University of Wisconsin, 1956.

Waters, H. S., & Andreassen, C. Children's use of memory strategies under instruction. In M. Pressley & J. R. Levin (Eds.), *Cognitive strategy research: Psychological foundations.* New York: Springer-Verlag, 1983.

Watkins, M. J., Ho, E., & Tulving, E. Context effects in recognition memory for faces. *Journal of Verbal Learning and Verbal Behavior,* 1976, *15,* 505–518.

Wattanawaha, N., & Clements, M. A. Qualitative aspects of sex-related differences in performances on pencil-and-paper spatial questions, grades 7–9. *Journal of Educational Psychology,* 1982, *74,* 878–887.

Webb, N. M. A process-outcome analysis of learning in group and individual settings. *Educational Psychologist,* 1980, *15,* 69–83.

Webb, N. M. Peer interaction and learning in cooperative small groups. *Journal of Educational Psychology,* 1982, *74,* 642–655.

Webb, N. M., & Cullian, L. K. Group interaction and achievement in small groups: Stability over time. *American Educational Research Journal,* 1983, *20,* 411–423.

Wechsler, D. *Manual: Wechsler Intelligence Scale for Children.* New York: Psychological Corporation, 1949.

Wechsler, D. *Range of human capacities* (2d ed.). Baltimore, Md.: Williams & Wilkins, 1952.

Wechsler, D. *The measurement and appraisal of adult intelligence* (4th ed.). Baltimore, Md.: Williams & Wilkins, 1958.

Wechsler, D. *Manual: WISC-R. Wechsler Intelligence Scale for Children* (Revised). New York: Psychological Corporation, 1974.

Wechsler, D. Intelligence defined and undefined: A relativistic appraisal. *American Psychologist,* 1975, *30,* 135–139.

Wegner, N., & Zeaman, D. Team and individual performances on a motor learning task. *Journal of General Psychology,* 1956, *55,* 127–142.

Weiner, B. A theory of motivation for some classroom experiences. *Journal of Educational Psychology,* 1979, *71,* 3–25.

Weiner, B. *Human motivation.* New York: Holt, Rinehart and Winston, 1980a.

Weiner, B. May I borrow your class notes: An attributional analysis of judgments of help giving in an achievement-related context. *Journal of Educational Psychology,* 1980b, *72,* 676–681.

Weinstein, C. E. Elaboration skills as a learning strategy. In H. F. O'Neil, Jr. (Ed.), *Learning strategies.* New York: Academic Press, 1978.

Weiss, R. J. Understanding moral thought: Effects on moral reasoning and decision making. *Developmental Psychology,* 1982, *18,* 852–861.

Welch, W. W., Anderson, R. E., & Harris, L. J. The effects of schooling on mathematics achievement. *American Educational Research Journal,* 1982, *19,* 145–153.

West, L. J. *Acquisition of typewriting skills* (2d ed.). Indianapolis: Bobbs-Merrill, 1983.

White, R. W. Motivation reconsidered: The concept of competence. *Psychological Review,* 1959, *66,* 297–333.

Wickelgren, W. A. Human learning and memory. In M. R. Rosenzweig & L. M. Porter (Eds.), *Annual Review of Psychology.* Palo Alto, Calif.: Annual Reviews, 1981.

Williams, P. A., Haertel, E. H., Haertel, G. D., & Walberg, H. J. The impact of leisuretime television on school learning. A research synthesis. *American Educational Research Journal,* 1982, *19,* 19–50.

Wine, J. D. Cognitive-attentional theory of test anxiety. In I. G. Sarason (Ed.), *Test anxiety: Theory, research, and application.* Hillside, N.J.: Erlbaum, 1980.

Wingfield, A. *Human learning and memory: An introduction.* New York: Harper & Row, 1979.

Witkin, H. A. Perception of body position and of the position of the visual field. *Psychological Monographs,* 1949, *63* (1, Whole No. 302).

Witkin, H. A., Moore, C. A., Goodenough, D. R., & Cox, P. W. Field-dependent and field-independent cognitive styles and their educational implications. *Review of Educational Research,* 1977, *47,* 1–64.

Wittrock, M. C. Set to learn and proactive inhibition. *Journal of Educational Research,* 1963, *57,* 72–75.

Wittrock, M. C., & Lumsdaine, A. A. Instructional psychology. *Annual Review of Psychology.* Palo Alto, Calif.: Annual Reviews, 1977.

Wiviott, S. *Bases of classification of geometric concepts used by children of varying characteristics.* Unpublished doctoral dissertation, University of Wisconsin, 1970.

Wixson, K. K. Postreading question-answer interactions and children's learning from text. *Journal of Educational Psychology,* 1983, *75,* 413–423.

Wlodkowski, R. J. *Motivation and teaching: A practical guide.* Washington, D.C.: National Education Association, 1978.

Wohlwill, J. F. *The study of behavioral development.* New York: Academic Press, 1973.

Workman, E. A., & Hector, M. A. Behavioral self-control in classroom settings: A review of the literature. *Journal of School Psychology,* 1978, *16,* 227–236.

Yamamoto, K. Relationships between creative thinking abilities of teachers and achievement and adjustment of pupils. *Journal of Experimental Education,* 1963, *32,* 3–25.

Zajonc, R. B. Feeling and thinking: Preferences need no inferences. *American Psychologist,* 1980, *35,* 151–175.

Zellman, G. L. Antidemocratic beliefs: A survey and some explanations. *Journal of Social Issues,* 1975, *31,* 31–53.

Zellman, G. L., & Sears, D. O. Childhood origins of tolerance for dissent. *Journal of Social Issues,* 1971, *27,* 109–136.

Zimmerman, B. J., & Blotner, R. Effects of model persistence and success on children's problem solving. *Journal of Educational Psychology,* 1979, *71,* 508–513.

NAME INDEX

SUBJECT INDEX